Wireless Digital Communications

Modulation and Spread Spectrum Applications

Wireless Digital Communications

Modulation and Spread Spectrum Applications

DR. KAMILO FEHER

Director, Digital & Wireless Communication Laboratory
Professor, Electrical and Computer Engineering Department
University of California, Davis
Davis, California 95616

President, Consulting & Licensing Group, DIGCOM, Inc.
FQPSK Consortium–Dr. Feher Associates

Prentice-Hall of India Private Limited
New Delhi - 110 001
2000

This Second Indian Reprint—Rs. 275.00
(Original U.S. Edition—Rs. 3539.00)

WIRELESS DIGITAL COMMUNICATIONS: Modulation and Spread Spectrum Applications (with Diskette)
by Kamilo Feher

ISBN-81-203-1472-7

The export rights of this book are vested solely with the publisher.

This Eastern Economy Edition is the authorized, complete and unabridged photo-offset reproduction of the latest American edition specially published for sale only in Bangladesh, Bhutan, India, Malaysia, Nepal, Pakistan and Sri Lanka.

Reprinted in India by special arrangement with Prentice-Hall, Inc., One Lake Street, Upper Saddle River, New Jersey 07458, U.S.A.

Second Printing ... ... **August, 2000**

Published by Asoke K. Ghosh, Prentice-Hall of India Private Limited, M-97, Connaught Circus, New Delhi-110001 and Printed by Mohan Makhijani at Rekha Printers Private Limited, New Delhi-110020.

In Loving Memory

of my father Camillo Feher, Sr. and
of my mother Melanija Feher

for their unlimited love and continuous encouragement to learn, to be inventive, and to become active in the "American Dream"

Dedicated to the
Constitution of the United States
Article 1, Section 8, Clause 8:

"The Congress shall have power: ...to promote the progress of science and useful arts, by securing for limited times to authors and inventors the exclusive right to their respective writings and discoveries."

The Constitutional basis of the US Patent Law motivated me and provided the means to describe my inventions and patents in the text and Appendix 3 of this book, with the hope of encouraging extraordinary engineering talents to invent and create.

Contents

Preface

You may be a self-motivated and ambitious engineer. Perhaps you are a student or professor. Regardless of your position or occupation, we have one goal in common: the desire or the need to be at the forefront of the fascinating field of wireless digital communications.

Are you reading this preface to find out why you should read this book or what you will learn from it? How is this book unique? Should you use it as a reference text in your courses? Is it necessary to read complete sections, or is it effective to use the book as a reference text? Should you use the CREATE-1 software diskette contained in this book? Please continue to read this preface and allow me to respond to the preceding questions.

My goal is to cooperate with you in the learning process. I wish to share my product and system design experience and enthusiasm in order to improve our joint understanding of wireless communications systems.

The following quotation summarizes one vision of the importance and tremendous potential of wireless computer and phone systems as:

> … a new era of human communications where wireless technologies become information skyways, a new avenue to send ideas and masses of information to remote locations in ways most of us would never have imagined. Wireless hand-held computers and phones will deliver the world to our fingertips wherever we may be, with speed and flexibility.
>
> William Clinton
> President of the United States of America

Users' opinions, understanding, and learning of wireless communications applications, particularly those of future communications customers, are of utmost importance to all of us. The following quotation illustrates the opinion and understanding of a 12-year-old:

> Wireless Communications: Communications in our world is very important. We could not have as many things going on around this world as we do now. Police, for example, would have a much tougher job. They could not tell each other what is going on where and no dispatcher could tell them if there is a call. Communications makes it easier to build big buildings. They need to have it because then they could tell each other to do this or that. This world would be quite chaotic. There are two types of communications. Wired communications and wireless communications. Wireless communications includes examples such as hand held CB radio, or a hand held cellu-

lar phone. Wired communications are like house phones, or faxes. Today I am going to be talking about Wireless Communications...

Antoine-Kamilo Feher, Sixth-Grade Student, 1994
Pioneer Elementary School Report
Davis, California

The size of the annual cellular communications business in the United States has grown from $100 million to more than $30 billion in less than 10 years. Cellular, wireless-cable, and other telecommunications and broadcasting corporations are increasing the voice (telephony) capacity of their networks and are adding new data features so that customers with wireless modulation-demodulation devices (modems) in portable personal computers and workstations can access electronic mail and facsimile, written, graphic, audio, and video messages. For the cellular industry, selection of the most appropriate access method is a challenging task. This task is focused on the choice between time division multiple access (TDMA) and spread-spectrum code division multiple access (CDMA) architectures. Both of these access methods have the capability to increase the capacity of analog cellular systems by approximately 10 to 40 times. Already in 1995, more than five million cellular subscribers are using second-generation TDMA digital technology. Spread-spectrum systems have the promise of further increasing the capacity of TDMA-based cellular and wireless systems. Both of these architectures will be extensively used during the next decade.

The ultimate wireless information-communication advances will have to achieve truly unlimited capabilities and services. New satellite communications projects, such as the multibillion dollar IRIDIUM project of Motorola, which uses 66 satellites, could guarantee the "anytime, anywhere" promise; however, whether it could reach a broad consumer market at a reasonable price is questionable.

The business fields affected by the wireless computer information and communications revolution are broad and challenging. To meet this challenge, managers, engineers, students, and professors will have to become very familiar with the technologies and system architectures described in this book. I do not know of another book of comparable scope and depth in the wireless digital communications field. Most modern digital communications techniques required for the comprehension, analysis, design, and maintenance of digital wireless systems are described in this book. An introductory overview of basic material is included. After the description of principles of operation and concepts we proceed with the study of modern techniques, architectures, products, and standards. In-depth material on some of the most advanced digital modulation, spread-spectrum, and wireless radio engineering research, business developments, and worldwide applications is also included.

I assume that, to understand this book, you have a reasonable background in the foundations of basic communications engineering and technology. Selected chapters from this book have been taught at the University of California, Davis, in undergraduate and graduate courses. Sections of this text have also been presented at numerous professional "short courses" around the world to practicing engineers, managers, and system operators. The enthusiastic feedback received from hundreds of participants of these courses and from readers of my previously published books motivated me to formalize my notes and write this text. I believe that university professors will find educational and intellectually challenging material for senior undergraduate and graduate level courses.

If you are a practicing engineer and already have a generally broad knowledge of some of the topics covered in this volume, I hope that reading this text will motivate you to read the more advanced subjects. Even if you do not have the time, energy, or interest to study all of the derivations and mathematical and theoretical concepts, you could benefit from the more than 300 figures, graphs, tables, photographs, and original measurement results. Numerous comparisons of system specifications and standards of the 1990s should be of considerable value to the system architect and design engineer. Thus this volume could be used for your in-depth studies or as a professional reference. It is my intent to motivate you to be "inventive" in this fascinating field. In my courses I devote considerable time and effort to help students develop inventive, cost-efficient solutions. In some cases in this text I felt that I needed to become "provocative" in order to really challenge you and to uncover and encourage your inventive mind. Although the principal objective of this text is to provide general "knowledge transfer" and "technology transfer" to you, I believe that the general educational material should be complemented by research achievements. Research, particularly research and development from my university and industry-based teams, is reported extensively in this book.

In several sections, combined modulation and nonlinearly amplified, power-efficient and spectrally efficient radio developments, implementations, and technology transfer and licensing activities for a broad family of patented GMSK, GFSK, FQPSK, FBPSK, and FQAM (Dr. Feher, Engineering Associates-Digcom, Inc., El Macero, California) wireless systems are described. These systems have a spectral efficiency advantage of more than 200% as compared with internationally standardized (GMSK) and Gaussian frequency shift keying (GFSK) systems, are compatible with GMSK systems, and have a radio frequency (or infrared) power efficiency advantage of more than 300% as compared with standardized $\pi/4$-DQPSK and other conventional QPSK systems

Unique features of this book include its pragmatic, down-to-earth treatment of some of the most complex and advanced digital wireless communications concepts. "Physical layer" (PHY) wireless system designs, advanced baseband processing, filtering, modulation, radio frequency amplification, efficient radio architecture, demodulation, and synchronization subsystems are given a comprehensive treatment for the first time in a book. Most important, critical interaction among these subsystems and essential joint system and hardware design, optimization, implementation, and testing of components is thoroughly discussed. In-depth mathematical and analytical treatment of radio propagation, cellular interference, digital modem, error-control, spread-spectrum, and diversity wireless systems is presented for the advanced reader; however, the busy professional could skip the derivations and use the final performance charts and tables.

For computer-aided analysis and design, our software package CREATE-1 is appended to the back cover. The software adds to the uniqueness and value of this book. It is a software package that you could install on your personal computer and meaningfully use with a minimal investment of time. This package enables you to design standard modulation, linear and nonlinear wireless systems and to "create" and analyze your own waveforms and modulated systems in a relatively complex linearly or nonlinearly amplified environment.

Chapter 1 is an introduction to cellular, digital personal communications systems and to the wireless mobile radio environment. Brief sections on the evolution of mobile communications and mobile communication fundamentals are followed by descriptions of the cellular concept and first, second, third, and subsequent generations of digital cellular and wireless systems. The importance of national and international standards and standardization efforts is highlighted. Tremendous market opportunities, demands, and forecasts are presented.

In Chapter 2, digital signal processing techniques for wireless telephone and broadcast systems are highlighted. We progress from the basics of pulse code modulation (PCM) toward the description of advanced vocoders and linear predictive coding concepts and devices. The performance of reduced data rate (4.8 kb/s range) and of conventional 64 kb/s PCM systems is compared. Standardized American, European, and international speech coders and decoders (codecs) are highlighted.

In Chapter 3 you learn the most significant cellular engineering concepts and practical characteristics of radio propagation. After a basic treatment of radio propagation, including envelope fading, Doppler spread, time delay spread, shadowing, and path loss, antenna directional and omnidirectional fundamentals and radiation patterns are described. Propagation characteristics for free-space line-of-sight (LOS) and non-line-of-sight (NLOS) wireless systems are discussed. Frequently used empirical formulas and numerous path loss charts are presented. I provide a study of the mathematical model of multipath faded radio signals and include a simple theoretical delay spread bound. This delay spread bound is useful for a simple, effective prediction of the maximal delay spread to be anticipated in a new system design, without the requirements for extensive and time-consuming field measurements. Conventional and original instrumentation and measurement setups, including the design and construction of low-cost delay spread field measurement apparatus, are described for the first time in a book. Extensive field measurement results of personal communications systems (PCS), cellular, and land-based mobile radio applications are presented in numerous charts. Industry standards for propagation models are also described. These standards highlight the differences for various bit-rate mobile applications.

Chapter 4 places a strong emphasis on the treatment of modem and combined modulation and radio engineering design techniques for wireless applications. This chapter presents original, in-depth coverage of modulation topics. Comprehensive study of propagation-interference and synchronization of modem and combined modem-radio equipment is provided, as these have a critical importance in the overall wireless radio and PHY architecture and performance. The wide range of modulation choices is beneficial, since it allows us to select and design the best new and emerging systems. The challenge we face is that we have to take a fair amount of time to study these choices in order to standardize these systems and to design compatible systems that can interact with previously standardized systems.

After the study of essential principles of baseband premodulation, techniques of spectral density, eye diagrams, and Nyquist transmission theorems, we describe modem principles and architectures. These include coherent and noncoherent conventional binary phase shift keying (BPSK), quadrature phase shift keying (QPSK), and π/4-DQPSK modems and radio systems that have been adopted as some of the major U.S. and Japanese standards. You will find it interesting and thought-provoking that I dare to question the wisdom of standardizing π/4-DQPSK and of GFSK modulated wireless systems in the United States and internationally. Some of the standardized modulated systems have substantially inferior performance as compared with existing alternatives. In hindsight, it is easy for me to criticize some of the specifications of U.S. and international standards in the cellular and wireless local area network fields, such as the Institute of Electrical and Electronic Engineers (IEEE) 802.11 standard. In this book you learn the strengths and pitfalls of the specifications of standardized systems, and you will be in a position to design better systems and standards and to create improved-performance systems that are compatible with previously standardized systems. Detailed study of Chapter 4 in regard to QPSK, GMSK, FQPSK, and GFSK wireless systems operated in an interference environment is expected to lead to more efficient future system designs. Complex cellular interference environment, including in-band carrier and adjacent channel interference and their relation to the newest, most powerful modulated system performance, is described for the first time in a book. Fundamental and practical definitions of spectral and power efficiency, as well as specifications, are presented. A thorough study of advantages of coherent demodulation over noncoherent systems is also included in this chapter.

In Chapter 5, error correction and detection methods and techniques are highlighted. By adding redundancy to the information (customer or source) bits, errors induced by a noisy or interference-limited wireless system can be detected and corrected. Block coding concepts and definitions, repetition codes, Hamming distance and codes, BCH, and Golay, Reed-Solomon, and convolutional coding methods are briefly described. In addition to bit-error-rate performance, also known as probability of error (P_e), word-error-rate, false-alarm-rate, and throughput of wireless systems are studied. Performance studies of repetition codes and of majority voting systems, as well as automatic repeat request or query (ARQ), are reviewed.

In Chapter 6 you learn spread-spectrum system fundamentals and applications. These systems have been used in government and military systems for at least 50 years. Large-scale commercial applications, promoted by many industry and academic engineering leaders, were triggered by the far-sighted and innovative approach of the Federal Communications Commission (FCC) of the U.S. government, which authorized wireless applications in the popularly known "FCC-15" 900 MHz, 2.4 GHz, and 5.7 GHz bands. These bands, also known as instrumentation scientific and medical (ISM) bands, initiated completely new business applications and engineering research and development. The FCC stipulated that as much as 1 watt of power can be transmitted in these bands if spread-spectrum techniques, frequency hopping, or direct sequencing is employed. In addition to the regulatory leadership of the FCC, Qualcomm, Inc., of San Diego, California, pioneered the introduction of CDMA spread-spectrum cellular and wireless systems. The founders of Qualcomm, including Drs. Viterbi and Jacobs, used extraordinary knowledge of communication theory, practical engineering and technology, and business entrepreneurship skills to demonstrate America's leadership in advanced CDMA communications technology. Industry leaders such as Air Touch (formerly PacTel), led by its vice-president and chief engineer, Dr. William Lee, embraced the CDMA concept and with the cooperation of an increasing number of corporations contributed to the successful implementation and use of CDMA techniques, systems, and standards.

Fundamental concepts of spread-spectrum systems, including direct-sequence spread-spectrum and frequency-hopped spread-spectrum systems, are described. Important pseudonoise (PN) sequences are reviewed. Performance of direct-sequence CDMA and frequency-hopped systems is analyzed in a complex interference environment. A comparison of frequency-hopped and direct-sequence CDMA spread-spectrum systems is presented, and some of their applications are illustrated. In Chapter 9, additional spread-spectrum applications, developments, and standards are presented.

In Chapter 7, diversity techniques, particularly antenna diversity systems that are used extensively in wireless radio systems, are described. You learn that in a multipath Rayleigh fading environment various combining and switching diversity methods improve the probability of error versus carrier-to-noise performance by orders of magnitude. Advanced mathematical concepts and performance derivations are given. The theoretical part of the chapter is of particular benefit to the advanced research engineer and graduate student, whereas the numerous performance graphs and results are intended as an easily read reference for the practical-minded applications engineer.

Chapter 8 highlights satellite mobile communications and broadcasting systems. These systems have the unique capability of providing both multipoint-to-point, that is, multiple access, and point-to-multipoint, that is, broadcast, modes of transmitting voice, high-quality audio, image, broadcast-quality television (TV), and other data simultaneously. This capability can be turned into a universal, global mobile network system application and service. The traditional geosynchronous (GEO) satellite systems have a two-hop radio propagation delay of approximately 500 ms. This amount of delay is considered excessive for several voice and data applications of toll-grade quality. The emergence of low earth orbit (LEO) and medium earth orbit (MEO) satellite systems in the mid-1990s mitigated the impact of large-delay GEO satellites. Emerging personal wireless satellite communication programs such as the National Aeronautics and Space Administration (NASA) Advanced Communications Technology Satellite (ACTS), the Canadian Advanced Satellite Program, Advanced Intelsat, TRW's Odyssey, and Motorola's IRIDIUM program are briefly described in Chapter 8, as are integrated satellite and terrestrial mobile systems and services.

Chapter 9 presents some of the most important principles and applications of integrated cellular and wireless systems. A brief review is made of access methods, including TDMA time division duplex (TDD) and frequency division duplex (FDD) methods, frequency division multiple access (FDMA) methods, and spread-spectrum systems. A performance comparison of frequently used GMSK, GFSK, FQPSK, and $\pi/4$-DQPSK systems is followed by radio link design of wireless cellular systems. Spectrum utilization of cellular systems, including geographical cochannel reuse and capacity/throughput of various systems, is studied. Mature standards, as well as emerging standards for cellular, mobile, and personal networks and wireless local area networks (WLANs), are presented.

Problems are listed at the end of several chapters, and worked-out examples are contained within the text. These, combined with the CREATE-1 software, provide educational and practical experience to motivate the reader to further explore this challenging field. This book contains basic tutorial and advanced material. The copyright of my four previous Prentice Hall books has reverted to me, and I have permission of Prentice Hall to use material previously published in these books. The tutorial material contained in Chapter 5 has been extracted predominantly from Dr. Tranter's chapter in *Digital Communications Satellite Earth Station Engineering*. I used extensively the results originally published by Dr. Hirade in *Advanced Digital Communications*. I had to rely on the contributions and publications of hundreds of engineers who are active in this field, and I have quoted the reference source wherever possible and practical.

In Chapters 4, 9, and Appendix 3 my filter, DSP, GMSK, GFSK, FBPSK, and FQPSK patents and inventions are also described.

It is a real challenge to produce a "high-tech" book within a reasonable time limit in a very rapidly evolving field. Within my constraint of time, I did my best to write an authoritative and comprehensive book. I hope that you will be motivated and challenged and that you may even "fall in love" with this fascinating field as I have throughout the last years. For myself, the largest professional gratification I can receive is to see this book contribute to engineering knowledge and achievements and to be able to foster worldwide development of digital wireless communications.

Dr. Kamilo Feher, Fellow, IEEE
Professor, Electrical and Computer Engineering
University of California, Davis
Davis, CA 95616
President, Dr. Feher Associates-Digcom, Inc.
FQPSK Consortium & Consulting, El Macero, CA 95618

Kamilo Feher
Lake Tahoe, California
March, 1995

Acknowledgments

I thank the University of California for giving me the opportunity to undertake the most challenging digital wireless communications research, development, and teaching projects. Dr. Hakimi, Chair, Department of Electrical and Computer Engineering, and Dean M. Ghausi encouraged me to develop one of the most productive and best equipped experimental research and teaching laboratories in the United States. My colleagues Professors Soderstrand and Wang cooperated in several projects. Zoss, Golanbari, and Dr. Borowski reviewed and improved the manuscript. In several chapters, research and development achievements of our talented group of graduate students, research engineers, scholars, and visiting professors are highlighted. Marilyn Todd's devoted work and meticulous typing of the manuscript is acknowledged. Dr. Lender and other reviewers provided invaluable technical suggestions. Goodwin, vice president and publisher, and Gettman, senior editor, of Prentice Hall helped and motivated me during all phases of the preparation of my book.

Extraordinary research cooperation, consulting tasks, and partnerships with industrial allies, combined with our FQPSK Consortium's international technology transfer, patent licensing, and industry training programs have generated new inventions and led to new generations of cost, power, and spectrally efficient products that are described in this book. I wish to thank the following organizations for their valuable support, licensing agreements, and cooperation: Hewlett-Packard, Motorola, Marquette Electronics, Tellabs, Inc., Advanced Fiber Communications, Siemens, Intel, Nippon Telegraph & Telephone, NHK Japan, Matsushita/National-Panasonic, UBBB Germany, Telecommunications Technology Inc., Karkar Electronics, Inc., DSP Inc., RCA, DRL, CNET-PTT France, Telebras and Autel Brazil, CRC/DOC Canada, Comtel, Comdev, Teleglobe, GTE, National Semiconductor, CTIA, EIA/TIA, IUSA Mexico, IDC Canada, AirTouch (formerly PacTel), Ericsson-GE, TRW, NASA, Telebit, Harris-Farinon, Raynet, Raytheon, RCA, SPAR, and Qualcomm.

I wish to thank my wife, Elisabeth, and four children, Catherine, Valerie, Antoine-Kamilo, and Alexis-Joseph Feher, for their help (typing, drafting, and editing), understanding, encouragement, and love during the preparation and writing phases of this book. Catherine prepared most of the original artwork and technical drawings. Antoine helped debug the enclosed CREATE-1 software. I thank God that I recovered after my 1993 life-threatening ski injury and had the health, energy, and stamina to complete this project.

Dr. Kamilo Feher
El Macero and Lake Tahoe, California
January, 1995

LICENSE AGREEMENT AND LIMITED WARRANTY

READ THE FOLLOWING TERMS AND CONDITIONS CAREFULLY BEFORE OPENING THIS DISK PACKAGE. THIS LEGAL DOCUMENT IS AN AGREEMENT BETWEEN YOU AND PRENTICE-HALL, INC. (THE "COMPANY"). BY OPENING THIS SEALED DISK PACKAGE, YOU ARE AGREEING TO BE BOUND BY THESE TERMS AND CONDITIONS. IF YOU DO NOT AGREE WITH THESE TERMS AND CONDITIONS, DO NOT OPEN THE DISK PACKAGE. PROMPTLY RETURN THE UNOPENED DISK PACKAGE AND ALL ACCOMPANYING ITEMS TO THE PLACE YOU OBTAINED THEM FOR A FULL REFUND OF ANY SUMS YOU HAVE PAID.

1. **GRANT OF LICENSE:** In consideration of your payment of the license fee, which is part of the price you paid for this product, and your agreement to abide by the terms and conditions of this Agreement, the Company grants to you a nonexclusive right to use and display the copy of the enclosed software program (hereinafter the "SOFTWARE") on a single computer (i.e., with a single CPU) at a single location so long as you comply with the terms of this Agreement. The Company reserves all rights not expressly granted to you under this Agreement.

2. **OWNERSHIP OF SOFTWARE:** You own only the magnetic or physical media (the enclosed disks) on which the SOFTWARE is recorded or fixed, but the Company retains all the rights, title, and ownership to the SOFTWARE recorded on the original disk copy(ies) and all subsequent copies of the SOFTWARE, regardless of the form or media on which the original or other copies may exist. This license is not a sale of the original SOFTWARE or any copy to you.

3. **COPY RESTRICTIONS:** This SOFTWARE and the accompanying printed materials and user manual (the "Documentation") are the subject of copyright. You may *not* copy the Documentation or the SOFTWARE, except that you may make a single copy of the SOFTWARE for backup or archival purposes only. You may be held legally responsible for any copying or copyright infringement which is caused or encouraged by your failure to abide by the terms of this restriction.

4. **USE RESTRICTIONS:** You may *not* network the SOFTWARE or otherwise use it on more than one computer or computer terminal at the same time. You may physically transfer the SOFTWARE from one computer to another provided that the SOFTWARE is used on only one computer at a time. You may *not* distribute copies of the SOFTWARE or Documentation to others. You may *not* reverse engineer, disassemble, decompile, modify, adapt, translate, or create derivative works based on the SOFTWARE or the Documentation without the prior written consent of the Company.

5. **TRANSFER RESTRICTIONS:** The enclosed SOFTWARE is licensed only to you and may *not* be transferred to any one else without the prior written consent of the Company. Any unauthorized transfer of the SOFTWARE shall result in the immediate termination of this Agreement.

6. **TERMINATION:** This license is effective until terminated. This license will terminate automatically without notice from the Company and become null and void if you fail to comply with any provisions or limitations of this license. Upon termination, you shall destroy the Documentation and all copies of the SOFTWARE. All provisions of this Agreement as to warranties, limitation of liability, remedies or damages, and our ownership rights shall survive termination.

7. **MISCELLANEOUS:** This Agreement shall be construed in accordance with the laws of the United States of America and the State of New York and shall benefit the Company, its affiliates, and assignees.

8. **LIMITED WARRANTY AND DISCLAIMER OF WARRANTY:** The Company warrants that the SOFTWARE, when properly used in accordance with the Documentation, will operate in substantial conformity with the description of the SOFTWARE set forth in the Documentation. The Company does not warrant that the SOFTWARE will meet your requirements or that the operation of the SOFTWARE will be uninterrupted or error-free. The Company warrants that the media on which the SOFTWARE is delivered shall be free from defects in materials and workmanship under normal use for a period of thirty (30) days from the date of your purchase. Your only remedy and the Company's only obligation under these limited warranties is, at the Company's option, return of the warranted item for a refund of any amounts paid by you or replacement of the item. Any replacement of SOFTWARE or media under the warranties shall not extend the original warranty period. The limited warranty set forth above shall not apply to any SOFTWARE which the Company determines in good faith has been subject to misuse, neglect, improper installation, repair, alteration, or damage by you.

EXCEPT FOR THE EXPRESSED WARRANTIES SET FORTH ABOVE, THE COMPANY DISCLAIMS ALL WARRANTIES, EXPRESS OR IMPLIED, INCLUDING WITHOUT LIMITATION, THE IMPLIED WARRANTIES OF MERCHANTABILITY AND FITNESS FOR A PARTICULAR PURPOSE. EXCEPT FOR THE EXPRESS WARRANTY SET FORTH ABOVE, THE COMPANY DOES NOT WARRANT, GUARANTEE, OR MAKE ANY REPRESENTATION REGARDING THE USE OR THE RESULTS OF THE USE OF THE SOFTWARE IN TERMS OF ITS CORRECTNESS, ACCURACY, RELIABILITY, CURRENTNESS, OR OTHERWISE.

IN NO EVENT, SHALL THE COMPANY OR ITS EMPLOYEES, AGENTS, SUPPLIERS, OR CONTRACTORS BE LIABLE FOR ANY INCIDENTAL, INDIRECT, SPECIAL, OR CONSEQUENTIAL DAMAGES ARISING OUT OF OR IN CONNECTION WITH THE LICENSE GRANTED UNDER THIS AGREEMENT, OR FOR LOSS OF USE, LOSS OF DATA, LOSS OF INCOME OR PROFIT, OR OTHER LOSSES, SUSTAINED AS A RESULT OF INJURY TO ANY PERSON, OR LOSS OF OR DAMAGE TO PROPERTY, OR CLAIMS OF THIRD PARTIES, EVEN IF THE COMPANY OR AN AUTHORIZED REPRESENTATIVE OF THE COMPANY HAS BEEN ADVISED OF THE POSSIBILITY OF SUCH DAMAGES. IN NO EVENT SHALL LIABILITY OF THE COMPANY FOR DAMAGES WITH RESPECT TO THE SOFTWARE EXCEED THE AMOUNTS ACTUALLY PAID BY YOU, IF ANY, FOR THE SOFTWARE.

SOME JURISDICTIONS DO NOT ALLOW THE LIMITATION OF IMPLIED WARRANTIES OR LIABILITY FOR INCIDENTAL, INDIRECT, SPECIAL, OR CONSEQUENTIAL DAMAGES, SO THE ABOVE LIMITATIONS MAY NOT ALWAYS APPLY. THE WARRANTIES IN THIS AGREEMENT GIVE YOU SPECIFIC LEGAL RIGHTS AND YOU MAY ALSO HAVE OTHER RIGHTS WHICH VARY IN ACCORDANCE WITH LOCAL LAW.

ACKNOWLEDGMENT

YOU ACKNOWLEDGE THAT YOU HAVE READ THIS AGREEMENT, UNDERSTAND IT ,AND AGREE TO BE BOUND BY ITS TERMS AND CONDITIONS. YOU ALSO AGREE THAT THIS AGREEMENT IS THE COMPLETE AND EXCLUSIVE STATEMENT OF THE AGREEMENT BETWEEN YOU AND THE COMPANY AND SUPERSEDES ALL PROPOSALS OR PRIOR AGREEMENTS, ORAL, OR WRITTEN, AND ANY OTHER COMMUNICATIONS BETWEEN YOU AND THE COMPANY OR ANY REPRESENTATIVE OF THE COMPANY RELATING TO THE SUBJECT MATTER OF THIS AGREEMENT.

Should you have any questions concerning this Agreement or if you wish to contact the Company for any reason, please contact in writing at the address below.

Robin Short
Prentice Hall PTR
One Lake Street
Upper Saddle River, New Jersey 07458

CHAPTER 1

Introduction to Wireless, Cellular, Digital, PCS-Mobile Radio

1.1 SUMMARY

In this introductory chapter the evolution and fundamental engineering design concepts of analog and digital mobile, cellular, wireless, and personal communications systems or services (PCSs) are described. The importance of the standardization process and U.S. and international market trends are also highlighted.

1.2 MOBILE COMMUNICATIONS: EVOLUTION AND FUNDAMENTALS

The evolution of mobile communications, including cellular personal communications systems (PCSs), personal communications networks (PCNs), and land mobile and mobile satellite radio systems, is described in this chapter. We highlight major developments and achievements, from inception and development of the first generations of analog and digital cellular systems and PCSs of the early 1990s to the system and equipment plans for the second- and third-generation universal/integrated cellular wireless PCSs with national and international infrastructures. Major world standardization efforts and the importance of standards and well-defined radio interfaces are also briefly discussed (Subasinghe-Dias, 1992). A more detailed description of emerging standards is presented in Chapter 9.

The revolutionary growth in new developments in the market demand and an ever-increasing number of new applications led to tremendous demands for additional capacity and for new radio frequency (RF) band allocations. This section on "evolution" and on technology "revolution" is provided to assist in the comprehension of the new technological requirements and challenges ahead of us. Many old, pioneering concepts are revisited and applied in the newest designs and implementations. Evolution and history may teach us some interesting lessons.

1.2.1 The Pioneer Phase (1921 to 1947)

The pioneering experiments in land mobile communications were carried out in the early 1920s in Detroit. One-way broadcasts were made to receivers in mobile police cars. Many problems were encountered in the design of reliable mobile receivers. In 1928 a Purdue University student was able to develop a receiver based on a super-heterodyne design that operated with reasonable success in the mobile environment. With this receiver the Detroit Police Department demonstrated the first operational mobile radio system in the 2-MHz RF band.

In the early 1930s mobile transmitters were developed, and the first two-way mobile system was placed in operation by the Bayonne, New Jersey, police department. The bulky radio equipment occupied most of the trunk of a typical vehicle. Around this time the propagation vagaries of the mobile environment were first observed by the operators. Experimenters recognized that these problems had to do in part with the movement of the receiver and the inconsistent nature of the transmission path. Performance was not always satisfactory. However, the utility of two-way mobile radio for police and fire departments was immediately recognized, and the demand for such systems grew rapidly. By 1934 there were 194 municipal police radio systems and 58 state police radio stations serving more than 5000 police cars.

This provoked the first spectrum crisis for the recently established U.S. radio frequency regulatory body known as the Federal Communications Commission (FCC). Only 11 channels were allocated for police use at this time, and after extensive hearings the FCC granted 29 new channels to law enforcement agencies.

Up to the early 1930s all mobile radio systems in operation used amplitude modulation (AM). In the late 1930s the Connecticut police department implemented the first two-way frequency modulation (FM) mobile system, which proved to be much more resistant to the peculiar propagation problems of mobile radio transmission. By 1940 almost all police systems in the United States had converted to FM.

World War II was an enormous stimulus to mobile communications. Several hundred thousand mobile radios were built for military use. Almost every manufacturer of radio equipment in the United States undertook the production of mobile radio systems. Most of these used FM. Great strides were made in development, packaging, reliability, and cost reduction. The foundations had been built for the development of a commercial mobile communications market in the United States.

1.2.2 The Initial Commercial Phase (1946 to 1968)

The end of the Second World War saw the expansion of mobile telephone services to the commercial arena. Demand was strong, and the beginnings of chronic spectrum congestion were soon apparent. Technological improvements were oriented toward two principal goals: reduction of transmission bandwidth by channel splitting and introduction of automatic "trunking" or multiplexing systems.

In 1949 the FCC officially recognized mobile radio as a new class of service. The number of mobile users exploded from a few thousand in 1940 to 86,000 by 1948, about 700,000 by 1958, and 1.4 million by 1963.

True mobile telephone services—interconnection of mobile users to the public telephone network to allow calls from fixed stations to mobile users—were introduced in 1946, when the FCC granted a license to the American Telephone and Telegraph company (AT & T) to operate in St. Louis. This system used three channels at 150 MHz. These channels were based on FM and utilized a wide area architecture. A single powerful transmitter provided coverage to an area up to 50 miles or more from the base station. The first systems used operators to manually patch radio calls to the land telephone network. The first fully automatic mobile telephone system was put into operation in 1948 in Richmond, Indiana.

As the demand for mobile services grew, it stayed ahead of available capacity in many large urban markets. Loading of 50, 100, or more subscribers per channel was common. Blocking probabilities, that is, probabilities that indicate unsuccessful attempts to obtain a connection or find an available radio channel, rose to as high as 65% or more. The usefulness of mobile communications services diminished as users found it more and more difficult to find an available channel in which to initiate a call. It was obvious that the handful of channels available would not be enough for mobile communications to develop further.

The original FM mobile telephone channels required 120 kHz of RF bandwidth to transmit 3-kHz voiceband signals. By 1950 the FCC decided to split the original channels into 60 kHz channels. However, the FM receivers at that time could not handle this narrow bandwidth. At first, therefore, only every other channel or alternate channels were allocated to a given service area.

The FCC authorized 12 new mobile telephone channels in the ultrahigh frequency (UHF) band (around 450 MHz) in 1956. A bandwidth of 50 kHz was specified for these channels. By the early 1960s FM receiver technology had advanced, and the channel bandwidth was reduced again to 30 kHz. It was also possible to use adjacent channels in the same service area. The spectral efficiency of analog FM systems effectively quadrupled between the end of the Second World War and the mid-1960s.

Other important technological developments after World War II were the invention and application of automatic *trunking,* or multiplexing (grouping of) radio systems. The ability of the user to choose an available channel from a group of channels in service caused a significant increase in spectral efficiency and system capacity.

1.2.3 Cellular, Wireless, Mobile, and Personal Communications Systems (1947 to 2010)

The cellular concept began to appear in Bell system proposals during the late 1940s. This idea introduced a new model for mobile radio. Instead of the previously used "broadcast model" of a high-power transmitter, placed at a high elevation, transmitting the signal to a large area, the new model called for many lower-power transmitters, each specifically designed to serve only a small area called a *cell* (Subasinghe-Dias, 1992).

For example, a large city like New York with a single, powerful mobile transmitter would be divided into a large number of small cells, each equipped with a low-power transmitter. The same frequencies (channels) could be reused in different cells with sufficient distance, where the effects of interference between users of the same channel were negligible.

The concept of *frequency reuse in a cellular system* is illustrated in Figure 1.1. In each cell, illustrated by a hexagon, a group of radio "channel" frequencies is utilized. Cells designated with the same letter are assigned the same radio channels. For example,

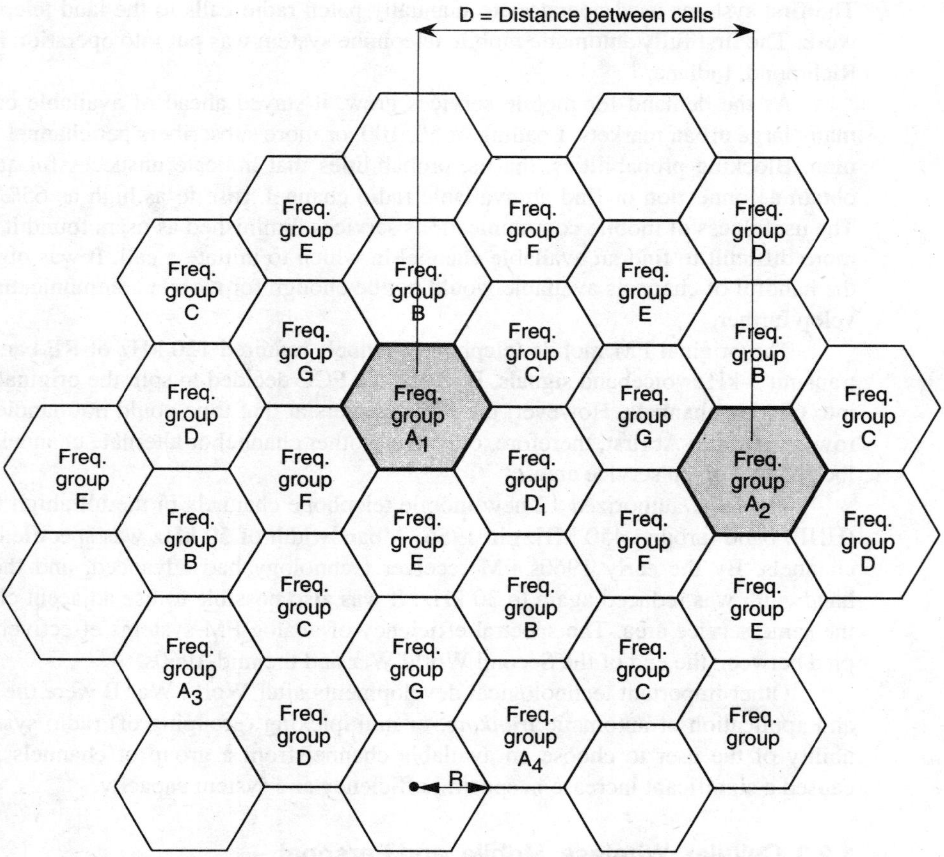

Figure 1.1 Frequency reuse in a seven-cell-pattern cellular system. In this configuration the same frequencies are reused in frequency groups A, B, C, D, E, F, and G. In geographical locations designated by the same letter, such as groups A_1 to A_4, the same group of frequencies is reused. Adjacent locations, such as locations A_1 and D_1, do not reuse the same frequencies. *D* is the distance between cells which use (reuse) the same group of frequencies; *R* is the radius of the cell. (From Lee, 1993).

frequency group A is assigned to all cells (hexagons) designated by *Freq. group A* in Figure 1.1. Thus the same frequencies are "reused" many times. The actual radio coverage depends on radio link parameters and propagation conditions. It is not hexagonal. However, for drafting convenience and to illustrate a complete geographical coverage, hexagonal representations are frequently used in current literature.

The real power of the *cellular idea* is that *interference is not related to the absolute distance between cells* but to the ratio of the distance between same-frequency cells (D) to the cell radius (R) (Figure 1.1). The cell radius is determined by the transmitter power and cell-site antenna height. It is under the control of the system engineer. Therefore it is the system engineer's responsibility to decide how many radio channels or "circuits" would be created through reuse.

Another attractive feature of the cellular concept is *cell splitting.* Larger cells can be easily reduced into smaller-radius cells over a period of time through cell splitting. When the traffic reaches the point in a particular cell such that the existing allocation of channels in that cell could no longer support a good grade of service, that cell would be subdivided into a number of smaller cells—with even lower transmitter power—fitting within the area of the former cell. The reuse pattern of channels could be repeated on a new, smaller scale, illustrated by the smaller hexagons in Figure 1.2.

Another fundamental cellular idea led to the possibility of *hand-off control.* In a

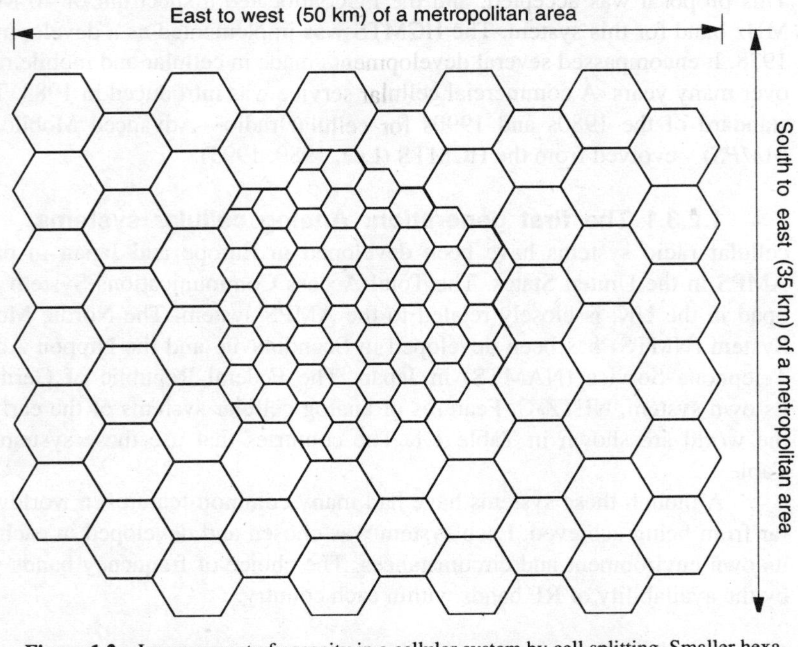

Figure 1.2 Improvement of capacity in a cellular system by cell splitting. Smaller hexagons illustrate reduced-size cell radius and cell coverage area architectures. With smaller cells the same frequencies are more often reused, and the overall capacity of the illustrated metropolitan area is increased.

cellular system, not all mobile calls may be completed within the boundaries of a single, relatively small cell. To deal with this, the cellular system is equipped with its own system-level switching and control capability. Through continuous monitoring of signal strength or of other digital parameters received from individual cell sites, the cellular system can sense when a mobile unit with a call in progress passes from one cell to another and can switch the call to the new cell without interruption.

Essential principles of the cellular architecture include the following:

- Low-power transmitters and small coverage zones
- Frequency reuse
- Cell splitting to increase capacity
- Hand-off and central control

Hence cellular radio represents a very different approach to structuring a radio-telephone network, as compared with the first-generation, high-power, large-coverage mobile radio systems applications. Cellular (digital as well as analog) radio is not so much a new technology as it is a new idea for organizing old technology.

In December 1971 the Bell system submitted a proposal for a new analog cellular FM radio system to the FCC—the High-Capacity Mobile Telephone System (HCMTS). This proposal was accepted, and the FCC allocated a spectrum of 40 MHz in the 850-MHz band for this system. The HCMTS was implemented as a developmental system in 1978. It encompassed several developments made in cellular and mobile radio technology over many years. A commercial cellular service was introduced in 1983. The U.S. analog standard of the 1980s and 1990s for cellular radio—Advanced Mobile Phone Service (*AMPS*)—evolved from the HCMTS (Lee, 1989, 1993).

1.2.3.1 The first generation: Analog cellular systems. Several analog cellular radio systems have been developed in Europe and Japan in parallel with the AMPS in the United States. The Total Access Communications System (TACS), developed in the UK, is closely related to the AMPS system. The Nordic Mobile Telephone System (NMTS) has been developed in Scandinavia, and the Nippon Advanced Mobile Telephone Service (NAMTS) in Japan. The Federal Republic of Germany developed its own system, NETZ-C. Features of analog cellular systems of the early 1990s around the world are shown in Table 1.1. The countries that use these systems are shown in Table 1.2.

Although these systems have had many common features, a worldwide standard is far from being achieved. Each system was chosen and developed in each country to suit its own environment and circumstances. The choice of frequency bands was determined by the availability of RF bands within each country.

1.2.3.2 The second generation: Digital cellular systems. Although the cellular concept promised virtually unlimited capacity through cell splitting, the industry encountered practical limits as the popularity of cellular radio escalated in the 1990s.

Table 1.1 Characteristics of several major analog, first-generation cellular systems. ETACS (extended TACS) is an extension to TACS that includes a larger bandwidth. *m*, mobile unit; *b*, base station (or access point). The AMPS system uses analog FM modulation.

Name of system	Began operations (year)	Channel width (kHz)	Frequency (MHz)	Number of channels	Characteristics
NAMTS	1978	25	870–885 b-m	600	Later increased to 1000 channels
NMT-450	1981	25	453–457.5 m-b 463–467.5 b-m	180	Low channel capacity, good radio coverage, suitable for rural areas
AMPS	1983	30	825–845 m-b 870–890 b-m	666	City based; higher capacity than NMT, but smaller cells
C-450/ NETZ-C	1985		451.3–455.74 m-b 461.3–465.74 b-m		
TACS plus ETACS	1985	25	890–915 m-b 935–960 b-m 872–888 m-b 917–933 b-m	1000 plus 640	50% greater capacity than AMPS, but smaller cells
NMT-900	1986	12.5	890–915 m-b 935–960 b-m	1999	Designed for cities, caters to hand held portables

From Subasinghe-Dias, 1992.

Table 1.2 First-generation analog cellular system types used in 1992 in various countries.

Name of system	Countries
AMPS	Australia, Canada, Hong Kong, New Zealand, Thailand
C-450/NETZ-C	Germany
NAMTS	Japan, Kuwait
NMT-450 and NMT-900	Austria, Belgium, China, Denmark, Finland, France, Iceland, Indonesia, Luxembourg, Malaysia, Netherlands, Norway, Oman, Saudi Arabia, Spain, Sweden, Switzerland, Thailand, Tunisia, Turkey
TACS	China, Republic of Ireland, Hong Kong, United Arab Emirates, Malta, United Kingdom

From Subasinghe-Dias, 1992.

With cells becoming progressively smaller, it has become increasingly difficult and expensive to place base stations at the best physical locations. This is particularly true of large, congested cities where capacity requirements are most pressing. Also, there appear to be fairly strict limits imposed by interference on just how small the cells of first-generation analog FM systems can be made. These practical limitations have *capped cellular capacity well below initial targets and below market demands.*

In addition to capacity bottlenecks, the utility of the first-generation cellular system in Europe has been diminished by the proliferation of incompatible standards, which make it impossible for a person to use the same cellular phone in different countries. These limitations motivated the development of second-generation cellular systems with the goals of achieving higher capacity and improved compatibility.

The choice of analog or digital technology is a fundamental and probably an irreversible decision that defines the next generation of cellular systems. The standardization committees for second-generation cellular systems worldwide have opted for digital systems. One of the most attractive aspects of digital transmission techniques is that they function better in high-interference environments and have a higher capacity potential than their analog counterparts. Digital signal processing (DSP) and digital communications techniques also lead to new applications, including mobile computer, facsimile, and other mobile information processing services. Better interference performance allows the next generations of cellular systems to surpass capacity limits of analog systems significantly. The advantages of digital implementations are also based on the fact that digital techniques are undergoing rapid and dramatic performance improvements and decrease in cost and power consumption. The *advantages of digital techniques* in cellular systems applications are summarized as follows:

- Advances in digital modulation techniques: By the use of new generations of digital modulation techniques, the spectral utilization can be improved beyond that achieved with analog techniques.
- Lower bit-rate digital voice coding: The recent improvements in low bit-rate voice coding, together with digital modulation techniques, enable the inclusion of several voice channels onto one carrier, therefore improving spectral utilization.
- Reduction of overhead for signaling: Analog systems are inefficient in this regard. Of the 333 channels originally allocated for AMPS, about 21 were required for call setup. This overhead reduces the usable capacity of a bandwidth-limited system. By using digital techniques for synchronization, control messages, and performance monitoring, overhead could be greatly reduced.
- Robust source and channel coding techniques: These techniques, which are available for digital voice or data transmission, enhance performance in the mobile environment.
- More robust to interference: Digital systems have an improved performance in high–cochannel-interference (CCI) and adjacent-channel interference (ACI) environments as compared with analog systems. This is one of the overwhelming reasons for adopting digital technology for second and third generations of cellular

systems. Digital systems are likely to operate under conditions of much higher cochannel interference, which will enable designers to bring the cell size and the reuse distance down, and even to reduce the reuse pattern. These key parameters and reductions increase the overall capacity of mobile-cellular networks.

- Flexible bandwidth: A predetermined fixed RF bandwidth could lead to inefficient use of the spectrum by not permitting users to adjust their bandwidth and timing to meet their actual communications needs. Digital systems, in principle, are capable of implementing flexible bandwidth architectures with relative ease.
- Inclusion of new services: Digital technology makes it possible to introduce new services that are not supported by AMPS or other analog systems, for example, authentication, data services, encryption of speech and data, and other integrated services digital network (ISDN) capabilities.
- Improved efficiency of access and hand-off control: For a fixed allocation of spectrum a large increase in capacity implies corresponding reductions in cell size. This means that signaling activity increases as more rapid hand-offs occur. The base stations are required to handle more access requests and registrations from the community of portables and mobiles in each cell. The functions may be carried out easily and swiftly by digital methods, whereas they may be cumbersome for analog techniques to handle.

Tables 1.1, 1.3, and 1.4 illustrate the incompatibility of analog and digital cellular systems that are used throughout the world. The first generation of analog systems include the narrowband AMPS (25-kHz spacing) and the Advanced Mobile Phone System (AMPS) of the 1980s (Arredondo, 1979). The second-generation digital cellular systems conform to at least three standards: one for Europe and international applications, *Group Special Mobile (GSM),* also known as the "Global Mobile System;" one for

Table 1.3 Second-generation digital frequency division multiple access (FDMA) and time division multiple access (TDMA) cellular system characteristics. *m,* Mobile unit; *b,* base station (or access point).

Name of system	Frequency (MHz)	Channel width (kHz)	Bit rate (kb/s)	Modulation scheme	Access scheme
IS-54 (North American Digital Cellular [NADC])	824–849 m-b 869–894 b-m	30	48.6	π/4-DQPSK	TDMA, 3/6 ch/carrier
Japanese Digital Cellular (JDC)	810–915 m-b 940–960 b-m	25	42	π/4-DQPSK	TDMA, 3/6 ch/carrier
GSM	890–915 m-b	200	270.8	GMSK	TDMA, 8/16 ch/carrier
CT-2		100	72	Binary FSK	FDMA
DECT		1728	1152	GMSK	TDMA, 12/24 ch/carrier

From Subasinghe-Dias, 1992.

Table 1.4 Low earth orbit (LEO) mobile satellite communications systems proposed to the International Telecommunications Union World Administrative Radio Conference 1992.

Characteristics of proposed systems	IRIDIUM (Motorola)	ODYSSEY (TRW)	ELLIPSAT (Ellipsat Corp.)	GLOBAL STAR (Loral and Qualcomm)	ARIES (CCI Constellation Comm. Inc.)
No. of satellites	77	12	6	24	48
Class	LEO	MEO	LEO	LEO	LEO
Lifetime (in years)	5	10	3	7.5	5
Orbit altitude (km)	755	10,600	2903/426	1390	1000
Orientation	Circular	Circular	Elliptical	Elliptical	Circular
Initial geographical coverage	Global	CONUS, Offshore United States, Europe, Asia-Pacific region	CONUS, Offshore United States	CONUS	CONUS, Offshore United States
Service markets	Cellular-like voice, positioning-RDSS, paging, messaging, data transfer	Cellular-like voice, positioning-RDSS, paging, messaging, data transfer	Cellular-like voice, positioning-RDSS, paging, messaging	Cellular-like voice, positioning-RDSS, paging, messaging	Cellular-like voice, positioning-RDSS, paging, messaging
Voice cost per min	$3.00	$0.60	$0.40–0.50	$0.30	Not Applicable
User terminal types	Handheld, vehicular, transportable	Handheld, vehicular, transportable	Vehicular, transportable	Handheld, vehicular, transportable	Vehicular, transportable
Estimated cost, wattage	$3500, 0.4	$250 to $350, 0.5	$1000 or $300, 6	$500 to $700, 1	$1500, 2
Uplink bands	L-band (1616.5–1626.5 MHz)	L-band	L-band	L-band	L-band
Downlink bands	L-band	S-band (2483.5–2500 MHz)	S-band	L-band with C-band (5199.5–5216 and 6525–6541 MHz) feeder links; L-band S-band; L-band, L-band with C-band and some S-band feeder links	S-band
CDMA	CDMA	CDMA	CDMA	CDMA	CDMA
Launch vehicle class	TBD	Atlas 2	Delta or Pegasus	Delta or Ariane	Delta or Atlas
Projected operational	1997	Mid-1996	Late 1993, first phase	Mid-1997	Early 1996

*C.M. Rush, "How WARC '92 will affect mobile services," *IEEE Communications Magazine,* (©1992 IEEE)

North America, *IS-54;* and a third for Japan, *Japanese Digital Cellular (JDC).* Second-generation cordless telephone standards include *Cordless Telephone-2 (CT-2)* and *Digital European Cordless Telephone (DECT).* A summary of characteristics of these second-generation digital systems is presented in Table 1.3. The numerous abbreviations, concepts, and techniques listed in this table, as well as recent developments, are explained in later chapters of this book.

While the second generation European and Japanese cellular standards have been designed for new cellular systems operating in dedicated new frequency bands and partially overlapped old bands, the North American standard specifies dual mode operation. It incorporates the first-generation standard AMPS and adds a digital voice transmission capability to new subscriber equipment. Thus IS-54, the North American Digital Cellular (NADC) standard, is an enhancement to, rather than a replacement for, present cellular technology.

The GSM system has been operational in Europe since the early 1990s. The NADC system has also carried traffic since 1992. Second-generation wireless information networks conforming to the CT-2 standard are presently in operation in the UK. Frequency allocations for the DECT standard are scheduled to be in place during the early 1990s. Meanwhile, at least one business cordless system with a transmission technique similar to that of the DECT standard has appeared in the market.

1.2.3.3 The third generation and subsequent generations of cellular, wireless, and personal mobile communication systems (1995 to 2010).

Third-generation cellular systems use advanced time division multiple access (TDMA), code division multiple access (CDMA), and collision sense multiple access (CSMA) spread-spectrum and narrow-band digital frequency division multiple access (FDMA) system architectures (Donaldson, 1994; Schilling, 1994; Viterbi, 1994). Third and subsequent generations of personal communications services are described in later chapters, particularly in Chapter 9.

1.2.4 Noncellular Mobile Communications Services

In addition to the analog and the emerging digital cellular communications systems, numerous other mobile communications services are in operation today. Their users include, among others, small taxi companies, utility companies, fire, police, medical, and emergency personnel, and national operators of large-vehicle fleets based on land and sea.

1.2.5 Paging

Paging is the simplest communication concept of all the major organized mobile radio services. It is a limited form of mobile radio in that two-way communication is not available. A paging system notifies the receiving party with an alarm, a defined voice, or an alphanumeric message. This signals that the person is required to report by telephone or other means to a known location. Simple instructions are occasionally conveyed.

Paging systems may be classified into two categories: private (local) and public (wide area) systems. Private systems, for example, one serving a hospital, carry a light data load and use one or a few low-power transmitters. Message input is via a manual operator or a private branch exchange (PBX), and transmission takes place immediately. On the other hand, private wide area paging systems could also carry a high data load, with messages originating from the public switched telephone system or a data network. The messages are queued and then transmitted in batches. A large number of medium- or high-power transmitters may also be used for wide area coverage.

The first paging systems were installed in a hospital in London in 1956. The first wide area systems were developed in the United States and Canada in the early 1960s. In Europe, wide area paging systems were introduced in Holland, Belgium, and Switzerland between 1964 and 1965.

The earliest paging systems used audio frequency loops that were placed around the buildings. Later, the system was changed to use a 35-kHz carrier modulated by audio tones. As the demand increased for wide area coverage, the carrier frequency changed from 35 kHz to radio frequencies in the 80- to 1000-MHz region.

British Telecom is probably the largest national operator in Europe, with more than 400,000 pagers in service. By 1988 there were well over 2 million wide area pager users in the United States and more than 1.5 million in Japan. During the early 1990s it was estimated that there were more than 9 million pagers in the world.

Paging may be combined with or overlayed on cellular or other mobile communications systems. A user might be paged for incoming telephone calls and could return the call later at the user's convenience. Further, the pager may be combined into a portable receiver. A combined service may also be used to contact drivers who are distant from their vehicles.

1.2.6 Private Mobile Radio

Private mobile radio (PMR) systems operate in parts of the very high frequency (VHF) and ultrahigh frequency (UHF) bands with transmitter effective radiated power (ERP) ranging from 5 to 25 watts depending on the operating area. Both AM and FM are used, although only FM is used in the UHF band. In a typical PMR system a fixed base station communicates with a number of mobile units. If the operation area is small, contrary to cellular systems, direct contact between mobile units is common. A number of base stations are used to cover a wide area.

Wide area coverage is not achieved by a cellular frequency reuse scheme but by the use of all available channels by all base stations. Synchronous base station operation (all base stations using exactly the same frequencies) is possible but requires specialized, expensive equipment. Also, stationary constructive and destructive interference patterns are created in areas of overlapping coverage, so a vehicle parked in such an area may experience a complete loss of reception. Hence, quasi-synchronous operation is often used among the multiple base stations, that is, the transmitters at each site are offset in frequency by 0.5 to 40 kHz. Although a beat note is heard in overlapping areas, it is well below the mobile audio response. Constructive and destructive interference patterns are also not stationary but move around the overlapping coverage areas, and stationary vehicles experience only a fluctuation of the received signal level.

1.2.7 Satellite Mobile Systems

Mobile satellite communications are particularly significant to long-distance travelers over parts of the world that cannot be covered by conventional land-based communications systems. For aircraft and ships, mobile satellite links greatly improve air traffic control, navigation, and rescue requirements for transoceanic crossings that were served by unreliable high-frequency (HF) communications.

Experiments in mobile satellite communications were conducted in the 1960s and the early 1970s, but not until 1979 was the International Maritime Satellite Organization (INMARSAT) formed to provide the first mobile satellite service. Technical feasibility of mobile satellite communications for aeronautical systems was proved during the early 1970s using the National Aeronautics and Space Administration (NASA) ATS-6 satellite. In 1983 the International Civil Aviation Organization (ICAO) set up a committee to study potential air navigation and communications systems. By the early 1990s standards for land mobile satellite communications were far less developed than were those for either aeronautical or maritime systems (Subasinghe-Dias, 1992).

Services in aeronautical mobile satellite communications include data services for the aircraft crew, cockpit voice communications, and passenger telephony. INMARSAT is a leader in the development of a worldwide aeronautical satellite communications system.

The INMARSAT maritime communications system, *Standard-A,* provides telephone and telex services. Standard-A is primarily an analog FM system, although a 56-kb/s data service is also available. The size and the cost of Standard A terminal equipment is large, and the cost is high, so it is installed only on large ships. A low-rate data service that provides telex and broadcast facilities, known as Standard-C, will be introduced in the future; its smaller size and reduced cost enable it to be installed on smaller ships. A fully digital system, Standard-B, was developed during the early 1990s to allow for additional services and connection into the ISDN.

Geostar's Radio Determination Satellite System (RDSS) began initial operations in 1988 and was the first domestic satellite system to provide regular service to mobile users within the United States. This system integrates radio navigation, radio location, and messaging within a single satellite system. Direct-sequence spread-spectrum binary phase shift keying (BPSK) signals over an RF bandwidth of 16 MHz are transmitted via this system.

The OmniTracs system operated by Qualcomm, Inc., a two-way mobile satellite communications and vehicle position reporting system in the United States and Europe, began operations in 1989. Direct-sequence spread-spectrum techniques, which are described in Chapter 6, are used in this system. The signal occupies a 1-MHz bandwidth. The Australian MOBILESAT system provides circuit-switched voice and data services and packet-switched data services for land, aeronautical, and maritime users. The system supports digital voice modulation at 4.8 kb/s in 5-kHz channels.

Telesat Mobile, Inc. (TMI) and the American Mobile Satellite Corporation (AMSC) are authorized to provide mobile satellite services in Canada and the United States. Operational systems using trellis-coded 16 quadrature amplitude modulation (16-QAM) QAM, also for 4.8 kb/s voice modulation in 5 kHz channels, are expected by 1995.

1.3 INTERNATIONAL MOBILE SATELLITE, LOW EARTH ORBIT, AND MEDIUM ALTITUDE ORBIT SATELLITE FREQUENCY BANDS

During the 1992 World Administrative Radio Conference (WARC'92), under the auspices of the International Telecommunications Union (ITU), it was decided to allocate additional spectrum to services that support mobile and mobile-satellite applications (Rush, 1992). Many of the decisions of WARC'92 will have far-reaching effects on the manner in which future mobile telecommunication services will be provided to the United States and throughout the world.

A key element of the U.S. proposals to WARC'92 was to obtain additional spectrum allocations for a variety of mobile satellite services. These services depend on technologies such as satellite manufacturing and launch, semiconductor design, and computer software application. Along with the flexibility that the United States enjoys with its current terrestrial mobile service allocations, these mobile satellite service (MSS) allocations will provide the framework required for the efficient introduction of new mobile service (MS) and MSS (Rush 1992).

WARC'92 resulted in a number of modifications to the tables of frequency allocations that form a major part of the Radio Regulations. These tables are used to govern the manner in which assignments and licenses for radio services are granted worldwide.

The WARC'92 decisions are described according to the types of telecommunications services considered, including MSS and MS. Proposed low earth orbit (LEO) satellite mobile communications systems for bands above 1 GHz are given in Table 1.4. In Table 1.5 a comparison matrix and WARC'92 decisions are highlighted.

Mobile LEO satellite communications could offer a cost-efficient solution for cellular-like mobile voice and data users, as well as for emerging PCSs. For example, TRW's ODYSSEY system (Table 1.4) could have an initial coverage in Europe, Asia, and the Pacific region with handheld or vehicular mobile-user voice and data terminals in the estimated $250 to $350 cost range. This cost estimate is competitive with the cost of numerous conventional land-based digital, cellular, and mobile handheld terminals.

1.4 PERSONAL COMMUNICATION SYSTEMS (PCS) UNIVERSAL DIGITAL PCS

During the last decade of the twentieth century and the first decade of the twenty-first century we are poised to confront the final frontier of telecommunications: location-independent communications. The emerging concept of personal communications ser-

Table 1.5 Mobile satellite frequency band allocations by the International Telecommunications Union World Administrative Radio Conference 1992 committee. Partial list of available radio frequency bands.

US Proposal	WARC '92 Decision
1850–1900 MHz ↑↓ (primary) Mobile-satellite	1930–1970 MHz ↑ (region 2) Mobile-satellite primary Coordination under resolution COM 5/8
	1970–1980 MHz[2] ↑ (region 2) Mobile-satellite primary Coordination under resolution COM 5/8
	1980–2010 MHz[2] ↑ Mobile-satellite primary Coordination under resolution COM 5/8
2110–2130 MHz ↓ (primary) Mobile-satellite	2120–2160 MHz ↓ (region 2) Mobile-satellite secondary
2160–2180 MHz ↓ (primary) Mobile-satellite	2160–2170 MHz[2] ↓ (region 2) Mobile-satellite primary Coordination under resolution COM 5/8
	2170–2200 MHz[2] ↓ Mobile-satellite primary Coordination under resolution COM 5/8
2390–2430 MHz ↑ (primary) Mobile-satellite	Not agreed
2483.5–2500 MHz ↓ (primary)	2483.5–2500 MHz ↓ primary Coordination under resolution COM 5/8
2500–2535 MHz ↓ (primary) Region 1 mobile-satellite	2500–2520 MHz[2] ↓ Mobile-satellite primary Coordination under resolution COM 5/8
2655–2690 MHz ↑ (primary)	2670–2690 MHz[2] ↑ Mobile-satellite primary Coordination under resolution COM 5/8

From Rush, 1992.

vices (PCS) and personal communication networks (PCN) allows the users the freedom of communicating any type of information between any two points, regardless of where the users are physically: indoors, outdoors, in an automobile in a crowded city, in a rural area, in an airplane, at sea, at standstill, or when traveling hundreds of miles per hour on a high-speed train.

Through an international group of connectivity standards now in development, the various PCS networks in various countries would be linked into one global system (Rush, 1992). The global system development of the Future Public Land Mobile Telecommunications System (FPLMTS) is coordinated by the WARC, a standing committee of the ITU.

The actual implementation and operation of such a global system is planned for the twenty-first century. However, cellular and cordless telephone systems are a major step toward this goal. The scarcity of usable spectrum squeezes the development of PCSs in many ways. It is impossible to say how much spectrum will be required to provide global PCSs. The answer depends on the type of technology employed, the services offered, and the usage demands made on the system. A solution to the problem of spectrum scarcity is to find alternatives that use the current spectrum more efficiently.

Time division multiple access (TDMA) techniques combined with slow frequency hopping spread-spectrum (SFH-SS) and direct-sequence spread-spectrum–based multiple access techniques, such as code division multiple access (CDMA) are receiving a great deal of attention as promising technologies for future generations of mobile communications systems. The efficiency of these techniques is exemplified in the capacity of the analog AMPS standard cellular system in Los Angeles, which is about 500,000 customers and may theoretically be increased to between 5 and 10 million customers by the use of CDMA or advanced TDMA, without using any new spectrum. Digital multiple access methods, include the following, are also considered for use in several increased-capacity digital PCS applications:

- Time division duplexed TDMA (TDMA-TDD)
- Frequency division duplexed TDMA (TDMA-FDD)
- Slow frequency hopped TDMA (SFH-TDMA)
- Code division multiple access (CDMA)

As the wireline networks evolve toward ISDNs, the expanding range of services made possible by end-to-end digital connectivity would be available to cellular and PCS customers. New PCS customers would be able to use laptop computers, portable facsimile (FAX) machines, and other, similar data devices, including the telephone, as efficiently as today's wireline networks are being used.

During the 1990s several visions of personal communications were developed, such as those shown in Figures 1.3, 1.4, and 1.5. In a global sense a PCS should embrace the integration of many concepts, products, and systems into one interconnected, interworking network (Bellcore, 1990). Several different *tetherless,* or *cordless,* devices and wireline communications networks should be interconnected and optimized for their specific

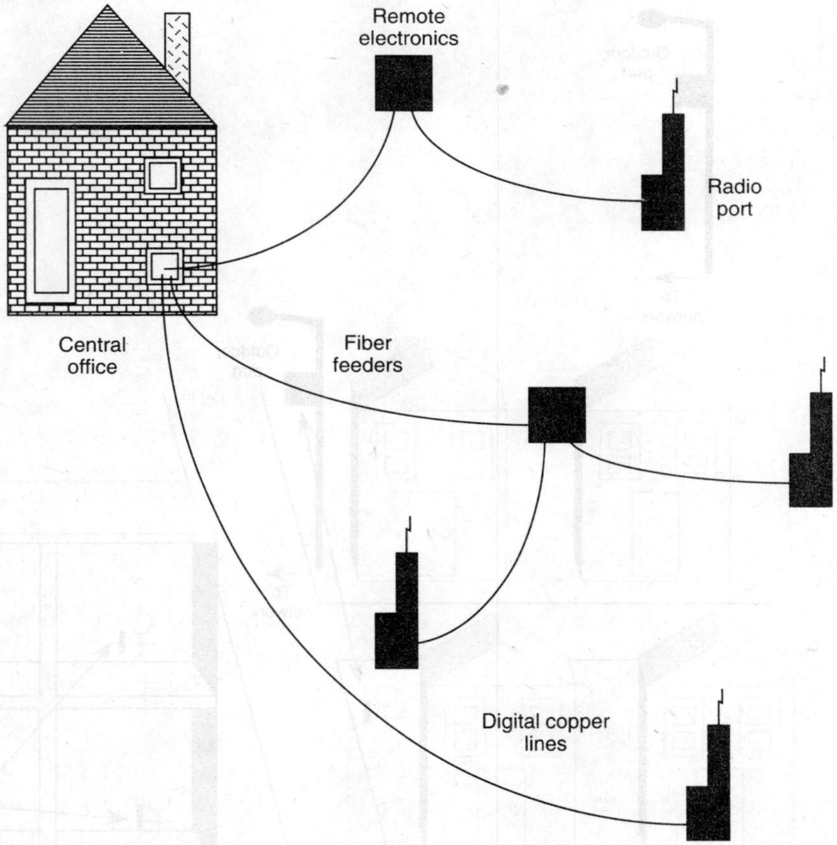

Figure 1.3 Fixed radio equipment that provides portable communications as part of the telephone network. Based on Bellcore's "Generic Framework Criteria." (From Bellcore, 1990.)

applications and environments. The terms *tetherless* and *cordless* imply that users are free of the wireline tether or cord. The term *wireless* refers to connection by radio. The PCS vision of Bellcore and several other corporations and engineers includes the capability for a person to initiate or receive calls (voice) and other information, including computer data and faxes, within areas that have reasonable population densities or along highways interconnecting such areas. Some large regions of the world are too sparsely populated to be economically served by terrestrial mobile cellular communications. Such areas may eventually be covered and interconnected by highly specialized mobile satellite systems well suited to this application, which should also be integrated into the overall interworking network. In Figure 1.5 the ODYSSEY global PCS-satellite-mobile constellation, the vision of TRW, is illustrated (Rush, 1990). The personal communications vision includes tetherless access to the interworking network within large buildings,

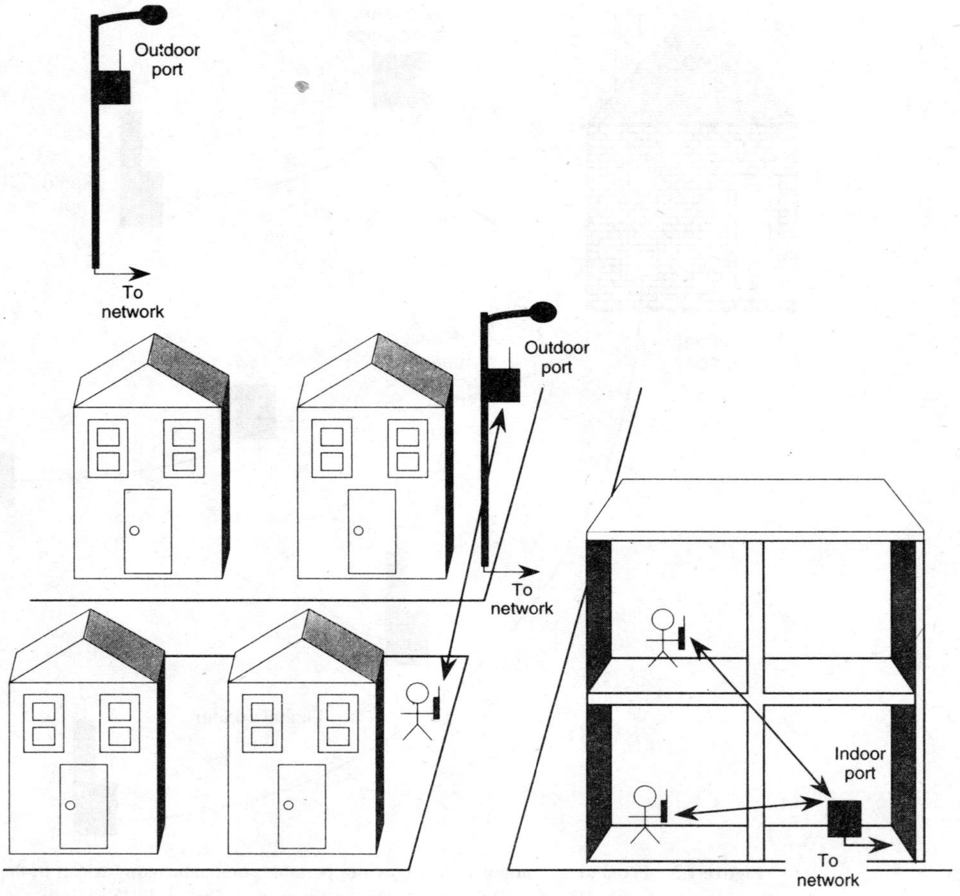

Figure 1.4 Wireless access using multiuser radio port, based on one of the Bellcore visions. (From Bellcore, 1990.)

shopping malls, airports, automobiles, trains, airplanes, and satellites and in residences. This concept of an integrated, interworking network does not imply that all subnetworks, systems, or elements of this overall network are owned or operated by the same business entity. However, the efficient interconnection of subnetworks will require standardization of interfaces and protocols.

Voluntary standards greatly enhance the overall market and customer acceptability of communications services and equipment. This technology is essential because it is used to provide PCSs, standards for channel allocation, critical power levels, spectrum access mode and other physical parameters, and signaling protocols at all levels (Bellcore, 1990).

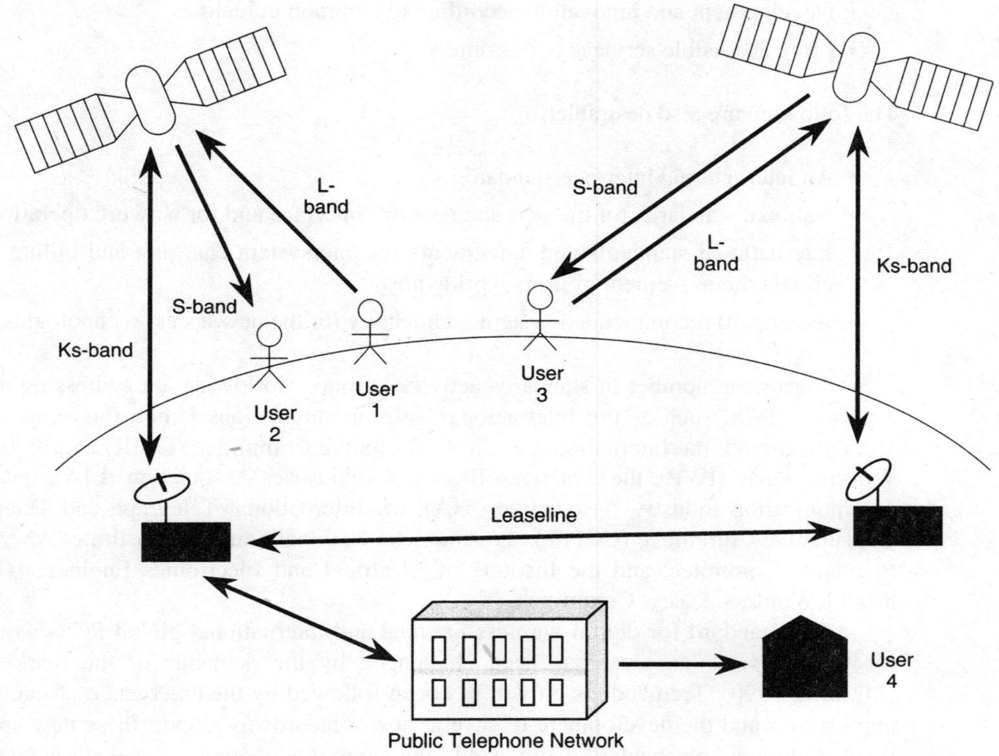

Figure 1.5 Global personal communications service (PCS) mobile communications vision by a constellation of medium altitude orbit (MEO) satellites of TRW known as ODYSSEY. The subscriber service charge is priced in line with terrestrial service charges. High-quality voice, data, radio location, and messaging services are provided. (From Rusch et al., 1992.)

1.5 STANDARDS: THE IMPORTANCE OF NATIONAL AND INTERNATIONAL STANDARDIZATION

In general, standards help to ensure or promote the following:

- Wide variety of products and services to customers
- Interoperability between products and services made by different vendors
- Easier introduction of PCS products into the national market
- Healthy competitiveness among vendors, which in turn may lead to reduced cost and improved product quality

- Development and innovation according to common guidelines
- More accessible services to customers

The following are also desirable:

- An international interface standard
- National standards for the port and network interface and for network operation
- International standards and agreements for intersystem charging and billing to facilitate the movement of users worldwide
- A standard recommended system architecture for the new access technologies

A growing number of standards activities groups worldwide are addressing unique aspects of PCS, such as the International Telecommunications Union (an entity of the United Nations), the International Radio Consultative Committee (CCIR) and its Interim Working Party (IWP), the American Electronic Industries Association (EIA), the Telecommunication Industry Association (TIA), the International Telegraph and Telephone Consultative Committee (CCITT), the American National Standards Institute (ANSI) T-1 Standards Commitee, and the Institute of Electrical and Electronics Engineers (IEEE) 802.11 Wireless Access Committee.

One standard for digital wireless national and international global PCSs would be ideal. However, this ideal has been challenged by the demands of the marketplace (Macario, 1990). Tremendous growth has been followed by the emergence of many new applications and the development of several new standards to support these new applications. Although one standard could lead to the greatest economies of scale, it would slow down the fast pace of new, innovative solutions and applications. The development of new standards takes several years, and if a standard is not adopted by all parties concerned, several de facto standards—noncompatible and compatible solutions—could be used by the same consumer.

1.6 MOBILE PERSONAL COMPUTERS (PC) AND PERSONAL COMMUNICATION SYSTEMS (PCS)

Mobile computers are small, generally handheld units that are used away from the typical office desktop. They represent the fastest-growing segment of the computer industry and, according to several projections, could make up half of all computer shipments by the late 1990s (Figure 1.6).

Other computers are becoming even smaller and more mobile than laptop computers. Notebooks, subnotebooks, palmtops, handhelds, and personal digital assistants that combine the functions of personal organizers, pagers, and cellular phones are all popular, modernized computers.

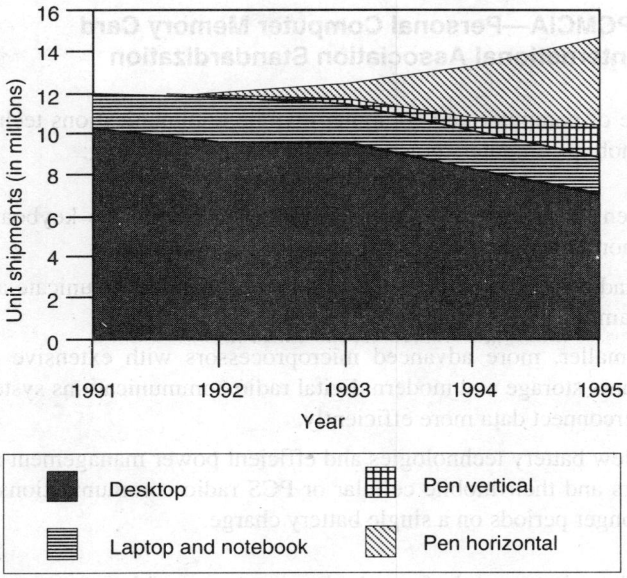

Figure 1.6 Growth rate of U.S. unit shipments of mobile computers by packaging type. Small, portable, frequently handheld units and palmtops represent the fastest-growing segment of the computer industry. According to several projections, these units could make up half of all computer shipments (PCMCIA, B. McGuire, 1995). Most of these computers require a mobile radio communications link for PCSs.

Analysts project tremendous market growth for these new personal computers (PCs). Laptop computers, although portable, cause great inconvenience and still function predominantly as desktop computers, whereas the new mobile computers are designed to be used conveniently by those who are mobile in the process of their work. Sales executives meeting with clients, engineers designing review meetings, researchers recording laboratory and field measurement data, doctors and nurses making hospital rounds, insurance claims adjusters reviewing damage sites, truck drivers and warehouse workers performing inventory control, and attorneys retrieving data during court hearings could all greatly benefit from the availability of the new mobile computers.

Mobile computers are frequently in operation while a person is standing or walking. The user can hold the computer in one hand, as a clipboard, notepad, or cellular phone would be held, and operate it with the other hand. This is not possible with laptops. To be practical and to meet the needs of the workers, mobile computers must be smaller, lighter, more rugged, and simpler. Frequently, users will need equally portable and flexible access to remote databases and host computers via wireless networks. These mobile radio (wireless) networks form parts of PCSs are connected to national and international public switched telephone networks (PSTNs).

1.6.1 PCMCIA—Personal Computer Memory Card International Association Standardization

A range of computer and computer–mobile communications technologies is available to make mobile computers practical, including the following:

- Pen computing and voice recognition can replace keyboards, making computers more practical and functional.
- Radio-based communications allow users to communicate across a room, building, campus, city, country, or the world.
- Smaller, more advanced microprocessors with extensive compact memories for mass storage and modern digital radio communications systems can process and interconnect data more efficiently.
- New battery technologies and efficient power management software allow computers and their mobile cellular or PCS radio communications systems to operate for longer periods on a single battery charge.

The primary goal of standardization is to enable system and card manufacturers to create products that can be operated by the end users who lack knowledge of the underlying technology. An additional significant goal of emerging standards is to enable a variety of computer types and noncomputer consumer products, including radio communications, electronic book players, and digital cameras, to exchange PC cards freely.

To ensure efficient standardization of these objectives and of system, product, and technology requirements, industry participants formed the Personal Computer Memory Card International Association (PCMCIA) in 1989. The association's goals are to establish and maintain a worldwide standard for PC cards.

1.7 U.S. AND WORLD CELLULAR MARKETS

The U.S. cellular market showed impressive gains during the early 1990s, despite widely held expectations that the economic recession in principal end-user industries (such as real estate, sales, and construction) would slow the growth. Even as the cellular industry continued to pursue its goal of a fully covered, interconnected U.S. network, pressures grew to replace analog cellular systems with new digital technology to alleviate capacity shortages and permit future growth. The analog-to-digital conversion within the same assigned spectrum is one of the most significant challenges this industry has faced (Golding, 1992; Goodman, 1991).

According to the Cellular Telecommunications Industry Association (CTIA), the number of U.S. subscribers reached 6.4 million as of mid-1991. With a growth rate amounting to more than 180,000 new subscribers per month (up nearly 30% from 1990), the number of subscribers rose to about 7.4 million by the end of 1991, an annual in-

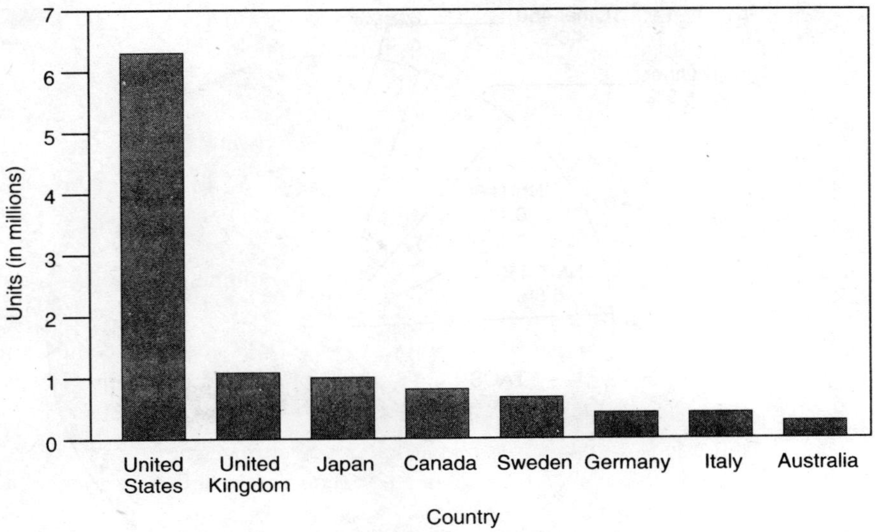

Figure 1.7 Leading world cellular markets. Number of subscribers during 1992, in millions of units. (Based on Gossack, 1992.)

crease of 40%. Cumulative capital investment increased by more than 30% in 1991, surpassing $8 billion. This sudden rise was due to the costs of expansion in metropolitan areas and new system construction in rural markets.

In the United States, two licensed carriers have been operating in all 305 metropolitan areas, serving more than 75% of the U.S. population. In addition, more than half of the rural service areas (RSAs) now have service. The average cost of local cellular service declined by 8% in 1991 to an average of about $75 per month, and the average cellular call lasted nearly 2.4 minutes (Gossack, 1992).

Leading world cellular markets, indicated by the number of subscribers (in millions) during 1991, and the system types are shown in Figures 1.7 and 1.8. Handheld portable cellular telephones have gained in popularity and compose a greater share of the U.S. cellular market, exceeding 50% of sales during the 1990s.

The phenomenal and unparalleled historical growth of the world cellular market is illustrated in Figure 1.9 (Gossack, 1992). The estimated number of cellular subscribers in the 20 largest international cellular markets, which is presented in Table 1.6 (Malarkey Taylor Associates, 1993), indicates that during 1993 the total number of subscribers increased to more than 24 million. Based on a market forecast published in *Time Magazine* (McCarroll, 1993), the largest U.S. cellular operators have a potential customer base that exceeds 100 million subscribers (Figure 1.10).

Market studies published by *Microwaves & RF* (Schneiderman, 1994) indicate that in 1993, 117 countries had cellular service, while in 1995, 130 countries will have cellular service. The number of countries that offer cellular and other wireless services is

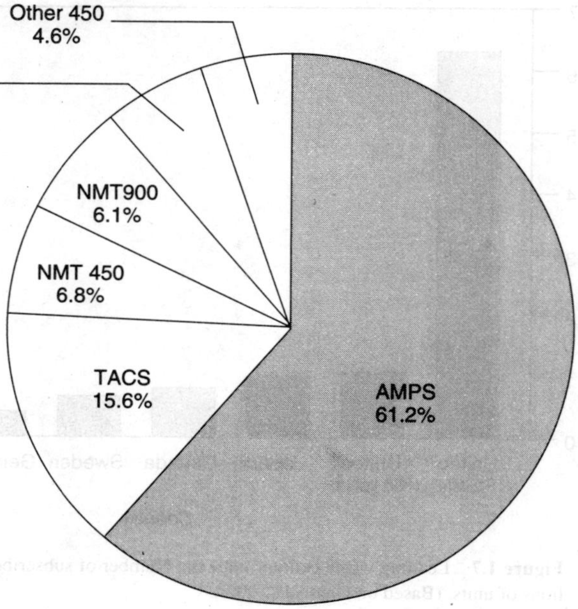

Figure 1.8 Distribution of world cellular markets by system type. (Based on Gossack, 1992.)

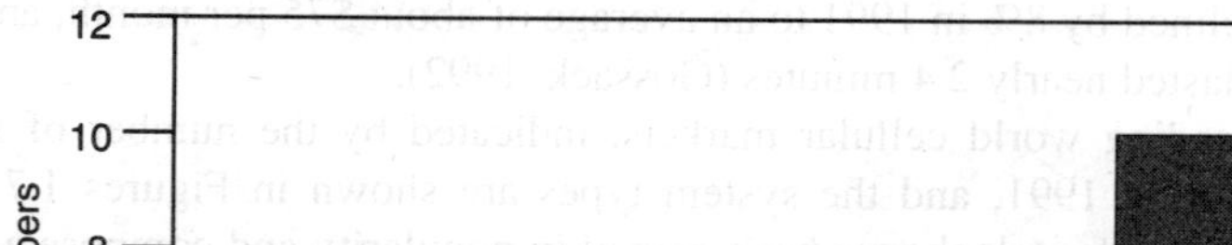

Figure 1.9 Growth of the world cellular market, from the U.S. Department of Commerce. (Based on Gossack, 1992.)

Table 1.6 The top 20 international cellular markets and estimated numbers of subscribers as of June 30, 1993.

Country	Number of subscribers	System(s)
United States	12,554,300	AMPS
Japan	2,264,500	J-TACS, N-TACS, NTT
United Kingdom	1,552,100	TACS, GSM
Germany	1,146,200	C-Netz, GSM
Canada	1,134,800	AMPS
Italy	878,200	RTMS, TACS-900, GSM
Sweden	725,500	NMT 450, NMT-900, GSM
Australia	638,700	AMPS
France	482,800	RC-2000, NMT-450, GSM
Mexico	414,800	AMPS
Taiwan	410,000	AMPS
Finland	385,300	NMT-450, NMT-900, GSM
South Korea	348,400	AMPS
Thailand	332,700	AMPS, NMT-450, NMT-900
Norway	311,200	NMT-450, NMT-900, GSM
Hong Kong	287,200	TACS, AMPS
Malaysia	239,000	NMT-450, TACS
Switzerland	237,800	NMT-900, GSM
Spain	228,400	NMT-450, TACS-900
Denmark	225,500	NMT-450, NMT-900, GSM
	Total: 24,797,000	

From Malarkey Taylor Associates, 1993.

rapidly increasing. During 1993 the United States had more than half of the world's cellular phones. The U.S. cellular and wireless markets are growing fast, but Europe, the Asia-Pacific region, and the rest of the world are not far behind. In Europe mobile communications is the fastest-growing area within the telecommunications sector. Between 1991 and 1994 Europe doubled its total number of analog and digital cellular subscribers to more than 8 million. During this period cellular business accounted for about 90% of the total European mobile communications market.

Bright forecasts for American PCSs and personal wireless businesses have also been predicted by other U.S. organizations. The Personal Communications Industry Association (PCIA) projects that by the year 2003 there could be nearly 31 million domestic PCS subscribers (Colmenares, 1994). Motorola, Inc., envisions more than 150 million domestic wireless users in the long run. American Personal Communications (APC) and California Microwave, Inc., estimate that PCSs will become an international industry worth $195 billion (in U.S. dollars) by the end of the decade.

A European Commission–sponsored market study predicts that ". . . the market po-

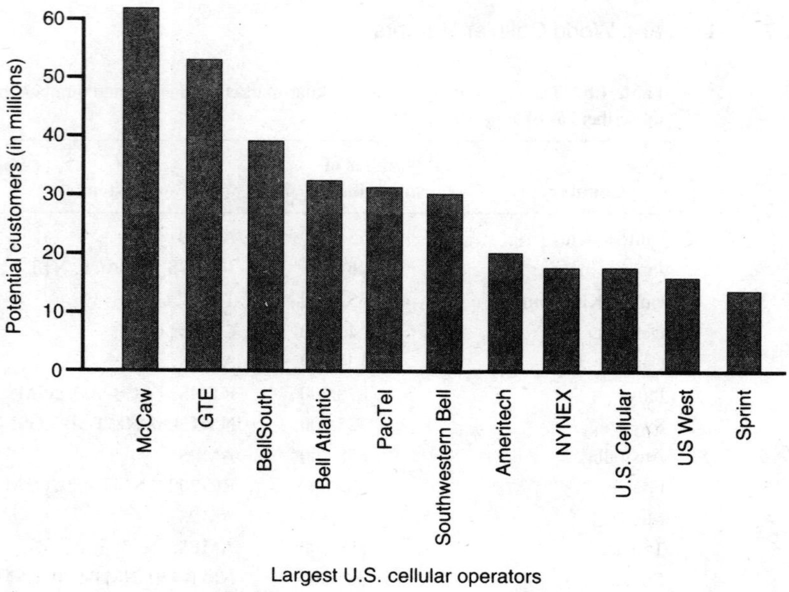

Figure 1.10 Largest U.S. cellular operators' potential customer bases. (From McCarroll, 1993.)

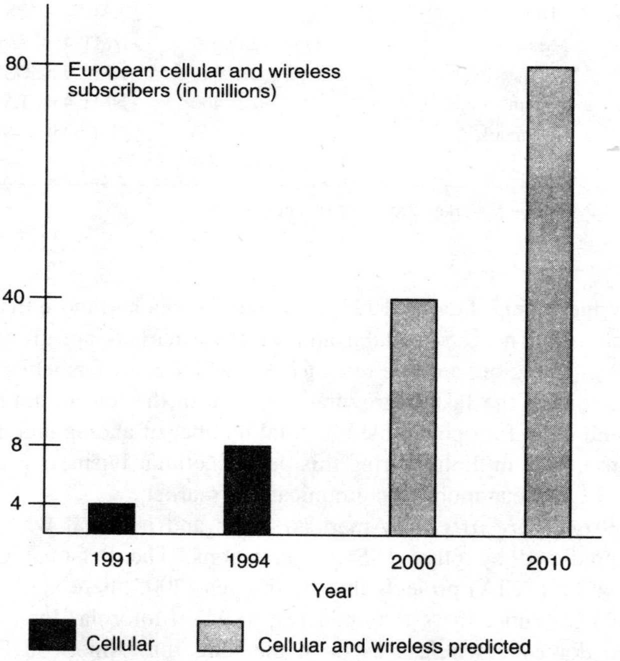

Figure 1.11 European Commission projections of number of wireless users for the European Union for the years 2000 and 2010. The 8 million users (1994) are cellular subscribers. (From Schneiderman, 1994.)

tential for PCS is huge" (Figure 1.11 [Schneiderman, 1994]). This study predicts nearly 40 million users of wireless communications by the year 2000. It is also predicted that with growing expansion into PCSs the number of European users could increase to about 80 million by 2010.

European Commission publications confirm that digital cellular technology, in particular, the GSM standard (a second-generation cellular system) based on TDMA architecture, has been adopted worldwide (Table 1.7). During 1994 there were 4 million TDMA digital GSM standard phones in use. Based on Frost and Sullivan studies

Table 1.7 Worldwide adoption of the Groupe Speciale Mobile (GSM) standardized time division multiple access (TDMA) technology. The GSM system specifications, a second-generation digital cellular standard, are based on the GMSK modulation format, described in later chapters of this book. For third- and subsequent-generation cellular and wireless standards, and also nonstandardized or special mobile, cellular, and wireless PCS applications, GMSK-compatible FQPSK systems have been licensed by Dr. Feher Associates-Digcom, Inc. El Macero, California. New generations of FQPSK-modulated radio systems are compatible with GMSK and have the potential to increase the system capacity by 200%. (See Chapters 4 and 9.) Feher's patented GMSK is described in Appendix 3.

Place of Adoption	Countries allocating one license	Countries allocating two licenses	Countries allocating more than two licenses
European Union	Luxembourg	Belgium, Denmark, France, Germany, Greece, Ireland, Italy, Netherlands, Portugal, Spain, United Kingdom	
Other European countries	Andorra, Austria, Croatia, Czech Republic, Estonia, Iceland, Latvia, Romania, Slovakia, Slovenia, Switzerland, Ukraine	Finland, Hungary, Norway	Sweden, Russia
Other countries	Bahrain, Brunei Darussalam, Cameroon, Cyprus, Egypt, Fiji, Iran, Israel, Kuwait, Lebanon, Morocco, Nigeria, Oman, Pakistan, Qatar, Saudi Arabia, Singapore, Sri Lanka, Syria, Taiwan, United Arab Emirates, Vietnam	China, Indonesia, Malaysia, New Zealand, Philippines, South Africa, Thailand, Turkey	Australia, Hong Kong, India
Total	35 licenses and countries	44 licenses in 22 countries	29 licenses in 5 countries

By permission of Penton Publishing (Schneiderman, 1994.)

(Schneiderman, 1994), the number of GSM-based digital TDMA cellular phones in use in Europe by 1998 is expected to exceed 8 million.

In later chapters, emerging standards for third- and subsequent-generation cellular and wireless systems and PCSs are described. Several of these systems are based on the GSM standardized Gaussian Minimum Shift Keying (GMSK) modulation technique. New generations of modulation and power-efficient Feher's Quadrature Phase Shift Keying (FQPSK) and other radio techniques, described in Chapters 4 and 9, are compatible with GMSK modulation and radio techniques. These GMSK-compatible wireless systems have a considerably simpler hardware requirement and have a 200% spectral efficiency advantage over the GMSK standardized systems. Technology transfer and licensing of the FQPSK systems for standard compatible and nonstandard special mobile wireless applications is coordinated by Digcom, Inc.–Dr. Feher Associates, 44685 Country Club Drive, El Macero, CA 95618. Quadrature modulated GMSK patented systems are described in Appendix 3.

CHAPTER 2

Speech Coding for Wireless Systems Applications

2.1 INTRODUCTION TO DIGITAL SIGNAL PROCESSING (DSP) TECHNIQUES IN WIRELESS TELEPHONE AND BROADCAST SYSTEMS

The implementation of sophisticated telephone grade, relatively narrow-band (300 Hz to 3.4 kHz) speech and fascimile (fax), wideband audio (10 Hz to 20 kHz), and video (direct current to 15 MHz) *coding algorithms* is increasingly cost-effective and economical in numerous wireless systems applications. Low-power, very large-scale integration (VLSI) led to the use of these coding algorithms in handheld transportable telephone sets and is paving the road to wireless digital broadcast applications. The purpose of most of these algorithms is to convert the analog source signal to a digital signal (A/D conversion), either to process it for data transmission or storage or to synthesize and reconstruct the noise- and interference-corrupted bandlimited or distorted signal with the fewest bits possible. The bit reduction (compression) is achieved by removing the redundancy of the A/D-converted signal. The compressed binary baseband signal is modulated, upconverted, and transmitted. At the receiver the radio signal is downconverted and demodulated into a digital baseband signal. This digital signal may contain errors, which are introduced by the wireless transmission system. The signal decoding algorithm combined with the digital-to-analog (D/A) subsystem reconstructs the analog source signal. Typical locations of digital signal processing (DSP) of A/D, D/A, and echo control subsystems are illustrated in Figure 2.1.1.

Frequently used, relatively simple conversion (coding and decoding) techniques are described in this chapter. These include pulse code modulation (PCM), differential pulse code modulation (DPCM), and delta modulation (DM). Basic concepts of advanced

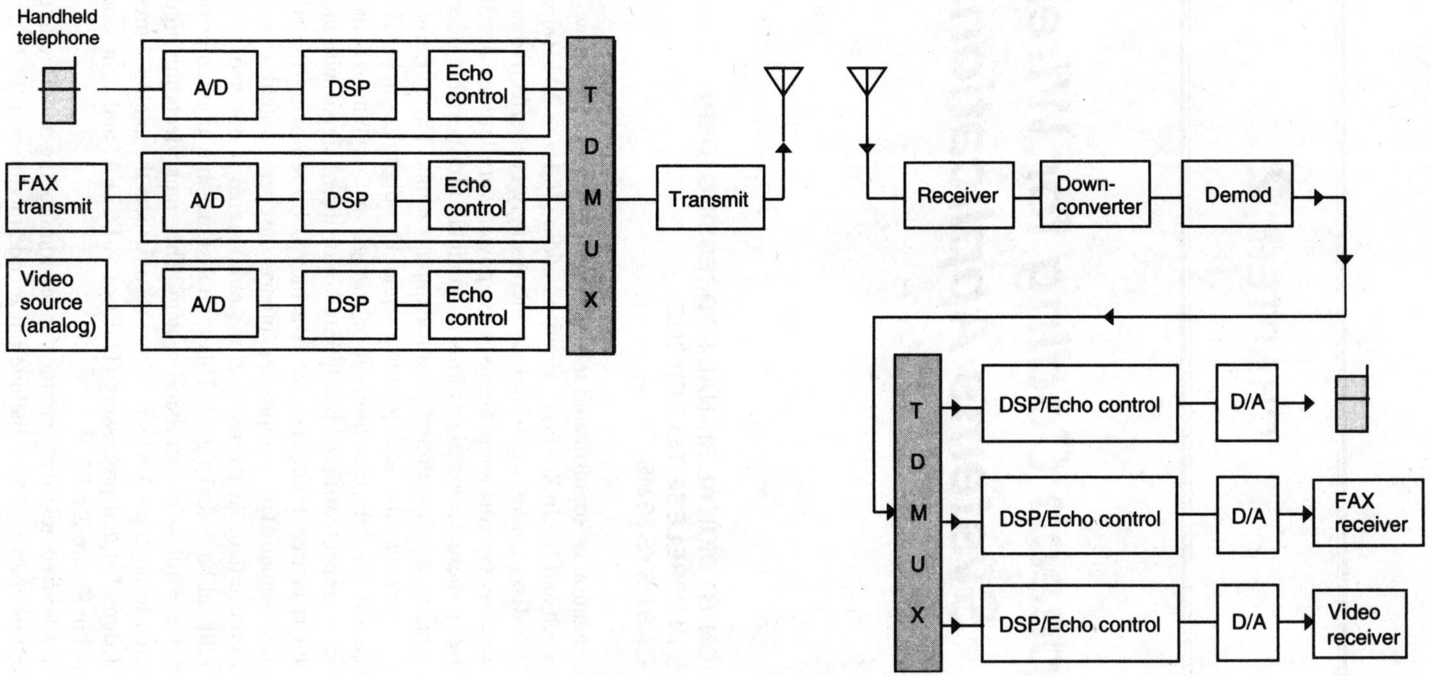

Figure 2.1.1 Digital signal processing (DSP) in an illustrative wireless network.

vocoders and of linear predictive codecs (LPCs) are also reviewed. A brief performance, bit-rate, and complexity comparison of the various DSP voice processing methods is presented. The importance of delay and combined echo and delay control in wired and wireless systems is also discussed. For an in-depth study of advanced DSP techniques, several outstanding reference books are recommended. (See Bibliography for additional references.) Illustrative U.S. and European wireless voice processing applications and standards are highlighted.

2.2 SPEECH CODING TECHNIQUES FOR AUDIO AND VOICE

The principles of frequently used digital signal processing and analog-to-digital conversion methods are described in the following section (Feher, 1983).

Basic analog-to-digital (A/D) and digital-to-analog (D/A) conversion methods used in communications systems include the following:

Delta modulation (DM)
Differential pulse code modulation (DPCM)
Pulse code modulation (PCM)

The analog-to-digital converter, located in the transmitter, is also known as the *encoder* or simply, *coder*. The digital-to-analog converter, located in the receiver, is known as the *decoder*. The word *codec* is derived from "coder/decoder."

In addition to the basic conversion methods previously listed, more involved codecs have been developed. Frequently used techniques and acronyms include the following:

ADM	Adaptive DM
ADPCM	Adaptive DPCM
APCM	Adaptive PCM
CDM	Continuous DM
DCDM	Digitally controlled DM
LDM	Linear (nonadaptive) DM
LPC	Linear predictive codec(s)
CELP	Code excited linear predictive coding
RELP	Residual excited vocoders
VQ	Vector quantization, subband coding, vocoder(s)

An in-depth study of the theoretical fundamentals, the detailed principles of operation, and the wireless and cellular applications of these advanced systems are described in such sources as Feher (1987), Sklar (1988), and Tuttlebee (1990). The following section highlights the principles of operation of basic codec methods.

2.2.1 Pulse Code Modulation

The principal functions performed by PCM encoders are illustrated in Figures 2.2.1 to 2.2.3. These include sampling, quantizing (linear and logarithmic compression), and encoding. The simplified *sampling theorem* is stated as follows.

Sample Theorem If the highest-frequency spectral component of a magnitude-time function $m(t)$ is f_m, then the instantaneous samples taken at a rate $f_s > 2f_m$ contain all the information of the original message.

Figure 2.2.1 illustrates a typical telephony application of the sampling theorem, where the voice or fascimile signal is bandlimited to $f_m = 3.4$ kHz and is sampled at a rate of $f_s = 8$k samples per second. The sampled output signal $m(t)s(t)$ has an infinite number of amplitude states. To encode this signal, the amplitude levels must be quantized.

For simplicity, only eight quantization levels are shown in Figure 2.2.2. The contin-

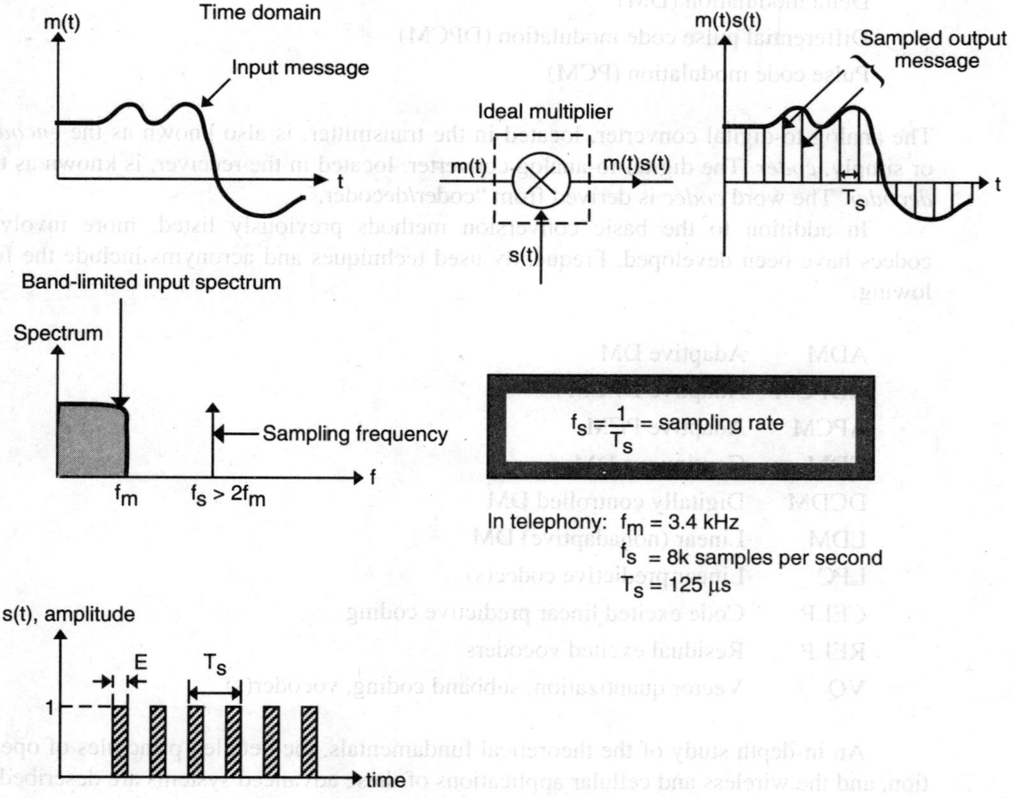

Figure 2.2.1 Instantaneous sampling of a bandlimited signal m(t).

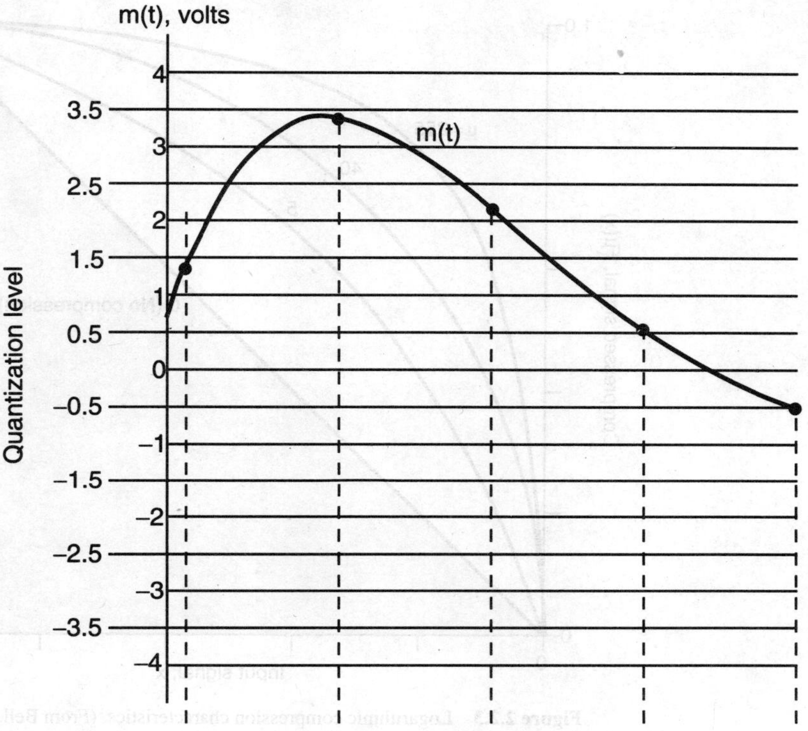

Sample value	1.3	3.6	2.3	0.7	−0.7
Nearest quantization level	1.5	3.5	2.5	0.5	−0.5
Code number	5	7	6	4	3
Binary representation	101	111	110	100	011

Figure 2.2.2 Quantization and binary encoding for PCM systems. A message signal is regularly sampled. Quantization levels are indicated. For each sample, the quantized value is given and its binary representation is indicated (From Taub and Schilling, 1986.)

uous signal *m(t)* has the following sample values: 1.3, 3.6, 2.3, 0.7, . . . , − 3.4 V. The quantized signal takes on the value of the nearest quantization level to the sampled value. The eight quantized levels are represented by a 3-bit *code* number. (Note: With 3 bits, $2^3 = 8$ distinct levels can be identified.) The amplitude difference between the sampled value and the quantized level is called the *quantization error*. This error is proportional to the step size, d, that is, the difference between consecutive quantization levels. With a higher number of quantization levels (smaller d), a lower quantization error is obtained. On experimentation it has been found that, to achieve an acceptable signal-to-noise ratio

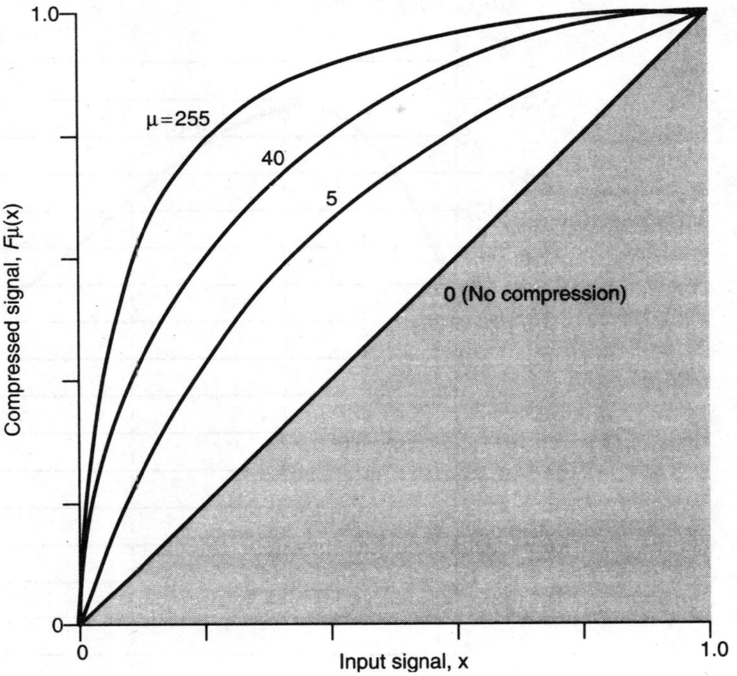

Figure 2.2.3 Logarithmic compression characteristics. (From Bell, 1982.)

of a telephone "toll-grade quality" voice, 2^8 or 256 quantization levels are necessary. (The term *toll-grade quality* is explained in Section 2.3.2.) This result requires 8 bits of information per quantized sample.

If the number of quantizer levels is large (>100), it may be assumed that the quantization error has a *uniform* probability density function given by

$$p(E) = \frac{1}{d}, \quad -\frac{d}{2} \le E < \frac{d}{2}. \tag{2.1}$$

This uniform error distribution assumption is true if the signal $m(t)$ does not overload the quantizer. For example, in a quantizer such as that shown in Figure 2.2.2, the quantizer output might saturate at level 5 for $|m(t)| > 5$. The quantization error during such *overload* is a linearly increasing function of $m(t)$. In the linear region of operation the mean-square value of the quantization error is

$$\int_{-d/2}^{d/2} E^2 p(E)dE = \int_{-d/2}^{d/2} E^2 \frac{1}{d} dE = \frac{d^2}{12}. \tag{2.2}$$

If the root-mean-square (rms) value of the input signal $m(t)$ is M_{rms}, then the *signal-to-quantization error* ratio is

$$S/N = \frac{M_{rms}^2}{d^2/12} = 12\frac{M_{rms}^2}{d^2}. \tag{2.3}$$

From this equation we conclude that the signal-to-quantization error ratio is dependent on the rms value of the input signal M_{rms}; that is, for larger input signals, a larger S/N is obtained. This is an undesirable effect in telephony systems, since some speakers have a considerably lower volume than others. It would be a nuisance to the listener to listen to a very low-volume signal corrupted by a relatively high quantization error (low S/N_q). To achieve the same signal-to-noise ratio for a small-amplitude signal as for a large-amplitude signal, a quantizer with a nonuniform step size is necessary. To achieve this nonuniform step-size quantization, given a uniform step-size quantizer such as that shown in Figure 2.2.2, it is essential to precede with a nonlinear input-output device known as a PCM *compressor/compandor,* or *companding system.* The compandor followed by the linear quantizer amplifies the low-volume signals more than the high-volume signals.

Compression characteristics used in North American and Japanese digital PCM networks are illustrated in Figure 2.2.3. The μ-law codecs are defined for a normalized coding range of ±1 by the equation

$$F_\mu(x) = \sin(x)\frac{ln(1+\mu\,|x|)}{ln(1+\mu)}, \qquad -1 \le x \le 1. \tag{2.4a}$$

Note that for small x, F_μ (x) approaches a linear function, whereas for large x it approaches a logarithmic function.

While the μ-law has found acceptance in the North American and Japanese digital networks, the standard compression law in Europe (CEPT) is the A-law, which is defined by

$$\begin{aligned} F_A(x) &= \sin(x)\frac{1+lnA\,|x|}{1+lnA} \qquad && \frac{1}{A} \le |x| \le 1 \\ F_A(x) &= \sin(x)\frac{A\,|x|}{1+lnA} && 0 \le |x| \le \frac{1}{A}. \end{aligned} \tag{2.4b}$$

Note that F_A(x) is truly logarithmic for $|x| > 1/A$ and truly linear for $|x| < 1/A$. The result is that the A-law gives somewhat flatter signal-to-distortion (S/D) performance than the μ-law over the range $1/A \le |x| \le 1$ at the expense of poorer S/D performance for low-level signals.

Both the μ- and A-laws satisfy the objective of maintaining relatively constant S/D performance over a wide dynamic range. If, however, the objective is to maximize the S/D ratio for the more probable speaker volumes, compression laws based on hyperbolic functions may be used. These laws give better S/D ratios for average speakers at the expense of poorer performance for the smaller population of weaker and louder speakers. However, the μ- and A-laws are the only laws in common use for digital transmission systems (Bell, 1982).

We may conclude that in telephony systems the speech, fascimile, or other modulated voice-band data signal is bandlimited to $f_m = 3.4$ kHz. To convert this analog signal into a binary PCM data stream, a sampling rate of $f_s = 8$k samples per second is used. Each sample is quantized into one of the 256 quantization levels. For this number of quantization levels, 8 information bits are required ($2^8 = 256$). Thus one voice channel being sampled at a rate of 8k samples per second and requiring 8 bits per sample will have a transmission rate of 64 kb/s.

Broadcast-quality *color television* signals have an analog baseband bandwidth of somewhat less than 5 MHz. For conventional PCM encoding of these video signals, a sampling rate of $f_s = 10$M samples per second and a 9-bit-per-sample coding scheme are utilized. Thus the resulting transmission rate is 90 Mb/s. Most television pictures have a large degree of correlation, which can be exploited to *reduce* the transmission rate. It is feasible to predict the color and brightness of any picture element (pel) based on values of adjacent pels that have already occurred. Digital broadcast-quality color television DSP techniques requiring only 10- to 45-Mb/s transmission rates, obtained by means of predictive techniques, are described in Feher 1987(a)]. For wireless video-teleconferencing, compressed video signals in the 20 kb/s-to-200 kb/s range are used (Ang et al, 1991).

2.2.2 DPCM—Differential Pulse Code Modulation

Differential pulse code modulation (DPCM) is a *predictive coding scheme* that exploits the correlation between neighboring samples of the input signal to reduce statistical redundancy and thus lower the transmission rate. Instead of quantizing and coding the sample value, as is done is PCM, is done in PCM, in DPCM *an estimate is made of the next sample value based on the previous samples.* This estimate is subtracted from the actual sample value. The difference of these signals is the prediction error, which is quantized, coded, and transmitted to the decoder. Basically this technique attempts to remove blatant redundancies from the signal before transmission. The decoder performs the inverse operation; it reconstructs the original signal from the quantized prediction errors.

The block diagram of a DPCM system is shown in Figure 2.2.4. Here $\{s_i\}$ is the sequence of input sample values, $\{\hat{s}_i\}$ is the prediction sequence, and

$$\{e_i\} = \{s_i - \hat{s}_i\} \tag{2.5}$$

is the prediction error sequence that is quantized, encoded, and transmitted. When the number of quantizing levels N is large ($N \geq 8$ is considered sufficiently large) and linear prediction is used, each $\{\hat{s}_i\}$ can be expressed as

$$\hat{s}_i = a_i s_{i-1} + a_i s_{i-2} + a_3 s_{i-3} + \ldots \tag{2.6}$$

where the a_i's are predictor coefficients.

If the quantizer or both the quantizer and predictor adapt themselves to match the signal to be encoded, considerable signal-to-noise improvement can be attained. The dynamic range of the encoder can be extended by adaptive quantization if a nearly optimum step size is generated over a wide variety of input signal conditions.

The two most frequently used quantizer adaptation methods include the syllabic or

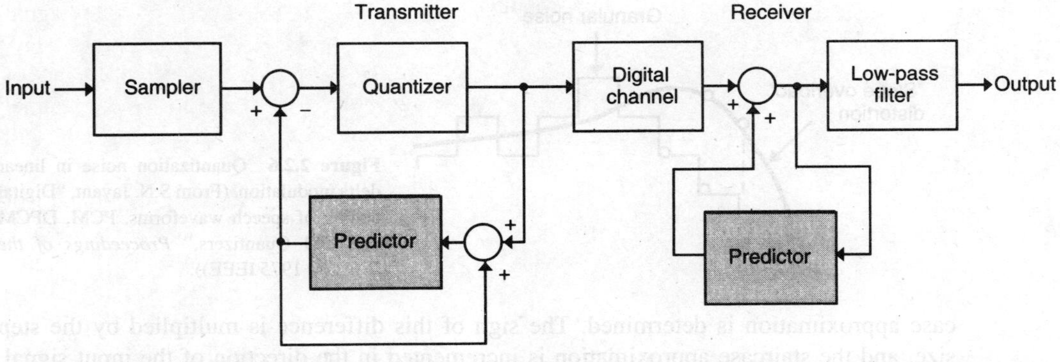

Figure 2.2.4 Differential PCM system (DPCM) block diagram. (From J.B. O'Neal, "Waveform encoding of voiceband data signals," *Proceedings of the IEEE* (© 1980 IEEE)).

slow-acting adaptation and the fast-acting or instantaneous companding, with only one sample memory.

2.2.3 Delta Modulation

The exploitation of signal correlations in DPCM suggests the further possibility of oversampling a signal to increase the adjacent sample correlations and thus to permit a simple quantizing strategy. Delta modulation (DM) is a 1-bit version of differential PCM. The DM coder approximates an input time function by a series of linear segments of constant slope. Such an analog-to-digital converter is therefore referred to as *linear delta modulator* (Figure 2.2.5).

At each sample time the difference between the input signal $x(t)$ and the latest stair-

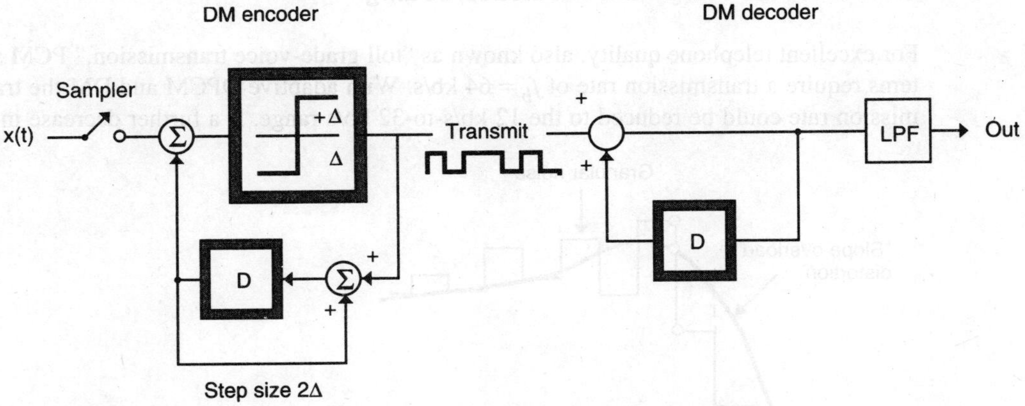

Figure 2.2.5 Linear delta modulator (DM). Step size = 2Δ. (From Feher, 1983.)

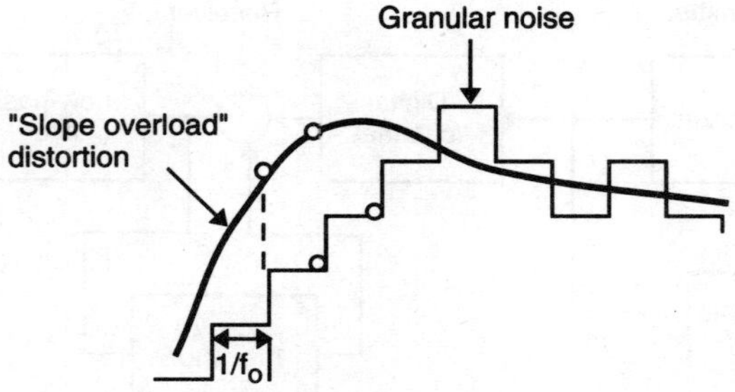

Figure 2.2.6 Quantization noise in linear delta modulation. (From S.N. Jayant, "Digital coding of speech waveforms. PCM, DPCM and DM Quantizers," *Proceedings of the IEEE* (© 1975 IEEE)).

case approximation is determined. The sign of this difference is multiplied by the step size, and the staircase approximation is incremented in the direction of the input signal. Therefore the staircase signal $y(t)$ tracks the input signal. The signs of each comparison between $x(t)$ and $y(t)$ are transmitted as pulses to the decoder, which reconstructs $y(t)$ and then low-pass filters $y(t)$ to obtain the output signal. The quantization noise is defined as

$$n(t) = x(t) - y(t) \tag{2.7}$$

The *slope overload* distortion region (Figures 2.2.6 and 2.2.7) occurs for large and fast signal transitions. It occurs because the maximum slope that can be produced by a linear delta modulator is $SS \cdot f_r$, where SS is the step size and f_r is the sampling rate. The *granular noise* is introduced because the staircase is hunting around the input x(t).

The use of adaptive techniques reduces the quantization noise and increases the dynamic range of delta modulators. The idea of adaptive step-size delta modulators is illustrated in Figure 2.2.7, and one of the first integrated-circuit hardware realizations is shown in Figure 2.2.8. Many methods for suitable adaptive step-size variation exist (Jayant, 1974; O'Neal, 1980). Monolithic integrated-circuit adaptive delta modulators using advanced digital algorithms are available from a number of manufacturers. The cost (in large quantities) of one of these high-performance ADM codecs is approximately $1.

2.2.4 Vocoder and Linear Predictive Coding

For excellent telephone quality, also known as "toll grade-voice transmission," PCM systems require a transmission rate of $f_b = 64$ kb/s. With adaptive DPCM and DM the transmission rate could be reduced to the 12 kb/s-to-32 kb/s range. If a further decrease in the

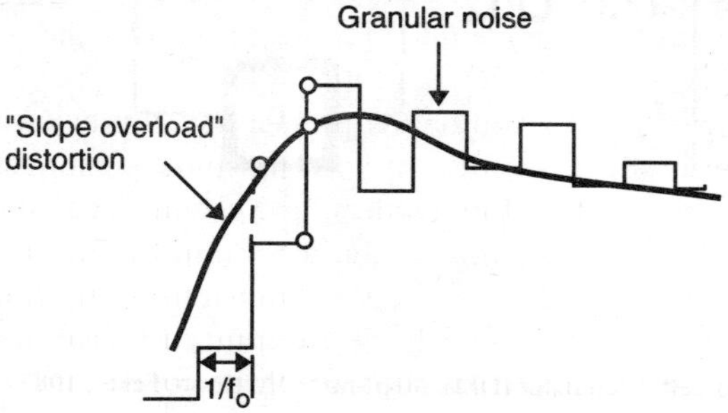

Figure 2.2.7 Quantization noise in adaptive delta modulation (ADM) [Jayant, 1975].

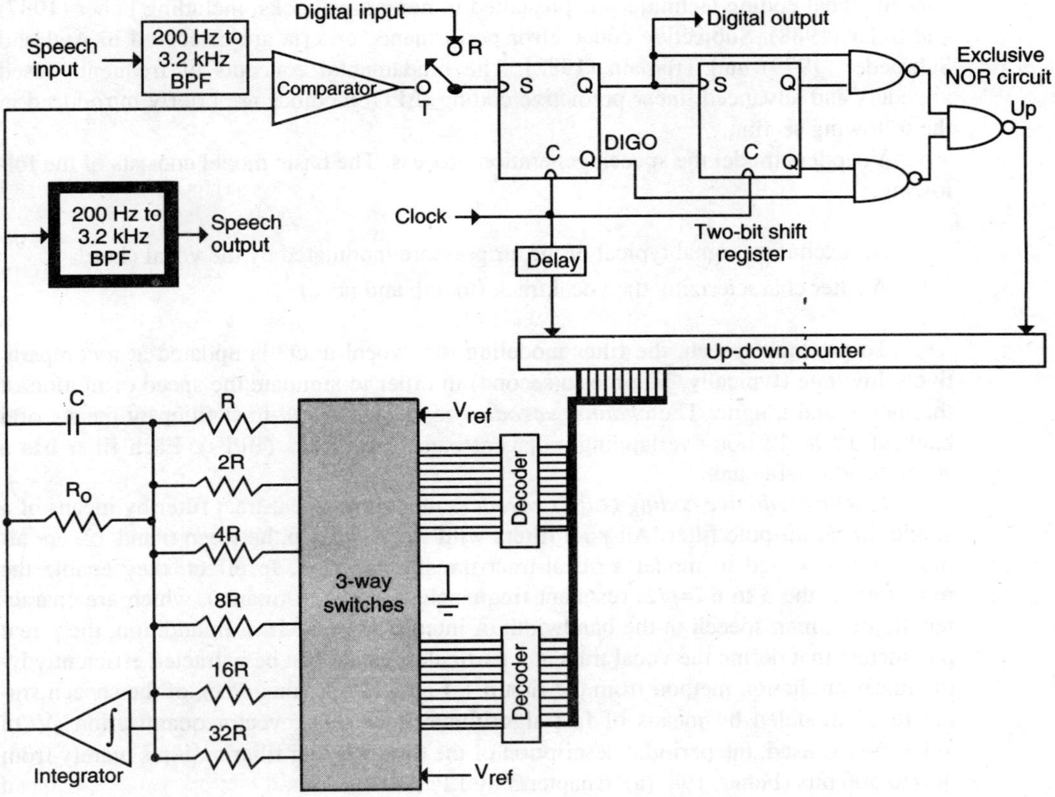

Figure 2.2.8 Realization of adaptive delta modulation (ADM) with integrated-circuit hardware. (From S.N. Jayant, "Digital coding of speech waveforms: PCM, DPCM and DM Quantizers," *Proceedings of the IEEE* (© 1975 IEEE)).

nominal transmission rate is desired and the telephony "toll-grade" quality, or nearly toll quality, speech encoding has to be retained, more advanced signal coding techniques must be used.

Block coders are advanced speech encoding/decoding systems (Feher, 1987(a)). The encoders used in conventional PCM and adaptive DPCM and DM systems have *scalar quantizers.* Scalar quantizers provide a single output sample based on the present input sample and the *N* previous output samples (in conventional PCM systems $N = 0$). Block coders form a *vector* of output samples based on the present and N previous input samples. Block coding techniques are often classified by their mapping techniques, including vector quantizers, various orthogonal transform coders, and channelized coders such as the subband coder. They are further described by their algorithmic structures, including codebook coders, tree coders, trellis coders, discrete Fourier transform, discrete cosine transform, discrete Walsh-Hadamard transform, discrete Karhunen-Loeve transform, and quadrature mirror filter bank. A detailed description of block codecs and of other advanced signal coding techniques is presented in numerous books, including Feher (1987) and Sklar (1988). Subjective codec error performance criteria are discussed in Atal and Schroeder (1979) and Tremain (1982). The fundamental concepts of frequently used vocoders and advanced linear predictive coding (LPC) methods are briefly introduced in the following section.

Vocoders model the speech generation process. The basic model consists of the following:

1. An excitation signal typical of the air pressure modulated by the vocal chords
2. A filter characterizing the vocal track (mouth and nose)

To produce speech, the filter modeling the "vocal tract" is updated at a comparatively low rate (typically, 50 times a second) in order to simulate the speed of motion of the mouth and tongue. The *channel vocoders* model the vocal-tract filter by means of a bank of 12 to 32 non-overlapping, adjacent band-pass filters (BPFs). Each filter has a separate adjustable gain.

Linear predictive coding (*LPC*) *vocoders* model the vocal-tract filter by means of a single, linear all-pole filter. All-pole filters with small-order p, between 6 and 12, are almost ideally suited to model a vocal-tract transfer function. In effect, they enable the modeling of the 3 to 6 ($=p/2$) resonant frequencies (that is, formants), which are characteristic of human speech in the bandwidth of interest (0 to 5 kHz). In addition, the p real parameters that define the vocal tract at a particular instant can be extracted efficiently by the linear prediction method from the first $p + 1$ autocorrelations, $R(k)$, of the speech signal to be modeled by means of fast algorithms or by using vector quantization (VQ). When VQ is used, the periodic description of the time-varying filter requires merely from 400 to 500 bits (Feher, 1987(a), Chapter 3 by J.P. Adoul).

Representation of the excitation signal. Once a particular vocal-tract filter has been retained for transmission of a particular speech segment, the ideal excitation can be obtained by inverse filtering of the speech segment, as shown in Figure 2.2.9. By definition, cascading a filter to its inverse filter amounts to a pure delay (that is, the total impulse response is a delayed unit impulse). It is particularly easy to obtain the inverse filter of an all-pole filter by taking the all-zero filter, which has zeros in place of the poles. The signal that results from inverse filtering of the speech (that is, the ideal excitation) is

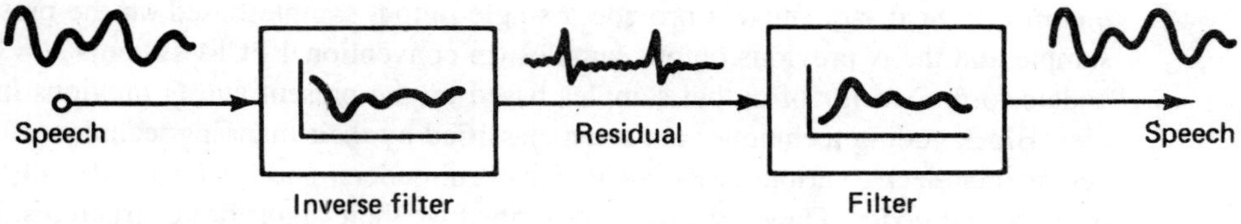

Figure 2.2.9 Excitation signal obtained by inverse filtering. (From Feher, 1987; chapter by J.P. Adoul.)

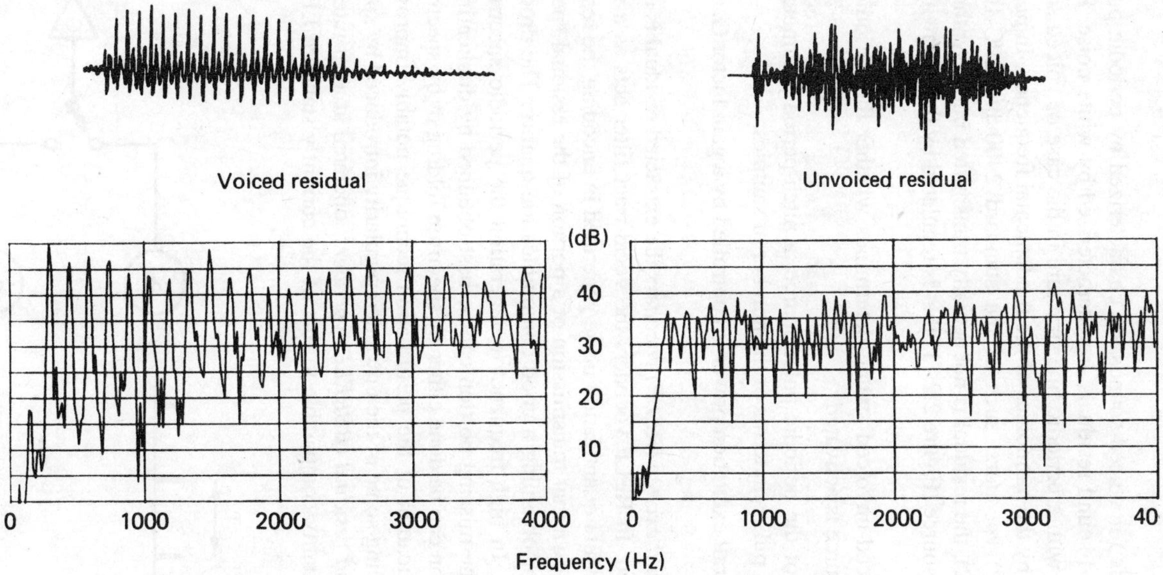

Figure 2.2.10 Typical voiced and unvoiced residual signals with their respective flat spectrum. Note that in the voiced case the spectrum retains its periodic fine structure [Feher, 1987; chapter by J.P. Adoul].

called the *residual.* The residual contains a significant redundancy, which led to the development of several encoding schemes. A typical residual signal is shown in Figure 2.2.10.

Residuals for voiced sounds are characterized by periodic pulses at the pitch rate, while unvoiced-sound residuals are characterized by white noise. Both types have a flat spectrum, but with a periodic fine structure in the case of voiced sounds. The fine structure is caused by the harmonics of the fundamental frequency. In *pulse excited linear predictive (PELP) vocoders,* such as the standard 2400 b/s LPC-10 codec (Atal, 1979; Tremain, 1982), the residual is not actually transmitted but is synthesized by means of an artificial dual source (Figure 2.2.11) that is regulated by the following parameters:

1. The voiced-unvoiced switch determines whether the periodic pulses or the white noise source is activated.
2. In case of the periodic pulse source, a pitch-period parameter defines the spacing between pulses in terms of the number of samples.
3. The overall excitation power is controlled by a gain factor G.

In *residual excited (RELP) vocoders* the extracted residual is economically encoded and transmitted. In RELP vocoders the vocal-tract filter acts as a noise-shaping mechanism for any white quantization noise generated in encoding the residual. Several experiments have shown that transmission of a portion of the residual spectrum (0 to 1000 Hz) is sufficient for obtaining a good communication quality. The procedure is described in Figure 2.2.12. In high-frequency regeneration the periodic spectrum of the residual is used. Hence the missing portion can be best obtained by duplicating the known portion. This duplication can be done either by spectrum folding or by spectrum translation.

An application of the perturbation technique notably improves the subjective results by removing some of the unwanted regularity introduced by spectrum duplication.

Baseband residual (BBRELP) vocoders, operated at a bit rate of 2400 bits per second, have a quality comparable to that of the currently standard LPC-10 and have a sig-

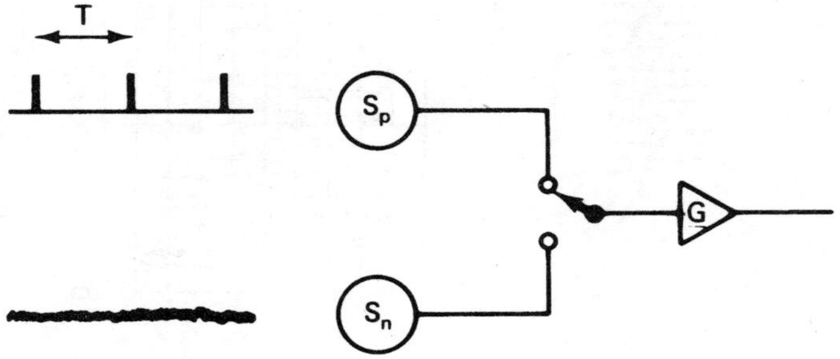

Figure 2.2.11 Excitation mechanism in P excited linear predictive (PELP) vocoders. The mechanism has a voiced-unvoiced switch that selects either a periodic-pulse source (S_p) or a noiselike source (S_n).

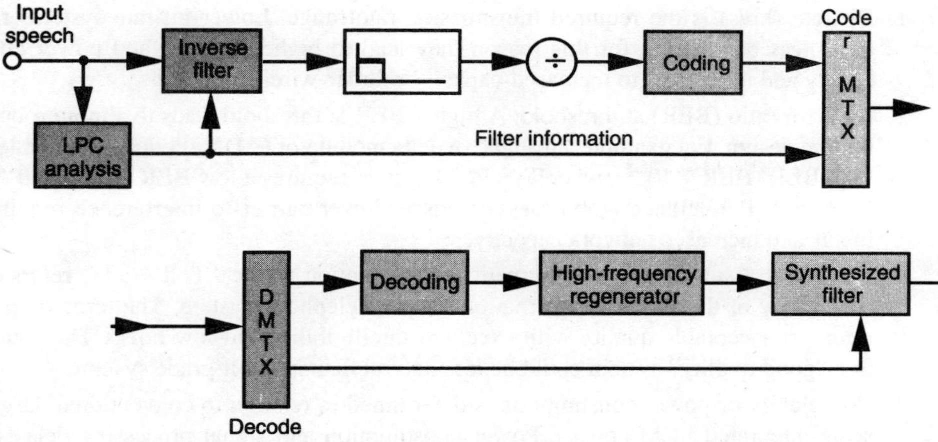

Figure 2.2.12 Block diagram of a R excited linear predictive (RELP) vocoder. A linear predictive coding analysis determines the spectrum of the input speech, thereby determining the inverse filter to be used. The residual is then low-pass filtered, decimated, and time-domain encoded. Both residual and filter information is multiplexed. (From Feher, 1987).

nificantly improved background-noise immunity. This immunity is possible through the application of efficient vector quantization schemes to the time-domain coding of the baseband residual.

2.2.5 Performance Comparison of Speech Processing Techniques

Rigorous and fair performance comparisons of various codec methods are complex, elaborate tasks. Because the voice "quality" is subjective, statistical opinion scores of several hundred listeners are frequently required. Detailed speech-quality codec and transmission/reception requirements have been standardized by several U.S. and international organizations. In Table 2.2.1 a basic performance comparison of several speech-processing codecs is presented. The most important parameters include the following:

Table 2.2.1 Performance comparison of various speech processing codec techniques.

Codec type	Required transmission bit rate	Bit error ratio (BER) at threshold	Subjective quality	Relative complexity and power consumption
PCM	64 kb/s	10^{-4}	Toll grade	simple, low
ADPCM	10–40 kb/s	10^{-3} – 10^{-4}	Almost toll grade	simple, low
ADM	10–40 kb/s	10^{-2}	Almost toll grade	simple, low
Vocoder	1–15 kb/s	10^{-2}	Good	complex, high
LPC	1–15kb/s	10^{-2}	Good	complex, high

1. Bit rate (kb/s) is the required transmission rate range. Lower bit-rate systems require less bandwidth; for this reason they lead to higher spectral and power efficiency and ultimately to increased-capacity cellular-wireless systems.
2. Bit error ratio (BER) at threshold. A higher BER at threshold leads to a more robust system design. For example, an adaptive delta modulator (ADM) codec can tolerate a high BER (BER = 10^{-2}), whereas a PCM system requires a low BER (BER = 10^{-4}). Higher BER tolerance (robustness) leads to lower carrier-to-interference requirements and increased network capacity.
3. Quality is a subjective measurement and evaluation result. "Toll grade" refers to the quality of the U.S. and international wired telephone system. The term "good" refers to acceptable quality with excellent intelligibility and low noise. The sound in a "good-quality" system could be less natural than in a toll-grade system.
4. Complexity or power consumption is determined in relation to conventional, large-scale integrated PCM codecs. Power consumption and signal processing delay of advanced LPCs or vocoders are several times higher than for PCMs.

The principal advantage of the advanced codecs is that they can attain good- to toll-grade quality with a significantly reduced bit rate. Reduced bit-rate systems lead to increased capacity or lower radio power requirements, or both.

2.2.6 Echo and Delay Control

Echo of transmitted speech or of data signals occurs in virtually all telephone networks. The longer the echo is delayed, the more disturbing it is and the more it must be attenuated before it becomes tolerable.

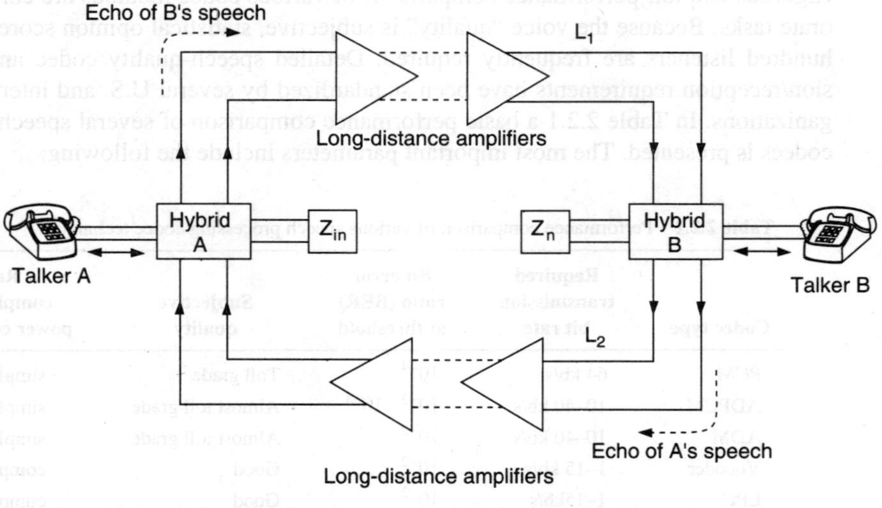

Figure 2.2.13 Typical long-distance telephone circuit. The hybrids are located in central office *A* and *B*. (From Feher, 1983.)

An illustrative segment of a wired long-distance network is illustrated in Figure 2.2.13. At any location in this circuit, if the transmitted signal encounters an impedance mismatch, a fraction of this signal is reflected as an echo. Telephone, data, and facsimile sets are connected by a two-wire line to a hybrid transformer located in the central office. For both transmission and reception to and from the central office, only two wires are used, which results in considerable savings of wire and local switching equipment.

The circuit diagram of a hybrid located at the place of talker *B* in Figure 2.2.13 is shown in Figure 2.2.14. If the two transformers are identical and the balancing impedance, Z_n, *equals* the impedance of the two-wire circuit, then the signal originating on the "in" side is transferred to the two-wire circuit of B but produces no response at the "out" terminal. Yet, if the signal originates in the two-wire circuit (talker B is active), the signal is transferred to both paths of the four-wire circuit. This signal has no effect on the "in" signal path, since the amplifiers shown in Figure 2.2.13 only amplify signals in the opposite direction. Echoes are generated whenever the "in" side is coupled (has a leak-through) to the "out" side. Unfortunately, this occurs in almost all networks, since the Z_n network is not identical to the distributed time-variable impedance of the two-wire circuit. In addition, a four-wire circuit may be connected to a large number of two-wire circuits. Thus the need for echo control (suppression or cancellation) in long-distance systems is imminent.

Wireless systems are frequently connected with wired public switched telephone networks (PSTNs) or with integrated services digital networks (ISDNs). The echo and delay, introduced in the network, must also be controlled in the wireless network units,

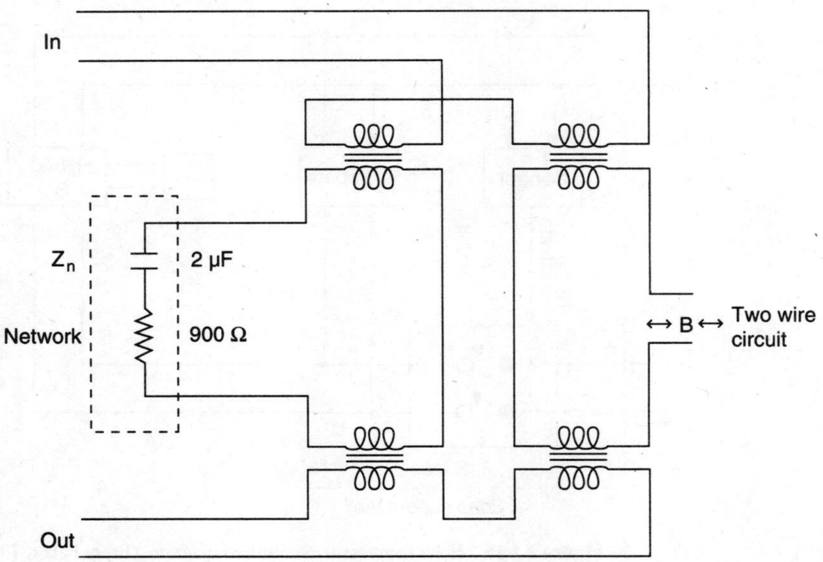

Figure 2.2.14 Circuit diagram of hybrid located at *B* in Figure 2.2.13. (From Feher, 1983.)

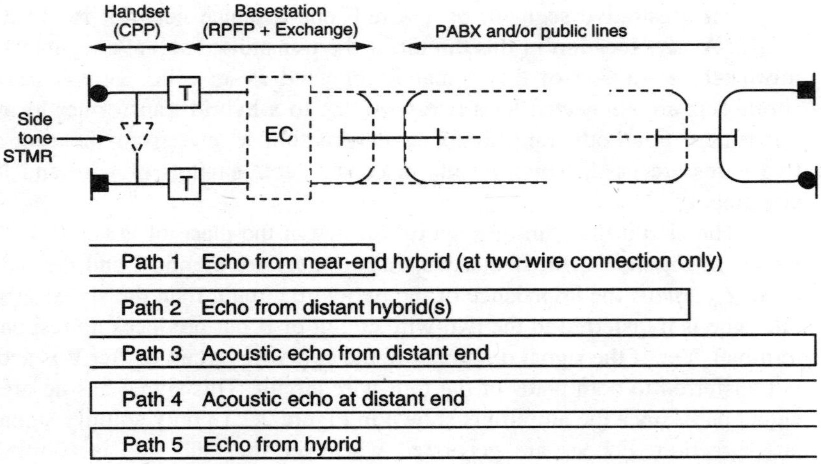

Figure 2.2.15 Echo paths relevant for a cordless telephone system. (From Tuttlebee, 1990.)

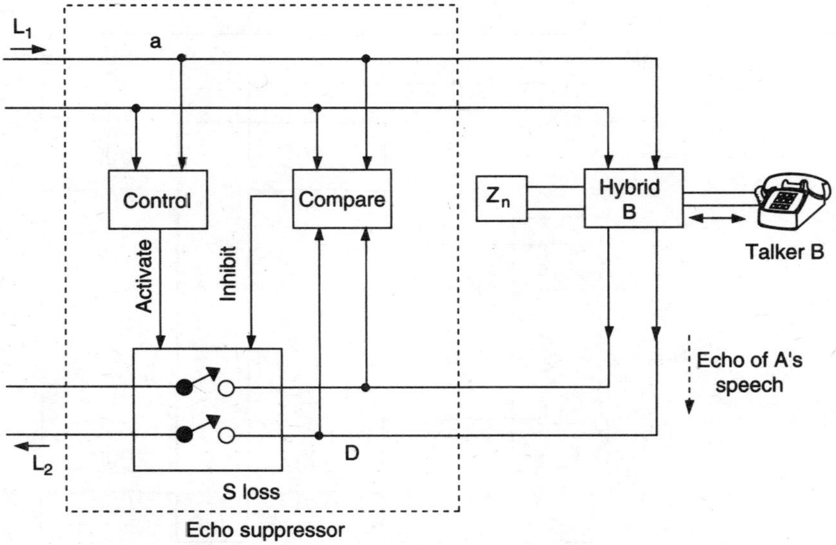

Figure 2.2.16 Echo suppressor. Simplified diagram. (From Feher, 1983.)

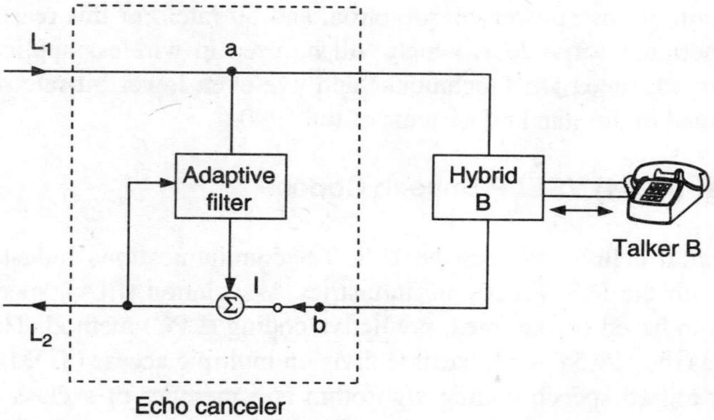

Figure 2.2.17 Echo canceler. Conceptual diagram.

including base stations and mobile units. Echo and delay paths relevant to a wireless telephone system are illustrated in Figure 2.2.15.

One-way signal processing and transmission delays (without echo) of up to 100 ms result in no subjective interference to a telephone conversation. Larger delays are noticeable and may be annoying for the user. An example is a 260-ms one-way delay caused by a satellite link. Delayed echoes are significantly more degrading to the perceived speech than the delay itself is. In powerful echoes a delayed signal of only a few milliseconds could be very annoying. For this reason, echo control must to be implemented in wired as well as wireless systems.

Echo control is achieved by echo suppressors and cancelers. Echo suppressors insert an attenuation into the return path, providing an attenuated echo signal. Alternatively, they prevent the echo from returning to the source by disconnecting the return path during intervals when only transmitter "A" is talking. This type of disconnection degrades the speech quality during simultaneous conversation, that is, during intervals when both parties are talking at the same time. A simplified block diagram of an echo suppressor is shown in Figure 2.2.16.

The basic intent of echo cancellation is to generate a synthetic replica of the echo and subtract it from the leaked-through echo signal that is returned through the hybrid unit, as shown in Figure 2.2.17. A detailed description of advanced echo cancelers is presented in (Feher, 1987a, Chapter by Messerschmidt). Criteria for acceptable echoes and delay-echo control requirements for wireless systems are described in Tuttlebee (1990).

2.3 AMERICAN AND EUROPEAN SPEECH CODECS

In this section standardized speech codes for several American and European wireless systems applications are briefly reviewed. Detailed, up-to-date requirements are presented in the most recent issues of the official specifications. The standardized codec algorithms of the early 1990s include simple ADPCM, advanced code excited linear predictive coding, and vector sum excited linear prediction. Ongoing speech codec research contributes to further reduction of cost, power consumption, and bit rate. For this reason it is likely that the next generations of codecs, which will be used in wireless applications, will make use of more advanced DSP techniques and hve even lower bit-rate requirements than those described in the standard systems of the 1990s.

2.3.1 U.S. Digital Cellular (IS-54) VSELP Speech Codec

For the North American digital cellular system the U.S. Telecommunications Industry Association (TIA), jointly with the U.S. Electronic Industries Association (EIA), specified a speech coding algorithm based on the linear predictive coding (LPC) method. This EIA specification is known as the "IS-54" cellular time division multiple access (TDMA) system (EIA, 1990). The specified speech coding algorothm is a member of a class of speech coders known as *code excited linear predictive coding (CELP),* stochastic coding, or vector excited speech coding. With these techniques code books are used to vector-quantize the excitation (residual) signal. The specific speech coding algorithm adopted for the IS-54 standard, specified by the TIA and the EIA, is a variation on CELP called *vector sum excited linear predictive coding (VSELP).* In VSELP a code book is used; the code book has a predefined structure in which the computations required for the code book search process can be significantly reduced (EIA, 1990).

The block diagram of the digital speech decoder (Figure 2.3.1) indicates the various parameters that must be determined and encoded by the speech coder. The speech decoder utilizes two VSELP excitation code books. Each of the two code books has its own gain. The two code-book excitations are each multiplied by their corresponding gains and

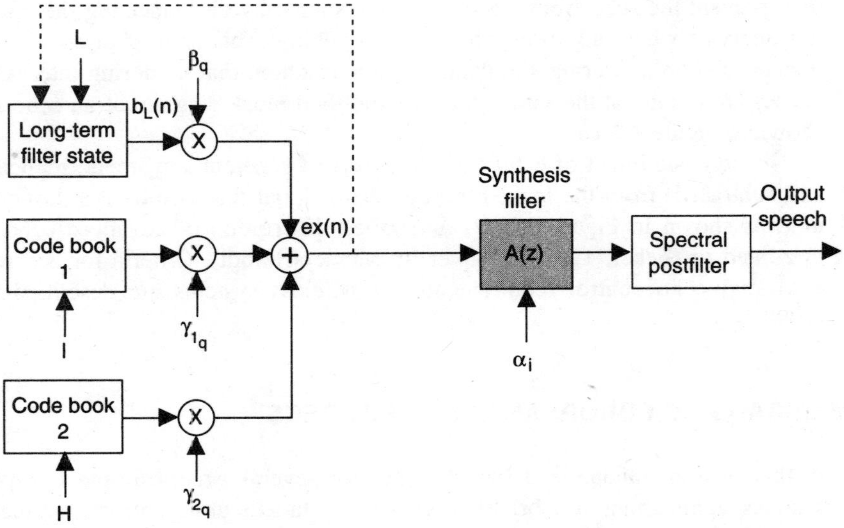

Figure 2.3.1 Speech decoder based on the U.S. digital cellular draft standard (EIA 1990). This $f = 7.95$ kb/s rate voice codec, known as CELP and also as VSELP codec, is based on linear predictive coding methods.

Table 2.3.1.1 Principal parameters of the $f_b = 7.95$ kb/s rate Vector-Sum Excited Linear Predictive (VSELP) coding, also known as Code Excited Linear Predictive (CELP) coding, speech coder, based on an early version of the U.S. digital cellular system draft specifications [EIA, 1990].

Parameter	Sampling rate	8 kHz
N_F	frame length	160 samples (20 msec)
N	subframe length	40 samples (5 msec)
N_P	short term predictor order	10
	# of taps for long term predictor	1
M_1	# of bits in code word 1 (# of basis vectors)	7
M_2	# of bits in code word 2 (# of basis vectors)	7
The basic data rate of the speech coder is 7950 b/s. There are 159 bits per speech frame (20 msec) for the speech coder. These 159 bits are allocated as follows:		
Short-term filter coefficients, α_i's		38 bits per frame
Frame energy, R(0)		5 bits per frame
Lag, L	7 bits per subframe	28 bits per frame
Code words, I, H	7 + 7 bits per subframe	56 bits per frame
Gains β, γ_1, γ_2	8 bits per subframe	32 bits per frame
The following is a list of all the parameter codes transmitted for each 20-ms speech frame:		
Ro	5 bits	Frame energy
LPC1	6 bits	First reflection coefficient

(From EIA, 1990.)

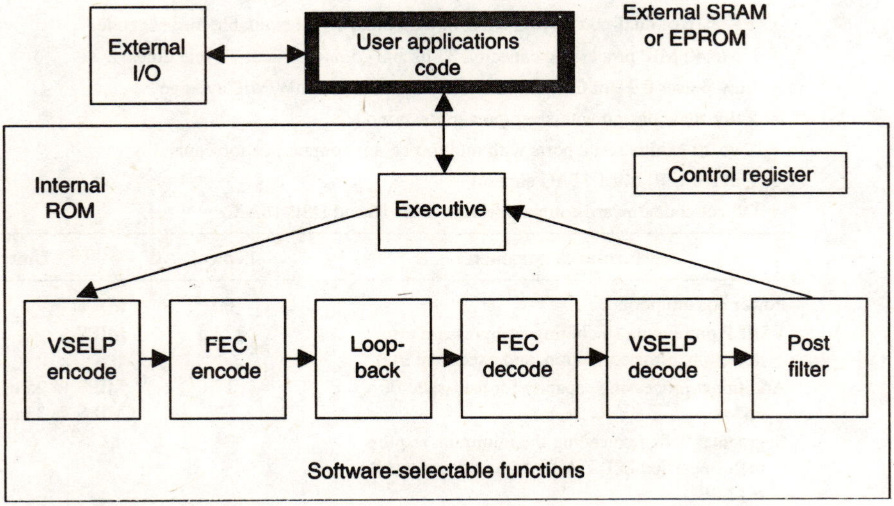

Figure 2.3.2 Software architectural diagram based on the AT&T DSP-1616 VSELP engine.

summed to create a combined code-book excitation. The transmission rate of this codec is f_b = 7.95 kb/s. Principal parameters are listed in Table 2.3.1.1. For detailed, up-to-date specifications, consult the respective TIA or EIA "Is-54" document (EIA, 1990).

A complete, self-contained VSELP speech encoder-decoder with speech-error correction that adheres to the requirements specified in the EIA IS-54 standard has been implemented in very large-scale integration (VLSI) chips, for example, as illustrated in Figure 2.3.2, in the AT&T digital signal processor VSELP engine.

The implementation of the VSELP speech codec algorithm utilizes less than 60 mA of current from a 5-V battery when driven with a 20-MHz clock. When power consumption is a critical factor for portable applications, the DSP-1616 hardware platform may be effective: it has a typical power consumption of less than 14 mW per MIP.

The AT&T DSP-1616 VSELP has additional processing capability. The VSELP speech encoder-decoder with error correction utilizes 22.5 MIP of the 40-MIP bandwidth available on the DSP-1616. This additional processing capacity provides more capability for the end application. The VSELP engine leaves an additional 3K of ROM and 1K of temporary RAM for user code. Features and performance of this advanced VLSI processor are summarized in Table 2.3.1.2.

Table 2.3.1.2 Features and illustrative performance highlights of the AT&T DSP1616 advanced VSELP-VLSI digital signal processor based on a data sheet.

Illustrative Features of the DSP-1616

- Optimized for digital-cellular applications with a bit manipulation architecture expansion
- 12 K × 16 of ROM (with secure option); 3 K available for user code
- 2 K × 16 of dual-port RAM; >1 K of temporary RAM available for user code
- Up to 40 MIP processing capacity, 33 ns and 25 ns instruction cycle times
- Low-power 0.9 μm CMOS technology, less than 14 mW/MIP average
- Fully static design with sleep/power down mode
- Two 20-Mbit/s serial ports with multiprocessor communication capability
- Full IEEE P1149.1 JTAG support
- Object-code upward compatible with DSP-16 and DSP-16A/C

Performance parameter	Typical	Unit
Power consumption	60	MA at 5 V
VSELP processing (including compression error detection, error correction, and executive I/O)	22.5	MIPS
Additional processing capacity for user-specific code	17 7	MIPS @ 25 ns clock MIPS @ 33 ns clock
Segmental SNR (exceeding the minimum requirement specified in DTIA IS-54 lockdown test by > 12 dB	>34	dB
ROM available to user	3	Kwords
Temporary RAM available to user	1040	Words

2.3.2 ADPCM Codecs for the European CT-2 and DECT Systems

The specified speech coding algorithm for the common interface standards of the second-generation cordless telephone (CT-2) and the Digital European Cordless Telecommunications (DECT) is a 32-kb/s-rate adaptive differential pulse code modulation (ADPCM) algorithm (CT-2, 1989; DECT, 1991). For the basic functional diagram of these codecs, see Figures 2.3.3 and 2.3.4. At the input of this standardized encoder is an A-law or a μ-law standard 64-kb/s PCM input. First, this signal is converted into a uniform PCM. The uniform PCM data stream is converted into a 32-kb/s-rate ADPCM signal. In the decoder the reverse signal processing is performed, and a 64-kb/s-rate A-law (for American requirements) or μ-law (for European and other international requirements) PCM output stream is generated. The detailed coding algorithms must conform to International Telegraph and

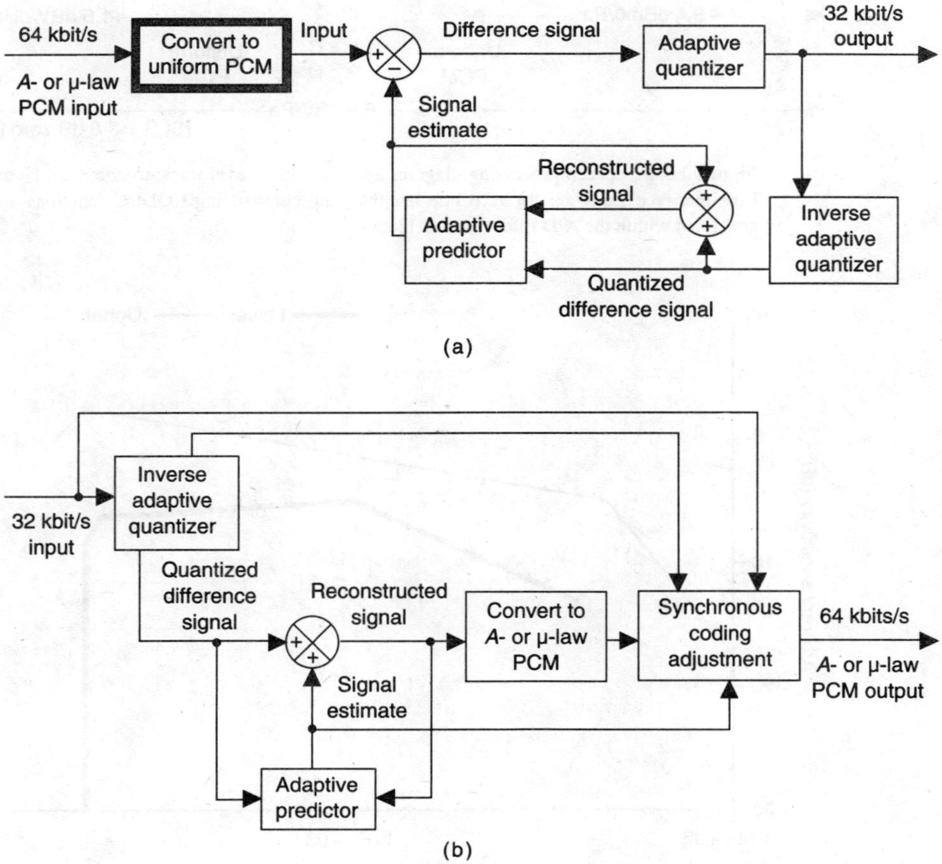

Figure 2.3.3 The ADPCM encoder and decoder: (a), encoder; (b), decoder. (From Townsend, 1988.)

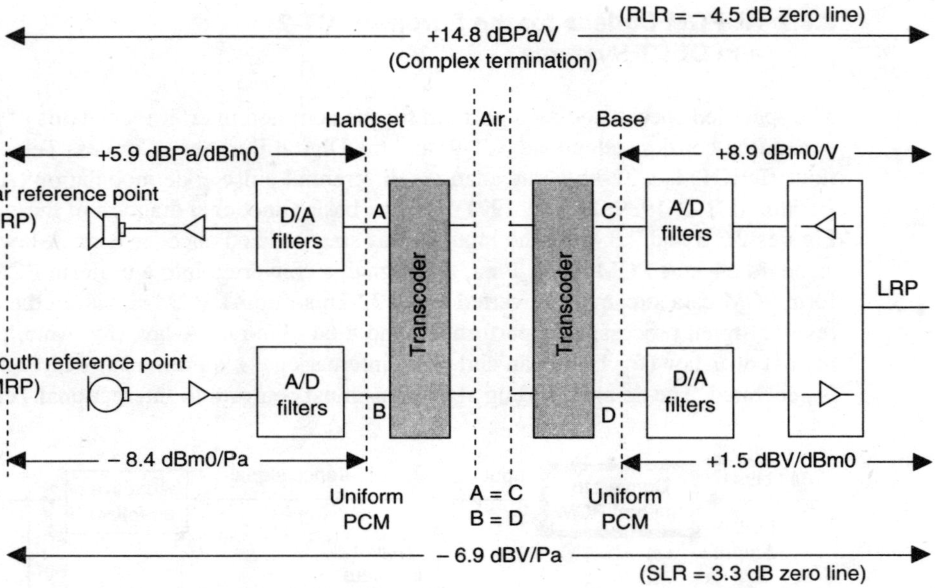

Figure 2.3.4 Speech processing diagram and CT-2 high-level transmission plan. Note: Line interface gains are for zero line lengths. Any companding CODEC functions are contained within the A/D filter function blocks.

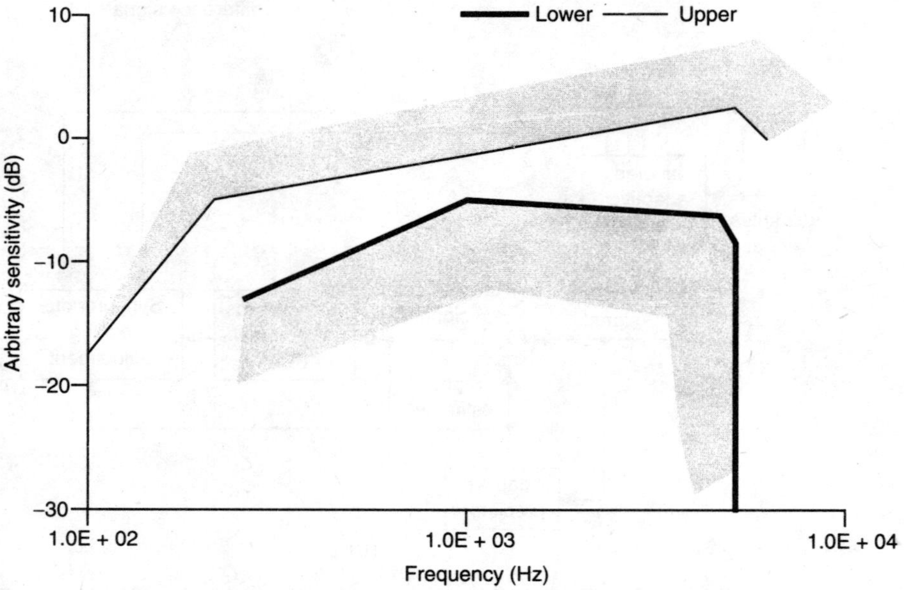

Figure 2.3.5 Handset send frequency masks of CT-2.

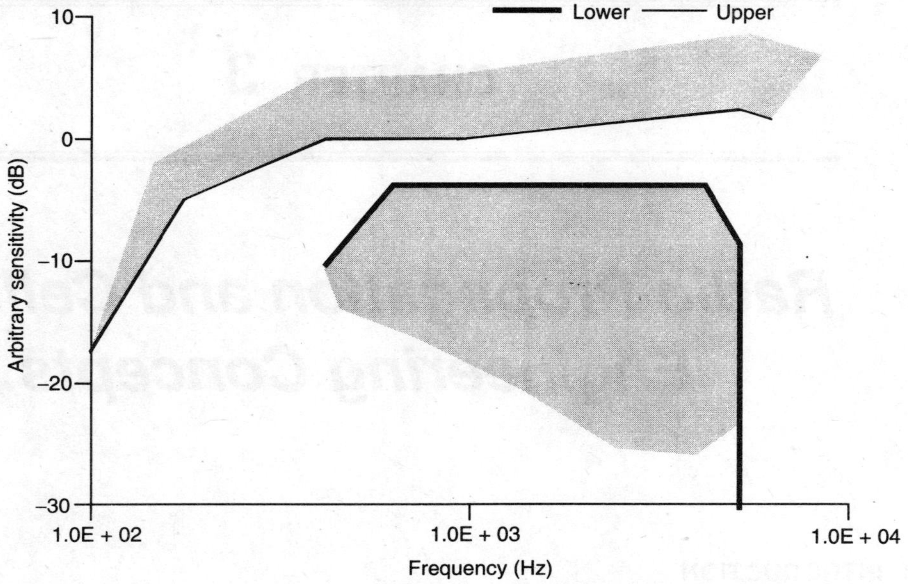

Figure 2.3.6 Handset receive frequency masks of CT-2.

Telephone Consultive Committee (CCITT) recommendation G.721 for 32-kb/s-rate ADPCMs. The G.721 codecs support use of telephone-grade voice and use of the voice channel for facsimile (telefax) of "Group 2 and Group 3." For Group 3 the data speed is limited to 4.8 kb/s (CCITT-G.721).

Frequency responses of the A/D, transcoder (ADPCM), and D/A systems (Figure 2.3.4) are specified in Figures 2.3.5 and 2.3.6. Instead of partitioning the frequency mask width equally between the telephone handset and the base station unit, a greater percentage is allocated to the handset to reflect the greater tolerance contribution, that is, the lower cost requirement of the handset transducers.

The CT-2 voice path performance requirements include specifications for high-level transmission plans (Figure 2.3.4), sending and receiving loudness ratings, sidetone rating, clipping, distortion, noise, delay, and echo loss. The signal- to total-distortion ratio must exeed 35 dB.

CHAPTER 3

Radio Propagation and Cellular Engineering Concepts

3.1 INTRODUCTION

This chapter describes radio propagation principles and models for cellular, personal communication systems (PCSs), and public land mobile radio (PLMR) communications systems applications. For typical non–line-of-sight (NLOS) cellular and PCS systems the random multiple radio propagation path is characterized by its principal parameters: multipath fading, shadowing, and path loss. A discussion of the cause and practical values of Doppler spread (time-selective fading) and time-delay spread (frequency-selective fading) is included. A physical insight of several mathematical propagation models and of the corresponding simulation (hardware and software) tools is described. Basic cellular engineering concepts and design principles related to radio propagation and network optimization are highlighted.

Instrumentation and measurement setups for Rayleigh fade tests, including "quasi-Rayleigh" or slow fading, having Doppler frequencies in the 1-Hz range and for fast Rayleigh-faded systems are explained. Final equations for maximal range-coverage distance are highlighted. A simple yet powerful upper bound for delay spread is described. Numerous delay-spread field test results and propagation models specified by American and European mobile and cellular standardization committees are also highlighted.

3.2 FUNDAMENTAL RADIO PROPAGATION AND SYSTEM CONCEPTS

A typical model of a land mobile radio, including PCS and digital cellular transmission link, consists of an elevated base-station antenna (or multiple antennas) and a relatively short distance line-of-sight (LOS) propagation path, followed by many NLOS reflected propagation paths and a mobile antenna or antennas mounted on the vehicle or more generally on the transmitter/receiver (T/R) or *transceiver* of the mobile or portable unit. In most applications, no complete, direct LOS propagation exists between the base-station antenna, also known as the *access point,* and the mobile antennas because of natural and constructed obstacles (Figures 3.2.1 and 3.2.2). In such environments the radio transmission path, or *radio link,* may be modeled as a *randomly varying propagation path.* In many instances there may exist more than one propagation path, and this situation is referred to as *multipath propagation.* The propagation path changes with the movement of the mobile unit, the base unit, and/or the movement of the surroundings and environment.

Even the smallest, slowest movement causes time-variable multipath, thus random time-variable signal reception. For example, assume that the cellular user is sitting in an automobile in a parking lot, near a busy freeway. Although the user is relatively stationary, part of the environment is moving at 100 km per hour (km/h). The automobiles on the freeway become "reflectors" of radio signals. If during transmission or reception the user is also moving, (for example, driving at 100 km/h, the randomly reflected signals vary at a faster rate. The rate of variations of the signal is frequently described as *Doppler spread.*

Radio propagation in such environments is characterized by three partially separable effects known as *multipath fading, shadowing,* and *path loss.* Multipath fading is described by its *envelope fading* (nonfrequency-selective amplitude distribution), *Doppler spread* (time-selective or time-variable random phase noise), and *time-delay spread* (variable propagation distance of reflected signals causes time variations in the reflected signals). These signals cause frequency-selective fades. These phenomena are summarized in Figure 3.2.3 and described in the following subsections.

3.2.1 Fundamentals of Envelope Fading

To illustrate the fundamental concepts of envelope fading, we refer to Figure 3.2.4. It is assumed that the base station is transmitting a constant-envelope phase-modulated signal $s_T(t)$ given by

$$s_T(t) = Ae^{j(\omega t + \psi_s(t))} \tag{3.2.1}$$

where A is a constant, ω is the angular radio frequency (RF), $\psi_s(t)$ is the phase- or frequency-modulated information-bearing signal, also known as *baseband* signal. The time-variable random "propagation medium" $p(t)$ is expressed as

$$p(t) = r(t)e^{j\psi_r(t)} \tag{3.2.2}$$

where $r(t)$ is the time-variable envelope and $\psi_r(t)$ the time-variable random phase of the propagation medium. The envelope of the random propagation medium $r(t)$ can be separated into *long-term* or *average fading* $m(t)$ and *short-term* or *fast multipath fading* $r_0(t)$ parts defined by

$$r(t) = m(t) \cdot r_0(t) \tag{3.2.3}$$

where $r_0(t)$ has unit mean value. (Otherwise, this definition does not hold).

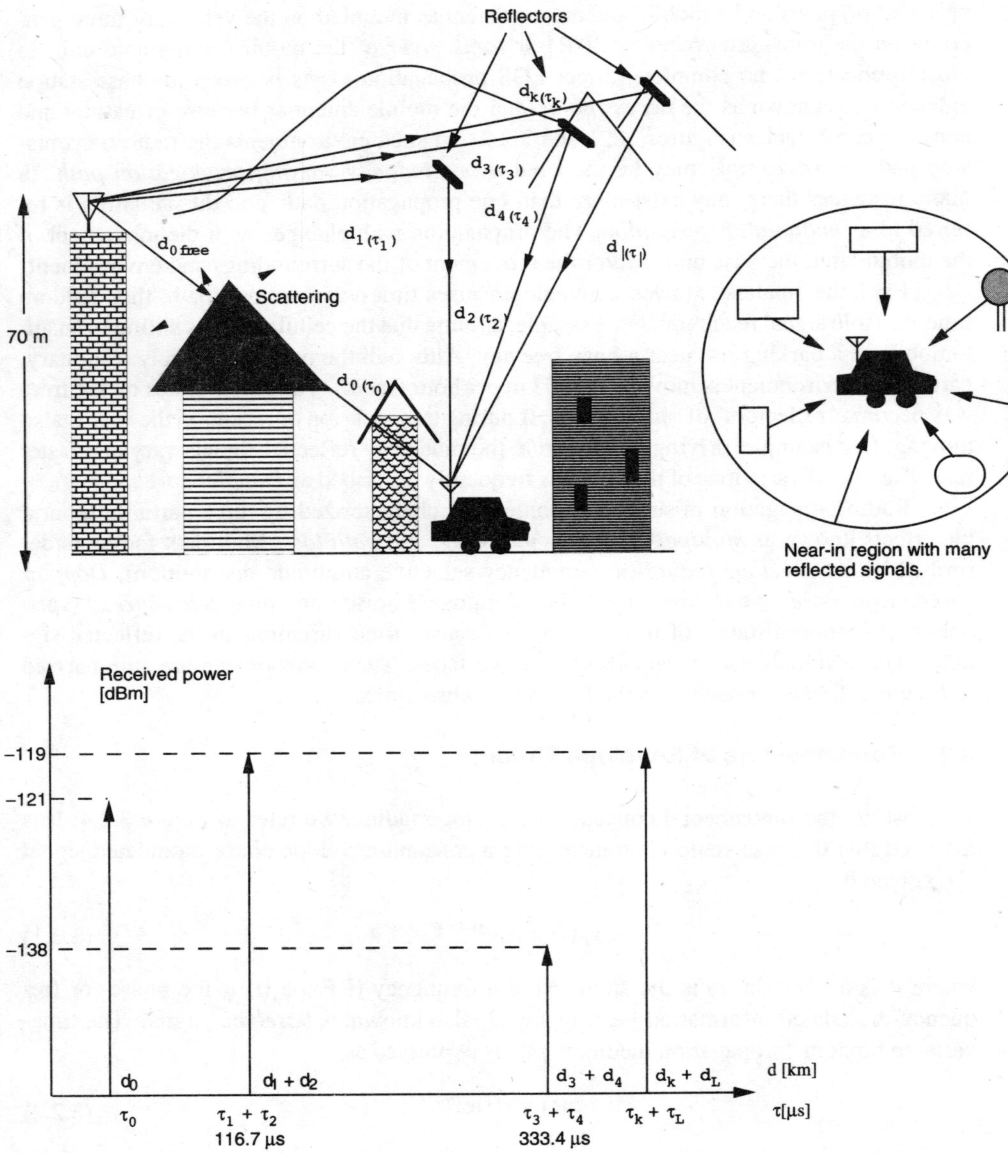

Figure 3.2.1 Propagation environment of a land-mobile line-of-sight (LOS) and non-line-of-sight (NLOS) radio system. The base station antenna in this illustrative example is at a height of 70 m, i.e., top of tallest building. The direct LOS free space path "d_{0free}" is between the base antenna and the first building. Afterwards the direct d_0 path is attenuated. The distant mountains reflect the signals. The reflected delayed signals could be received at a comparable power level to the attenuated direct path signals.

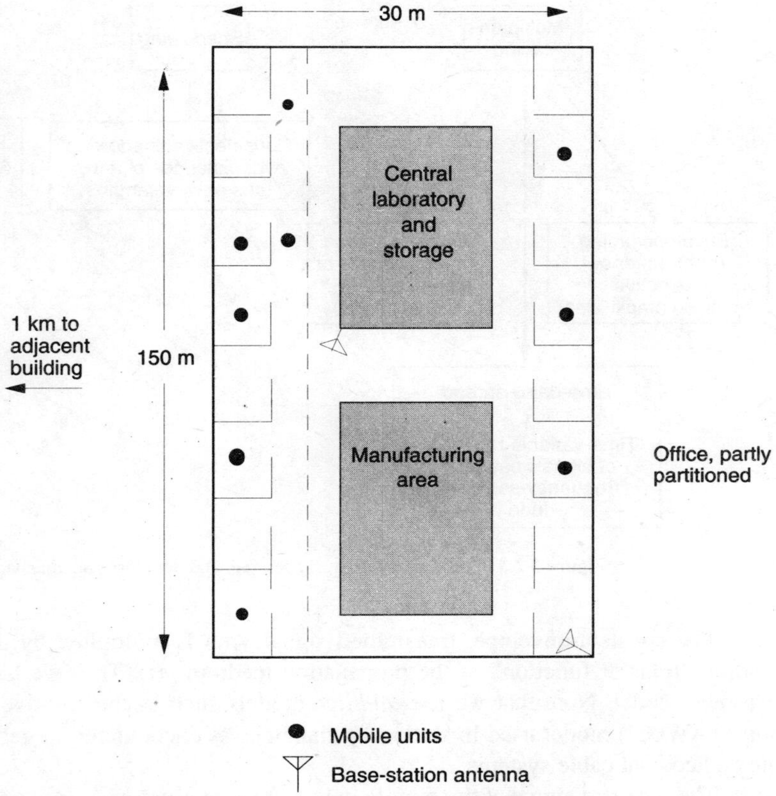

Figure 3.2.2 Indoor propagation environment of a *microcell,* having a coverage radius of r = 1 km, or a *nanocell,* having a coverage of 1 m ≤ r ≤ 50 m. The base station (access point) antenna height is approximately 3 m; the mobile unit antenna height, located on top of an office desk, is about 1 m. Office cubicles are partly partitioned. Central laboratory, storage, and manufacturing areas are isolated by walls and partial metal shields.

If the base station and mobile units are both stationary but the environment is moving (this is almost always the practical case, since even the smallest or slowest movement causes time-variable random reflections in an NLOS system), then we use equation 3.2.3 with time t as the random variable. If the mobile unit is moving at a speed of v (m/s or km/h), then the propagation distance x between the base station and mobile path is given by

$$x = v \cdot t(m). \qquad (3.2.4)$$

In this case we can write equation 3.2.3 as

$$r(x) = m(x) \cdot r_0(x).$$

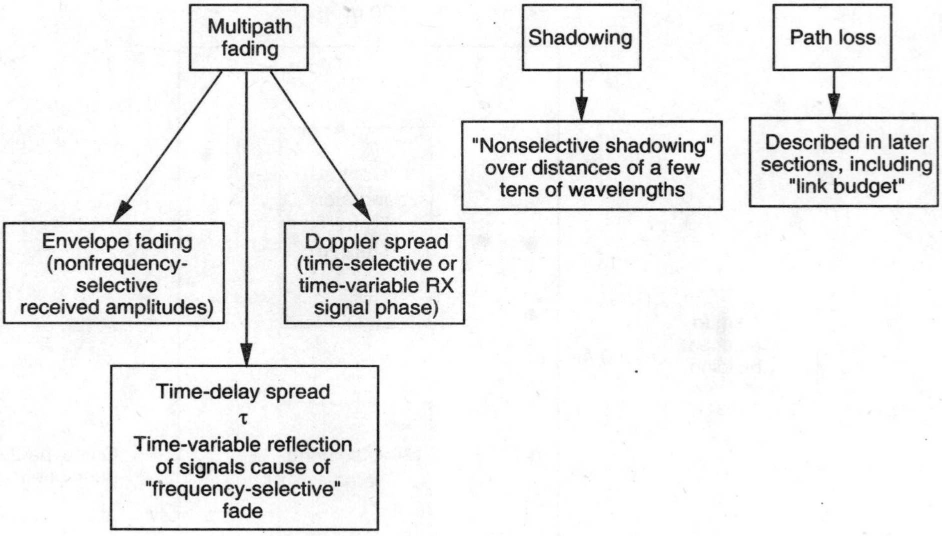

Figure 3.2.3 Multipath fading, shadowing, and path loss phenomena.

The constant-envelope, transmitted signal $s_T(t)$ is multiplied by the time-variable random "transfer function" of the propagation medium $p(t)$. Thus we have a *multiplicative* fade model. Note that we use *additive* models such as the additive white Gaussian noise (AWGN) model used in stationary channels, as encountered in geostationary satellite and coaxial cable systems.

The received signal at the mobile unit, $s_R(t)$ is as given by

$$\begin{aligned} s_R(t) &= s_T(t) \cdot p(t) = Ae^{j[\omega t+\psi_s(t)]} \cdot r(t)e^{j\psi_r(t)} = Ae^{j[\omega t+\psi_s(t)]} \cdot m(t)r_0(t)e^{j\psi_r(t)} \\ s_R(t) &= Am(t) \cdot r_0(t) \cdot e^{j[\omega t+\psi_s(t)+\psi_r(t)]}. \end{aligned} \tag{3.2.5}$$

Recall that the transmitted signal $s_T(t)$ (equation 3.2.1), is a constant-envelope (A = constant) phase-modulated signal having a phase modulation given by $\psi_T(t)$. The received signal $s_R(t)$ (equation 3.2.5), has an envelope given by $r(t) = m(t) \cdot r_0(t)$ (long-term "average" component $m(t)$ multiplied by a short-term, fast-fading component $r_0(t)$. A time-variable random-phase modulation component $\psi_r(t)$ has been introduced by the mobile propagation medium. The speed variation of $\psi_r(t)$ is dependent on the speed of the mobile unit and the changes in the propagation medium, for example, the relative speed of two automobiles traveling in opposite directions. The $\psi_r(t)$ random-phase variation is the cause of frequency spreading (recall phase-modulation correspondence with frequency modulation), also known as *Doppler spread.*

When the receiver, the transmitter, or the surroundings are moving, even slightly, the effective movement exceeds a few hundreds of wavelength. For example, in a 2-GHz radio system the wavelength "λ" is

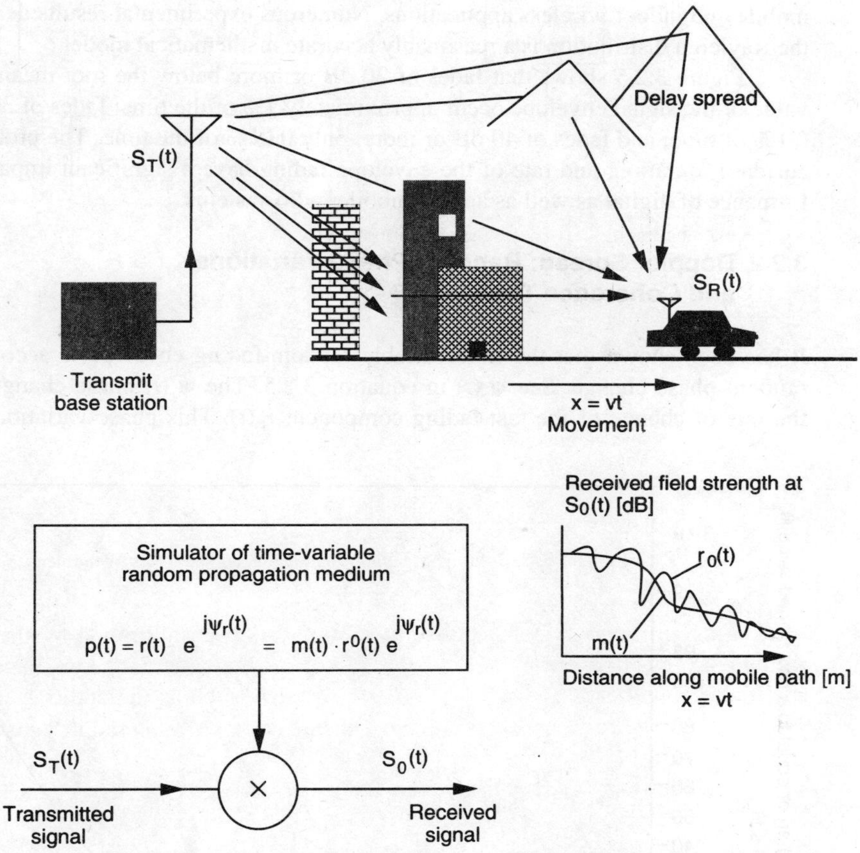

Figure 3.2.4 Fading fundamentals-illustration of a time variable envelope faded channel.

$$\lambda = \frac{c}{f} = \frac{3 \cdot 10^8 \, m/s}{2 \cdot 10^9 \,\text{Hz}} = 15 \text{ cm}. \tag{3.2.5a}$$

Thus, if the receiver is moving over a range of only 1.5 cm, it moves at a rate of 1.5:15 = 0.1 or more than 10 hundredths of a wavelength. Movement greater than a few hundreths of wavelengths could lead to signal envelope fluctuations. This situation is illustrated in Figure 3.2.4.

It has been theoretically shown (Jakes, 1974; Lee, 1989; Proakis, 1989) that the received fluctuating signal envelope has a *Rayleigh* distribution when the number of incident plane waves propagating randomly from different directions is sufficiently large and when there is no predominant LOS component. The Rayleigh distribution is the most frequently used distribution function for land-mobile channels, including outdoor land-mobile and indoor wireless applications. Numerous experimental results demonstrate that the Rayleigh distribution is a reasonably accurate mathematical model.

Figure 3.2.5 shows that fades of 20 dB or more below the root-mean-square (rms) value of the signal envelope occur approximately 1% of the time; fades of 30 dB or more, 0.1% of time; and fades of 40 dB or more, only 0.01% of the time. The probability of occurrence, duration, and rate of the envelope fading have a significant impact on the performance of digital as well as analog mobile radio systems.

3.2.2 Doppler Spread: Random Phase Variations and Coherence Time

It has been shown that the time-variable random-fading envelope is accompanied by a random phase change. See $\psi_r(t)$ in equation 3.2.5. The $\psi_r(t)$ phase change is related to the rate of change of the fast-fading component $r_0(t)$. This phase variation induces ran-

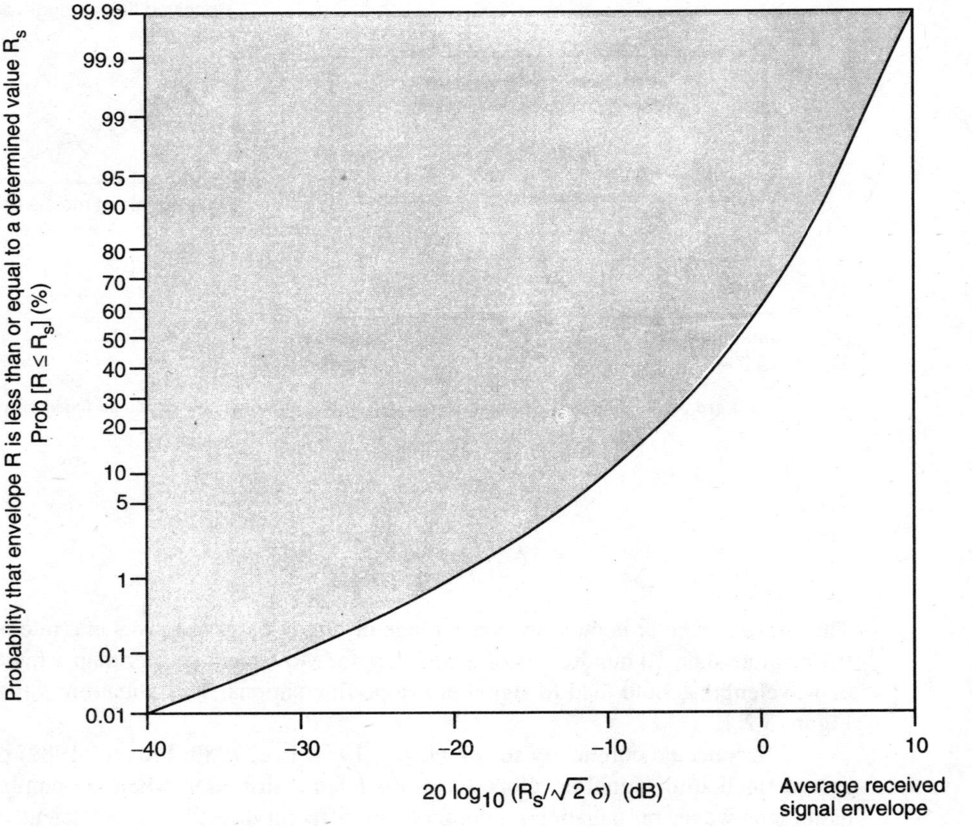

Figure 3.2.5 Rayleigh-faded envelope distribution function of an unmodulated carrier. (a) and (b) represent two different vertical scales [Feher, 1987].

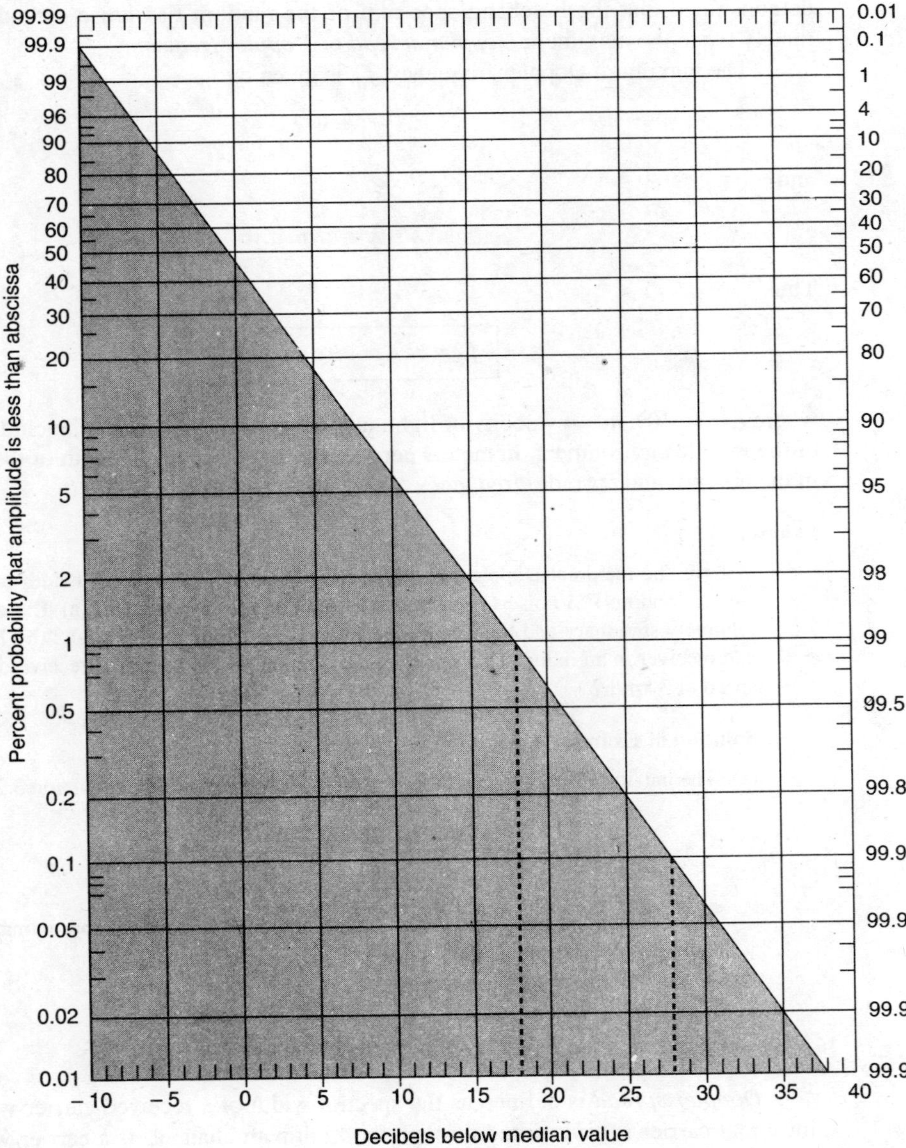

(b)

Figure 3.2.5 (continued)

dom frequency-modulation (FM) noise on the received carrier. In Jakes (1974) it was demonstrated that the baseband spectrum of the random FM noise extends to approximately twice the maximum *Doppler spread* or *Doppler frequency.*

The maximum Doppler frequency, f_d, is given by

$$f_d = v / \lambda \tag{3.2.6}$$

and

$$\lambda = c / f. \tag{3.2.7}$$

Thus

$$\boxed{f_d = v / \lambda = v / (c / f) = vf / c} \tag{3.2.8}$$

where $c = 3 \cdot 10^8$, *m/s* = velocity of light, and v = speed of the mobile, including the speed of the mobile environment, in meters per second (*m/s*); λ = wavelength of the radio signal in meters (*m*); and f = radio frequency.

Example 3.2.1

What is the maximal Doppler spread and the baseband spectral bandwidth of the Doppler-caused random FM noise for an 850-MHz mobile radio system, if: (a) The environment is relatively stationary and the mobile transmitter is travelling at 80 km/h? (b) The transmitter and receiver in an indoor PCS are stationary but one person near the receiver is walking at a speed of 3 km/h?

Solution of Example 3.2.1

(a) The maximal Doppler spread for v = 80 km/h is obtained from equation 3.2.8. It is

$$f_d = \frac{vf}{c} = \frac{(80 \cdot 10^3 / 3600) \cdot 850 \cdot 10^6}{3 \cdot 10^8} \approx 63 \text{ Hz}.$$

The baseband spectral bandwidth of the random FM noise is approximately twice the maximal Doppler spread, that is, 126 Hz.

(b) For v = 3 km/h, we have from (a)

$$f_d = 63 \cdot (3/80) = 2.36 \text{ Hz}.$$

Doppler spread is defined as the spectral width of a received carrier when a single sinusoidal carrier is transmitted through the multipath channel. If a carrier wave (an unmodulated sinusoidal tone) having a radio frequency f_c is transmitted, then because of Doppler spread f_d we receive a smeared signal spectrum with spectral components between $f_c - f_d$ and $f_c + f_d$. This effect may be interpreted as a *temporal decorrelation* effect of the random multipath-faded channel and is known as *time-selective fading.*

Coherence time (C_T) is usually defined as the required time interval to obtain an envelope correlation of 0.9 or less. It is inversely proportional to the maximum Doppler frequency and is defined (Lee, 1993; Proakis, 1989; Steel, 1992) as

$$C_T = 1/f_d. \tag{3.2.9}$$

3.2.3 Time-Delay Spread: Physical Cause and Concept

The physical cause of time-delay spread "τ" is illustrated in Figure 3.2.1. The direct line-of-sight (LOS) signal path d_0, having a propagation time τ, is severely attenuated by high rise buildings. Assume that the attenuated LOS signal power is −121 dBm. The mobile unit also receives reflected signals through the $d_1 + d_2$ path, $d_3 + d_4$ path $d_k + d_1$ path, and a large number of other reflected signal paths (not shown in Figure 3.2.1). If it is assumed that the strength of the signal received through the path with total distance $d_1 + d_2$ = −119 dBm, then we have an approximately equal direct strength (attenuated LOS) and reflected LOS pattern. In this illustrative example, if $d_1 + d_2$ = 36 km and d_0 = 1 km, there is a path delay or delay spread of

$$\tau = \frac{d_1 + d_2 - d_0}{c} = \frac{36 \text{ km} - 1 \text{ km}}{3 \cdot 10^8 \text{ m/s}} = 116.7 \mu s. \tag{3.2.9a}$$

In later sections the concept of delay-spread upper-bound τ_{max}, the practical importance of this bound, and various delay-spread definitions are highlighted. The *rms value of delay spread,* as well as the peak delay spreads, are among the most frequently used practical system specifications.

The effect of time-delay spread can also be interpreted as a *frequency-selective fading* effect. This effect may cause severe waveform distortions in the demodulated signal and may impose a limit on the bit-error-ratio (BER) performance of high-speed digital radio systems.

Coherence bandwidth (C_B) is the frequency spacing required for an envelope correlation of 0.9 or less. This bandwidth is inversely proportional to the rms value of time-delay spread, defined by

$$C_B = \frac{1}{\tau_{rms}}. \tag{3.2.10}$$

3.2.4. Shadowing and Path Loss

In Section 3.2.1 we stated that envelope fading can be separated into long-term or average fading and short-term or fast multipath fading. After the fast multipath fading is removed by averaging over distances of a few tens of wavelengths, *nonselective shadowing* still remains. Shadowing is caused mainly by terrain features of the land-mobile radio propagation environment. It imposes a slowly changing average on the Rayleigh fading statistics. Although there is no comprehensive mathematical model for shadowing, a *log-normal* distribution with a standard deviation of 5 to 12 dB has been found to best fit the experimental data in a typical urban area (Feher, 1987; Lee, 1993; Steel, 1992). *Path loss* is the average value of log-normal shadowing, which is also called the *area average.*

3.3 FUNDAMENTALS OF ANTENNA GAIN

To facilitate the comprehension of *line-of-sight* (*LOS*) and *non–line-of-sight* (*NLOS*) path loss, received signal power, and *link budget* calculations, we present a brief review of omnidirectional and directional antenna gain fundamentals. (For more details see Lee 1982, 1989, and 1993]).

A transmission line connects the radio transmitter and its radio frequency (RF) power amplifier (PA) to the transmit antenna. In the receiver the antenna is connected to the front-end low-noise amplifier (LNA). The amplified received signal is fed to a down converter and demodulated (see Figure 3.3.1). In the mobile or handheld transmitter/ receiver, the same antenna is used for transmission and reception. The transmit RF power amplifier excites the transmit antenna to radiate electromagnetic waves.

An isotropic antenna is an ideal lossless antenna that radiates power equally well in all directions. In mobile communications, omnidirectional antennas are most frequently used. These transmit/receive antennas are an approximation of ideal isotropic antennas. As transmit antennas they radiate well in all directions, and as receiving antennas they receive signals from all directions equally well. These antennas have an approximate unity *gain* G = 1, or 0 dB.

Assume that the transmit RF amplifier provides P_t watts of power to an isotropic

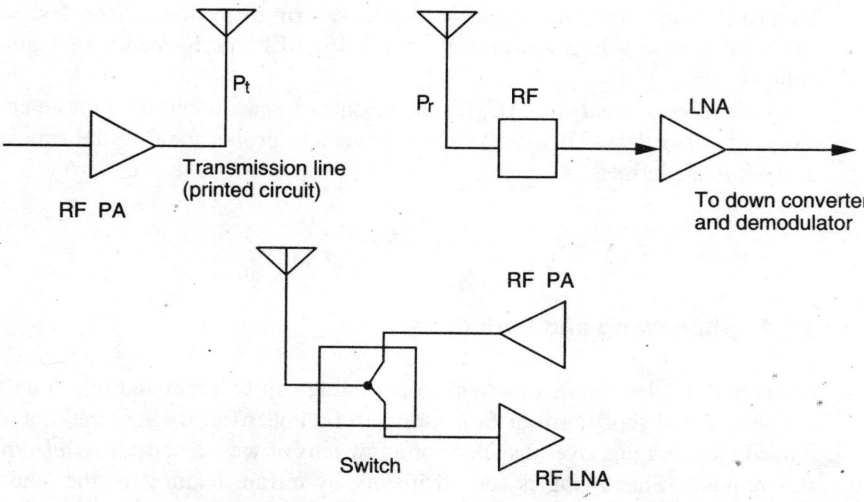

Figure 3.3.1 Transmit radio frequency (RF) power amplifier (PA), transmit antenna, receive antenna, RF subsection, and low-noise amplifier (LNA) parts of a transceiver. Switch is for standby or diversity operation.

transmit antenna illustrated in Figures 3.3.1 and 3.3.2). The radiated power density, ρ, or the outward flow of electromagnetic energy, measured at a distance r from antenna is

$$\rho = \frac{P_t}{4\pi r^2}[W/m^2]. \tag{3.3.1}$$

Directional antennas concentrate the radiated power in a particular direction. Antenna directivity (*D*) of a directional antenna is defined as

$$D = \frac{\text{Power density at distance } r \text{ in direction of maximum radiation}}{\text{Mean power density at distance } r}. \tag{3.3.2}$$

To use the antenna directivity definition (equation 3.3.2), we require knowledge of the power actually transmitted by the antenna. This power differs from the power supplied at the transmitter and receiver terminals by the losses in the antenna itself (Parsons and Gardiner, 1989).

A receiving antenna with an effective aperture A and at distance *r* from the omnidirectional transmitting antenna receives a power of P_r (watts) given by

$$P_r = \rho A = \frac{P_t A}{4\pi r^2}[W]. \tag{3.3.3}$$

Antenna gain *G* is related to the aperture of the antenna and the wavelength λ (in meters) of the radio signal. From Jordan and Balmain (1968) and other books on antennas and radiation.

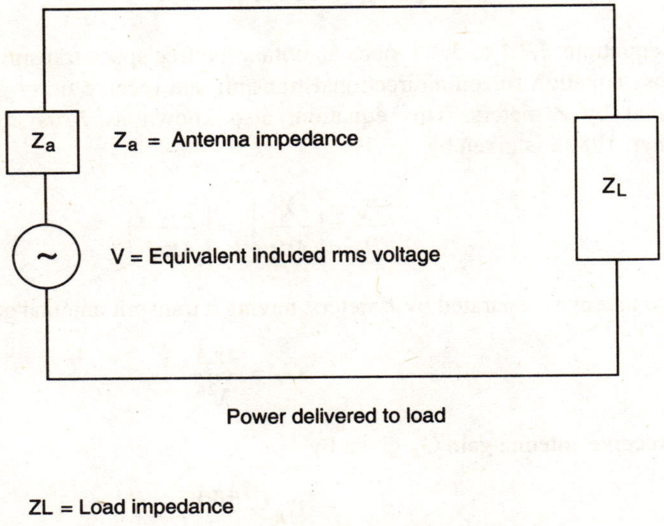

Figure 3.3.2 Antenna equivalent circuit.

$$G = \frac{4\pi A}{\lambda^2} \tag{3.3.4}$$

where

$$\lambda = c / f \tag{3.3.5}$$

and

$$\begin{aligned} c &= 3 \times 10^8 \text{ m/s (velocity of light)} \\ f &= \text{frequency of tranmitted carrier}. \end{aligned} \tag{3.3.6}$$

Ideal omnidirectional antennas have a unity gain $G = 1$; thus from equation 3.3.4 we have

$$A = \frac{\lambda^2}{4\pi}. \tag{3.3.7}$$

3.4 PROPAGATION CHARACTERISTICS

In this section the following propagation path loss characteristics of line-of-sight (LOS) and non–line-of-sight (NLOS) systems are described: the free space equations, path loss models, and the empirical path loss formula.

3.4.1 Free Space Propagation Loss Equation

From equations 3.3.1 to 3.3.7, one can obtain the free space transmission loss or propagation loss equation for omnidirectional transmit and receive unity gain ($G = 1$) antennas separated by r meters. This equation, also known as *Friis equation* (Parsons and Gardiner, 1989), is given by

$$\frac{P_R}{P_T} = \left(\frac{\lambda}{4\pi r}\right)^2 = \left(\frac{c}{4\pi r f}\right)^2. \tag{3.4.1}$$

For two antennas separated by r meters, having a transmit antenna gain G_T given by

$$G_T = \frac{4\pi A}{\lambda^2} \tag{3.4.2}$$

and a receive antenna gain G_R given by

$$G_R = \frac{4\pi A}{\lambda^2} \tag{3.4.3}$$

the free space propagation loss equation is

$$\frac{P_R}{P_T} = G_T G_R \left(\frac{\lambda}{4\pi r} \right)^2 . \tag{3.4.4}$$

The propagation loss (L_F), expressed in dB, is obtained from this *free space propagation loss equation.* It is given as

$$\begin{aligned} L_f[\text{dB}] &= 10\log\frac{P_R}{P_T} = 10\log G_T + 10\log G_R + 10\log\left(\frac{\lambda}{4\pi r}\right)^2 \\ &= 10\log G_T + 10\log G_R + 20\log\left(\frac{c/f}{4\pi r}\right). \end{aligned} \tag{3.4.5}$$

$$\boxed{L_f[\text{dB}] = 10\log G_T + 10\log G_R - 20\log f - 20\log r + 147.56 \text{ dB}} \tag{3.4.6}$$

For unity-gain, isotropic (that is, ideal omnidirectional) transmit and receive antennas and unobstructed LOS transmission, the basic transmission loss L_B is given by

$$\boxed{L_B[\text{dB}] = +27.56 - 20\log f[MHz] - 20\log r[m]} \tag{3.4.7}$$

or

$$\boxed{L_B[\text{dB}] = -32.44 - 20\log f[\text{MHz}] - 20\log r[\text{Km}]} \tag{3.4.8}$$

From this basic LOS transmission loss equation, note that the received power (relative to the transmitted power) *decreases by 6 dB for every doubling of distance and also for every doubling of the radio frequency.*

3.4.1.1 dBμV ↔ dBm relation. In equation 3.3.1 it is noted that the unit for radiated power density is [W/m^2]. Transmit and receive power is normally expressed in watts (W) or in dBm, whereas path loss is expressed in dB. Here we define the relations and conversion factors between these frequently used quantities.

Assume that a dipole or a monopole receiving antenna is used (Jordan, 1968; Lee, 1989). The induced voltage is related to field strength E as

$$V = \frac{E\lambda}{\pi}[V/m]. \tag{3.4.9}$$

V is expressed in volts per meter. The maximum power P_r delivered to a load impedance R_L in a system with a matched termination is

$$P_r = \frac{V^2}{4R_L}[W/m^2]. \tag{3.4.10}$$

It is assumed that the equivalent induced voltage by the antenna is V. The antenna impedance Z_a equals the load impedance Z_L and R_L is the real-load resistance of Z_L, as shown in Figure 3.3.2. Thus the received power can be expressed in W/m^2.

From the above equations we derive

$$P_r = \frac{V^2}{4R_L} = \frac{(E\lambda/\pi)^2}{4R_L} = \frac{E^2\lambda^2}{4\pi^2 R_L}. \tag{3.4.11}$$

Expressed in dBW, the power relative to 1 W, we obtain

$$P_r[\text{dB}W] = 10\log E^2[V^2] + 10\log\left(\frac{\lambda}{\pi}\right)^2[\text{dB}] + 10\log\frac{1}{4R_L}[R_L \text{ in } \Omega].$$

For a standard load resistance, $R_L = 50$ ohm, $10\log\frac{1}{4R_L} = -23$ dB; thus

$$P_r[\text{dB}W] = 10\log E^2[\mu V]^2 - 10\log(10^6)^2 + 10\log\left(\frac{\lambda}{\pi}\right)^2 - 23\text{dB}$$

where μv = microvolts. In units of dBm, relative to 1 mW (0 dBm = 1 mW) we have

$$P_r[\text{dBm}] = 10\log E^2[\mu V]^2 + 10\log 1000 - 10\log(10^6)^2 + 10\log\left(\frac{\lambda}{\pi}\right)^2 - 23\text{dB}$$

$$\boxed{P_r[\text{dBm}] = E^2[\text{dB}\mu V] - 113\text{dBm} + 10\log\left(\frac{\lambda}{\pi}\right)^2} \tag{3.4.12}$$

or in terms of radio frequency *f*, where $\lambda = c/f$

$$P_r[\text{dBm}] = E[\text{dB}\mu V] - 113\text{dBm} + 10\log(3\cdot 10^8/f\pi)^2$$
$$P_r[\text{dBm}] = E[\text{dB}\mu V] + 46.6[\text{dBm}] - 20\log f[\text{Hz}]$$
$$P_r[\text{dBm}] = E[\text{dB}\mu V] + 46.6[\text{dBm}] - 120\text{dB} - 20\log f[\text{MHz}]$$

$$\boxed{P_r[\text{dBm}] = E[\text{dB}\mu V] - 73.4 - 20\log f[\text{MHz}]} \tag{3.4.13}$$

Example 3.4.1

Find the relation between the received measured field strength, specified in [dBµV] and received power in [dBm] for a wireless system operated at an RF frequency of *f* = 1.9 GHz.

Solution of Example 3.4.1

From equation 3.4.13 we have

$$\begin{aligned} P_r[\text{dBm}] &= E[\text{dB}\mu V/m] - 73.4 - 20\log f[\text{MHz}] \\ &= E[\text{dB}\mu V] - 73.4 - 65.57 \\ &= E[\text{dB}\mu V] - 139\text{dB}. \end{aligned} \tag{3.4.14}$$

3.4.2 Path Loss of Non–Line-of-Sight (NLOS) and Line-of-Sight (LOS) Systems

The majority of land-mobile cellular systems and PCSs operate in a non–line-of-sight (NLOS) environment, such as those illustrated in Figure 3.2.1 and 3.2.2. From equation 3.4.8 it is noted that for the line-of-sight (LOS) operation the received power decreases by $1/r^2$ as the distance r between antennas increases. In summary, mean path loss increases exponentially with distance. The exponent n for unobstructed LOS systems is $n = 2$.

Based on empirical data a fairly general model has been developed for NLOS propagation and is used by most engineers (Cox et al, 1984; Rappaport, 1989). This model is given as

$$L(d) \propto L_B * \left(\frac{d}{d_0}\right)^{-n} \tag{3.4.15}$$

and indicates that the mean path loss L increases exponentially with distance d, where α is an abbreviation for "proportional to," as follows:

n = Path loss exponent; typical range of n is $3.5 \le n \le 5$.
d = Distance (separation) between transmit and receive antennas.
d_0 = Reference distance or free space propagation corner distance.
L_B = Propagation loss of the LOS path for d_0[m], based on equations 3.4.7 and 3.4.8.
L = Loss (propagation loss) of the combined NLOS and LOS signal path.

The path loss exponent n indicates how fast path loss increases with distances. The reference distance d_0 assumes that there is free space propagation (unobstructed) between the antenna and d_0. Practical values for indoor free space propagation corner distance d_0 typically range between 1 and 3 m.

Absolute mean path loss in dB is defined as the path loss in dB from the transmitter to the reference distance, abbreviated $L(d_0)$, plus the additional path loss described by equation 3.4.15. Thus the absolute mean path loss $L(d)$[dB] is given by

$$L(d)[\text{dB}] = L(d_0) - 10 * n * \log_{10}(d / d_0). \tag{3.4.16}$$

Experimental results indicate that typical NLOS outdoor cellular mobile systems have a path loss of $3.5 \le n \le 5$ and that indoor channels have a path loss of $2 \le n \le 4$, as shown in Figure 3.4.1. Additional experimental mean path loss results at 900 MHz and 17.5 GHz, obtained by Vannucci of AT&T Bell Laboratories (Vannucci and Roman, 1992, are illustrated in Figure 3.4.2.

Example 3.4.2

Compute the absolute mean path loss at $d_0 = 3$ m and at $d = 22$ m for a mobile radio system operated in the 2.4- to 2.48-GHz authorized band (FCC, 1990). Assume the path

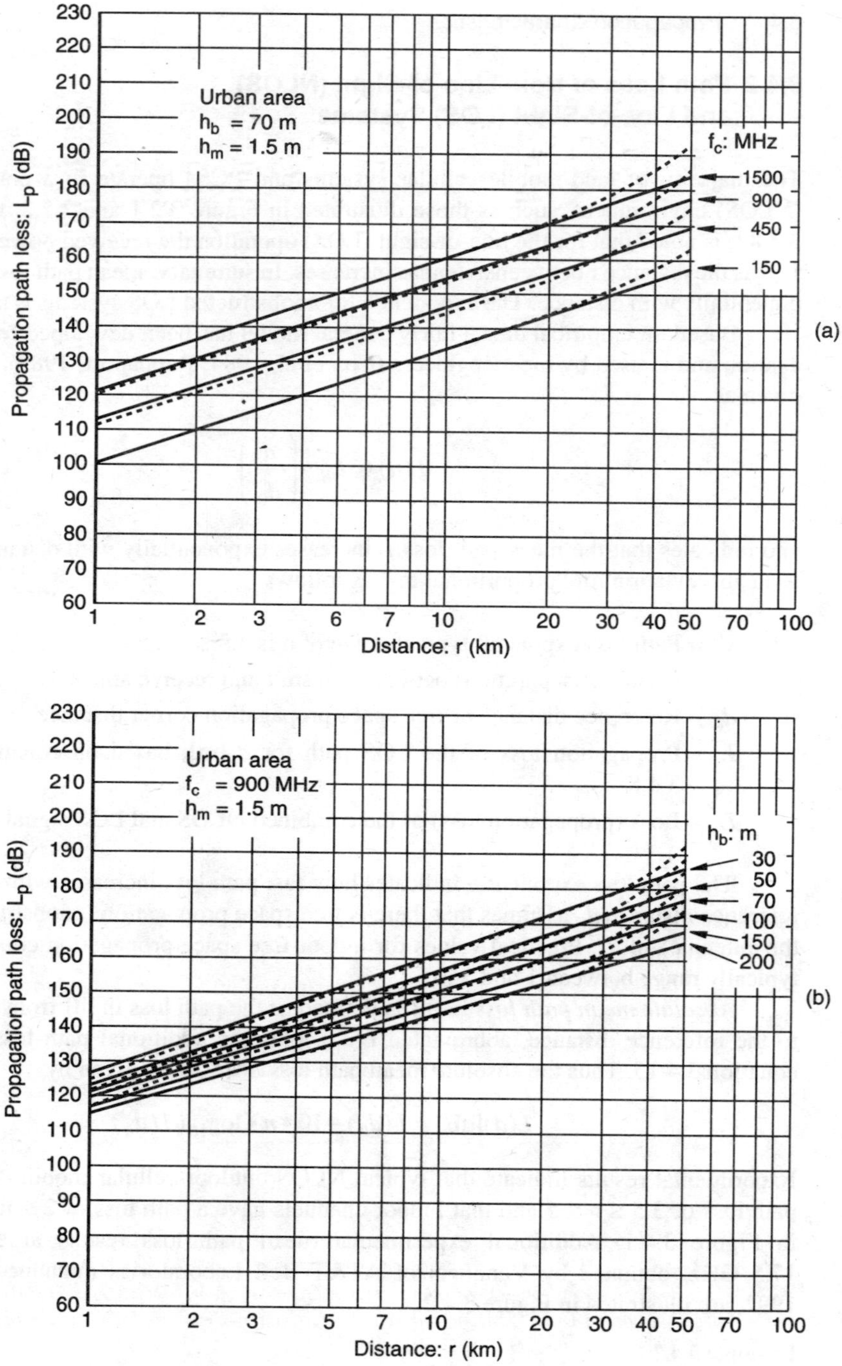

Figure 3.4.1 Propagation path loss in urban area. Solid lines are obtained by empirical formula, dashed lines by Okomura's prediction method. (a), f_c is a parameter; (b), base station height h_b is a parameter. (From Feher, 1987a).

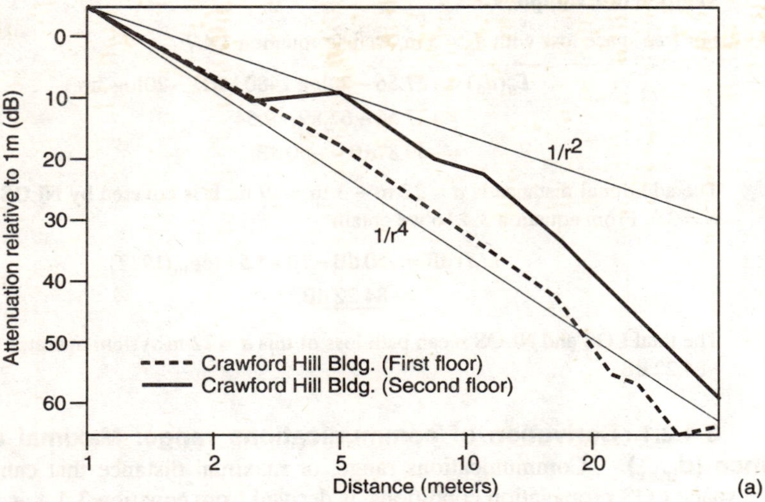

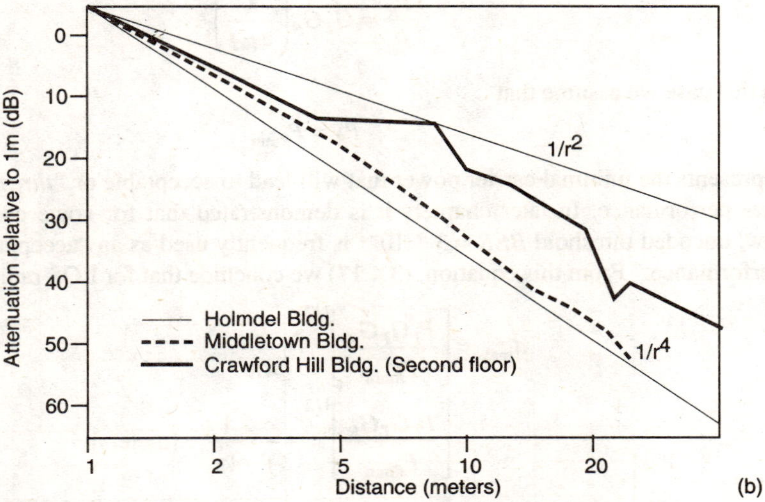

Figure 3.4.2 Propagation attenuation measurements at (a) 900 MHz and at (b) 1.75 GHz in a mobile PCS environment for radius of 1 to 30 m. G. Vanucci and R. S. Roman, "Measurement results on indoor radio frequency re-use at 900 MHz and 18 GHz," *Proceedings of the Third IEEE International Symposium on Personal, Indoor and Mobile Radio Communications*, (© 1992 IEEE).

loss exponent is $n = 3.5$. Assume the first two meters are LOS, afterwards NLOS propagation should be assumed.

Solution of Example 3.4.2

For free space loss with $d_0 = 3$ m, we use equation 3.4.7:

$$\begin{aligned} L_B(d_0) &= +27.56 - 20\log 2480\text{ MHz} - 20\log 3\text{m} \\ &= +27.56 - 67.89 - 9.54 \\ &= -49.87\text{dB} \approx -50\text{ dB}. \end{aligned}$$

The additional distance is $d = 22$ m − 3 m = 19 m. It is covered by NLOS propagation with $N = 3.5$. From equation 3.4.16 we obtain

$$\begin{aligned} L(d)\text{ dB} &= -50\text{ dB} - 10 * 3.5 * \log_{10}(19/2) \\ &= \underline{-84.22}\text{ dB}. \end{aligned}$$

The total LOS and NLOS mean path loss of this $d = 22$ m system operated at $f = 2.48$ GHz is −84.22 dB.

3.4.2.1. Derivation of communications range: Maximal coverage distance (d_{max}). Communications range, or maximal distance that can be covered for free space LOS propagation conditions, is derived from equation 3.4.4 as follows:

$$\frac{P_R}{P_T} = G_T G_R \left(\frac{\lambda}{4\pi d}\right)^2. \tag{3.4.17}$$

In this case we assume that

$$P_R = P_{R\min}$$

represents the minimal carrier power that will lead to acceptable or *"threshold" bit-error-rate* performance. In later chapters it is demonstrated that for voice communications a raw, uncoded threshold $BER = 3 * 10^{-2}$ is frequently used as an "acceptable or threshold performance." From this equation, (3.4.17) we conclude that for LOS radio systems

$$\begin{aligned} d_{\max} &= \left[\frac{P_T G_T G_R}{P_{R\min}}\right]^{1/2} * \frac{\lambda}{4\pi} \\ &= \left[\frac{P_T G_T G_R}{P_{R\min}}\right]^{1/2} * \frac{c}{f} \cdot \frac{1}{4\pi} \quad \text{[meters]}. \end{aligned} \tag{3.4.18}$$

For more general NLOS conditions, we assume that there is a reference distance, or free space propagation corner distance, between the antenna of the transmitter and the nearest obstacles. As illustrated in Figure 3.2.1, the radio waves cover the initial distance "d_0" in an LOS mode, and afterwards the waves are scattered and propagate in an NLOS mode.

The maximal distance or communications range of the combined LOS and NLOS radio path is derived as

$$P_R = P_T * G_T * G_R * L_{TOT} \tag{3.4.19}$$

where

$$L_{TOT} = \text{Combined LOS and NLOS loss}$$
$$L_{TOT} = L_{d_0} * L_{NLOS} \tag{3.4.20}$$

has two components, the LOS loss (L_{d_0} or $L_{d_0\text{free}}$) and the NLOS loss (L_{NLOS}). The LOS loss is abbreviated as L_{d_0} to remind us that the radio waves propagate only a distance "d_0" in an LOS mode and the remainder of the distance "d" is in an NLOS mode. Typically $d - d_0 \approx d$, as d_0 is much smaller than "d." From the preceding equations we conclude that

$$L_{TOT}(d) = \underbrace{\left(\frac{\lambda}{4\pi d_0}\right)^2}_{\substack{\uparrow \\ \text{LOS component}}} * \underbrace{\left(\frac{d_0}{d}\right)^n}_{\substack{\uparrow \\ \text{NLOS component}}}. \tag{3.4.21}$$

Note that this equation is practically the same as equation 3.4.15. In this subsection the notation is somewhat changed to lead to a more convenient communications range equation.

The communication range (maximal distance d_{max}) is derived below as follows:

$$P_R = P_T * G_T * G_R * L_d \tag{3.4.22}$$

$$L_d = L(d_0) * L(\text{NLOS}) = \left(\frac{\lambda}{4\pi d_0}\right)^2 * \left(\frac{d_0}{d}\right)^n \tag{3.4.23}$$

$$P_R = P_T * G_T G_R \left(\frac{\lambda}{4\pi d_0}\right)^2 \left(\frac{d_0}{d}\right)^n \tag{3.4.24}$$

$$d^n = \left[\frac{P_T G_T G_R \left(\frac{\lambda}{4\pi d_0}\right)^2}{P_R}\right] d_0^n \tag{3.4.25}$$

$$d = \left[\frac{P_T G_T G_R \left(\frac{\lambda}{4\pi d_0}\right)^2}{P_R}\right]^{1/n} d_0 \tag{3.4.26}$$

3.4.2.2 Definition of system gain (G_s). System gain is a useful measure of performance because it incorporates many parameters of interest to the designer of radio systems. In its simplest form, applying only to the equipment, it is the difference between transmitter output power and the receiver threshold sensitivity. The receiver threshold sensitivity is the minimum received power required to achieve an acceptable level of performance such as a maximum BER. Its value must be greater than or at least equal to the sum of the gains and losses that are external to the equipment (Feher, 1981). Mathematically, it is

$$G_s = P_t - C_{\min} \geq FM + |L_p| + |L_f| + |L_b| - G_t - G_r \quad (3.4.27)$$

where

G_s = System gain (dB)

P_t = Transmitter output power [dBm], excluding antenna branching network or other antenna connectivity losses

$C_{\min}$ = $P_{r\min}$ = received carrier level (dB) for a minimum quality objective. The $C_{\min}$ in dBm is usually specified for a maximal BER. For a mobile voice telephony link this BER = $3 \cdot 10^{-2}$ (in several standards). For mobile data links it could be BER = $1 \cdot 10^{-6}$. This is also called the *receiver threshold.*

$P_{r\min}$ = $C_{\min}$ as defined above

L_p = Line-of-sight (LOS) or free space path loss attenuation between isotropic radiators.

$$L_p = -92.4 - 20 \log d\,[\text{km}] - 20 \log f[\text{GHz}] \quad (3.4.28)$$

where

d = Path length, in km

f = Carrier frequency (GHz)

L_F = Feeder loss

L_B = Branching loss, that is, the total filter and circulator loss when transmitters and receivers are coupled to a single line

G_T, G_R = Gain of transmitter and receiver antennas over an isotropic radiator. Although antenna gains are frequency dependent, for the sake of simplicity, midband gains as published in manufacturers' catalogs are typically assumed.

FM = Radio hop fade margin (dB) of a nondiversity system required to meet the reliability objective.

Equation 3.4.28 is similar to equations 3.4.7 and 3.4.8. The RF frequency is specified in units of GHz instead of MHz.

3.4.2.3 Empirical formula for path loss. Empirical models based on extensive field measurements are used to predict the average path loss along the radio path. This path is from the base-station antenna to the mobile antenna. Experimental path loss curves are generated by measuring the received signal strength (RF carrier) and subtracting it from the transmitted signal power. For example, if we have unity gain omnidirectional antennas, the transmit power $P_T = +30$ dBm, and at a given location the received carrier power $P_R = -105$ dBm, then the path loss Lp is

$$L_P = P_T - P_R = +30\text{ dBm} - (-105\text{ dBm}) = 135\text{ dB}. \tag{3.4.29}$$

(*Note:* Since P_T and P_R are in the same units, L_P can be expressed in dB.)

Extensive measurements performed by *Okomura* (summarized and described in Feher [1987] and Hata [1980] led to an empirical formula for the *median path loss Lp* (in decibels) between two isotropic (ideal omnidirectional) unity-gain base and mobile antennas. This formula, also known as the *Okomura prediction method,* is given as

$$L_P = \begin{cases} A + B\log_{10}(r) & \text{for urban area} \\ A + B\log_{10}(r) - C & \text{for suburban area} \\ A + B\log_{10}(r) - D & \text{for open area} \end{cases} \tag{3.4.30}$$

where r (kilometers) is the distance between base and mobile stations. The radio carrier frequency is f_c (MHz), the base station antenna height is h_b (meters), and the mobile station antenna height is h_m (meters). The values of A, B, C, and D are given, respectively, by

$$\begin{aligned} A &= A(f_c, h_b, h_m) = 69.55 + 26.16\log_{10}(f_c) - 13.82\log_{10}(h_b) - a(h_m) \\ B &= B(h_b) = 44.9 - 6.55\log_{10}(h_b) \\ C &= C(f_c) = 2\left[\log_{10}\left(\frac{f_c}{28}\right)\right]^2 + 5.4 \\ D &= D(f_c) = 4.78\left[\log_{10}(f_c)\right]^2 - 19.33\log_{10}(f_c) + 40.94 \end{aligned} \tag{3.4.31}$$

where

$$a(h_m) = \begin{cases} [1.1\log_{10}(f_c) - 0.7]h_m - [1.56\log_{10}(f_c) - 0.8] \\ \qquad\qquad \text{for medium or small city} \\ \begin{cases} 8.28[\log_{10}(1.54\,h_m)]^2 - 1.1 & \text{for } f_c \geq 200\text{ MHz} \\ 3.2[\log_{10}(11.75\,h_m)]^2 - 4.97 & \text{for } f_c \geq 400\text{ MHz} \end{cases} \\ \qquad\qquad \text{for large city} \end{cases} \tag{3.4.32}$$

Equation 3.4.31 can be used if the following conditions are satisfied:

f_c: 150 to 1500 (MHz)
h_b: 30 to 200 (m); extended range, 1.5 to 400 (m)
h_m: 1 to 10 (m)
r: 1 to 20 (km); extended range, 2 m to 80 km.

The path loss L_p (dB) in an urban area, where the carrier frequency f_c (MHz) and the base station antenna height h_b (meters) are variable parameters, is illustrated in Figure 3.4.1.

The solid lines are obtained by the empirical formula, and the dashed lines by the Okomura's prediction method. These figures show that the maximum error is only about 1 dB within the distance range of $r = 1$ to 20 km (Feher, 1987). Experimental propagation attenuation measurements for short-distance PCS environments (in the range of 1 to 30 meters) are illustrated in Figure 3.4.2, based on experimental data of Vanucci of AT&T Bell Laboratories (Vanucci and Roman, 1992). A comparison of experimental data with equations 3.4.30 to 3.4.32 indicates that these equations can also be used for systems operating at a range of up to 3 meters.

3.5 MODELS OF MULTIPATH-FADED RADIO SIGNALS

In previous sections we described fundamental concepts and presented a physical insight into line-of-sight (LOS) and non–line-of-sight (NLOS) radio propagation. Here we describe a useful mathematical model of an unmodulated sinusoidal carrier, transmitted through random multiple propagation paths between a stationary base station and a moving mobile receiver. This theoretical model is used in our later studies of Rayleigh faded carrier envelope (signal strength) distributions, signal level crossing rate, and fade duration. These parameters and concepts are required for link design issues such as error control and system design issues such as access methods. For instance, fade durations and zero crossing rates relate BER and word-error rate (WER).

3.5.1 Unmodulated Carrier: Theoretical Models

Assuming that the *vehicle speed* v is sufficiently small compared to the product of the *carrier center frequency* f_c and *carrier wavelength* λ, that is, $v << f_c\lambda$, the *received faded carrier* $e(t)$ can be represented as

$$e(t) = \sum_{n=1}^{N} e_n(t) = Re\left[\sum_{n=1}^{N} z_n(t)e^{j2\pi f_c t}\right] \tag{3.5.1}$$

where $e_n(t)$ is an elementary wave, $Re[\cdot]$ is the real part of $[\cdot]$, and $j = \sqrt{-1}$. Furthermore, $z_n(t)$ is the complex random modulation of $e_n(t)$, which is caused by the random variation of propagation paths resulting from the vehicle movement (Hirade, in Feher, 1987).

Provided that N is sufficiently large and that all the $|z_n(t)|$ are equal, then by the central limit theorem, $e(t)$ can be expressed by the following narrow-band Gaussian process

$$e(t) = Re\left[z(t)e^{j2\pi f_c t}\right] \tag{3.5.2}$$

where $z(t)$ is a complex zero-mean stationary baseband Gaussian process having the following properties:

$$\langle z(t)\rangle = 0$$
$$\frac{1}{2}\langle z(t)z*(t-\tau)\rangle = \psi_z(\tau) \tag{3.5.3}$$
$$\frac{1}{2}\langle z(t)z(t-\tau)\rangle = 0.$$

In the previous equation, $\langle\cdot\rangle$ represents an ensemble average, $(\cdot)^*$ is the complex conjugate of $(\cdot)$, and $\psi_z(\tau)$ is the autocorrelation function of $z(t)$ given by

$$\psi_z(\tau) = \int_{-\infty}^{\infty} W_z(f)e^{j2\pi f\tau}df \tag{3.5.4}$$

where $W_z(f)$ is the power spectrum of the process $z(t)$.

In a typical system the moving vehicle has an antenna with an omnidirectional pattern in the horizontal plane, and the propagation angle of each elementary wave is uniformly distributed. The faded signal spectrum $W_z(f)$ is derived in Arredondo (1979), Clark (1992), Ganesh (1981) and Gans (1972) and is given by

$$w(f) = \begin{cases} \dfrac{\sigma^2}{\pi\sqrt{f_D^2 - f^2}} & |f| \le f_D \\ 0 & |f| > f_D \end{cases} \tag{3.5.5}$$

where σ^2 is the average power of $e(t)$ and f_D is the maximum Doppler frequency, given by $f_D = v/\lambda$. Theoretical and experimentally obtained power spectra of the faded unmodulated carriers are illustrated in Figure 3.5.1. Substituting equation 3.5.5 into equation 3.5.4, $\psi_z(\tau)$ is

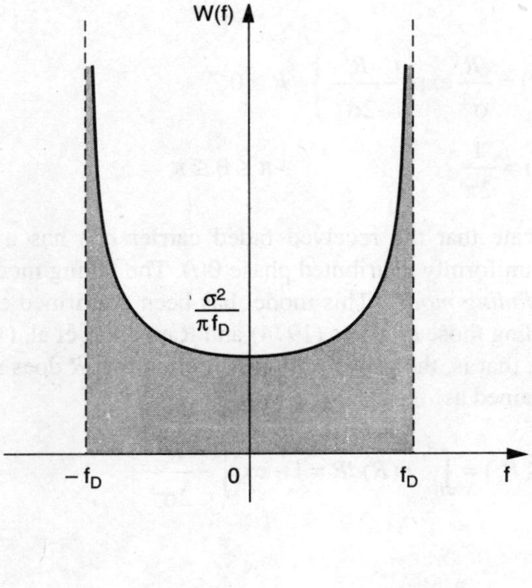

Figure 3.5.1 Theoretical faded power spectrum of a single sinusoidal (unmodulated carrier), having a maximum Doppler frequency $f_D = v/\lambda = f_c \times v/c$.

$$\psi_z(\tau) = \sigma^2 J_0(2\pi f_D \tau) \tag{3.5.6}$$

where $J_0(\cdot)$ is the zero-order Bessel function of the first kind. Several types of faded-signal spectra other than the one defined above have been observed and derived for land-mobile radio applications. Their properties are described in detail in Section 3.8 and in Gans (1972).

From the preceding equations it can be shown that multipath fading can be regarded as a multiplicative complex stationary Gaussian process characterized by $W_z(f)$ and $\psi_z(\tau)$. This fundamental property is used in the design of fade simulators, which are described in Sections 3.6 and 3.8.

3.5.1.1 Envelope and phase of the faded, unmodulated carrier. The received faded carrier $e(t)$, given by equation 3.5.2, can also be represented as

$$e(t) = R(t)\cos\{2\pi f_c t + \theta(t)\}. \tag{3.5.7}$$

where $R(t)$ and $\theta(t)$ are the envelope and phase of $e(t)$ given, respectively, by

$$\begin{aligned} R(t) &= |z(t)| \\ \theta(t) &= \angle z(t). \end{aligned} \tag{3.5.8}$$

Here $\angle z(t)$ denotes the angle of $z(t)$. At any particular time instant, $z = z(t)$ is a complex Gaussian random variable, and the joint probability density function (pdf) of $R = R(t)$ and $\theta = \theta(t)$ can be written as

$$p(R,\theta) = \frac{R}{2\pi\sigma^2}\exp\left(-\frac{R^2}{2\sigma^2}\right) \qquad R \geqq 0,\ -\pi \leqq \theta \leqq \pi. \tag{3.5.9}$$

Consequently, the probability density functions (pdf) of R and θ are given, respectively, by

$$\begin{cases} p(R) = \dfrac{R}{\sigma^2}\exp\left(-\dfrac{R^2}{2\sigma^2}\right) & R \geq 0 \\ p(\theta) = \dfrac{1}{2\pi} & -\pi \leq \theta \leq \pi \end{cases} \tag{3.5.10}$$

The preceding equations indicate that the received faded carrier $e(t)$ has a Rayleigh-distributed envelope $r(t)$ and a uniformly distributed phase $\theta(t)$. The fading model just described is called the *Rayleigh fading model.* This model has been confirmed experimentally by many field tests, including those of Jakes (1974) and Rappaport et al. (1990).

The cumulative pdf of R, that is, the probability distribution that R does not exceed a specified level Rs, can be obtained as

$$\text{Prob}[R \leq R_s) = \int_0^{R_s} p(R)dR = 1 - \exp\left(-\frac{R_s^2}{2\sigma^2}\right). \tag{3.5.11}$$

Computed results of these theoretical Rayleigh distributions are presented on two different vertical scales in Figure 3.2.5. From this figure it is noted that the envelope of a Rayleigh-faded carrier fluctuates within a dynamic range of about 40 dB to 50 dB with a probability of 99.9%. The probability density function of θ, that is, the probability that θ does not exceed a specified valued θ_s, can be described by

$$\text{Prob}[\theta \le \theta_s] = \int_{-\pi}^{\theta_s} p(\theta)d\theta = \frac{\theta_s + \pi}{2\pi}. \quad (3.5.12)$$

The rate of change (speed) of envelope and of phase fluctuation of a Rayleigh-faded unmodulated carrier is a function of the maximal Doppler shift, that is, the rate of change of the Rayleigh fade. If the Doppler shift of the Rayleigh fade is very small, for example, $f_d < 1$ Hz, the fade is called *Quasi-Rayleigh* or *Quasi-Stationary Rayleigh* fade (Figure 3.5.1).

3.5.1.2 Level crossing rate and fade duration. In the design of high-speed digital mobile radio transmission systems, it is important to know the characteristics of multipath fading that induce burst errors. Provided that burst errors occur when the signal envelope fades below a specific threshold value, the level crossing rate can be used as an appropriate measure for the burst error occurrence rate. The fade duration may also be used to estimate the burst error length.

The level crossing rate, which is generally defined as the expected rate at which the envelope R crosses a specified level R_s in the positive direction, is given by Gans (1972) as follows:

$$N_{R_s} = \int_0^{\infty} \dot{R}p(R_s,\dot{R})d\dot{R} \quad (3.5.13)$$

where the dot denotes a time derivative, $p(R_s, \dot{R})$ is the joint pdf of R, and $\dot{R}$ for $R = R_s$. It can be shown that the *level crossing rate* N_{R_s} for a signal received by a vertical monopole antenna (Feher, 1987, Gans, 1972) is

$$N_{R_s} = \sqrt{2\pi} f_D \left(\frac{R_s}{\sqrt{2}\sigma} \right) \exp\left(-\frac{R_s^2}{2\sigma^2} \right). \quad (3.5.14)$$

Computed results of the normalized level crossing rate N_{R_s}/f_D of a Rayleigh-faded, unmodulated carrier are shown in Figure 3.5.2. Since R_s and $\dot{R}$ are statistically independent, for the Rayleigh fading model, $p(R_s, \dot{R})$ can be written (Rice, 1974) as

$$p(R_s, \dot{R}) = p(R_s)p(\dot{R}) \quad (3.5.15)$$

where $p(\dot{R})$ is the probability density function (pdf) of $\dot{R}$. Further, $\dot{R}$ has a Gaussian pdf given by

$$p(\dot{R}) = \frac{1}{2\pi f_D \sigma \sqrt{\pi}} \exp\left[-\left(\frac{\dot{R}}{2\pi f_D \sigma} \right)^2 \right]. \quad (3.5.16)$$

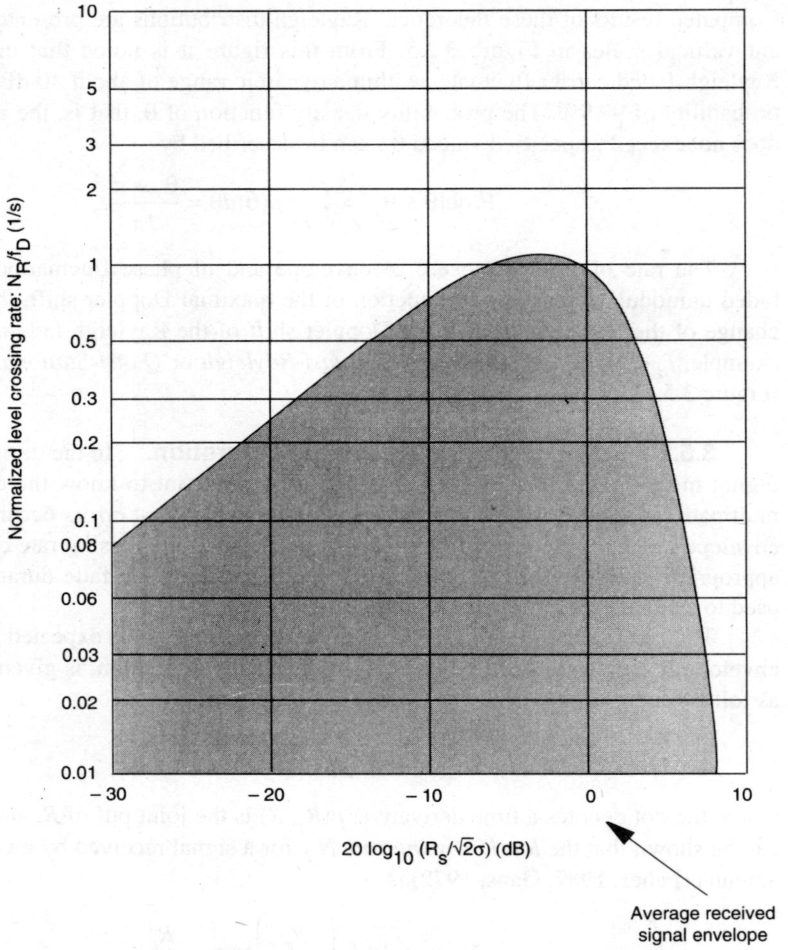

Figure 3.5.2 Level crossing rate N_R of a Rayleigh-faded carrier, normalized by the Doppler frequency f_D.

The statistical distribution function of the *fade duration* of the Rayleigh-faded channel has not been derived in a closed form. However, the average value of the fade duration can be expressed (Gans, 1972) by

$$\langle T_f \rangle = \frac{1}{N_{R_s}} \text{Prob}[R \le R_s]. \tag{3.5.17}$$

Using equations 3.5.11 and 3.5.14 in equation 3.5.17, the average duration is given by

$$\left\langle T_f \right\rangle = \frac{1}{\sqrt{2\pi}\left(R_s/\sqrt{2\sigma}\right)f_D}\left[\exp\left(\frac{R_s^2}{2\sigma^2}\right) - 1\right]. \tag{3.5.18}$$

A plot of this equation is shown in Figure 3.5.3.

3.5.2 Delay Spread: Theoretical Concepts and Terminology

The physical cause of delay spread is illustrated in Figure 3.2.1. We assume that at $t = 0$, one very short RF burst at 150 MHz is transmitted from the base station, located on the 70-m rooftop of a highrise building. The "direct" LOS signal path has a length of $d_0(m)$ and a propagation time (delay) of τ_0. In our illustrative example we assumed that the LOS path is obstructed by several buildings and has an obstruction-caused signal attenuation of 96 dB. If $d_0 = 1000$ m = 1 km, then the free space LOS loss at 150 MHz, obtained from equation 3.4.8, is 65 dB. Thus the total path loss of the direct signal path is 96 dB + 65 dB = 161 dB, as shown in Table 3.5.1. The reflected multipath RF signals travel along

$$d_1 + d_2, d_3 + d_4, \ldots, d_k + d_L.$$

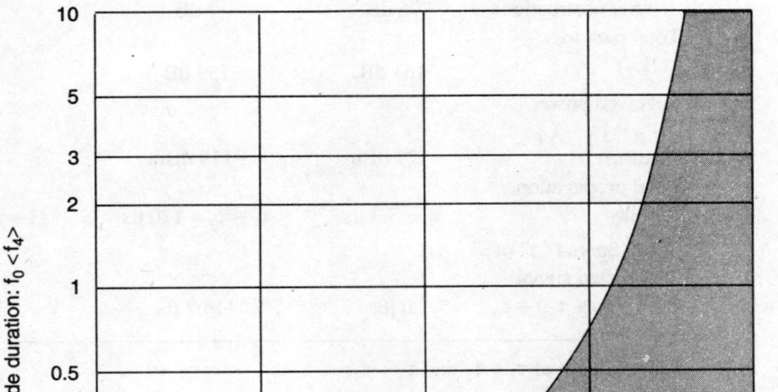

Figure 3.5.3 Average fade duration of a Rayleigh-faded carrier. (From Feher, 1987.)

Table 3.5.1 Delay spread "τ" and illustrative propagation loss values of a 3-kHz narrowband 150-MHz radio frequency Public Land Mobile Radio (PLMR) system. Values in this Table correspond to those in Figure 3.2.1.

Value	Direct LOS path "d_0"	First reflected path "$d_1 + d_2$"	Second reflected path "$d_3 + d_4$"
Total propagation distance	$d_0 = 1km$	$d_1 + d_2 = 36$ km	$d_3 + d_4 = 101$ km
Transmit power $P_T = 10$ Watt	40 dBm	40 dBm	40 dBm
Propagation path loss (based on Figure 3.4.2 at 150 MHz)	65 dB	152 dB	168 dB
Path loss due to buildings and other obstructions	96 dB	7 dB	10 dB
Total path loss (L_T)	161 dB	159 dB	178 dB
Received power $P_R = P_T - L_T$ (dBm)	−121 dBm	−119 dBm	−138 dBm
Total propagation delay	$\tau_0 = 3.3\ \mu s$	$\tau_1 + \tau_2 = 120\ \mu s$	$\tau 3 + \tau 4 = 336.7\ \mu s$
Delay Spread "τ" of reflected signal $\tau = (\tau_N + \tau_m) - \tau_0$	0 μs	116.7 μs	333.4 μs

Computation of $\tau_1 + \tau_2$ and $\tau_3 + \tau_4$:

$$\tau_1 + \tau_2 = \frac{d_1 + d_2}{c} = \frac{36 \times 10^3 m}{3 \times 10^8 m/s} = 120 \mu s$$

$$\tau_3 + \tau_4 = \frac{d_3 + d4}{c} = \frac{101 \times 10^3 m}{3 \times 10^8 m/s} = 336.7 \mu s$$

If the signal obstruction-caused attenuation along these longer signal paths is not very large, for example, assuming 7 dB and 10 dB in Table 3.5.1., then the received reflected signals, having an considerably longer propagation delay than the LOS signal arriving along the d_0 path, are received at the mobile with powers of comparable magnitude to the power of the LOS signal path. In this example we assume that the signal received by the mobile, through the reflected delayed path $d_1 + d_2$, having a propagation delay of $\tau_1 + \tau_2$, is −119 dBm, that is, 2 dB higher than the obstructed LOS signal.

The reflected signal path $d_1 + d_2$ has a total delay of $\tau_1 + \tau_2$. The delay relative to the direct LOS signal is $\tau_A = \tau_1 + \tau_2 - \tau_0$. This is called the first arrival delay. The second reflected signal, path $d_3 + d_4$, arrives at $\tau_3 + \tau_4$ and has a delay interval (relative to the d_0 direct signal path) of $\tau_B = \tau_3 + \tau_4 - \tau_0$ and a received power of −138 dBm. The received power of this delayed signal is 17 dB lower than the power of the direct path signal. In a realistic multipath environment a large number of delayed components are added. These components form a power delay profile. The extent of the power delay profile is called delay spread.

In the literature, several definitions have been used for exact mathematical analysis of delayed signals. The most frequently used definition and terminology, described in the following subsections are extracted from Chennakeshu (1988).

3.5.2.1 Delay terminology and mathematical definitions

1. *Power delay profile.* Multipath propagation causes severe dispersion of the transmitted signal. The expected degree of dispersion is determined through the measurement of the power delay profile of the channel. The power delay profile provides an indication of the dispersion or distribution of transmitted power over various paths of the multipath structure. The mobile radio channel exhibits a continuous multipath structure, hence the power delay profile can be thought of as a density function

$$P(\tau) = \frac{S(\tau)}{\int S(\tau)d\tau} \tag{3.5.19}$$

where $S(\tau)$ is the measured power delay profile (Figure 3.5.4).

2. *First arrival delay* (τ_A). This is the delay of the first arriving path, which is measured at the receiver. This delay is usually set at approximately the minimum possible propagation path delay from the transmitter to the receiver (Cox, 1972). This delay serves as a reference, and all delay measurements are taken in relation to it. Any delay measured to the right of this reference delay is called an *excess* delay.

3. *Mean excess delay* (τ_e). This is the average delay measured with respect to the first arrival delay and is expressed as

$$\tau_e = \int (\tau - \tau_A)P(\tau)d\tau . \tag{3.5.20}$$

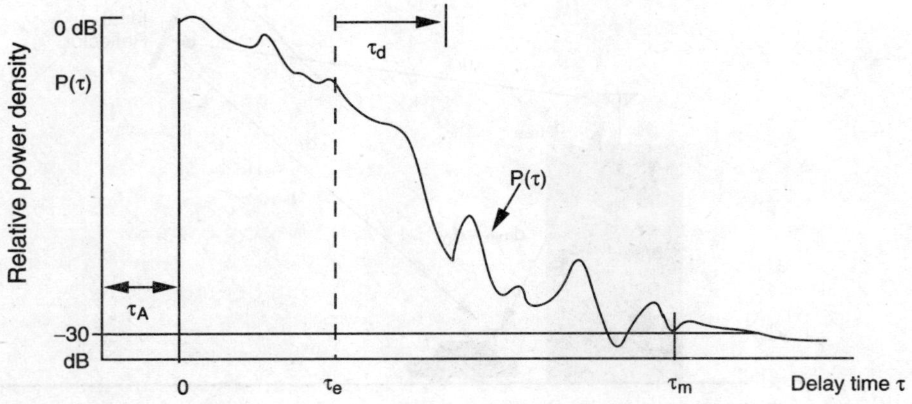

Figure 3.5.4 Illustration of a typical delay power profile, $P(\tau)$, measurement and of the delay parameters and terminology: τ_A = first arrival delay; τ_e = mean excess delay; τ_d = root-mean-square (rms) delay; τ_m = maximum excess delay with respect to a certain power level.

4. *RMS delay* (τ_d). This term is normally used as a measure of delay spread. It is the standard deviation about the mean excess delay and is expressed as

$$\tau_d = \left[\int (\tau - \tau_e - \tau_A)^2 P(\tau) d\tau\right]^{1/2}. \qquad (3.5.21)$$

5. *Maximum excess delay* (τ_M). This is measured with respect to a certain power level. For example, the maximum excess delay spread can be specified as the excess delay (τ) for which $P(\tau)$ falls to −30 dB of its peak value (Figures 3.5.4 and 3.5.5).

3.5.2.2 Mathematical models of delay profiles. Power delay profile models and channel transfer function models are often used to facilitate simulation and experimental study of BER performance of a digital system in a multipath environment. Typically, average power delay profiles are used for semianalytic simulations, while channel transfer function and impulse response models are used for experimental and full simulation studies. Models of delay profiles include the following:

1. *One-sided exponential profile*

$$P(\tau) = \frac{1}{\tau_d} \exp\left(-\frac{\tau}{\tau_d}\right); \qquad \tau_d > 0 \qquad (3.5.22)$$

2. *Gaussian profile*

$$P(\tau) = \frac{1}{\sqrt{2\pi}\tau_d} \exp\left[-\frac{1}{2}\left(\frac{\tau}{\tau_d}\right)^2\right] \qquad (3.5.23)$$

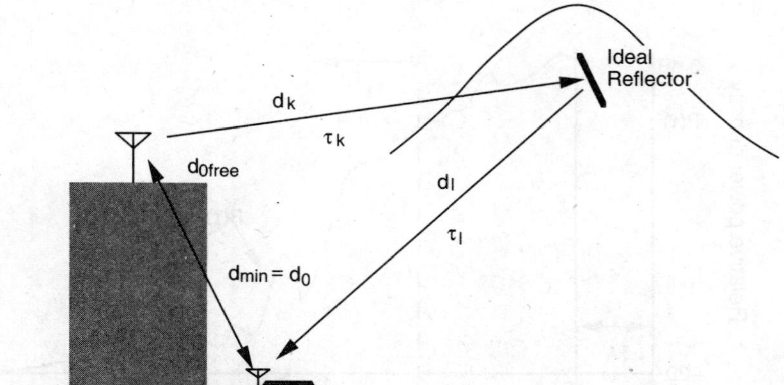

Figure 3.5.5 Feher's theoretical delay-spread upper bound (Feher, 1993) and model for worst-case delay-spread prediction of any type of radio system. For this simple and powerful one-delayed ray "limit" prediction, only knowledge of *system gain* G_S, defined by $G_S = P_T : P_{R\,\min}$ (P_T = transmit power; $P_{R\,\min}$ = receiver sensitivity threshold) and of the radio frequency is required.

3. *Equal-amplitude two-path or double-spike profile*

$$P(\tau) = \frac{1}{2}[\delta(\tau) + \delta(\tau - 2\tau_d)] \tag{3.5.24}$$

$$P(\tau) = \frac{1}{2}[\delta(\tau - \tau_d) + \delta(\tau + \tau_d)] \tag{3.5.25}$$

4. *Rummler's two-ray model.* This model, unlike the previous three, is specified in terms of the channel transfer function

$$H(f) = 1 - b\exp[-j2\pi(f - f_0)\tau] \tag{3.5.26}$$

where f_0 is the frequency offset from the band within the center of the notch, τ is the relative delay between the two rays (paths,) and b is the amplitude of the second ray with respect to the main ray ($b \leq 1$).

When the stronger of the two rays occurs first ($\tau > 0$), then the channel is in the *minimum phase* condition. When the stronger of the two rays follows the weaker ray ($\tau < 0$), the channel is said to be in the *nonminimum phase* condition (Walker, 1990).

The one-sided exponential profile often models the general trend of field-measured profiles, as illustrated in Figures 3.7.1 and 3.7.4. The Gaussian power delay profile is essentially a theoretical model. The double-spike profile is more severe on BER performance because of the equal amplitude of the two paths. Most measured profiles appear to exhibit exponential profiles with superimposed spikes, as illustrated in the field-measurement results shown in Figure 3.7.2. The previously listed models 1 to 3 have been used extensively in simulation-based BER studies of portable systems. The Rummler two-ray model has been used extensively for testing the performance of equalizers for digital microwave (D'Aria et al., 1988; D'Avella et al., 1987; Walker, 1990). Modifications of the Rummler model and other models used for study of equalizers can be found in D'Avella et al. (1987) and Walker (1990). Also refer to GSM, (1988–1990) for further details.

3.5.3 A Simple Delay-Spread Bound—Feher's Upper Bound

A simple bound of "worst-case" delay spread is introduced in Feher (1993). The derivation of this bound is summarized next. Maximal delay spread, abbreviated as τ_{max}, is difficult to measure and estimate, and it can have a devastating effect by increasing the BER.

This delay-spread bound leads to a simple estimation of "worst-case" delay spread, based on knowledge of basic system parameters: transmit power (P_T), receive power at threshold (P_{Rmin}), and radio frequency (f_c). This bound applies to all wireless radio communications.

3.5.3.1 Derivation of the delay-spread bound. To derive the delay-spread upper bound, we take a closer look at Figures 3.2.1 and 3.5.5. In this "physical-engineering derivation" it is assumed that the "d_k" and "d_1" signal paths having "τ_k" and "τ_1" propagation delays are the longest line-of-sight (LOS) signal paths and that the reflection coefficient is 100%, that is, the total signal energy is reflected. Furthermore, we assume that the "direct" or shortest path is LOS for a short distance d_{0free}, and afterwards scattering and severe signal attenuation occurs in this direct path. For upper-bound derivation, it is assumed that the delayed signal energy could have a significant impact on the system performance, (for example, BER = *f*(S/N), if the received power of the delayed path is at threshold level, that is,

$$P_{r\,\min} = P_{r\,\text{threshold}}.$$

Thus we have

$$d_{\max} = r_{\max} = d_k + d_l.$$

For LOS propagation, the path loss is stated by equation 3.4.4 as the ratio of $P_{R\min}/P_{\text{transmit}}$, or

$$\frac{P_{R\min}}{P_T} = G_T G_R \left(\frac{\lambda}{4\pi d_{\max}}\right)^2.$$

From this expression we obtain Feher's bound

$$\boxed{d_{\max} = \left[\frac{P_T G_T G_R (\lambda/4\pi)^2}{P_{R\min}}\right]^{1/2}} \tag{3.5.27}$$

Feher's bound on the round-trip propagation delay is given by

$$\boxed{\tau_{\max} = \frac{d_{\max}}{c}} \tag{3.5.28}$$

where P_T = transmit power; G_T and G_R represent the transmit and receive antenna gains; λ and c the wavelength ($\lambda = c/f$) and velocity of light respectively; and f = radio carrier frequency.

The *maximal delay spread bound* equations 3.5.27 and 3.5.28 can be further simplified if omnidirectional unity gain ($G_T = G_R = 1$) transmit and receiver antennas are assumed. This simplified delay spread bound is

$$\tau_{\max} = \frac{d_{\max}}{c} = \left[\frac{P_T}{P_{R_{\min}}}\right]^{1/2} \frac{\lambda}{4\pi}\frac{1}{c} = \left[\frac{P_T}{P_{R_{\min}}}\right]^{1/2} \frac{c}{f}\frac{1}{4\pi c}$$

$$\boxed{\tau_{\max} = \frac{1}{4\pi}\frac{1}{f}\sqrt{\frac{P_T}{P_{R_{\min}}}}} \quad \text{[seconds].} \tag{3.5.29}$$

The following examples illustrate the simple and powerful estimation method offered by this bound.

Example 3.5.4

What is the delay spread bound τ_{max} of a 220-MHz public land-mobile radio (PLMR) system if $P_T = 1$ watt (+30 dBm) and $P_{Rmin} = -90$ dBm? How much is τ_{max} if the sensitivity of the receiver is improved to $P_{Rmin} = -100$ dBm? Why does increased sensitivity or increased system gain, $G_s = P_T P_{Rmin}$, lead to a higher delay-spread bound?

Solution of Example 3.5.4

We use Feher's bound with unity gain omnidirectional antennas, equation 3.5.29, and the specified parameters:

$$\tau_{max} = \frac{1}{4\pi}\frac{1}{f}\sqrt{\frac{P_T}{P_{R_{min}}}}.$$

For $P_T = 1$ watt $= 10^3$ mW and PRmin $= -90$ dBm $= 10^{-9}$ mW, we have $P_T/P_R = 10^{12}$, thus

$$\tau_{max} = \frac{1}{4\pi}\frac{1}{220\cdot 10^6}\sqrt{10^{12}} = 361.7\,\mu s.$$

For the improved sensitivity receiver with $P_{Rmin} = -100$ dBm, (10^{-10} mW) we obtain $P_T/P_R = 10^{13}$, thus

$$\tau_{max} = \frac{1}{4\pi\, 220.10^6}\sqrt{10^{13}} = 1143.8\,\mu s.$$

The computed delay-spread bound for the $P_{Rmin} = -90$ dBm receiver is $\tau_{max} = 361.7$ μs, while for the 10-dB (10 times) increased sensitivity receiver the bound increased $\sqrt{10}$ times to $\tau_{max} = 1143.8$ μs. Increased sensitivity or increased system gain leads to an increased delay spread because reflected signal paths from larger distances (larger delays) have a more significant impact on the overall measured delay spread profile. In Figure 3.7.4, with an increased transmit power of $P_T = 10$ W, we illustrate measured delay spread results in the 350-μs range. In this case an increased transmit power is equivalent to improved sensitivity. The sensitivity of the receiver in this experimental delay-spread measurement setup is about −90 dBm. Note the actual data receiver sensitivity in 3 kHz is −110 dBm. However, to measure with sufficient resolution, we require a 300-kHz bandwidth. Thus the sensitivity amounts to −110 dBm + 10log 300 kHz/3 kHz = −90 dBm. The 350-μs measured result is about three times lower than the predicted upper bound of 1143.8 μs.

Example 3.5.5

How much is the delay-spread bound for the European standard Digital European Cordless Telephone (DECT) system, having a transmit power of $P_T = +24$ dBm (250 mW), a receiver bandwidth of 1.1 MHz, and a carrier frequency of $f_c = 1.8$ GHz? The receiver sensitivity is controlled by the receiver noise figure (F). This low-cost system is designed for an $F = 11$ dB overall noise figure and requires a threshold (minimum) C/N of 23 dB.

Solution of Example 3.5.5

To use equation 3.5.29, first we have to compute P_{Rmin}. It is given by

$$P_{Rmin} = P_{R\,threshold} = kTBF + C/N \qquad (3.5.30)$$

where

$$kT = -174 \text{ dBm/Hz} \tag{3.5.31}$$

B = Receiver noise bandwidth

F = Noise figure of the receiver

C/N = Required carrier-to-noise ratio in the receiver bandwidth.

First we obtain the total noise N_T in the receiver

$$N_T = kTBF = -174 \text{ dBm/Hz} + 10\log 1.1 \cdot 10^6 \text{ Hz} + 11$$

$$= -174 \text{ dBm/Hz} + 60.041 + 11 = -103 \text{ dBm}$$

$$P_{R\min} = N_T + \text{C/N} = -103 \text{ dBm} + 23 \text{ dB} = -80 \text{ dBm } (10^{-8} \text{ mW}).$$

Thus

$$\tau_{\max} = \frac{1}{4\pi}\frac{1}{f}\sqrt{\frac{P_T}{P_{R\min}}} = \frac{1}{4\pi \cdot 1.8 \cdot 10^9}\sqrt{\frac{250\text{mW}}{10^{-8}\text{mW}}} \tag{3.5.32}$$

$$\tau_{\max} = 6.99\ \mu s.$$

Note: This computed upper bound $\tau_{\max} = 6.99\ \mu s$ is about 20 times higher than the indoor measurements illustrated in Figure 3.7.5. However, our predicted bound is similar to the measurements in Figure 3.7.1 for a distance (coverage) of several km.

3.6 INSTRUMENTATION AND MEASUREMENTS FOR LABORATORY AND FIELD TESTS

3.6.1 From Laboratory Tests to Product Release

Mobile radio channel simulators are essential for repeatable system tests in a development, design, or test laboratory. Field tests in a mobile environment are considerably more expensive and may require permission from the Federal Communications Commission (FCC) or other regulatory authorities. Because of the random, uncontrollable nature of the mobile propagation path, it is difficult to generate repeatable field test results.

Most product and system designs follow the conceptual and architectural development phase computer-aided simulation and design. An initial breadboard is built and tested in the laboratory. Following initial tests, improvements, and modifications, which are all frequently required, a newly created breadboard is tested in the laboratory. Following extensive laboratory evaluations, such as comparison with the system specifications, design goals and field tests are performed. Upon completion of successful field tests, comparison of field test results with laboratory measurements, computer predictions, and final approval from marketing, the design engineering team forwards the drawings and documentation to the production department.

Instrumentation principles and requirements for Rayleigh-faded land-mobile cellular PCSs are described in this section. We introduce simple, low-cost architectures suitable for in-house instrumentation design for small- to medium-size design groups. The described concepts are also extensively utilized in sophisticated complex instrumentation available from Hewlett-Packard (HP) and other companies. We focus on the following groups of tests in the laboratory as well as in the field:

Rayleigh simulator and instrumentation

Delay-spread tests and measurements

Numerous other measurements and instruments are required for comprehensive testing of mobile communications systems. For a detailed description of measurement methods and instrumentation, you may wish to refer to Feher and Engineers of Hewlett-Packard (1987).

3.6.2 Rayleigh Fade Tests, Simulators, and Measurements

Figure 3.6.1 illustrates conceptual instrumentation block diagrams for multiplicative Rayleigh-faded channels with additive white Gaussian noise (AWGN) and time-delay spread "τ_n" reflected signals. The Rayleigh *field-propagation test* environment is depicted in Figure 3.6.1(a). Front-end receiver amplifiers, also know as low-noise amplifiers (LNA), generate a "flat-spectrum" Gaussian noise. For this reason we indicated "additive white Gaussian noise" (AWGN) under the LNA. The oscillator down converts the received RF signal to a convenient intermediate frequency (IF). The demodulator output contains the desired information signal or "data out" signal.

To enable repetitive measurements and tests in a laboratory environment, the transmit and receive antennas must be disconnected. The amplified RF transmit (*Tx*) signal is attenuated, typically by about 40 to 120 dB. This variable-step attenuator simulates average RF propagation losses and provides the appropriate signal levels to the receive LNA. For *stationary* AWGN tests the noise generated in the receiver front end may not be sufficient. In this case, additional AWGN could be added at IF, as shown in Figure 3.6.1(b), or it could be added at RF. The second band-pass filter (BPF_2) protects the demodulator from excessive wideband noise and could be used as the calibrated "receiver noise bandwidth" filter.

As shown in Figure 3.6.1(c), the transmitted RF signal is connected through a Rayleigh hardware simulator known as the "test instrument." The modulated, transmitted RF signal "RF In" is fed to quadrature (90-degree shifted) multipliers. The baseband "BB Control" signals multiply the "RF In" and 90-degree shifted (quadrature) "RF In" signals by two independent Gaussian-bandlimited signals (Figure 3.6.2). In the set up of Figure 3.6.1(c), multiplicative Rayleigh fading and additive AWGN are simulated.

A detailed implementation concept of the Rayleigh fade simulator is illustrated in Figures 3.6.2 and 3.6.3. The theoretical foundation and justification for the implementation of such simulators has been explained in previous sections' references. From our derivations and results, we note that the in-phase $i(t)$ and quadrature-phase $q(t)$ baseband

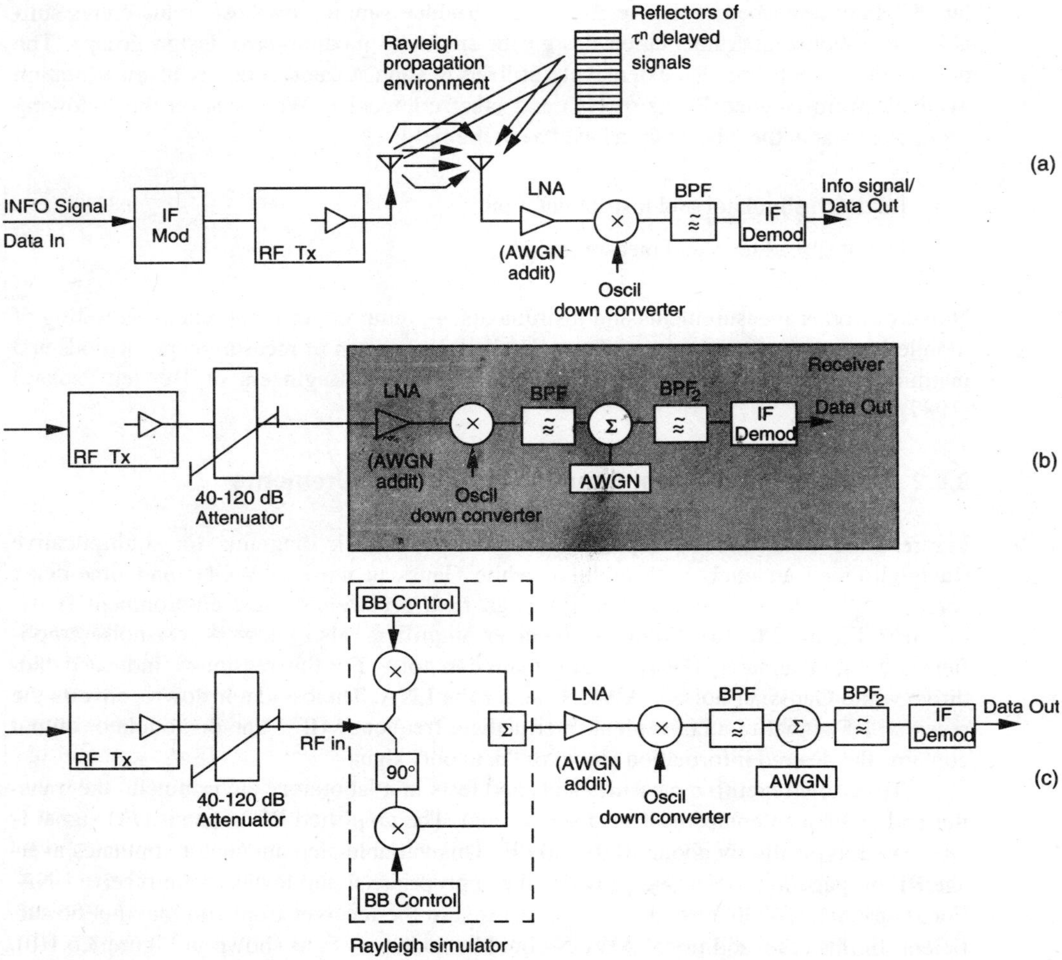

Figure 3.6.1 Conceptual diagrams of measurement with multiplicative Rayleigh fading with and without delay spread and additive white Gaussian noise (AWGN). (a), Field tests in a Rayleigh-faded and delay-spread environment. (b), Laboratory tests with a "hardwired RF connection" and AWGN. (c), Laboratory RF (or equivalent IF) tests with Rayleigh simulator and AWGN. For Rayleigh-faded delay-spread and cochannel interference (CCI) simulation and measurements, multi-tap Rayleigh fade simulators are required.

control signals must be band-limited Gaussian sources with a power spectral density $W(f)$. This density is proportional to

$$W(f) = \begin{cases} C \cdot 1/(f_D^2 - f^2)^{1/2} & |f| \le f_D \\ 0 & |f| \le f_D \end{cases} \tag{3.6.1}$$

where f_D is the maximal Doppler frequency and C is a proportionality constant.

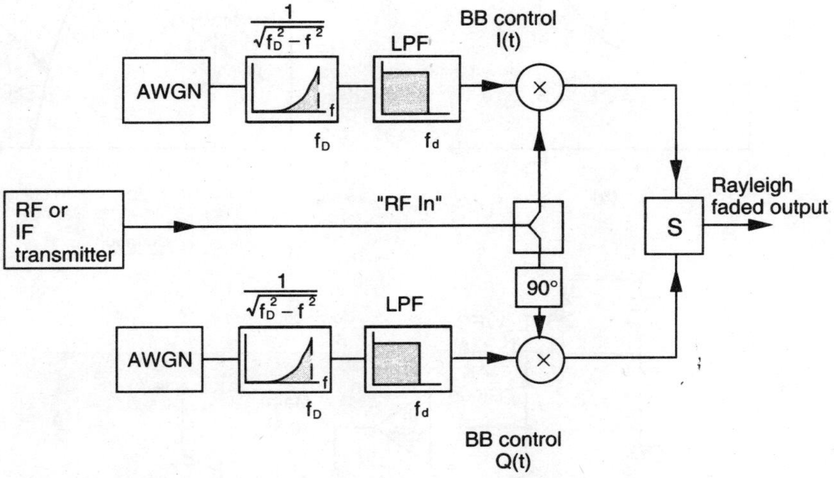

Figure 3.6.2 Rayleigh fade simulator, Detailed conceptual diagram for "Single Rayleigh channel" without significant delay spread. For delay spread and Rayleigh-faded cochannel interference (CCI) simulation, multitap Rayleigh fade simulators are required.

Analog and/or digital components have been used for various implementations of Rayleigh fade simulators. Most designers generate the AWGN drive signals through digital pseudo random binary sequences (PRBS). In Feher (1987b) it has been demonstrated that if a sufficiently long synchronous PRBS is low-pass filtered (LPF) with an arbitrary LPF, having a 3-dB cut-off frequency of at least 10 to 100 times below the bit rate of the PRBS, then a "practically ideal" Gaussian noise source is obtained. If we wish to simulate Doppler frequency variations between 0.01 Hz (minimum) and 10 kHz (maximum), the PRBS source should have a bit rate 100 times higher or a rate of 1 bit per second to 1 Mbit per second. In most land-mobile applications at the 900-MHz band, the practical Doppler rate of interest reaches approximately 100 to 125 Hz. For low earth orbiting (LEO) satellite mobile systems and other nonland-mobile applications, the Doppler shift could be as high as 50 kHz in the 1.6- to 2.4-GHz band on mobile up and down links. *Note: The amount of Doppler shift depends on the frequency band.*

The $1/(f_D^2 - f^2)^{1/2}$ spectral shaping can be approximated with an active analog high-pass filter (HPF), that is, a peaking amplifier, as shown in Figure 3.6.3, followed by a band-limiting low-pass filter (LPF) having a cut-off frequency f_d. In our experimental setup at the University of California, Davis, we found that a reasonably accurate Rayleigh envelope fade probability distribution is obtained with LPFs having $f_{3dB} = f_D$ in the I and Q baseband drive signal path without the need for the "high-pass shaping." However, this high-pass shaping does modify the duration of fade crossings and other higher-order fade statistics.

The multipliers or "mixers" are double-sideband suppressed-carrier amplitude modulators (DSB-SC-AMs) (Feher, 1983). For a high-quality Rayleigh-fading simulation the unmodulated carrier (carrier leakage) should be suppressed by 50 dB or more in order to obtain an accurate Rayleigh envelope with a 40-dB or larger dynamic range, as illustrated in Figure 3.6.4. The component cost of an "in-house built" low-cost hardware simulator

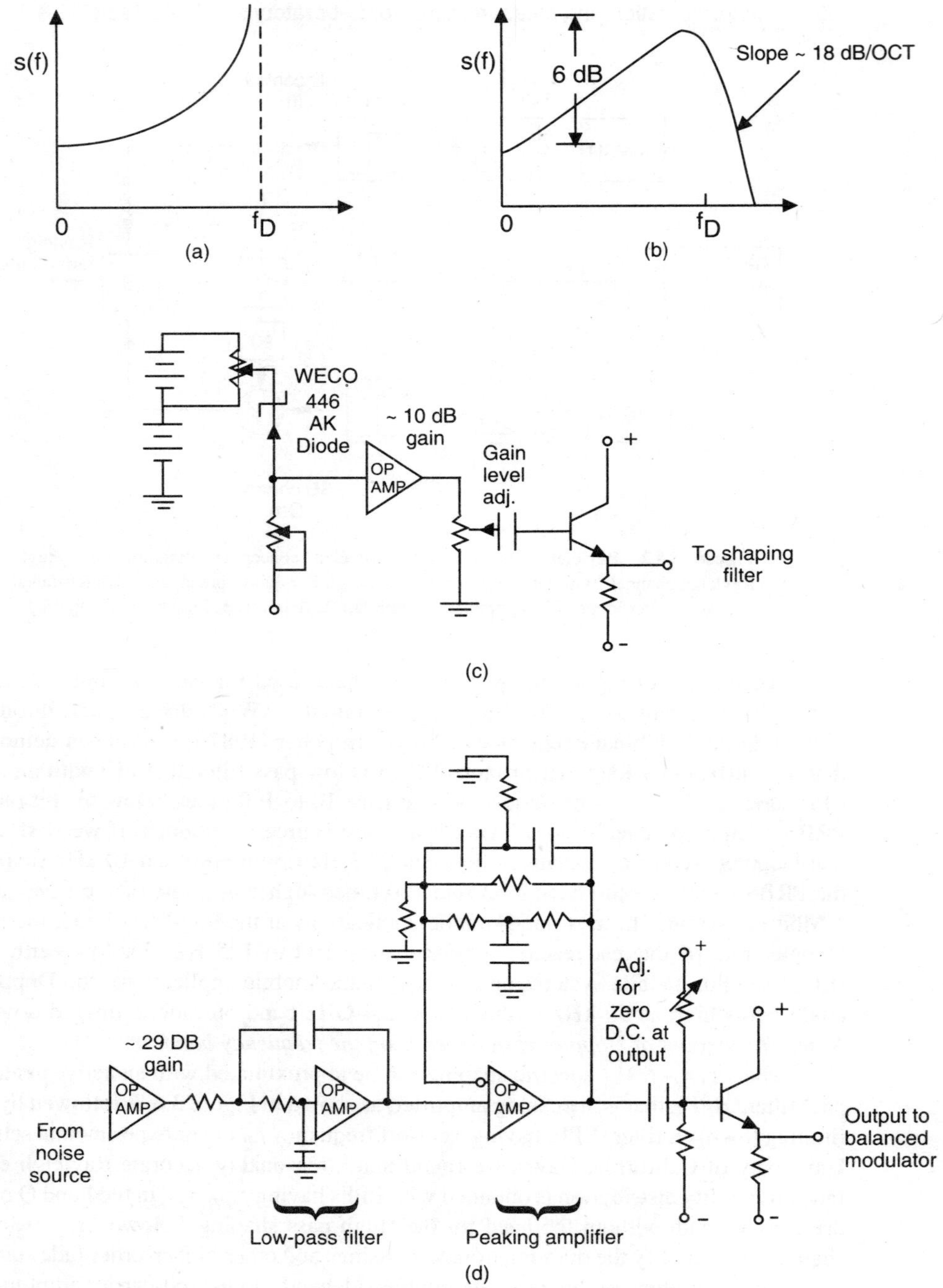

Figure 3.6.3 (a), (b), (c), and (d), Circuit diagrams for analog implementation of a Rayleigh fade simulator and corresponding theoretical and practical shaped frequency-spectral response. (From G. Arredondo, W. Chriss and E. Walker, "A multipath fading simulator for mobile radio," *IEEE Transactions on Vehicular Technology* © 1973 IEEE).

unit is about $40 (Figure 3.6.3). A comprehensive Rayleigh simulator instrument has a market value in the $20,000 to $70,000 range.

Digital Rayleigh fading simulators have been designed by several organizations. A simple implementation and evaluation of such a simulator is described in Casas (1990). Figure 3.6.4 presents a comparison of measured and theoretical Rayleigh cumulative probability distribution functions (CPDFs) and level crossing rates for Doppler frequen-

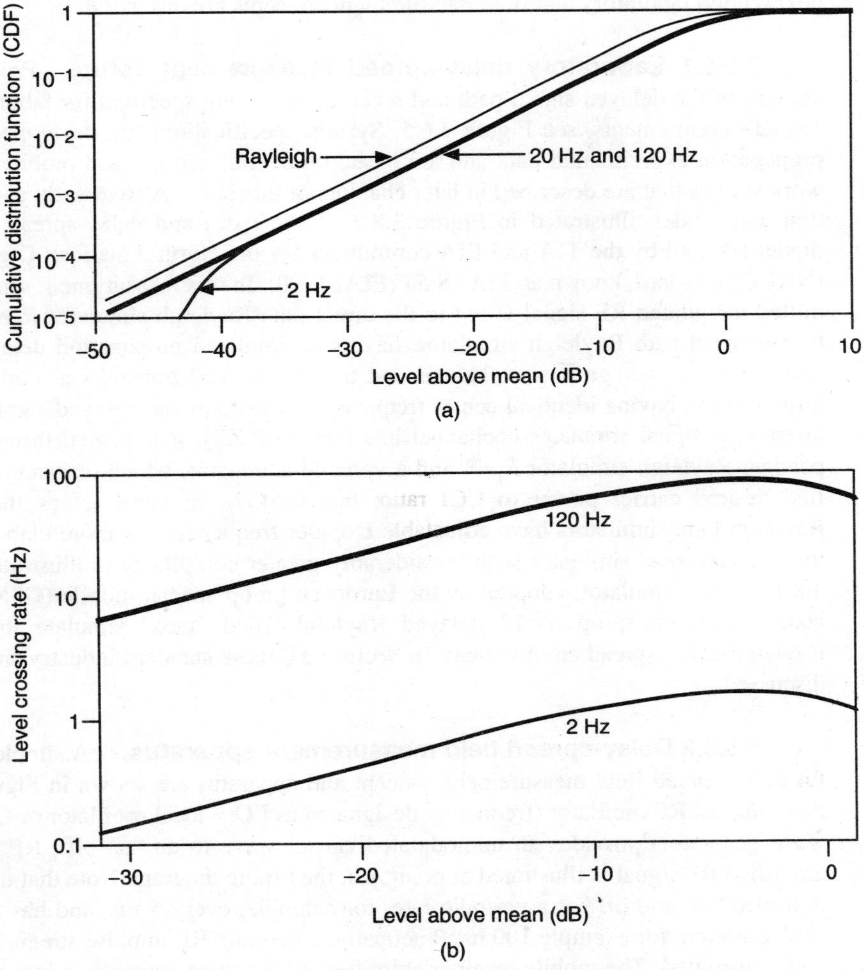

Figure 3.6.4 Experimental and theoretical Rayleigh envelope cumulative probability distribution function (CDF) and level crossing rate results for preset Doppler frequencies between 2 Hz and 120 Hz, over a 50-dB range. (From E. Casas and C. Leung, "A simple digital fading simulator for mobile radio," *IEEE Transactions on Vehicular Technology* (*© 1990 IEEE*).

cies in the 2- to 120-Hz range. The practical and theoretical results are within approximately 1% over a 50-dB Rayleigh-faded range.

3.6.3 Delay Spread Measurements

The impact of delay spread (τ) on the performance of mobile systems can be evaluated analytically and predicted by means of computer simulations. It can be measured in the laboratory or in the field in a realistic or actual multipath propagation environment. In the next section laboratory and field measurement concepts are discussed.

3.6.3.1 Laboratory delay-spread measurement setup. Profile and the amount of the delayed signal path and received levels are specified for laboratory delay-spread measurements, see Figure 3.6.5. System specifications are developed from field propagation experimental data and are based on overall cellular and mobile system network studies that are described in later chapters of this book. A frequently used specification and model, illustrated in Figure 3.8.2, is the radio and delay-spread propagation model adopted by the TIA and EIA committees for the North American Digital Cellular (NADC) standard, known as TIA-IS 54 (EIA, 1990). In this measurement setup the transmitted modulated RF signal is fed to the direct-path Rayleigh simulator $R_0e^{j\phi_0}$, and also to a delayed-path Rayleigh simulator, having a simulated propagation delay of τ_1 [μs] and the same average power. The second transmitter Tx2 transmits a modulated interfering signal, having identical center frequency to the main and delayed signal path. This interfering signal simulates cochannel interference (CCI). It is passed through an independent Rayleigh simulator $R_ie^{j\phi_i}$ and a variable attenuator, which determines the specified desired carrier power to CCI ratio, that is, C/I_c. In these setups the individual Rayleigh fade simulators have adjustable Doppler frequencies. A more elaborate laboratory delay spread simulator with considerably greater complexity is illustrated in Figure 3.8.1. In this simulator, adopted by the European group special mobile (GSM) standardization committee, up to 12 delayed Rayleigh-faded "taps" simulate the multipath Rayleigh delay-spread environment. In Section 3.8 these standard industry simulators are discussed.

3.6.3.2 Delay-spread field measurement apparatus. A simple yet powerful delay-spread field measurement concept and apparatus are shown in Figure 3.6.5. In this setup an RF oscillator (frequently designated as LO = local oscillator or CW = carrier wave generator) provides an unmodulated carrier wave to an "on-off" RF switch. The amplified RF signal is illustrated at point A in the timing diagram. Note that the RF signal is turned "on and off" at a periodic rate, for example, every 5 ms, and has a very short "on" duration, for example 100 ns. Practically, a periodic RF impulse stream is generated and transmitted. The mobile receiver amplifies the received signal by a low-noise amplifier (LNA) and down converts it to a suitable intermediate frequency (IF), such as 140 MHz. The LNA and down converter could be included in the low-noise RF spectrum analyzer. By setting the RF-IF spectrum analyzer to a "zero IF" position, the spectrum analyzer envelope detects the received carrier burst. The "resolution" bandwidth, also known

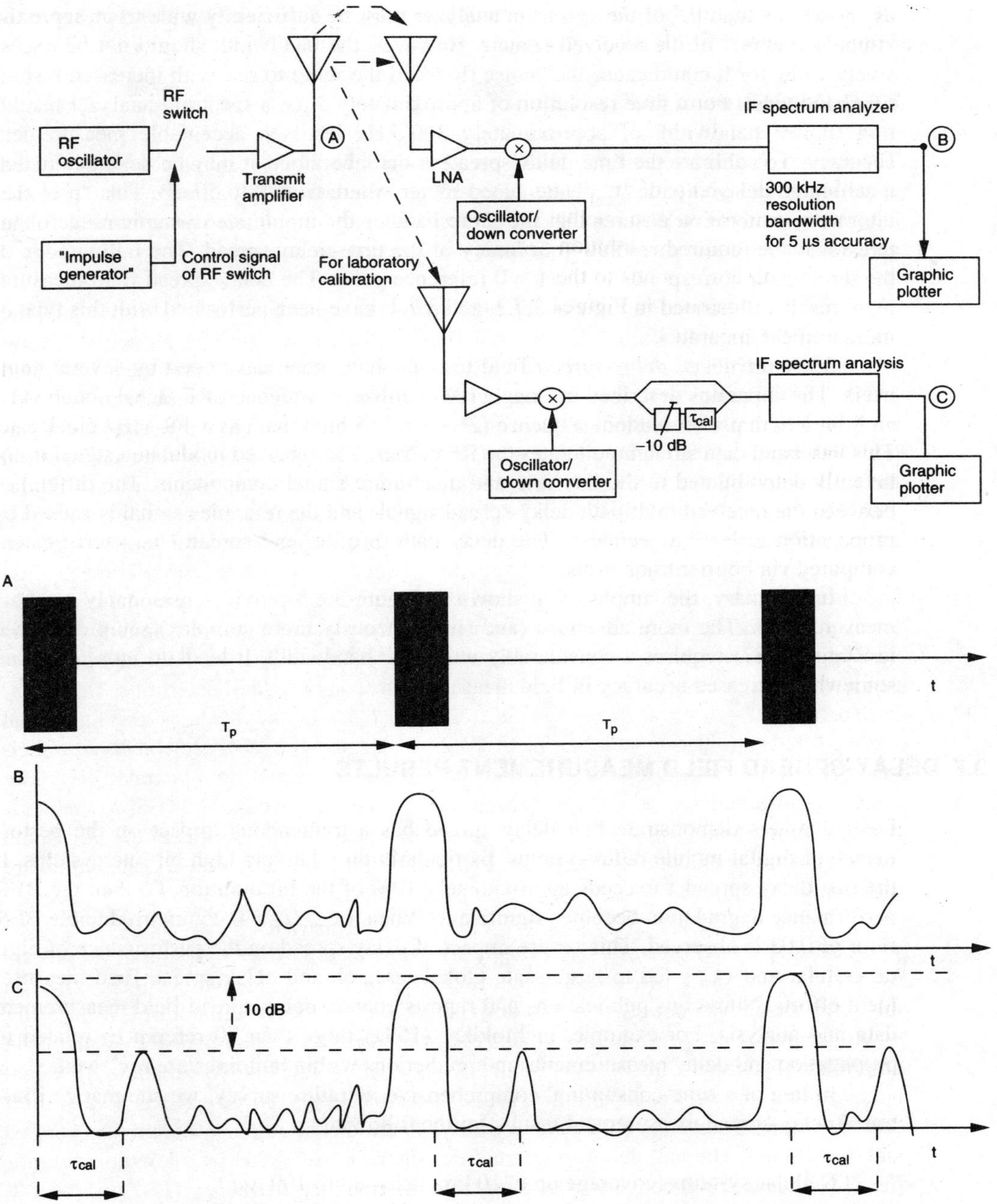

Figure 3.6.5 Delay-spread measurement apparatus for simple field measurements. At point *A*, a wide-band short burst having a repetition time of T_p is illustrated. At point *B*, a band-limited pulse pattern with noise floor is measured. At point *C*, 10-dB attenuated and delayed signals are observed.

as "noise bandwidth," of the spectrum analyzer must be sufficiently wide to preserve the "impulse nature" of the received signals. However, the bandwidth should not be excessively wide, for it could cause the "noise floor" of the setup to rise with increased resolution bandwidth. For a time resolution of approximately 5 μ*s*, a spectrum analyzer resolution (noise) bandwidth of approximately 300 kHz leads to acceptable measurement accuracy. To calibrate the time-delay spread in the laboratory, it may be desirable to add a calibrated delayed path "τ_{cal}" attenuated by anywhere from 0 to 50 dB. This "prefield" laboratory calibration ensures that the setup handles the amplitude dynamic range of interest and the required resolution accuracy of the time-delay spread. The falling edge of the direct path corresponds to the $\tau = 0$ reference point. The delay-spread field measurement results, illustrated in Figures 3.7.3. and 3.7.4, have been performed with this type of measurement apparatus.

More advanced delay-spread field test sets have been developed by several engineers. The apparatus described in Zogg, (1987) utilizes a wideband RF signal obtained by an 8-bit length pseudorandom sequence ($2^8 - 1 = 255$ bits) that has a 4.9-MHz clock rate. This baseband data stream modulates the RF carrier. The received modulated signal is coherently demodulated to the in-phase and quadrature signal components. The difference between the received multipath delay-spread signals and the reference signal is caused by propagation reflection "echoes." The delay path, profile, and spread characteristics are computed via Fourier transforms.

In summary, the simple setup shown in Figure 3.6.5 provides reasonably accurate measurements. The more advanced (and simultaneously more complex) setup described in Zogg, (1987) requires a considerably wider RF bandwidth. It leads to more data and somewhat increased accuracy in field measurement.

3.7 DELAY-SPREAD FIELD MEASUREMENT RESULTS

Later chapters demonstrate that delay spread has a tremendous impact on the performance of digital mobile radio systems, particularly on relatively high bit-rate systems. If the rms delay spread τ exceeds approximately 10% of the bit duration T_b, then the BER performance degradation becomes significant. When a $\tau_{rms}/T_b = 0.25$, an irreducible BER floor of 0.03 is observed. This severe impact of delay spread on the performance of digital cellular and PCSs led to large-scale global research and delay-spread field measurement efforts. Numerous publications and reports contain delay-spread field measurement data and analysis. For example, in Moldkar (1991) more than 70 references related to propagation and delay measurements and predictions within buildings are reviewed.

In lieu of a time-consuming, comprehensive literature survey, we summarize illustrated delay-spread measurement results for the following:

Cellular systems (coverage up to 10 km, delay up to 100 μs)

Land-mobile radio (coverage up to 70 km, delay up to 350 μs)

Indoor/outdoor PCSs (coverage up to 30 m, delay up to 300 ns)

3.7.1. Delay Spread in PCS, Cellular, and Land-Mobile Radio Applications

Figure 3.7.1 illustrates a delay profile measured during the 1970s by Cox (1977) on Manhattan Island, New York, for a cellular application. Figures 3.7.2 and 3.7.3 illustrate other 900-MHz delay profiles, also for cellular applications, with maximal coverage area of approximately $r = 10$ km (Drucker, 1988; Rappaport, 1990). Profiles measured in San Francisco and Salt Lake City, respectively, are illustrated. The measurement results in the relatively flat terrain of New York City indicate that the maximal significant excess delay spread (down to only 30 dB relative to the direct path) is about 9 μs, while the measurements in the hilly, mountainous cities of San Francisco and Salt Lake City indicate that the delay-spread excess delay values are in the 100-μs range. Delayed signal values at 10 dB below the main (direct) path are of interest because in a time-variable environment the direct path could be attenuated and the delayed path received at the same level as the main path.

Our experimental results that were obtained in mountains and hilly areas, shown in Figure 3.7.4, indicate excess delay spreads of up to 350 μs. In these field measurements, we found maximal delay spreads for digital PLMR (public land mobile radio) applications with a coverage radius of up to 80 km.

Figure 3.7.5 highlights delay profiles and delay-spread measurements for coverage distances in the 30-m range. We note that the maximal delay spread is approximately 300 ns.

A summary of delay-spread measurement results for the indoor/outdoor LOS

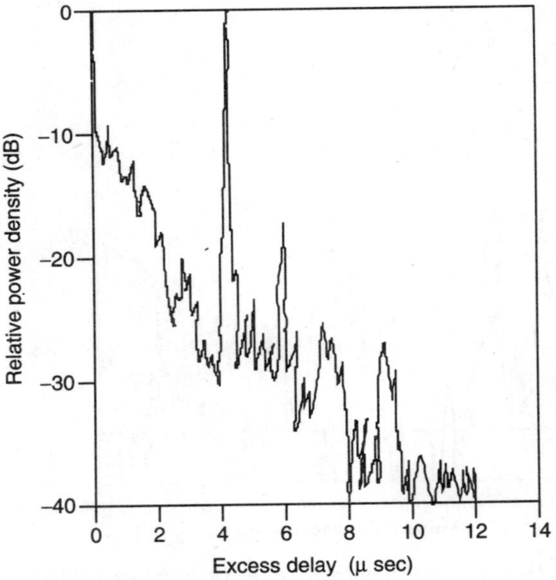

Figure 3.7.1 Delay profile measured on Manhattan Island, New York, for a cellular application having a radius of 3 km. (From D. C. Cox et al., "Correlation bandwidth and delay spread multipath propagation statistics for 910-MHz urban mobile radio channels," *IEEE Transactions on Communications*, (© 1975 IEEE).

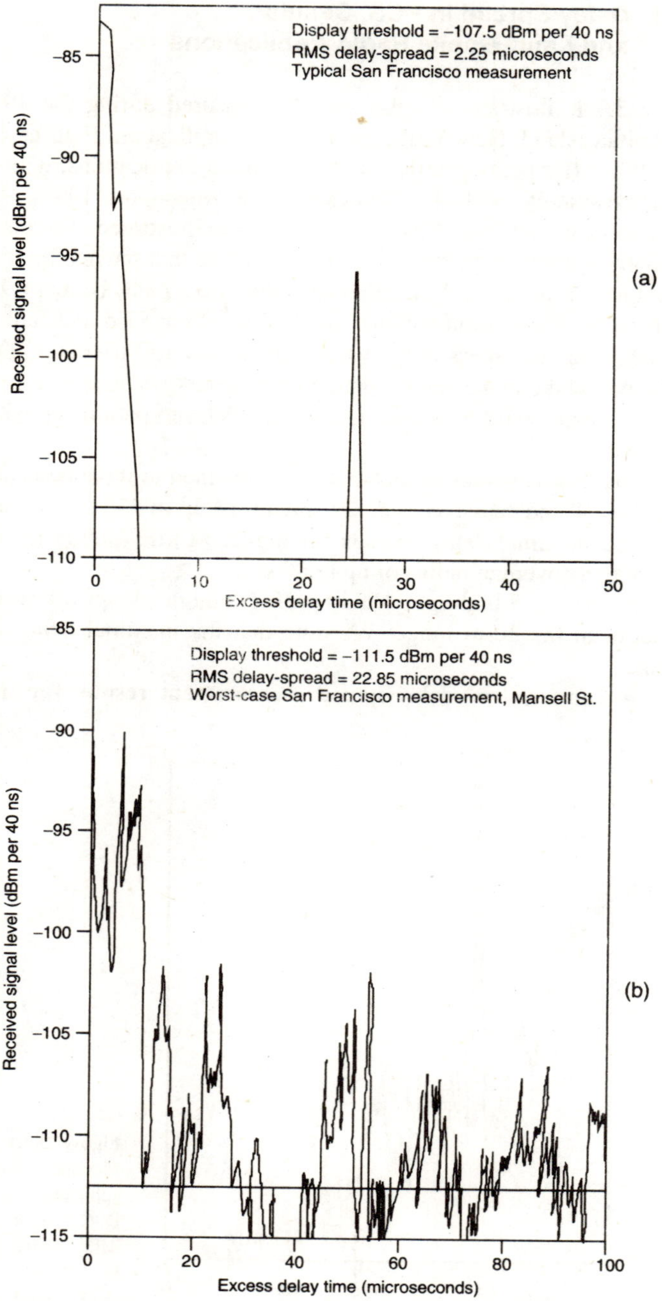

Figure 3.7.2 (a) and (b), Delay profiles. Measured results in San Francisco, California, at 900 MHz. (From Rappaport et al., 1990).

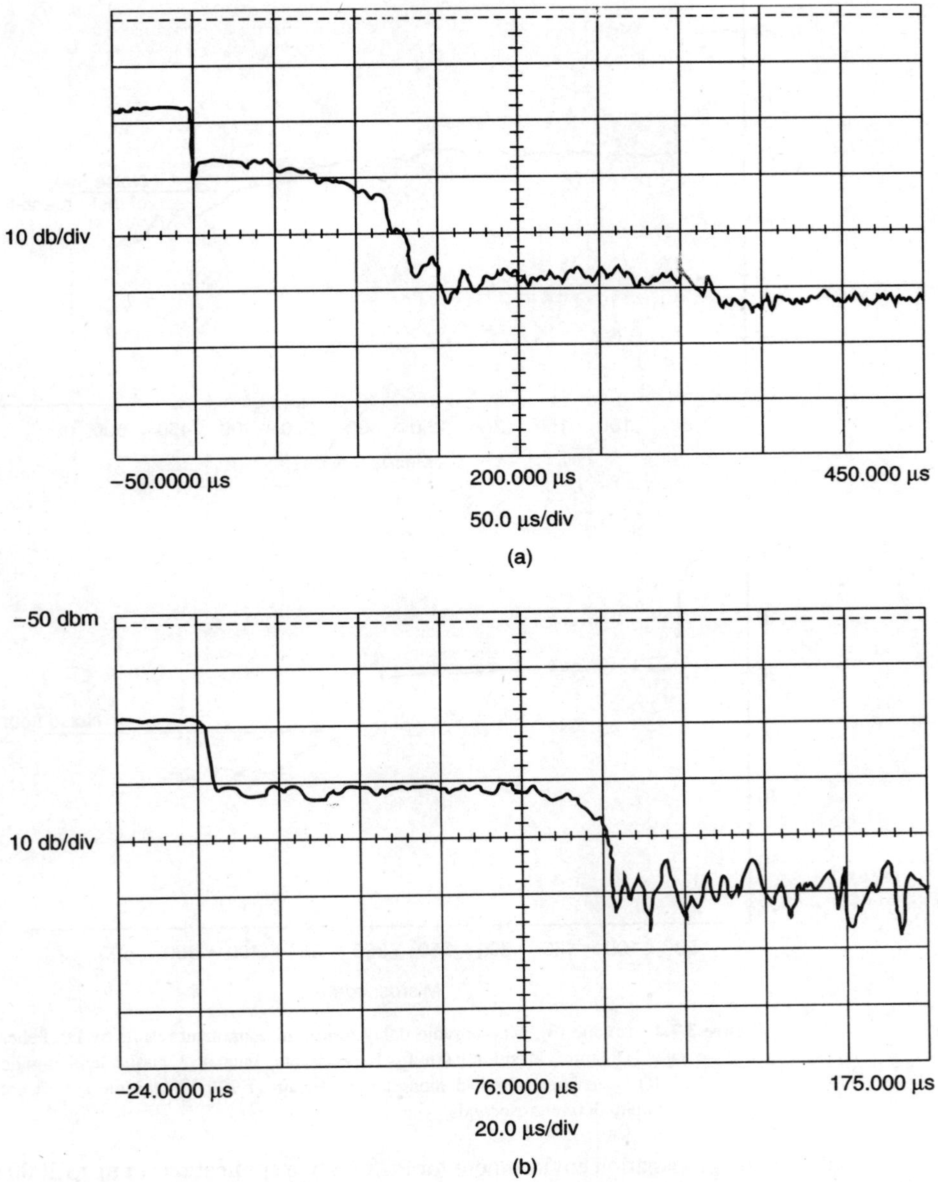

Figure 3.7.3 Cellular mobile radio delay-spread measurement results, (a) and (b), in Salt Lake City, Utah. (From Drucker, 1988.)

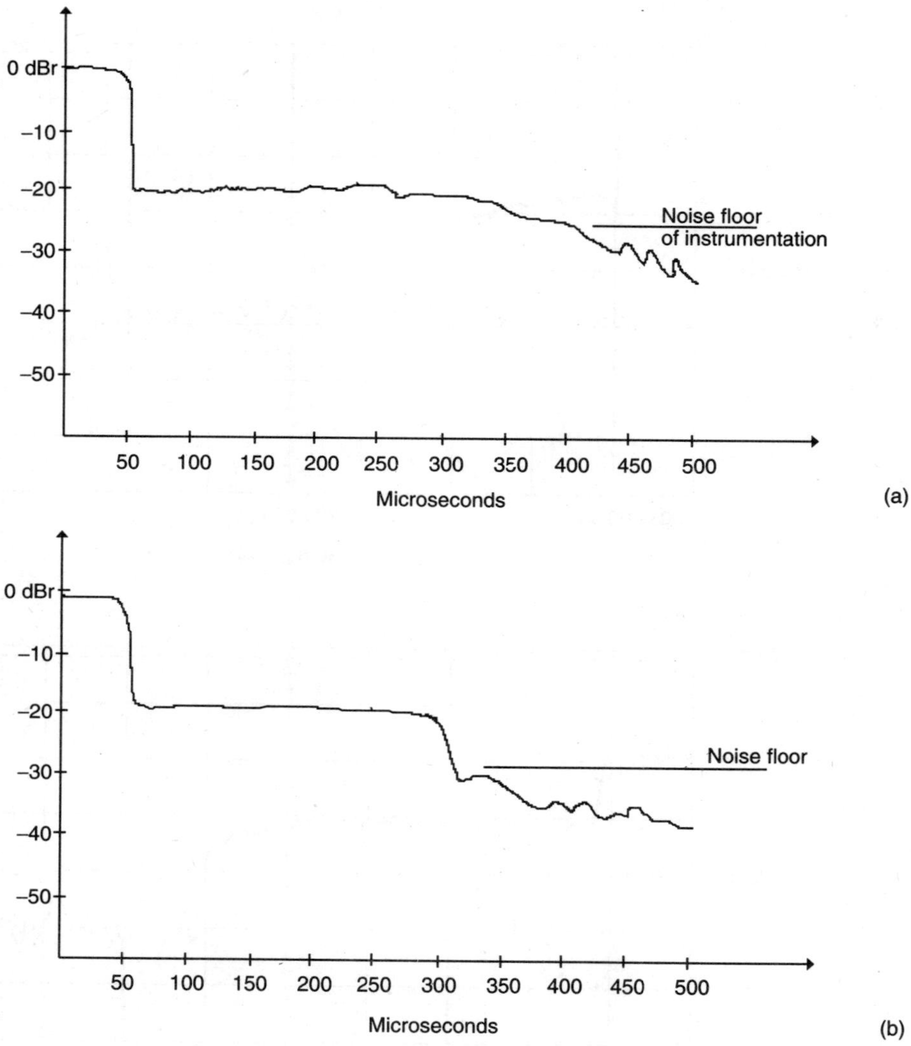

Figure 3.7.4 (a) and (b), Mobile radio delay-profile measurement results by Dr. Feher & Associates, Digcom Consulting Group. Experimental data of a public land mobile radio (PLMR) system measured in mountainous terrain at 220 MHz. Note significant delay spread up to 300 microseconds.

mobile radio propagation environment for PCS mobile applications of up to 2000 m (2 km) is given in Table 3.7.1. Table 3.7.2 provides additional delay-spread measurement results.

From the measured data, a general observation in regard to the "insensitivity" of delay spread to RF frequency is of interest. The delay spread is controlled by the coverage area and the nature of the terrain and is bounded by the system gain, as demonstrated in Section 3.5.3.

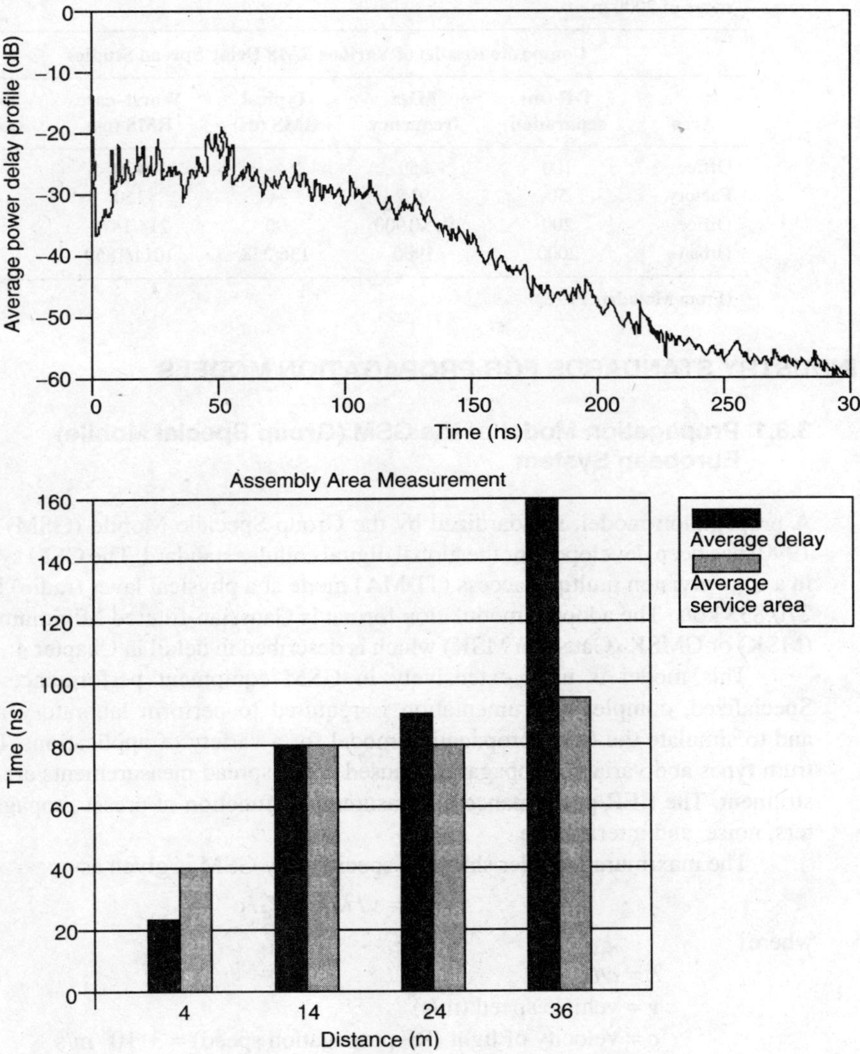

Figure 3.7.5 Delay profile measurement results for an indoor personal communications system (PCS) having a coverage of $r = 2$ to 34 m at $f = 1.8$ GHz. (From Pickering et al., 1992; Smulders and Wagemans, 1992.) (From L. W. Pickering, E. N. Barnhart, M. L. Witten, and R. C. Lu, "Trends in multipath delay spread from frequency domain measurements of the wireless indoor communications channel," *Proceedings of the third IEEE International Symposium on Personal, Indoor and Mobile Radio Communications* (© 1992 IEEE).

Table 3.7.1 Delay-spread measurements for PCS applications with a maximal coverage range of 2000 m.

Composite Results of Various RMS Delay Spread Studies

Area	T-R (m) separation	MHz frequency	Typical RMS (ns)	Worst–case RMS (ns)	Multipath spread (ns)
Office	100	850	—	420	1000
Factory	50	915	—	150	—
Office	200	915/1900	90	214/1470	8000
Urban	2000	1900	136/258	1011/1859	—

(From Molkdar, 1991.)

3.8 INDUSTRY STANDARDS FOR PROPAGATION MODELS

3.8.1 Propagation Model of the GSM (Group Special Mobile) European System

A propagation model, standardized by the Group Speciale Mobile (GSM) (GSM, 1988, 1990) has been developed for the global digital cellular standard. The GSM system operates in a time division multiple access (TDMA) mode at a physical layer (radio) bit rate of f_b = 270.833 kb/s. The adopted modulation format is Gaussian-filtered Minimum Shift Keying (MSK) or GMSK (Gaussian MSK) which is described in detail in Chapter 4.

This model is used extensively in GSM equipment performance verifications. Specialized, complex instrumentation is required to perform laboratory measurements and to simulate the GSM propagation model for a variety of applications. Doppler spectrum types and variable propagation-caused delay-spread measurements are set on the instrument. The BER performance is measured as a function of preset propagation parameters, noise, and interference.

The maximum Doppler shift (f_d) specified by GSM is given as

$$f_d = v / \lambda = v \cdot f_c / c$$

where

$\lambda = c/f_c$
v = vehicle speed (m/s)
c = velocity of light (RF propagation speed) = $3*10^8$ m/s

Table 3.7.2 Measured excess delays for Public Land Mobile Radio (PLMR), cellular, and microcellular systems.

Application coverage range	Measured excess delay	Assumed transmit power/ receiver sensitivity/ system gain (G_s)
r = 70 km (PLMR)	400 μs	+40 dBm/–110 dBm/140 dB
r = 10 km (cellular)	100 μs	+30 dBm/–100 dBm/130 dB
r = 30m (PCS-microcel)	200 ns	+10 dBm/–80 dBm/90 dB

λ = wavelength of the RF signal (m) = c/f_c

f_c = carrier frequency (RF signal).

The *time-delay spread* specified by GSM is up to 16 μs. Larger delay spreads of several hundred μs have been measured in the same frequency band in mountainous terrain (Drucker, 1988). The f_b = 270.833 kb/s rate GMSK modulation-demodulation subsystem of the GSM mobile radio, which utilizes adaptive equalizers, is designed to equalize delay spreads of up to 16 μs. For geographic areas where the measured delay spread exceeds the specified 16 μs delay spread, more base stations or antenna directivity "cell site engineering" techniques, or both, must be used. In some delay-spread analyses it is assumed that an infinite number of reflected delayed signal components are added (integrated). For *practical simulation,* however, a finite number of discrete taps must be assumed. For GSM simulators such as the one shown in Figure 3.8.1, NLOS conditions with Rayleigh-distributed amplitudes of each tap, varying according to a Doppler spectrum $S(f)$, are specified. Partial LOS is simulated with the RICE function, which is discussed in the next section.

3.8.1.1 Doppler spectrum types for GSM acceptance tests. Four kinds of Doppler spectra are specified for the modeling and acceptance testing of the GSM system. In these specifications, the following abbreviations are used:

f_d represents the maximum Doppler shift.

$G(A,f_1,f_2)$ is the Gaussian function

$$G(f) = A\exp[-(f-f_1)^2/2f_2^2]. \tag{3.8.4}$$

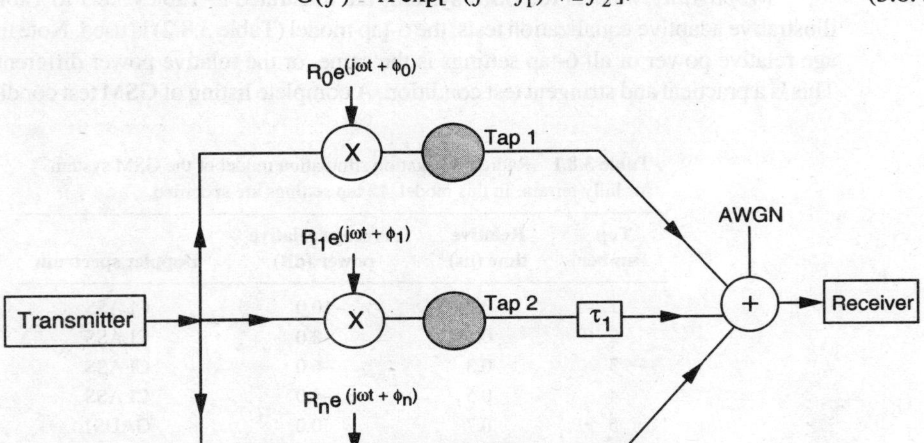

Figure 3.8.1 Multitap Rayleigh/Rician fade simulator, conceptual implementation diagram. In the GSM system, up to 12 taps have been specified. For the IS-54 standard TDMA North American Digital Cellular (NADC) system, only two taps (worst case is two taps) have been simulated (Gurunathan, 1992). In this diagram, each tap represents a Rayleigh-faded signal that could be generated by a block diagram as illustrated in Figure 3.6.2.

The following kinds of Doppler spectra are used for GSM measurements and models:

1. CLASS is the classic Doppler spectrum, which will be used for paths with delays not in excess of 500 ns:

$$\text{(CLASS)} \qquad S(f) = A/\sqrt{(1-(f/fd)^2)} \quad \text{for } f \in [-fd, f]. \tag{3.8.5}$$

2. GAUS1 is the sum of two functions and is used for excess delay times in the range of 500 ns to 2 μs:

$$\text{(GAUS1)} \qquad S(f) = G(A, -0.8fd, 0.05fd) + G(A_1, 0.4fd, 0.1fd). \tag{3.8.6}$$

where A_1 is 10 dB below A.

3. GAUS2 is also the sum of two functions and is used for paths with delays in excess of 2 *μs*:

$$\text{(GAUS2)} \qquad S(f) = G(B, 0.7fd, 0.1fd) + G(B_1, -0.4fd, 0.15fd) \tag{3.8.7}$$

where B_1 is 15 dB below B.

4. RICE is the sum of a classic Doppler spectrum and one direct path. This spectrum is used for the shortest path of the GSM model:

$$\text{(RICE)} \qquad S(f) = 0.41/2\pi fd/\sqrt{(1-(f/fd)^2)} + 0.91\,\delta(f-0.7fd) \quad \text{FOR } f \in [-FD, FD]. \tag{3.8.8}$$

Propagation models for GSM systems are illustrated in Tables 3.8.1 to Table 3.8.3. For illustrative adaptive equalization tests, the 6-tap model (Table 3.8.2) is used. Note that the average relative power of all 6-tap settings is the same, or the relative power differential is 0 dB. This is a practical and stringent test condition. A complete listing of GSM test conditions is pre-

Table 3.8.1 Radio propagation simulation model of the GSM system for hilly terrain. In this model, 12 tap settings are specified.

Tap number	Relative time (μs)	Average relative power (dB)	Doppler spectrum
1	0.0	−10.0	CLASS
2	0.1	−8.0	CLASS
3	0.3	−6.0	CLASS
4	0.5	−4.0	CLASS
5	0.7	0.0	GAUS1
6	1.0	0.0	GAUS1
7	1.3	−4.0	GAUS1
8	15.0	−8.0	GAUS2
9	15.2	−9.0	GAUS2
10	15.7	−10.0	GAUS2
11	17.2	−12.0	GAUS2
12	20.0	−14.0	GAUS2

(From GSM, 1990.)

Table 3.8.2 GSM propagation model for adaptive equalization tests.

Tap number	Relative time (μs)	Average relative power (dB)	Doppler spectrum
1	0.0	0.0	CLASS
2	3.2	0.0	CLASS
3	6.4	0.0	CLASS
4	9.6	0.0	CLASS
5	12.8	0.0	CLASS
6	16.0	0.0	CLASS

(From GSM, 1990.)

sented in GSM (1990) and in the revised GSM specifications. These tables specify the GSM propagation models, or the delay spread and Doppler shift (spectrum) settings. Using these models, performance specifications for various conditions have been developed (GSM, 1990).

3.8.2. Delay-Spread Propagation and Laboratory Test Models of the North American Digital Cellular and Japanese Digital Cellular Systems

For the second-generation cellular systems, also known as the North American Digital Cellular (NADC) (EIA, 1990) and second-generation Japanese Digital Cellular (JDC) systems (Kinoshita et al., 1991), a considerably simpler delay spread–radio propagation model than that of the GSM system has been developed. A Rayleigh fade simulator based on one RF signal and one delayed signal, as illustrated in Figure 3.8.2, is specified. In this

Table 3.8.3 Bit-error rate (BER) under noise performance. Propagation delay-spread specification of the IS-54 North American Digital Cellular (NADC) system in a noise-controlled environment.

Simulated vehicle speed (km/h)	Delay-interval (ms)	Total power (dBm)	Bit-error rate (BER)
8	10.3	−103	3%
8	20.6	−103	3%
8	41.2	−103	3%
50	10.3	−100	3%
50	20.6	−100	3%
50	41.2	−100	3%
100	10.3	−100	3%
100	20.6	−100	3%
100	41.2	−100	3%

(From EIA, 1990.)

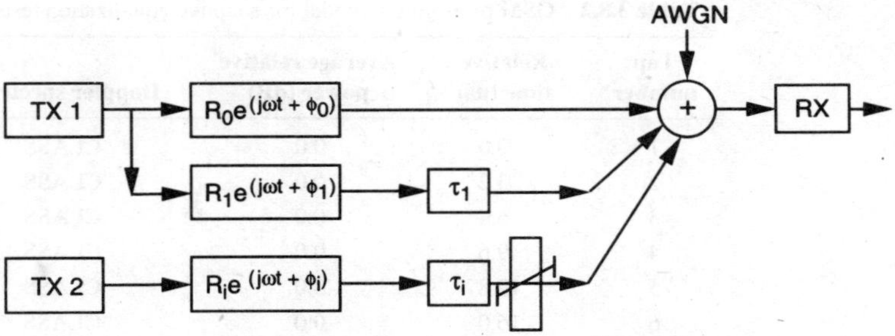

Figure 3.8.2 Radio propagation simulator model specified by TIA and EIA committees for the IS-54 North American Digital Cellular (NADC) standard (EIA, 1990; Gurunathan, 1992). Cochannel interference comes from the adjacent cell transmitting at the same frequency. R_X is an independent Rayleigh fade simulator with a given rms power gain. The specified rms delay τ_X is smaller than the symbol duration T_S.

simulator the upper Rayleigh simulator represents the predominant signal path, which consists of an infinite summation of radio paths that have a negligible delay among individual radio signals. The second path represents the summation of delayed signals, while the third path is for cochannel interference (CCI) simulation.

In this simulation model, delay interval is defined as the difference in μs (microseconds) between an RF signal and a delayed version of the same RF signal. In a two-ray

Table 3.9.1 Path loss computation by LINK1 for a sample mobile noise–limited link budget computation.

Parameters entered	Values entered
NLOS cell coverage radius	35.0 m
RF frequency band	890.0 MHz
RF bandwidth	30.0 kHz
Bit rate	48.0 kb/s
Modulation selected	Coherent QPSK
Channel selected	Rayleigh without diversity
E_bN_o	15.5 dB
Additional degradation	2.0 dB
Noise figure NF	7.0 dB
Margin for outage %	11.0 dB
Transmit antenna gain	0 dB
Receiver antenna gain	0 dB
Transmitter hardware loss	1.0 dB
Receiver hardware loss	1.5 dB
Rx bandpass filter loss	1.0 dB
Base station antenna height	30.0 m
Mobile antenna height	1.0 m
The answers are:	
Propagation pathloss	–76.3 dB
Minimum required transmit power	–13.9 dBm

Rayleigh model where both rays are of equal magnitude, these two RF signals are referred to as the first and last ray.

Table 3.8.3 specifies the BER for simulated vehicle speeds in the 8-km/h to 100-km/h range, corresponding to Doppler frequencies up to 20 Hz and delay spread in the 10.3-μs to 41.2-μs range. The relationships between various parameters in this table are explained in Chapter 4.

3.8.2.1 Method of measurement. Measurement and verification of the previously mentioned specifications are relatively precise. The BER is measured for a mean signal level under simulated Rayleigh fading conditions with a simulated vehicle (signal source) speed and delay interval under noisy conditions, as listed in Table 3.8.3. In the measurement setup the specified $\pi/4$ shifted DQPSK test signal, described in Chapter 4, and an identical delayed signal are equally (with equal power) coupled through two independent, uncorrelated Rayleigh fading simulators to the receiver antenna input. Transmitted data bits consist of pseudorandom data. All tests have to be performed with specified delay interval compensation. The base station should provide a monitoring means for "data field" bits without correction.

In Tables 3.9.1 to 3.9.5 path loss computations, coverage, link budget examples and the effect of diversity on cell radius is illustrated.

Table 3.9.2 Coverage (radius) computation of a cell with the LINK1 computer program.

C:\LINK1>print link1 **Name of list device (PRN)**	**Values entered**
E_bN_o:	15.5 dB
Additional degradation:	2.0 dB
Transmit power:	30.0 dBm
Noise figure NF:	7.0 dB
Margin for outage %:	11.0 dB
Transmit antenna gain:	0 dB
Receiver antenna gain:	0 dB
Transmitter hardware loss:	1.5 dB
Receiver hardware loss:	1.0 dB
Rx bandpass filter loss:	0.5 dB
Base station antenna height:	30.0 m
Mobile antenna height:	2.0 m
The answers are:	
Cell NLOS coverage radius	17.6 dB
Cell LOS coverage radius	32343.9 m
Press enter to continue . . .	
Carrier-to-noise (CNR)	17.6 dB
Sensitivity (Cmin or pth)	−104.6 dBm
Propagation pathloss	121.6 dB
STOP **Program terminated**	

Table 3.9.3 Link budget example for GMSK modulation. No diversity, 2.4 GHz, 1 Mb/s. Impact of external channel interference (ECI) not included. Patents in Appendix 3.

Parameters				
RF frequency (MHz)	2400			
RF bandwidth (kHz)	1000			
Bit rate (kbs)	1000			
Modulation	GMSK (BT = 0.5)			
Diversity	no			
Propagation parameters	σ = 6dB	α = 3.5		
BER				
Required E_b/N_o	16	26	36	46
Required C/N	18	28	38	48
Tx power (dBm)	10	10	10	10
Tx antenna gain (dB)	0	0	0	0
Tx hardware loss (dB)	1	1	1	1
Rx antenna gain (dB)	0	0	0	0
Rx hardware loss (dB)	1	1	1	1
Rx BPF loss (dB)	1	1	1	1
Noise figure (dB)	8	8	8	8
Margin (dB), for 99% coverage	15	15	15	15
Sensitivity, Pth (dBm)	–88	–78	–68	–58
Path loss (dB)	80	70	60	50
NLOS distance (m)	17	10	6	3
LOS distance (m)	99	31	9	3

3.9 PROBLEMS

3.1 How much is the maximal Doppler spread in a 2.4-GHz mobile system if the user is traveling at 200 km/h in a high-speed train? Explain why the Doppler spread is dependent on the velocity of the mobile unit, and provide detailed physical reasoning or an analogy, or both. If the radio frequency is changed, for example, reduced to 1 GHz, how will it impact the Doppler spread?

3.2 How much is the mean path loss (in dB) at a distance of 25 km from the base station of a public land-mobile radio (PLMR) system operating in (a) the 150-MHz frequency and (b) the 900-MHz frequency bands if the base station elevation is h_b = 70 m and the mobile antenna height is h_m = 1.5 m. How much is the path loss if h_b = 30m? Assume operation in an urban area. Use Okomura's prediction method and equations.

3.3 Compute the average fade duration for Rayleigh signal envelopes of less than 20 dB below the average signal envelope. The Doppler spread is 20 Hz. Assume that an f_b = 1 Mb/s rate binary signal is transmitted, and the 20-dB faded signal represents an approximate threshold between "error free" and error containing seconds. How many bits (on the average) will contain errors within one transmitted packet? Assume a packet length of 10,000 bits.

3.4 How much is the theoretical delay-spread upper bound for a mobile system operated at f_c = 220 MHz, having a transmit power of P_T = + 10 dBm and a receiver sensitivity of P_R = –110 dBm?

Table 3.9.4 Link budget FQPSK modulation example. No diversity, 2.4 GHz, 1 Mb/s. Impact of ECI not included. Feher's FQPSK and GMSK Patents, see Appendix 3.

RF frequency (MHz)	2400			
RF bandwidth (kHz)	1000			
Bit rate (kbps)	1000			
Modulation	F-QPSK			
Diversity	no			
Propagation parameters	$\sigma = 6$dB	$\alpha = 3.5$		
BER				
Required E_b/N_o	13.5	23.5	33.5	43.5
Required C/N	15.5	25.5	35.5	45.5
Tx power (dBm)	10	10	10	10
Tx antenna gain (dB)	0	0	0	0
Tx hardware loss (dB)	1	1	1	1
Rx antenna gain (dB)	0	0	0	0
Rx hardware loss (dB)	1	1	1	1
Rx BPF loss (dB)	1	1	1	1
Noise figure (dB)	8	8	8	8
Margin (dB), for 99% coverage	15	15	15	15
Sensitivity, Pth (dBm)	–90	–80	–70	–60
Path loss (dB)	82	72	62	52
NLOS distance (m)	19	11	7	4
LOS distance (m)	132	41	13	4

How much is the "worst-case" delay spread measured result as described in this book? Discuss the predicted bound and measured values. Why is there such a large (or small) discrepancy?

3.5 Determine the communications range (maximal distance "d") of a wireless system having a transmit power of 1 watt, ideal omnidirectional transmit and receive antennas, and a receiver sensitivity for a specified threshold uncoded (raw) BER = $3 * 10^{-2}$ of (a) –80 dBm and (b) –90 dBm. Assume that $d_0 = 2$ m for this indoor wireless system application, and assume a transmit carrier center frequency of 2.48 GHz.

3.6 What is the level crossing rate N_{R_s} and the average fade duration $\langle T_f \rangle$ of a mobile wireless system operated at $f_c = 900$ MHz? Assume that the speed of the mobile unit is v = 48 km/h, corresponding to a Doppler shift of $f_D = 40$ Hz, and that the average signal level is 30 dB higher than the threshold level, that is, $20\log_{10} (R_s/\sqrt{2}\sigma) = -30$ dB.

Table 3.9.5 Effect of diversity on cell radius at BER = 10^{-4} and BER = 10^{-5} at 900 MHz, for GMSK (BT = 0.5) modulation.

BER	Non-diversity NLOS distance (m)	Diversity NLOS distance (m)
10^{-4}	14	30
10^{-5}	8	23

3.7 What is the maximum Doppler shift for the GSM mobile cellular system on the "downlink" from the base station to the mobile unit (935 to 960 MHz RF band)? What is it on the "uplink" direction, or mobile to base (890 to 915 MHz RF band)? Assume that the automobile is driven at a speed of $v = 180$ km/h, a speed permitted on the German expressways known as *autobahn.*

3.8 (a) Find the propagation loss L_F for a system operating at 2.7 GHz when the mobile unit is 213 meters from the base station. Assume that the transmit antenna has an aperture of 1 meter and the receive antenna's aperture is 10 cm.

(b) Now assume that the antennas have unity gain and that LOS transmission takes place. Find the basic path loss.

3.9 Explain concisely the three effects that impair the propagating signal in the mobile/cellular environment. Also give typical values where appropriate. (Since "typical" can be open to interpretation, briefly justify your choice of values.)

3.10 Describe the conceptual design of a "test bed" or instrument for the measurement of the maximum Doppler shift of a wireless system operated at 1.9 GHz. The assumed bit rate is $f_b = 1$ Mb/s. The maximal spread of the handheld portable unit is 7 km/hour.

3.11 Design a detailed Rayleigh fade simulator based on Figure 3.6.2. Assume that the RF frequency is between 902 and 928 MHz.

CHAPTER 4

Digital Modulation-Demodulation (MODEM) Techniques

4.1 INTRODUCTION

Principles of digital transmission and binary baseband transmission techniques are described in this chapter. A thorough knowledge of these techniques is essential for the study of digitally modulated systems. Physical interpretation of power spectral density (PSD) equations of binary signals is followed by a study of band-limiting effects and a description of the frequently used "eye diagram" concept. The most important Nyquist transmission theorems for intersymbol interference-free, band-limited transmission systems are described. The probability of error (P_e), or bit-error-rate (BER), performance in an additive white Gaussian noise (AWGN) environment is studied.

Section 4.3 describes modulation-demodulation (modem) principles and architectures. Frequently used, nationally and internationally standardized modulation methods such as Binary Phase Shift Keying (BPSK), Quadrature Phase Shift Keying (QPSK), π/4-DQPSK, and patented Gaussian Minimum Shift Keying (GMSK), as well as improved-performance, increased-capacity Feher's FBPSK and FQPSK modem-wireless transmission techniques, are described. Concepts and definitions of interferences, including cochannel, adjacent channel, and externally caused interference, are presented in Section 4.4.

The spectral and power efficiency of linearly amplified systems and of their more power-efficient nonlinearly amplified counterparts are discussed in Section 4.4. Performance of digitally modulated radio systems in complex mobile interference environments is analyzed in Section 4.6. Bit-error-rate (BER) performance and degradations caused by fast Rayleigh-faded channels, interference, and delay-spread and frequency-selective propagation are studied. Coherent and noncoherent systems are compared in Section 4.7. Brief descriptions of advanced modulation and adaptive equalization techniques are presented in Sections 4.8 and 4.9. In Section 4.10 fast-burst demodulation-synchronization techniques for carrier and symbol timing acquisition are highlighted.

4.2 BASEBAND TRANSMISSION SYSTEMS

Particular attention is given to *binary* baseband systems, that is, systems in which only two signaling levels are used. In later sections we will see that binary systems are more power efficient, but less spectrally efficient, than multistate *M-ary* systems. Spectral efficiency (the alternative term *bandwidth efficiency* is also frequently used) may be expressed in terms of transmitted bits per second per Hertz (*b/s/Hz*). This normalized quantity is a valuable system parameter. For instance, if data are transmitted at a rate of 1 Mb/s in a 0.6-MHz-wide baseband system, the spectral efficiency is 1 Mb/s/0.6 MHz, or 1.67 b/s/Hz.

The study, analysis, and filter implementations of coherent digital *modem* systems are frequently performed in the simpler *equivalent baseband model*. The block diagram of a binary modem is shown in Figure 4.2.1, and its corresponding equivalent baseband model in Figure 4.2.2. A brief description of the major functional blocks of both of these systems follows.

The local oscillator (LO) signal $c(t)$ is multiplied by the band-limited baseband signal $b(t)$. This multiplication is the actual modulation process. When a baseband transmit low-pass filter (LPF_T) significantly band-limits the spectrum of the binary source, $a(t)$, we say that *premodulation* filtering has been employed. However, when the transmit bandpass filter (BPF_T) is the major band-limiting element, we have a *postmodulation* filtered signal. A linear wideband channel simulator is provided to simulate the system noise. The noise generated in the receiver's radio frequency (*RF*) amplifier is frequently the predominant cause of noise. If the noise bandwidth is significantly wider, for instance, 10 times wider than the modulated carrier bandwidth, then the noise spectrum is flat or "white." In such a case the probability density of the noise approaches the theoretical Gaussian density (see Appendix A). In such a case we have an *additive white Gaussian noise* (AWGN) model. The receive bandpass filter eliminates out-of-band noise and interference. The carrier recovery (CR) subsystem generates a pure carrier wave from the received modulated carrier. The multiplier in the receiver, followed by the receive

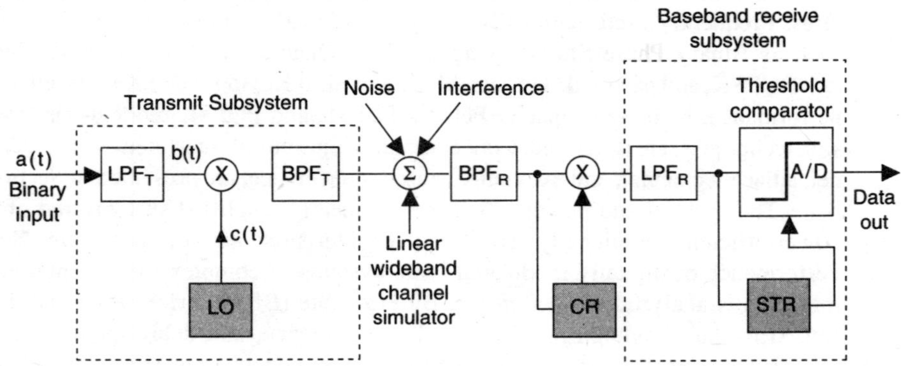

Figure 4.2.1 Block diagram of a coherent modulator-demodulator (modem). *LO*, local oscillator; LPF_T, low-pass filter (transmitter); BPF_T, bandpass filter (transmitter); BPF_T, bandpass filter (receiver); *CR*, carrier recovery circuit; LPF_R, low-pass filter (receiver); *STR*, symbol timing recovery circuit; *A/D*, one-bit analog-to-digital converter (threshold comparator). (From Feher, 1983.)

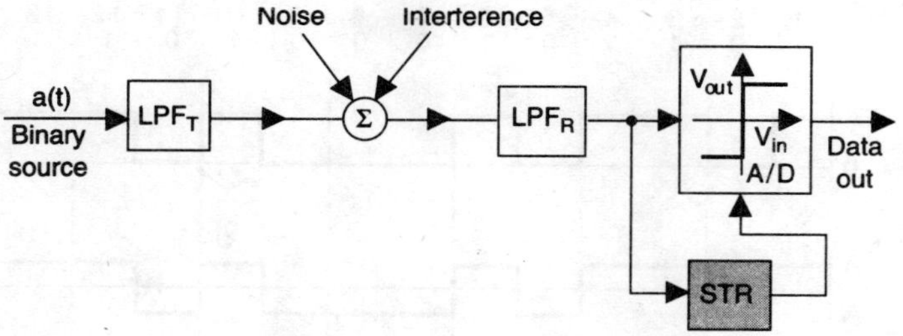

Figure 4.2.2 Equivalent baseband model of the coherent modem shown in Figure 4.2.1.

low-pass filter, demodulates the received signal. The demodulated, bandlimited signal is fed to a threshold comparator, which is gated by the recovered clock. This clock is generated by the symbol timing recovery (STR) circuitry.

The transmission characteristics of filters and of the complete transmission channel may be described in terms of their respective amplitude and phase responses. The terms *filter* and *channel* may be used interchangeably. In *binary* transmissions systems, the term *symbol* is synonymous with *bit* and the term *symbol rate* (f_s) is synonymous with *bit rate* (f_b). That is, $f_s = f_b$ only in binary transmission; otherwise, a symbol may consist of several bits. In QPSK systems, as we will see later, $f_s = f_b/2$ and $T_s = 2T_b$, implying that one symbol contains two bits of information.

4.2.1 Spectral Density of Digital Baseband Signals

In Figure 4.2.3 various binary baseband waveforms are illustrated and defined. The most frequently used basic signaling format is known is as *Nonreturn to zero* (NRZ). Return to zero (RZ) signaling is also in frequent use. The baseband minimum shift keyed (MSK) signaling elements are defined in Figure 4.2.3, (f). In all cases we assume that the signaling is for random *synchronous* systems; that is, zero crossings may occur only at integer multiples of the symbol interval nT_s, where $n = 0, 1, 2, 3, \ldots$, and T_s is the unit symbol interval.

Spectral density derivations are fairly long and beyond the scope of this book. A comprehensive derivation is presented in Feher (1983). The final result for the spectral density $w_s(f)$ is given by

$$\underbrace{w_s(f) = w_u(f)}_{\text{continuous}} \quad \underbrace{+\, w_v(f)}_{\text{dc term and harmonics}}$$

$$= 2 f_s p(1-p)\left|G_1(f) - G_2(f)\right|^2 \qquad \leftarrow \text{continuous spectrum}$$

$$+ f_s^2 [pG_1(0) + (1-p)G_2(0)]^2 \delta(f) \qquad \leftarrow \text{dc component}$$

$$+ 2 f_s^2 \sum_{m=1}^{\infty} \left|pG_1(mf_s) + (1-p)G_2(mf_s)\right|^2 \delta(f - mf_s) \qquad \leftarrow \text{harmonics.} \tag{4.2.1}$$

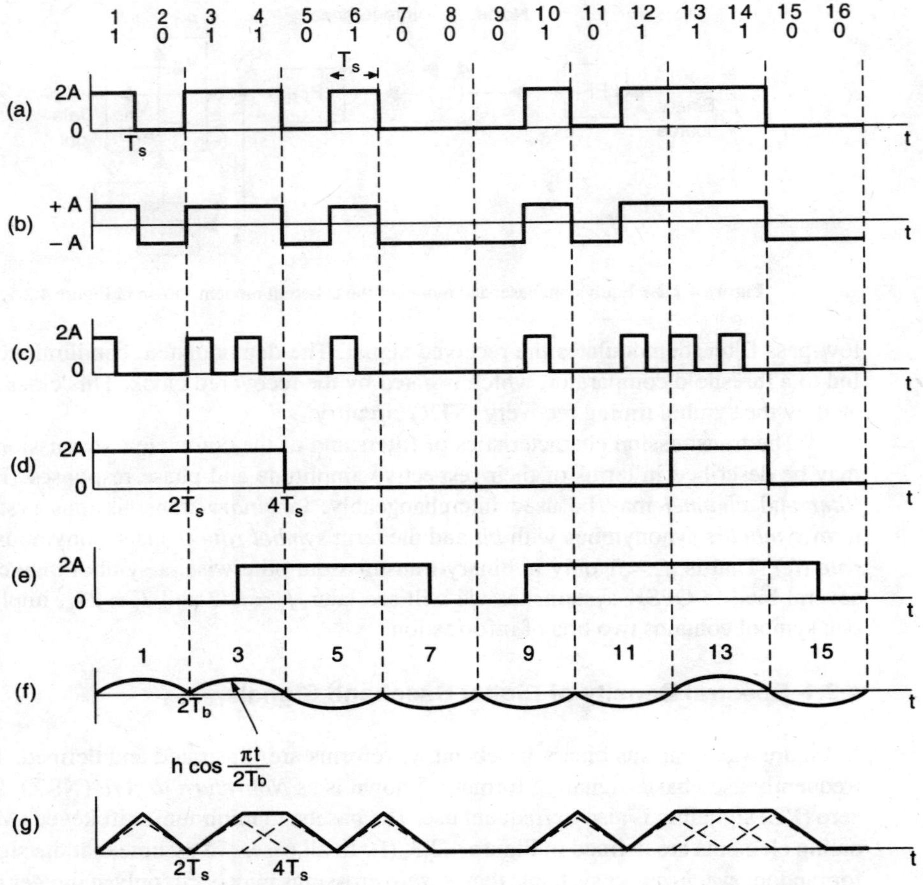

Figure 4.2.3 Time domain representation of various baseband waveforms. (a), NRZ (with dc comp.); (b), NRZ (with zero dc); (c), RZ with dc; (d), half-rate NRZ; (e), half-rate shifted or offset NRZ; (f), half-rate solid line represents the resulting wave of MSK; (g), FQPSK-triangular baseband.

In the spectral density $w_s(f)$ equation the following terms and notations are used:

$w_s(f)$ = The complete power spectral density (including the continuous and the discrete spectral components) of the binary synchronous data system
$w_u(f)$ = The continuous part of the power spectral density
$w_v(f)$ = The discrete part of the spectrum and may include the dc term
$G_1(f)$ = The Fourier transform of the symbol $g_1(t)$
$G_2(f)$ = The Fourier transform of the symbol $g_2(t)$
m = An integer number ($m = 1, 2, 3, \ldots$)

p = Probability of occurrence of the $g_1(t)$ symbol
$1-p$ = Probability of occurrence of the $g_2(t)$ symbol

The baseband spectral density equation 4.2.1 applies to a large class of signals. In the following examples we derive the spectrum of synchronous NRZ data and calculate the power spectral density of an f_s = 100 kb/s rate signal.

Example 4.2.1

Derive the power spectral density of synchronous binary NRZ data stream. Assume that the probability of the "0" logic state equals the probability of the "1" logic state and that the dc component is zero. Use spectral equation 4.2.1.

Solution for Example 4.2.1

For balanced $+A$ or $-A$ volt NRZ signaling states we have

$$g_1(t) = \begin{cases} +A \text{ volts} & -\frac{T_s}{2} < t \leq \frac{T_s}{2} \\ 0 \text{ volts} & \text{elsewhere} \end{cases}$$
$$g_2(t) = \begin{cases} -A \text{ volts} & -\frac{T_s}{2} < t \leq \frac{T_s}{2} \\ 0 \text{ volts} & \text{elsewhere} \end{cases} \tag{4.2.2}$$

and

$$p = 1 - p = 0.5 \tag{4.2.3}$$

The Fourier transform of the $g_1(t)$ symbol is

$$\begin{aligned} G_1(f) &= \int_{-\infty}^{\infty} g(t) e^{-j2\pi ft}\,dt = \int_{-T_s/2}^{T_s/2} A e^{-j2\pi ft}\,dt \\ &= \frac{A}{-j2\pi f} \int_{-T_s/2}^{T_s/2} e^{-j2\pi ft}\,d(-j2\pi ft) \\ &= \frac{A}{\pi f} \sin(\pi f T_s). \end{aligned} \tag{4.2.4}$$

Similarly,

$$G_2(f) = \int_{-T_s/2}^{T_s/2} (-A) e^{-j2\pi ft}\,dt = \frac{-A}{\pi f} \sin(\pi f T_s). \tag{4.2.5}$$

As $G_1(f) = -G_2(f)$, we obtain $G_1(f = 0) = -G_2(f = 0)$. At integer multiples of the signaling frequency ($f = mf_s$), we have

$$\begin{aligned} G_1(f = mf_s) &= \frac{A}{\pi f} \sin(\pi f T_s) = \frac{A}{\pi m f_s} \sin(\pi m f_s T_s) \\ &= \frac{A}{\pi m f_s} \sin(\pi m) = 0. \end{aligned} \tag{4.2.6}$$

Similarly,

$$G_2(f = mf_s) = 0 \tag{4.2.7}$$

By inserting the terms from equations 4.2.4 to 4.2.7 into equation 4.2.1 we obtain

$$w_s(f) = 2f_s p(1-p)\left|\frac{A}{\pi f}\sin(\pi f T_s) - \frac{-A}{\pi f}\sin(\pi f T_s)\right|^2 \tag{4.2.8}$$

+ zero ← dc component

+ zero ← harmonics

$$= 2f_s \cdot 0.5 \cdot 0.5\left(2\frac{A}{\pi f}\sin\pi f T_s\right)^2 \frac{2A^2}{f_s}\left(\frac{\sin\pi f T_s}{\pi f T_s}\right)^2 = 2A^2 T_s\left(\frac{\sin\pi f T_s}{\pi f T_s}\right)^2. \tag{4.2.9}$$

The complete *spectral density of equiprobable p(+ A) = p(−A) = 0.5 balanced NRZ random data,* as shown in Figure 4.2.3, (b), is given by

$$\boxed{w_s(f) = 2A^2 T_s\left(\frac{\sin\pi f T_s}{\pi f T_s}\right)^2} \tag{4.2.10}$$

Comparing this result with equation 4.2.1, we conclude that the dc component is zero and that there are no discrete components. The *first spectral zero* occurs for $f = 1/T_s = f_s$, that is, at the signaling frequency.

Even though the dc component is zero, the spectral density has its maximum value $2A^2 T_s$ at dc, that is, for $f = 0$. (Here you should *stop for a minute* and again read the previous sentence and equation 4.2.10. It is important that you *grasp the difference* between the missing dc component and the maximal spectral density at zero frequency.)

Throughout the derivation we assumed that the voltage values of the signaling elements have been specified across a 1Ω normalized resistance.

Example 4.2.2

(a) Calculate the power spectral density of an $f_s = 100$ kb/s rate, random, equiprobable NRZ signal. Assume that logic state 1 is represented by a + 100 mV signal and logic state 0 by a −100 mV signal. These voltages are measured across a 75-Ω termination matched to the characteristic impedance of the transmission line. The probability of a logic 0 state is the same as the probability of a logic 1 state.

(b) Assume the same impedance and voltage levels as in part (a), but increase the signaling rate to 10 Mb/s.

Solution for Example 4.2.2

(a) In equation 4.2.10 a normalized 1-Ω resistance is assumed. For the 75-Ω system operating at a rate of 100 kb/s ($T_s = 1/f_s = 1/f_s = 10^{-5}s$), we have

$$w_s(f) = \frac{2A^2T_s}{75}\left(\frac{\sin\pi fT_s}{\pi fT_s}\right)^2 = \frac{2(0.1)^2 \times 10^{-5}}{75}\left(\frac{\sin\pi f \times 10^{-5}}{\pi f \times 10^{-5}}\right)^2$$

$$= 2.666 \times 10^{-9}\left(\frac{\sin\pi f \times 10^{-5}}{\pi f \times 10^{-5}}\right)^2 \quad \text{W/Hz.}$$

For practical calculations the power spectral density is expressed in dBm/Hz. Remember that 0 dBm corresponds to 1 mW of power as follows:

$$\boxed{0\text{dBm} = 1\text{mW} \qquad \text{and} \qquad 0\text{dBW} = 1\text{W}} \tag{4.2.11}$$

The continuous power spectral density represents the signal power in a bandwidth of 1 Hz. The power spectral density in a 1-Hz bandwidth centered around *dc* ($f = 0$ Hz) is w_s ($f = 0$) = w_s ($f = 0$) = 2.66×10^{-9} W/Hz. (Note that $\lim_{\varepsilon\to 0} \sin\varepsilon/\varepsilon = 1$.) Expressed in dBm/Hz,

$$w_s(f = 0) = 10 \log 2.66 \times 10^{-9}\,\text{dBW/Hz} = 10 \log 2.66 \times 10^{-6}\,\text{dBm/Hz}$$

$$= -55.76\,\text{dBm/Hz} = -85.76\,\text{dBW/Hz.}$$

The measured power spectral density of the described NRZ signal is shown in Figure 4.2.4. Note that the maximum density of the first sidelobe is 13.5 dB below the maximal density of the main lobe If this signal is measured on a spectrum analyzer whose noise bandwidth is set to 3 kHz, the measured results will be approximately 10 log (3 kHz/1 Hz) = 35 dB higher than the calculated spectral density.

(b) In this case f_s = 10 Mb/s or T_s = 100 ns. The total power of the signal does not change. (Verify this statement in the time domain!) From equation 4.2.10 it follows that

$$w_s(f) = \frac{2(0.1)^2 \times 10^{-7}}{75}\left(\frac{\sin\pi f \times 10^{-7}}{\pi f \times 10^{-7}}\right)^2 \quad \text{W/Hz.}$$

As additional exercises, solve Problems 4.1 and 4.2 (at the end of this chapter). In these problems the RZ signal and the signaling element used in the baseband of MSK systems are considered. Note from your solutions that the RZ signal contains discrete spectral lines, in addition to the continuous signal spectrum, and that the first spectral null of the MSK signaling element is at 1.5 times the frequency of the first spectral null of the identical-rate NRZ signal (Figure 4.2.4, [b]).

4.2.2 Fundamentals of Band Limiting and Eye Diagrams

A band-limited digital transmission system becomes more spectrally efficient if it has the capability of transmitting a greater number of bits per second (b/s) in a given bandwidth. The bandwidth is frequently normalized to 1 Hz so that the spectral efficiency can be ex-

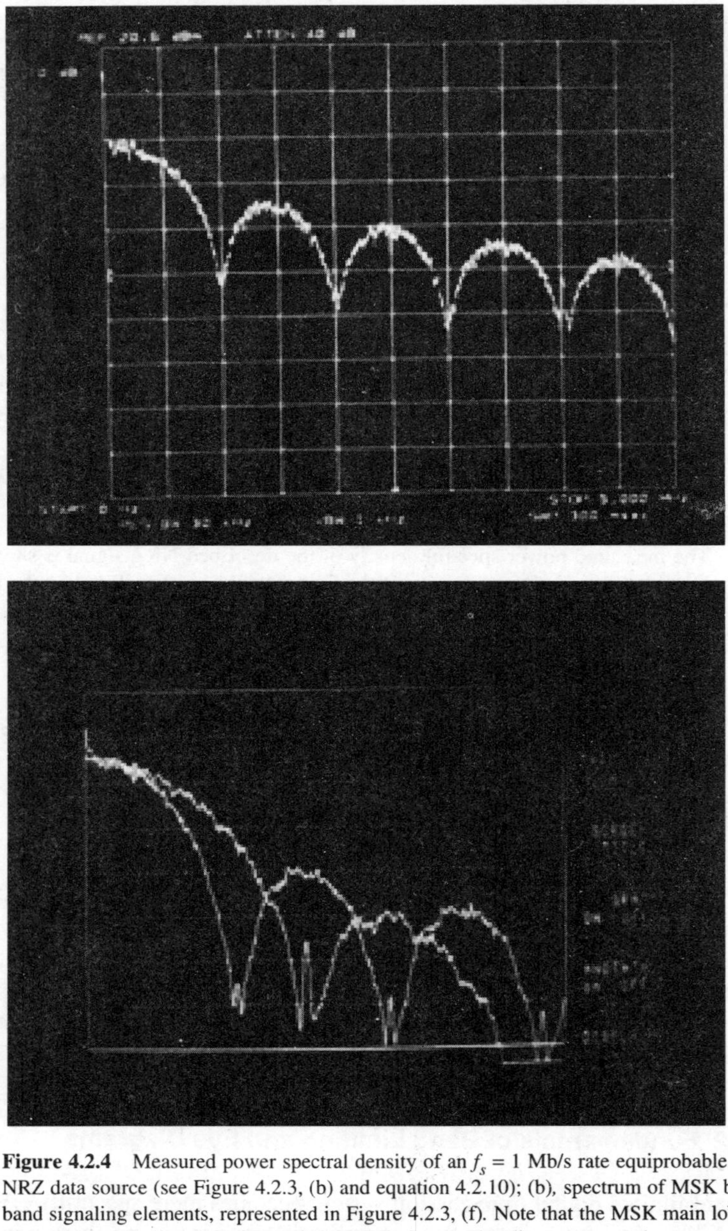

(a)

(b)

Figure 4.2.4 Measured power spectral density of an $f_s = 1$ Mb/s rate equiprobable. (a), NRZ data source (see Figure 4.2.3, (b) and equation 4.2.10); (b), spectrum of MSK baseband signaling elements, represented in Figure 4.2.3, (f). Note that the MSK main lobe is 50% wider than the main lobe of the NRZ signal. The discrete spectral component's "spikes" are due to nonsymmetry and other imperfections.

pressed in b/s/Hz. The rectangular wave is the most frequently used signaling element. For example, the NRZ and RZ signals (Figure 4.2.3) consist of rectangular, infinite bandwidth signals.

In his landmark paper on channel characteristics, Nyquist (1928) derived the minimum channel bandwidth requirements for synchronous impulse streams, the NRZ format, and other signals. He proved that it is possible to have both a deformed, band-limited wave and a receiving device that receives and regenerates a perfect signal. A brief description of ideal, minimum-bandwidth brick-wall channels and a study of eye diagram fundamentals are presented here.

Consider the ideal brick-wall channel model in Figure 4.2.5. The cut-off frequency, also known as the *Nyquist frequency,* is defined to equal $f_N = 1/2T_s = f_s/2$, where T_s is the unit symbol duration and f_s is the symbol rate. *Note:* In binary systems the symbol rate equals the bit rate; thus $T_s = T_b$, where T_b is the unit bit duration. In multilevel or multistate systems $T_s = T_b \log_2 M$, where M is the number of signaling levels.

The impulse response of the channel, $h(t)$, is given by the inverse Fourier transform of the transfer function, $H(f)$:

$$H(f) = \begin{cases} T_s & |f| \le \dfrac{1}{2T_s} \\ 0 & |f| > \dfrac{1}{2T_s} \end{cases} \tag{4.2.12}$$

$$h(t) = F^{-1}\{H(f)\} = \int_{-\infty}^{\infty} H(f) e^{j2\pi ft}\, df \tag{4.2.13}$$

$$h(t) = \frac{\sin(2\pi f_N t)}{2\pi f_N t} = \frac{\sin(\pi t/T_s)}{\pi t/T_s}. \tag{4.2.14}$$

A linear-phase filter is assumed. The phase of $H(f)$ equals 0 for all frequencies. From this impulse response, note that

$$h(nT_s) = \begin{cases} 1 & \text{for } n = 0 \\ 0 & \text{for } n = \pm 1, \pm 2, \pm 3, \ldots \end{cases} \tag{4.2.15}$$

Thus the impulse response attains its full value for $t = nT_s = 0$ and has zero crossings for all other integer multiples of the symbol duration. If the ideal brick-wall channel has a nonzero but linear phase (*dashed line*, Figure 4.2.5), the impulse response is shifted by an amount that equals the channel delay. This delay is $\tau = d\phi/d\omega$ and for linear-phase filters is constant over all frequencies. Because the shape of the impulse response is the same as with $\tau = 0$, no further distortion will be introduced.

Note that the channel input (also known as the filter excitation), $\delta(t)$, has an infinitesimally short duration, whereas the output (that is, the impulse response) has an *infinite duration.* The band-limited channel stretches the impulse response beyond the T_s interval and deforms the input signal. A desirable property of the described impulse response is

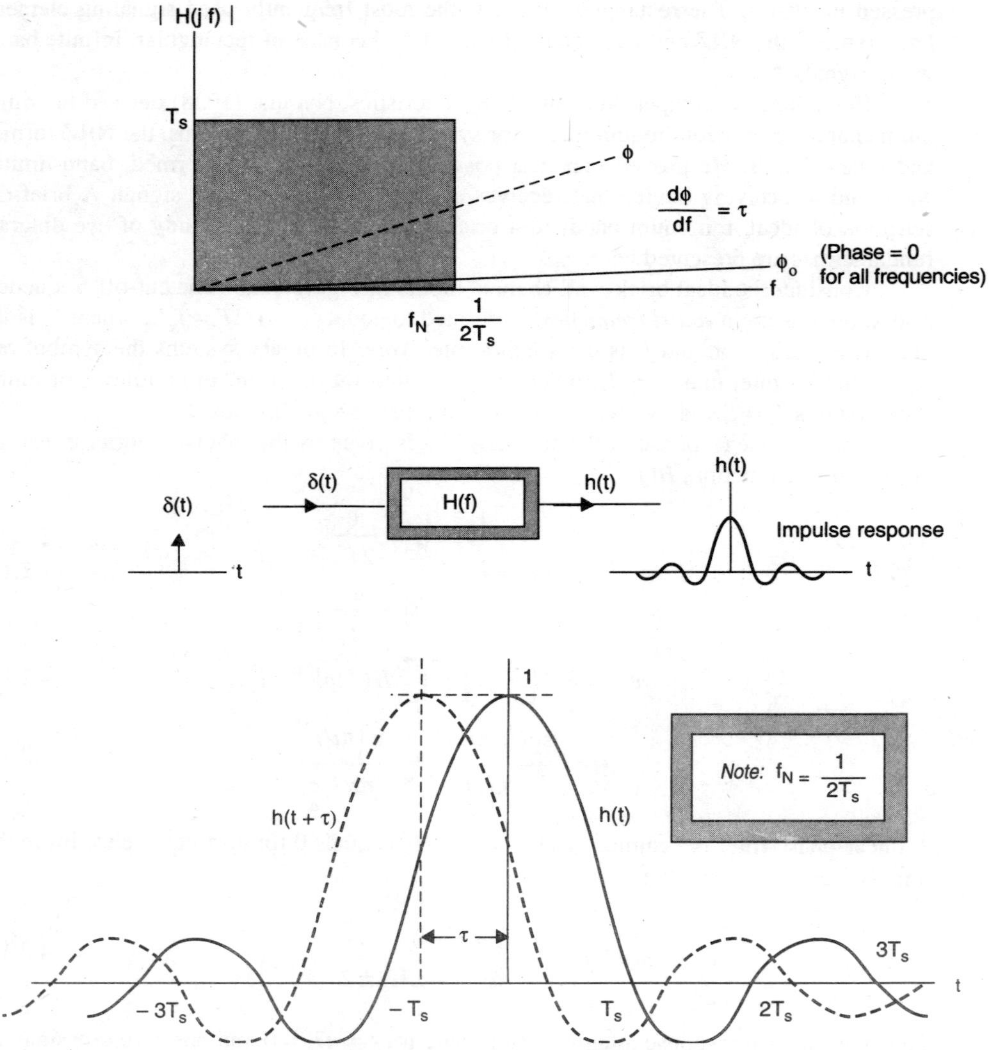

Figure 4.2.5 Ideal "brick wall" channel and its corresponding impulse response. The anticipatory impulse response of the "brick wall" channel is nonrealizable. T_s = Time duration of unit signaling element. For binary systems, $T_s = T_b$, that is, the symbol duration equals the bit duration.

that it has zero values for integer multiples of T_s. Thus in an $f_N = 1/2T_s$–wide brick-wall channel it is possible to transmit and detect synchronous, random impulses at a rate of $f_s = 1/T_s = 2f_N$. Theoretically the detection of any of these symbols can be performed without any interference from the previously sent or subsequent impulse patterns. This situation is known as *intersymbol interference–free* (SIS-free) transmission.

Eye diagrams or *eye patterns* are frequently used in the evaluation of channel and signal imperfections. These patterns may be obtained on an oscilloscope if a signal such as $v_o(t)$ (in Figure 4.2.6) is fed to the vertical input "y" of an oscilloscope. The symbol clock $c(t-nT_s)$ is fed to the external trigger of the oscilloscope. The front trigger-delay adjustment, conveniently available on most oscilloscopes, ensures that the displayed eye pattern is centered on the screen. The horizontal time base is set to be approximately equal to the symbol duration. The inherent persistence of the cathode-ray tube displays the superimposed segments of the $v_o(t)$ signal. The eye pattern of the *pseudorandom binary sequence* (PRBS) generator is displayed if the data output of this generator is directly connected to the vertical input of the oscilloscope.

Computer-generated eye diagrams are described in later sections. The "information content" of experimentally obtained and computer-generated eye diagrams is important for the comprehension of most digital wireless transmission systems. For example, the experimentally obtained (that is, observed in a hardware laboratory experiment) eye diagram of a *non–phase-equalized, conventional* fourth-order Butterworth filter is shown in

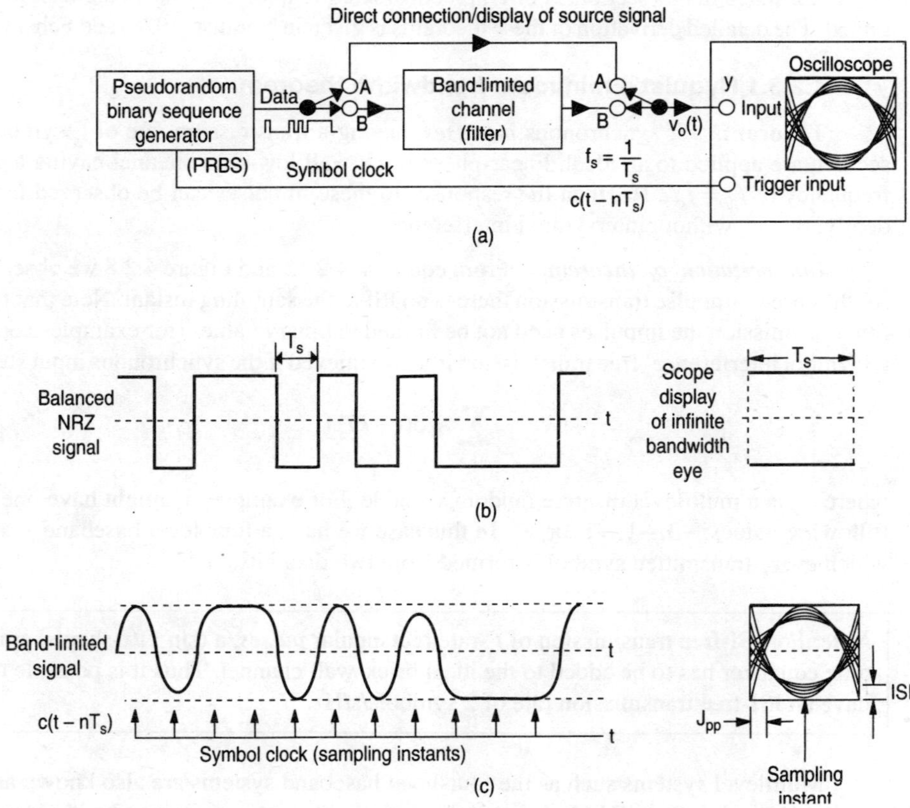

Figure 4.2.6 Eye diagram measurement setup and display. (a), setup; (b), NRZ signal (c), bandlimited eye diagram.

Figure 4.2.7. The applied symbol rate of the PRBS source is set at f_s = 1 Msymbols/second = 1 MBaud, and the 3-dB cut-off frequency for this filter is 550 kHz. Because of the ISI of the unequalized channel, the eye is open approximately 85% (instead of 100%) at the sampling instant. To maintain an equal decision margin, the same P_e as in the ISI-free case, the signal level must be increased by 20 log(1/0.85) = 1.4 dB. For the systems engineer this ISI-caused degradation could be a serious drawback.

From the observed eye diagram it is noted that the overlapped signal pattern does not cross the horizontal 0 line at exact integer multiples of the symbol clock. The deviation from the nominal crossing points is known as the peak-to-peak *data transition jitter* (J_{pp}). This jitter has an effect on the symbol timing recovery circuits and may significantly degrade the performance of cascaded regenerative sections (Takasaki, 1991).

4.2.3 Nyquist's Transmission Theorems and Spectral Efficiency

Nyquist's frequently used minimum-bandwidth, ideal brick-wall, and vestigial symmetry theorems are stated in this section. A brief, practical interpretation of these theorems is also presented. The detailed derivation of these theorems is given in Nyquist (1928) and Feher (1983).

4.2.3.1 Nyquist's minimum-bandwidth theorem

Theorem. If synchronous *impulses,* having a transmission rate of f_s symbols per second, are applied to an ideal, linear-phase brick-wall low-pass channel having a cut-off frequency of $f_N = f_s/2$ Hz, then the responses to these impulses can be observed independently, that is, without intersymbol interference.

Interpretation of theorem. From equation 4.2.15 and Figure 4.2.8 we observe that for the case of impulse transmission there is no ISI in the sampling instant. Note that for ISI-free transmission the impulses need not be limited to binary values (for example, $\pm\delta(t)$). Intersymbol interference–free transmission is also achieved if the synchronous input stream is

$$\sum_k A_k \delta(t - kT_s) \tag{4.2.16}$$

where A_k is a multilevel discrete random variable. For example, A_k might have one of the following values: −3, −1, +1, or +3. In this case we have a four-level baseband system in which every transmitted symbol is formed from two data bits.

> *Note:* For ISI-free transmission of f_s-rate rectangular *pulses*, a (sin x)/x-shaped amplitude equalizer has to be added to the ideal brick-wall channel. Thus it is possible to have an ISI-free transmission rate of 2 symbols/s/Hz.

Multilevel systems such as the four-level baseband systems are also known as *pulse amplitude modulation* (PAM) baseband systems. Now we explain why the (x/sin x)-shaped amplitude equalizer is essential for the ISI-free transmission of rectangular pulses, as used in the case of binary NRZ transmission (shown in Figure 4.2.3, (a) or (b)). For an

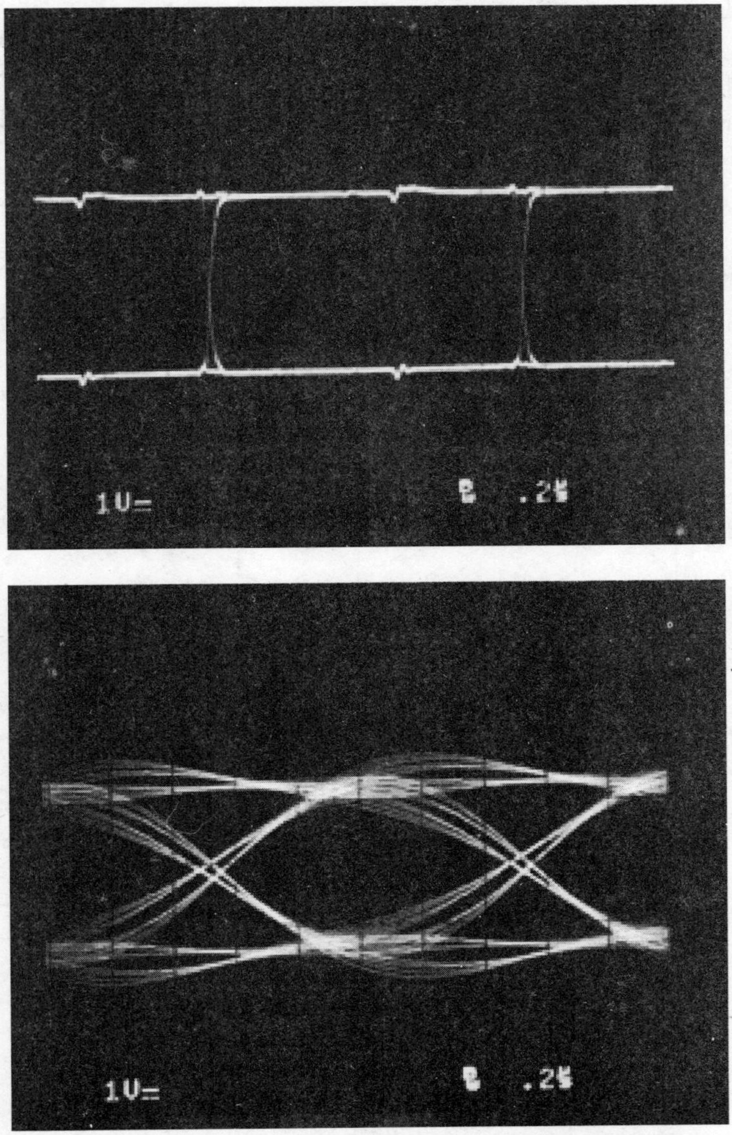

(a)

(b)

Figure 4.2.7 Measured eye diagrams. A conventional fourth-order, unequalized-phase Butterworth filter having a 3 dB corner frequency at 550 kHz is used as channel simulator. The applied symbol rate is f_s = 1 MBaud. (a), Infinite-bandwidth eye diagram; (b), band-limited eye diagram.

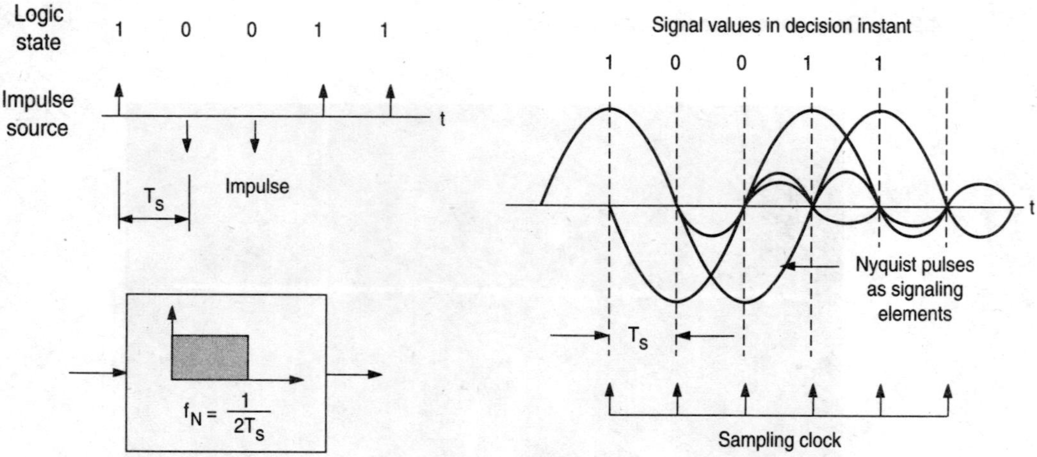

Figure 4.2.8 Intersymbol interference–free transmission concept of band-limited impulses.

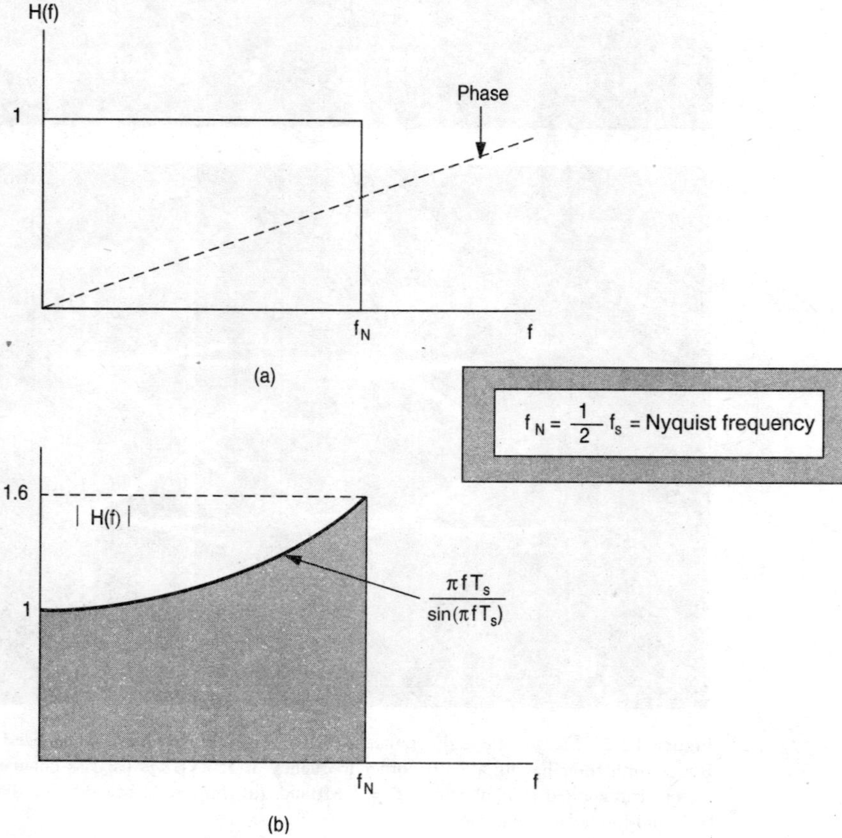

Figure 4.2.9 Minimum-bandwidth Nyquist channel models for impulse and pulse transmission. (a), Amplitude response of an ideal minimum-bandwidth filter that has no ISI for the conceptual case of impulse transmission. (b), Amplitude response of minimum-bandwidth channel for NRZ rectangular pulse transmission.

impulse, the amplitude of the Fourier transform is constant over all frequencies while it has a (sin x)/x shape for rectangular pulses. To keep the same system response (that is, no ISI for both the impulse and the rectangular excitation), it is required that the Fourier transform for both cases be identical. The output Fourier transform is obtained by multiplying the Fourier transform of the excitation by the channel transfer function. In the rectangular pulse transmission case the brick-wall channel transfer function is modified by an x/sin x amplitude equalizer. The ideal minimum-bandwidth Nyquist channel characteristics for the conceptual synchronous impulse and for the practical, rectangular (NRZ) pulse transmission case are summarized in Figure 4.2.9.

Unfortunately the described minimum-bandwidth Nyquist channels are not realizable. An infinite number of filter sections would be required to synthesize the infinite-attenuation slope of the brick-wall channel. Additionally, the decay in the lobes of the time-domain response is very slow. This in turn would cause a prohibitively large ISI degradation (that is, the P_e may approach 0.5) for the smallest filtering or symbol timing imperfections.

To alleviate these problems and to define more practical channel characteristics, Nyquist introduced a theorem on vestigial symmetry.

4.2.3.2 Nyquist's vestigial symmetry theorem: raised-cosine filters

Theorem. The addition of a skew-symmetrical, real-valued transmittance function $Y(\omega)$ to the transmittance of the ideal low-pass filter maintains the zero-axis crossings of the impulse response. These zero-axis crossings provide the necessary condition for ISI-free transmission. The symmetry of $Y(\omega)$ about the cut-off frequency ω_N (Nyquist radian frequency $\omega_N = 2\pi f_N$) of the linear-phase brick-wall filter is defined by

$$Y(\omega_N - x) = -Y(\omega_N + x) \qquad 0<x<\omega_N$$

where $\omega_N = 2\pi f_N$.

Perhaps one of the simplest interpretations of this formal vestigial symmetry theorem is illustrated in Figure 4.2.10. In simple terms, the resultant amplitude transfer function has a symmetry around the Nyquist frequency f_N. This vestigial-symmetry amplitude response, combined with a linear phase, ensures ISI-free transmission. One of the frequently used functions that satisfies this vestigial theorem is the *raised cosine* function. Filter designers frequently approximate the raised-cosine channel characteristics for ISI-free impulse transmission (Tröndle and Söder, 1987). The amplitude response of this channel is given by

$$|H(j\omega)| = \begin{cases} 1 & 0 \le \omega \le \dfrac{\pi}{T_s}(1-\alpha) \\ \cos^2\left\{\dfrac{T_s}{4\alpha}\left[\omega - \dfrac{\pi(1-\alpha)}{T_s}\right]\right\} & \dfrac{\pi}{T_s}(1-\alpha) \le \omega \le \dfrac{\pi}{T_s}(1-\alpha) \\ 0 & \omega > \dfrac{\pi}{T_s}(1+\alpha) \end{cases} \qquad (4.2.17)$$

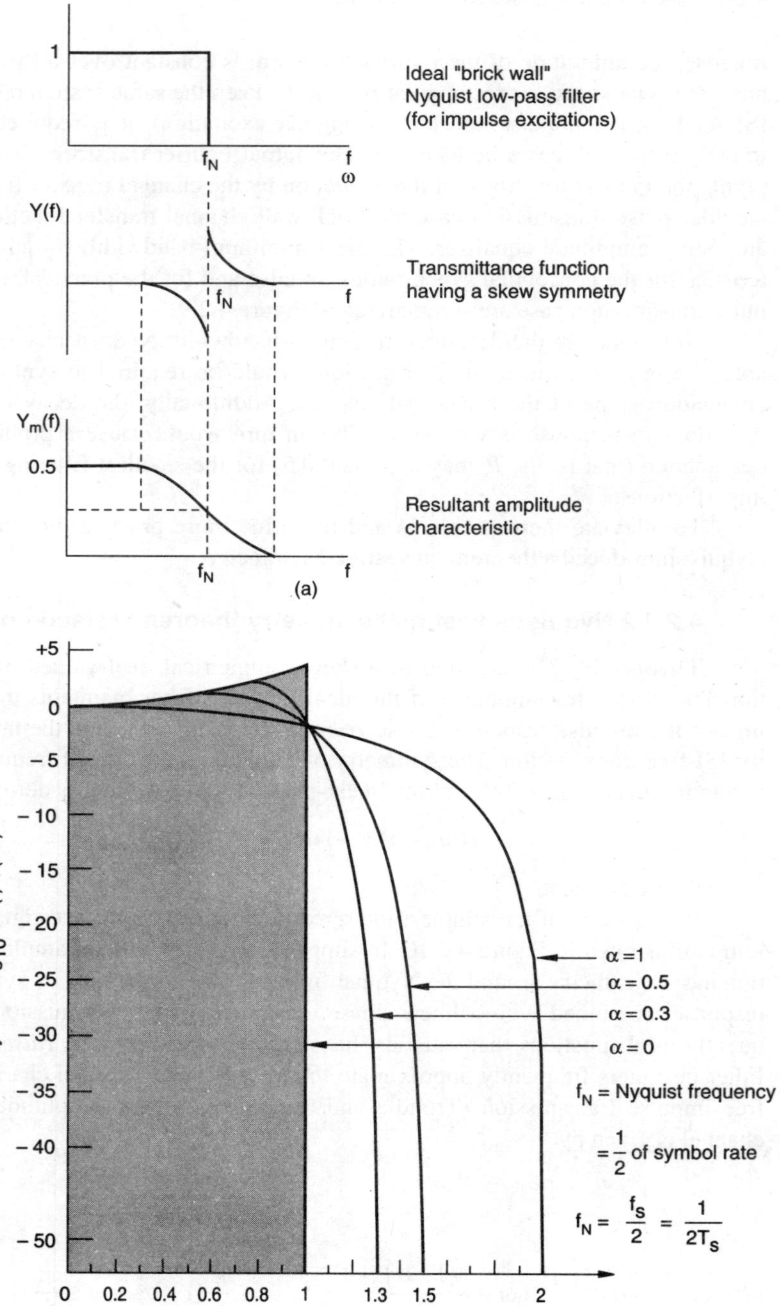

Figure 4.2.10 Nyquist vestigial symmetry theorem. (a), Amplitude characteristics with linear scale; (b), amplitude characteristics plotted on dB scale, including *x*/sin *x*-shaped aperture equalizer and raised-cosine Nyquist filters for rectangular synchronous pulse transmission. The roll-off parameter is α.

where $\omega = 2\pi f$ and α is the channel *roll-off* factor.

An alternative form of this raised-cosine equation, also frequently used in the literature, is

$$H(f) = \begin{cases} 1 & 0 < f < f_N - f_x \\ \frac{1}{2}\left\{1 - \sin\frac{\pi}{2\alpha}\left[\frac{f}{f_N} - 1\right]\right\} & f_N - f_x < f < f_N + f_x \\ 0 & f > f_N + f_x \end{cases} \quad (4.2.18a)$$

$$\phi(f) = kf \quad (4.2.18b)$$

where $\alpha = f_x/f_N$ is the roll-off factor and k is a constant. For practical systems that are employed for the transmission of $f_s = 1/T_s = 2f_N$ rate synchronous rectangular pulses, an (x/sin x)-shaped amplitude equalizer must be added to the channel characteristics described by equation 4.2.17. Thus the desired channel response for *ISI-free pulse transmission* (such as that of NRZ signals) is given by

$$H(j\omega) = \begin{cases} \dfrac{\omega T_s/2}{\sin(\omega T_s/2)} & 0 \le \omega \le \dfrac{\pi}{T_s}(1-\alpha) \\ \dfrac{\omega T_s/2}{\sin(\omega T_s/2)} \cos^2\left\{\dfrac{T_s}{4\alpha}\left[\omega - \dfrac{\pi(1-\alpha)}{T_s}\right]\right\} & \dfrac{\pi}{T_s}(1-\alpha) \le \omega \le \dfrac{\pi}{T_s}(1+\alpha) \\ 0 & \omega \le \dfrac{\pi}{T_s}(1+\alpha) \end{cases} \quad (4.2.19)$$

where α is the roll-off factor. For $\alpha = 0$, an unrealizable minimum-bandwidth filter having a bandwidth equal to $f_N = 1/2T_s$ is obtained. For $\alpha = 0.5$ a 50% excess bandwidth is used, whereas for $\alpha = 1$ the transmission bandwidth is twice the theoretical minimum bandwidth. The amplitude characteristics for various values of the bandwidth parameter α are shown in Figure 4.2.10. Theoretically, at the frequency $f = (1 + \alpha)f_N$ the attenuation has an infinite value. For practical realizations an attenuation of 20 to 50 dB is specified, depending on the allowed amount of adjacent channel interference.

The square root of

$$\cos^2\left\{\frac{T_s}{4\alpha}\left[w - \frac{\pi(1-\alpha)}{T_s}\right]\right\}$$

in equation 4.2.19 is known as the "square root of raised-cosine filters with roll-off factor α." We use the abbreviation $\sqrt{\alpha}$ or $\sqrt{RC}$ for the same term.

Example 4.2.3

Determine the frequency at which the theoretical raised-cosine channel has a 30-dB attenuation. Assume that the transmitted NRZ data rate is $f_s = 1$ Mb/s and that $\alpha = 0.3$ and, $\alpha = 0.5$ filters are specified.

Solution for Example 4.2.3

The Nyquist frequency of the ideal brick-wall filter is at $f_N = f_s/2 = 500$ kHz. From Figure 4.2.10, note that the 30-dB attenuation point is only at a slightly lower frequency than the ∞-dB attenuation point. We assume as a first approximation that these frequencies are equal. For the case of $\alpha = 0.3$ this attenuation is at $(1 + 0.3)$ 500 kHz = 650 kHz, whereas for the case of $\alpha =$ 0.5 it is at $(1 + 0.5)$ 500 kHz = 750 kHz. It could be helpful to go back and solve equation 4.2.18 and obtain the exact frequencies. Solve Problem 4.6 (at the end of this chapter).

Computer-generated eye diagrams for synchronous NRZ data filtered by raised-cosine channel filters, including the (x/sin x) aperture equalizers, are illustrated in Figure 4.2.11. We note that the $\alpha = 0.3$ filtered system has a significant data transition jitter, $J_{pp} = 36\%$ of T_s, whereas for the $\alpha = 1$ filtered, wider-band system, $J_{pp} = 0\%$. The $ISI = 0$ in both cases. The spectral efficiency is inversely proportional to α.

4.2.4 Baseband QPSK, MSK, GMSK, and FQPSK Signal Generation

Most American, Japanese, and European cellular-wireless standardization committees adopted relatively simple, robust modulation techniques by the 1990s. A modification of conventional quadrature phase shift keying (QPSK) has been adopted as standard for the North American and Japanese digital cellular systems (EIA, 1990). For European and several international applications, a minimum shift keying (MSK) Gaussian-premodulation filtered system known as GMSK has been adopted as standard (GSM, 1990).

This section presents concepts of baseband signal generation and processing for conventional QPSK and MSK modulated systems. A simple yet powerful baseband filter (that is, signal processor) invented by Dr. Feher and Associates (Feher, 1982; Feher, 1987a; Kato and Feher [patent], 1986) is also described. This processor, in a QPSK structure, generates Feher's patented or "FQPSK" modulated signal. For a detailed implementation see Appendix A.3. In Section 4.5 and Chapter 9 we demonstrate that FQPSK doubles the capacity of Global Speciale Mobile (GSM) standardized GMSK modulated systems, increases the battery lifetime, and reduces the radiation of the U.S. digital "π/4-DQPSK" cellular system (EIA, 1990). The baseband signal processor requirements for quadrature modem architectures are described in Section 4.3 and illustrated in Figure 4.2.12. For QPSK implementations the transmit baseband signal processor has an (x/sin x)-shaped amplitude equalizer where $x = \pi T_s f$. It is followed by a square root of raised-cosine ($\sqrt{RC}$) transfer function. The processor, abbreviated as x/sin x $\sqrt{RC}$, is defined by equation 4.2.18. The square root of equation 4.2.18 without the x/sin x is $\sqrt{RC}$. In the receiver it is used as a matched Nyquist-receive filter. The resultant eye diagrams at the threshold detector input in Figure 4.2.12, (a), are illustrated in Figure 4.2.11.

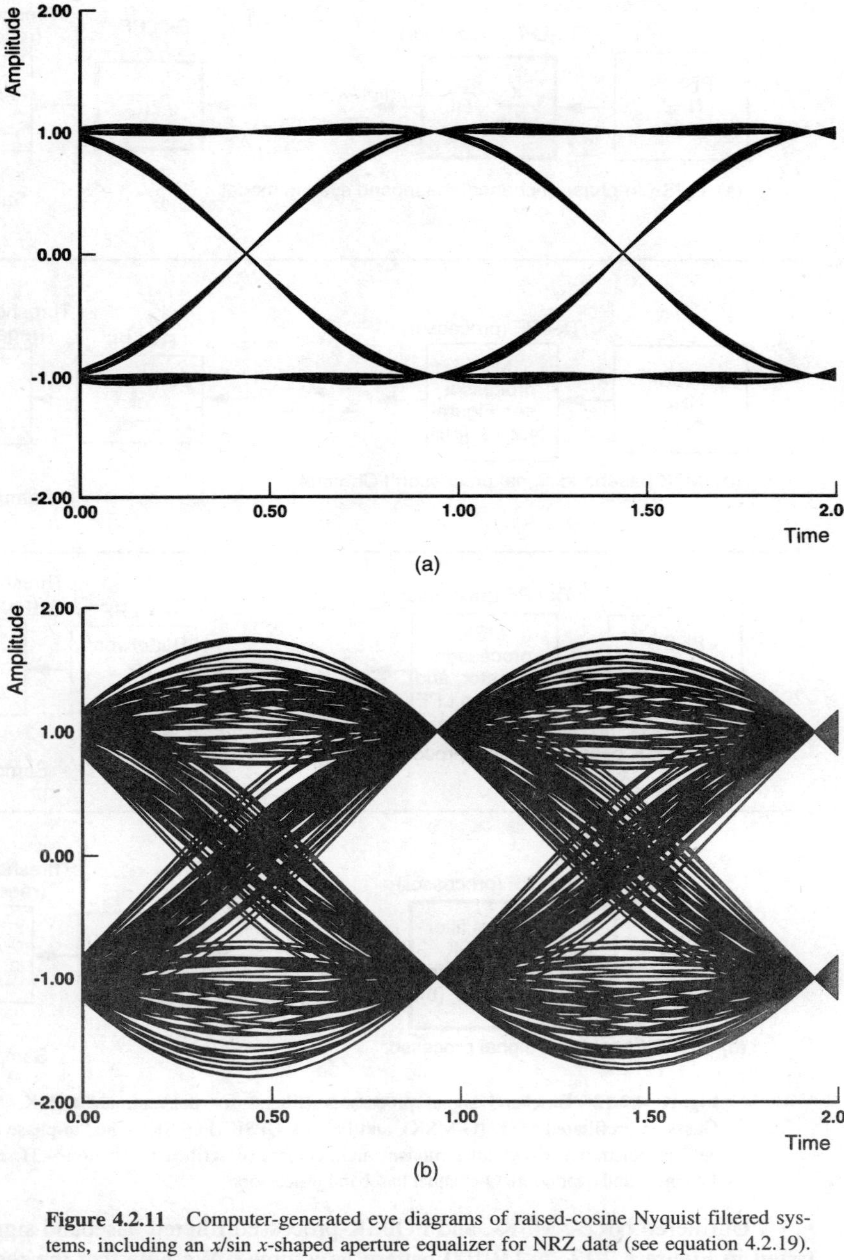

Figure 4.2.11 Computer-generated eye diagrams of raised-cosine Nyquist filtered systems, including an $x/\sin x$-shaped aperture equalizer for NRZ data (see equation 4.2.19). (a), $\alpha = 1$ roll-off factor; (b), $\alpha = 0.3$ roll-off factor. CREATE-1 program, Appendix 2, generates this type of diagrams.

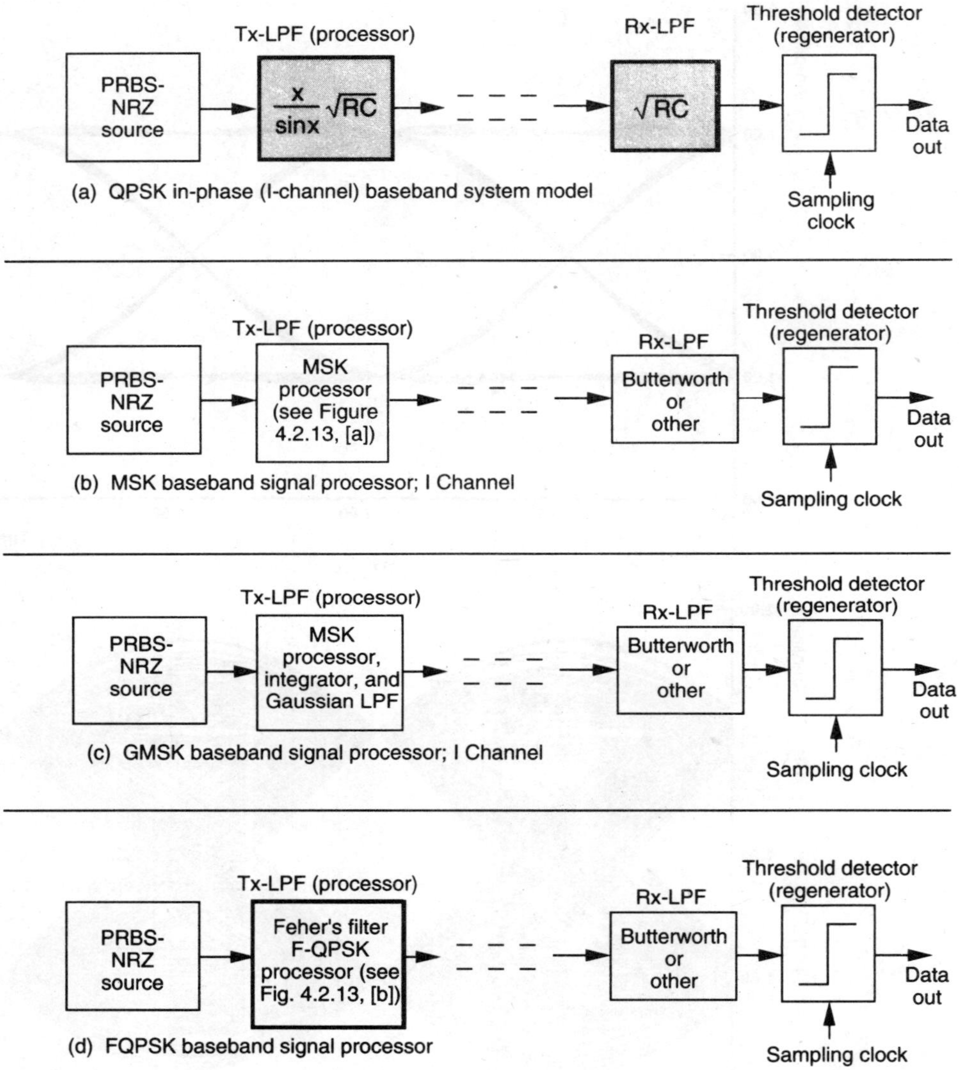

Figure 4.2.12 Baseband signal processors (filters) for conventional QPSK, MSK, Gaussian prefiltered MSK (G-MSK), and Feher's QPSK (FQPSK). The "in-phase channel" is illustrated. Quadrature modem architectures (described in Section 4.3) require I-channel and quadrature Q-channel baseband processors.

Unfiltered NRZ-, MSK-, and FQPSK-processed filtered baseband signals are illustrated in Figure 4.2.13. A 110100 pattern is assumed. We note that the resultant output signals of the transmit low-pass filter (Tx-LPF) are similar, with the exception of Feher's FQPSK baseband processor, which generates only smooth signal transitions; in contrast, the MSK processor has abrupt changes and discontinuities. See Feher, 1982, U.S. Patent No. 4,339,724.

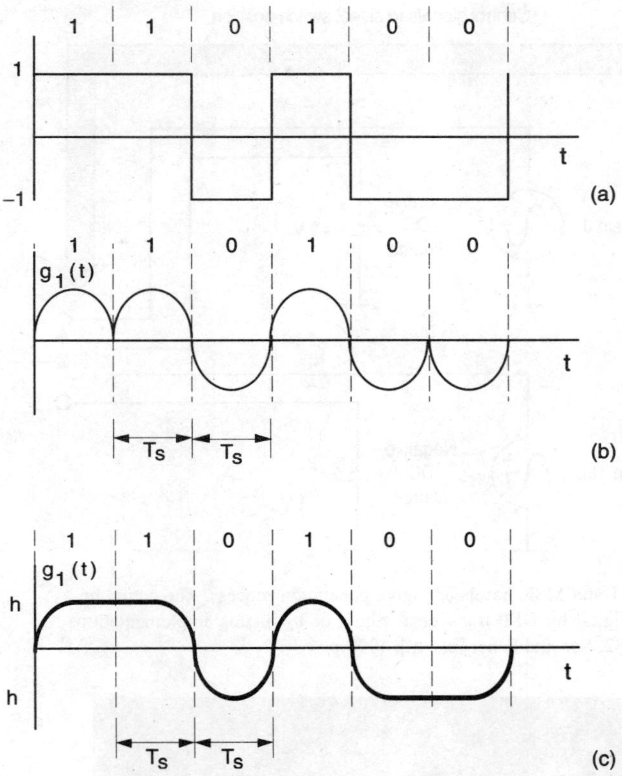

Figure 4.2.13 Baseband signal patterns for, (a), unfiltered NRZ; (b), MSK (minimum shift keying); and (c), FQPSK-1 (Feher's patented USA Patents 4,339,724 and 4,567,602) QPSK modulated systems.

The baseband MSK and FQPSK waveshapes could be generated by a conceptual diagram, as illustrated in Figure 4.2.14. The actual implementation could be in digital signal processing (DSP) and/or by means of analog processing and filtering techniques. An experimental f_b = 32-kb/s rate eye diagram and the corresponding baseband spectrum of an FQPSK baseband signal are illustrated in Figure 4.2.15. The eye diagram illustrates that an ISI- and jitter-free (IJF) band-limited signal is obtained.

The power spectral density of the FQPSK baseband signal (Le-Ngoc et al., 1982) is

$$S(x) = T_s\left(\frac{\sin 2\pi x}{2\pi}\,\frac{1}{1-4x^2}\right)^2 \tag{4.2.20}$$

where $x = fT_s$ and T_s = symbol duration.

The baseband spectrum of the MSK-processed signal (Feher, 1983) is given by

$$w_s(f) = \frac{4h^2T_s}{\pi^2}\,\frac{1+\cos 2\pi fT_s}{(1-4f^2T_s^2)^2} \tag{4.2.21}$$

where h is a constant.

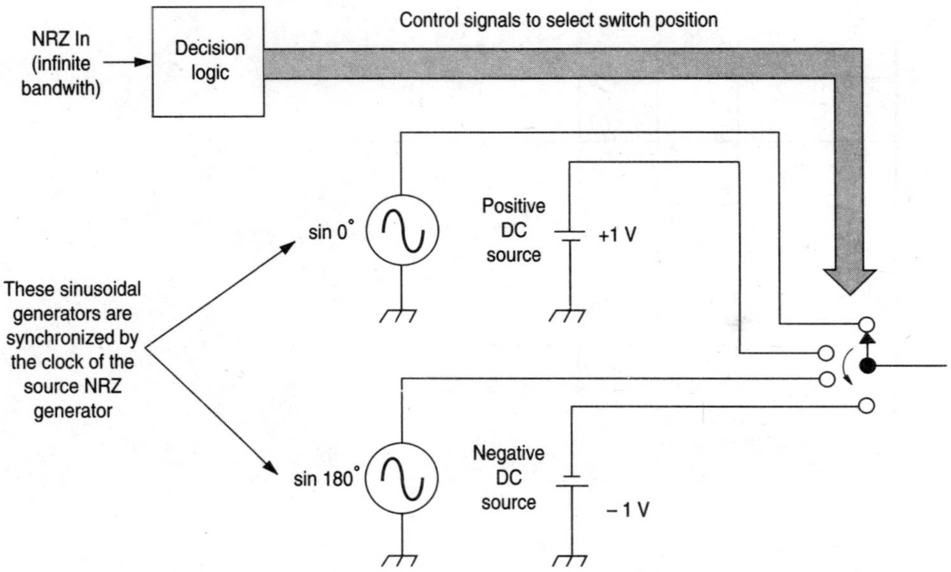

Figure 4.2.14 FQPSK-1 and MSK baseband signal generation process. The actual implementation could be digital by DSP transversal filters or by analog implementation. (From Feher [patent], 1982; Seo and Feher [patent], 1990.)

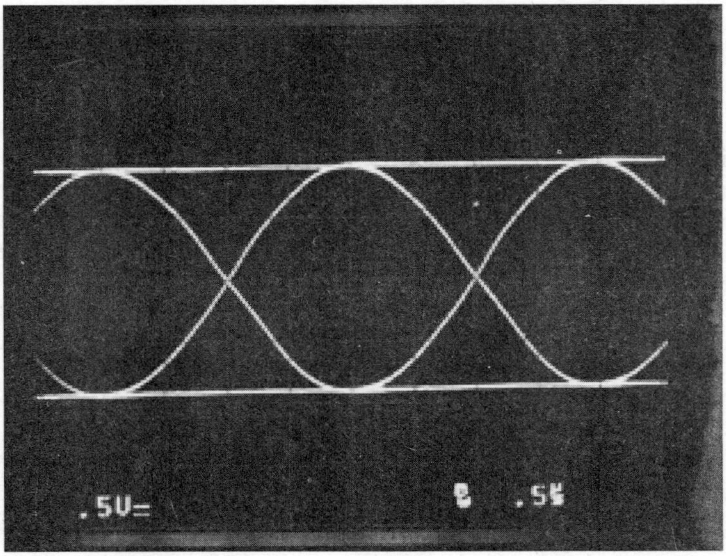

Figure 4.2.15 Intel 740-FPGA (field programmable gate array) generated FQPSK-1, for f_b = 1 Mb/s (500 kBaud) rate baseband eye diagram. This intersymbol interference- and jitter–free (IJF) eye is the signal used as the in-phase (I) and quadrature (Q) channel baseband drive of quadrature modulators. More advanced FQPSK processors and signal wave shapes with further increased efficiency are illustrated in Figures 4.3.35 to 4.3.40.

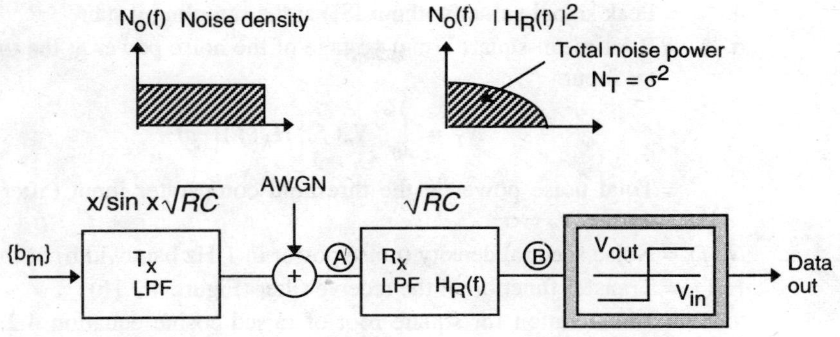

Figure 4.2.16 Additive White Gaussian Noise (AWGN) in a binary baseband Nyquist channel. At the sampling instants the signal equals $+A$ or $-A$ volts. The rms noise voltage is σ volts. The noise bandwidth is limited by the receive low-pass filter. If optimal ISI-free raised-cosine filters are used, the total signal power equals A^2. Abbreviation for square root of raised-cosine transfer function $\sqrt{RC}$ is defined by the square root of equation 4.2.17 and $x = \omega T_s/2$ in equation 4.2.19. An optimal band-limited Nyquist-shaped matched filter system is illustrated. (From Feher, 1983.)

4.2.5 Bit-Error-Rate Performance of Baseband Systems

This section describes the bit-error-rate (BER) performance of ideal binary baseband systems in an additive white Gaussian noise (AWGN) environment. Instead of BER, the term "probability of error," that is, P_e or $P(e)$, is used in several references. The fundamental statistical properties of the AWGN channel are highlighted in Appendix A. Here we focus on the relationship of baseband systems, as follows:

$$\text{BER} = P_e = f(\text{S/N}). \tag{4.2.22}$$

The average signal power is S and the average AWGN power is N. The average signal-to-noise (S/N) power ratio is specified at the threshold detector (regenerator input). See point B in Figure 4.2.16.

In the BER = f(S/N) derivation (Feher, 1983) an ideal raised-cosine Nyquist-filtered channel is assumed with matched optimal filtering (Figures 4.2.12, [a], and 4.2.16). The results of the derivation are

$$P_e = \int_{A/\sqrt{N_T}}^{\infty} \frac{1}{\sqrt{2\pi}} e^{-\omega^2/2}\, d\omega = Q\left(\frac{A}{\sqrt{N_T}}\right) = Q\left(\frac{A}{\sigma}\right) \tag{4.2.23}$$

where

$$Q(y) = \int_{y}^{\infty} \frac{1}{\sqrt{2\pi}} e^{-\omega^2/2}\, d\omega \tag{4.2.24}$$

and

A = Peak signal value (without ISI) at the sampling instant

σ = Root-mean-square (rms) voltage of the noise power at the threshold detector input

$$N_T = \int_0^{\infty} N_o(f) \left| H_R(f) \right|^2 df \qquad (4.2.25)$$

= Total noise power at the threshold comparator input (after the Rx-LPF), that is, $N_T = \sigma^2$

$N_o(f)$ = Noise spectral density (noise power in 1-Hz bandwidth) of the AWGN

$H_R(f)$ = Transfer function of the receive filter (Figure 4.2.16)

$\sqrt{RC}$ = Abbreviation for square root of raised-cosine equation 4.2.17; this is the assumed implementation of the receive low-pass filter (Rx-LPF)

The $Q(y)$ function is tabulated in many mathematics handbooks and also in Feher (1983). It is sketched in Figure 4.2.17. We should remember the following, as a frequently used practical reference point:

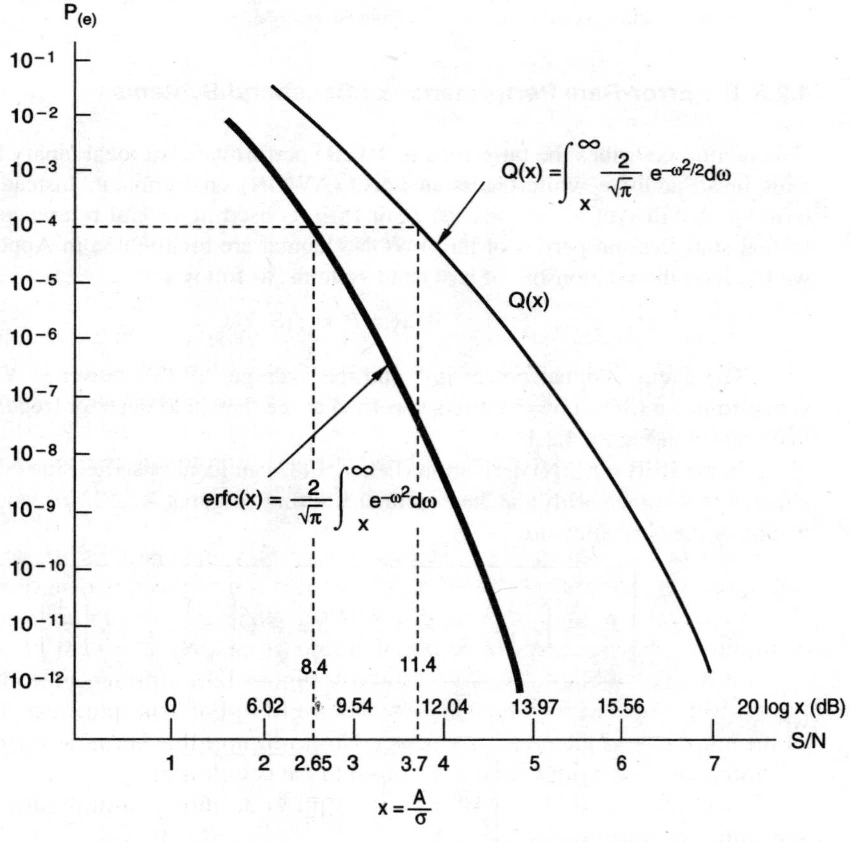

Figure 4.2.17 $P_e = f$(S/N) of binary baseband signals. *A*, Signal voltage; σ, rms noise voltage at threshold comparator input.

For a $P_e = 10^{-4}$, an $A/\sigma = 3.7$, or $S/N = 11.4\ dB$, is required.

This signal-to-noise (S/N) ratio is obtained for $\alpha = 0$ (brick-wall) channels. The rms signal-to-noise ratio requirement depends on the raised-cosine channel filter roll-off factor α. The derivation of optimal receive filters that satisfy the Nyquist ISI-free transmission criteria is a fairly complex task and is beyond the scope of this text. Detailed derivations are presented in Bennett and Davey (1965) and Morais and Feher (1979). The final theoretical result is that the rms S/N ratio for the optimal receive filter ($\alpha = 1$ roll-off channel) specified *at the threshold comparator input* is as follows:

$$(S/N)_{rms_{opt}} = 10.2 \text{ dB} \qquad \text{then} \qquad P_e = 10^{-4} \tag{4.2.26}$$

We have already mentioned that noise samples exceeding the signal level A may cause errors. The signal power at the receive filter input equals A^2. This power is independent of the roll-off factor α of the Nyquist-filtered raised-cosine channel. Solve problem 4.10 (at the end of this chapter).

4.3 MODEM PRINCIPLES AND ARCHITECTURES

4.3.1 Coherent Modem-Baseband Equivalence

For a large class of modulated and coherently demodulated systems, complex and frequently unrealizably narrow RF and intermediate frequency (IF) bandpass filters may be replaced by simple baseband low-pass filters (LPFs). This "baseband equivalence" of *linearly modulated* (IF and RF) bandpass-filtered (BPF) signals with premodulation-filtered and postdemodulation-filtered baseband LPFs is derived in this section. Linearly modulated signal implies that the spectrum is linear, or double-sideband, suppressed-carrier amplitude modulation (DSB-SC-AM) that is modulated or translated so as to be centered around the desired carrier frequency (Figure 4.3.1). A profound understanding of the appropriate equivalence conditions enables the engineer to design simple LPFs instead of the more complex BPFs.

For *coherent* demodulation the carrier frequency and phase of the received modulated signal must be precisely established. Here it is assumed that perfect carrier and symbol timing synchronization signals are available. The principles of operation of the synchronization subsystems and their possible impact on overall system performance are discussed in later sections. The BPF shown in Figure 4.3.1 represents the cascade of the transmit BPF, the channel filters, and the receive BPF. For conceptual simplicity assume that the noise is negligible on the channel. However, note that because of the linearity of the system, the conclusions are not restricted to the noiseless case.

If the linear modulator contains only a premodulation low-pass filter, LPF_T, then the modulated signal is represented by

$$s_1(t) = [a(t) * h_L(t)]c(t) \tag{4.3.1}$$

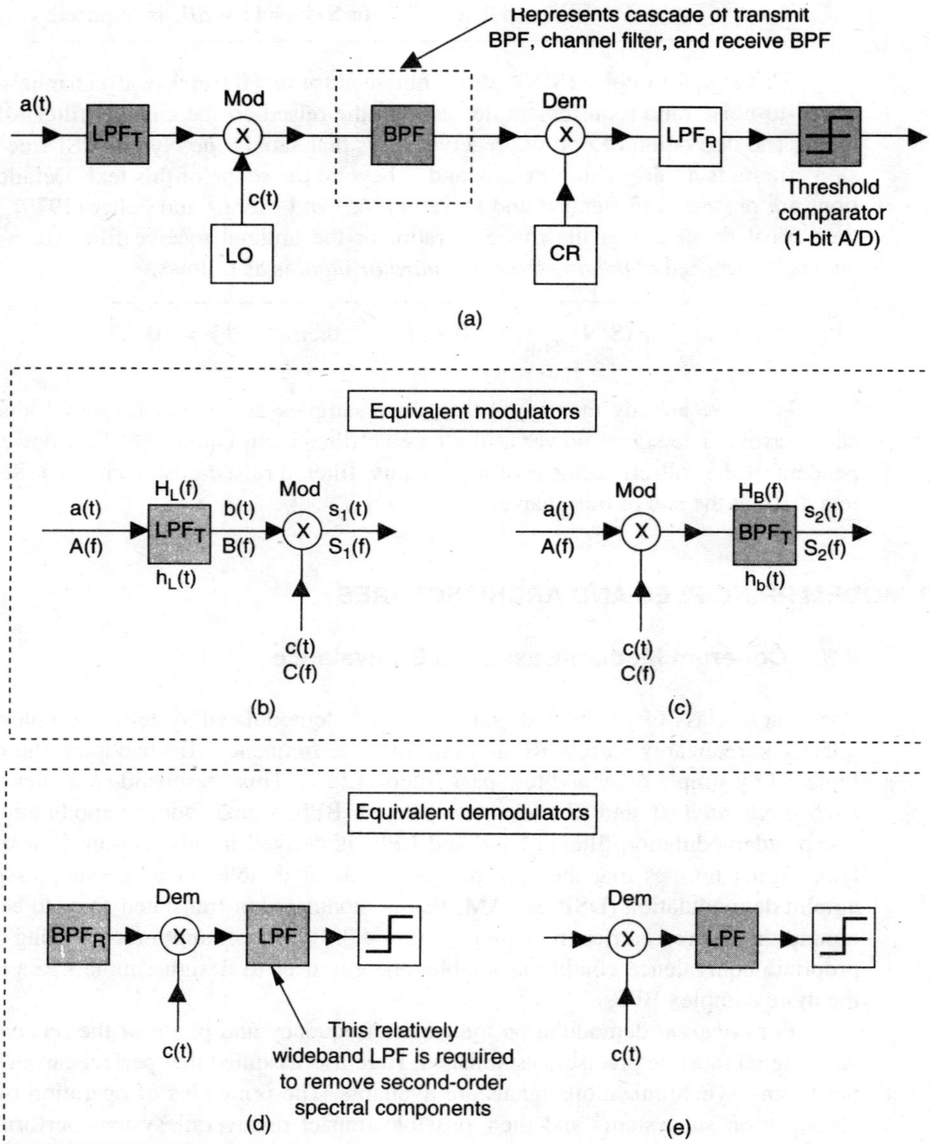

Figure 4.3.1 Baseband equivalent model of bandpass modulated signals. (a), Modulator, channel, demodulator. *LO,* Local oscillator; *CR,* carrier recovery. (b), Linear modulator having a premodulation LPF only. (c), Modulator having a postmodulation BPF only. $h_L(t)$ and $h_b(t)$, Impulse response of the low-pass and the bandpass filters. (d), Demodulator having a predetection BPF. (e), Demodulator having a postdetection LPF only.

where * denotes the convolution, defined by

$$b(t) = a(t) * h_L(t) = \int_{-\infty}^{\infty} a(\tau)h_L(t-\tau)d\tau. \qquad (4.3.2)$$

Taking the Fourier transform of equation 4.3.1 and noting that convolution in the time domain corresponds to multiplication in the frequency domain and that convolution in the frequency domain corresponds to multiplication in the time domain, we obtain

$$S_1(f) = [A(f)H_L(f)] * C(f). \qquad (4.3.3)$$

Convolution of a baseband spectrum with a sinusoidal carrier results in a double-sideband (DSB) spectrum centered around the carrier frequency. If the baseband signal does not contain a dc component, that is, if $dc = 0$, then the resultant signal is a DSB-SC-AM signal. This statement applies to analog and digital baseband input signals. The signal that is filtered before being modulated is given by

$$S_1(f) = A(f-f_c)H_L(f-f_c) + A(f+f_c)H_L(f+f_c). \qquad (4.3.4)$$

If the linear DSB modulator contains only a postmodulation BPF, then

$$s_2(t) = [a(t)c(t) * h_B(t) \qquad (4.3.5)$$

and the corresponding Fourier transform is

$$\begin{aligned} S_2(f) &= [A(f) * C(f)]H_B(f) \\ &= [A(f-f_c) + A(f+f_c)]H_B(f). \end{aligned} \qquad (4.3.6)$$

The amplitude spectra of the premodulation- and postmodulation-filtered signals, represented by equations 4.3.4 and 4.3.6, respectively, are equivalent if $S_1(f) = S_2(f)$, or

$$H_L(f-f_c) + H_L(f+f_c) = H_B(f). \qquad (4.3.7)$$

From equation 4.3.7 we conclude that the equivalence condition is satisfied if the BPF $H_B(f)$, has the same transfer function as the LPF, $H_L(f)$, shifted so as to be centered around the carrier frequency. *For the equivalence condition, the BPF must be symmetrical around the carrier frequency.* For the coherent receiver, the derivation of the band- and low-pass channel model equivalence conditions is almost identical to the derivation for the transmitter. The advantage of the equivalent low-pass filtering approach for systems with a relatively low bit-rate is discussed next.

Example 4.3.1

Design a DSB binary modulator for a transmission rate of f_b = 10 kb/s. Assume that the source information is in NRZ format and that direct baseband-to-RF modulation is required. The carrier frequency, f_c, is specified as 2 GHz, and a 30% excess bandwidth is permissible (30 dB attenuation point).

Solution for Example 4.3.1

The DSB modulator consists of a mixer preceded by an LPF or followed by a BPF. Either a low-pass *or* a bandpass filter having a roll-off factor of $\alpha = 0.3$; that is, an excess bandwidth of 30% must be designed. In Figure 4.3.2 the amplitude characteristics of these filters are illustrated. The (x/sin x)-shaped amplitude equalizers are included to meet the ISI-free transmission requirements stipulated in the Nyquist theorems. For ISI-free transmission, linear phase characteristics are required. A careful examination of the BPF reveals that it would be difficult or even impossible to design the narrow, phase-equalized BPF illustrated in Figure 4.3.2. In addition, the slightest drift of the filter center frequency would cause an intolerable asymmetry. However, the equivalent LPF could be designed by relatively simple analog or digital signal processing (DSP) techniques.

4.3.2 Coherent and Differentially Coherent Binary Phase Shift Keying (PSK) Systems (BPSK)

Discrete phase modulation, known as M-ary phase shift keying, is among the most frequently used digital modulation techniques. Biphase or binary phase shift keying (BPSK) systems are considered the simplest form of phase shift keying ($M = 2$). The modulated signal has two states, $m_1(t)$ and $m_2(t)$, given by

$$m_1(t) = +C \cos \omega_c t \tag{4.3.8}$$

$$m_2(t) = -C \cos \omega_c t. \tag{4.3.9}$$

These signals can be generated by a system such as that shown in Figure 4.3.1. The modulated signal is given by

$$m(t) = b(t)c(t) = Cb(t) \cos \omega_c t. \tag{4.3.10}$$

If $b(t)$ represents a synchronous random binary baseband signal having a bit rate of $f_b = 1/T_b$ and levels -1 and $+1$, then equation 4.3.10 represents the antipodal (180-degree) phase-shifted signaling elements $m_1(t)$ and $m_2(t)$. Thus the information is contained in the *phase* of the modulated signal, or

$$m(t) = C \cos [\omega_c t + \theta(t)] \tag{4.3.11}$$

where

$$\theta(t) = 0° \text{ or } 180°.$$

Time-domain multiplication is equivalent to double-sideband, suppressed-carrier amplitude modulation (DSB-SC-AM). The representation in equation 4.3.11 implies that a phase-shift keyed (PSK) signal is obtained. We should remember that time-domain multiplication may correspond to digital phase modulation. In other words, an *equivalence*

$$\boxed{\mathbf{DSB - SC - AM = PSK}} \tag{4.3.12}$$

exists in this case.

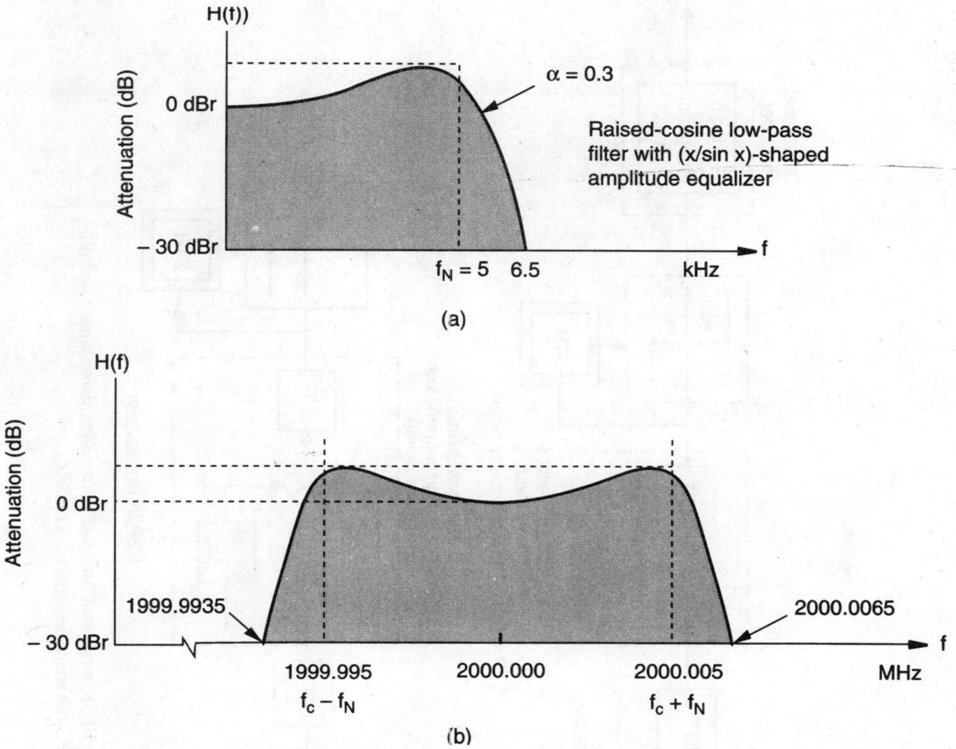

Figure 4.3.2 (a), Low-pass and, (b), equivalent bandpass attenuation characteristics for a 30% excess bandwidth 10 kb/s double-sideband binary system. The frequency scale is in MHz.

For *coherent demodulation,* a carrier frequency that is in synchronism with the received modulated wave is required. In the recovered-carrier system shown in Figure 4.3.3 the upper signal path provides the receive multiplier with a sinusoidal frequency that has the identical center frequency and phase as the transmitted carrier wave, modified by the radio propagation environment and receiver equipment delay.

Coherent phase demodulation, or coherent demodulation, is implemented by multiplication of the modulated received band-limited RF or IF signal $r(t)$ by the recovered unmodulated carrier $k \cos \omega_c t$. The phase modulation is removed in the carrier recovery subsystem.

The baseband demodulated output signal, before low-pass filtering, is given by

$$\begin{aligned} p(t) &= r(t)\, K \cos \omega_c t = C_r\, K \cos[\omega_c t + \theta(t)] \cos \omega_c t \\ &= \frac{1}{2} C_r K \cos[\omega_c t + \theta(t) - \omega_c t] + \frac{1}{2} C_r K \cos[\omega_c t + \theta(t) + \omega_c t] \\ &= \frac{1}{2} C_r K\, [\cos \theta(t) + \cos[2\omega_c t + \theta(t)]]. \end{aligned} \tag{4.3.13}$$

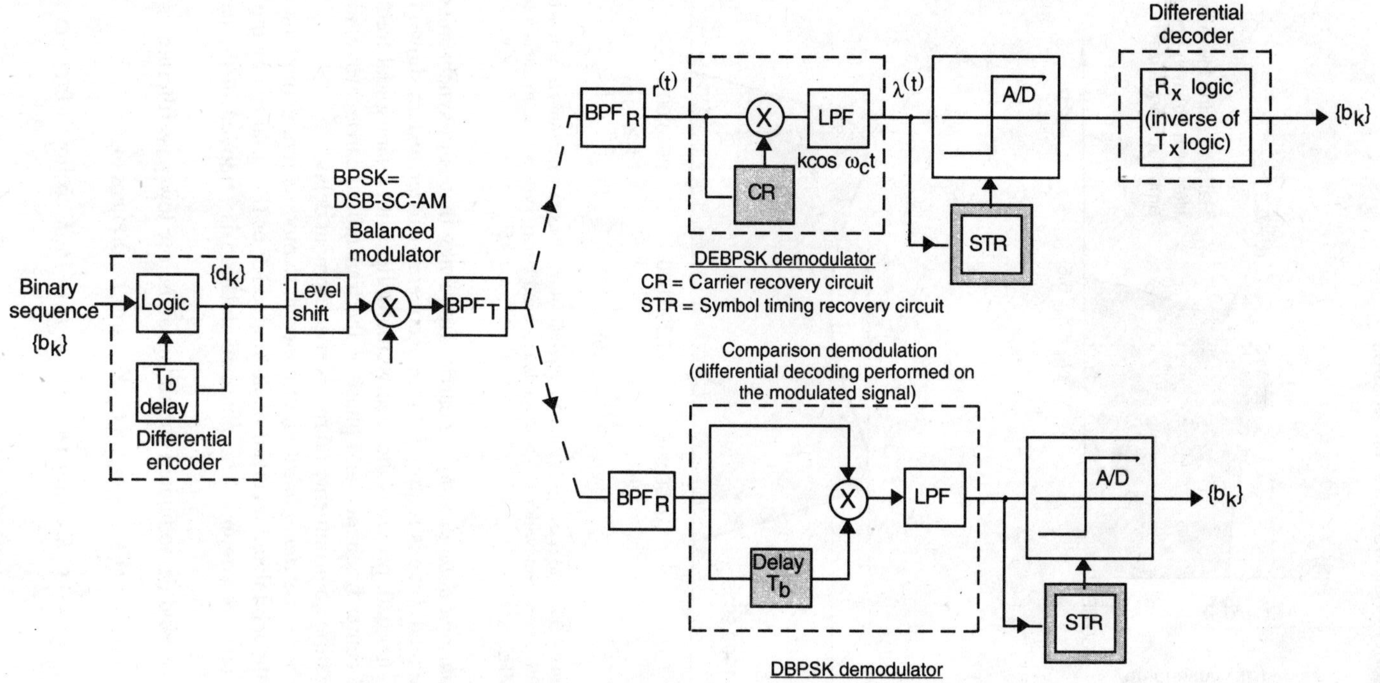

Figure 4.3.3 Differentially encoded BPSK modulator followed by coherent demodulator and differential decoder (*DEBPSK*) and differential phase demodulator (*DBPSK*).

The receive LPF removes the double-frequency spectral components. At the *threshold comparator input,* we have

$$q(t) = \frac{1}{2} C_r K \cos[\theta(t)]. \tag{4.3.14}$$

In this equation, $C_r K/2$ represents a gain constant; cos $[\theta(t)]$ is the time-variable band limited baseband signal. For $\theta(t) = 0°$ or $180°$, this signal equals +1 or −1, respectively. This baseband voltage is proportional to the cosine of the phase angle differential between the received modulated carrier and the recovered carrier; thus the term *coherent phase comparator* or *phase demodulator* is justified for the multiplier or LPF subsystem. The threshold comparator provides the digital output $\{\hat{b}_k\}$. If the system interference and noise are negligible, then $\hat{b}_k(t) = b_k(t - \tau)$, meaning that the demodulated or regenerated output equals the source information delayed by the equipment and propagation delay, τ.

Differentially coherent demodulation is illustrated in the lower part of the receive signal path in Figure 4.3.3. The differential BPSK demodulator performs a comparison detection (a demodulation) directly on the modulated signal and thus does not require a carrier recovery circuit. The modulated signal is multiplied by a 1-bit delayed replica and then band-limited with an LPF. The differentially encoded modem equipped with a carrier-recovery circuit is designated *DEBPSK*; the one without carrier recovery is designated *DBPSK.*

4.3.3 Synchronization: Carrier Recovery (CR) and Symbol Timing Recovery (STR)

Carrier recovery (CR) and Symbol timing recovery (STR) synchronization circuits provide essential signal processing functions for coherent demodulation and baseband signal regeneration. Some of the simplest CR and STR methods that are frequently used in BPSK demodulation are described in this section. These methods are also used in an extended form in the demodulation of QPSK, **Feher's QPSK or FQPSK**, O-QPSK, minimum shift keying (MSK) Gaussian Minimum Shift Keying (GMSK) and other, more complex modulated systems. A detailed description of synchronization subsystems is presented in Feher (1983), Lee and Messerschmitt (1988), and many other books and journal papers. A fast-burst synchronizer is described in Section 4.10.

The simple CR circuit shown in Figure 4.3.4 consists of a multiplier, a phase-locked loop (PLL) or tracking BPF, a frequency halver (represented by ":2"), and a delay line τ_{cd}. The received BPSK-modulated IF carrier signal is

$$\begin{aligned} m_1(t) &= C \cos(w_c t + 0°) \\ \text{or} \quad m_2(t) &= C \cos(w_c t + 180°). \end{aligned} \tag{4.3.15}$$

Assuming that the baseband data are random and equiprobable, the spectrum at point *A* is continuous. The carrier recovery is required to generate a discrete spectral line at point *C*. (See the spectral sketch in Figure 4.3.4 of $S_c(f)$.) This discrete spectral line is obtained by

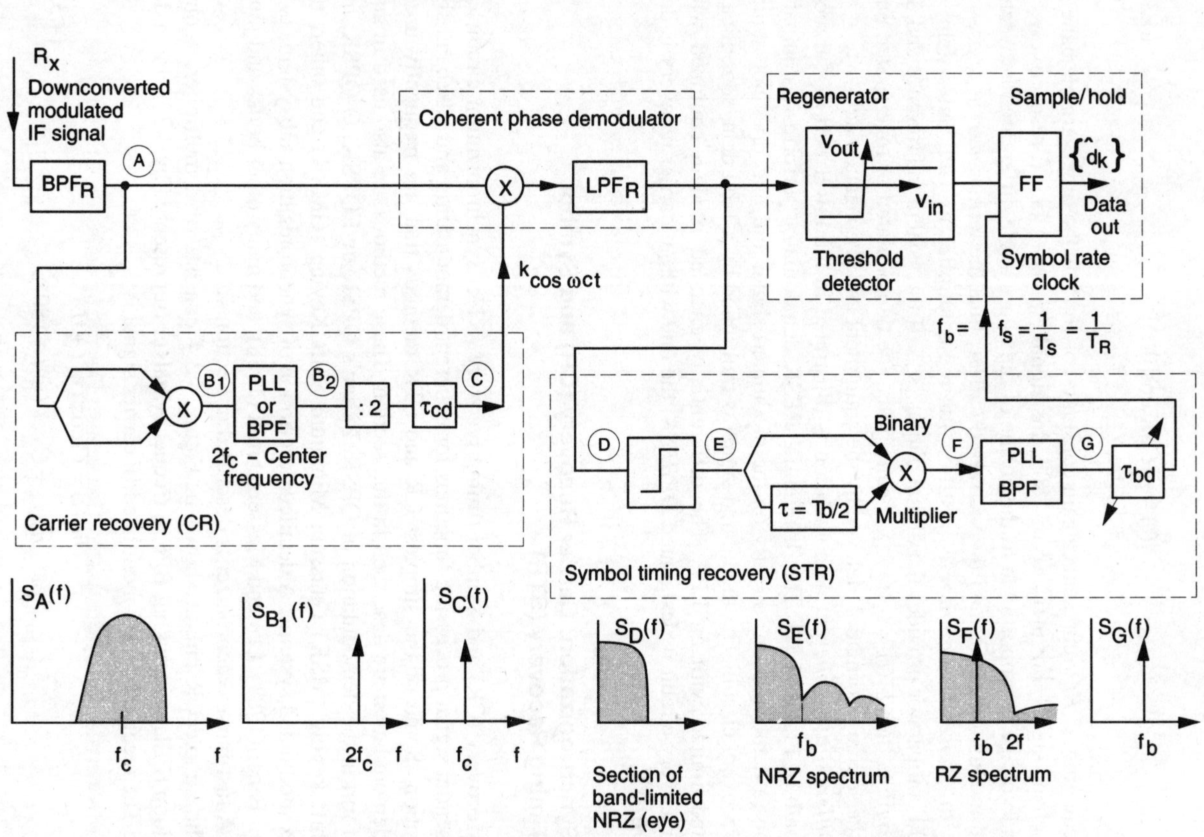

Figure 4.3.4 Carrier recovery (CR) and symbol timing recovery (STR) conceptual BPSK implementations and corresponding continuous and discrete spectra.

multiplication of the received signals $m_1(t)$ or $m_2(t)$ by themselves, that is, by "squaring of the signals." We obtain at point B_1

$$m_1(t)\cdot m_1(t) = [C\cos(w_c\cdot(\omega_c t + 0°)]\cdot[C\cos(\omega_c t + 0°)]$$
$$= \frac{1}{2}C^2[1+\cos(2\omega_c t + 2\cdot 0°)] = \frac{1}{2}C^2[1+\cos 2\omega_c t] \quad (4.3.16)$$
$$m_2(t)\cdot m_2(t) = [C\cos(\omega_c t + 180°)]\cdot[C\cos(\omega_c t + 180°)]$$
$$= \frac{1}{2}C^2[1+\cos(2\omega_c t + 2\cdot 180°)] = \frac{1}{2}C^2[1+\cos 2\omega_c t]. \quad (4.3.17)$$

From equations 4.3.16 and 4.3.17, we conclude that at point B_1 in Figure 4.3.4 the phase modulation, that is, 0° or 180°, is removed. The dc component is removed, and the output spectrum of the PLL or tracking BPF is a discrete spectral line having a frequency of $2f_c$. After frequency division by a factor of 2 and static delay compensation τ_{cd}, an unmodulated phase-aligned carrier tone $k\cos\omega_c t$ is fed into the coherent phase demodulator.

Note: For QPSK, Offset QPSK (O-QPSK), and FQPSK applications, "quadrupling" is used instead of a "squaring" signal for carrier recovery implementations. Quadrupling removes the QPSK phase modulation, since $4\cdot 0° = 4\cdot 90° = 4\cdot 180° = 4\cdot 270° = 0°$.

The multiplication and frequency division process introduces a 180-degree phase ambiguity. During and after carrier acquisition, such a carrier recovery circuit could provide the correct absolute frequency and phase, or a 180-degree phase-shifted carrier. This ambiguity could lead to a bit-error rate of 100%, an unacceptable scenario. To mitigate the CR-introduced ambiguity problem, differential encoding and decoding are used in many applications.

Symbol timing recovery circuit implementation concepts are similar to CR methods. At point D in Figure 4.3.4, we have the band-limited eye diagram of the demodulated signal. This eye diagram has a continuous spectrum, $S_D(f)$. A simple threshold detector (not clocked) provides a wideband output, NRZ spectrum, $S_E(f)$. The $\tau = T_b/2 = T_s/2$ delay line "staggers" or offsets the input data patterns. At the binary multiplier output an RZ signal such as the one depicted in Figure 4.2.3, (c), is obtained. This spectrum $S_F(f)$ contains a discrete spectral line. The PLL or tracking BPF, having a center frequency of $f_s = f_b$, provides a filtered clear spectral line at the bit rate f_b. The bit rate (or symbol rate f_s) clock is fed to a flip-flop (FF), which provides the sample-hold function and the regenerated baseband data output stream $\{\hat{d}_k\}$.

4.3.4 Differential Encoding and Decoding Requirement

The simple squaring (frequency doubling) and frequency quadrupling (used for QPSK) CR circuits, as well as most other practical carrier-recovery circuits, introduce a *phase ambiguity* into the recovered carrier. In binary PSK demodulators a steady 180-degree phase error in the recovered carrier is possible. This error inverts (multiplies by cos 180° = −1) the demodulated data stream and causes a 100% error rate. Fortunately, the insertion of a simple *differential encoder* into the transmitter and a *differential decoder* into the receiver prevents errors that could be introduced by this phase ambiguity. The basic principles of operation of such encoders are now described.

The differential encoding process is illustrated in Figure 4.3.5. In the generation of a differentially encoded bit, the d_k of the encoded sequence $\{d_k\}$, the present bit b_k of the message sequence $\{b_k\}$, and the previous bit d_{k-1} are compared. *If there is no difference between* b_k *and* d_{k-1}, *then* $d_k = 1$; *otherwise* $d_k = 0$. This can be expressed as

$$d_k = \overline{b_k \oplus d_{k-1}} = b_k d_{k-1} + \bar{b}_k \bar{d}_{k-1} \tag{4.3.18}$$

where ⊕ represents the *Exclusive -OR* operation. An arbitrary reference binary digit may be assumed for the initial bit of the $\{d_k\}$ sequence.

Both differential demodulators in Figure 4.3.3 perform the inverse function to that of the encoder. In the case of DEBPSK demodulation the differential decoding is performed by means of logic circuitry. In the case of the DBPSK demodulator the phase angles of the received signal (which may be corrupted by noise) and its one-bit delayed version are compared.

4.3.5 Quadrature Phase Shift Keying: Coincident and Offset Types

Quadriphase or quadrature phase shift keying (QPSK) modems are used in systems applications where the 1-b/s/Hz theoretical spectral efficiency of BPSK modems is insufficient for the available bandwidth. The various demodulation techniques used in BPSK systems also apply to QPSK systems. In addition to the straightforward extensions of the binary modem techniques, a technique known as *offset-keyed* or *staggered* (O-QPSK or SQPSK) quadriphase modulation is also in use.

The various QPSK modem architectures and the BPSK modems are similarly defined and abbreviated. Several analogies are listed in Table 4.3.1.

In QPSK systems the modulated signal has four distinct phase states (Figure 4.3.6). These states are generated by a unique mapping scheme of consecutive *dibits* (pairs of bits) into symbols. The corresponding phase states are maintained during the signaling interval T_s. This interval has a two-bit duration (that is, $T_s = 2T_b$). The four possible dibits are frequently mapped in accordance with the *Gray code.* An important property of this code is that *adjacent symbols* (phase states) *differ by only one bit.* In transmission systems corrupted by noise and interference, the most frequent errors are introduced by making decision errors between adjacent states. In such cases the Gray code ensures that a single symbol error corresponds to a single bit error. These Gray codes are advantageous, particularly when QPSK systems are followed by single-error-correcting decoders.

A block diagram of a conventional or "coincident" and a staggered or offset QPSK modulator is illustrated in Figure 4.3.6, (a). For coincident QPSK applications the $T_b = T_s/2$ offset delay line is removed (short-circuited) from the quadrature channel. The NRZ data stream entering the modulator is converted by a serial-to-parallel converter into two separate NRZ streams. One stream, $I(t)$, is in phase, and the other, $Q(t)$, is quadrature

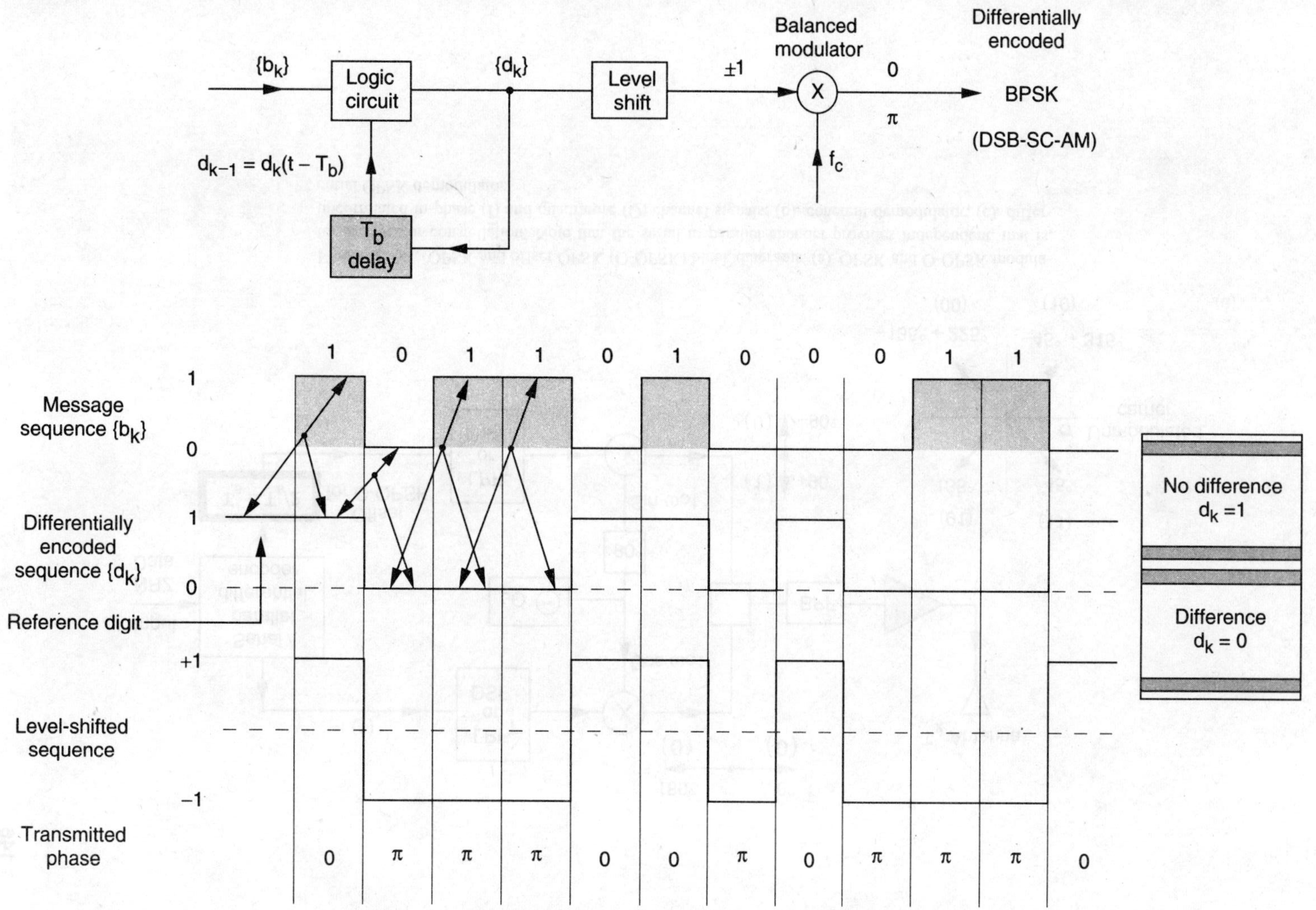

Figure 4.3.5 Differential encoding. If there is no difference between the signal states of b_k and d_k−1 (same logic states), then the logic output state $d_k = 1$; otherwise, $d_k = 0$.

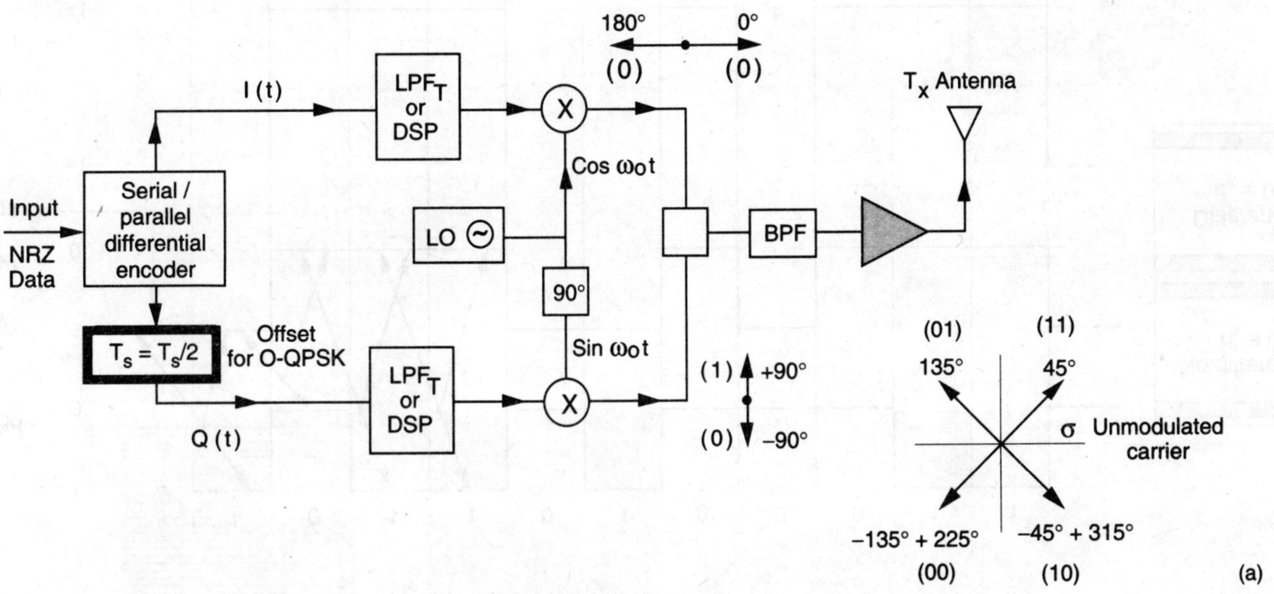

Figure 4.3.6 QPSK and offset QPSK (O-QPSK) block diagrams. (a), QPSK and O-QPSK modulator and vector constellation. Note that the serial to parallel encoder provides independent, that is, uncorrelated in-phase (I) and quadrature (Q) channel signals; (b), coherent demodulator; (c), differential QPSK demodulator.

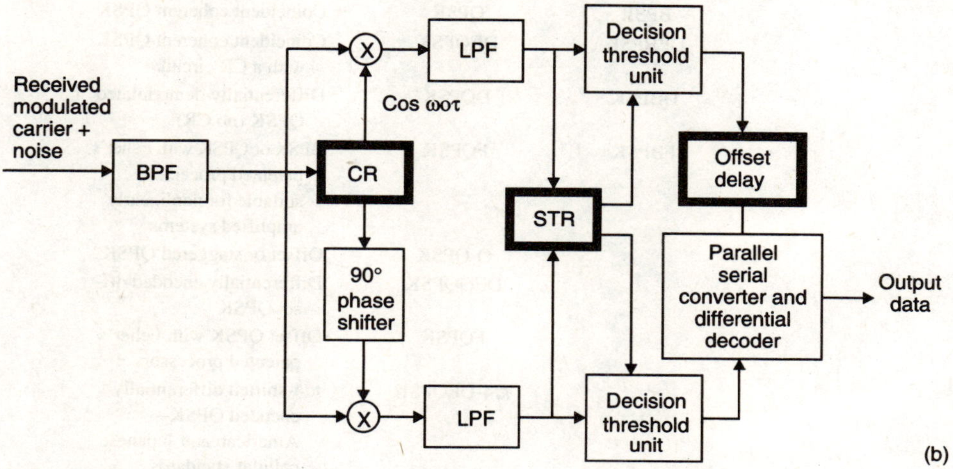

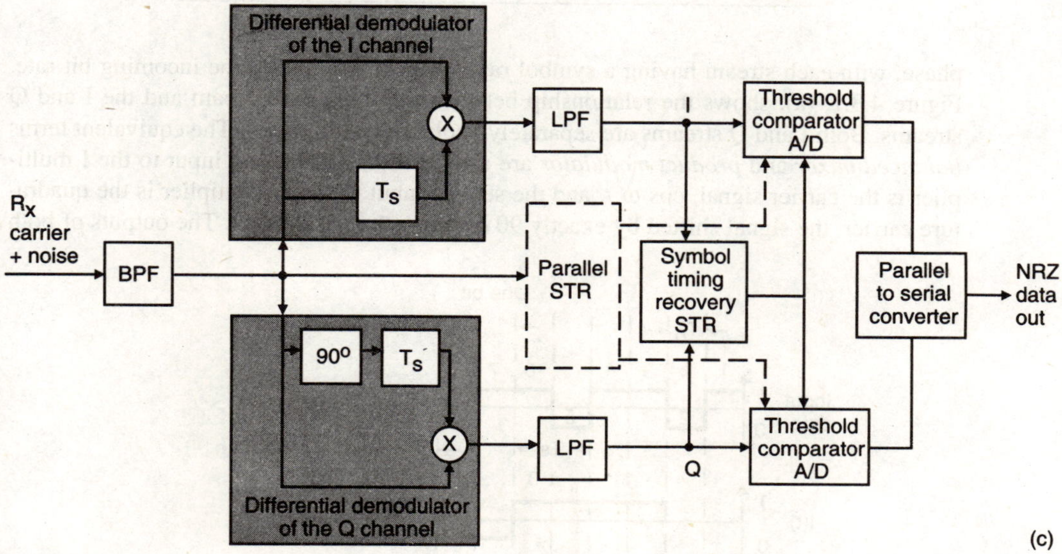

Figure 4.3.6 (continued)

Table 4.3.1 Brief description of QPSK and BPSK nomenclature. Carrier recovery (CR) is used in coherent demodulators.

Binary PSK	Quadriphase PSK	Brief description
BPSK	QPSK	Coincident coherent QPSK
DEBPSK	DEQPSK	Coincident coherent QPSK with a CR circuit
DBPSK	DQPSK	Differentially demodulated QPSK (no CR)
FBPSK	FQPSK	BPSK or QPSK with Feher's patented processor suitable for nonlinearly amplified systems
	O-QPSK	Offset or staggered QPSK
	DEOQPSK	Differentially encoded offset QPSK
	FQPSK	Offset QPSK with Feher's patented processors
	π/4-DEQPSK	π/4-shifted differentially encoded QPSK—American and Japanese cellular standards

phase, with each stream having a symbol rate equal to *half* that of the incoming bit rate. Figure 4.3.7, (a), shows the relationship between the input data stream and the I and Q streams. Both I and Q streams are separately applied to multipliers. (The equivalent terms *balanced mixer* and *product modulator* are also in use.) The second input to the I multiplier is the carrier signal, cos $\omega_o t$, and the second input to the Q multiplier is the quadrature carrier, the signal shifted by exactly 90 degrees (that is, sin $\omega_o t$). The outputs of both

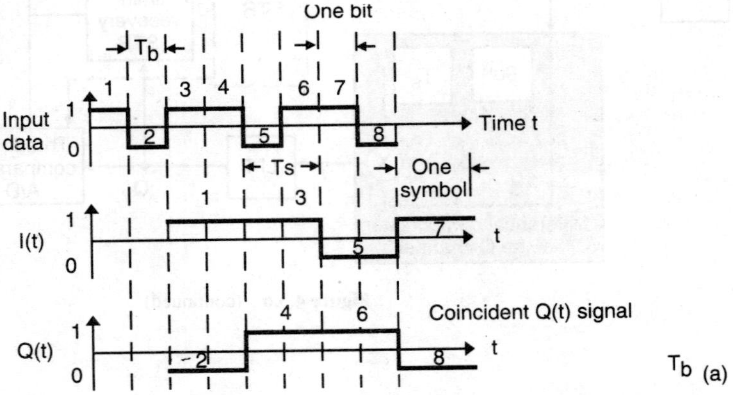

Figure 4.3.7 Timing and constellation diagrams of unfiltered signals. (a), Coincident I and Q transitions and, (b), offset I and Q transitions. (c), QPSK, (d), O-QPSK, (e), MSK, and, (f), FQPSK constellation diagrams.

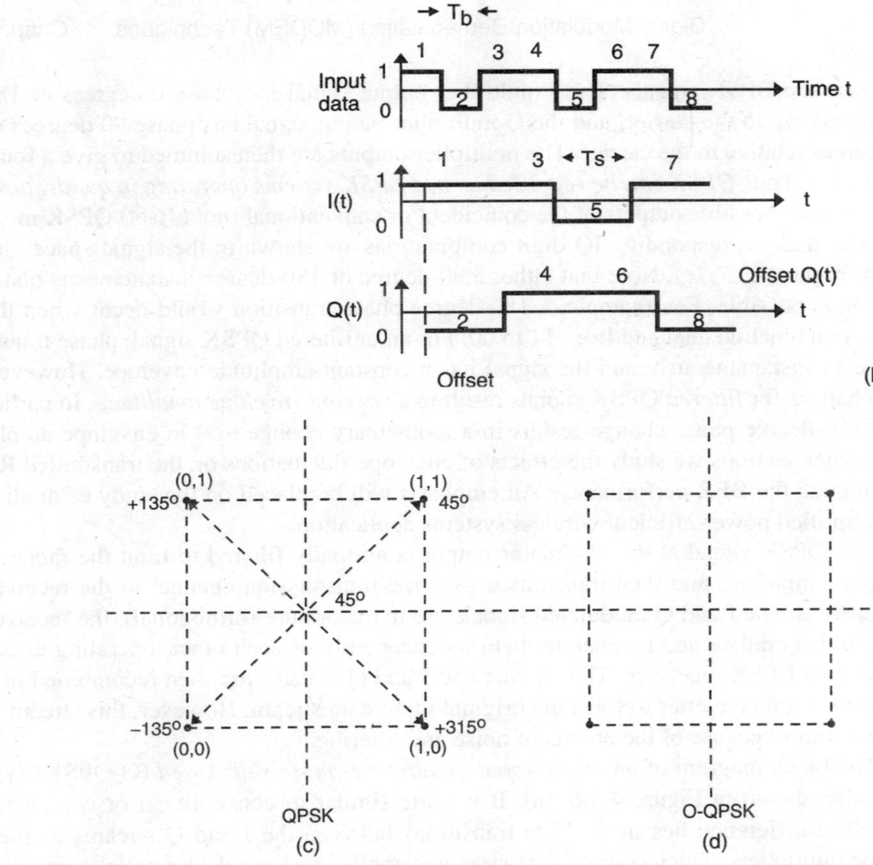

Figure 4.3.7 (continued)

multipliers are BPSK signals. The I multiplier output signal has phase 0 degrees or 180 degrees relative to the carrier, and the Q multiplier output signal has phase 90 degrees or 270 degrees relative to the carrier. The multiplier outputs are then summed to give a four-phase signal. Thus *QPSK can be regarded as two BPSK systems operating in quadrature.*

The four possible outputs of the coincident or conventional (not offset) QPSK modulator and their corresponding IQ digit combinations are shown in the signal space diagram of Figure 4.3.7, (c). Note that either a 90-degree or 180-degree instantaneous phase transition is possible. For example, a 180-degree phase transition would occur when the IQ digit combination changed from 11 to 00. For an unfiltered QPSK signal, phase transitions occur instantaneously and the signal has a constant-amplitude envelope. However, phase changes for *filtered* QPSK signals result in a *varying envelope amplitude.* In particular, a 180-degree phase change results in a momentary change to 0 in envelope amplitude. In later sections we study the effects of envelope fluctuations on the transmitted RF spectrum and the BER performance. An emphasis will be placed on the study of nonlinearly-amplified power-efficient wireless systems applications.

The QPSK signal at the modulator output is normally filtered to limit the radiated spectrum, amplified, and then transmitted over the transmission channel to the receiver input. Because the I and Q modulated signals are in quadrature (orthogonal), the receiver is able to demodulate and regenerate them independently of each other, operating effectively as two BPSK receivers. The regenerated I and Q streams are then recombined in a parallel-to-serial converter to form the original input data stream. However, this stream is subject to error because of the effects of noise and filtering.

The block diagram of an *offset-keyed quadrature-phase shift keyed* (O-QPSK) system is also shown in Figure 4.3.6, (a). It is quite similar to conventional or coincident QPSK. The difference lies in the data transitions between the I and Q streams as they enter the multipliers. The incoming data stream is applied to a serial-to-parallel converter. One of the converter output streams (the Q stream in the case show in Figure 4.3.7, (b) is then *offset* from the other by delaying it by an amount equal to the incoming signal bit duration, $T_b = T_s/2$. The resulting instantaneous phase states at the modulator output are the same as for QPSK. However, because both data streams that are applied to the multipliers can never be in transition simultaneously, only one of the vectors that make up the offset-keyed quadriphase modulator output signal can change at any one time. The result is that only 90-degree phase transitions occur in the modulator output signals. Similarly to QPSK, an *unfiltered* O-QPSK signal has a *constant-amplitude envelope.* For filtered O-QPSK signals, however, the transmitted signal has an amplitude envelope variation of 3 dB (30%), as compared with the 100% amplitude envelope variation for conventional QPSK systems. In later sections we demonstrate that this lower-amplitude envelope variation imparts significant advantages to O-QPSK, as compared with QPSK, in nonlinearly amplified, Power-efficient cellular and other wireless system applications. For example, when a band-limited O-QPSK signal is transmitted through an amplitude-limiting device, there is only partial regeneration of the spectrum amplitude back to the unfiltered level. For QPSK under identical circumstances, however, there is an almost complete regeneration to the unfiltered level (Figure 4.3.8).

The O-QPSK receiver shown in Figure 4.3.6, (b), is identical to that for coincident

QPSK, except that the regenerated I data stream is delayed by a unit bit duration of $T_b = T_s/2$ so that, when combined with the regenerated Q stream, the original "input data" stream is recreated. This process is subject to error because of the effects of noise and filtering. Details of differential encoding and decoding subsystems of QPSK and O-QPSK modems are described in Feher (1983).

Differential QPSK Demodulation. The design of coherent QPSK and O-QPSK demodulators is a difficult task, particularly if very fast modem synchronization is required. To avoid the need for a complex carrier recovery circuit and to improve the synchronization speed of the demodulator, differential QPSK (DQPSK) demodulation may be employed instead of coherent demodulation. Architecture for a DQPSK is illustrated in Figure 4.3.6, (c). It is a straightforward extension of previously described DBPSK demodulators.

4.3.6 π/4-DQPSK Modems for U.S. and Japanese Digital Cellular Standards

A modem method known as π/4-shifted, differentially encoded quadrature phase shift keying (π/4-DQPSK) has been adopted for U.S. and Japanese digital cellular time division multiple access (TDMA) radio standards. For detailed references see Akaiwa and Nagata (1987), EIA (1990), Kinoshita et al. (1991), and Liu and Feher (1991a). This modulation method was introduced in 1962 by Baker of AT&T Bell Laboratories (Baker, 1962). The π/4-DQPSK modulation technique represents a *compromise* solution between the conventional or coincident transition QPSK and offset-keyed QPSK (O-QPSK) methods (Table 4.3.2). Instantaneous phase transitions are as follows:

For QPSK: 0°, ±90°, ±180°

For O-QPSK and FQPSK: 0°, ±90°

For π/4-DQPSK: 0°, ±45°, ±135°

Table 4.3.2 Phase change of $\Delta\phi$ in π/4-DQPSK systems. The signals A_k, B_k at the output of the differential phase encoding block can take one of five values, 0, ±1, $\pm 1/\sqrt{2}$, resulting in the "unfiltered" constellation.

I_k	Q_k	$\Delta\phi$
1	1	$\frac{-3\pi}{4}$
0	1	$\frac{3\pi}{4}$
0	0	$\frac{\pi}{4}$
1	0	$\frac{-\pi}{4}$

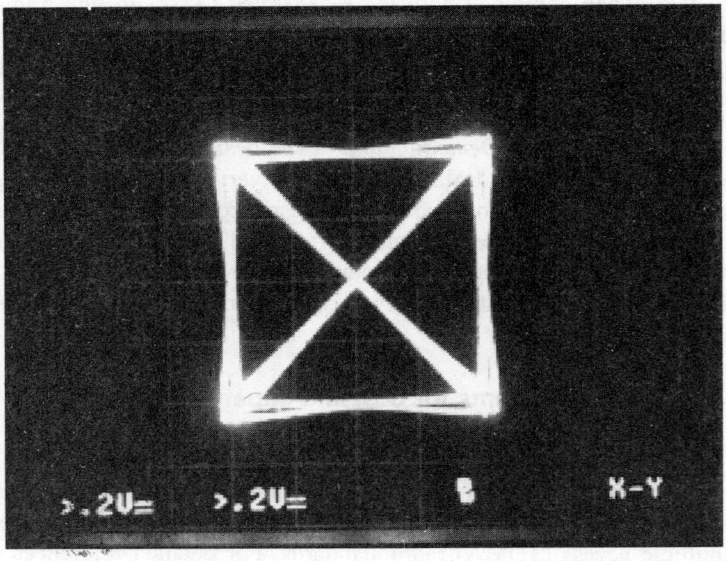

(a)

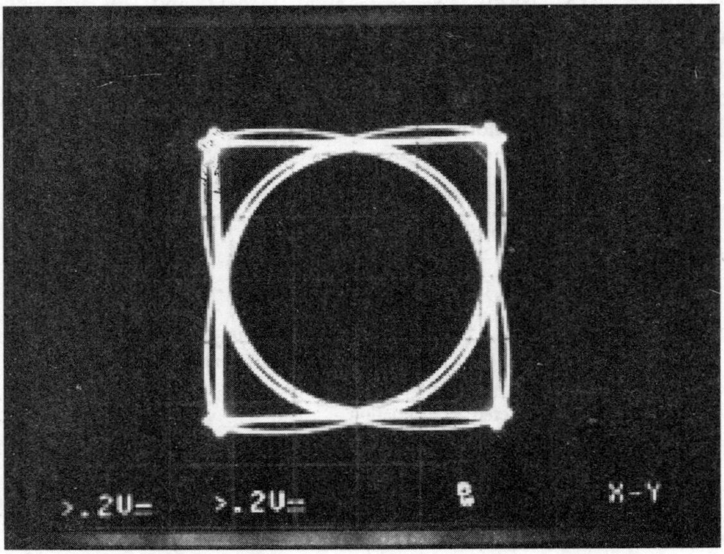

(b)

Figure 4.3.8 Measured constellation signal space vector diagrams of QPSK, O-QPSK, and FQPSK-1 modulated signals. (a), Conventional QPSK (coincident signal transition); (b), offset or O-QPSK; (c), Feher's patented FQPSK-1.

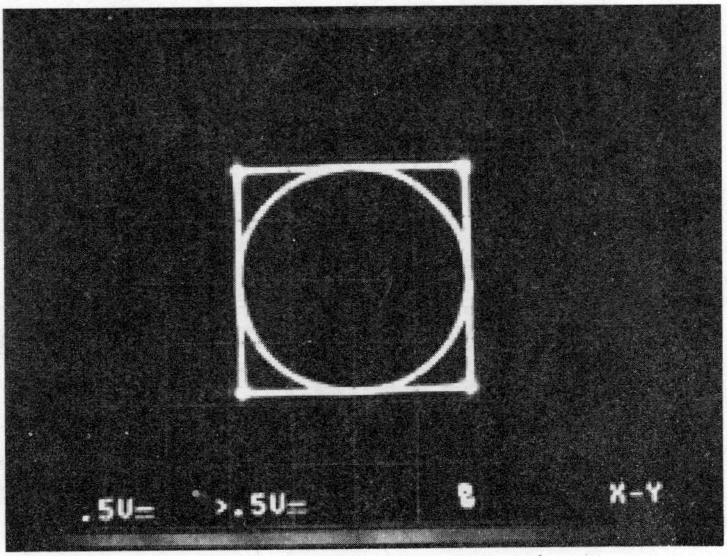

(c)

Figure 4.3.8 (continued)

In power-efficient, *nonlinearly amplified* (NLA), fully saturated, C-class or hard-limited cellular-mobile systems, the instantaneous 180-degree phase shift of conventional QPSK systems lead to a significant spectral regrowth and thus has a low spectral efficiency (Figure 4.3.8). In Feher (1987) it is demonstrated that conventional C-class amplifiers and hard-limited amplifiers or preamplifiers lead in practice to the same spectral regrowth and BER performance degradation. With $\pi/4$-DQPSK the spectral restoration (regrowth) is somewhat reduced, since the instantaneous phase transitions are limited to $\pm 135°$ (Figure 4.3.9). In the O-QPSK family of modems the instantaneous phase transition is limited to only $\pm 90°$. Offset QPSK modems, particularly the offset FQPSK modems described in Section 4.3.9, have the lowest spectral restoration.

4.3.6.1. Why is $\pi/4$-DQPSK the U.S. and Japanese standard? Power efficiency and spectral efficiency are among the most important requirements of digital personal communication system (PCS) mobile cellular radio systems. For cost-efficient, small-size solutions, nonlinear amplifiers are used. Figures 4.3.8 and 4.3.9 show that the NLA spectrum (spectral restoration) of $\pi/4$-DQPSK is much higher than that of O-QPSK. To reduce the harmful adjacent channel interference (ACI), that is, restored spectral power overlap into the adjacent channels, we must space the channels wider apart. However, wider channel spacing means reduced spectral efficiency. To increase the spectral efficiency of $\pi/4$-DQPSK, a linear amplifier is required. During the 1990s this increase has been achieved with a 6- to 9-dB output backoff (OBO) of the RF amplifiers (Table 4.3.3). In other words, an RF amplifier of 4 watts (at saturation) must be "backed off" to a maximal output power of 1 watt. (*Note:* 6 dB = 4 times; 4 watt reduced 4 times

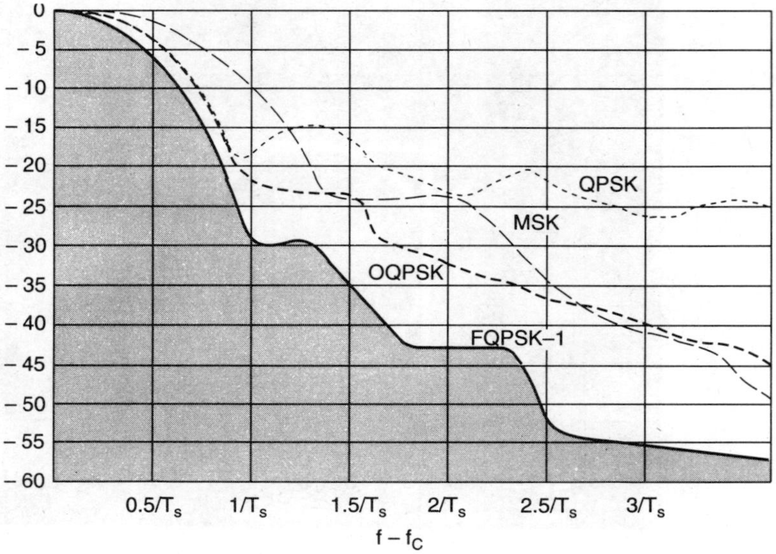

(a)

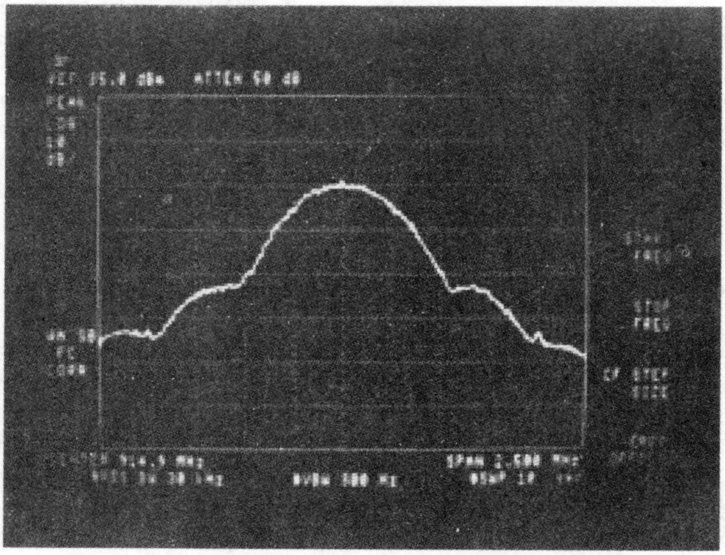

(b)

Figure 4.3.9 Nonlinearly amplified (NLA) hard-limited spectral density of, (a), conventional (coincident) QPSK, MSK, O-QPSK, and FQPSK-1 (computer simulation by CREATE software enclosed in this book); (b), experimental FQPSK-1 saturated 914.9 MHz amplified signal measured with Minicircuit's amplifiers; (c), experimental FQPSK-1 saturated MMIC of Teledyne model TFE-1050 at 2.452 GHz with +28 dBm power. Bit rate is 1 Mb/s in both FQPSK-1 measurements.

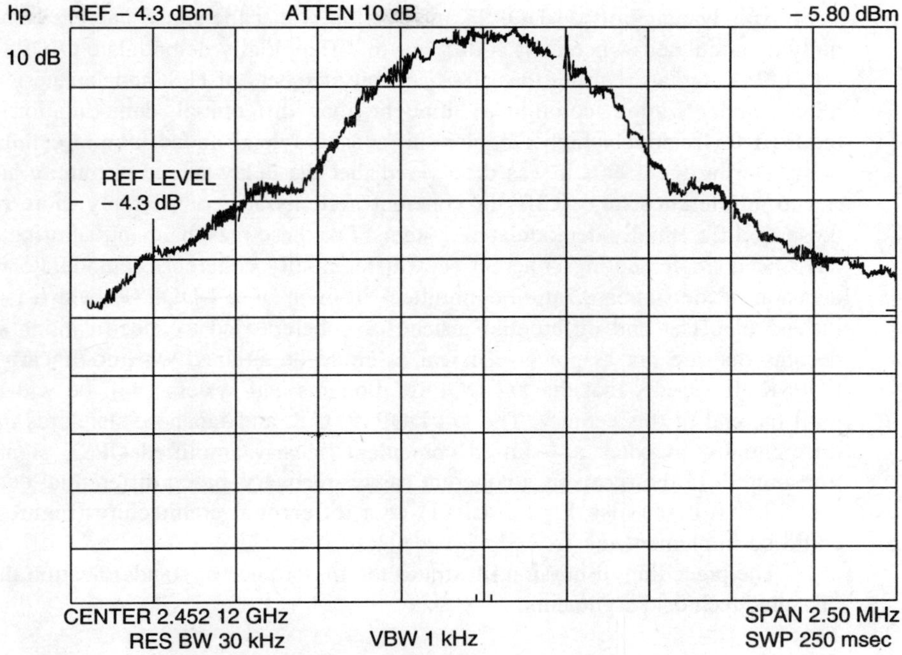

(c)

Figure 4.3.9 (continued)

= 1 watt). This spectrally efficient solution leads to a very low power efficiency and has an impact on the *reduced battery lifetime* of portable devices. The measured NLA spectra in Figure 4.3.9 indicate that the patented FQPSK subclass of O-QPSK modems (described in Section 4.3.9) has a spectral efficiency that is 60% to 90% higher than that of nonlinearly amplified π/4-DQPSK. In Section 4.5 we provide a detailed definition of spectral efficiency. Chapter 9 highlights the importance of spectral efficiency and integrated ACI on the performance and capacity of PCS and cellular systems.

Table 4.3.3 Output backoff (OBO) requirements in decibels for illustrative π/4-DQPSK linearly amplified wireless systems operated at 2.4 GHz.

Requirement	Amount (dB)
OBO required to avoid spectral regeneration of π/4-DQPSK filtered signals, assuming ideal linearized "soft-limited" amplifiers	1.5 to 2.5
Additional OBO required because of nonideal (nonlinear soft-limited) RF amplifiers	2 to 4
Additional OBO required because of gain variations, gain setting level changes, and output power variations	1.5 to 2.5
Total output backoff (OBO) required	5 to 9

An advantage of π/4-DQPSK modulation is that the signal can easily be differentially demodulated, whereas it is difficult to differentially demodulate O-QPSK and offset FQPSK signals. During the 1980s several members of U.S. and Japanese digital cellular standardization committees thought that differential demodulation might be required for relatively high Doppler-shift, fast Rayleigh-faded mobile cellular applications. During the 1990s it was discovered that the delay-spread immunity and the carrier-to-interference ratio (CIR) of coherent systems are considerably more robust than those of differentially demodulated systems. For these reasons manufacturing companies have been implementing coherent (not differentially coherent) demodulators. Thus the decision of the standardization committees in favor of π/4-DQPSK, which is coincident instead of offset and differential instead of coherent, led to specifications and system designs that are not as power-efficient as could be attained with nonlinearly amplified FQPSK. It appears that the π/4-DQPSK modems and systems will be with us at least until the end of this century. The π/4-DQPSK U.S. and Japanese standards imply that a differentially encoded, π/4-shifted coincident linearly amplified QPSK signal must be transmitted. In the receiver, a coherent carrier-recovery–based differential decoder (Figure 4.3.6, (b); see also Figure 4.10.1) or a differential architecture (Figure 4.3.6, (c)) could be implemented.

The preceding discussion illustrates the importance of standardization that is based on sound technical arguments.

4.3.6.2 π/4-DQPSK transmitter architecture. A conceptual implementation block diagram of basic π/4-DQPSK modulator architecture and constellation is given in Figure 4.3.10. Gray code is used in the mapping; two dibit symbols corresponding to adjacent signal phases differ only in a single bit. Since the most probable errors caused by noise result in the erroneous selection of an adjacent phase, most dibit symbol errors contain only a single bit error. In Figure 4.3.11, note the rotation by π/4 of the basic QPSK constellation for odd (denoted ⊕) and even (denoted ⊗) symbols (Liu and Feher, 1991a; Liu, 1992).

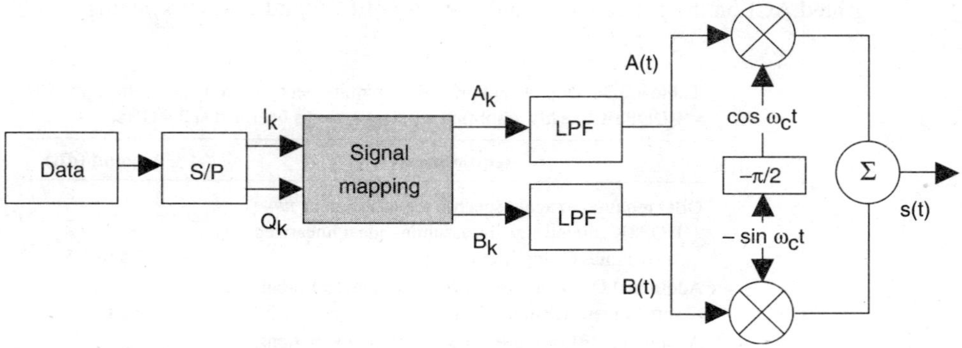

Figure 4.3.10 π/4-DQPSK and π/4-QPSK modulator block diagram.

The information is differentially encoded; symbols are transmitted as changes in phase rather than as absolute phases. Let A_k and B_k denote the amplitudes of the unfiltered baseband NRZ pulses in the I and Q channel, respectively, during $kT \le t < (k+1)T$ (Liu, 1992). The signal levels A_k and B_k are determined by the signal levels of the previous pulses and the current information symbol denoted by θ_k, as follows:

$$\begin{aligned} A_k &= A_{k-1}\cos\theta_k - B_{k-1}\sin\theta_k \\ B_k &= A_{k-1}\sin\theta_k + B_{k-1}\cos\theta_k . \end{aligned} \tag{4.3.19}$$

In equation 4.3.19, θ_k is determined by the current symbol of the carrier phase denoted by (I_k, Q_k) of the information source. The relationship between θ_k and the input symbol is given in Table 4.3.2. Note that A_k and B_k can take the amplitudes of ±1, 0, and $\pm 1/\sqrt{2}$. However, they are either "two-level" or "three-level" at any sampling instant. A "five-level" eye diagram of the π/4-QPSK signal is shown in Figure 4.3.12. Initially, let us assume that the transmit low-pass filters (LPFs) are absent and that the phase of the carrier is 0 during $0 \le t < T$, that is, $A_0 = 1$, $B_0 = 0$. At $t = T$, the symbol (1,1) is sent from the information source; then θ_1 is π/4. From equation 4.3.19 we have $A_1 = 1/\sqrt{2}$, and $B_1 = 1/\sqrt{2}$, the phase of the carrier, "jumps" to π/4. In equation 4.3.19 the output is actually a linear transformation (rotation) of the input in the complex-envelope plane. θ_k is the rotated angle and the angle between the complex envelope. The in-phase axis is the phase of the carrier. From Table 4.3.2 and equation 4.3.19 it follows that if the carrier is at one of the four states denoted by x in Figure 4.3.11 during the present symbol duration, it shifts (or rotates) to one of the four states denoted by + during the next symbol duration, and vice versa. Hence the carrier always shifts its phase between two symbols, but the phase shift can only be $k\pi/4$ where k is ±1 or ±3. If the pulses are band-limited, the phase

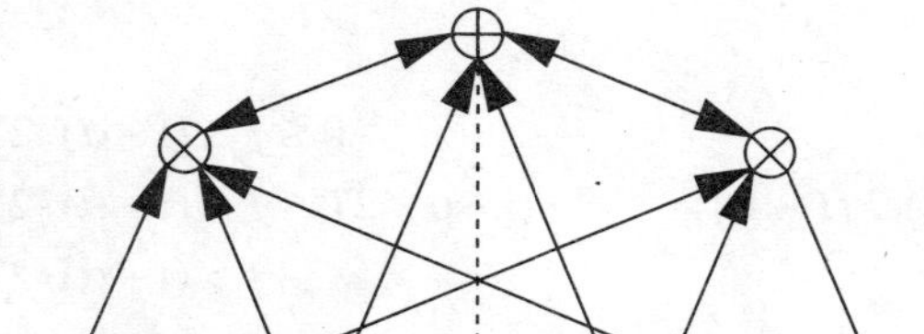

Figure 4.3.11 Constellation diagram of π/4-DQPSK transmitter without filtering.

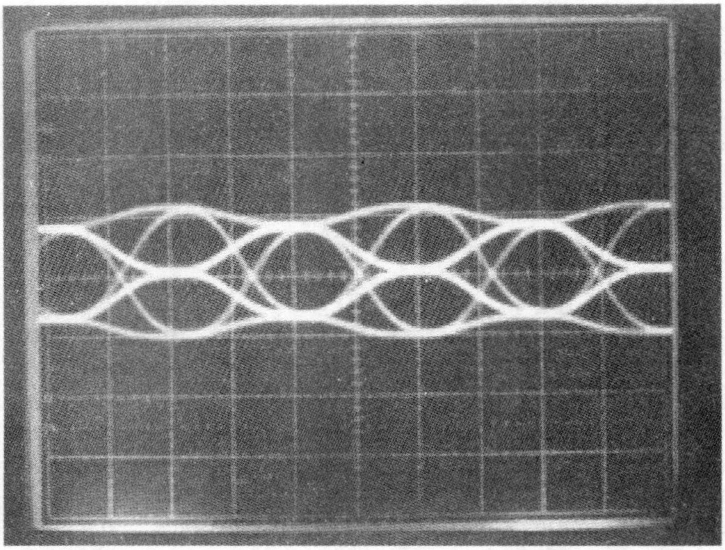

Figure 4.3.12 Eye diagram of a coherently demodulated π/4-QPSK signal. At alternate sampling instants the signal has two levels; in-between signals have three levels. The bit rate in this experimental setup is 2 Mb/s. Horizontal: 0.5 μs/div; vertical: 0.5 V/div. (Courtesy Hongying Yan, University of California, Davis.)

transition becomes smoother. However, if ISI-free filters are used, the phase of the carrier is preserved at sampling instants.

The premodulation transmit LPFs shown in Figure 4.3.10 have been standardized in the United States by the Electronic Industries Association (EIA, 1990). These baseband filters, for input *impulses,* have a square-root raised-cosine frequency response of the following form

$$\begin{cases} & 0 \le f \le (1-\alpha)/2T \\ \sqrt{\dfrac{1}{2}\{1-\sin[(\pi/2\alpha)(2fT-1)]\}} & (1-\alpha)/2T \le f \le (1+\alpha)/2T \\ & f > (1+\alpha)/2T \end{cases} \qquad (4.3.20)$$

where T is the symbol duration. Linear phase filters are specified. For the U.S. digital cellular system the roll-off parameter is $\alpha = 0.35$.

Note: The preceding transfer function is defined for a synchronous stream of impulses. For NRZ inputs (T second duration symbols), as explained in previous sections, a $\pi fT/\sin(\pi fT)$ aperture equalizer should be inserted.

4.3.6.3. Design strategies for π/4-DQPSK modulation and demodulation. The modulation architecture of π/4-DQPSK and π/4-QPSK systems is essentially the same as that of conventional DQPSK and QPSK systems (described in previous sections), assuming that IF band differential demodulation is implemented (Figures 4.3.10

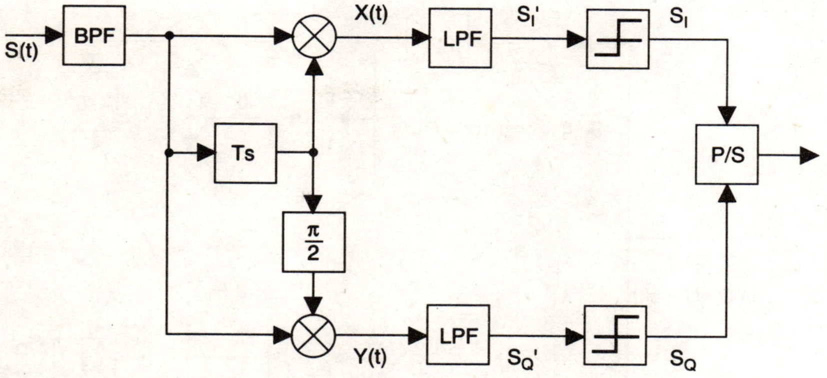

Figure 4.3.13 Block diagram of IF band differential π/4-QPSK demodulator. (From Guo and Feher, 1994.)

and 4.3.13). For fully digital implementations, baseband π/4-DQPSK demodulators (Figure 4.3.15) provide alternative efficient, low-power solutions. At the transmit end, all-digital π/4-DQPSK modulator implementations (as illustrated in Figure 4.3.14) provide an architectural alternative to the premodulation-filtered quadrature implementation illustrated in Figure 4.3.10. The "all-digital" implementation is suitable for relatively high

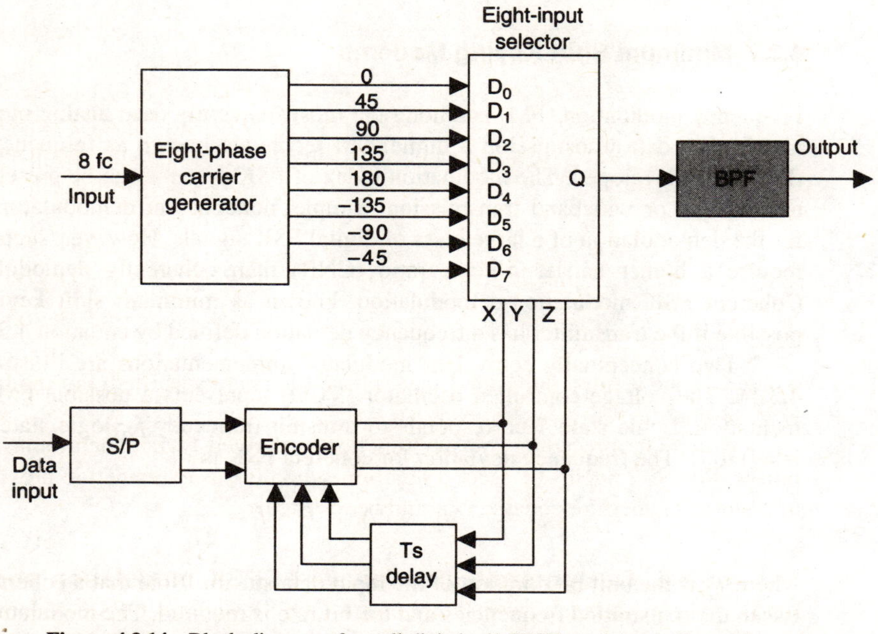

Figure 4.3.14 Block diagram of an all-digital π/4-QPSK modulator. (From Guo and Feher, 1994.)

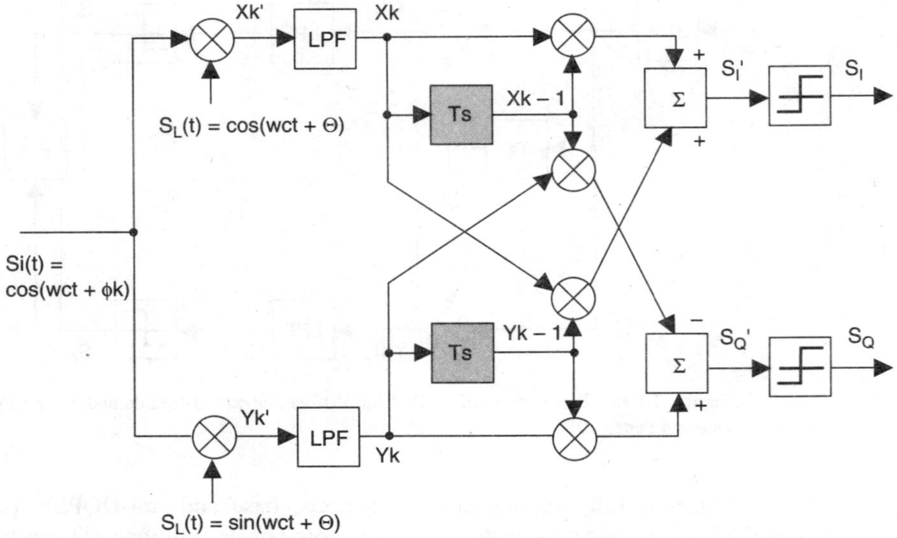

Figure 4.3.15 Block diagram of baseband differential π/4-QPSK demodulator that is suitable for all digital implementation. (From Guo and Feher, 1994.)

bit-rate, low IF-carrier applications where practical low-cost, small-size band-pass filters (BPFs) are commercially available.

4.3.7 Minimum Shift Keying Modems

Frequency modulation (FM) is among the most frequently used analog modulation techniques. For data transmission a digital FM technique known as frequency shift keying (FSK) was developed. The modulation index of FSK systems can be preset to give either narrowband or wideband transmission. Simple, noncoherent demodulators can be used for the demodulation of a large class of digital FSK signals. However, such demodulators require a higher carrier-to-noise ratio (CNR) than coherently demodulated systems. Coherent FSK modulation-demodulation, known as minimum shift keying (MSK), is possible if the transmitter has a frequency deviation defined by equation 4.3.21.

Two conceptually equivalent modulator implementations are illustrated in Figure 4.3.16. The voltage-controlled oscillator (VCO) represents a possible FM-based implementation. Logic state 1 corresponds to transmit frequency f_2, logic state 0 (–1 V data level) to f_1. The frequency deviation for coherent FSK is

$$\Delta f_{pp} = 2\Delta f = f_2 - f_1 = \frac{1}{2T_b} \tag{4.3.21a}$$

where T_b is the unit bit duration of the input data stream. Note that a coherent relation between the transmitted frequencies and the bit rate is required. The modulation index is defined by

$$m = \Delta f_{pp} \cdot T_b = \frac{1}{2}. \tag{4.3.21b}$$

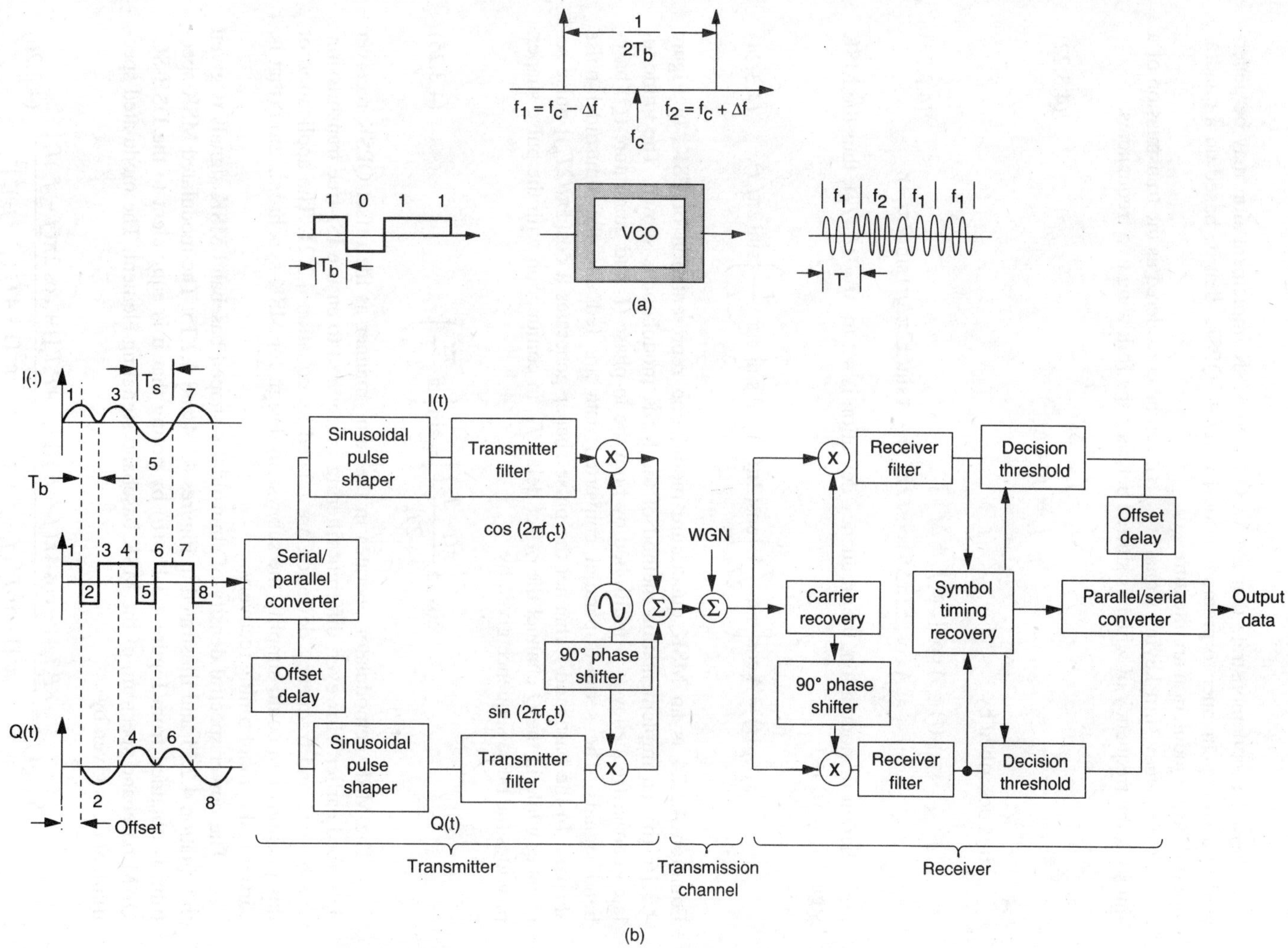

Figure 4.3.16 MSK modem architectures. (a), A voltage-controlled oscillator (VCO) FM modulator with a frequency deviation defined by equation 4.3.21 is a possible MSK architecture. (b), A QUAD based (quadrature O-QPSK) transmitter-coherent MSK receiver architecture. Note that the serial to parallel converter provides independent thus noncorrelated I and Q data streams.

Now let us demonstrate that the VCO-based MSK implementation may be generated in a similar manner to premodulation-filtered O-QPSK, that is, based on a quadrature (QUAD) modulation architecture.

A frequency shift-keying signal, $s_{FSK}(t)$, can be considered as the transmission of a sinusoid, the frequency of which is shifted between the following two frequencies:

$$\begin{aligned} f_1 &= f_c - \Delta f \\ f_2 &= f_c + \Delta f. \end{aligned} \tag{4.3.22}$$

It is described by

$$\begin{aligned} s_{FSK}(t) &= A\cos[2\pi(f_c \pm \Delta f)t] \\ &= A\cos(\pm 2\pi\Delta f t)\cos(2\pi f_c t) - A\sin(\pm 2\pi\Delta f t)\sin(2\pi f_c t). \end{aligned} \tag{4.3.23}$$

For coherent demodulation, the frequency deviation is set to $\Delta f = 1/(4T_b)$; thus the MSK signal $s_{MSK}(t)$ is

$$s_{MSK}(t) = A\cos\left(\pm\pi\frac{t}{2T_b}\right)\cos(2\pi f_c t) - A\sin\left(\pm\pi\frac{t}{2T_b}\right)\sin(2\pi f_c t). \tag{4.3.24}$$

Equation 4.3.24 is an MSK quadrature modulation representation of FSK. In Figure 4.3.16, (b), an implementation method of the MSK modulator is shown. The unmodulated carrier frequency f_c is multiplied by both the in-phase (I) and quadrature (Q) baseband signals. The serial-to-parallel converted data are fed into the sinusoidal pulse shapers. In the baseband I channel the pulse shaper generates a $\cos[\pm\pi t/2T_b)]$ pulse sequence, while in the Q channel the offset delay T_b, in conjunction with the pulse shaper, provides the pulse sequence given by

$$\cos\left[\pm\frac{\pi(t - T_b)}{2T_b}\right] = \sin\left(\pm\frac{\pi t}{2T_b}\right). \tag{4.3.25}$$

The MSK demodulator operates in the same manner as the offset QPSK receiver described earlier. However, different filtering is required to ensure ISI-free transmission. The bit rate and frequency deviation are related by equation 4.3.21. The application of this phenomenon could simplify the subsystem design for MSK synchronization (that is, carrier and symbol timing recovery).

The power spectral density of sinusoidally shaped baseband MSK signals is given in Equation 4.2.21 and illustrated in Figures 4.2.4 and 4.2.15. The modulated MSK spectrum is obtained from Figure 4.3.16, (b) by noting that it is equivalent to the DSB-SC-QAM baseband spectrum of the MSK baseband signaling element. The modulated spectrum, $S(f)$, is given by

$$S_{MSK}(f) = \frac{8P_cT_b[1 + \cos 4\pi(f - f_c)T_b]}{\pi^2[1 - 16T_b^2(f - f_c)^2]^2} = \frac{4P_cT_s[1 + \cos 2\pi(f - f_c)T_s]}{\pi^2[1 - 4T_s^2(f - f_c)^2]^2} \tag{4.3.26}$$

where

f_c = Unmodulated carrier frequency
P_c = Total power in modulated waveform
$T_b = 1/f_b$ = Bit duration
$T_s = 1/f_s = 2T_b$ = Symbol duration

The normalized power spectral density of conventional QPSK, O-QPSK, and MSK as a function of frequency, and normalized to the binary bit rate $R_b = 1/T_b$, is shown in Figure 4.3.17. The QPSK main lobe has a width of $\pm 1/2\ T_b$. The width of the main lobe of the MSK signal is $\pm 3/4\ T_b$, that is, the MSK signal has a 50% wider main lobe than the QPSK signal. However, for larger values of $(f - f_c)/f_b$, the unfiltered MSK spectrum falls

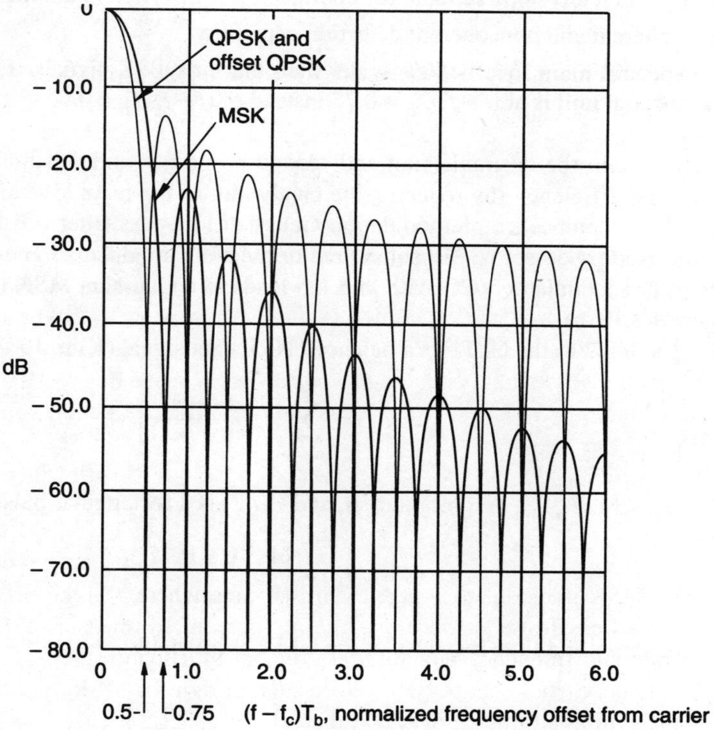

$$G_{MSK}(f) = \frac{8P_cT_b(1 - \cos 4\pi (f - f_c)T_b]}{\pi^2(1 - 16T_b^2(f - f_c)^2]^2}$$

$$G_{OKQPSK}(f) = 2P_cT \left[\frac{\sin 2\pi (f - f_c)T_b}{2\pi(f - f_c)T_b}\right]^2$$

Figure 4.3.17 Normalized power spectral densities of unfiltered QPSK, O-QPSK, and MSK systems. Because the modulated spectrum is symmetrical around the carrier frequency, only the upper sideband is shown.

off at a rate proportional to f^{-4}, whereas the unfiltered QPSK spectrum decays at a rate proportional to f^{-2}. The unfiltered *infinite bandwidth* spectral properties are of particular importance in radio transmitter designs and applications where the output amplifier is frequently operated in a nonlinear (saturated) power efficient mode. It is not practical to have a postamplification, spectral-shaping RF filter.

4.3.8 GMSK and GFSK Wireless Modems

Minimum shift keying is a binary-digital FM modulation technique with a modulation index of $m = 0.5$. It has the following fundamental properties:

1. Constant envelope suitable for nonlinear, power-efficient amplification
2. Coherent and noncoherent detection capability
3. Spectral main lobe is 50% wider than that of QPSK signals (Figure 4.3.17). First spectral null is at $(f-f_c)T_b = 0.75$ instead of $(f-f_c)T_b = 0.5$.

To retain the desirable first and second properties and to simultaneously increase the spectral efficiency (by reducing the bandwidth of the main lobe and the spectral density of the sidelobes), a premodulation Gaussian low-pass filter (GLPF) is inserted into the baseband processor (BBP) subsystem of the MSK modulator. The cascade of a GLPF with an FM modulator VCO with $m = 0.5$ leads to a Gaussian MSK (GMSK) modulator (Figure 4.3.18, (a)).

The input to the GLPF is a balanced NRZ data signal (Kim, 1988) given by

$$a(t) = \sum_{n=-\infty}^{\infty} a_n \Pi\left(\frac{t-nT}{T}\right) \tag{4.3.27}$$

where $a_n = \pm 1$, T_b is a unit bit interval, and $\Pi(t/T)$ is a rectangular pulse

$$\Pi(t/T_b) = \begin{cases} 1 & 0 \le t \le T_b \\ 0 & \text{elsewhere} \end{cases}. \tag{4.3.28}$$

The frequency and time response of the GLPF is given by

$$G(f) = \exp\left[-\left(\frac{f}{B}\right)^2 \frac{\ln 2}{2}\right] \tag{4.3.29}$$

$$g(t) = B\sqrt{\frac{2\pi}{\ln 2}} \exp\left[-\frac{2\pi^2 B^2}{\ln 2} t^2\right] \tag{4.3.30}$$

where B is the 3-dB bandwidth of the GLPF. The output of the GLPF is

$$b(t) = \sum_{n=-\infty}^{\infty} a_n r(t-nT) \tag{4.3.31}$$

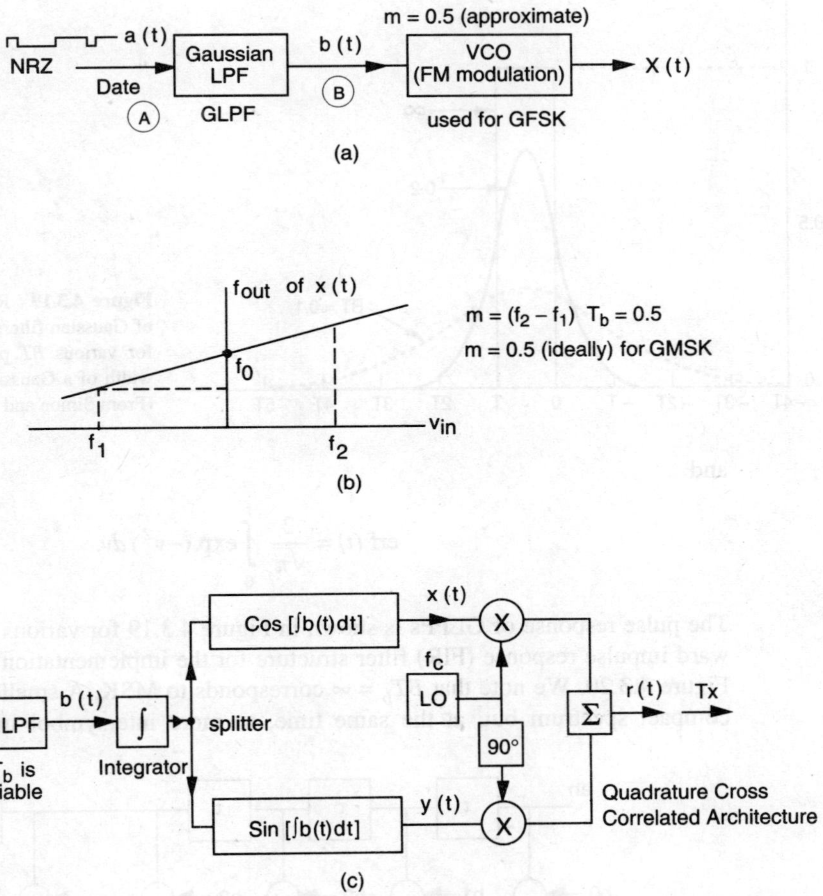

Figure 4.3.18 Gaussian prefiltered MSK (GMSK) and Gaussian FSK (GFSK) implementation. The GMSK modulation index is $m = 0.50$ (exact value). For GFSK, the modulation index m is a variable, typically $0.1 \le m \le 1$. (a). Voltage controlled oscillator (VCO) FM modulator implementation of GFSK. (b), Transmit frequency as a function of baseband voltage. (c), Quadrature (QUAD) modulator and baseband GMSK processing subsystems. The simplest and most efficient Gaussian low-pass filter (LPF) design is by means of Dr. Feher Associates patented and licensed technologies, described in Appendix 3. The cross-correlated GMSK Quadrature Modulation Architecture (US Patent No 4,567,602) of Fig. 4.3.18(c) is described in Appendix 3 which covers Feher's inventions and licensed technologies.

where

$$r(t) = \Pi(t/T) * g(t) = \int_t^{t+T} g(v)\,dv = B\sqrt{\frac{2\pi}{\ln 2}} \int_t^{t+T} \exp\left(-\frac{2\pi^2 B^2 v^2}{\ln 2}\right) dv$$
$$= \frac{1}{2}\left\{\text{erf}\left[-\sqrt{\frac{2}{\ln 2}}\,\pi B\,(t)\right] + \text{erf}\left[\sqrt{\frac{2}{\ln 2}}\,\pi B\,(t+T)\right]\right\} \tag{4.3.32}$$

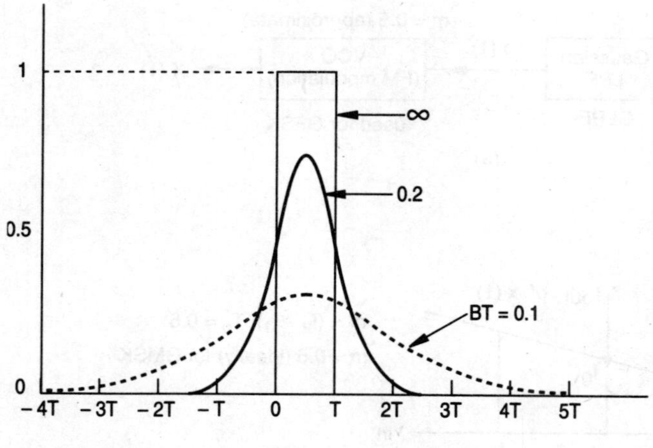

Figure 4.3.19 Rectangular pulse response of Gaussian filters $r(t)$ (see equation 4.3.32) for various BT products. B = 3 dB bandwidth of a Gaussian filter; T = bit duration. (From Simon and Wang, 1984.)

and

$$\operatorname{erf}(t) = \frac{2}{\sqrt{\pi}} \int_0^t \exp(-v^2)\, dv. \tag{4.3.33}$$

The pulse response of GLPFs is shown in Figure 4.3.19 for various BT_b products. A forward impulse response (FIR) filter structure for the implementation of $h(t)$ is depicted in Figure 4.3.20. We note that $BT_b = \infty$ corresponds to MSK. A smaller BT_b leads to more compact spectrum but, at the same time, to more intersymbol interference (ISI) (see

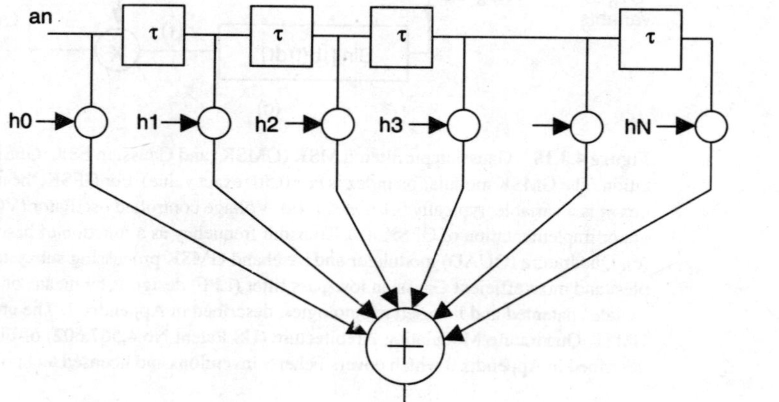

Figure 4.3.20 GMSK Quadrature Rom and Finite Impulse Response (FIR) filter implementation of $h(t)$ of Figure 4.3.19. (a), FIR filter with $\tau = T/n$; n = upsample rate. (b) GMSK modern IC-chip implementation of Quadrature Cross-Correlated GMSK. ROM based Gaussian filter and Integrator [Feher USA Patents 4,339,724 and Kato/Feher USA Patent No 4,567,602] and cross correlator analyzed and described in Appendix A.3.

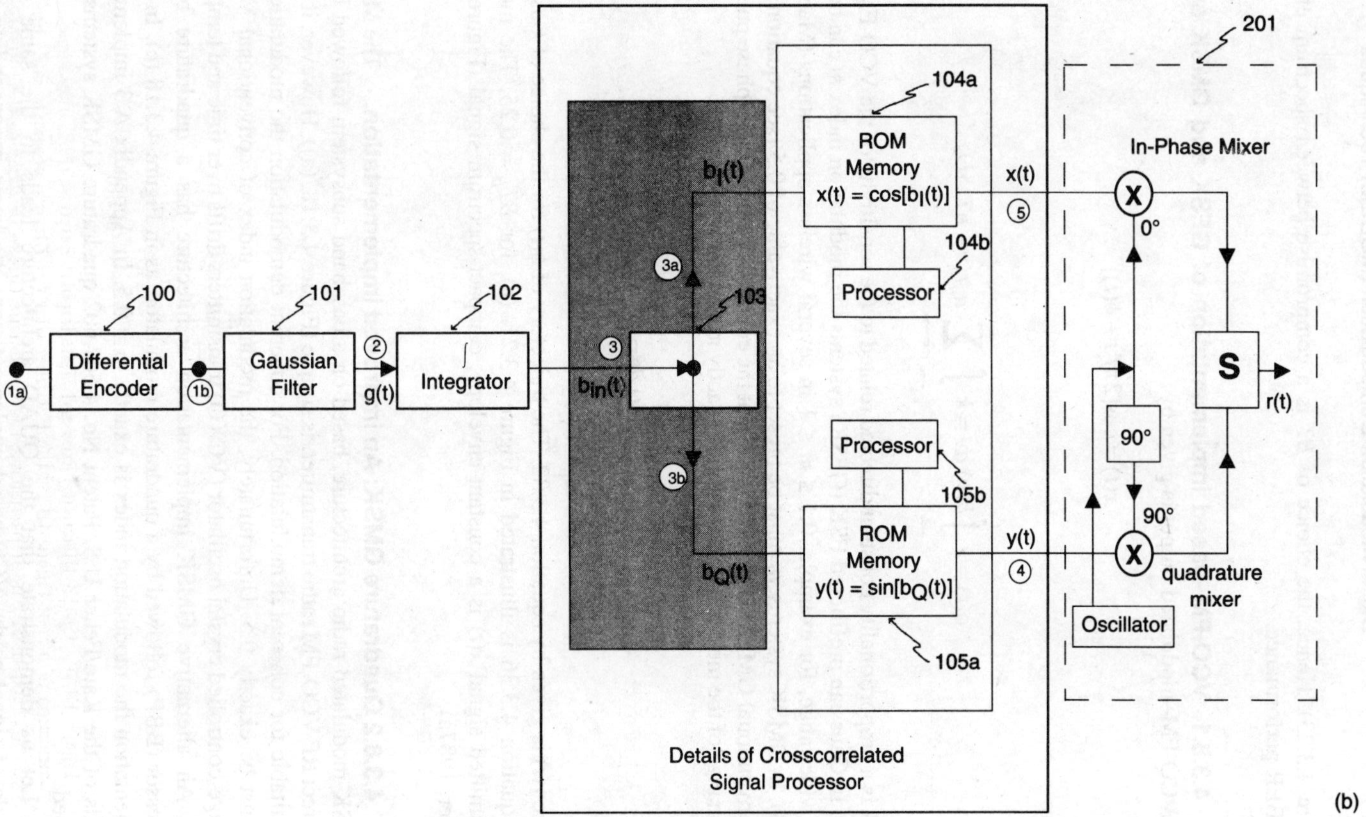

Figure 4.3.20 (continued)

Figure 4.3.23). Hence, the choice of BT is a compromise between spectrum efficiency and BER performance.

4.3.8.1. VCO-FM–based implementation of GFSK and GMSK systems The VCO-FM–modulated output is given by

$$x(t) = \cos[2\pi f_c t + \phi(t)] \tag{4.3.34}$$

where

$$\phi(t) = k \int_{-\infty}^{t} b(v)\, dv = k \int_{-\infty}^{t} \sum_{n=-\infty}^{\infty} a_n r(v - nT)\, dv, \tag{4.3.35}$$

and k is a proportionality constant directed related to the sensitivity of the VCO-FM modulator. In Gaussian prefiltered FSK (GFSK) systems the modulation index m can be chosen in a wide range, for example, $0.1 \le m \le 1$ in several wireless applications (MacDonald, 1993). In GMSK systems, m must be preset to an exact value of 0.5 (see equation 4.3.21b. In conventional GMSK, k is chosen such that the contribution of a single-phase pulse $r(t)$ to the change of the modulated phase $\phi(t)$ is exactly $\pi/2$ as follows:

$$k \int_{-\infty}^{\infty} r(t)\, dt = \pi/2 \tag{4.3.36}$$

where $r(t)$ is given by equation 4.3.32. The trajectory of $\phi(t)$ for the choice of k as defined by equation 4.3.36 is illustrated in Figure 4.3.21, (a), for $BT_b = 0.25$, The modulated transmitted signal $x(t)$ is a constant-envelope, compact-spectrum signal (Figure 4.3.22) (Feher, 1987a).

4.3.8.2 Quadrature GMSK: An improved implementation. The MSK- and GMSK-modulated radio architecture, based on a baseband subsystem followed by an IF or direct RF VCO-FM radio transmitter, is simple (Figure 4.3.18, (a)). However, it may not be suitable for coherent demodulation. For coherent demodulation the modulation index m must be exactly 0.5. Unfortunately, the modulation index of conventional VCO and voltage-controlled crystal oscillator (VCXO) transmitters drifts over time and temperature.

An alternative GMSK implementation architecture has a quadrature baseband processor (BBP) followed by a quadrature modulator, as in Figure 4.3.18 (c). In this implementation the modulation index is exactly $m = 0.5$. In Appendix A.3 implementation details of the Kåto/Feher U.S. Patent No. 4,567,602 quadrature GMSK systems are described.

Let us demonstrate that the QUAD architecture leads to the same GMSK-modulated signal as the VCO-based implementation. We begin by expanding equation 4.3.34 as follows:

$$x(t) = \cos\,[2\pi f_c t + \phi(t)] = \cos\,2\pi f_c t\,\cos\,\phi(t) - \sin\,2\pi f_c t\,\sin\,\phi(t)$$
$$= \cos\,2\pi f_c t\,\cos\left[k\int_{-\infty}^{t} b(v)\,dv\right] - \sin\,2\pi f_c t\,\sin\left[k\int_{-\infty}^{t} b(v)\,dv\right]. \tag{4.3.37}$$

The quadrature structure implements the last part (right-hand side) of equation 4.3.37. From equation 4.3.35 we have $\phi(t) = k\int_{-\infty}^{t} b(v)dv$, where $b(t)$ is the output of the GLPF. Note that the in-phase and quadrature baseband channels are crosscorrelated, have a resultant constant envelope and are practically intersymbol and jitter free.

4.3.8.3. Noncoherent demodulation of GFSK and GMSK signals. Numerous noncoherent GMSK implementations have been investigated and described in the literature (Feher, 1987). Here we present one of the simplest techniques: the limiter-discriminator method (Figure 4.3.24). Conventional FM limiter-discriminator ICs provide

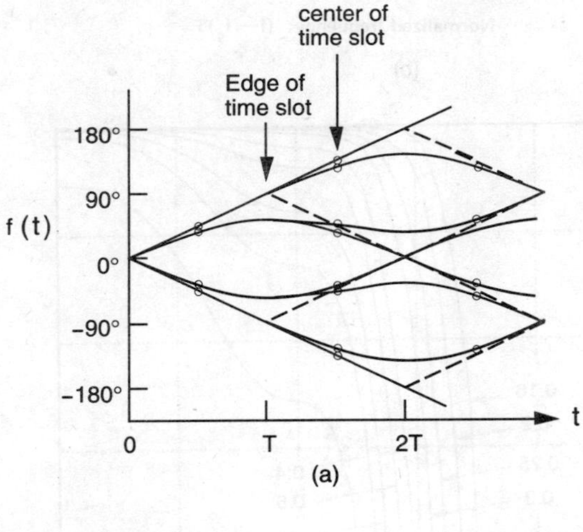

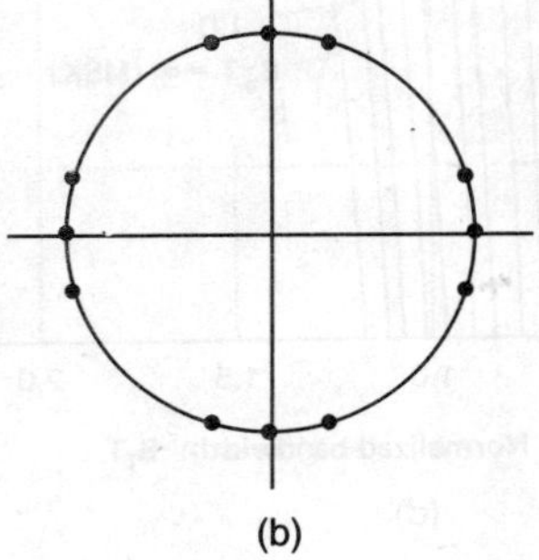

Figure 4.3.21 Phase trajectory, constellation diagram, and spectra of GMSK. (a), Phase trajectory. (b), Constellation diagram of a GMSK system with $BT_b = 0.25$; B is the 3 dB bandwidth of the Gaussian LPF; T_b is the bit duration (Ishizuka and Yasuda, 1984). (c), Computer-generated GMSK power spectral density by "CREATE-1" enclosed (Appendix 2) software. (d), Fractional power (Feher, 1987a).

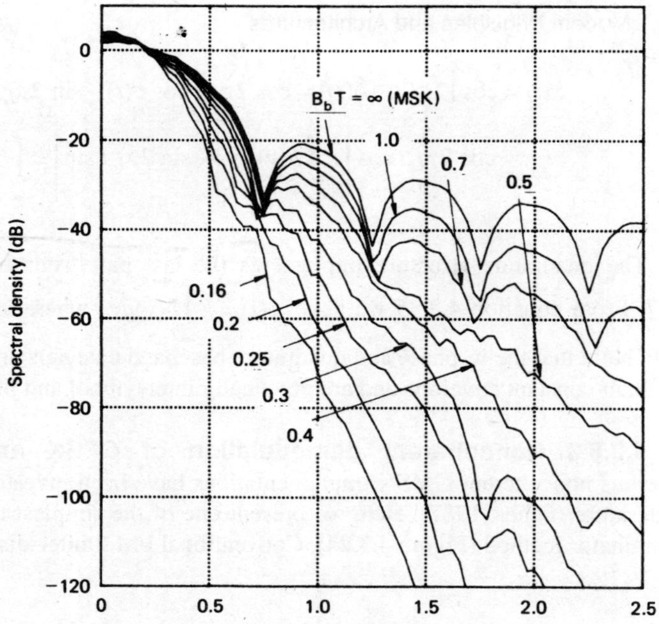

(c)

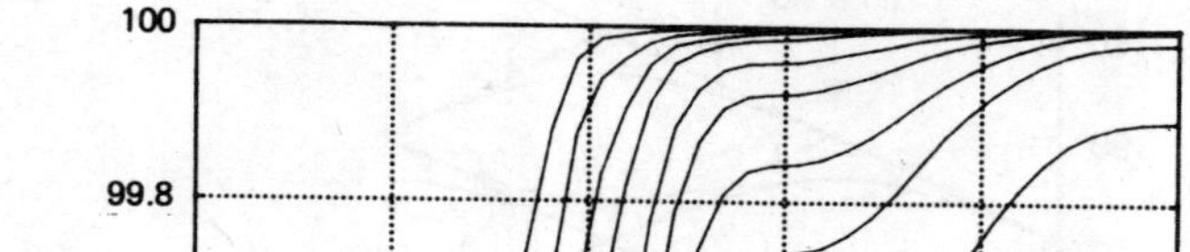

(d)

Figure 4.3.21 (continued)

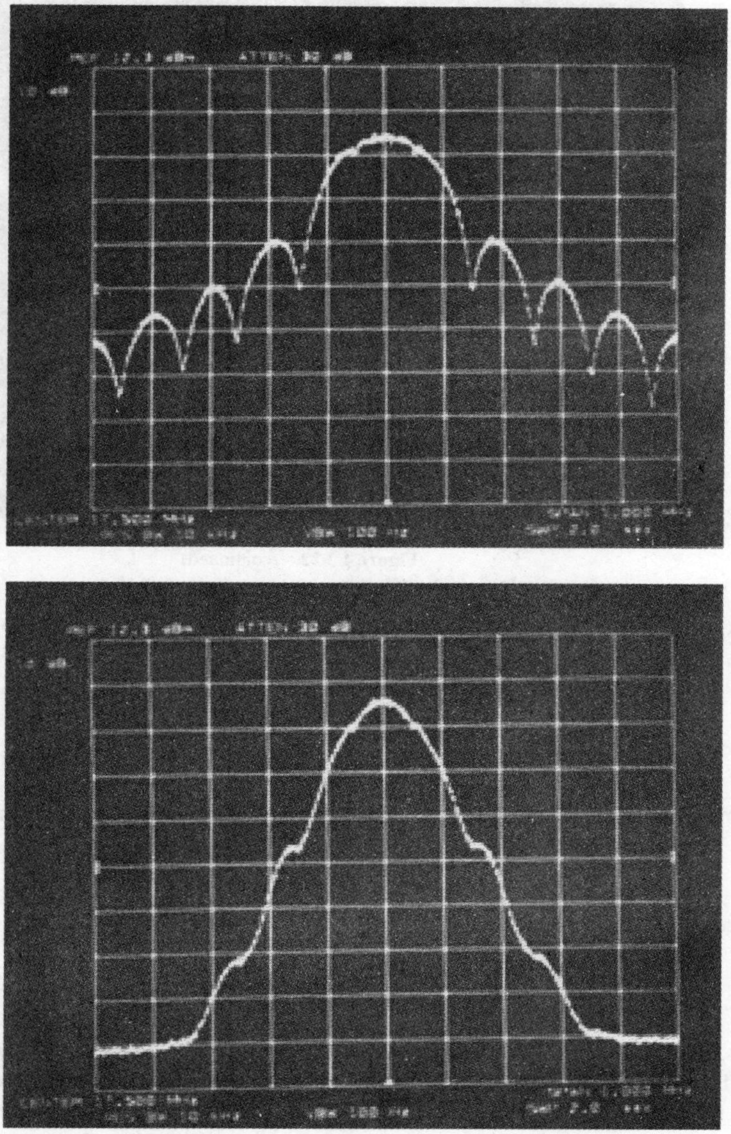

(a)

(b)

Figure 4.3.22 Illustrative MSK and GMSK spectral results. Bit rate: $f_b = 100$ kb/s. IF center: $f_c = 17.5$ MHz. (a), MSK (corresponds to GMSK with $BT_b = \infty$); (b), GMSK with $BT_b = 0.5$; (c), $BT_b = 0.2$. Premodulation Gaussian filters and deviation index were not optimized in this setup. (Courtesy Huajing Fu, University of California, Davis.)

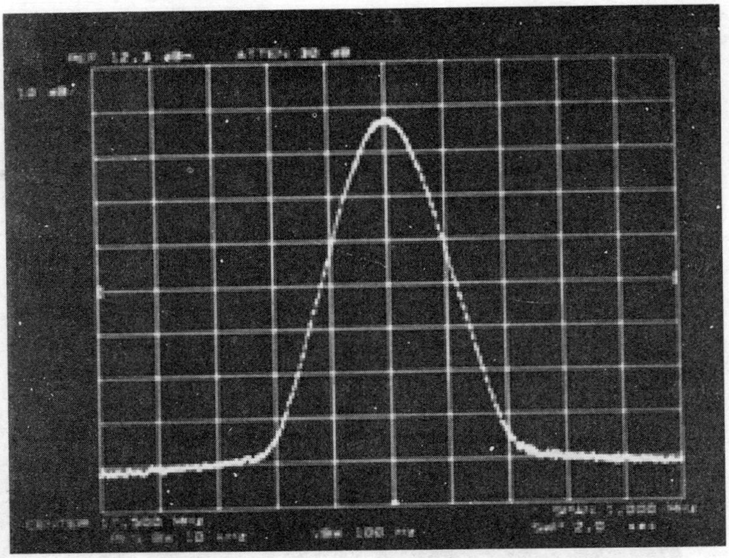

(c)

Figure 4.3.22 (continued)

the estimated baseband $\hat{b}(t)$ signal, which is the time derivative of the transmitted modulated phase, $\phi(t)$, given by equation 4.3.35. It is as follows:

$$\hat{b}(t) = \phi'(t) = k \sum_{n=-\infty}^{\infty} a_n r(t - nT). \tag{4.3.38}$$

From Figure 4.3.23 we observe that sampling should occur at the maximal eye opening:

$$\hat{b}(t) = \hat{b}(t - T/2) = k\left[a_0 r\left(\frac{T}{2}\right) + \sum_{\substack{n=-\infty \\ n\neq 0}}^{\infty} a_n r\left(nT + \frac{T}{2}\right)\right]. \tag{4.3.39}$$

The sampled baseband signal $\hat{b}(t)$ contains a desired signal component and the ISI term, represented by the Σ term in equation 4.3.39. Thus the discriminator-detected baseband eye diagram is very similar to the transmitted eye diagram, measured at point B, before the VCO (Figures 4.3.18, (a), and 4.3.23, (a) to (d). Note that k, the modulation proportionality constant directly related to the modulation index, does not have any role in determining the ISI level. For this reason the performance of the discriminator detector is not very sensitive to the inaccuracy of the modulation index. This is a definitive advantage of simple discriminator detectors (MacDonald, 1993). Simple and power efficient Gaussian filter designs, based on ROM look-up tables are described in Appendix A.3. These designs are based on Feher's 1982 patent U.S. No. 4,339,724.

4.3.8.4 Coherent GMSK demodulation. For coherent demodulation a quadrature O-QPSK structure is assumed (Figures 4.3.6, (b), and 4.3.16, (b)). The $I(t)$ and $Q(t)$ demodulated baseband signals are cos $\phi(t)$ and sin $\phi(t)$, respectively. The quadrature architecture provides a GMSK-modulated signal given by

$$x(t) = \cos \phi(t) \cos 2\pi f_c t - \sin \phi(t) \sin 2\pi f_c t. \qquad (4.3.40)$$

The demodulated baseband signals $\hat{I}(t)$ and $\hat{Q}(t)$ are obtained by multiplication of the received modulated signal $x(t)$ by the recovered, unmodulated carrier wave cos $\omega_c t$ and sin $\omega_c t$, respectively, and by eliminating (low-pass filtering) the higher-order spectral components. In the sampling instants we obtain

$$\cos\phi(2mT) = \pm 1 \pm \Delta \qquad m = 1, 2, \ldots \qquad (4.3.41)$$

$$\sin\phi[(2m-1)T] = \pm 1 \pm \Delta \qquad m = 1, 2, \ldots \qquad (4.3.42)$$

where Δ represents an ISI component. The decision rules are as follows:

$$d_{2m} = \begin{cases} 1 & \cos\phi(2mT) > 0 \\ -1 & \cos\phi(2mT) < 0 \end{cases} \qquad (4.3.43)$$

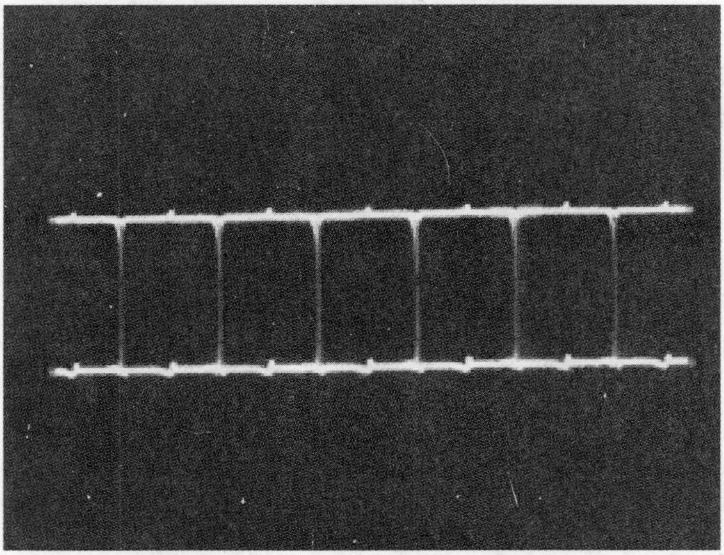

(a)
$BT_b = \infty$ (MSK)

Figure 4.3.23 GMSK and MSK baseband eye diagrams. Drive signals of digitally controlled VCO FM-based implementation with bit rate = 1 Mb/s. (a), $BT_b = \infty$ (MSK); (b), $BT_b = 0.3$ (GMSK); (c), $BT_b = 0.2$ (GMSK). Coherently demodulated eye diagrams: (d), $BT_b = 0.5$; (e), $BT_b = 0.3$. These eye diagrams are offset by half a symbol and are practically the same as those of demodulated FQPSK systems. This is an indication of GMSK and FQPSK compatible operation. Hardware initial test at University of California, Davis.

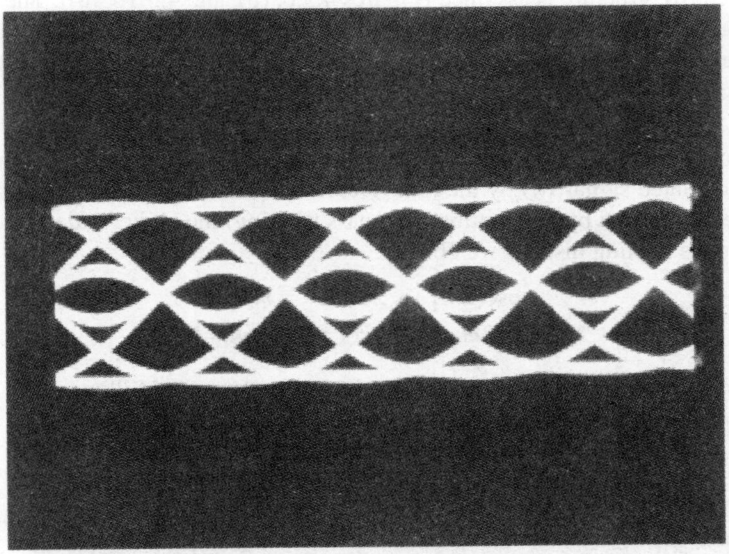

(b)
$BT_b = 0.3$

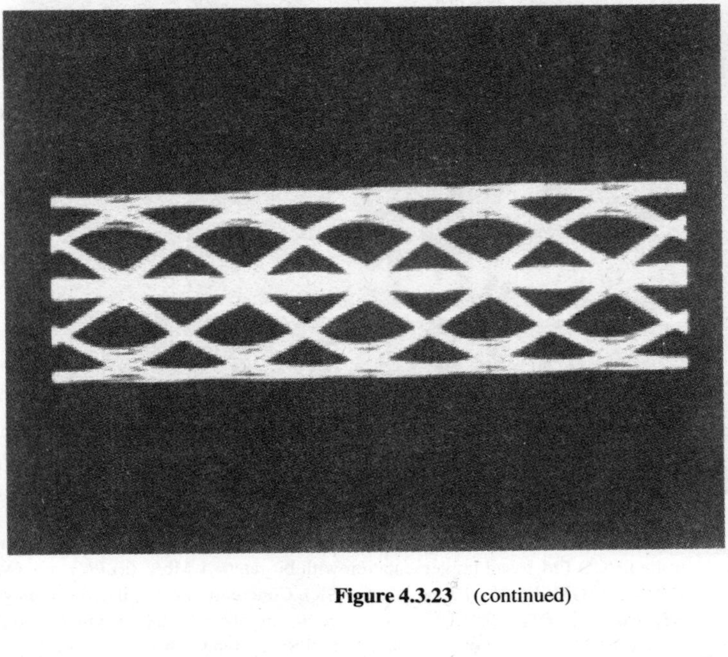

(c)
$BT_b = 0.2$ (GMSK)

Figure 4.3.23 (continued)

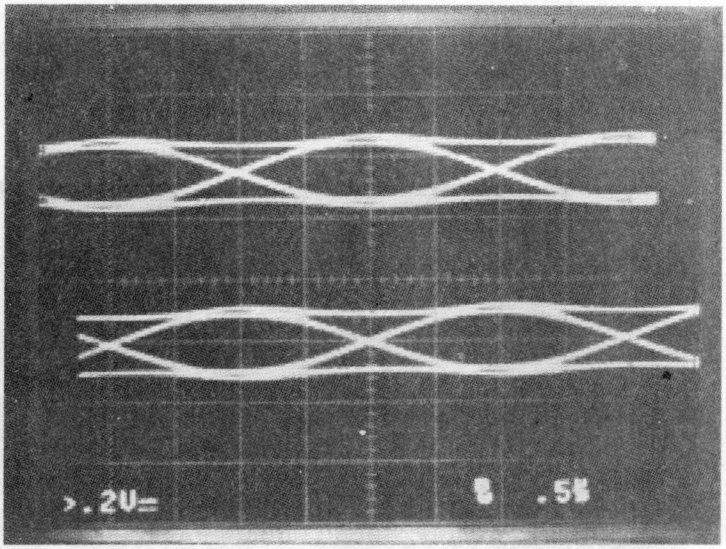

(d)
$BT_b = 0.5$

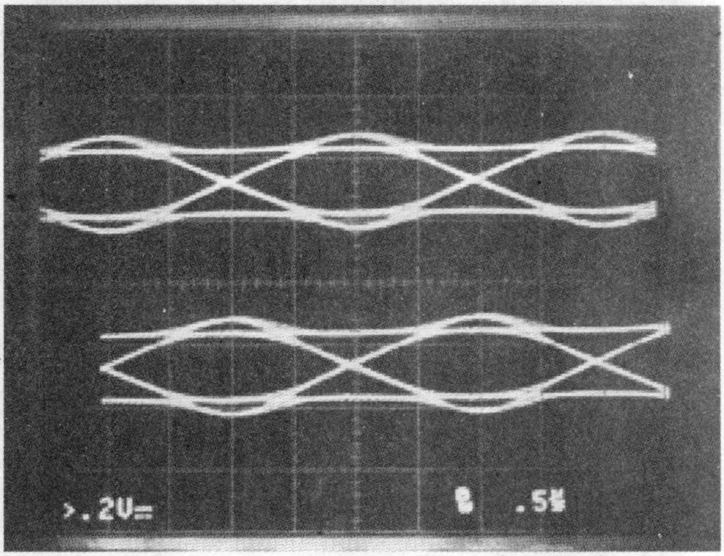

(e)
$BT_b = 0.3$

Figure 4.3.23 (continued)

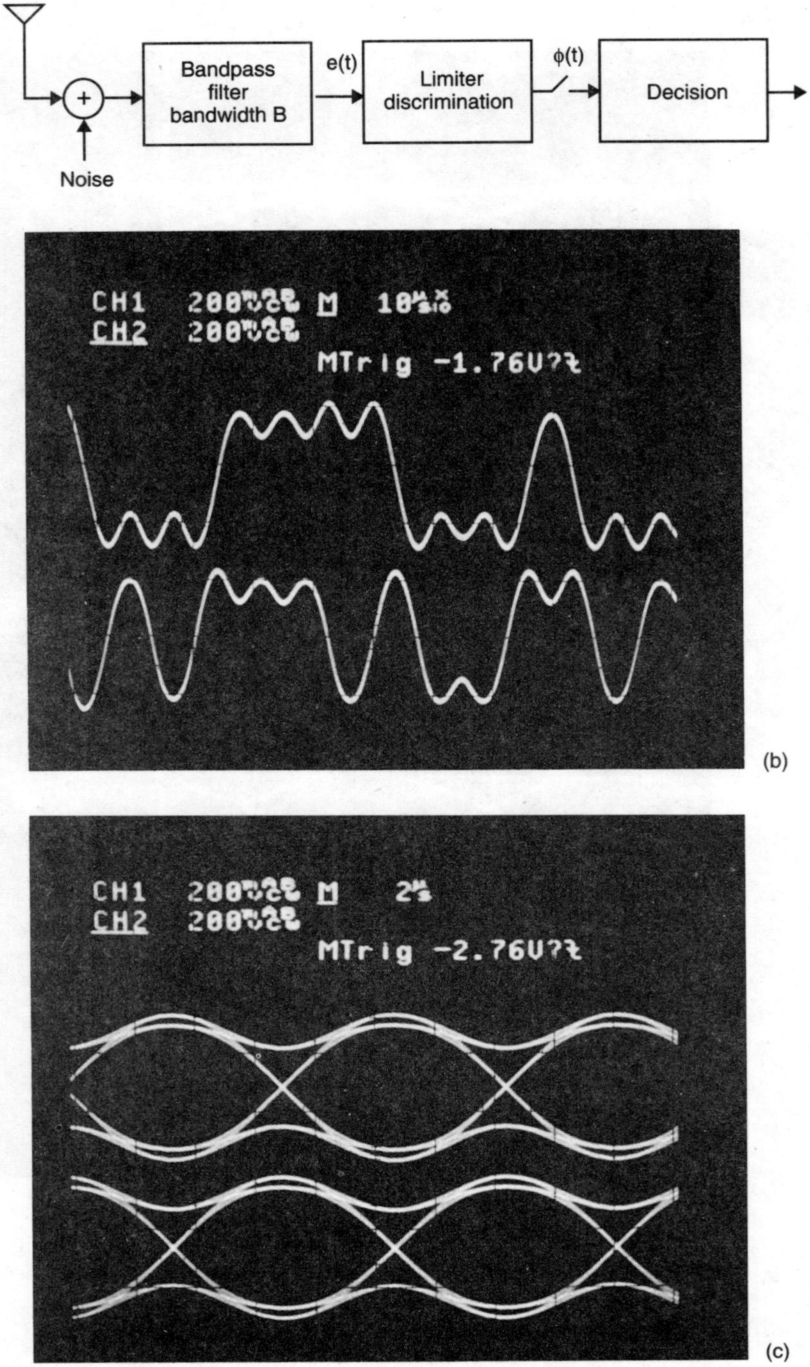
Bandpass filter bandwidth B
e(t)
Limiter discrimination
ϕ(t)
Decision
Noise
(a)
CH1
CH2
(b)
CH1
CH2
(c)

$$d_{2m-1} = \begin{cases} 1 & \sin\phi((2m-1)T) > 0 \\ -1 & \sin\phi((2m-1)T) < 0 \end{cases}. \quad (4.3.44)$$

The coherently demodulated baseband signals $\cos[\phi(t)]$ and $\sin[\phi(t)]$ contain considerably less ISI than the premodulation low-pass filtered transmitted signal. From Figure 4.3.23 we note that for $BT_b = 0.3$ and $BT_b = 0.2$, the transmitted eye diagrams contain large ISI, whereas the corresponding quadrature coherently demodulated I and Q channel eye diagrams each have two levels with much less ISI. The ideal BER performance of coherent GMSK systems is better than that of noncoherent ones (Figure 4.3.25 and see Figures 4.6.2 to 4.6.13).

4.3.9 FQPSK, FQAM, and FBPSK: Patented, Increased-Capacity, Improved Power-Efficiency Modems and Wireless Systems of Dr. Feher and Associates–Digcom, Inc.

Increased "talk time," that is, more efficient battery power utilization, is one of the most essential requirements of new generations of wireless systems. Increased capacity and increased spectral efficiency are also important requirements. Dr. Feher and Associates–Digcom, Inc., invented and developed several modem and wireless radio transceiver (transmitter/receiver) techniques and products that meet the most stringent power and spectral efficiency requirements of present and future generations of wireless and cellular mobile systems. These systems and products, known as FQPSK, FQAM, and FBPSK, which are described in the following sections, have been licensed in the United States and internationally through the "FQPSK Consortium" managed by Dr. Feher and Associates–Digcom, Inc.* Small, mid-size, and large international organizations have joined this technology transfer, licensing, education, and training consortium. For a description of Feher's licensed/patented GFSK, GMSK, FBPSK, FQPSK and FQAM technology, see Appendix 3.

To reduce battery power consumption, simpler and lower-power digital signal processing (DSP) baseband subsystems have been invented. To generate a specified RF power, for example, 1 watt at 2.4 GHz, permitted by the FCC for spread-spectrum systems, the RF subsystems should operate with maximal power efficiency, that is, minimal dc power consumption. In the FQPSK family of inventions, we describe "FQPSK-1," Feher's first and simplest patented baseband processor and wireless system, and "FQPSK-KF," a somewhat more advanced concept and patent invented by Dr. S. Kato

*44685 Country Club Drive, El Macero, CA 95618, USA.

Figure 4.3.24 GMSK and GFSK discriminator detection and quadrature correlated signal generation. (a) Block diagrams of discriminator detector; (b) Quadrature signals generated by a crosscorrelated baseband signal processor of a GSM (Global System Mobile) communication standardized chip set. The crosscorrelation of the I and Q signals is evident from the data pattern and from the eye diagrams of Fig. 4.3.24(c). Details of the Feher patented and licensed technology are described in Appendix 3. Illustrative measurement at standardized f_b = 270.833 kb/s rate on Philips "PCD5071" integrated circuit chip.

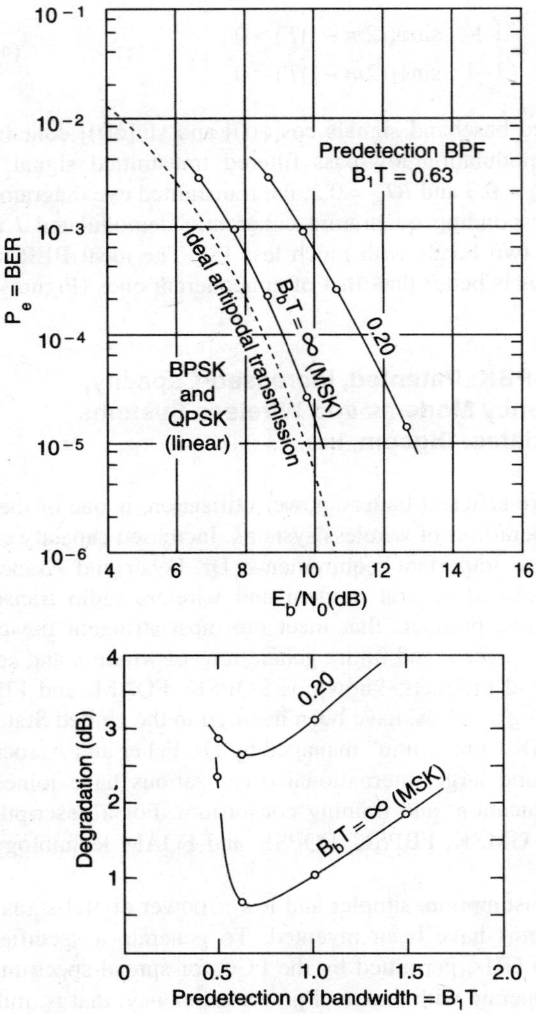

Figure 4.3.25 Performance of coherent GMSK and MSK systems in a stationary AWGN environment. (a), BER = $f(E_b/N_o)$ performance for an optimized experimental system with a Gaussian predetection BPF having B_iT_b = 0.63. (b), E_b/N_o requirement (degradation) to maintain BER = 10^{-3}. (From Murota and Hirade, 1981.)

and Dr. Feher (thus the KF abbreviation). Other power-efficient and spectrally efficient wireless solutions within the same family of products include FQAM and FBPSK.

4.3.9.1 FQPSK-1: A superior modulation for personal communications systems (PCS) and mobile cellular radio. The baseband signal and corresponding eye diagram of the FQPSK-1 processor at the I and Q inputs of a conventional offset QPSK (O-QPSK) or quadrature amplitude modulator (QAM) are illustrated in Figures 4.2.13 and 4.2.15, respectively.

The block diagram of a generic FQPSK modulator, including a nonlinear RF power amplifier, is illustrated in Figure 4.3.26. It is a conventional O-QPSK structure achieved by the $T_b = T_s/2$ digital element in the Q channel. An illustrative circuit diagram of the

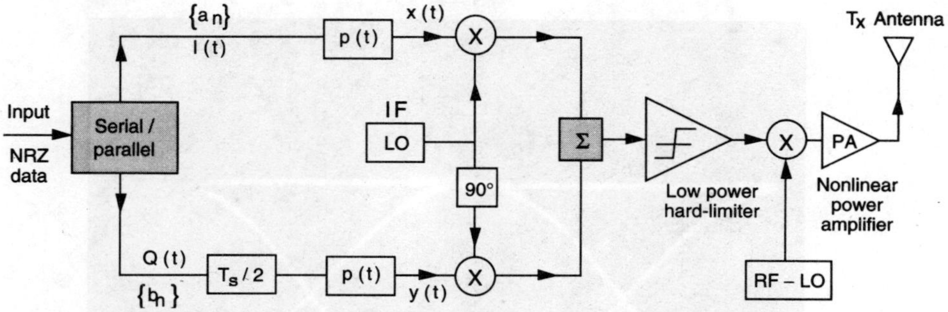

Figure 4.3.26 FQPSK block diagram. Pulse-shaping filter concept and a circuit diagram are illustrated in Figures 4.2.13 and 4.3.27. The lower-power, intermediate frequency (IF), hard-limited FQPSK constant envelope signal is upconverted and amplified by a nonlinear radio frequency (RF) power amplifier. A direct baseband to RF implementation and nonlinear amplification of FQPSK is an alternative practical architecture.

$p(t)$ pulse-shaping elements is shown in Figure 4.3.27. The resultant transmit and received or demodulated eye diagrams are illustrated in Figure 4.3.28. At the output of the low-power hard limiter, the FQPSK signal is constant envelope. This hard limiter could be implemented at an IF frequency or directly at RF. Alternately, for direct baseband to RF architectures, a conventional nonlinear (class C or saturated) amplifier can be used.

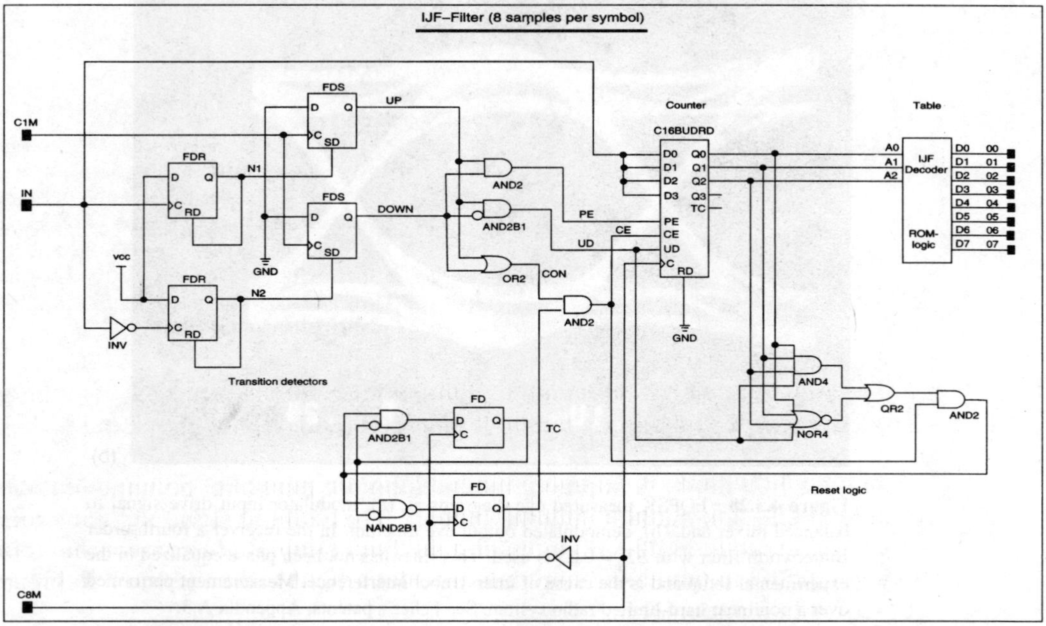

Figure 4.3.27 Illustrative circuit diagram of an FQPSK-1 pulse-shaping mixed digital/analog filter. Field Programmable Gate Array (FPGA) implementation with low-power solution up to 40 Mb/s. [Feher patents]

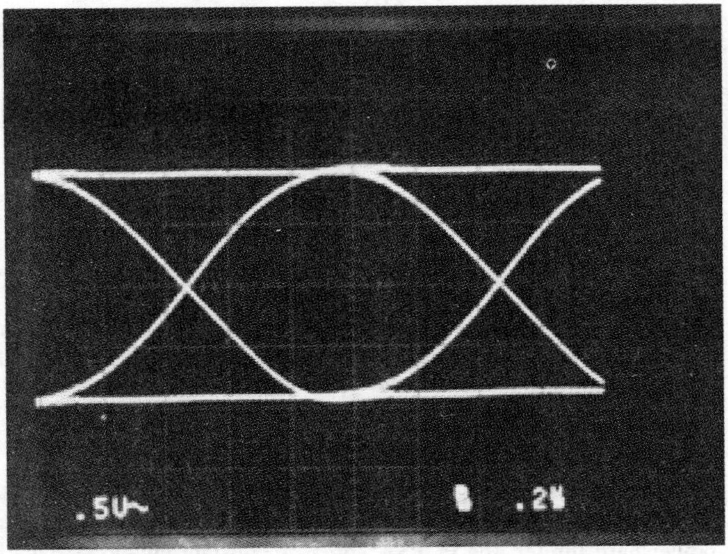

(a)

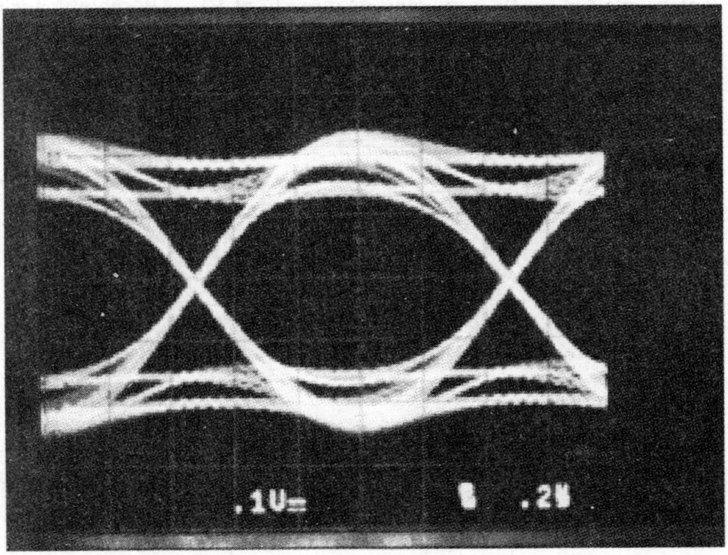

(b)

Figure 4.3.28 FQPSK measured eye diagrams at, (a), modulator input drive signal to balanced mixer and, (b), demodulated output eye diagram. In the receiver a fourth-order Butterworth filter with $BT_s = 0.55$ is used. This filter has not been phase equalized in the experimental setup and is the cause of intersymbol interference. Measurement performed over a nonlinear hard-limited radio system. See Feher's patents, Appendix A.3.

The input binary data sequence $\{a_n\}$ is first converted into two independent I/Q channel symbol streams $\{a_n\}$ and $\{b_n\}$ before being processed by the pulse-shaping filter, which has an impulse response

$$p(t) = \begin{cases} 0.5\left[1+\cos\left(\dfrac{\pi t}{T_s}\right)\right] & \text{for } |t| \le T_s \\ 0 & \text{otherwise} \end{cases} \tag{4.3.45}$$

where T_s is symbol duration. After the quadrature modulator and hard limiter, we obtain the following FQPSK signal:

$$S_o(t) = \frac{x(t)\cos 2\pi f_c t}{\sqrt{x^2(t)+y^2(t)}} + \frac{y(t)\sin 2\pi f_c t}{\sqrt{x^2(t)+y^2(t)}} \tag{4.3.46}$$

where

$$x(t) = a_n p(t-nT_s) + a_{n-1}p[t-(n-1)T_s]$$

and

$$y(t) = b_n p[t-0.5](T_s) + b_{n-1}p[t-(n+0.5)T_s] + b_{n-2}p[t-(n+1.5)T_s] \tag{4.3.47}$$

are the I and Q channel baseband signals, respectively.

Diagrams of radio and modern transmitter/receiver circuits suitable for FQPSK-1, FQPSK-KF, FQAM, conventional QPSK, MSK, GFSK, and GMSK implementations are given in Figures 4.3.29 and 4.3.30. In these figures a slow frequency-hopping, spread-spectrum (SFH-SS) configuration is illustrated. A direct baseband processor (BBP) to radio frequency modulation architecture is depicted. The transmitter implementation is practically the same for GMSK and FQPSK-1 systems. In the FQPSK-1 BBP implementation of $p(t)$, equation 4.3.45 is somewhat simpler than that of GMSK systems.

Coherent generic FQPSK and GMSK receivers are similar (Figure 4.3.30). The overall optimal channel shaping filter (receiver band-pass filters [BPFs] in cascade with the equivalent postdemodulation LPFs is as follows:

For GMSK: Gaussian with $BT_b = 0.6$ (Murota and Hirade, 1981)
For FQPSK-1: Butterworth with $BT_b = 0.55$ (Leung and Feher, 1993)

Figure 4.3.31 illustrates the power spectral density (PSD) of nonlinearly amplified (hard-limited or class-C amplified) FQPSK-1 and GMSK systems. The out-of-band integrated adjacent channel interference (ACI) of these nonlinearly amplified systems is shown in Figure 4.3.32. The computed ACI ratio is defined by

$$\text{ACI ratio} = A(W) = \frac{\int_{-\infty}^{\infty} G(f)\left|H(f-w)\right|^2 df}{\int_{-\infty}^{\infty} G(f)\left|H(f)\right|^2 df} \tag{4.3.48}$$

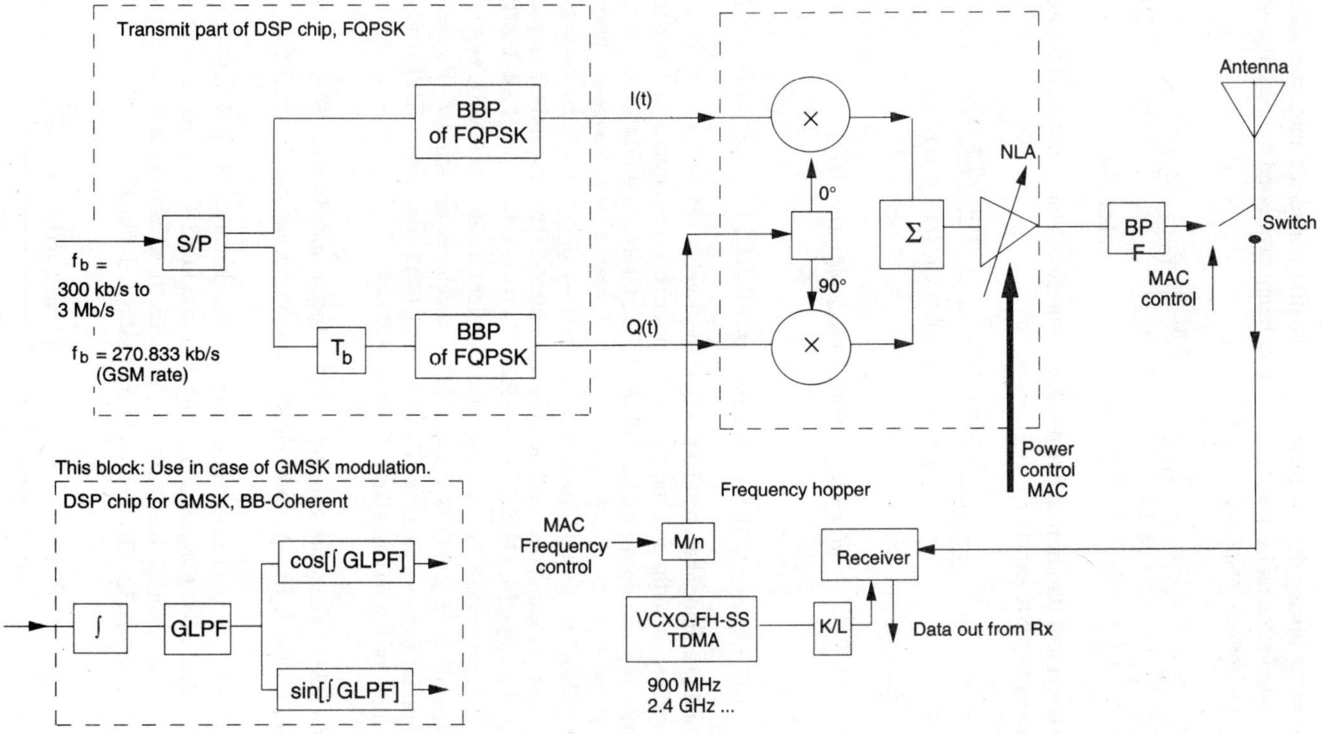

Figure 4.3.29 Spread-spectrum slow frequency-hopping application diagram of GMSK and FQPSK transmitter wireless systems. Both systems are implemented by means of compatible Feher's patents, see Appendix A.3.

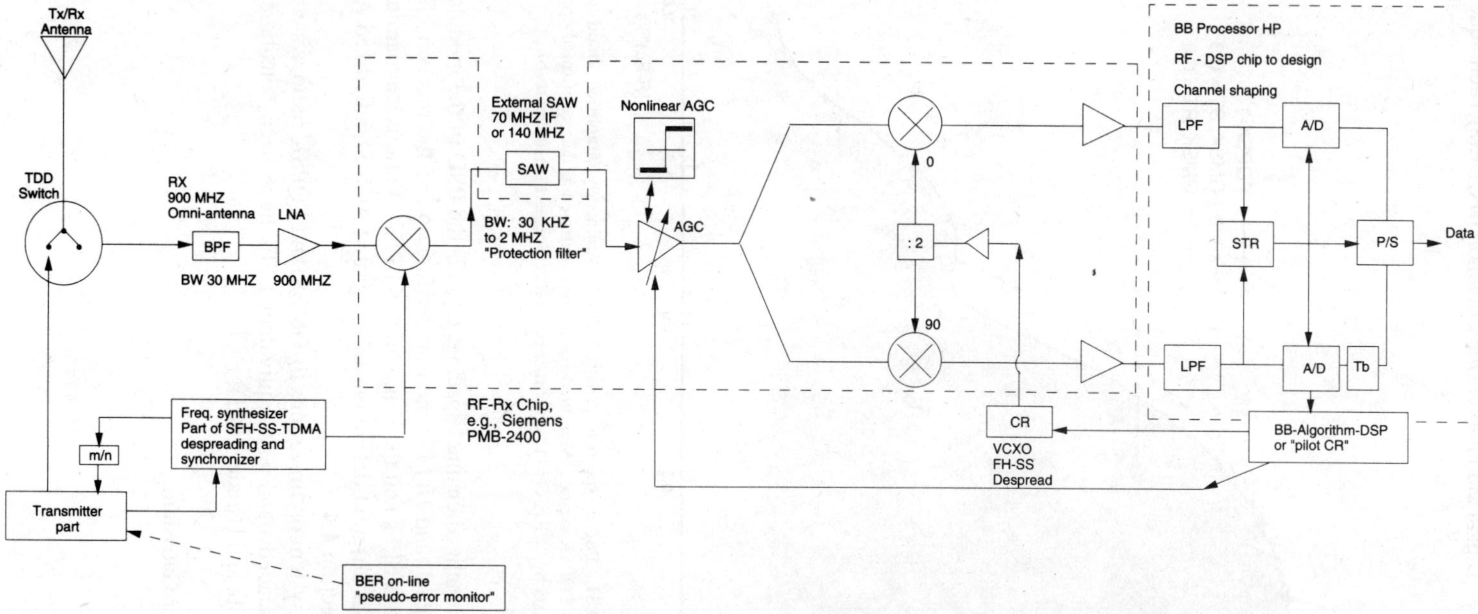

Figure 4.3.30 Receiver with one IF stage for coherent FQPSK or GMSK system for time division multiple access (TDMA) time division duplex (TDD), slow frequency-hopping spread-spectrum (SFH-SS) applications.

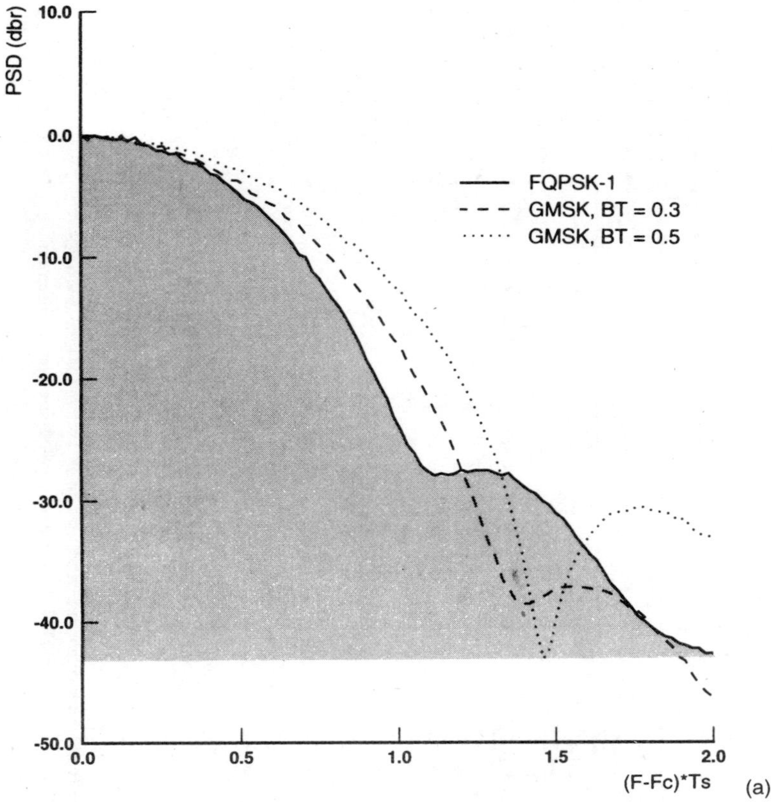

Figure 4.3.31 Power spectral density (PSD) nonlinearly amplified (hard-limited) GMSK and FQPSK signals. Measured hardware experimental data confirmed computer generated data by "CREATE-1" and other programs. See part (a) and part (b).

where W is the normalized channel spacing. $G(f)$ is the PSD of the modulated or nonlinearly amplified signal, and $H(f)$ is the transfer function of the receiver channel shaping filter (cascade of the BPFs and the demodulated LPFs). Various standardization committees have somewhat different definitions of integrated ACI. Standardized ACI definitions are described in Section 4.4.

In practical system optimizations of GMSK and FQPSK radio systems, the following classes of cascaded band-pass–equivalent LPFs have been considered (Leung and Feher, 1993; Murota and Hirade, 1981):

1. Infinite-order Gaussian:

$$H(f) = e^{ln\left(\frac{1}{\sqrt{2}}\right)\left(\frac{f}{0.5B_i}\right)^2} \tag{4.3.49}$$

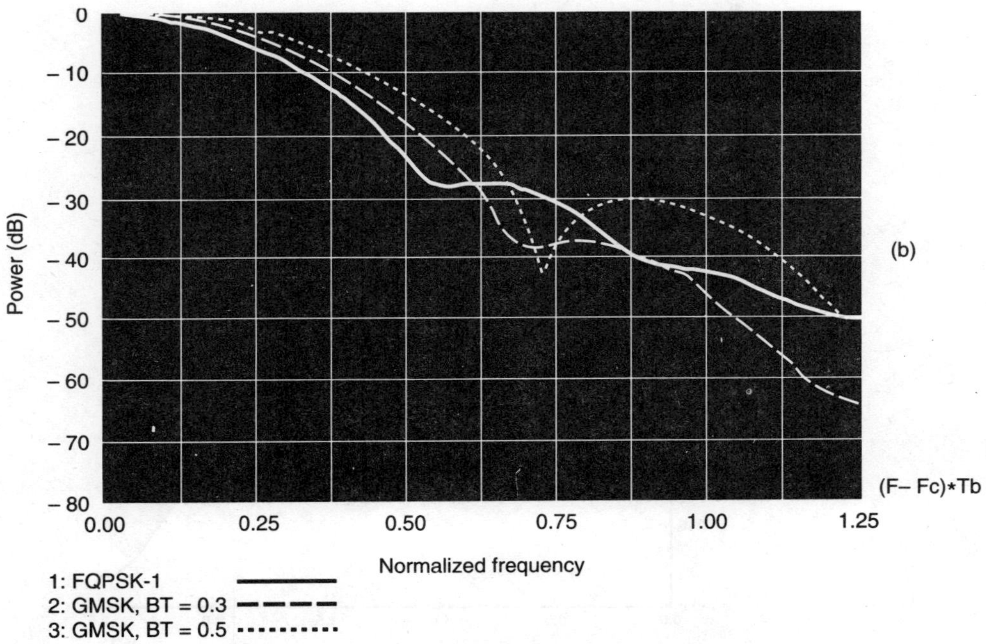

Figure 4.3.31 (continued)

2. Fourth-order Gaussian:

$$H(j\omega) = \prod_{i=1}^{2} \frac{\omega_i^2}{\omega_i^2 + 2j\xi_i\omega_i\omega - \omega^2} \tag{4.3.50}$$

where $\omega = 2\pi f$, $\omega_1 = 1.9086$, $\omega_2 = 1.6768$, $\xi_1 = 0.7441$, $\xi_2 = 0.9721$.

3. Eighth-order Gaussian:

$$H(j\omega) = \prod_{i=1}^{4} \frac{\omega_i^2}{\omega_i^2 + 2j\xi_i\omega_i\omega - \omega^2} \tag{4.3.51}$$

where $\omega_1 = 2.7240$, $\omega_2 = 2.3584$, $\omega_3 = 2.1821$, $\omega_4 = 2.1061$, $\xi_1 = 0.5492$, $\xi_2 = 0.7761$, $\xi_3 = 0.9201$, $\xi_4 = 0.9911$

4. Fourth-order Butterworth:

$$H(j\omega) = \frac{1}{(\omega^4 - 3.4142\omega^2 + 1) - j2.6131\omega(\omega^2 - 1)} \tag{4.3.52}$$

In Figure 4.3.32 the computed integrated ACI ratio $A(\omega)$ as a function of normalized channel spacing WT_b for FQPSK and GMSK systems is illustrated. From the results we note that FQPSK-1 causes far less ACI than GMSK does for WT_b <1.5. To obtain this re-

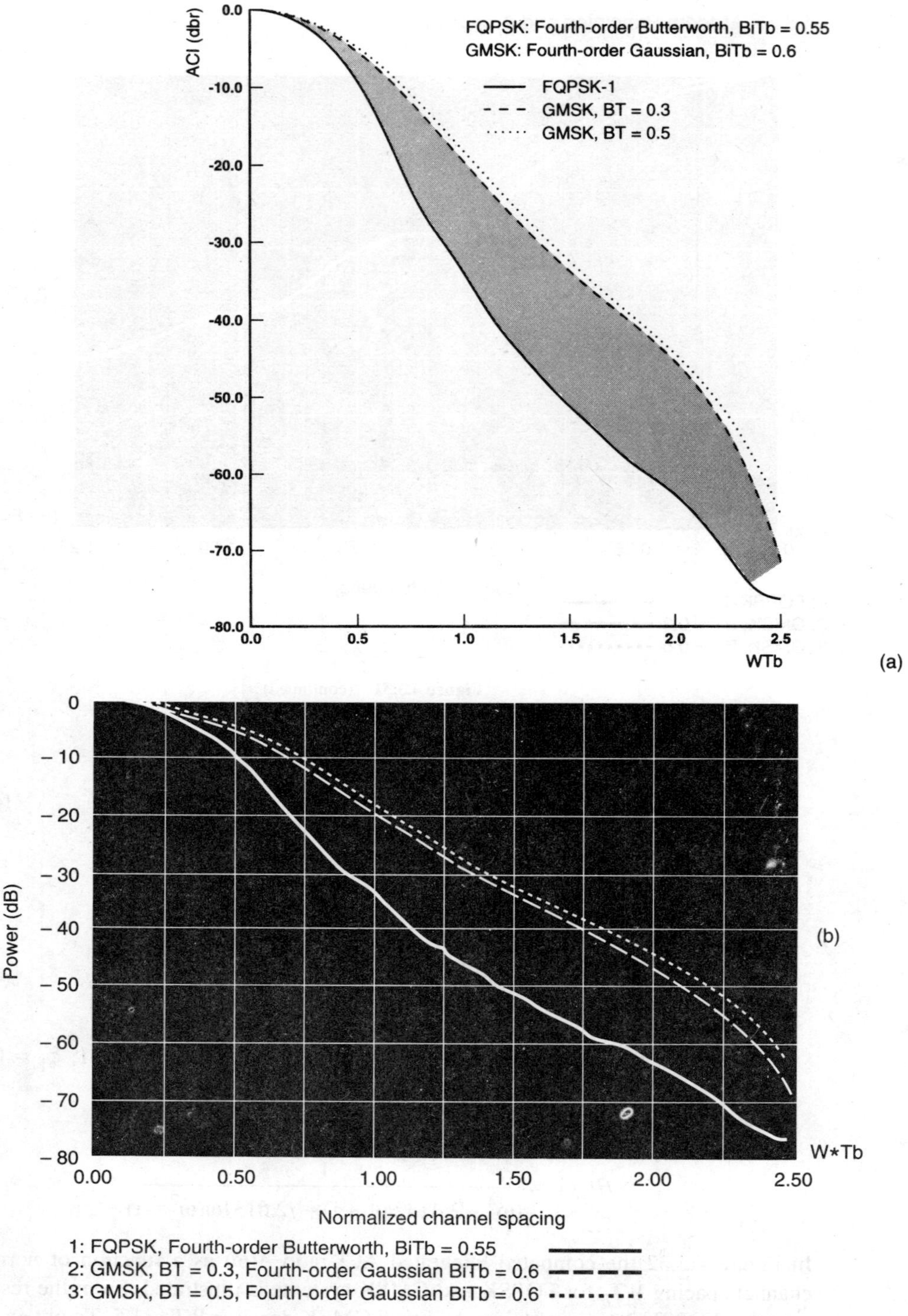

Figure 4.3.32 Integrated adjacent channel interference (ACI) of FQPSK-1 and GMSK systems. W is the channel spacing and $f_b = 1/T_b$ is the bit rate. (a) ACI of FQPSK and GMSK; (b), ACI generated by CREATE program.

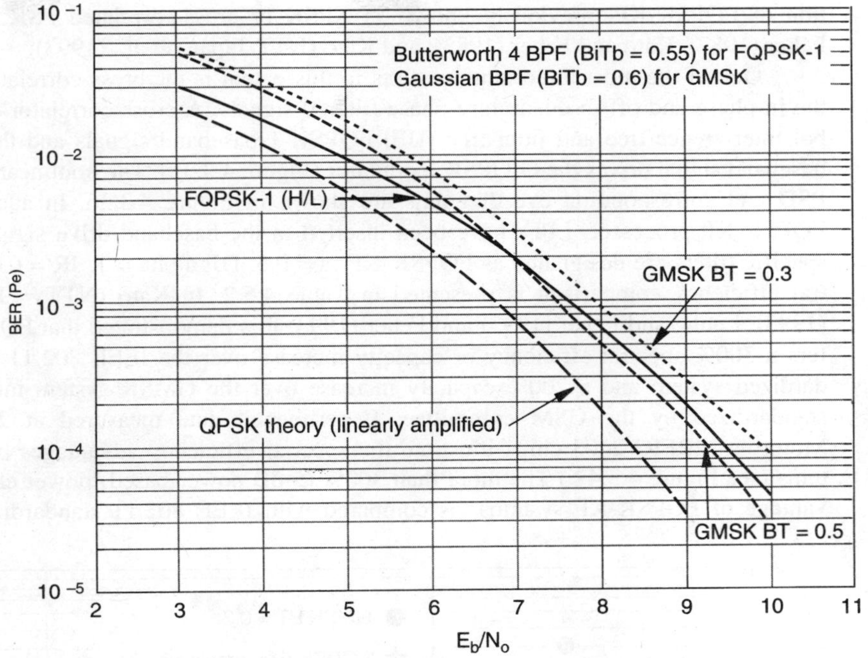

Figure 4.3.33 BER performance of nonlinearly amplified FQPSK and GMSK in an AWGN channel. FQPSK employs Butterworth (fourth order) receive BPF with BiTb = 0.55. GMSK employs Gaussian (fourth order) receive BPF with BiTb = 0.6. The BER performance of linearly amplified QPSK systems is also illustrated.

sult, we employ a fourth-order Butterworth BPF with normalized 3-dB bandwidth B_iT_b = 0.55 for FQPSK-1 and a fourth-order Gaussian BPF with B_iT_b = 0.6 for GMSK. From the ACI graphs we note that FQPSK has a 50% spectral advantage over standardized GMSK systems with B_iT_b = 0.5 and 0.3. These filters are chosen for their optimized BER performances in Gaussian noise channels.

The BER = $f(E_b/N_o)$ performance curves (Leung and Feher, 1993) in stationary AWGN and mobile, slow Rayleigh-faded channels are highlighted in Figures 4.3.33 and 4.3.34, respectively. In these graphs the performance of ideal, linearly amplified QPSK and practical, nonlinearly amplified FQPSK-1 and GMSK modems is presented. From Figure 4.3.34 we note that the performance of FQPSK is practically equal to that of the linearly amplified QPSK, whereas the performance of GMSK is about 2.5 dB worse than that of QPSK.

4.3.9.2 FQPSK-KF invention offers a 200% spectral efficiency increase over standardized GMSK and GFSK and a 300% power efficiency improvement over conventional DQPSK and π/4-DQPSK. The "FQPSK-KF" invention (Kato and Feher [patent] 1986) led to even more significant performance improvements than did the FQPSK-1 invention described in the previous subsection. A detailed description of FQPSK-KF, previously known as XPSK or cross-correlated PSK, is given in Feher (1987), Kato and Feher (1983), and Kato (NTT-Japan) et al., (1993).

One of the most important concepts in this patent is the cross-correlation between the in-phase and offset quadrature-phase filtered signals. A cross-correlator of intersymbol interference-free and jitter-free (IJF) FQPSK-1 baseband signals and the processed baseband signal drives the O-QPSK modulator (Figure 4.3.35). The nonlinearly amplified PSD and corresponding eye diagrams are shown in Figure 4.3.36. In addition to the FQPSK-KF processor, LPFs have been inserted in the baseband drive signal path. The specific filters are designated as FQPSK-KF (a = 0.5, DJ, alpha = 1, JR = 0.01). A spectral efficiency comparison is presented in Table 4.5.2. In Kato (NTT = Japan) et al. (1993), Leung and Feher (1993) and Feher (1993) it is demonstrated that FQPSK-KF offers a 300% spectral efficiency or capacity increase over the IEEE 802.11 GFSK standardized system and a 200% capacity increase over the GMSK system internationally standardized by the GSM committee. Experimental data measured at 2.4 GHz on Motorola MRFIC 2403 chips illustrate the spectral efficiency advantages of these systems (see Figure 4.3.42.) The more than 300% (5-dB power-based) power efficiency advantage of FQPSK-KF systems, as compared with IEEE 802.11 standardized conven-

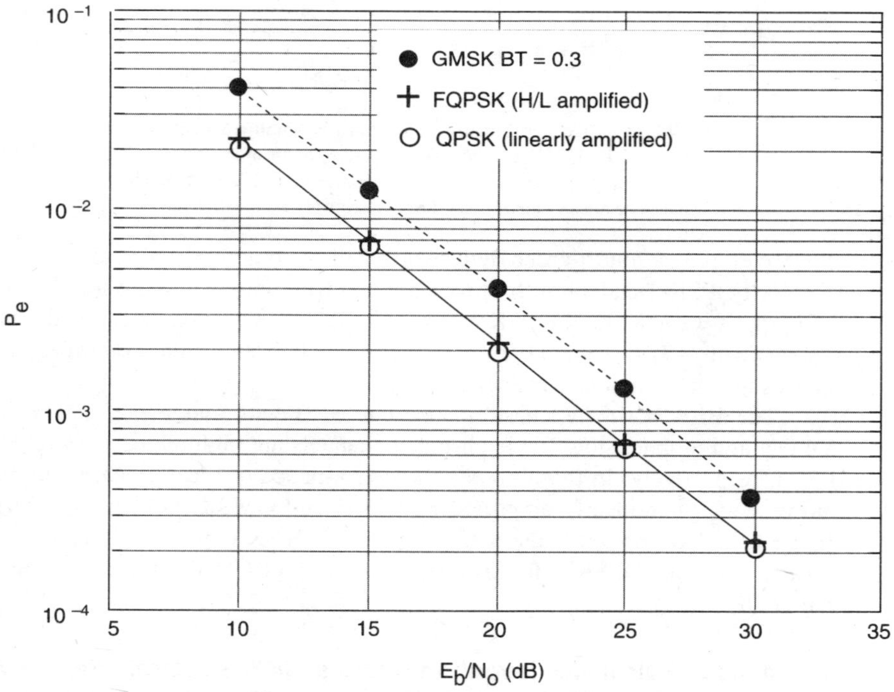

Figure 4.3.34 BER performance of nonlinearly amplified FQPSK and GMSK as a function of E_b/N_o in Rayleigh-fading channels. FQPSK employs Butterworth (fourth order) receive BPF with $BiTb = 0.55$. GMSK employs Gaussian receive BPF with $BiTb = 0.6$. Linearly amplified coherent QPSK performance is also shown.

tional DQPSK systems, is observed from the 2.4-GHz measurement results in Figures 4.3.41 and 4.3.42. Table 4.5.3 presents additional comparative data.

4.3.9.3. FQPSK family of QAM systems. In Figure 4.3.37 the baseband signal generation concept and a processed FQAM baseband signal pattern are illustrated (Seo and Feher [patent] 1987a). This baseband is obtained by superposition (S) of two

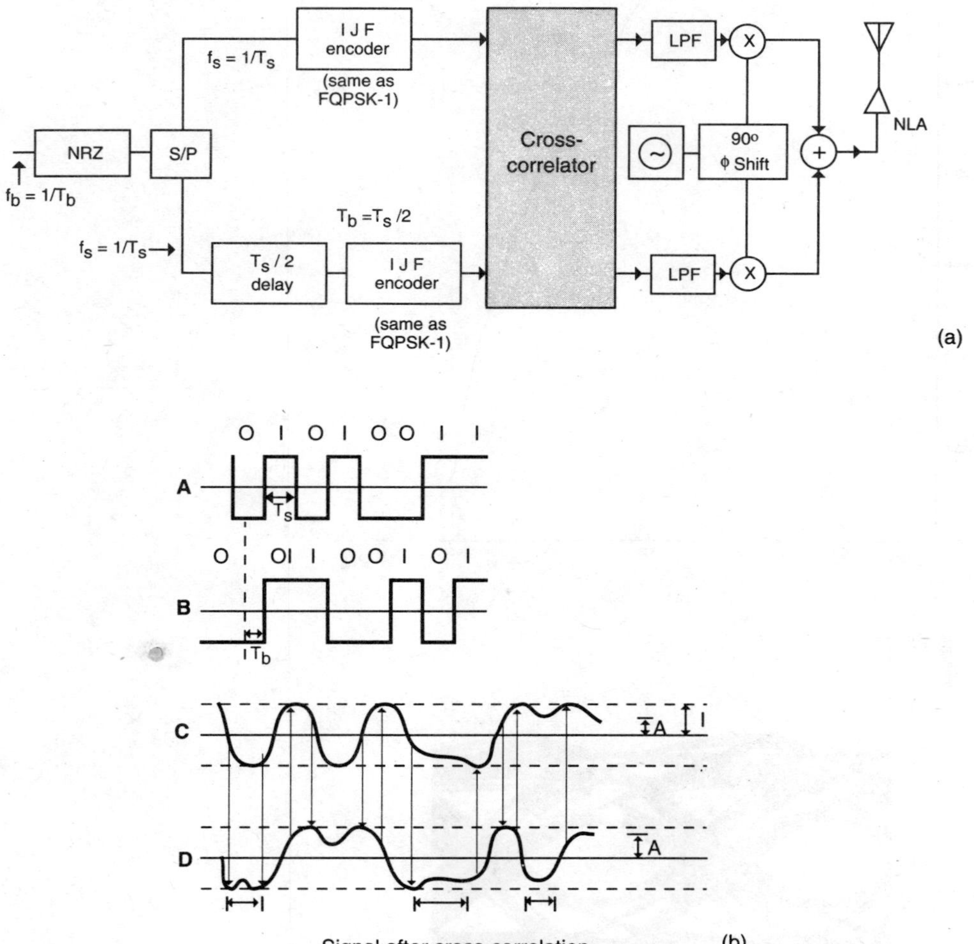

Figure 4.3.35 FQPSK-KF nonlinearly amplified (NLA) modem and radio invention. (a), One of the block diagrams of the invention, using intersymbol and jitter–free (IJF) I and Q signals. The patented IJF processor is the same as that used in FQPSK-1. (b), IJF cross-correlated signals, *A* to *D*, at the serial-to-parallel (S/P) output, after the correlator. The low-pass-filters (LPFs) following the cross-correlator lead to increased spectral efficiency. This Kato/Feher patent has been licensed also for cross-correlated quadrature GMSK implementations of Fig. 4.3.20 (b). It is described in Appendix 3. (From Feher, 1987; Kato/Feher [US Patent No. 4,567,602], 1986; Kato et al., 1993.)

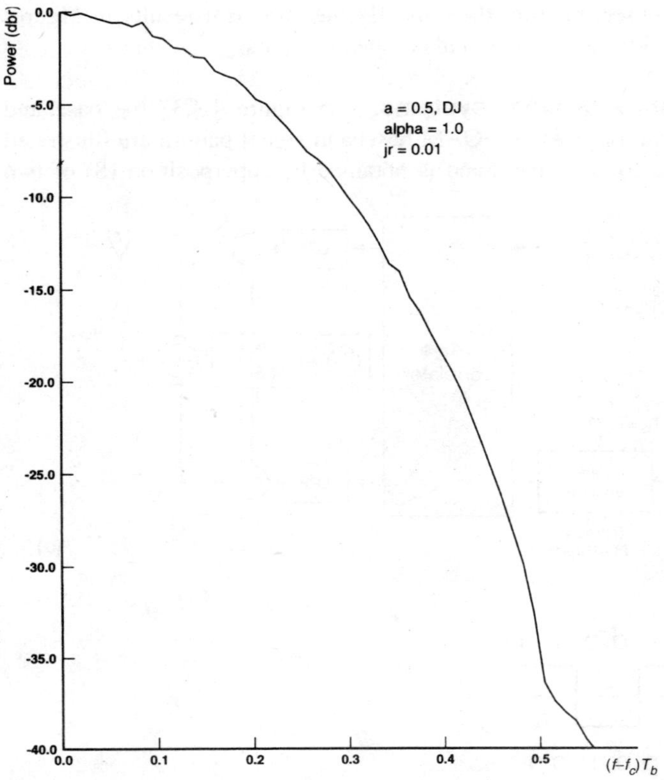

(a)

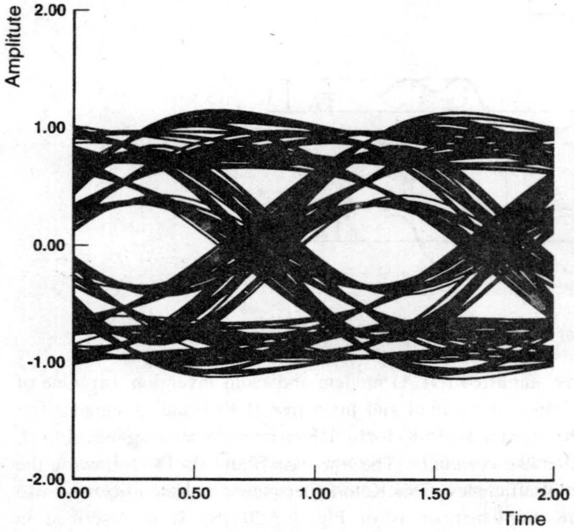

(b)

Figure 4.3.36 FQPSK-KF nonlinearly amplified (a) power spectral density, (b) demodulated eye diagrams [Kato, 1993; Kato and Feher, patent of, 1986; Kato and Feher, 1983]. In this case, low-pass-filters (LPF) after the crosscorrelator further increase the spectral efficiency.

basic signaling elements. For this reason it is also known as an SQAM signal (Feher, 1987a). The I and Q baseband signals are used as drive signals of conventional offset QAMs. In recent literature the term *SQAM* has been changed to FQAM to clearly indicate that these modulation techniques are patented techniques, licensed worldwide by Dr. Feher and Associates–Digcom, Inc. FQAM modem or nonlinearly amplified radio, satellite, and cellular products have been in use for several years. They have a power and spectral efficiency advantage similar to that of the FQPSK techniques described in the

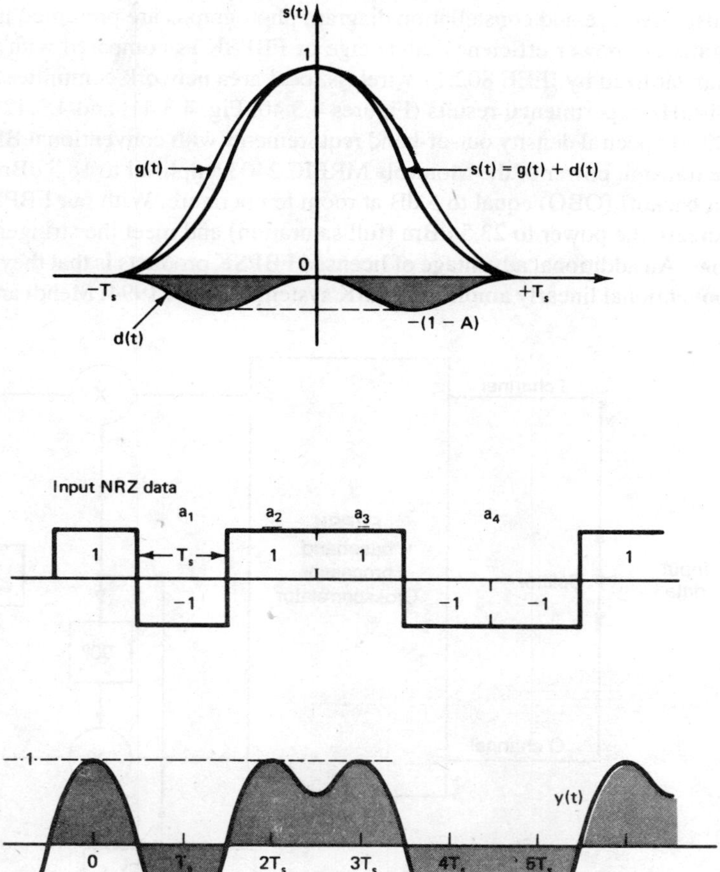

Figure 4.3.37 FQAM = SQAM. Signal wave shapes of Dr. Feher and Associates' patented *Superposed Quadrature Modulated* or *SQAM* double-interval signals. Modulated, nonlinearly and linearly amplified satellite, wireless, and cable systems have been licensed and implemented with the FQAM technology.

previous subsection. Multistate FQAM, increased spectral efficiency applications (Seo and Feher, 1991) are described in Section 4.8.

4.3.9.4. FBPSK: A nonlinearly amplified power-efficient invention that is compatible with conventional linearly amplified BPSK. In Figure 4.3.38 the basic architecture of a powerful BPSK system is illustrated. The FBPSK processor technologies patented by Dr. Feher and Associates of Digcom, Inc. enable the use of nonlinear amplifiers instead of linearized amplifiers, which are required for conventional BPSK (Feher [patent], 1982a; Feher, 1987; Kato and Feher [patent], 1986; Seo and Feher [patent], 1990). Illustrative eye and constellation diagram photographs are presented in Figure 4.3.39. The significant power efficiency advantage of FBPSK as compared with conventional BPSK (standardized by IEEE 802.11 wireless local area network committee) is noticed from the 2.4-GHz experimental results (Figures 4.3.40, Fig. 4.3.41, and 4.3.42). To meet the IEEE 802.11 spectral density out-of-band requirements with conventional BPSK, we had to limit the transmit power of the Motorola MRFIC 2403 amplifier to 18.5 dBm (that is, use an output backoff (OBO) equal to 5 dB at room temperature. With our FBPSK system we could increase the power to 23.5 dBm (full saturation) and meet the stringent spectral specifications. An additional advantage of licensed FBPSK products is that they are compatible with conventional linearly amplified BPSK systems (Feher, 1994; Mehdi and Feher, 1994).

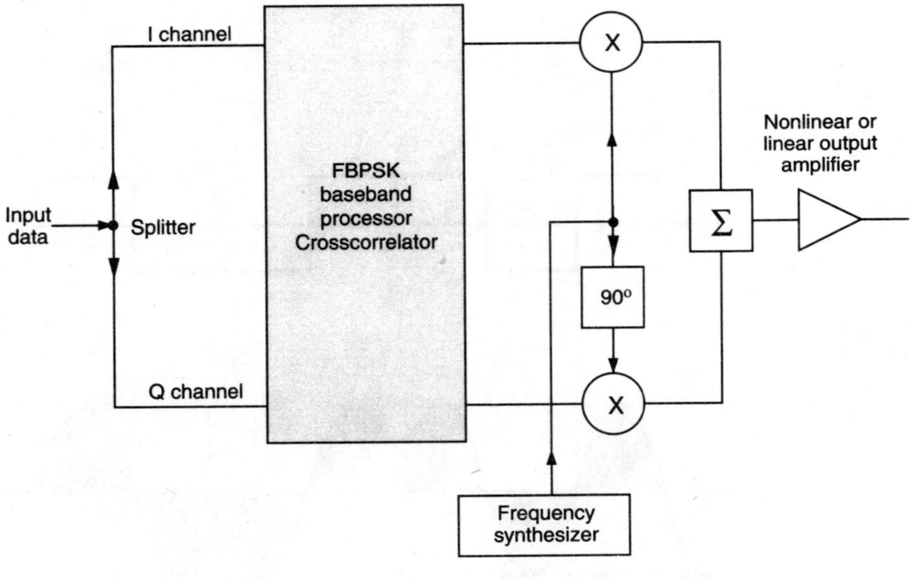

Figure 4.3.38 FBPSK (Feher's BPSK) modulator block diagram. The FBPSK modulated signal is used in nonlinearly amplified wireless systems. This spectral- and power-efficient system is fully compatible with conventional linearly amplified BPSK, such as the IEEE 802.11 standardized direct-sequence spread-spectrum system. For detailed technology transfer and licensing information of these patented systems, contact Dr. Feher Associates–Digcom, Inc. (From Feher and Mehdi, 1995.)

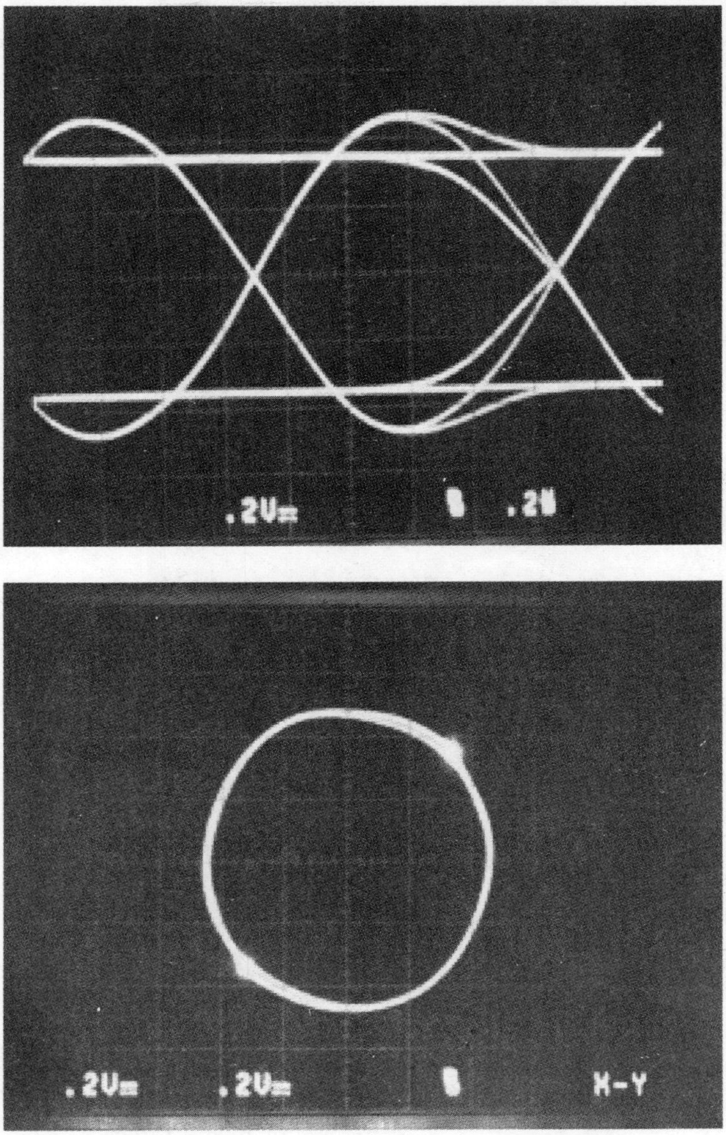

(a)

(b)

Figure 4.3.39 Experimental demodulated eye and constellation diagram of a nonlinearly amplified, coherently demodulated 1 Mb/s rate FBPSK signal. (Courtesy Hussein Mehdi, University of California, Davis.) Patented. See Appendix A.3.

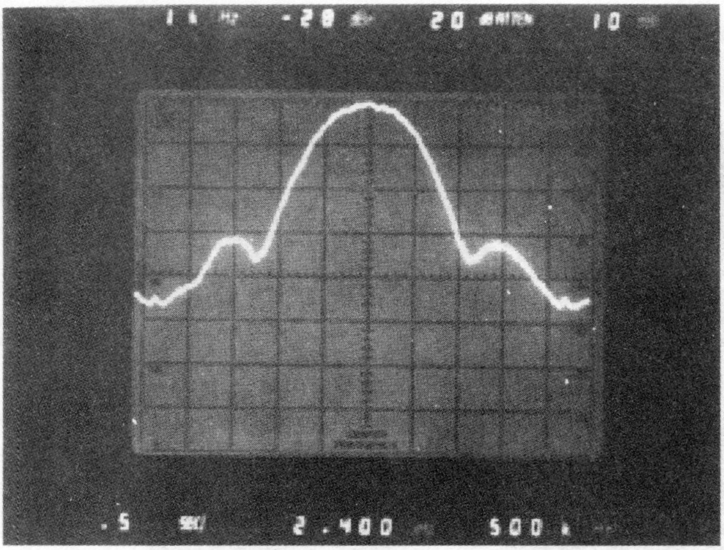

(a)
DBPSK with 18.5 dBm output power, MRFIC 2403

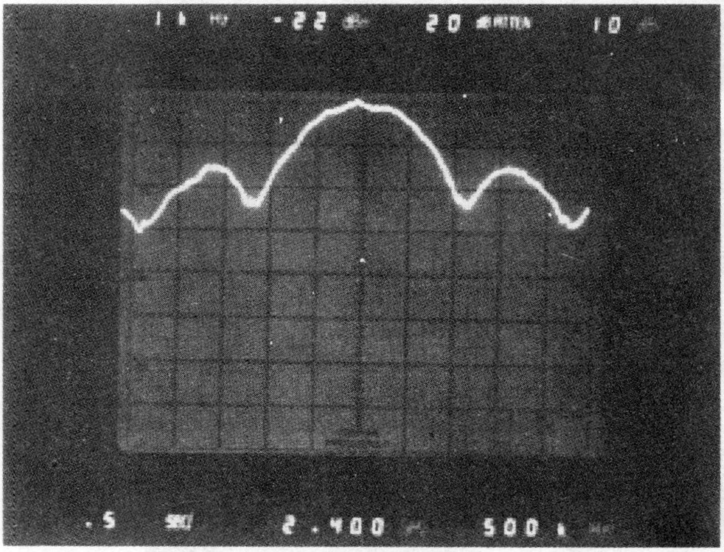

(b)
DBPSK with 23.5 dBm output power, MRFIC 240

Figure 4.3.40 Feher's patented FBPSK-2.4-GHz spectrum measurements. Conventional DBPSK and FBPSK systems. In all cases a normalized f_b = 1 Mb/s rate is used. The tested microwave integrated circuit is Motorola's MRFIC 2403. (a), The DBPSK signal is linearly amplified, with an output backoff (OBO) of 5 dB (saturated +23.5 dBm power minus power of backed-off amplifier +18.5 dBm is 5 dB, i.e., OBO = 5 dB). An OBO = 5 dB (at room temperature) is required to meet the out-of-band spectrum specifications, e.g., –30 dBr at ±1 MHz for 1 Mb/s. This corresponds to 11 Mchips for –30 dBr IEEE 802.11 specifications at ±11 MHz. (b), The premodulation filtered conventional DBPSK signal is operated at saturation. The spectral re-growth (restoration) is evident. The –30 dBr specification is not met. (c), The FBPSK modulated signal power is 23.5 dBm, i.e., full saturation; OBO = 0 dB. The FBPSK system is compatible with conventional BPSK. At room temperature of 20°C, this experimental result indicates a 5-dB power advantage over conventional DBPSK. The FBPSK advantage over a full operating range could be as much as 8 dB.

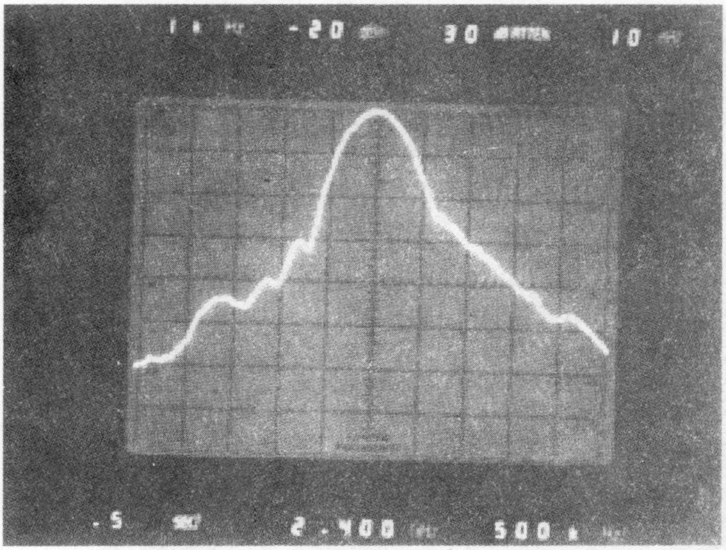

(c)
FBPSK with 23.5 dBm output power, MRFIC 240 (saturated amplifier OdB-OBO)

Figure 4.3.40 (continued)

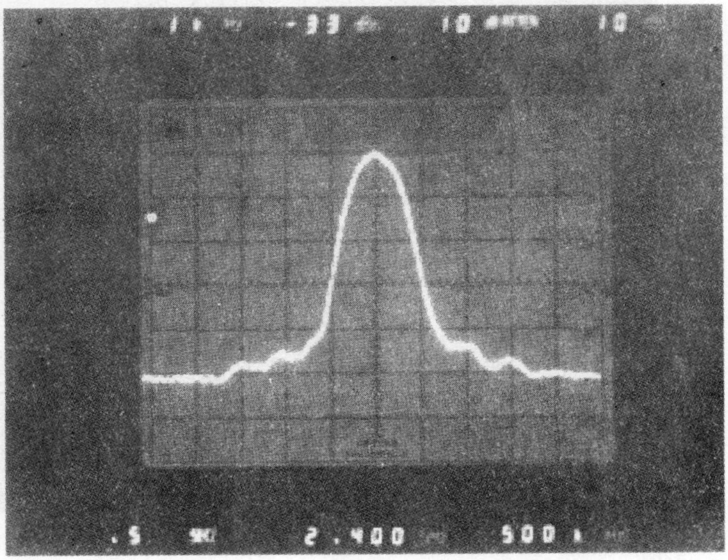

(a)

Figure 4.3.41 Linearly and nonlinearly amplified DQPSK measurement results over Motorola's MRFIC 2403. (a), ±15 dBm output. (b), ±23.5 dBm output. Bit rate in both cases is $f_b = 1$ Mb/s. Experiment indicates reduced output RF power requirement for conventional DQPSK.

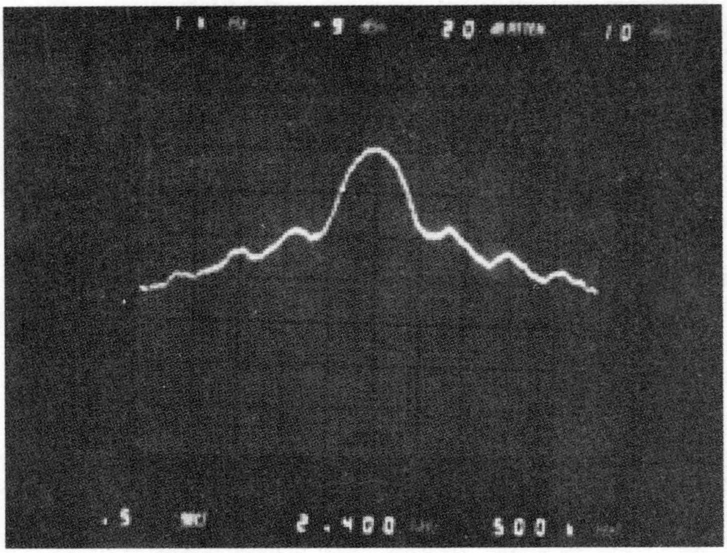

(b)

Figure 4.3.41 (continued)

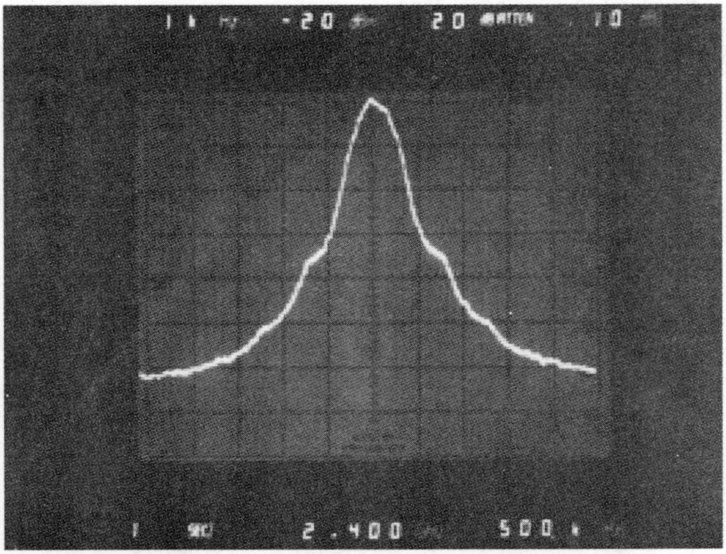

Figure 4.3.42 2.4-GHz, nonlinearly amplified (fully saturated) spectrum of an FQPSK-KF premodulation, low-pass-filtered wireless transmitter. In this experiment an $f_b = 1$ Mb/s rate is used. In this experiment the Motorola MRFIC 2403 microwave-integrated chip provides in saturation + 24.3 dBm. The measured FQPSK-KF bit rate normalized spectrum meets the increased $f_b = 2$ Mb/s rate stringent IEEE 802.11 WLAN standardized requirement at full saturation.

4.4 INTERFERENCE

Substantial radio frequency (RF) interference, abbreviated *I,* is inherent in all wireless systems and is one of the most significant design parameters of cellular and other mobile systems. The modulated-demodulated system BER performance is frequently controlled by interference. Demodulators provide a desirable (low) BER in relatively high carrier-to-noise (*C/N*) ratio and carrier-to-interference (*C/I*) ratio environments and may exhibit an undesirably high BER "floor" or "residual" BER in low *C/I* environments. In this section, we use the following terms in discussing interference and noise:

Adjacent channel interference (ACI)
Carrier-to-interference ratio (*C/I* or CIR)
Carrier-to-noise ratio (*C/N* or CNR)
Co channel interference (CCI)
Externally caused cochannel interference or noise (ECI)

A brief description of these interference sources is given. A detailed discussion of interference sources and of cellular-link and capacity-budgets systems design in an interference controlled environment is presented in Chapter 9.

4.4.1 Carrier-to-Interference and Carrier-to-Noise Limited Systems

4.4.1.1. Carrier-to-noise limited systems. If there is only one transmitter in operation, the receiver performance could be limited exclusively by noise. Assuming that the externally caused interference (ECI) is negligible, then the total noise power in the receiver bandwidth N_T is

$$N_T = kTB_wF \tag{4.4.1}$$

where

k = Boltzman constant (−228.6 dBW sec/°K)
T = Absolute temperature in degrees Kelvin
B_w = Double-sideband noise bandwidth of the receiver
F = Noise figure of the receiver

The following kT value at a room temperature of 17 °C (290 °K) is a frequently used system parameter:

$$\boxed{kT = -174\text{dBm}/\text{Hz}} \quad (4.4.2)$$

The E_b/N_o term, its relation to C/N, and the BER = $f(E_b/N_o)$ equations are described in Section 4.5.2. The following example illustrates the relation between noise figure (F), bandwidth E_b/N_o and corresponding C/N.

Example 4.4.1

How much is the required average faded carrier power, C, of an ideal, linearly amplified, coherently demodulated QPSK system if a BER = 10^{-3} is required and the mobile system operates in a noise-limited mobile Rayleigh-faded environment? Assume that the transmission rate is f_b = 48 kb/s and the receiver noise figure F = 8 dB. (These are practical bit rates and noise figure assumptions for the U.S. digital TDMA cellular system standard.) How much is the required received power for a nonlinearly amplified FQPSK system?

Solution for Example 4.4.1

From Figure 4.3.34 we note that for BER = 10^{-3}, a bit energy (E_b) to noise density (N_o) ratio (E_bN_o) equal to 23 dB is required. In Section 4.5.2 we demonstrate that

$$\frac{E_b}{N_o} = \frac{C}{N}\frac{B_w}{f_b}. \quad (4.4.3)$$

In ideal QPSK systems the receiver noise bandwidth is one half of the bit rate bandwidth, or 24 kHz. For this example.

$$\frac{E_b}{N_o} = \frac{C}{N} \cdot \frac{24\text{kHz}}{48kb/s}$$
$$\frac{E_b}{N_o}[\text{dB}] = \frac{C}{N}[\text{dB}] - 3\text{ dB} \quad (4.4.4)$$

and

$$\frac{C}{N} = \frac{E_b}{N_o} + 3\text{ dB}$$

Thus for a BER = 10^{-3}, a C/N = 23 dB = 26 dB is required.

The noise power in the B_w = 24 kHz receiver bandwidth is obtained from equation 4.4.1. It is

$$N_T = -174\text{dBm}/\text{Hz} + 10\log(24 \cdot 10^3) + 8\text{dB}$$
$$N_T = -122.7\text{dBm(in24kHz)}.$$

The C/N = 26 dB requirement leads to

$$C = N_T[\text{dBm}] + C/N[\text{dB}]$$
$$C = -122.7\text{dBm} + 26\text{dB} \quad (4.4.5)$$
$$C = -96.7\text{dBm}.$$

The linearly amplified QPSK and nonlinearly amplified FQPSK systems require the same received power. *Note:* In this example we assumed that there is a "slow" Rayleigh-fading channel, or the Doppler shift–caused degradation is negligible. We also assumed that the delay-spread impact of BER degradation is negligible. This computed carrier power, for a BER = 10^{-3}, is within a few decibels of the IS-54 specifications of the U.S. digital cellular (TDMA) standard.

Noise is always present in receivers. It is generated by front-end amplifiers, downconverters, and oscillators and by miscellaneous electronic devices, which are all part of the receiver. Receiver-generated noise has a relatively flat power spectral density (white) and a Gaussian probability density, termed additive white Gaussian noise (AWGN). The noise figure, F, is a measure of the amount of noise the receiver adds to the received carrier (Feher, 1981). In addition to noise, most signals are also corrupted by interference.

4.4.1.2. Carrier-to-interference ratio: Basic definition. Interference, in the broad sense, may be defined as any undesired signal within a band of interest. Interference often arises from many transceivers operating simultaneously in the same frequency band or in adjacent frequency bands. Interference could also be generated by "man-made noise" such as automobile ignition, any electromagnetic interference, including distortion products, and atmospheric noise. In this section we assume that intersymbol interference (ISI) is negligible. The carrier-to-interference ratio is defined as the ratio of average carrier power to average interference power in a specified bandwidth, frequently in bandwidth of the desired receiver.

4.4.2 Cochannel Interference

Cochannel interference (CCI) is generated when two or more independent signals (modulated or unmodulated) are transmitted simultaneously in the same frequency band. The same frequencies (frequency bands) are reused many times. Frequency reuse leads to CCI-limited system designs. In Figure 4.4.1, for example, frequency bands f_1 to f_7 are reused in a $k = 7$ cell reuse pattern. If the mobile unit is at location M_7, then it receives the desired signal on frequency f_7 from the nearest base station B_7. Simultaneously, the mobile unit at M_7 also receives, in the same frequency band, an independent interfering signal from base station A_7. The ratio of desired average carrier power (C) from the nearby base station (B_7) to average interference (I) power from the distant base station (A_7) the average C/I or cochannel interference (CCI) (Figures 4.4.2 and 4.4.3).

The CCI reduction factor "a" is defined by

$$a = \frac{D}{R} \tag{4.4.6}$$

where

D = Distance between base stations that transmit on the same frequencies, for example, distance A_7 to B_7 in Figure 4.4.3

R = Coverage radius of the base station transmitter of one cell

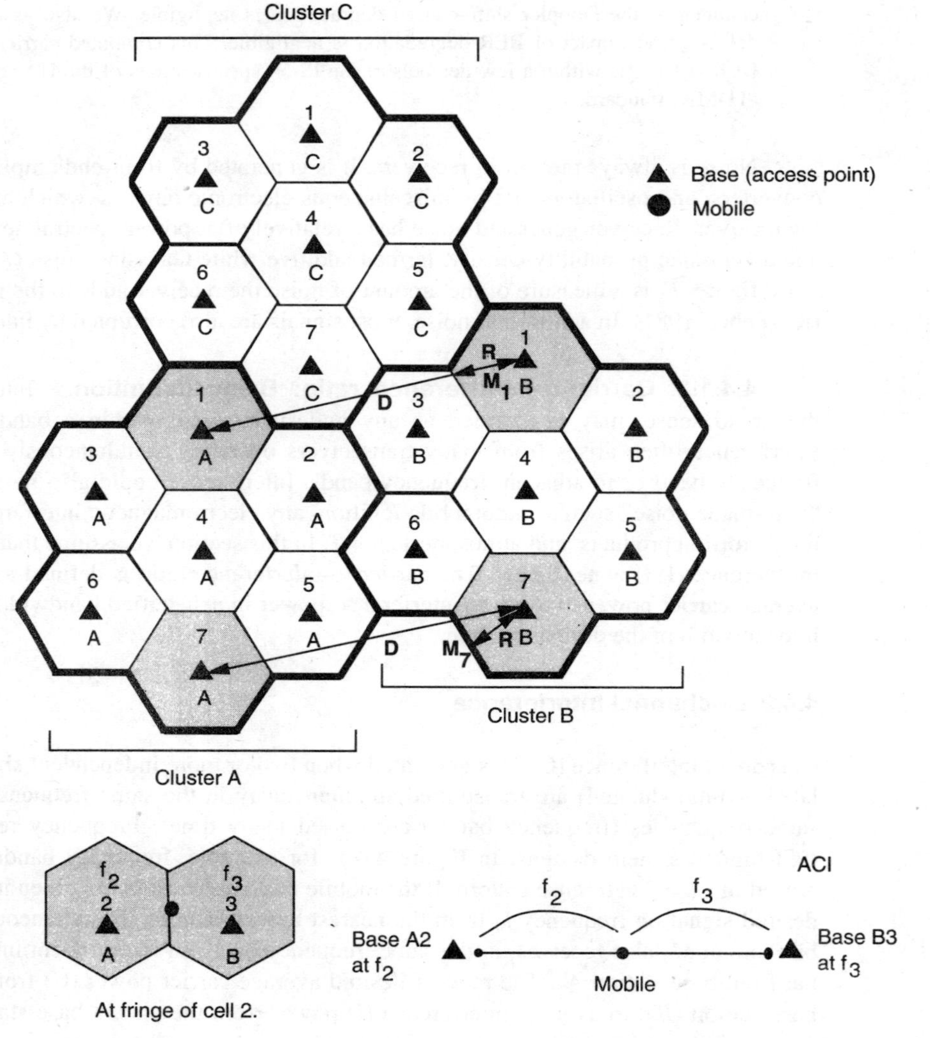

Figure 4.4.1 Cellular k = 7 reuse pattern system. Adjacent chanel interference (ACI) impact on cochannel interference (CCI) from first neighboring cell. Assume that first ACI is used in cells A2 and B3 (designated ACI-1).

A larger "a" factor leads to higher *C/I*, that is, higher CCI values. To obtain larger *C/I* values, the cell reuse factor must increase and the capacity is reduced. The relation between D and R_1 for hexagonal cells sharing k frequencies is given by

$$D = \sqrt{3k}\,R. \tag{4.4.7}$$

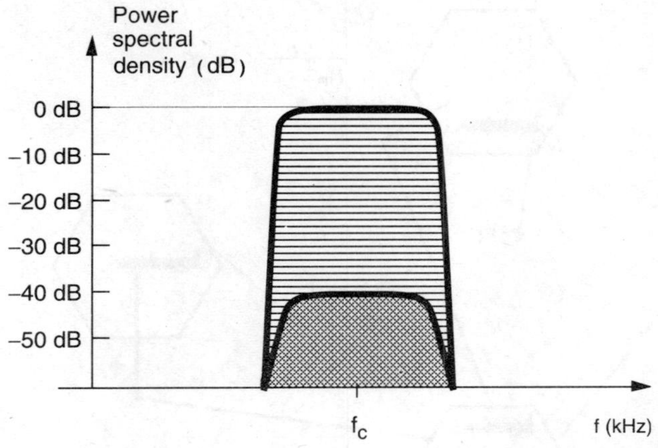

Figure 4.4.2 Cochannel interference for a $K = 7$ cell reuse pattern. Only one cochannel interference (*double-shaded surface*) is illustrated. Power spectral density is indicated in dB-relative (dBr), that is, relative to the power spectral density of the desired signal.

The CCI-caused *C/I* ratio received at a desired base station (cell site) for a $k = 7$ cell reuse pattern is illustrated in Figure 4.4.4. Assuming that we have all six, $M = 6$, cochannel interferers, the CCI at the base station is

$$CCI_b = \frac{C}{N_T + I} = \frac{C}{N_T + \sum_{i=1}^{M} I_i}. \tag{4.4.8}$$

If CCI is the predominant factor, or noise N_T is negligible, then we have

$$CCI_b = \frac{C}{\sum_{i=1}^{M=6} I_i}. \tag{4.4.9}$$

We assume, for example, that the non–line-of-sight (NLOS) path loss is at a slope of 40 dB/decade, that is, it is proportional to R^{-4}. In this case,

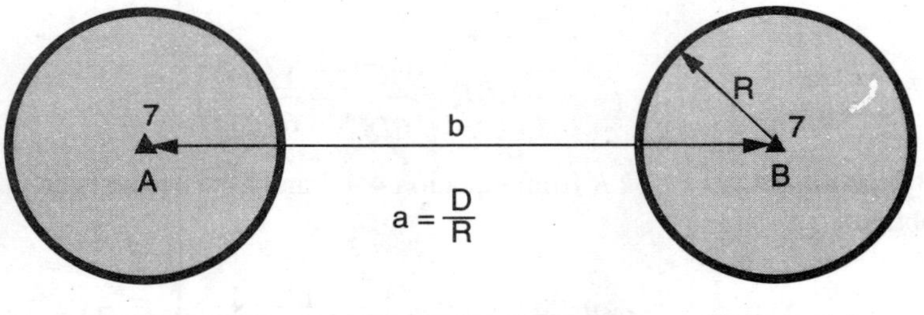

Figure 4.4.3 Cochannel interference reduction factor *a* for two cochannel cell sites operated at the same frequency.

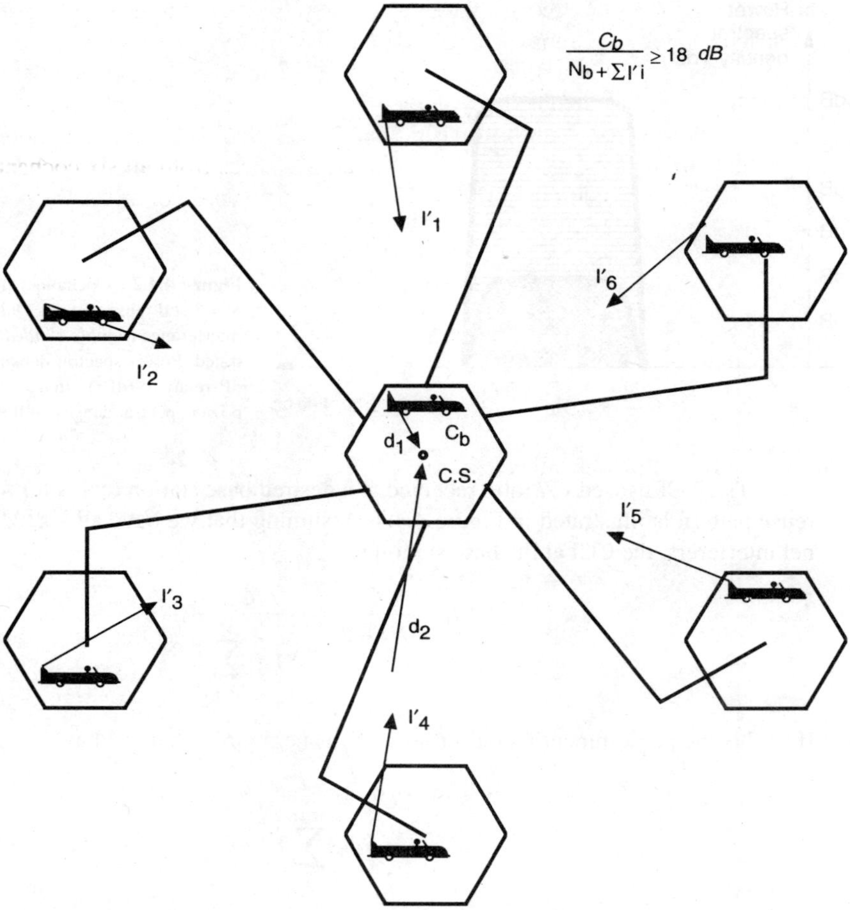

Figure 4.4.4 Cochannel interference at the base station caused by $M = 6$ interferes in a $k = 7$ cell reuse pattern. (From *Mobile Communications Design Fundamentals,* William C.Y. Lee, Copyright © J. Wiley and Sons, 1993. Reprinted by permission of J. Wiley & Sons, Inc.)

$$CCI_b = \frac{R^{-4}}{6D^{-4}} = \frac{1}{6}\left(\frac{R}{D}\right)^{-4} \tag{4.4.10}$$

By substituting $D = \sqrt{3k}\,R$ from equation 4.4.7 and $k = 7$ for a seven-cell reuse factor, we obtain

$$CCI_b = \frac{1}{6}\left(\frac{R}{\sqrt{3k}\,R}\right)^{-4} = \frac{1}{6}\left(\frac{1}{\sqrt{3\cdot 7}}\right)^{-4} = 73.5 \tag{4.4.11}$$

$$CCI_b = 18.7\text{dB}.$$

This computed C/I ratio, received at the base, assumes equal transmit power and equidistant spacing of the six remote interfering signals from the base. For an increased geographic coverage, for example, approximately 90% of a cell, the computed value of the CCI is lower, as illustrated in Table 4.4.1.

To obtain the C/I values listed in Table 4.4.1, we assume that the mobile unit is at the cell boundary. For the $k = 7$ cell pattern, the distances from all six cochannel-interfering sites will contribute to the overall C/I at the mobile unit. For an NLOS path loss slope of 40 dB/decade, we have

$$\begin{aligned}\frac{C}{I} &= \frac{R^{-4}}{2(D-R)^{-4} + 2(D)^{-4} + 2(D+R)^{-4}} \\ &= \frac{1}{2(a-1)^{-4} + 2(a)^{-4} + 2(a+1)^{-4}}.\end{aligned} \tag{4.4.12}$$

When $k = 7$, we obtain from equation 4.4.12 for the cell boundary $C/I = 15$ dB. When $k = 12$, we obtain 23 dB.

4.4.3 Adjacent Channel Interference

Adjacent channel interference (ACI) is caused by modulation, filter, and radio design imperfections. The transmitted signal is not band-limited to a "brick wall" spectrum, so some spectral power will be radiated into adjacent channels, as shown in Figure 4.4.5. If C_D is the desired signal power, then the shaded area represents ACI power falling into the desired bandwidth. Here we assume that only two adjacent channels are causing interference in each other. The spacing between channel center frequencies is

$$\Delta f = f_{c2} - f_{c1},$$

and the ideal "brick wall" receiver filter has a bandwidth of W_R. *Note:* $W_R \leq \Delta f$. Interference power caused by the first upper and lower interfering signals is designated as ACI-1. Transmitters having a larger frequency spacing also cause ACI, as illustrated in Figure 4.4.6.

Table 4.4.1 Cochannel interference CCI = C/I for $k = 7, 9, \ldots, 12$ cell reuse patterns assuming a propagation factor of $\alpha = 4$ and a 90% coverage.

No. of cell reuse patterns (k)	Cochannel interference reduction factor (a = D/R)	Average C/I for 90% coverage ($\alpha = 4$)
7	4.6	15 dB
9	5.2	19 dB
12	6	23 dB

$D = \sqrt{3K}\,R$

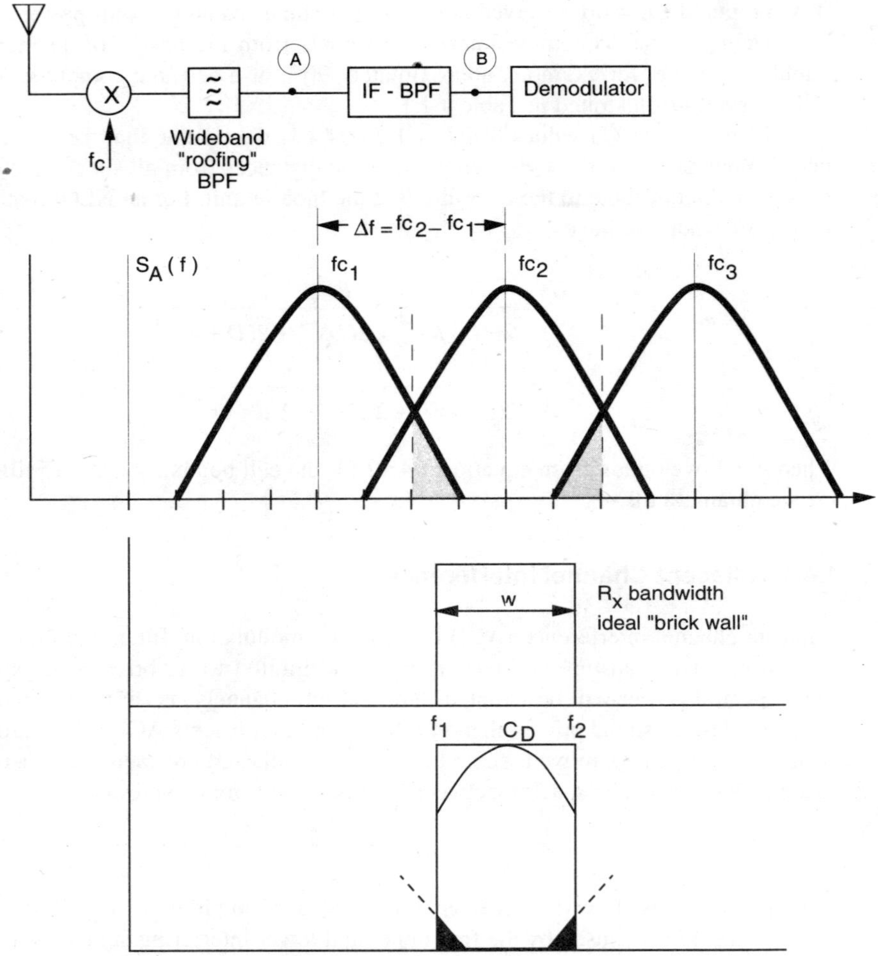

Figure 4.4.5 Adjacent channel interference (ACI) caused by two adjacent channels.

In several system specifications the receiver filter is assumed to be a "brick wall" filter. For example, in the U.S. digital cellular (IS-54) system, the first ACI is specified to be −26 dB below the desired carrier power, that is, first ACI = −26 dB, in a $W_R = 30$ kHz, "brick wall" channel. The closest frequency spacing in this system is $\Delta f = 30$ kHz, that is, $W = \Delta f$. In the Digital European Cordless Telephone (DECT) system the channel spacing is approximately $\Delta f = 1.8$ MHz, whereas the ACI is specified in a $W = 1.1$ MHz bandwidth.

The integrated (total) ACI power or *C/I* ratio in the demodulator—before threshold detector—determines the performance. For this reason we propose to use the following ACI definition:

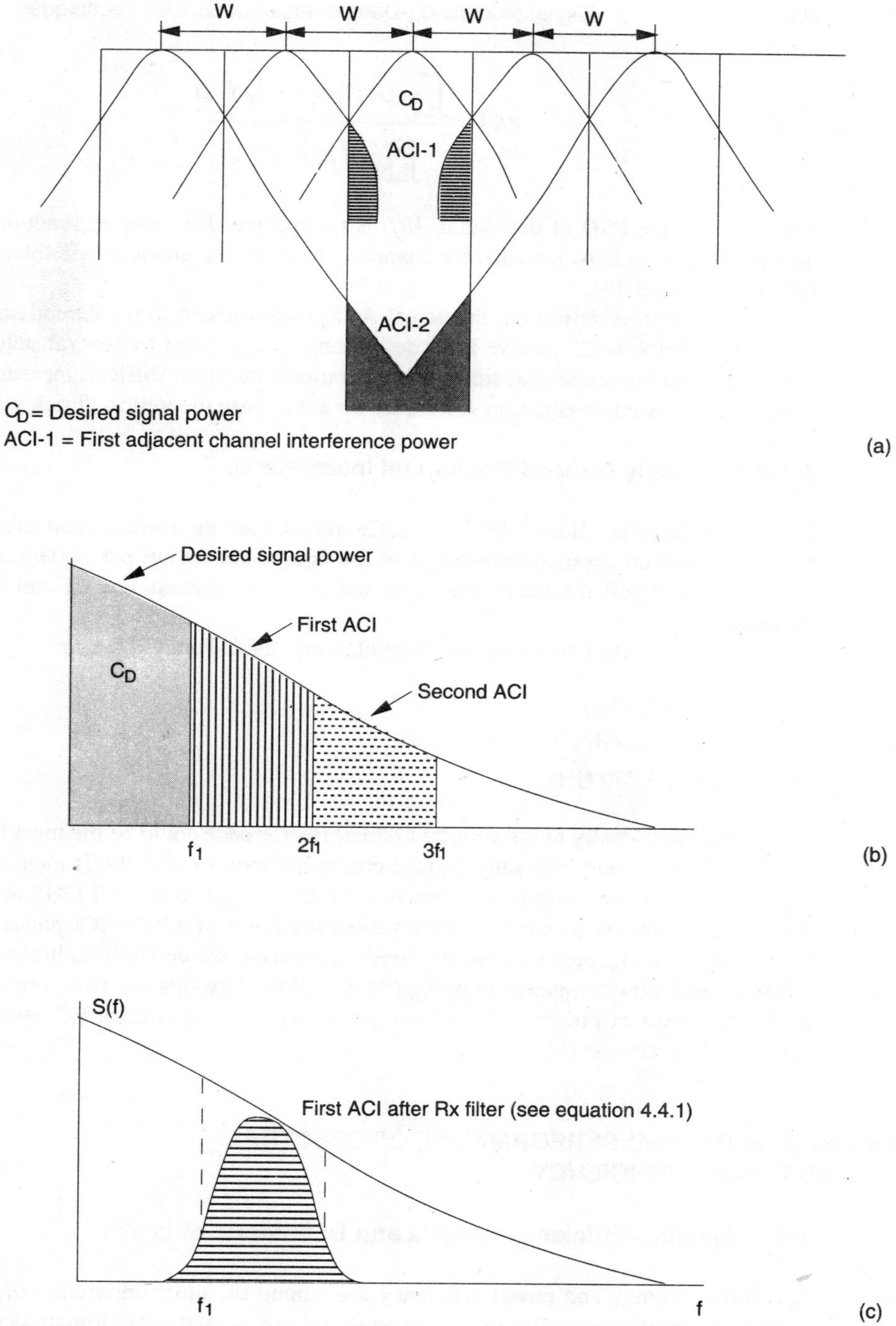

Figure 4.4.6 Adjacent channel interference (ACI) at radio frequency, intermediate frequency, and equivalent baseband using in (a) and (b) integrated "brick-wall" ACI definition; (c) after the Rx filter.

$$\text{ACI} = \frac{\int_{-\infty}^{\infty} G(f)\left|H(f-\Delta f)\right|^2 df}{\int_{-\infty}^{\infty} G(f)\left|H(f)\right|^2 df}. \tag{4.4.13}$$

where $G(f)$ is the PSD of the signal, $H(f)$ is the receive BPF transfer function, and Δf is the carrier spacing between adjacent channels. Also see the previously defined ACI equation (equation 4.3.48).

Based on this definition, the actual ACI power present in the demodulator is computed. The "brick wall" receive filter definition concepts used by several standardization committees lead to somewhat simpler computations, but more difficult measurements. To measure ACI based on equation 4.4.13, we do not require theoretical "brick wall" filters.

4.4.4 Externally Caused Cochannel Interference

In well-regulated or "clean" RF bands, CCI and ACI are the predominant causes of interference. Based on detailed knowledge of the equipment design parameters, propagation conditions, and cell frequency planning, the total *C/I* containing CCI and ACI is predictable.

For unregulated bands such as the following "FCC-Part 15" bands:

902 to 928 MHz

2.4 to 2.485 GHz

5.725 to 5.850 GHz

the external (externally to the cellular system) interference could be the most harmful.

In some of our externally caused cochannel interference (ECI) measurements we observed ECI power in the –40 dBm to –60 dBm range in the 2.4 GHz to 2.485 GHz band. Microwave ovens have frequently been the cause of a high ECI power. In the 902 to 928 MHz band, spread-spectrum, direct sequence-code division multiple access (DS-CDMA), and slow frequency hopping (SFH)-CDMA systems are also permitted to radiate up to 1 watt of power. Such a large power causes a significant ECI into geographically nearby receivers (FCC, 1990).

4.5 DEFINITIONS AND PERFORMANCE OF SPECTRAL AND POWER EFFICIENCY

4.5.1 Spectral Efficiency Criteria and Definitions of b/s/HZ

Spectral efficiency and power efficiency are among the most important requirements of digital communications systems in general and are of particular importance to cellular and other wireless applications. In this section a *basic* practical definition of spectral efficiency is presented. We use this definition extensively throughout the book. In Chapter 9 we demonstrate that the basic spectral efficiency, in addition to power, space, and time efficiency, has a significant impact on system performance and on the capacity of cellular networks. We use the term *basic spectral efficiency* to highlight the fact that spectral efficiency is only one of the elements of an efficient cellular system. We define the basic efficiency by the following:

$$n_s = \frac{R}{B_w} = \frac{\text{transmission rate}}{\text{required bandwidth}} \tag{4.5.1}$$

where

n_s = Spectral efficiency or bandwidth efficiency defined in b/s/Hz

R = Transmission rate in b/s

B_W = Bandwidth, including required guard band. The term *bandwidth* applies to baseband systems as well as to modulated systems

This definition of spectral efficiency is illustrated in the following example.

Example 4.5.1

What is the practical baseband and RF spectral efficiency of an f_b = 1.152 Mb/s rate system if a raised-cosine filtered system having (a) $\alpha = 0$ and (b) $\alpha = 0.5$ is used and the "out-of-band" spectral density has to be attenuated by 15 dB and 40 dB, respectively? In this example we use the standardized transmission rate of the DECT system (DECT, 1991).

Solution for Example 4.5.1

From the Nyquist transmission theorems we obtain

$$f_N = \frac{f_b}{2} = \frac{1.152 \text{ Mb/s}}{2} = 576 \text{ kb/s}.$$

For the ideal "brick wall" Nyquist channel having a cut-off frequency f_N, the basic spectral efficiency is based on equation 4.2.19, as follows:

$$n_s = \frac{R}{B_w} = \frac{R}{f_N} = \frac{1.152 \text{ Mb/s}}{576 \text{ kb/s}} = 2 \text{ b/s/Hz}.$$

For the $\alpha = 0$ roll-off "brick wall" case, the 0 dB, 15 dB and 40 dB filter attenuation is at f_N; thus we have for all spectral attenuation values an efficiency of 2 b/s/Hz.

For the $\alpha = 0.5$ case, we read from Figure 4.2.10 that the 15 dB attenuation is approximately at $1.3 f_N$, while the 40 dB attenuation is at $1.45 f_N$. For exact values, equation 4.2.19 should be used. Thus the practical spectral efficiency of an ideal $\alpha = 0.5$ filtered raised-cosine baseband binary channel is

$$n_s = \frac{1.152 \text{ Mb/s}}{1.3 \times f_N} = \frac{1.152 \text{ Mb/s}}{1.3 \times 57\ 6\text{kb/s}} = 1.54 \text{ b/s/Hz}$$

for a 15 dB spectral attenuation requirement. The efficiency for the higher out-of-band spectral attenuation specification of 40 dB is smaller. It is

$$n_s = \frac{1.152 \text{ Mb/s}}{1.45 \times f_N} = \frac{1.152 \text{ Mb/s}}{1.45 \times 576 \text{ kb/s}} = 1.38 \text{ b/s/Hz}.$$

These are baseband spectral efficiency values. For simplest double-sideband modulated systems the spectral efficiency values at RF are one half of the computed baseband (single-sideband) efficiencies. In other words, the practical RF efficiencies become the following:

$n_s = 1$ b/s/Hz for the $\alpha = 0$ filtered channel (−15 dB and −40 dB, respectively)

$n_s = 0.77$ b/s/Hz for the $\alpha = 0.5$ filtered channel, with 15 dB out-of-band spectral efficiency attenuation requirement

$n_s = 0.69$ b/s/Hz for the $\alpha = 0.5$ filtered channel, with 40 dB out-of-band spectral efficiency attenuation requirement

It is worthwhile to note that the DECT system in Europe has an RF channel spacing of 1.8 MHz and a transmission rate of 1.152 Mb/s. Thus the basic spectral efficiency of the DECT system is 1.152 Mb/s/1.8 MHz = 0.64 b/s/Hz.

Example 4.5.2

Determine the spectral efficiency of linearly amplified and nonlinearly amplified QPSK, FQPSK, and GMSK systems, assuming that a $BT_b = 0.5$ filtered GMSK and $\alpha = 0.2$ filtered QPSK are used. The out-of-band spectral components are required (specified) to be at least 25 dB attenuated relative to the in-band spectral components.

Solution for Example 4.5.2

For linearly amplified QPSK, the spectral efficiency of the $\alpha = 0.2$ roll-off filtered QPSK system is

$$\frac{2 \text{ b/s/Hz}}{1+\alpha} = \frac{2 \text{ b/s/Hz}}{1+0.2} = 1.67 \text{ b/s/Hz}$$

The $\alpha = 0.2$ filter attains the 26 dB as well as the ∞ dB attenuation point at 1.2 times the Nyquist frequency (see Figure 4.2.10). The GMSK and the FQPSK signals have practically identical spectra for linearly and nonlinearly amplified systems. From Figure 4.3.31 we note that the specified 26 dB spectral attenuation is obtained at $(f - f_c)\, T_b = 0.52$ for FQPSK and at $(f - f_c)T_b = 0.72$ for $BT_b = 0.5$ filtered GMSK. For conventional QPSK systems, we note from Figure 4.3.8 that the 26 dB attenuation point is attained at $2.8/T_s$, or $(f - f_c)T_b = 1.4$. The spectral efficiency of these linearly and nonlinearly amplified systems is summarized in Table 4.5.1.

The spectral efficiency of the modulated system is defined by

$$\text{Spectral efficiency [b/s/Hz]} = \frac{1}{2(f - f_c)T_b}. \tag{4.5.2}$$

The factor 2 is present because we are dealing with double-sideband quadrature modulated systems.

Table 4.5.1 Spectral efficiency of QPSK, GMSK and FQPSK systems. A −26 dB out-of-band integrated adjacent channel interference is specified. In power-efficient, nonlinearly amplified systems FQPSK has the highest spectral efficiency; in linearly amplified systems QPSK has the highest efficiency.

	Linearly amplified	Nonlinearly amplified	
	Spectral efficiency	$(f-f_c)T_b$	Spectral efficiency
QPSK (a = 0.2)	1.67	1.40	0.36
GMSK (BTb = 0.5)	0.70	0.72	0.69
FQPSK	1.00	0.52	0.96

We note that the spectral efficiency, based on our 26 dB specification of nonlinearly amplified QPSK systems, is only 0.36 b/s/Hz, whereas that of FQPSK is about 1 b/s/Hz. Although FQPSK is the most spectrally efficient nonlinearly amplified (power efficiency of RF amplifier) modulated system, it is less spectrally efficient than linearly amplified QPSK.

From this example we observe that while nonlinear power amplification is advantageous from the point of view of RF power amplifier efficiency, for some system applications it may not be as efficient from a b/s/Hz point of view.

4.5.2 Relationship of the Bit-Energy to Noise-Density Ratio and the Carrier-to-Noise Ratio

The ratio of required bit energy (E_b) to noise density (N_o) ratio (the E_b/N_o ratio) is a convenient quantity for system calculations and performance comparisons. However, in *practical* measurements it is more convenient to measure the average carrier–to–average noise (*C/N*) power ratio. Most tests are performed using power meters and root-mean-

Table 4.5.2 Spectral efficiency comparison of nonlinearly amplified GMSK, GFSK, FQPSK, and FQPSK-KF based on FCC Part 15.247 definition of 99% in-band power; this, efficiency criterion has been adopted by the IEEE 802.11 Wireless Local Area Network (WLAN) Standardization Committee (Feher, 1993a). Details of the GFSK standard are presented in MacDonald (1993). The FQPSK-KF nonlinearly amplified modulation techniques, invented by Kato and Feher (1986) are described in Section 4.3.9 and in Kato and Feher (1983). FQPSK-KF has also been known as XPSK or cross-correlated PSK. For design and patent details, see Appendix A.3.

System	Spectral efficiency
GMSK	0.8
GFSK	1.0
FQPSK	1.22
FQPSK-KF	1.48

square (rms) voltage meters, which are readily available. The following simple relations are useful for converting from E_b/N_o to C/N:

$$E_b = CT_b = C\left(\frac{1}{f_b}\right) \tag{4.5.3}$$

$$N_o = \frac{N}{B_w} \tag{4.5.4}$$

$$\frac{E_b}{N_o} = \frac{CT_b}{N/B_w} = \frac{C/f_b}{N/B_w} = \frac{CB_w}{Nf_b} \tag{4.5.5}$$

$$\boxed{\frac{E_b}{N_o} = \frac{C}{N}\cdot\frac{B_w}{f_b}} \tag{4.5.6}$$

The E_b/N_o ratio equals the product of the C/N ratio and the receiver *noise bandwidth*–to–bit rate ratio (B_w/f_b). It should be clearly noticed that any C/N measuring instrument can be recalibrated to read E_b/N_o directly, if required.

Example 4.5.3

A coherent QPSK modem operates at a rate of f_b = 1.152 Mb/s. A stationary AWGN environment is assumed. The unmodulated carrier frequency is f_c = 1914.5 MHz. What is the probability of error, P_e, performance of this system if the available E_b/N_o ratio is 8.4 dB? Assume that Nyquist channel shaping is employed. How much is the corresponding C/N ratio if it is measured at the receive bandpass filter output?

Solution for Example 4.5.3

The theoretical $P_e = f(E_b/N_o)$ curve (Equation 4.5.7) is shown in Figure 4.5.1. From the curve we conclude that an E_b/N_o ratio of 8.4 dB will yield a P_e of 10^{-4}. The double-sideband RF noise bandwidth of the QPSK Nyquist-filtered system equals one half of the bit rate (that is, 576 kHz). From equation 4.5.6 we have

$$\frac{C}{N} = \frac{E_b}{N_o}\frac{f_b}{B_w}$$

or, expressed in decibels,

$$\frac{C}{N} = \frac{E_b}{N_o} + 10\log\frac{f_b}{B_w}$$

$$= 8.4 + 10\log\frac{1.152\ \text{Mb/s}}{576\ \text{kHz}} = 11.4\ \text{dB}.$$

4.5.3 Power Efficiency and Bit-Error-Rate Performance in an Additive White Gaussian Noise Environment

The probability of error, P_e, performance as a function of available C/N ratio in a stationary additive white Gaussian noise (AWGN) environment is described in this section. The term "P_e" is most frequently used in theoretical references, whereas the prac-

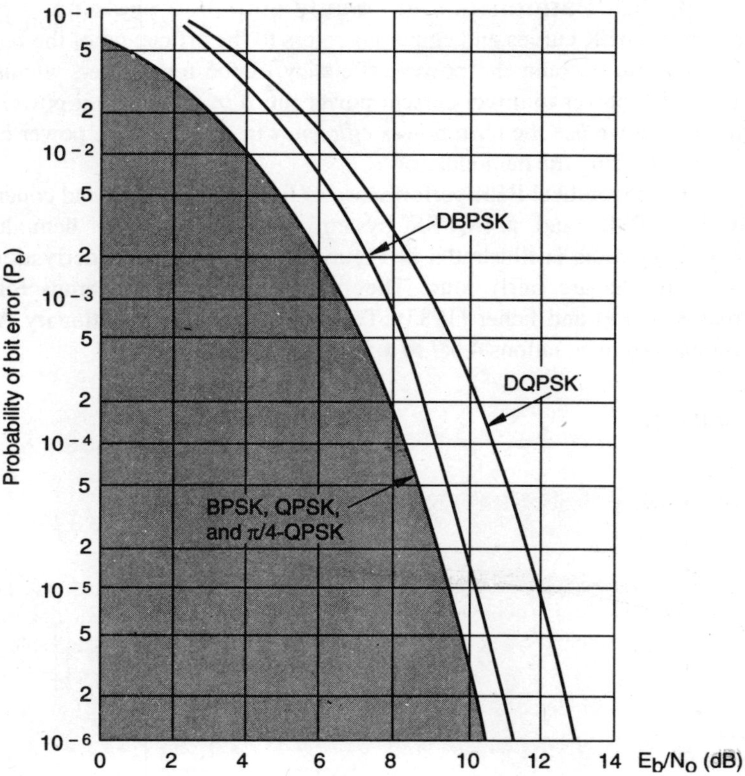

Figure 4.5.1 Theoretical $P_e = f(E_b/N_o)$ performance in a stationary additive white Gaussian noise (AWGN) environment. Ideal, linearly amplified coherent BPSK, QPSK, and differentially demodulated DBPSK systems are illustrated. The performance of non-linearly amplified FQPSK and GMSK is compared to ideal linearly amplified QPSK in Figures 4.3.33 and 4.3.34. (From Proakis, 1989.) See Appendix A.3.

tically equivalent term bit-error rate (BER) is used in applied references and specifications.

Power efficiency of modulated systems is defined as being inversely proportional to the

$$\text{BER} = f(C/N)$$

and/or

$$\text{BER} = f(E_b/N_o)$$

equations and performance curves, where E_b is the average energy of a modulated bit and N_o is the noise power spectral density (the noise power in a normalized 1-Hz bandwidth) at the demodulator input. The higher the probability of error, the lower the power efficiency, since transmitted power is "wasted" on more bad data.

4.5.3.1. Performance in linearly amplified systems. Power efficiency as defined by BER curves and equations refers to the efficiency of the receiver only. It does not take into account the power efficiency of the transmitter, which includes the efficiency (RF power to direct-current power ratio) of the transmit power amplifier. Thus in this section we use the term *power efficiency* to designate the power efficiency of the receiver, including the demodulator.

The theoretical BER performance of linearly amplified and coherently demodulated BPSK, QPSK, and π/4-QPSK systems and differentially demodulated DBSK and DQPSK systems is illustrated in Figure 4.5.1 The detailed derivations of these performance results are fairly long. They are presented in numerous references, including Proakis (1989) and Feher (1983). The *final results* for a stationary AWGN channel are summarized in equations 4.5.7 to 4.5.15).

For BPSK,
$$P_e = \frac{1}{2}\operatorname{erfc}\sqrt{\frac{E_b}{N_o}}. \tag{4.5.7}$$

For QPSK,
$$P_e = \frac{1}{2}\operatorname{erfc}\sqrt{\frac{E_b}{N_o}}. \tag{4.5.8}$$

For DPSK,
$$P_e = \frac{1}{2}e^{-E_b/N_o}. \tag{4.5.9}$$

For DQPSK,
$$P_e = Q(a,b) - \frac{1}{2}I_o(ab)\exp\left[-\frac{1}{2}\left(a^2+b^2\right)\right] \tag{4.5.10}$$

and

$$a = \sqrt{2\gamma_b\left(1-\frac{1}{\sqrt{2}}\right)} \tag{4.5.11}$$

$$b = \sqrt{2\gamma_b\left(1+\frac{1}{\sqrt{2}}\right)}. \tag{4.5.12}$$

$Q(a,b)$ is the Q function defined by

$$\begin{aligned} Q_m(a,b) &= \int_b^\infty x\left(\frac{x}{a}\right)^{m-1} e^{-(x^2+a^2)/2} I_{m-1}(ax)dx \\ &= Q(a,b) + e^{(a^2+b^2)/2}\sum_{k=1}^{m-1}\left(\frac{b}{a}\right)^k I_k(ab) \end{aligned} \tag{4.5.13}$$

where

$$Q(a,b) \equiv Q_1(a,b) = e^{-(a^2+b^2)/2}\sum_{k=0}^{\infty}\left(\frac{a}{b}\right)^k I_k(ab) \qquad b > a > 0 \tag{4.5.14}$$

and $I_0(x)$ is the modified Bessel function of order zero, defined by equation 4.5.15, the α-th order modified Bessel function of the first kind

$$I_\alpha(x) = \sum_{k=0}^{\infty} \frac{(x/2)^{\alpha+2k}}{k!\,\Gamma(\alpha+k+1)} \qquad x \geq 0. \tag{4.5.15}$$

These theoretical "optimal" performance results are valid for linearly amplified, ideal Nyquist-filtered, stationary AWGN environments. The theoretical performance curves (see Figure 4.5.1) indicate that the $P_e = f(E_b/N_o)$ performance of the coherent BPSK system is identical to that of coherent QPSK and π/4-QPSK systems. The following example presents a physical insight and interpretation.

Example 4.5.4

Assume that a line-of-sight (LOS) radio system has a relatively constant received *C/N* of 9.5 dB. This *C/N* ratio is measured in the Nyquist (minimum) bandwidth of a BPSK system, having a transmission bit rate of f_b = 4 Mb/s. The only disturbance in this "stationary" system is AWGN.

(a) How much is the BER of this system?
(b) How much would the BER of this radio system be if the 4 Mb/s rate BPSK modem was replaced by an ideal 4 Mb/s rate QPSK modem?
(c) Would this "upgrade" in QPSK reduce the required RF bandwidth and offer a more spectrally efficient solution?
(d) How much would the BER performance be of an f_b = 8 Mb/s increased-rate QPSK system, operated in the same RF bandwidth as the original BPSK 4 Mb/s rate system?

Solution of Example 4.5.4

(a) From the $P_e = f(E_b/N_o)$ performance curves of Figure 4.5.1 and equation 4.5.6 we obtain that

$$\frac{E_b}{N_0} = \frac{C}{N} \cdot \frac{B_w}{f_b} = \frac{C}{N} \cdot \frac{4\text{MHz}}{4\text{Mb/s}} = \frac{C}{N} = 9.5\text{dB}$$

and that the corresponding BER = 10^{-5}.
(b) The *BER* = 10^{-5} (same as for BPSK) because the E_b/N_o requirement of QPSK and BPSK systems is the same.
(c) The "upgrade" to a 4 Mb/s rate QPSK modem reduces the RF bandwidth requirement from 4 MHz to 2 MHz, thereby offering a more spectrally efficient solution.
(d) If the bit rate is increased to 8 Mb/s, then the available E_b/N_o will be reduced, as $E_b = CT_b$. The bit duration is reduced. We have

$$\frac{E_b}{N_o} = \frac{C}{N} \cdot \frac{4\text{MHz}}{8\text{Mb/s}} = 9.5\text{dB} - 3\text{dB}$$

$$\frac{E_b}{N_o} = 6.5\text{dB}.$$

The corresponding performance, from Figure 4.5.1, is

$$\text{BER} = 10^{-3}.$$

4.5.3.2 Nonlinearly amplified $P_e = f(E_b/N_o)$ performance Linearly amplified systems require linear amplifiers, linear up/down converters, and linear automatic gain control (AGC) circuits. The theoretical $P_e = f(E_b/N_o)$ performance of these systems is the best; however, linear amplification is neither as power efficient (as defined by RF power to battery power ratio) nor as inexpensive or simple as nonlinear amplifier and nonlinear AGC circuit implementations.

Conventional QPSK, DQPSK, and π/4-QPSK systems require linear amplifiers because in a nonlinearly amplified system their spectrum spreads into adjacent channels. For this reason we focus on the performance of nonlinearly amplified GMSK and FQPSK systems. The $P_e = f(E_b/N_o)$ performance of nonlinearly amplified MSK and GMSK systems in a stationary AWGN environment is given in Figure 4.3.25 (see Table 4.5.3).

Results optimized by computer simulation and computer-aided design indicate that an "optimal" $BT_b = 0.25$ filtered GMSK coherent system is approximately 1.6 dB degraded at BER = 10^{-4}, as compared with ideal, linearly amplified QPSK. The performance of nonlinearly amplified (a "hard-limited" amplifier has been used as a "simplest" nonlinear amplifier) FQPSK and GMSK systems is compared with that of linearly amplified QPSK in Figure 4.3.33. From this figure we note that at $P_e = 10^{-4}$ FQPSK and GMSK systems have very similar degradation, whereas at $P_e = 10^{-2}$ the FQPSK system is about 0.7 dB better than $BT_b = 0.3$ filtered GMSK. This 0.7-dB advantage is significant in Rayleigh-faded channels, where the threshold BER performance is approximately BER = 10^{-2}.

4.6 PERFORMANCE IN COMPLEX INTERFERENCE-CONTROLLED MOBILE SYSTEMS

Performance of QPSK, π/4-DQPSK, GMSK, and FQPSK systems in a complex mobile interference environment is studied in this section. First we study and derive the performance in a "quasi-static" or slow Rayleigh-faded environment, and afterwards we present BER degradations and BER "error floors" caused by fast Rayleigh fading, that is, by fast Doppler and frequency-selective fading and delay spread. In particular, we cite and illustrate results for the probability of a bit error for QPSK, π/4-DQPSK, FQPSK, and GMSK systems and the probability of a symbol error for M-ary PSK and DPSK systems. These illustrative results provide reference material for a relatively speedy comparison of modulated linearly or nonlinearly amplified system performance in complex-interference, slow-fading, fast-fading (large Doppler), and delay-spread controlled environments.

The general system model used in our performance studies is illustrated in Figure

Table 4.5.3 Comparison of FQPSK-1, GFSK, and QPSK, including more advanced FQPSK-KF, FQPSK 4*4, and FQPSK 8*8. Additional comparative data are presented in Chapter 9 and Appendix A.3.

GFSK, FQPSK-1, FQPSK-KF, 4*4, and FQPSK 8*8 comparison.

	Standardized	Proposed higher speed			
Feature	**GFSK**	**FQPSK-1**	**FQPSK-KF**	**FQPSK 4*4**	**FQPSK 8*8**
Maximum bit rate in 1 MHz	1 Mb/s	1.0 Mb/s	1.5 Mb/s	2.8 Mb/s+	4.2 Mb/s
Required E_b/N_o for BER = 10^{-5} in Gaussian noise	19.3 (15.5*)dB	10.5 dB	15.7 dB	15 dB	19.8 dB

*With more complex receiver baseband processor.

BER = f(C/I) in Rayleigh fading and BER = f(E_bN_o)k in AWGN (stationary) for GFSK, FQPSK, and 4-FM constant-envelope NLA systems. The π/4-DQPSK BER performance is similar to that of FQPSK, however, it requires linear amplifiers.

Feature	**GFSK**	**FQPSK**	**QPSK**	**4-FM**
Bit rate in 1 MHz (−20dB)	1.0 MB/s	1.6 Mb/s	1.6 Mb/s	2 Mb/s
RF power @ 2.4GHz (max)	1 Watt (NLA)	1 Watt (NLA)	150 mW (linear)	1 Watt (NLA)
Required C/I for BER = 10^{-2} Rayleigh	20 dB	16 dB	16 dB	23 dB
Increase in peak radiation	0 dB	0 dB	5 to 10 dB	0 dB
Capacity (relative to GFSK)	100%	300%	300%	50?%

GaAs MMIC, 2.4GHz power efficiency; newest generation of power amplifiers (Teledyne TAE-1010a) measurement result with 3-V dc battery power. Amplifier measured at Teledyne during March 1994 to meet IEEE 802.11 spectrum mask.

	Efficiency (%)	**RF out (dBm)**
FQPSK saturated (NLA)	19.8	+24
DQPSK linear*	8.6	+21

*With more complex receiver baseband processor.
(From IEEE P802.11-94/51, March 1994.)

4.6.1. This "physical layer" system model is practically the same as that illustrated in Figure 3.8.1 for the IS-54 EIA North American TDMA cellular standard (EIA, 1990). The transmitted modulated signals (*Tx* 1 and *Tx* 2) in Figure 4.6.1 could be linearly or nonlinearly amplified signals. *Tx* 1 is the desired signal; *Tx* 2 is the cochannel interference (CCI) signal, which has characteristics similar to those of the main desired signal. The delay spread "τ" is a parameter, and the attenuation "*A*" of the delayed signal is set by the attenuator in the block diagram. The average power of the direct undelayed path is *C*, that of the delayed path is *D*, and that of the CCI signal is *I*. It is assumed that all these re-

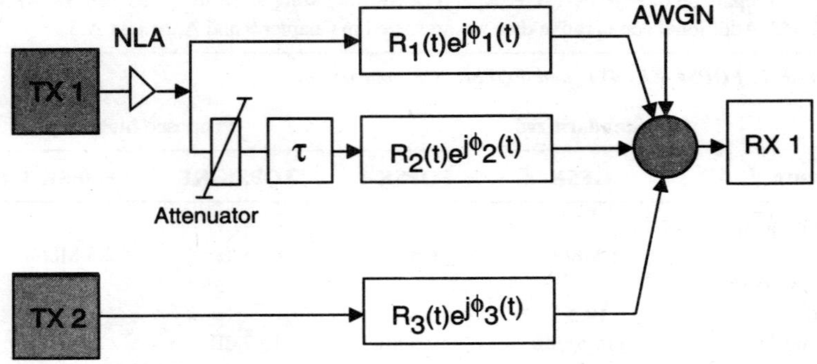

Figure 4.6.1 Rayleigh channel simulator for fast frequency-selective fades. This simulation model is used in the IS-54 standard (EIA, 1990). The desired transmitted signal Tx-1 could be linearly or nonlinearly amplified. The delayed Rayleigh signal has a delay spread of τ. This signal could be attenuated or amplified, relative to the desired signal. (a), TX1-RX1: The desired channel; (b), TX2: transmitter of cochannel interfering signal; (c), $R_i(t)$: Rayleigh envelope; (d), $\phi_i(t)$: uniform phase. For TX-1 a linear or nonlinear amplifier (NLA) may be used.

ceived signals C, D, and I are Rayleigh faded (each path has an independent Rayleigh fade simulator) and independent Doppler spread. For Doppler spread (f_D) bit rate products ($f_b = 1/T_b$) in the range of

$$f_D T_b \le 10^{-4}$$

we have a slow Raleigh-faded or "quasi-Rayleigh–faded" system because the phase shift during a bit duration is negligible. For high Doppler shift

$$f_D T_b \ge 10^{-2}$$

we have a fast Rayleigh-faded channel. In this case a BER degradation and even a BER floor may be caused by the fast Doppler shifts.

4.6.1 Rayleigh Fading and BER Performance in "Quasi-Static" Systems

We define a Rayleigh-faded system to be a "slow fading" or "quasi-static" Rayleigh channel if

$$f_D T_b < 10^{-4}.$$

For these slowly faded channels, Doppler shift (because of the speed of the mobile unit relative to the environment) has no degrading impact on the $P_e = f(E_b/N_o)$ performance. The terms "slowly faded" or "quasi-Rayleigh–faded" imply that the Rayleigh multiplicative process may be regarded as constant during at least one symbol interval.

The coherent receiver (demodulator) is assumed to "track out" all Doppler shifts, and the differential or discriminator receiver has no additional degradations relative to the case of $f_D = 0$ Doppler Rayleigh-faded systems.

The probability of *bit error*, P_e, as a function of E_b/N_o of ideal BPSK, FSK, QPSK, and π4-QPSK coherent systems, as well as of noncoherent DPSK and noncoherent, wideband, large-deviation index FSK systems, is illustrated in Figure 4.6.2. The performance of nonlinearly amplified FQPSK and GMSK systems with $BT_b = 0.3$ coherent demodulation is illustrated by dotted lines. We note that at high E_b/N_o, coherent PSK is 3 dB better than with DPSK on a slow Rayleigh-fading channel. The probability of *symbol error,* P_M, as a function of E_b/N_o of several coherent and differentially demodulated PSK (BPSK to 8-PSK) systems is presented in Figure 4.6.3.

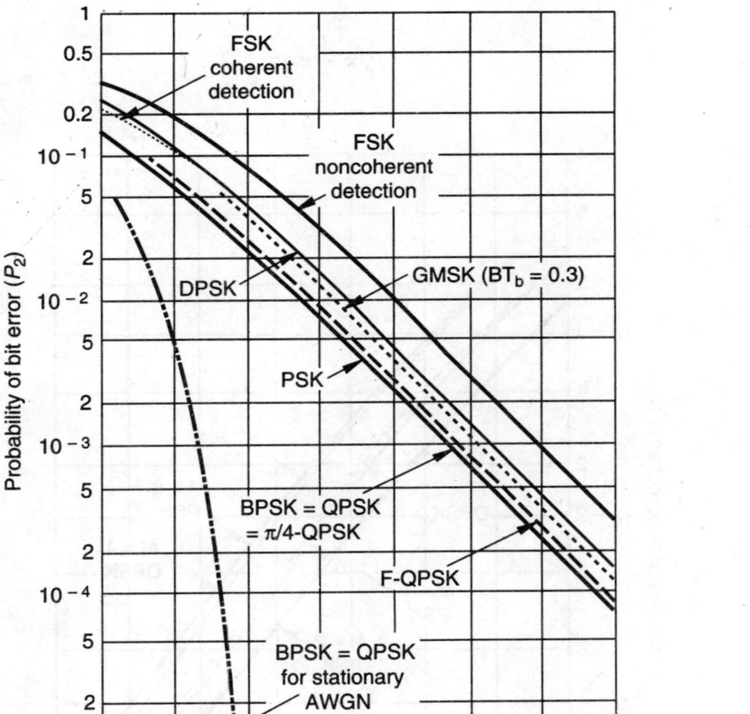

Figure 4.6.2 $P_e = f(E_b/N_o)$ performance of linearly amplified coherent BPSK, QPSK, π/4-QPSK, and wideband FSK and of noncoherent DPSK and FSK in a slow Rayleigh-faded system without delay spread (nonselective fading environment). Narrowband FSK and GFSK, such as specified by IEEE 802.11 has a much inferior performance, as illustrated in Appendix 3, Fig. A.3.9. Nonlinearly amplified coherent GMSK and FQPSK are also illustrated. The performance in an AWGN-stationary environment of BPSK and QPSK systems is also shown. (From Leung and Feher, 1990; Proakis, 1989.)

A comparison of Figures 4.6.2 and 4.6.3 reveals that the $P_e = f(E_b/N_o)$ and $P_M = f(E_b/N_o)$ performance curves of binary PSK (coherent or differentially coherent) systems are identical, whereas for QPSK (that is, 4-PSK) systems there is a 3 dB difference. This difference exists because in Gray-coded QPSK systems P_e (probability of bit error) is approximately two times lower than P_M (probability of symbol error). For a detailed explanation see Feher (1983).

4.6.1.1 Derivation of the $P_e = f(E_b/N_o)$ performance: BPSK and QPSK systems. Equations 4.5.7 and 4.5.8 represent the P_e performance of BPSK and QPSK signals for stationary AWGN environments. From these equations we note that the P_e performance as a function of E_b/N_o is the same for coherently demodulated BPSK and Gray-coded QPSK systems. It is given by

$$P_e = \frac{1}{2} \operatorname{erfc} \sqrt{\frac{E_b}{N_o}}. \tag{4.6.1}$$

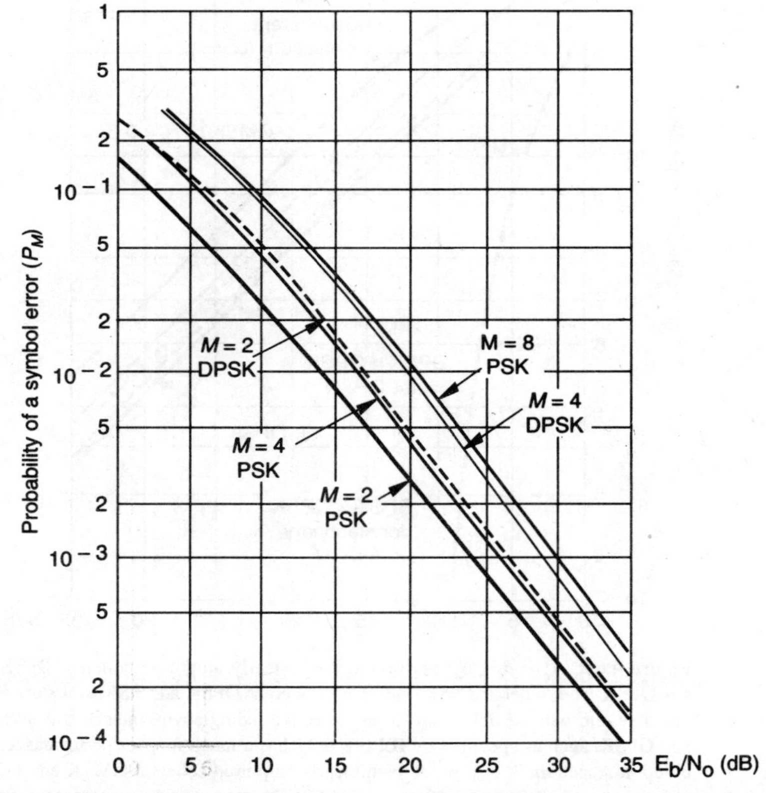

Figure 4.6.3 Probability of symbol error for PSK and DPSK in a slow Rayleigh-faded channel. (Based on Proakis, 1989.)

In this expression E_b/N_o represents the average bit energy ($E_b = C \cdot T_b$) to noise density (noise power in 1 Hz) ratio. The noise density N_o does not change with fading. The average received E_b in a stationary AWGN environment is constant, whereas it is a random variable in a multiplicative Rayleigh-faded environment. For this reason we must determine the average E_b/N_o, Γ in a Rayleigh-faded environment and use this faded "average E_b/N_o" in our derivation. In other words,

$$\Gamma = \bar{\gamma}_b = \frac{E_b}{N_o} E\left(\alpha^2\right) \tag{4.6.2}$$

where $E(\alpha^2)$ is the average value of α^2 and α is a Rayleigh-distributed random variable (representing the multiplicative fade).

To obtain the error probability in the slowly faded Rayleigh environment we note that

$$P_e\left(\gamma_b\right) = \frac{1}{2}\operatorname{erfc}\sqrt{\alpha^2 \frac{E_b}{N_o}} = \frac{1}{2}\operatorname{erfc}\sqrt{\gamma_b} \tag{4.6.3}$$

where

$$\gamma_b = \alpha^2 E_b / N_o. \tag{4.6.4}$$

To obtain the error probability for random α, we average $P_e(\gamma_b)$ over the probability density function of γ_b. That is, we compute the integral

$$P_e = \int_0^\infty P_e(\gamma_b) p(\gamma_b) d\gamma_b. \tag{4.6.5}$$

Since α is Rayleigh distributed, it follows that γ_b is chi-square distributed, and α^2 has a chi-square probability distribution with 2 degrees of freedom. It can be shown (Feher, 1987; Proakis, 1989) that

$$P_e(\gamma_b) = \frac{1}{\bar{\gamma}_b} e^{-\gamma_b/\bar{\gamma}_b} \tag{4.6.6}$$

where $\bar{\gamma}_b$ is the average E_b/N_o ratio defined by equation 4.6.2.

Substituting equation 4.6.6 into equation 4.6.5 and completing the integration for P_e of equation 4.6.1, we obtain the following final result:

$$P_e = \frac{1}{2}\left[1 - \sqrt{\frac{\Gamma}{1+\Gamma}}\right]. \tag{4.6.7}$$

For large values of Γ (average E_b/N_o) we simplify equation 4.6.7 and obtain

$$P_e \cong \frac{1}{4\Gamma}. \tag{4.6.8}$$

This expression is valid for coherently demodulated ideal BPSK and QPSK (Gray-coded) systems in a slow Raleigh-faded channel.

Example 4.6.1

How much is the P_e of a QPSK slow Rayleigh-faded system if average values of received E_b/N_o are 20 dB and 14.5 dB?

Solution for Example 4.6.1.

The average $E_b/N_o = \Gamma = 20$ dB. On a linear scale $\Gamma = 100$. Thus the average P_e based on equation 4.6.8 is

$$P_e = \frac{1}{4\Gamma} = \frac{1}{4*100} = 2.5\times10^{-3}$$

For $\Gamma = 13.0$ dB based on the simplified equation 4.6.8 for high E_b/N_o, we have:

$$P_e = \frac{1}{4\Gamma} = \frac{1}{4*19.95} = 2.5\times10^{-2}.$$

The accurate equation 4.6.7 for $\Gamma = 13$ dB (19.95 on a linear scale) leads to the following result:

$$P_e = \frac{1}{2}\left[1-\sqrt{\frac{\Gamma}{1+\Gamma}}\right] = \frac{1}{2}\left[1-\sqrt{\frac{19.95}{1+19.95}}\right] = 1.208\times10^{-2}.$$

Practically, both equations give the same results for relatively high Γ (average E_b/N_o). For Γ in the 10-dB range or below, equation 4.6.7 should be used. From Figure 4.6.2 we could also observe these results.

4.6.1.2 Theoretical performance comparison: slow Rayleigh-faded channels.

The $P_e = f(\Gamma) = f(\text{average } E_b/N_o)$ of coherent BPSK and QPSK systems is derived in Section 4.6.1.1. The derivations for differential and discriminator-detected DPSK and noncoherent MSK, including GMSK systems, are presented in Proakis (1989) and Feher (1987). The bit-error rates for sufficiently high Γ (≥ 10 dB) are given by the following simple final results:

$$P_e \approx \begin{cases} \frac{1}{4\Gamma} = \frac{1}{4\Lambda} \text{ coherent BPSK, QPSK, } \pi/4-\text{QPSK and MSK} \\ \frac{1}{2\Gamma} = \frac{1}{2\Lambda} \text{ coherent orthogonal FSK} \\ \frac{1}{2\Gamma} = \frac{1}{2\Lambda} \text{ DPSK and MSK with differential detection} \\ \frac{1}{\Gamma} = \frac{1}{\Lambda} \text{ noncoherent, orthogonal FSK} \end{cases}$$

In Feher (1987) and Liu (1992) it is demonstrated that for Rayleigh-faded channels the impact of Rayleigh-faded interference and noise on the P_e performance is the same. The average C/I (carrier-to-interference ratio) is

$$\left(\frac{C}{I}\right)_{\text{average}} = \Lambda = \text{average received carrier to interference ratio}$$

while

$$\left(\frac{E_b}{N_o}\right)_{\text{average}} = \Gamma = \text{average received carrier to noise ratio} = \frac{C}{N} \text{ in bit} - \text{rate bandwidth.}$$

4.6.2 BER Degradations and Error Floor Caused by Fast Doppler Spread

Let us consider the case of fast Rayleigh-faded channels, or environments in which the maximal Doppler shift (f_D) times bit duration (T_b) is relatively large, for example, $f_D T_b > 0.01$. In this case the FM noise caused by random Doppler shift of the unmodulated and the modulated carrier may be the predominant cause of bit errors.

For large $f_D T_b$ products, coherent demodulators tend to have a poor performance and exhibit high *error floors.* The error floor is defined as the persistent P_e (or BER) for even very large *C/N* and *C/I* ratios, that is, the errors are arising only from FM noise caused by fast Doppler effects. Ideally, coherent demodulators should "track out" this FM noise and thus cancel the impact of Doppler shift. However, for large $f_D T_b \geq 0.01$ it is very difficult to build carrier recovery and other synchronization loops because very wideband (relative to the data rate $f_b = 1/T_b$) phase-locked loops (PLLs) would have to be designed. Wideband PLLs could track the random phase variations caused by Doppler shifts, but such loops would also cause significant pattern jitter and intersymbol interference and thus P_e degradation. The analysis of coherent demodulation performance in a fast Doppler-fading channel is quite complex (Feher, 1987) and beyond the scope of this book.

The average P_e performance in slow Rayleigh-faded (quasi-Rayleigh) environments ($f_d T_b < 10^{-3}$), as well as fast Doppler, fast Rayleigh-fading environments, is illustrated in Figures 4.6.4 to 4.6.7. A performance comparison of differential and discriminator-detected MSK systems indicates that for fast Rayleigh-fading environments the P_e performance of the discriminator architecture is approximately 2.5 times better than that of the differential MSK demodulator. This can be explained by *physical-intuitive engineering* reasoning by observing that the discriminator detection mechanism (implementation) is practically equivalent to that of a differential detector having a delay line with very small ($d << T_b$) time delay. This implementation is able to track the Doppler-caused phase change faster than the conventional differential detector, having a delay of $d = T_b$ or $d = T_s$ (see Figures 4.3.3 and 4.3.6).

Example 4.6.2

How much is the average P_e performance, for short P_e, of (a) a differential and (b) a discriminator-detected ideal MSK system if the average $E_b/N_o = 40$ dB, the average $C/I = 40$

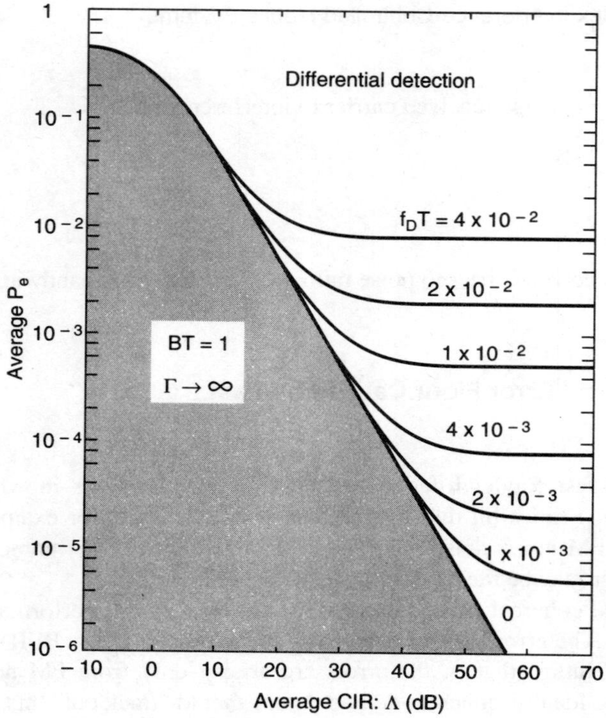

Figure 4.6.4 Average P_e versus Λ (carrier-to-interference ratio [CIR] of MSK in fast Rayleigh-faded channels. Normalized f_DT is a parameter. Γ is average carrier-to-noise (C/N) ratio. GMSK systems with $BT = 1$ are equivalent to differential-detection MSK. (From Feher, 1987a.)

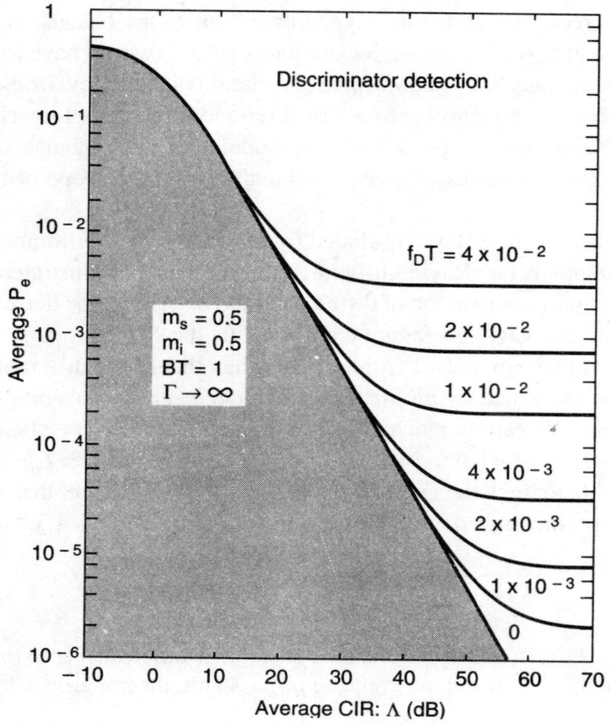

Figure 4.6.5 Average P_e versus CIR performance of MSK with discriminator detection in a Rayleigh-faded system. Normalized maximum Doppler frequency f_DT is a parameter. Γ is average carrier-to-noise ratio.

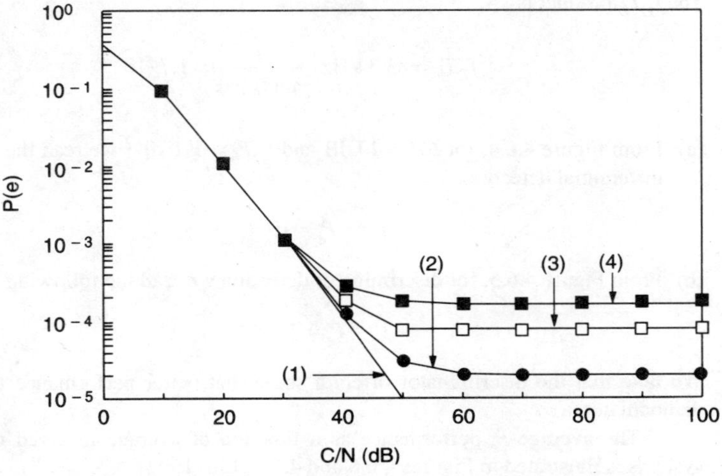

Figure 4.6.6 *P*(e) versus *C/N* of π/4-DQPSK in a flat, fast-fading, Rayleigh channel corrupted by AWGN; f_c = 850 MHz, f_s = 24 kBaud (48 kb/s), α = 0.2, *C/I* = ∞ dB, no time dispersion; *v* = (*1*), 0; (*2*), 25; (*3*), 50; (*4*), 75 (miles per hour). (From Liu, 1992.)

dB, the vehicle speed is v = 100 km/hour, the data transmission rate is f_b = 4.8 kb/s, and the transmitted carrier frequency if f_c = 900 MHz?

Solution for Example 4.6.2.

The Doppler frequency, from equation 3.2.8, is

$$f_D = \frac{vf}{c} = \frac{(3 \cdot 10^8[\mathrm{m/s}]:3600) \cdot 900 \cdot 10^6[\mathrm{Hz}]}{3 \cdot 10^8[\mathrm{m/s}]} = 83.34 \text{ Hz}.$$

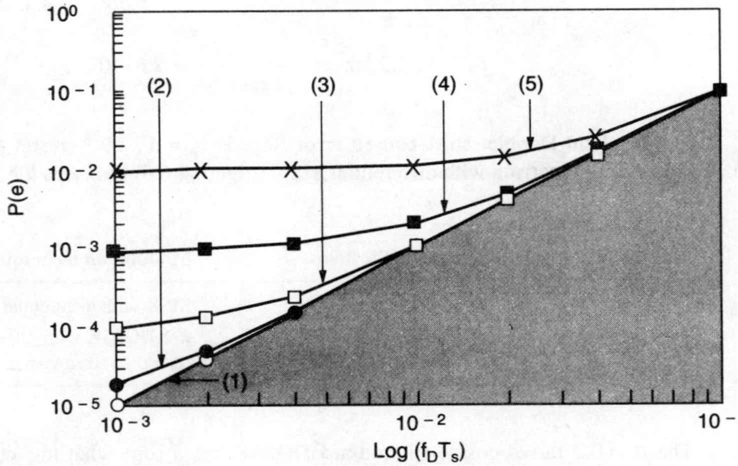

Figure 4.6.7 *P*(e) versus $f_D T_s$ of π/4-DQPSK in a flat, fast-fading, Rayleigh channel corrupted by CCI; f_c = 850 MHz, f_s = 24 kBaud, α = 0.2, *C/N* = ∞ dB, no time dispersion; *C/I* = (*1*), ∞; (*2*), 50; (*3*), 40; (*4*), 30; (*5*), 20 (dB).

The $f_D T_b$ product is

$$f_D T_b = 83.34 \text{ Hz} \cdot \frac{1}{4800 \text{ b/s}} = 1.7 \cdot 10^{-2}.$$

(a) From Figure 4.6.4, for $C/I = 40$ dB and $f_D T_b = 1.7 \cdot 10^{-2}$ we read the following result for differential detection:

$$P_e = 10^{-3}.$$

(b) From Figure 4.6.5, for discriminator detection we read the following result:

$$P_e = 7 \cdot 10^{-4}.$$

We note that the discriminator offers a somewhat better performance than the differential demodulator.

The average P_e performance as a function of average received C/N of $\pi/4$-DQPSK systems is illustrated in Figures 4.6.6 and 4.6.7 (Liu, 1992).

Example 4.6.3

An $f_s = 24$ kbaud, or $f_b = 48$ kb/s, rate system is assumed to operate at $f_c = 850$ MHz. How much is the P_e floor for a vehicle speed of 50 mph (approximately 80 km/hour)?

Solution for Example 4.6.3.

The corresponding Doppler shift, from equation 3.2.8, is

$$f_D = \frac{vf}{c} = 62.9 \text{ Hz}$$

and

$$f_D T_s = 62.9 \text{ Hz} \times \frac{1}{24\text{ksymb/s}} \approx 2.6 \cdot 10^{-3}.$$

The resultant Doppler shift–caused error floor is $P_e = 5 \cdot 10^{-5}$ (result from curve 3, Figure 4.6.6). A comparison with differential MSK (Figure 4.6.5) indicates the following:

	BER floor	**Modulation technique**
$f_D T_b = 1 \cdot 10^{-3}$	$5 \cdot 10^{-6}$	MSK with differential demodulation
$f_D T_s = 2.6 \cdot 10^{-3}$	$5 \cdot 10^{-5}$	$\pi/4$-DQPSK with differential demodulation ($\alpha = 0.2$ raised-cosine filtered)

The $\alpha = 0.2$ raised-cosine filtered $\pi/4$-DQPSK has a somewhat higher error floor than the MSK system. The average P_e degradation as a function of $f_D T_b$ for $\pi/4$-DQPSK systems is illustrated in Figure 4.6.7.

4.6.3 BER Performance and Fast-Fading, Delay-Spread, Frequency-Selective Systems

In relatively low symbol-rate systems (described in the previous section) the predominant cause of error floor and of P_e degradation is the large Doppler spread, or fast fading. In fast, flat faded Rayleigh systems, the symbol duration is much larger than the time delay spread; hence the impact of frequency selectivity on $P_e = f(C/I)$ or $P_e = f(E_b/N_o)$ degradation is negligible.

In high bit-rate systems the propagation-caused time delay spread τ may be a significant part of the symbol duration and contribute to significant intersymbol interference–caused P_e degradation and even to high error floors.

Figure 4.6.8 illustrates the average $P_{(e)}$ performance of coherent $\pi/4$-QPSK and differentially demodulated $\pi/4$-DQPSK systems for $\tau = 0.1\,T_s$ and $\tau = 0.4\,T_s$ (Liu and Feher, 1991 and 1992). In the graph in Figure 4.6.8, *C/D* denotes the ratio of average received

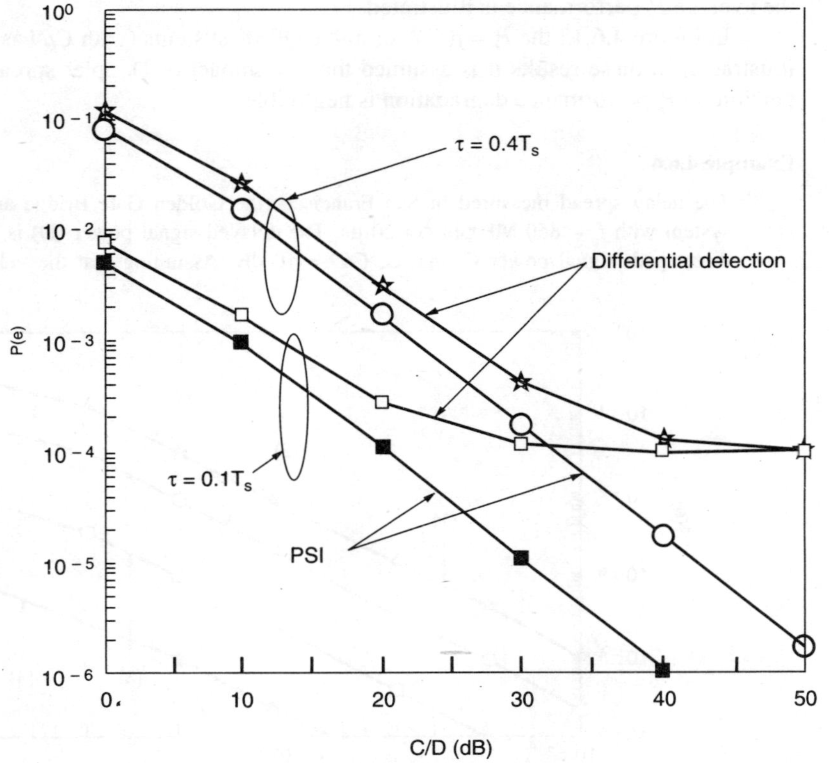

Figure 4.6.8 Error floors of fade-compensated $\pi/4$-QPSK and $\pi/4$-DQPSK in a frequency-selective fading channel as function of average desired carrier (*C*) to τ delayed carrier (*D*) ratio of *C/D* for $\tau = 0.1T_s$ and $0.4T_s$. The fading rate is assumed to be $f_D T_s = 3 \times 10^{-3}$. For the pilot symbol inserted (PSI) $\pi/4$-QPSK coherent receiver, the data power to pilot power ratio is $\beta = 10$. (From Liu and Feher, 1992.)

carrier power in the main carrier path to average delayed carrier power, corresponding to the system model in Figure 4.6.1. A coherent, pilot-symbol inserted (PSI), Doppler phase, noise-compensated receiver architecture is assumed. The PSI-compensated coherent demodulator has a "digital channel sounder" or "digital pilot" that is $B = 10$ times lower than the power of the modulated information data. From Figure 4.6.8 we observe that for $C/D = 0$ dB (in which case the delayed carrier has the same power as the direct path carrier) the BER *floor,* caused by delay spread, is 10^{-1} (approximately) for $\tau = 0.4\ T_s$, and it is 7×10^{-3} for $\tau = 0.1\ T_s$. For both cases the coherent demodulator is somewhat more robust with regard to time delay spread than the noncoherent demodulator. If the delayed signal path is attenuated, for example, $C/D = 20$ dB, then the degradation caused by delay spread (frequency-selective fading) is much lower. The $P_e = f(\tau/T_s)$ error floors of $\pi/4$-DQPSK systems for various values of C/D are presented in Figure 4.6.9.

In Figures 4.6.10 and 4.6.11 the $P_{(e)} = f(C/D)$ and $P_{(e)} = f(f_D T_s)$ are illustrated for an $f_s = 24$ kbaud, that is, $f_b = 48$ kb/s mobile system application (Liu, 1992). In these results the *combined* impact of Doppler spread (vehicle speed), delay spread, and C/D ratio on the average P_e performance is illustrated.

In Figure 4.6.12 the $P_e = f(C/I)$ of $\pi/4$-DQPSK systems (with C/N as a parameter) is illustrated. In these results it is assumed that the impact of Doppler spread and time dispersion on P_e performance degradation is negligible.

Example 4.6.4

The delay spread measured in San Francisco (the Golden Gate Bridge area) of a cellular system with $f_c = 850$ MHz is $\tau = 20$ μs. The delayed signal power (D) is 10 dB below the direct path signal power C, that is, $C/D = 10$ dB. Assuming that the vehicle speed is 80

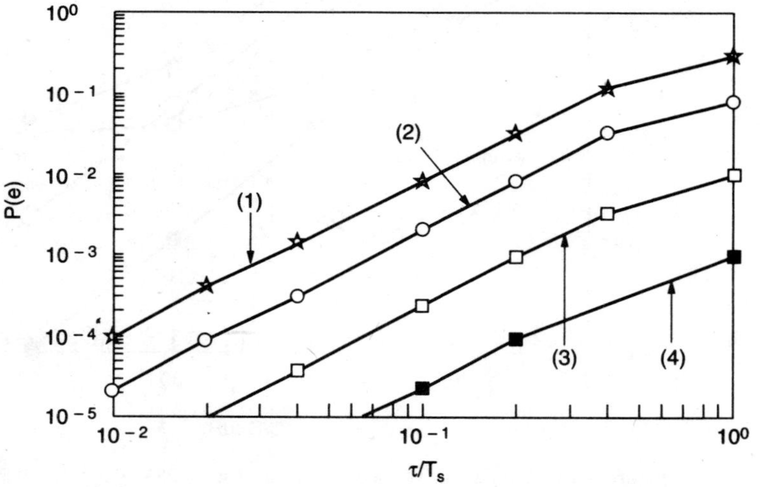

Figure 4.6.9 P(e) versus τ/T_s of $\pi/4$-DQPSK in a frequency-selective slowly fading channel. $f_c = 850$ MHz, $f_s = 24$ kBaud, $\alpha = 0.2$, $C/N = \infty$ dB, no Doppler spread. C/D = (*1*), 0; (*2*), 10; (*3*), 20; (*4*), 30 (dB). (From Liu, 1992.)

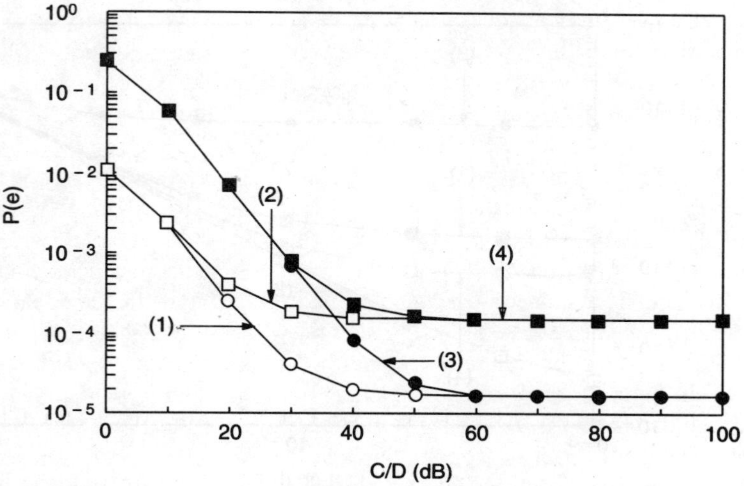

Figure 4.6.10 P(e) versus *C/D* of π/4-QPSK in a frequency-selective fast fading channel. $f_c = 850$ MHz, $f_s = 24$ kBaud, $\alpha = 0.2$, $C/I = \infty$ dB, $C/N = \infty$ dB. *(1)*, $\tau/T = 0.1$, $v = 25$ mph; *(2)*, $\tau/T = 0.1$, $v = 75$ mph; *(3)*, $\tau/T = 0.5$, $v = 25$ mph; *(4)*, $\tau/T = 0.5$, $v = 75$ mph. (From Liu, 1992.)

km/hour, determine the P_e performance of an $f_b = 8$ kb/s rate (approximate rate of a standard ADC system) operated in a $C/I = 30$ dB environment.

Solution for Example 4.6.4

For this complex mobile environment we must refer to Figure 4.6.11 and compute the $f_D T_s$ and τ/T_s parameters as follows:

$$f_D = vf/c = 62.9\text{Hz}; \quad T_s = 1/24\text{kBaud} = 41.7\mu\text{s}; \quad \tau/T_s = 20\mu\text{s}; \quad 41.7\mu s = 0.48;$$

$$f_D T_s = 62.9[\text{Hz}] \cdot \frac{1}{24\text{kBaud}} = 0.0026 = 2.6 \cdot 10^{-3}.$$

In Figure 4.6.11 we use curve No. 3 for $\tau/T_s = 0.5$ and $C/D = 10$ dB, since this curve presents the closest parameter values. For $f_D T_s = 2.6 \cdot 10^{-3}$, we read the P_e value, $P_e = 6 \cdot 10^{-2}$. This high error ratio is predominantly caused by the large delay spread τ. From curve No. 3 we note that the $f_D T_s$ parameter does not have such a significant factor as delay spread. Adaptive equalization would be required to reduce the $6 \cdot 10^{-2}$ error floor.

4.6.4 Optimal Bit Rate (f_b) in Delay-Spread and Fast Doppler Spread and Rayleigh Channels

In some applications, delay spread or fast Doppler, or both, may be the cause of error floors. The system architect may have the flexibility to optimize the bit rate of the system. An illustrative bit-rate optimization curve is shown in Figure 4.6.13. The average P_e should be optimized (minimized). An average $C/N = \Gamma = 30$ dB, a maximal Doppler shift of $f_D = 36$ Hz, and a delay spread $\tau = 1$ μs (with $C/D = 0$ dB) are assumed. Computer-

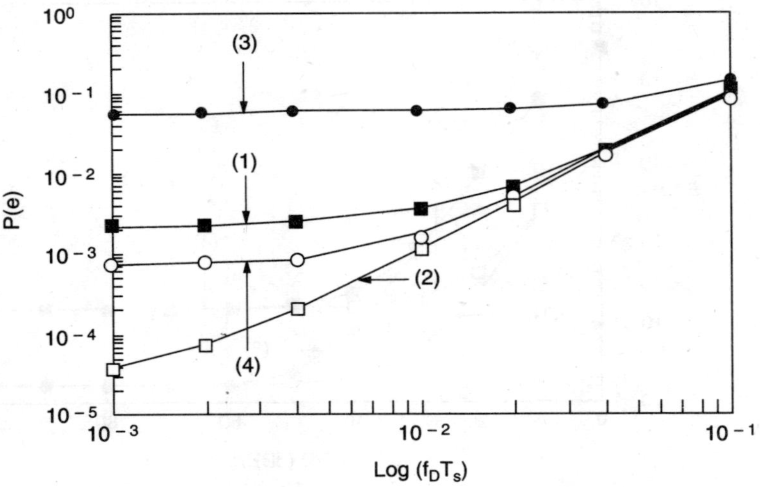

Figure 4.6.11 $P(e)$ versus $f_D T_s$ of $\pi/4$-DQPSK in a frequency-selective fast fading channel. $f_c = 850$ MHz, $f_s = 24$ kBaud, $\alpha = 0.2$, $C/I = \infty$ dB, $C/N = \infty$ dB. *(1)*, $\tau/T = 0.1$, $C/D = 10$ dB; *(2)*, $\tau/T = 0.1$, $C/D = 30$ dB; *(3)*, $\tau/T_s = 0.5$, $C/D = 10$ dB; *(4)*, $\tau/T = 0.5$, $C/D = 30$ dB. (From Liu and Feher, 1991.)

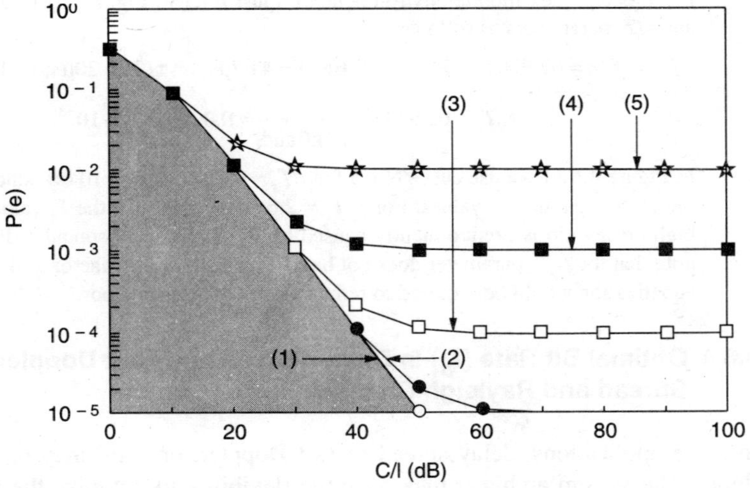

Figure 4.6.12 P(e) versus C/I of $\pi/4$-DQPSK in a flat slowly fading channel corrupted by AWGN and CCI. $f_c = 850$ MHz, $f_s = 24$ kBaud, $\alpha = 0.2$. Negligible Doppler spread and time dispersion. C/N = *(1)*, ∞; *(2)*, 50; *(3)*, 40; *(4)*, 30; *(5)*, 20 (dB) (From Liu and Feher, 1991.)

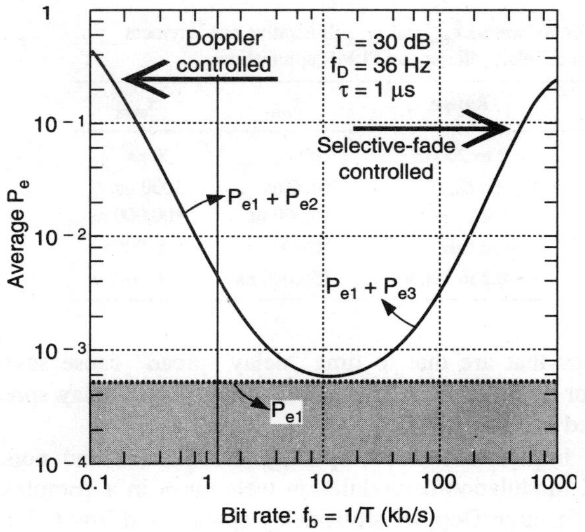

Figure 4.6.13 Average P_e versus transmission bit rate of MSK with differential detection. Γ is average CNR. f_D is maximum Doppler frequency. Selective fade (delay spread) and Doppler fade-controlled regions are shown. (From Feher, 1987a.)

aided design results indicate that for these system parameters an f_b = 10 kb/s rate, differential MSK would provide an optimal BER of 4×10^{-4}. For lower bit rates, for example, f_b = 1 kb/s, the BER becomes 9×10^{-3}. This increased BER is caused by relatively fast fades, that is, high $f_D T_b$ products. For larger bit rates, for example, f_b = 1000 kb/s, the BER = 2.5×10^{-1}. This large error floor is caused by the assumed τ = 1 μs delay spread. Similar graphs and optimizations have been derived for many other applications (Feher, 1987).

4.7 ADVANTAGES OF COHERENT DEMODULATION OVER NONCOHERENT SYSTEMS

In previous sections we described several coherent and noncoherent (discriminator and differential detection) demodulation systems. In this section we compare and demonstrate the performance advantages of coherent mobile radio systems and discuss integrated modem and radio architectures.

Our examples are for outdoor public land mobile radio (*PLMR*) (approximately 1 km to 80 km radius), *cellular* (about 1 km to 10 km radius), and *microcellular* (2 m to 1 km radius) *personal communications system* (PCS) applications. Relatively low bit-rate systems operated in a high Doppler-shift environment—for example, f_b = 4.8 kb/s, v = 100 km/h, and f_c = 900 MHz—have efficient Rayleigh fades and are described in Section 4.6.2, where we demonstrate that noncoherent systems are more effective than coherent ones. In this section we focus on relatively high bit-rate systems, for example, $f_b \geq 40$ kb/s (and up to 20 Mb/s), operated in a slow Rayleigh-fading environment, for example, v = 6 km/hour maximum and f_c = 2.4 GHz or f_c = 6 GHz. For these types of microcellular or other, longer distance (r = 100 m to 30 or even 50 km, such as wireless, "fixed point" "omni" applications) the Doppler- and carrier recovery–caused degradations are negligi-

Table 4.7.1 Delay-spread τ_{rms} and τ_{max} illustrative measurement results for microcellular, cellular and PLMR applications.

Application	Range	τ_{rms}	τ_{max}
Microcellular	r = 2 to 200 m	100 ns	500 ns
	"worst case"	1000 ns	3000 ns
Cellular	r = 0.2 to 10 km	10,000 ns	100,000 ns
	"worst case"	40,000 ns	200,000 ns
PLMR	r = 0.2 to 100 km	150,000 ns	600,000 ns

ble, whereas the degradations that are due to time "delay spread" cause severe BER floors or BER degradation, or both. Typical, reasonable "worst case" delay spread measurement results are illustrated in Table 4.7.1.

The performance and implementation complexity of coherent and noncoherent QPSK, FQPSK, and GMSK modulation/demodulation techniques in a complex mobile system environment, including large Doppler shift, delay spread, and low *C/I*, are compared. In Table 4.7.2 and in Feher (1993) we demonstrate that for large $f_D T_b$ products, where f_D is the Doppler shift and T_b is the bit duration, noncoherent (discriminator detector or differential demodulation) systems have a lower BER floor than their coherent counterparts. For significant delay spreads, for example, $\tau_{rms} > 0.4\ T_b$ and low *C/I*, coherent systems outperform noncoherent systems. However, the synchronization time of coherent systems is longer than that of noncoherent systems.

Spectral efficiency, overall capacity, and related issues of hardware complexity for these systems are also highlighted in Table 4.7.2. We demonstrate that coherent systems have a simpler overall architecture and are more robust in an RF drift environment. Additionally, the prediction tools, computer simulations, and analyses of coherent systems are simpler. In conclusion, we note that coherently demodulated radio or modem receivers have significant performance advantages as compared with noncoherent systems.

4.8 ADVANCED MODULATION METHODS

Numerous publications, patents, and books contain detailed descriptions of more advanced modulation techniques and concepts than the ones presented in the previous sections. The more advanced modulation techniques may be categorized as multistate or multilevel modems, including trellis-coded modems. Frequently used or referenced techniques are briefly reviewed in this section. See Table 4.8.1 Abbreviations, definitions, and illustrative reference books include the following:

QAM: Quadrature amplitude modulation (Lce and Messerschmitt, 1988)

M-QAM: Multi-state or Multi-ary (M-ary) QAM (for example, 16-QAM, 64-QAM, 256-QAM, and 512-QAM) (Feher, 1987; Wu and Feher, 1993)

Table 4.7.2 Performance and hardware comparison of coherent and differential systems.

Maximal bit-rate and delay-spread τ_{rms} issues	***Coherent QPSK or FQPSK (or GMSK, which is similar; however, performance is worse.)***	***Differential DQPSK (or DGMSK)***
τ_{rms} "worst case" 1μs		
$\tau_{rms} = 200$ ns		
BER = 10^{-2} floor due to τ_{rms}/T_s	$\tau_{rms}/T_s = 0.2$	$\tau_{rms}/T_s = 0.15$
$P_{(e)}$ = C/I degrad(addit) of 1 dB due to τ_{rms}/T (4*more sensitive than for "floor")	$\tau_{rms}/T_s = 0.075$ QPSK F-QPSK is higher abut 50%	$\tau_{rms}/T_s = 0.05$
Maximum bit rate f_b		
For 10^{-2} error floor 1μs (200 ns)	600 kb/s (3 Mb/s)	300 kb/s (1.5 Mb/s)
For 1 dB τ_{rms} caused degradation 1μs (200 ns)	150 kb/s (750 kb/s)	75 kb/s (375 kb/s)
Capacity issues based on C/I = 3 dB (CCI advantage)	BER = 10^{-2} C/I = 15 dB (Rayleigh)	BER = 10^{-2} C/I = 18 dB
Normalized Relative Capacity		
Based on $k = 9$ to $k = 7$ reuse	100%	70% (30% loss)
Based on WER and throughput	100%	20% (80% loss)
Spectral efficiency ACI and BPF versus LPF caused advantage, i.e., lower noise, BW-coherent receiver (normalized to coherent)	100%	60%
Increased bit rate or cell coverage/adaptive equalization	Relatively simple, low-cost DSP/SW adaptive equalizer could increase rate (coverage)	Very costly if at all feasible adaptive equalization technology (theory not well understood; requires original new research)
Bit rate (PHY) change without loss of performance (within range)	Automatic SW (software controlled) in BBP	Very difficult; could require change of IF-BPF
Spectral efficiency for ACI = −20 dB nonlinearly amplified radio	F-QPSK = 1.42 b/s/Hz GMSK = 0.94 b/s/Hz $BT_b = 0.5$ and 0.98 b/s/Hz for $BT_b = 0.3$	Approximately 0.7 b/s/Hz depending on BPF complexity
Synchronization time (CR) (relative to no CR—differential loss of frame efficiency for 1000 or 10,000 bit word (packet)	50 bits:1000 = 5% (max 100 bits = max 10% 50 bits:10,000 = 0.5% max 100 bits for CR = max. 1% a disadvantage. Parallel CR and STR design could eliminate this drawback.	Potential of 1% to 10% packet/synch time advantage(?); however, could be lost because of BPF transient ringing. Synchronization time advantage could be lost because of DC compensation to saturation time requirement.

(continued)

Table 4.7.2 (cont.) Performance and hardware comparison of coherent and differential systems.

Maximal bit-rate and delay-spread t_{rms} issues	***Coherent QPSK or F-QPSK (or GMSK, which is similar; however, performance is worse.)***	***Differential DQPSK (or DGMSK)***
Normalized Relative Capacity		
Threshold capture effect (discriminator-impulse noise)	No problem	Potential problem in the critical BER = 10^{-2} range with discriminator.
Tools (prediction)	Well known	Much more involved as IFBPF imperfect; impact of frequency tolerance GMSK $BT_b = 0.3$ very difficult.
RF oscillator drifts include synthesizer, impact on BER, DC restoration.	Simple	Very costly; potential danger, like in DECT
Additional down conversion/filters	Not required	Very costly. Extra stage could be required because of lower IF and BPF problems.
Carrier recovery requirements	Yes. Simple pilot in band and other Costas . . . well-known techniques. No Doppler problem. Low power solution. GSM, ADC, other cellular have it.	No need for CR; advantage
DC power, extra for CR	Could be marginally higher for demand alone	Discriminator power requirement is smaller than coherent. However, DC battery power advantage could be lost because of LO or synthesizer-DC compensation requirement.
IC Chips, Trend	Most manufact. companies developing QUAD (coherent struct.)	Noncoherent discrimination today cheaper however, overall radio extra IF, BPF, DC compensation not evident
Overall cost/DC or power estimate	About the same as noncoherent receiver (total radio) with new technology	About the same
Radio frequency 900 MHz; 1.9 GHz, 2.4 GHz bit rate variation	Same architecture for both radio frequencies; flexible bit rate	Could require in some applications extra expensive IF stage. Does not lead to software driven bit rate change

TCM: Trellis-coded modulation (Proakis, 1989)
CPM: Continuous phase modulation (Feher, 1987)
CPFSK: Continuous phase frequency shift keying (Lee and Messerschmitt, 1988)

The *objective* of these modems is to attain increased spectral efficiency or to reduce the *C/N* requirement for a specified BER, or both. In most cases, advanced M-state QAM and TCM systems are suitable for linearly amplified systems. Assuming a linear channel

Table 4.8.1 *C/N* and E_b/N_o requirements for BER = 10^{-4} in a stationary AWGN environment. *C/N* is specified in the double-sided Nyquist bandwidth. Theoretical and practical spectral efficiency data for conventional BPSK to 64-QAM and for FBSK, FQPSK, and FQAM patented systems are also presented.

Requirements	BPSK	QPSK	16-QAM	64-QAM
C/N in (dB) required for BER = 10^{-4}	8.4	11.4	19.2	25.5
E_b/N_o (in dB) required for BER = 10^{-4}	8.4	8.4	13.2	17.8
Theoretical spectral efficiency	1	2	4	6
Practical spectral efficiency in linearly amplified systems (b/s/Hz)	0.8	1.6	3.2	5
Practical spectral efficiency in nonlinearly amplified systems (b/s/Hz)	0.3	0.7	1–1.5	2–2.5
Practical spectral efficiency of FBPSK, FQPSK and FQAM nonlinearly amplified systems (b/s/Hz)	0.7	1.5	3	4.5

(transmitter/receiver), the theoretical Shannon limit could be approached with multistate signaling (Figure 4.8.1).

In general, linearly amplified M-ary QAM systems such as 16-QAM, 64-QAM, and 256-QAM are more spectrally efficient than theoretical, linearly amplified QPSK, which has a fundamental limit of 2 b/s/Hz. For example, we note from Figure 4.8.1 that a linearly amplified 256-QAM system has a theoretical spectral efficiency of 8 b/s/Hz. Nonlinearly amplified systems such as GMSK, while more battery efficient in terms of RF-to-DC (direct current power, have a much smaller practical spectral efficiency of about 1 b/s/Hz. We can ask ourselves the following question: Why are the American, European, and Japanese second-generation digital PCS and cellular systems using GMSK with only 1 b/s/Hz or linearly amplified $\pi/4$-DQPSK with about 1.5 b/s/Hz? In Chapter 9, detailed answers to this question can be found. Here it is sufficient to state that higher-state signaling systems such as 16-QAM and trellis-coded 64-QAM may require very linear amplifiers and a considerably higher *C/N* than the simpler QPSK or GMSK type of system. For increased spectral efficiency at a BER that equals 10^{-4}, significantly increased *C/N* and E_b/N_o are required (Figures 4.8.2 and 4.8.3). From Table 4.8.1 we note that 16-QAM has an approximately 8-dB (19.2 dB versus 11.4 dB) increased *C/N* when compared with QPSK. The corresponding increased E_b/N_o requirement is 13.2 dB – 8.4 dB = 4.8 dB.

In previous sections we explained that in Rayleigh-faded channels the BER = *f*(*C/N*) requirement is practically the same as the BER = *f*(*C/I*) requirement—in other words, that interference has the same impact as noise. An 8-dB higher *C/N* or *C/I* requirement could lead to reduced capacity of cell layouts because most systems are interference-controlled. Thus, increased spectral efficiency in b/s/Hz does not necessarily lead to increased overall system or network spectral efficiency in terms of b/s/Hz/m^2.

In several PLMR and mobile applications it may be essential to achieve a high spectral efficiency in terms of b/s/Hz, even if this increased efficiency leads to increased *C/N* or *C/I* requirements, or both, and affects cell configurations. In such cases, M-ary modulation techniques combined with trellis-coded modulation can be used.

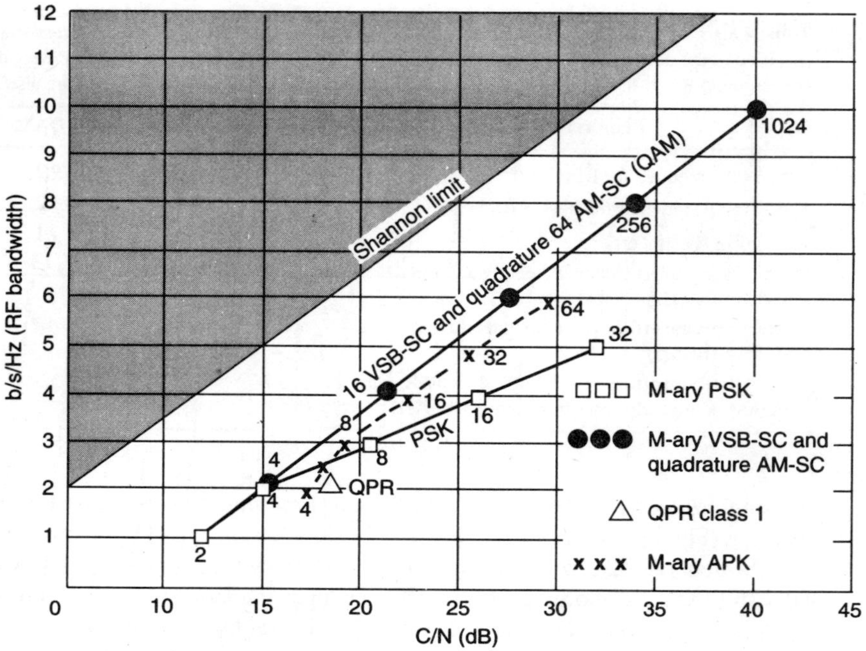

Figure 4.8.1 Bit rate efficiency (in bits per second per hertz) of M-ary coherent PSK, VSB-SC, quadrature AM-SC, APK, and QPR systems as a function of the available *C/N* at $P(e) = 10^{-8}$. The average *C/N* is specified in the double-sided Nyquist bandwidth, which equals the symbol rate. Ideal $\alpha = 0$ filtering and linearly amplified system is assumed. (From Feher, 1987a.)

In Figures 4.8.4 and 4.8.5, linearly and nonlinearly amplified architectures of various QAM or "multistate" QPSK systems are illustrated. For nonlinearly amplified power-efficient applications, patented FQAM (previously known as SQAM) systems by Feher and others are suitable (Subasinghe-Dias and Feher, 1994). In Figures 4.8.6 and 4.8.7 the spectrum and BER $= f(E_b/N_o)$ performance of nonlinearly amplified FQAM systems is illustrated (Feher, 1987). Illustrative measured eye diagrams of spectrally efficient 64-FQAM and 225-QPRS systems are shown in Figures 4.8.8 and 4.8.9.

Trellis-Coded Modulation. Signal constellations of trellis-coded modems contain more signal points, that is, have a larger constellation (more signaling states) than required for modulation schemes without trellis coding. For instance, a 16-state QAM architecture is converted to a trellis-coded 32-QAM constellation. The additional points in the constellation allow for redundancy and can be used for detecting and correcting errors. Convolutional coding, combined with the trellis-coded modulator, introduces dependency between successive signaling points (Yacoub, 1993).

Research of combined modulated and coded systems led to the development of *power-efficient systems that have a spectral efficiency of more than 2 bits/s/Hz.* Ungerboeck (1982) introduced channel coding with multilevel phase signals. Ungerboeck's ob-

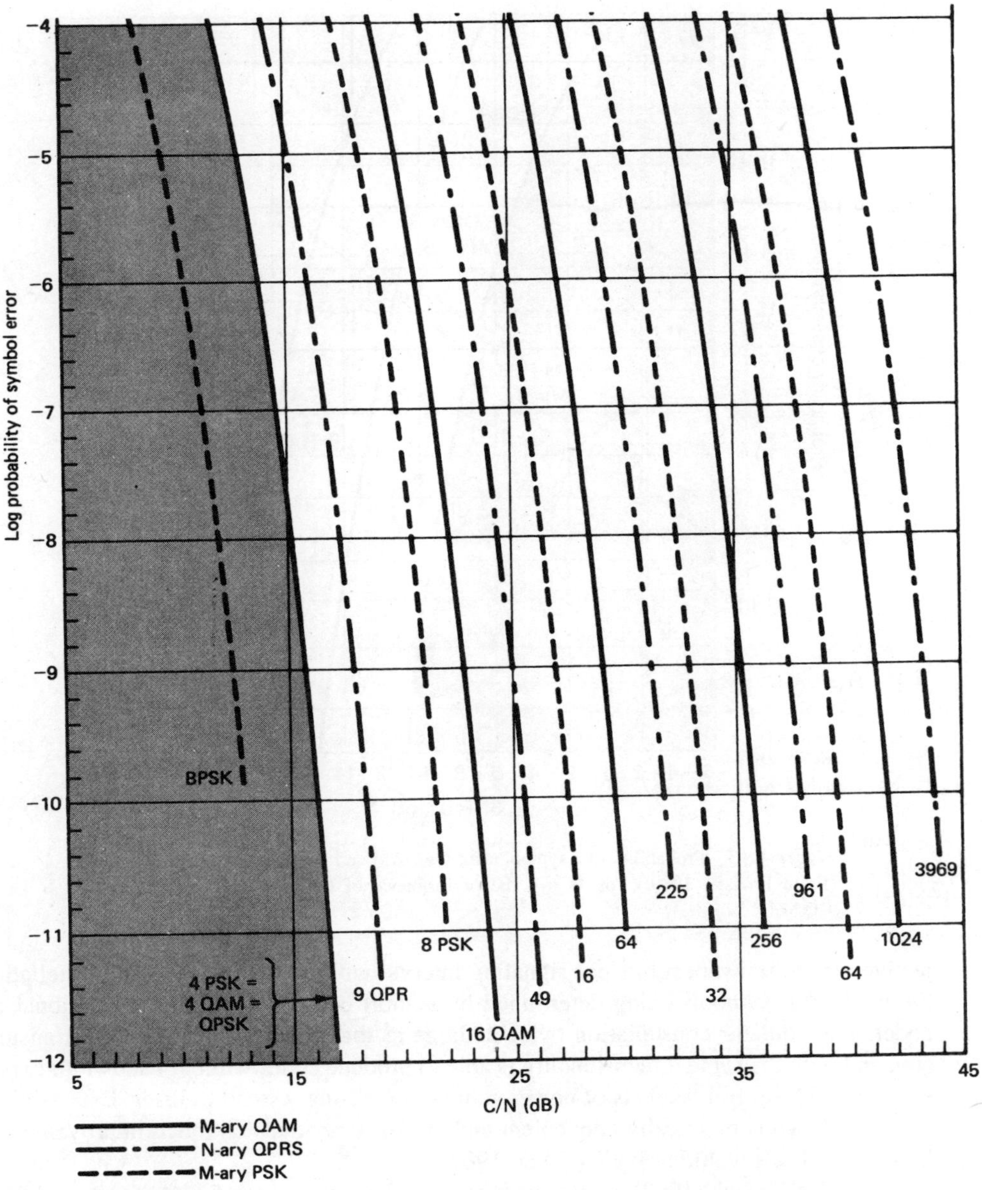

Figure 4.8.2 Probability of error performance curves of M-ary PSK, M-ary QAM, and N-ary QPR modulation systems versus the carrier-to-thermal noise ratio. White Gaussian noise in the double-sided Nyquist bandwidth in a linearly amplified system is specified. (From Feher, 1987a.)

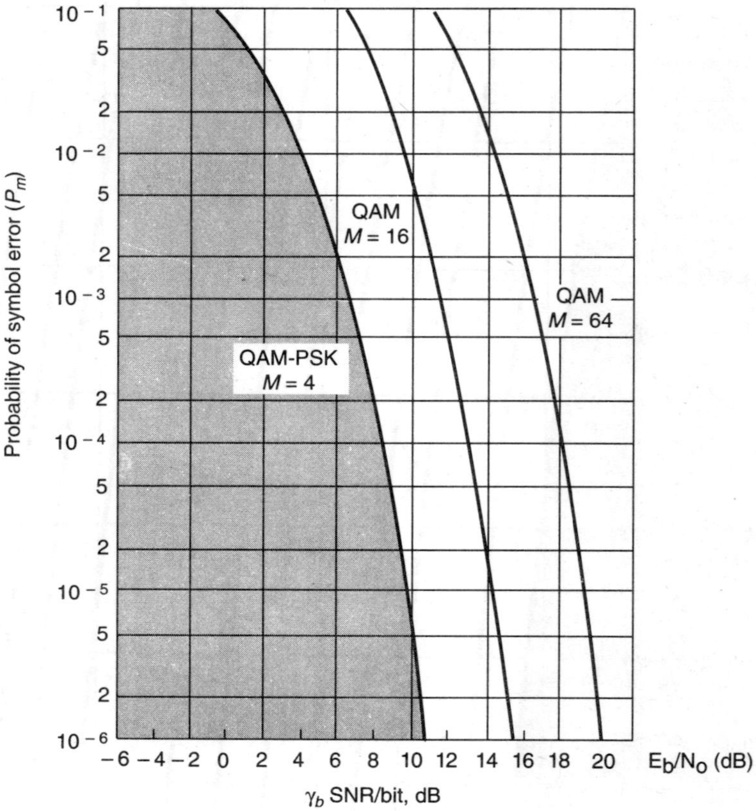

Figure 4.8.3 Probability of a symbol error for QAM and PSK in the 10^{-1} to 10^{-6} range. (From Proakis, 1989.) For $M = 4$ the performance of QPSK is the same as that of 4-QAM.

jective was to transmit n bits per signaling interval with a 2^{n+1}-ary QAM constellation, the modulator symbols being determined by a short constraint-length convolutional encoder. A modulator constellation twice as large as that necessary for uncoded transmission and with the same dimensionality is able to produce codes without bandwidth expansion and with several decibels of power gain for surprisingly small trellises. Expansion by a factor of two is practically convenient and affords essentially as much improvement as larger signal sets would provide (Feher, 1987).

In Ungerboeck (1982) a range of spectral efficiencies (up to 5 bits per interval) with expanded signal sets was analyzed. Lebowitz and Rhodes (1981) have studied a related special case (coded 8-PSK) for application in band-limited, nonlinear satellite channels and have found the scheme to have robust performance relative to its uncoded counterpart (QPSK). Taylor and Chan (1981) have also provided simulation results for rate 3/4–coded 8-PSK for various channel bandwidths and Travelling Wave Tube (TWT) operating points.

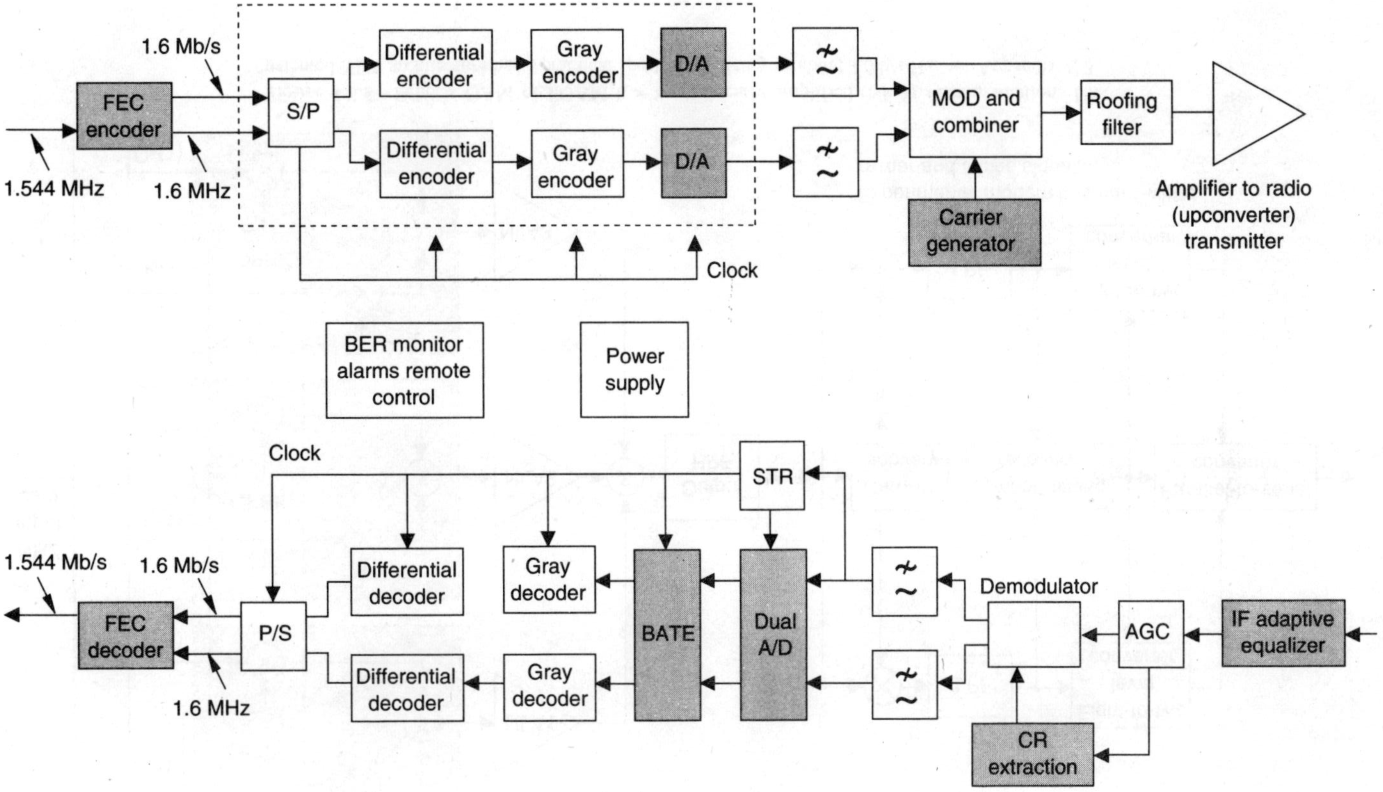

Figure 4.8.4 256-QAM block diagram of a 1.544 Mb/s rate system. With forward error correction we designed a transmission rate of 1.6 Mb/s. Our baseband adaptive transversal equalizer (BATE) has over 200 taps. A spectral efficiency of 6.66 b/s/Hz (at 55 dBr) is attained. Design by Dr. Feher and Associates, Digcom, Inc. for Karkar Electronics. (From Feher, 1987a.)

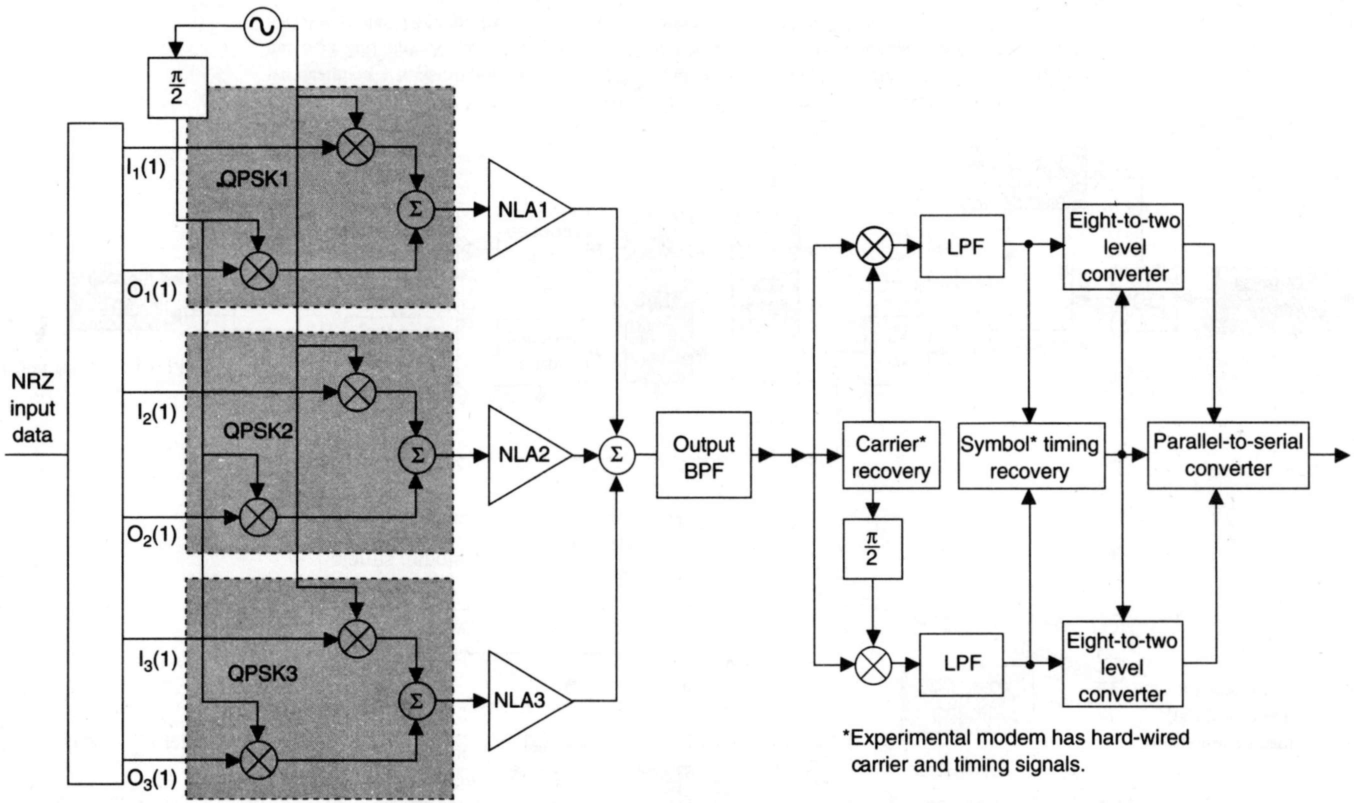

Figure 4.8.5 Feher's QAM or FQAM 8 × 8 nonlinearly amplified (NLA) system solution. This patented NLA architecture has a practical spectral efficiency of about 4.5 b/s/Hz; see Appendix A.3.

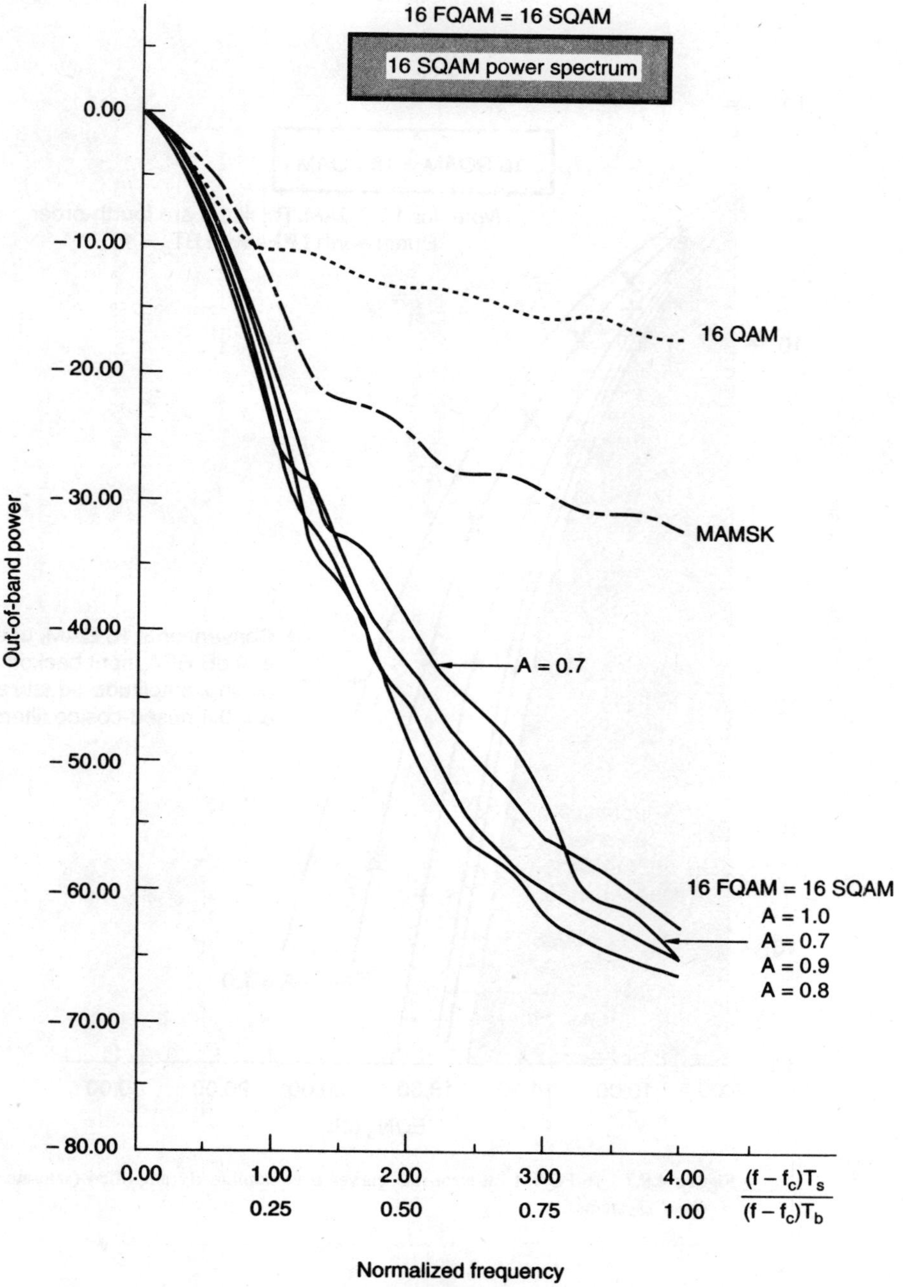

Figure 4.8.6 Nonlinearly amplified FQAM (previously known as SQAM [Feher, 1987]) spectrum. (Patented technology, see Appendix A.3.)

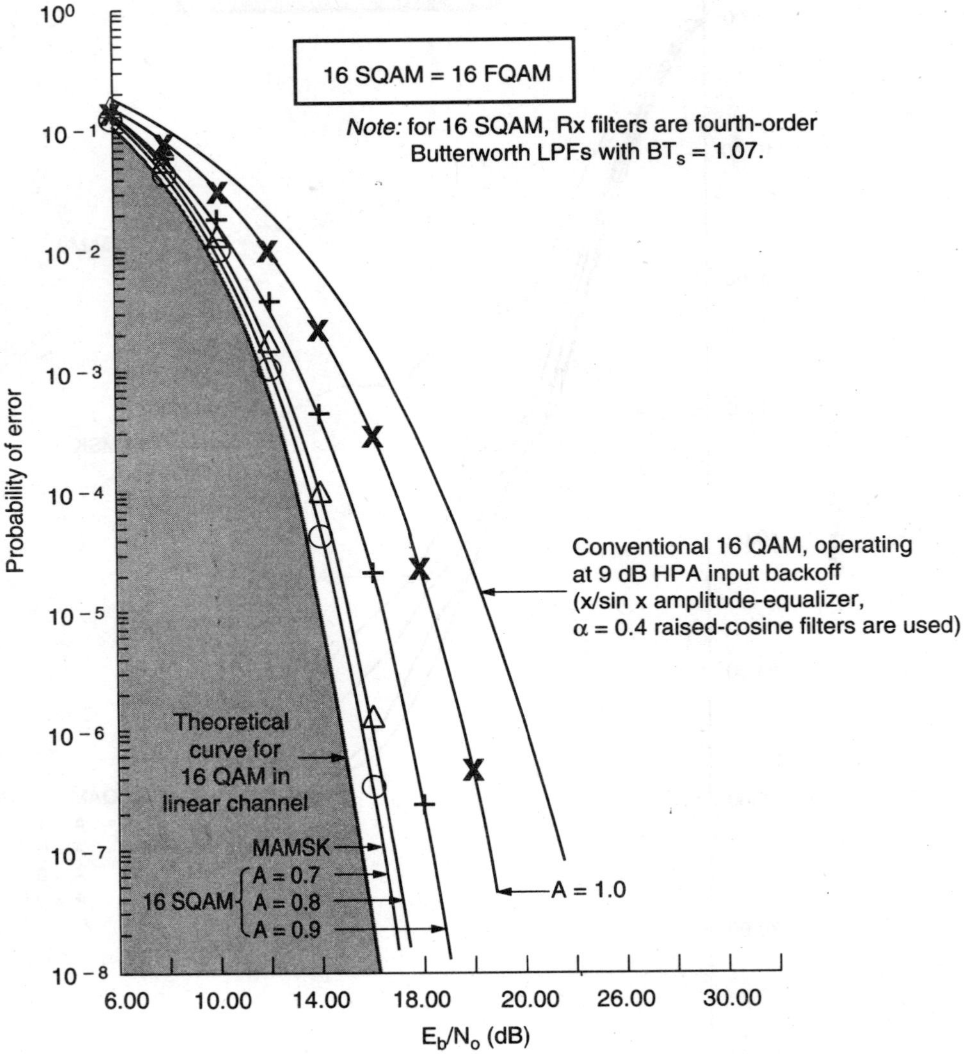

Figure 4.8.7 16-FQAM bit-error-rate curves over nonlinearly amplified (saturated or "C class") systems.

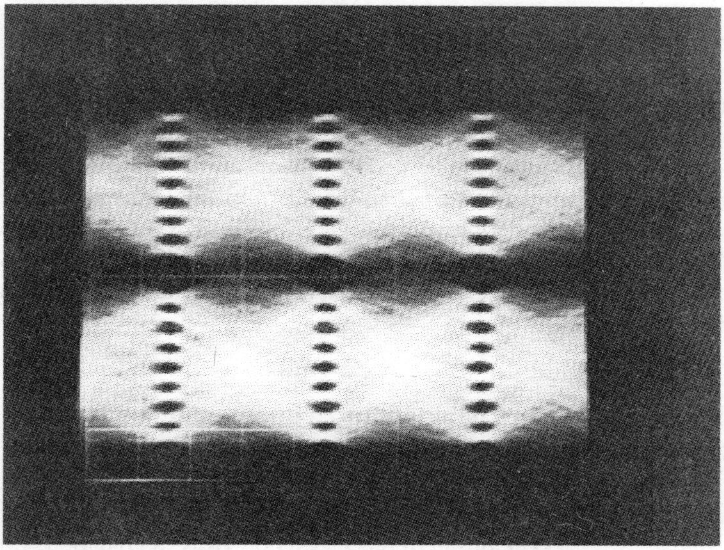

Figure 4.8.8 Photograph of experimental 64-QAM, 90 Mb/s rate, demodulated eye diagram. Hardware design by Dr. Feher Associates-Digcom, Inc.

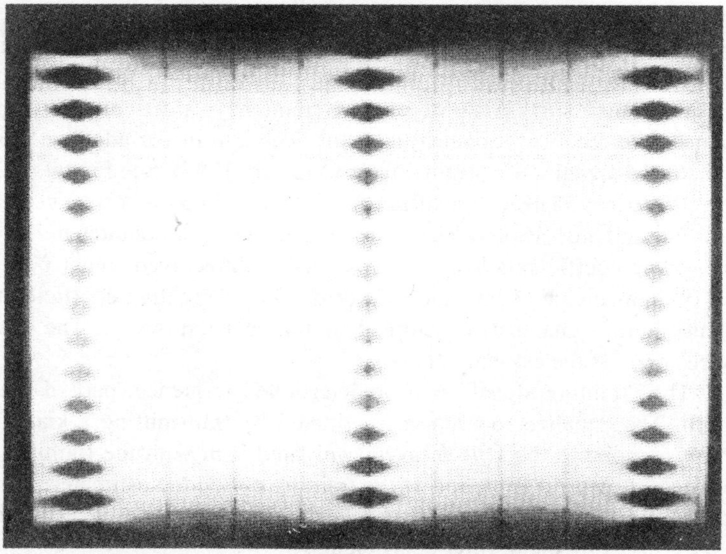

Figure 4.8.9 Eye diagram of experimental 225 QPRS. This system has a 6 b/s/Hz efficiency, a transmission rate of 1.6 Mb/s and spectral attenuation of 60dB. Hardware design by Dr. Feher Associates for Karkar Electronics.

Wilson et al. (1984) achieve the spectral efficiency of 8-PSK, or 50% higher than QPSK, yet without sacrificing the usual E_b/N_o penalty of 8-PSK, as compared with QPSK. This power-efficiency improvement is achieved by combined modulation and coding. A 3/4-rate convolutional encoder and a 16-PSK modem are combined in their investigation.

Combined modulated and coded systems are investigated by a number of research teams. Current issues of the *IEEE Transactions on Communications and Conferences* contain detailed descriptions of new developments in combined modulated and coded systems. Detailed descriptions of the very complex and lengthy trellis-coded modulation are also presented in several outstanding books (Lee and Messerschmitt, 1988; Proakis, 1989; Sklar, 1988).

4.9 ADAPTIVE EQUALIZATION FOR FREQUENCY-SELECTIVE FADED AND DELAY-SPREAD SYSTEMS

Equalization is a method of phase and amplitude compensation that is used to minimize the impact of intersymbol interference (ISI) on BER degradation. In earlier sections we noted that frequency-selective fading (radio wave time dispersion) is a major cause of ISI and thus of BER degradations and error rate floors. Adaptive equalizers are required to equalize the amplitude and phase variations caused by fading radio channels and by the implementation of less-than-ideal filters. In this section the fundamental concepts of adaptive equalization are briefly described. Detailed treatment of this subject is found in Feher (1987), Lee and Messerschmidt (1988), and Proakis (1988).

A simplified model of a digital communications system that highlights the functions of an adaptive equalizer is illustrated in Figure 4.9.1. The transmitted band-limited digital sequence $x(n)$ is distorted by the frequency-selective, time-dispersive propagation channel. The received sequence is $x''(n)$. The aim of the adaptive equalizer is to restore the distorted signal to its original form (Yacoub, 1993). See Figure 4.9.2.

The basic adaptive equalizer architecture contains a transversal filter, a summing amplifier, and a decision device. The transversal filter contains n delay elements "Δ" and n weighting coefficients $h_1 \ldots h_n$. The distorted received signal $x''(n)$ is delayed through a set of delay elements "Δ" and is multiplied by weighting coefficients $h_1 \ldots h_n$. The resultant "sum" signal $\hat{x}(n)$ is sampled by the decision device. The output of the decision device, $x'(n)$, is the estimate of $x(n)$.

The "training signal" is a predetermined sequence, part of the transmitted signal pattern. The equalizer operation is initiated by transmitting a known training sequence and by comparing the $\hat{x}(n)$-delayed, weighted sum with the training signal generated in the receiver. After completion of the training period the estimate $x'(n)$ approximates $x(n)$, and the "tracking mode" is initiated. In the tracking mode the error signal $x'(n) - \hat{x}(n)$ is used for updating the h_i filter coefficients.

The training sequence can be interleaved with data packets to update the tap settings on a sufficiently frequently basis.

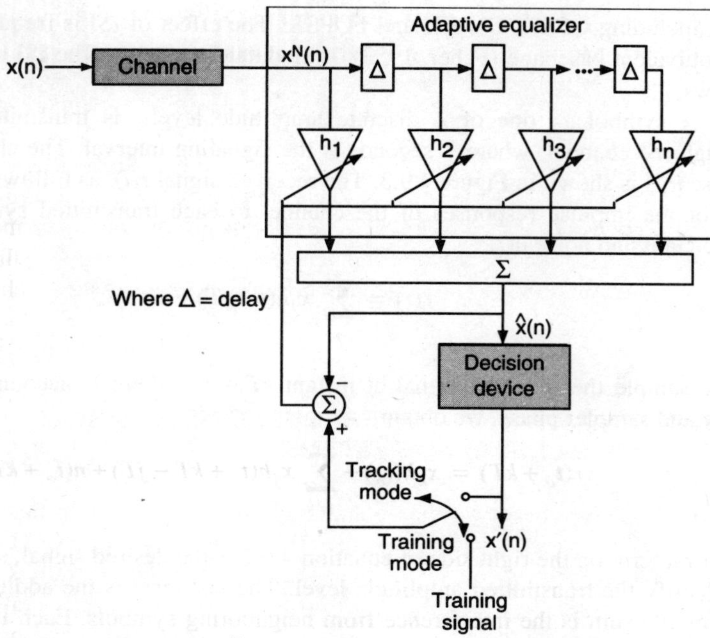

Figure 4.9.1 Digital system with adaptive equalizer. (Based on Yacoub, 1993.)

Another class of adaptive equalizers, known as blind equalizers, does not require a training sequence. Blind equalizers, or "self-adaptive equalizers," operate only in the tracking mode and with a slower convergence rate than adaptive equalizers, which do have training sequences.

Intersymbol interference is frequently caused by nonideal, or non-Nyquist, channel characteristics. In mobile systems the cascade of transmit and receive filters satisfies the Nyquist ISI-free transmission criteria. Frequency-selective fading (time-delay spread) distorts the amplitude and phase characteristics of the overall channel; for this reason ISI is observed at the input of the adaptive equalizer. This ISI degrades the $P_e(C/N)$ performance of the system. Intersymbol interference may arise in all digital transmission sys-

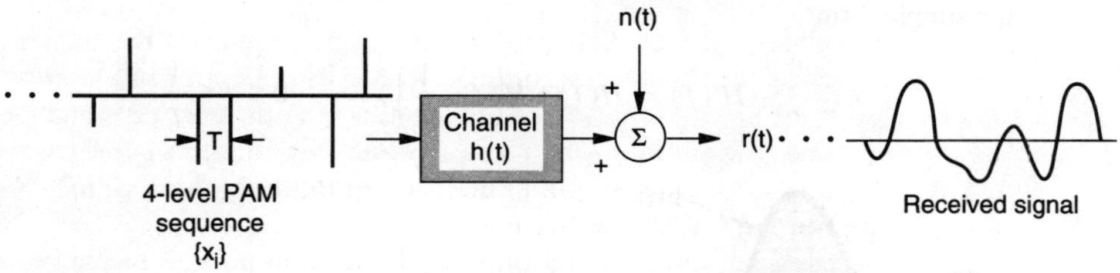

Figure 4.9.2 Baseband PAM system model. (From Feher, 1987a.)

tems, including QPSK, GMSK, and FQPSK. The effect of ISI is frequently described in the equivalent baseband (Feher, 1983) of modulated systems. The ISI term is obtained as follows.

A symbol x_j, one of L discrete amplitude levels, is transmitted at instant mT through the channel, where T seconds is the signaling interval. The channel impulse response $h(t)$ is shown in Figure 4.9.3. The received signal $r(t)$, as follows, is the superposition of the impulse responses of the channel to each transmitted symbol and additive white Gaussian noise $n(t)$:

$$r(t) = \sum_j x_j h(t - jT) + n(t). \tag{4.9.1}$$

If we sample the received signal at instant $kT + t_o$, where t_o accounts for the channel delay and sampler phase, we obtain

$$r(t_o + kT) = x_k h(t_o) + \sum_{j \neq k} x_j h(t_o + kT - jT) + n(t_o + kT). \tag{4.9.2}$$

The first term on the right side of equation 4.9.2 is the desired signal, since it can be used to identify the transmitted amplitude level. The last term is the additive noise, whereas the middle sum is the interference from neighboring symbols. Each interference term is proportional to a sample of the channel impulse response, $h(t_o - iT)$, spaced a multiple iT of symbol intervals T away from t_o, as shown in Figure 4.9.3. The ISI is zero if and only if $h(t_o + iT) = 0$, $i \neq 0$, or if the channel impulse response has zero crossings at T-spaced intervals (Feher, 1987).

When the impulse response has such uniformly spaced zero crossings, it is said to satisfy *Nyquist's first criterion.* In frequency domain terms, this condition is equivalent to

$$H'(f) = \sum_n H\left(f - \frac{n}{T}\right) = \text{constant for } |f| \leq \frac{1}{2T}. \tag{4.9.3}$$

$H(f)$ is the channel frequency response, and $H'(f)$ is the "folded" (aliased or overlapped) channel spectral response after symbol-rate sampling. The band $|f| \leq 1/(2T)$ is commonly referred to as the *Nyquist,* or *minimum, bandwidth.* When $H(f) = 0$ for $|f| > 1/T$ (the channel has no response beyond twice the Nyquist bandwidth), the folded response $H'(f)$ has the simple form

$$H'(f) = H(f) + H\left(f - \frac{1}{T}\right), \qquad 0 \leq f \leq \frac{1}{T}. \tag{4.9.4}$$

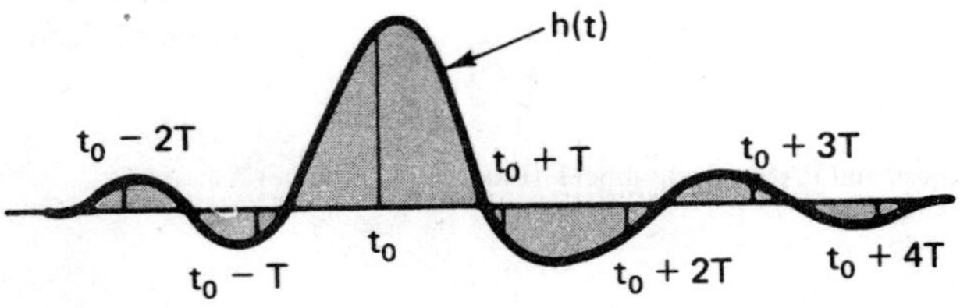

Figure 4.9.3 Channel impulse response. (From Feher, 1987a.)

All ISI terms add to produce the maximum deviation from the desired signal at the sampling time (Feher, 1987).

The purpose of an equalizer, which is placed in the path of the received signal, is to reduce the ISI as much as possible to maximize the probability of correct decisions.

4.9.1 Linear Transversal and Least-Mean-Square Equalizers

Among the many structures used for equalization the simplest is the transversal (also known as a tapped delay-line or nonrecursive) equalizer (Figure 4.9.4). In such an equalizer the current and past values $r(t - nT)$ of the received signal are linearly weighted by equalizer coefficients (tap gains) c_n and summed to produce the output. If the delays and tap-gain multipliers are analog, the continuous output of the equalizer $z(t)$ is sampled at the symbol rate and the samples go to the decision device. In the commonly used digital implementation, samples of the received signal at the symbol rate are stored in a digital shift register (or memory), and the equalizer output samples (sums of products) $z(t_o + kT)$ or z_k are computed digitally, once per symbol, according to

$$z_k = \sum_{n=0}^{N-1} c_n r(t_o + kT - nT)$$

where N is the number of equalizer coefficients and t_o denotes sample timing.

The equalizer coefficients, c_n, $n = 0, 1, \ldots, N-1$ may be chosen to force the samples of the combined channel and equalizer impulse response to zero at all but one of the N T-spaced instants within the span of the equalizer. Such an equalizer is called a *zero-forcing* (ZF) equalizer.

The *least-mean-squared* (LMS) equalizer is more robust. Here the equalizer coefficients are chosen to minimize the mean squared error (MSE), the sum of squares of all the ISI terms plus the noise power at the output of the equalizer. Therefore the LMS equalizer maximizes the signal-to-distortion (S/D) ratio at its output within the constraints of the equalizer time span and the delay through the equalizer.

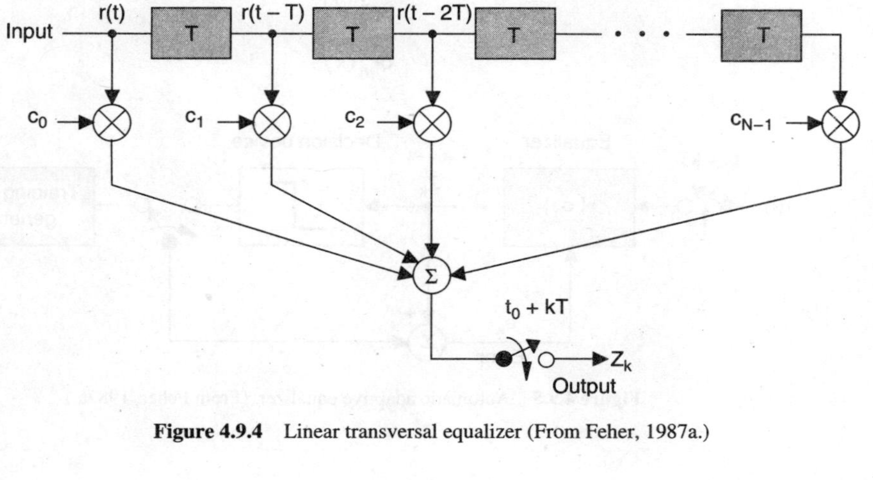

Figure 4.9.4 Linear transversal equalizer (From Feher, 1987a.)

The delay introduced by the equalizer depends on the position of the main or reference tap of the equalizer. Typically the tap gain corresponding to the main tap has the largest magnitude.

If the values of the channel impulse response at the sampling instants are known, the N coefficients of the ZF and the LMS equalizers can be obtained by solving a set of N linear simultaneous equations for each case.

Most current, high-speed voiceband telephone line modems use LMS equalizers because they are more robust in the presence of noise and large amounts of ISI and superior to the ZF equalizers in their convergence properties. The same is generally true of radio channel modems.

4.9.2 Automatic Synthesis

During the training period, a known signal is transmitted and a synchronized version of this signal is generated in the receiver to acquire information about the channel characteristics. The training signal may consist of periodic isolated pulses or a continuous sequence with a broad, uniform spectrum such as the widely used maximum-length shift-register or pseudonoise (PN) sequence.

Given a synchronized version of the known training signal, a sequence of error signals $e_k = z_k - x_k$ can be computed at the equalizer output and used to adjust the equalizer coefficients to reduce the sum of the squared errors (Figure 4.9.5). The most popular method of equalizer adjustment involves updates to each tap gain during each symbol interval. Iterative solution of the coefficients of the equalizer is possible because the MSE is a quadratic function of the coefficients. The MSE may be envisioned as an N-dimensional paraboloid (punch bowl) with a bottom or minimum. The adjustment to each tap gain is in a direction opposite to an estimate of the gradient of the MSE with respect to that tap gain. The idea is to move the set of equalizer coefficients closer to the unique optimum set corresponding to the minimum MSE. This symbol-by-symbol procedure developed by Widrow and Hoff is commonly referred to as the *stochastic gradient* method because, instead of the true gradient of the MSE,

$$\frac{\delta E\left[e_k^2\right]}{\delta c_n(k)},$$

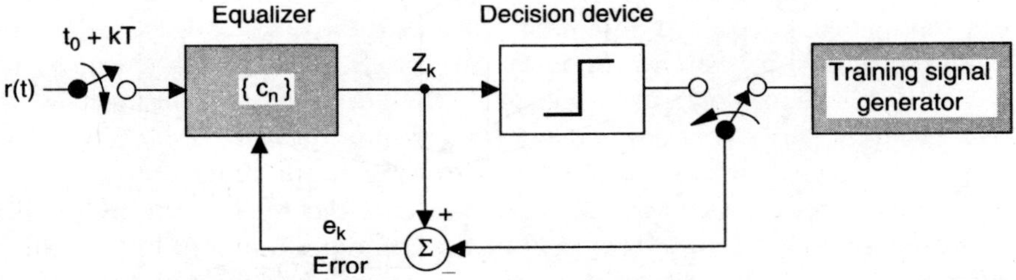

Figure 4.9.5 Automatic adaptive equalizer. (From Feher, 1987a.)

a noisy but unbiased estimate,

$$\frac{\delta e_k^2}{\delta c_n(k)} = 2e_k r(t_o + kT - nT),$$

is used. Thus the tap gains are updated according to

$$c_n(k+1) = c_n(k) - \Delta e_k r(t_o + kT - nT), \qquad n = 0, 1, \ldots, N-1,$$

where $c_n(k)$ is the nth tap gain at time k, e_k is the error signal, and Δ is a positive adaptation constant or step size.

4.9.3 Equalizer Convergence

The exact convergence behavior of the stochastic update method is difficult to analyze. However, for a small step size and a large number of iterations the behavior is similar to the steepest-descent algorithm, which uses the actual gradient rather than a noisy estimate.

General convergence properties include the following:

1. Fastest convergence (or shortest settling time) is obtained when the (folded) power spectrum of the symbol rate–sampled equalizer input is flat and when the step size Δ is chosen to be the inverse of the product of the received signal power and the number of equalizer coefficients.
2. The larger the variation in the folded power spectrum in property No. 1, the smaller the step size must be, and therefore the slower the rate of convergence.
3. For systems where sampling causes aliasing (channel foldover or spectral overlap), the convergence rate is affected by the channel delay characteristics and the sampler phase because they affect the aliasing. This influence will be explained later in more detail.

4.9.4 Adaptive Equalization

After the initial training period (if there is one) the coefficients of an adaptive equalizer may be continually adjusted in a *decision-directed* manner. In this mode the error signal $e_k = z_k - \hat{x}_k$ is derived from the final (but not necessarily correct) receiver estimate $\{\hat{x}_k\}$ of the transmitted sequence $\{x_k\}$. In normal operation the receiver decisions are correct with high probability, so the error estimates are correct often enough to allow the adaptive equalizer to maintain precise equalization. Moreover, a decision-directed adaptive equalizer can track slow variations in the channel characteristics or linear perturbations in the receiver front end, such as slow jitter in the sampler phase (Feher, 1987).

The larger the step size, the faster the equalizer tracking capability. However, a compromise must be made between fast tracking and the *excess MSE* of the equalizer. The excess MSE is that part of the error power in excess of the minimum attainable MSE (with tap gains frozen at their optimum settings). This excess MSE, caused by tap gains deviating from their optimum settings, is directly proportional to the number of equalizer coefficients, the step size, and the channel noise power. The step size that provides the fastest convergence results in an MSE that is, on the average, 3 dB worse than the minimum achievable MSE. In practice, the value of the step size is selected for fast convergence during the training period and then reduced for fine tuning during the steady-state operation (or data mode). A frequently used decision-feedback equalizer structure that is suitable for automatic adaptive equalizer implementations is illustrated in Figure 4.9.6.

The performance of an adaptively equalized digital cellular system is compared to that of an unequalized system in the following example.

Example 4.9.1

The measured time delay spread in one part of San Francisco, CA is approximately 16 μs. How much is the BER floor of unequalized π/4-QPSK and of π/4-DQPSK systems if the delayed signal power (Δ) equals the main signal power (*C*), or *C/D* = 0 dB and a bit rate f_b = 48.6 kb/s is used (the standardized bit rate of the U.S. cellular TDMA system, IS-54). How much is the BER floor with an advanced adaptive equalizer?

Solution of Example 4.9.1

First, we compute the τ/T_s ratio. It is

$$\frac{\tau}{T_s} = \frac{16\ \mu\text{s}}{1/f_s} = \frac{16\ \mu\text{s}}{1/(48.6{:}2\ \text{kb/s})} = \frac{16\ \mu\text{s}}{41.15\ \mu\text{s}}$$

$$\frac{\tau}{T_s} = 0.388 \approx 0.4.$$

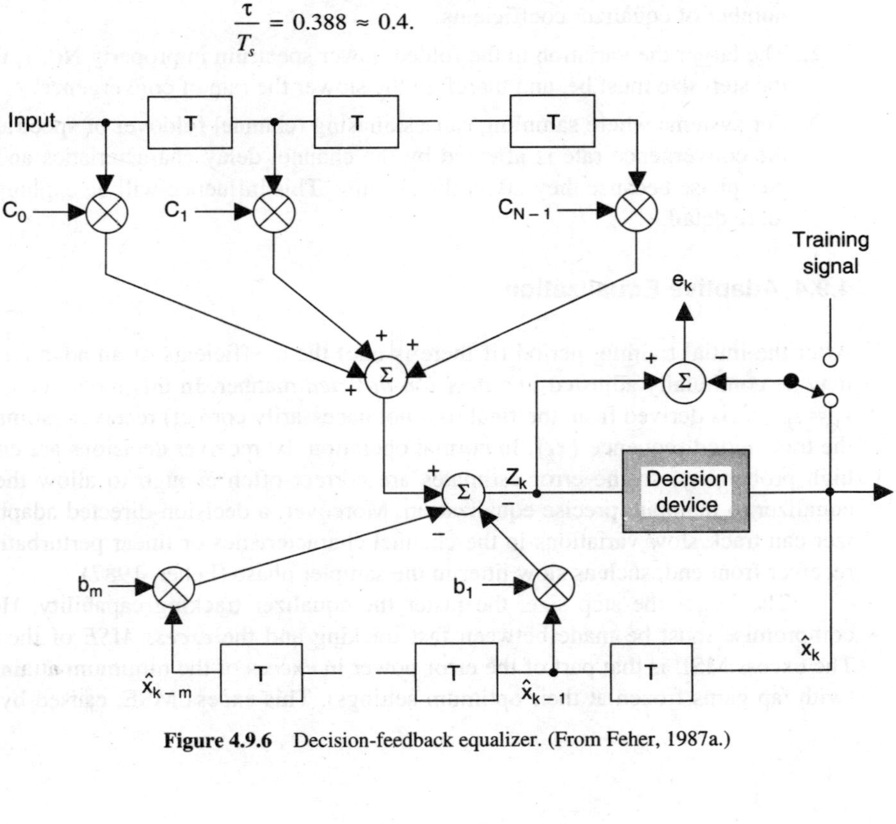

Figure 4.9.6 Decision-feedback equalizer. (From Feher, 1987a.)

From Figure 4.6.8 we observe that for $\tau/T_s = 0.4$ the BER floor for $C/D = 0$ dB is approximately BER = 10^{-1} for both the coherent and the noncoherent systems.
Advanced adaptive equalizers reduce this error floor to approximately BER = 10^{-1} or 10^{-4}.

4.10 SYNCHRONIZATION OF BURST DEMODULATORS: CARRIER RECOVERY AND SYMBOL TIMING RECOVERY

For many wireless system applications, fast burst acquisition is required. In time division multiple access (TDMA), code division multiple access (CDMA), and collision sense multiple access (CSMA) systems fast carrier recovery (CR) and symbol timing recovery (STR) circuits have been specified. In Section 4.3 a classic, simple synchronization concept is described. To meet fast synchronization requirements, newer, faster systems have to be designed.

In Figure 4.10.1 the adaptive carrier tracking (ACT) synchronizer is illustrated. In this fast-burst synchronizer the phase detector detects the phase of the received IF signal at t_o^- immediately before decision timing. If there is a phase error in the recovered signal (the eye diagram is not open), then the I and Q reference signals generated by the digital numerically controlled oscillator (NCO) are shifted to coincide instantaneously with the desired positions of these reference signals (Figure 4.10.2). In Saito and Takam: (1993) the details of this ACT joint CR and STR are described. Detection of the next symbol is performed by the instantaneously shifted reference vectors. Thus the acquisition is performed on a symbol-by-symbol basis. This is a remarkably fast synchronization achievement, having a speed comparable to that of differential demodulators and the performance of coherent systems.

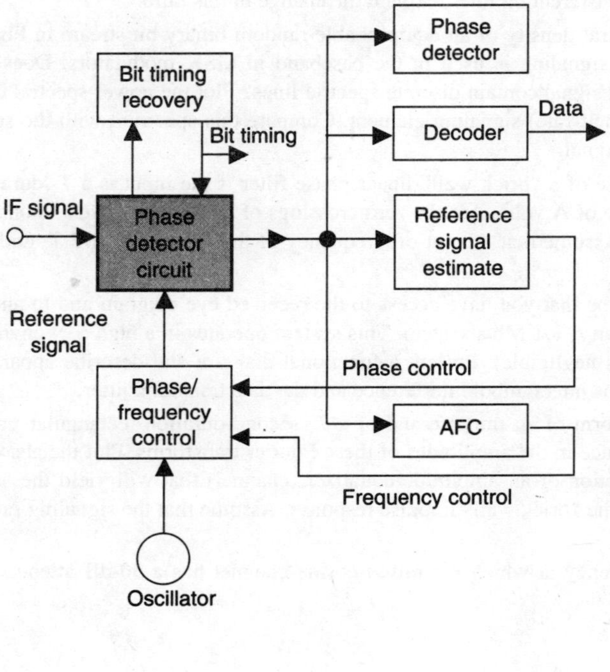

Figure 4.10.1 Synchronization of a burst QPSK and FQPSK demodulator: block diagram. The adaptive carrier tracking (ACT) concept, combined with simultaneous symbol timing recovery, may lead to complete demodulator synchronization time in less than 20 bits. (From Saito and Takami, 1993.) Recently developed hardware by Dr. Feher—UC Davis attained less than 10 bit carrier recovery speed.

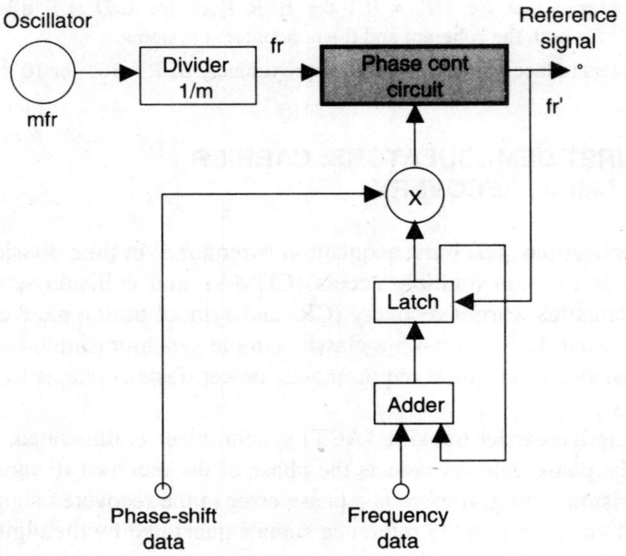

Figure 4.10.2 Implementation of fast frequency and phase acquisition-synchronization of the adaptive carrier tracking (ACT) subsystem, based on digital numerically controlled oscillator (NCO). Design at UC Davis—Dr. Feher's Laboratory.

4.11 PROBLEMS

4.1 Calculate the power spectral density of a return-to-zero (RZ) random data stream. Assume that the illustrated signal is measured across a 50-Ω termination. Note that a logic state 1 is represented by a 50% duty cycle pulse and a 0 state by a zero signal. Plot the computed spectrum on a logarithmic (dB) scale. How much is the discrete spectral component to the continuous spectrum ratio? For different bit rates, explain the change in this ratio.

4.2 Calculate the power spectral density of an equiprobable random binary bit stream in Figure 4.2.13, (b). This type of signaling is used in the baseband in MSK modulators. Does the spectrum of this baseband signal contain discrete spectral lines? Plot the power spectral density of an f_s = 100 kb/s (half-rate) signaling element. Compare this spectrum with the spectrum of a 100-kb/s NRZ signal.

4.3 Derive the output response of a "brick wall" linear phase filter if the input is a T_s duration pulse having an amplitude of A volts. Are the zero crossings of the output pulse response at integer multiples of T_s? Assume that the cut-off frequency of the filter is (a) 1/2 T_s and (b) $20/T_s$.

4.4 *Advanced problem.* Assume that you have access to the received eye diagram and to an external jitter-free clock of an f_s = 1 Mb/s system. This system operates in a high S/N environment (that is, the noise is negligible). Present a functional diagram and describe apparatus that would measure the rms intersymbol interference and the data transition jitter.

4.5 Obtain the Fourier transform of an impulse and of a T_s second-duration rectangular pulse. Note carefully the difference in the amplitudes of these Fourier transforms. Plot the absolute value of the transfer function of an amplitude equalizer (channel) that will yield the same output pulse response as the "brick wall" impulse response. Assume that the signaling rate is f_s = 10 kb/s.

4.6 Calculate the exact frequency at which the raised-cosine channel has a 30-dB attenuation.

Assume that $\alpha = 0.3$ and $\alpha = 0.5$ are roll-off factors and that the Nyquist frequency is at 500 KHz.

4.7 Obtain and sketch the impulse response of raised-cosine filters having $\alpha = 0$, $\alpha = 0.5$, and $\alpha = 1$ roll-off factors. Based on the obtained impulse responses, explain why a steeper filter has a larger peak-to-peak jitter. Explain why the ISI is not affected by the roll-off factor. *Note:* A synchronous stream of impulses (not pulses) is assumed.

4.8 Derive the power spectral density for an equiprobable random data stream for $\pm h \cos(\pi t/T_s)$ baseband signaling elements. Sketch the power spectral density in dB, and compare your result to the measured power spectral density result in Figure 4.2.15. Assume that the transmitted symbol rate is 32 kb/s.

4.9 The carrier recovery (CR) circuit of a BPSK demodulator contains a multiplier (see Figure 4.3.4, point *B*) followed by a phase-locked loop (PLL). What would happen if we did not use this multiplier? Is this nonlinear component (multiplier) an essential function of CR circuits?

4.10 The transfer function of the transmit and receive low-pass filters illustrated in Figure 4.2.12, (a), meet the Nyquist intersymbol interference–free transmission criteria. Assume that for low frequencies the attenuation of this baseband Nyquist channel is 0 dB. Let the transmit and receive filters be identical, with the exception of the $x/\sin x$ amplitude equalizer. This equalizer is an integral part of the transmit filter. If the input data sequence $\{b_m\}$ is an equiprobable random NRZ data stream having levels of + A or −A volts, show that the power, measured at the receive filter input, equals A^2. Assume a normalized 1-Ω impedance. Show that this power is independent of the roll-off factor, α, of the raised-cosine channel model. Give a physical interpretation of your results. Show that the power at the receive filter output (threshold comparator input) equals $A^2[(4 - \alpha)/4]$.

4.11 Describe the required conditions to satisfy the equivalence between the predetection bandpass filter, BPF_R, and postdetection (postdemodulation) low-pass filter, LPF_R, illustrated in Figure 4.2.1. Is a low-pass filter essential in both demodulators? (*Hint:* What would happen if the second-order spectral components were not removed?)

4.12 Sketch the unfiltered and filtered RF outputs of a BPSK modulator. Note the difference in the envelope fluctuation. What is the impact (a qualitative answer is sufficient) of the filter roll-off (steepness) and cut-off frequency on the envelope fluctuation?

4.13 Assume that the message sequence, $\{b_k\}$ (shown in Fig. 4.3.3), is differentially encoded and binary-phase modulated. A comparison demodulator (DBPSK in Fig. 4.3.3) is used. Show that the DBPSK demodulator recovers the $\{b_k\}$ bit sequence correctly. Assume that the channel noise is negligible.

4.14 Sketch the unfiltered power spectrum of a BPSK signal if the unmodulated carrier frequency $f_c = 70$ MHz and the bit rate is $f_b = 6$ Mb/s. Assume (a) that the data source is a periodic 101010 . . . data stream and (b) that the data source is an equiprobable random source. Highlight the difference between the discrete and continuous power spectra in cases (a) and (b). Sketch the corresponding transmit power spectra of the Nyquist filtered system. Assume an $\alpha = 0.5$ roll-off factor, and include the $(x/\sin x)$-shaped amplitude equalizer in your transmitter.

4.15 An integrate-sample-and-dump (ISD) circuit is a possible implementation of a matched filter receiver. Describe the type of signals for which the ISD receiver is an optimal receiver. Note that this receiver is not an optimal receiver for band-limited synchronous data transmission. Why? (*Hint:* The ISD circuitry is a possible implementation of $h_0(t) = s(T - t)$ if $s(t)$ is an infinite bandwidth signal.)

4.16 In an $f_b = 10$ Mb/s infinite bandwidth BPSK system (illustrated in Figure 4.3.3; the bandpass filters in the figure are bypassed) the receiver filter is a low-pass RC circuit of 3-dB bandwidth f_{3dB}. Calculate the value of f_{3dB} for which the signal-to-rms noise ratio is maximal. Show that for the RC network, the P_e is about 10 times larger than that for an ideal receiver. This corresponds to a 1-dB S/N difference in the $P_e = 10^{-6}$ range. *Note:* If there is no band-limitation in the channel, then the ideal receive filter is an integrator.

4.17 Explain in a few sentences the fundamental differences and similarities between the matched filter and the Nyquist receiver. When are these receivers equivalent? Try to answer this question without referring to the book. That is, take the courage to close your book and write down your answer.

4.18 The four phase states of a Gray-coded and binary-coded decimal (BCD) QPSK system are as follows:

State number	Dibits		Phase state Gray code	Phase state BCD
1	0	0	225°	225°
2	0	1	135°	135°
3	1	1	45°	–45°
4	1	0	–45°	45°

How many bit errors are generated as a result of adjacent symbol errors? Carefully analyze the Gray-coded and BCD systems. Is the number of bit errors caused by wrong decisions by adjacent symbols independent of the signal state?

4.19 Assume that the spectral shaping of a QPSK modulator is performed with premodulation low-pass filters. The spectral shaping of a second QPSK modulator is performed by post-modulation bandpass filters. Assume that both of these modulators transmit data at the same rate, f_b, and have the same carrier frequency, f_c. If both modulators have the same RF power spectra, which conditions do their respective filters satisfy?

4.20 Explain the difference between QPSK and offset-QPSK (O-QPSK) systems. Is the differential encoder/decoder of O-QPSK modems simpler or more complex than that of QPSK systems? Which system has larger envelope fluctuations?

4.21 Compare the P_e performance of DQPSK systems with that of DEQPSK systems. Both systems have differential encoders and decoders. What is the physical reason for the significant (about 2 dB) difference in the E_b/N_o requirement?

4.22 What is the *C/N* ratio requirement of an $f_b = 45$ Mb/s rate DQPSK modem if $P_e = 10^{-4}$ is required? Assume that the receiver noise bandwidth equals 30 MHz.

4.23 The amplitude slope of a QPSK system is 0.4 dB/MHz. The bit rate of the system is f_b 45 Mb/s. Calculate the required E_b/N_o if $P_e = 10^{-4}$ is specified and the only distortion in the system is caused by the amplitude slope.

4.24 The delay slope of an O-QPSK system is 0.6 ns/MHz. How much is the required E_b/N_o if $P_e = 10^{-4}$ is specified and the only system distortion is caused by the delay slope?

4.25 Explain the difference in phase transitions in conventional QPSK, offset QPSK, and MSK. Why are the phase transitions of offset QPSK (O-QPSK) limited to ±90 degrees? What is the reason that there are no abrupt phase transitions in MSK (that is, why is the MSK a phase continuous system)? (*Hint:* Note the coherence requirement between the frequency deviation and the bit rate (in equation 4.125.)

4.26 The main lobe of the MSK system equals $f_b \cdot 3/4$ where f_b is the bit rate. Explain why it is possible to achieve a 2-b/sHz radio frequency (RF) efficiency. Describe how it is possible to have a minimum-bandwidth RF filter that is narrower than one half that of the main lobe. (*Hint:* Revise Nyquist's generalized ISI-free transmission theorem and the equivalence of bandpass and low-pass channels.)

4.27 Compare the band-limited and hard-limited QPSK, O-QPSK, MSK, and FQPSK-1 spectra with the spectra of unfiltered systems. Determine which modulation scheme has the smallest sideband restorations. How much is the sideband restoration of conventional QPSK at $1.5/T_s$?

4.28 A QPSK modulated signal is band-limited by an ideal Nyquist filter. This filter has a roll-off factor $\sqrt{\alpha} = 0.3$ and includes the (x/sin x)-shaped amplitude equalizer. The filtered signal is hard-limited by an ideal memoryless infinite bandwidth limiter. Assume that an ideal coherent demodulator is used and that the transmission medium is infinite bandwidth, noise free. Is cross-talk generated in the I and Q channels? If so, explain why.

4.29 Explain the physical reason for large P_e degradation if the peak factor of the interference is larger.

4.30 A satellite system has to operate at $P_e \leq 10^{-9}$. The available C/N = 17 dB. What is the maximum interference power (that is, minimal C/I ratio) (a) if the interference consists of a single sinusoidal tone and (b) if the interference is the sum of two equal-power cochannel sinusoids? Assume that these sinusoids are independent of each other. (*Hint:* Compute the peak factor of two sinusoidal tones.)

4.31 How much is the E_b/N_o requirement of a nonlinearly amplified wireless digital system (a) if GMSK with $BT_b = 0.25$ and (b) if FQPSK-1 is used and a BER = 10^{-4} is required. Assume a stationary AWGN channel. Use the CREATE software to obtain your results.

4.32 Compute the spectral efficiency of nonlinearly amplified GMSK, MSK, and FQPSK-1 systems. Use the CREATE software. Assume that the spectral efficiency in [b/s/Hz] is defined at the (a) −20 dBr and (b) −30 dBr spectral density attenuation points. The term *dBr* refers to power spectral density attenuation relative to the center-in-band power spectral density value.

4.33 Create your own new waveform and modem with the CREATE software. Compare the spectral efficiency of your new modem and the BER = $f(E_b/N_o)$ performance with that of FQPSK-1, FQPSK-KF, and GMSK with $BT_b = 0.5$. *Note:* Your newly created waveform is most probably within the FQPSK family of patented signals and modems.

4.34 Plot the power spectrum of linearly and nonlinearly amplified DQPSK and FQPSK-1 systems. Use the CREATE program. For conventional DQPSK, assume square-root of raised-cosine filters with x/sin x transmit aperture equalizers and a roll-off factor $\alpha = 0.3$. Compare the resultant spectral densities.

CHAPTER 5

Coding: Error Correction and Detection

5.1 ERROR CONTROL REQUIREMENTS

In a remarkable paper published in 1948, **Shannon (1948) shattered the belief** that the performance of communications systems in a noisy environment was limited. He showed that by adding redundancy to the information, errors induced by a noisy channel can be reduced to any desired level without sacrificing the rate of information transmission, if the rate of information is smaller than the channel capacity. Conversely, he showed that if redundancy was not used in a noise-controlled environment, error-free performance was not possible. Since Shannon's work, succeeding coding and information theorists have devised many efficient encoding and decoding methods for error control, making the use of coding an important consideration in the design of highly reliable modern digital communications systems. In this chapter we describe several error correction and detection schemes for the wireless digital communications environment.

If error control is to be used, it is important to use codes with good burst-error detection and correction capabilities or to interleave the coded symbols, or to do both, since the wireless communications channel is often characterized by deep fades. *Interleaving* randomizes the bursty-error statistics resulting from deep fades, which makes the channel seem memoryless (Steele, 1992). In this case, most of the results of coding theory (which were formulated for memoryless channels) can be applied to the wireless communications channel. In most sections of this chapter, we assume that the code symbols are interleaved before transmission and that successive received bits are independent of each other.

We begin with a discussion of interleaving, followed by descriptions and numerical results of *block* and *convolutional* codes. We close with a discussion of error control by means of *automatic repeat request (ARQ).* We denote the group of information bits that are input to the encoder as the vector $u = (u_1, u_2, \ldots, u_k)$ or vector x, and the resulting group of symbols at the output of the encoder as vector $v = (v_1, v_2, \ldots, V_n)$ or vector y, where $n > k$; v is also called a code vector or a codeword.

5.2 INTERLEAVING

Interleaving is an effective method to combat error bursts occurring on a fading channel. The basic principle is to spread the codeword, positioning the bits one away from another so that they experience independent fading. In independent fading, the bits affected by the error bursts belong to several codewords. Therefore the effect of the error burst is spread over the message so that it may be possible to recover the data with the original error-correcting code (Yacoub, 1993).

Several types of interleavers have been proposed in the literature, such as diagonal (GSM, 1988–1990), convolutional (Forney, 1971; Ramsey, 1970), interblock (GSM, 1988–1990), and block (Lin and Costello, 1983; Steele, 1992) interleaving. Perhaps the simplest of these four kinds of interleavers is the block interleaver, which arranges λ code vectors in the original code into λ rows of a rectangular array and then sends them column by column to the transmitter, as shown in Figure 5.2.1 (Lin and Costello, 1983).

Regardless of where it starts, a deep fade resulting in an error burst of length λ will affect only one digit in each row. Thus, if the original code is capable of correcting single errors in a code vector, the interleaved code corrects single bursts of length λ or less (Lin and Costello, 1983). If the original code is capable of correcting any single burst of length ℓ or less, the interleaved code will correct any single burst of length $\lambda\ell$ or less.

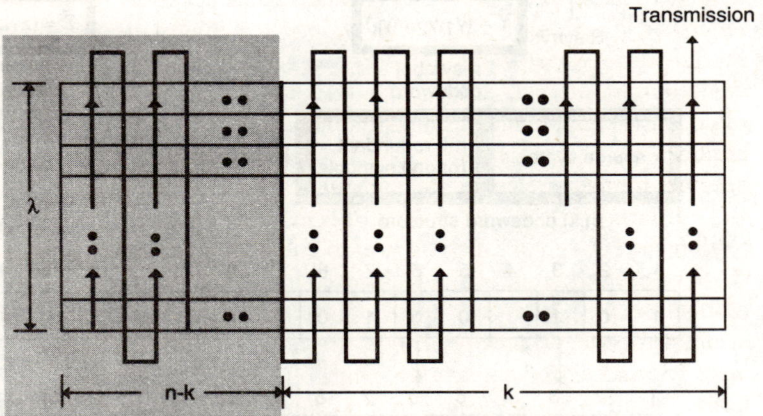

Figure 5.2.1 Transmission of a block-interleaved code. Each codeword is of length n symbols (k information bits plus n-k redundant bits). The rectangular array contains λ codewords. The parameter λ is the *interleaving degree.* (Based on Lin and Costello, 1983.)

The interleaving technique reduces the problem of implementing complex codes with a high burst-error-correcting capacity to the implementation of simpler codes with considerably smaller burst-error-correcting capacity (Berlekamp et al., 1987; Lin and Costello, 1983; Steele, 1992).

The following sections (5.3 and 5.4) are based on Chapter 6 by W. H. Tranter in Feher, K.: *Digital Communications: Satellite/Earth Station Engineering,* Prentice-Hall, Inc., Englewood Cliffs, N.J., 1983.

5.3 BLOCK CODING

5.3.1 Block Coding and Hamming Distance: Concepts and Definitions

The process of forming a *block code* is illustrated in Figure 5.3.1, (a). The binary source is assumed to generate a sequence of symbols (s) at a rate (R), that is, Rs. These symbols are grouped into blocks k symbols long. To each of these k-symbol blocks, $n - k$ redundant symbols are added to produce an n-symbol codeword. The $n - k$ redundant symbols

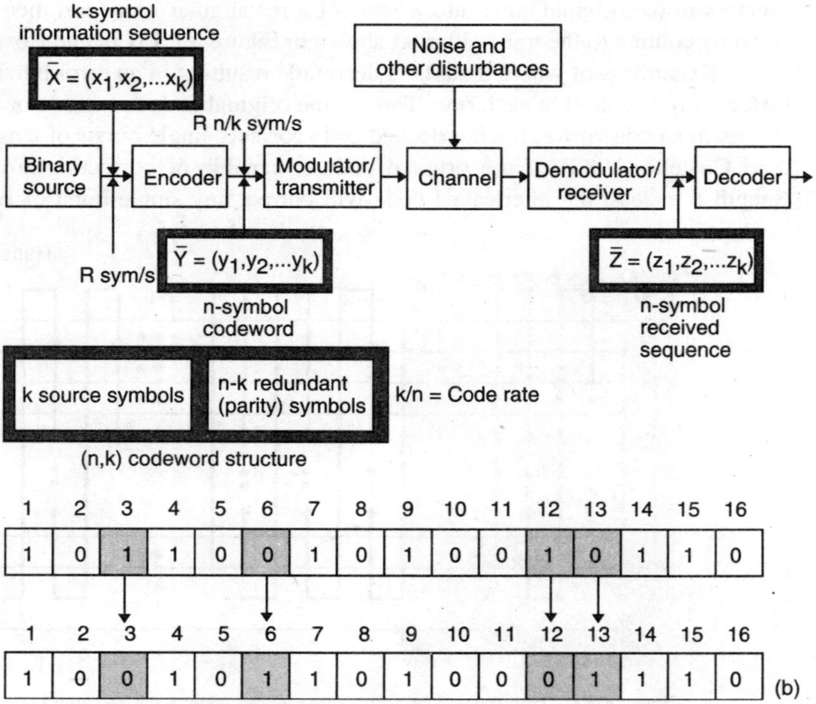

Figure 5.3.1 Block coding concept and encoding-decoding and Hamming distance. (a), Block diagram of an (n, k) block encoder-decoder (Feher, 1983). (b), Hamming distance: the four arrows indicate that the two 16-bit codewords differ by 4 bits, that is, they have a Hamming distance of 4.

are referred to as *parity symbols.* The result is denoted an (n, k) block code. Since each codeword contains n symbols and conveys k bits of information, the information rate of the encoder output is k/n bits per symbol. Thus k/n is referred to as the *code rate.*

The purpose of the encoder is to map the binary (101101 . . .) information sequence of k bits per block

$$\overline{X} = (x_1, x_2, \ldots, x_k) \tag{5.3.1}$$

onto the binary codeword

$$\overline{Y} = (y_1, y_2, \ldots, y_n) \tag{5.3.2}$$

having n bits per coded block. Decoding is accomplished by determining the most likely transmitted codeword, that is given the received binary sequence of n bits per block

$$\overline{Z} = (z_1, z_2, \ldots, z_n). \tag{5.3.3}$$

If all transmitted codewords are equally likely, this is accomplished by deciding that the transmitted codeword is most likely the codeword which is closest in *Hamming distance* to the received codeword.

Hamming distance between the sequence $\overline{Y}$ and $\overline{Z}$ is defined as the weight (the number of binary ones) in the modulo-2 sum of $\overline{Y}$ and $\overline{Z}$. Since $\overline{Y}$ and $\overline{Z}$ are written as vectors, the modulo-2 sum is taken component by component.

Example 5.3.1

Hamming distance between two codewords is illustrated in Figure 5.3.1, (b). The received codeword differs from the transmitted codeword in bit positions 3, 6, 12, and 13. Hence the Hamming distance is 4.

In typical applications, coding is used in environments in which the transmitter power is limited. Also, the n-symbol codewords must be transmitted in the same time span in which the k information symbols are generated by the source. If these conditions do not apply, there is little use for coding. Increasing the transmitter power almost always improves system performance in a noise-limited environment. In a cellular interference-limited environment, increase of transmitter power may not lead to performance improvement. Similarly, if the data stream can be read into a buffer and read out at a reduced rate, system performance is improved because of increased symbol energy.

Let the transmitter power be S watts, and assume that the k symbols are output from the source in T_w seconds. Thus the energy available for each codeword is ST_w joules. The received energy per symbol is ST_w/k without coding. With coding, the energy must be spread over the n-symbol codeword; therefore the received energy per symbol with coding is ST_w/n. Since $n > k$, the symbol energy is reduced with the use of coding; it follows that the symbol-error probability with coding is greater than without coding. If the code is properly designed, the redundancy induced with the $n - k$ parity symbols allows sufficient error-correction capability for the system to enjoy a net gain in performance.

A measure of coding effectiveness is obtained by comparing the *word-error probability* with coding, P_{wec}, to the word-error probability without coding, P_{weu}. The symbol-error probabilities with and without coding are denoted q_c and q_u, respectively. The word-error probability without coding is 1 minus the probability that all k information symbols are received correctly. This yields

$$P_{weu} = 1-(1-q_u)^k. \tag{5.3.4}$$

The word-error probability with coding is somewhat more complicated. Assume that a code has a minimum distance $d_{\min}$ so that e errors can be corrected, where

$$e = \frac{1}{2}(d_{\min}-1). \tag{5.3.5}$$

If more than e errors in a received codeword always lead to a word error, the word-error probability is

$$P_{wec} \le \sum_{i=e+1}^{n} \binom{n}{i} q_c^i (1-q_c)^{n-i} \tag{5.3.6}$$

in which $\binom{n}{i}$ represents the number of all possible patterns of i errors in an n-symbol codeword and is equal to $n!/i!(n-1)!$, and q_c denotes the symbol-error probability with coding. Codes for which equation 5.3.6 holds with equality are known as perfect codes. The only perfect codes are the single-error-correcting Hamming codes and the *Golay code,* both of which are explored in some detail in following sections. For other codes there are particular codewords for which correct decoding can occur with more than e errors. For these codes, equation 5.3.6 provides a useful upper bound.

Example 5.3.2

A particularly useful code is the (23, 12) code known as the Golay code. This code corrects all patterns of three errors. It follows from the preceding discussion that with coherent phase shift keyed (PSK) transmission, the uncoded symbol-error probability is

$$q_u = \frac{1}{2} erfc\left(\sqrt{\frac{ST_w}{12N_o}}\right)$$

and that with coding, the symbol-error probability is

$$q_u = \frac{1}{2} erfc\left(\sqrt{\frac{ST_w}{23N_o}}\right).$$

The word-error probability without coding is

$$P_{weu} = 1-(1-q_u)^{12},$$

and the word-error probability with coding is

$$P_{wec} = \sum_{i=4}^{23} \binom{23}{i} q_c^i (1-q_c)^{23-i}.$$

These results are plotted in Figure 5.3.2. The increase in symbol-error probability with coding is clear, as is the decrease in word-error probability. More will be said about the Golay code (Figure 5.3.3) throughout this chapter.

It should be noted that the q_u and q_c curves differ by 2.6 dB, which is, of course, 10 $\log_{10}$ (n/k) for $n = 23$ and $k = 12$.

5.3.2 Repetition Codes

A very simple block code, but one that points out very well the concept of error correction and code performance, is the $(n, 1)$ block code known as the repetition code. In the repetition code, each of the $n - 1$ parity symbols is equal to the information symbol. The code rate is $1/n$, which is very low for a large n. The relationship between the information symbols and the codewords is shown in Figure 5.3.4. The minimum distance of the code is n; therefore for a large n, repetition codes have very powerful error-correction capabilities. Since the minimum distance of the code is n, a total of $e = 1/2\ (n - 1)$ errors in a received codeword can be corrected. Figure 5.3.4 gives interesting results for repetition codes.

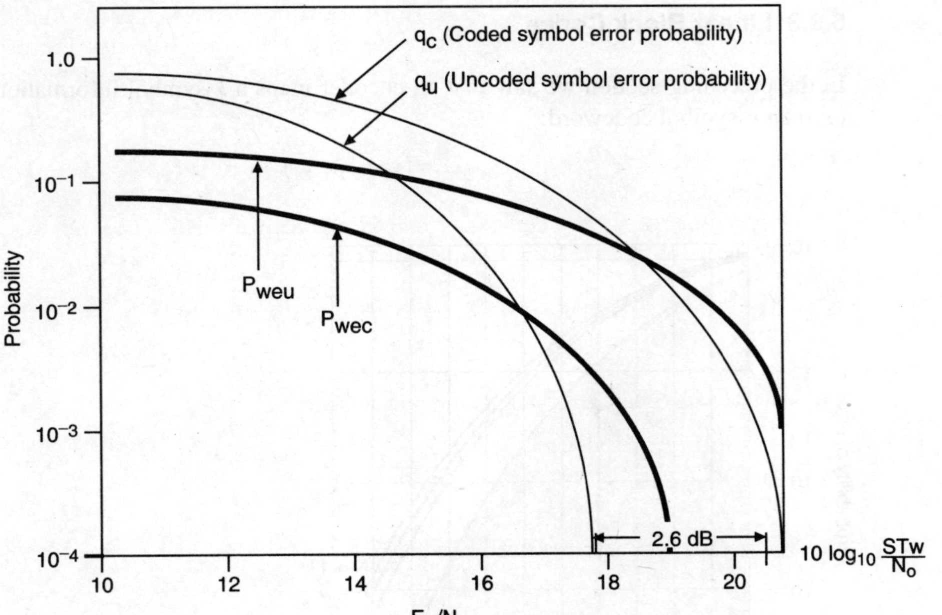

Figure 5.3.2 Symbol- and word-error probabilities of (23, 12) Golay code (Feher, 1983). As an exercise, you may add E_b/N_o to horizontal scale, being careful with bit error, symbol energy, and error conversion. Consider $T_w = 23\ T_b$, i.e., 10 log23 = 13.6 dB shift from coded and 10 log12 = 10.8 dB shift from uncoded word-error rate.

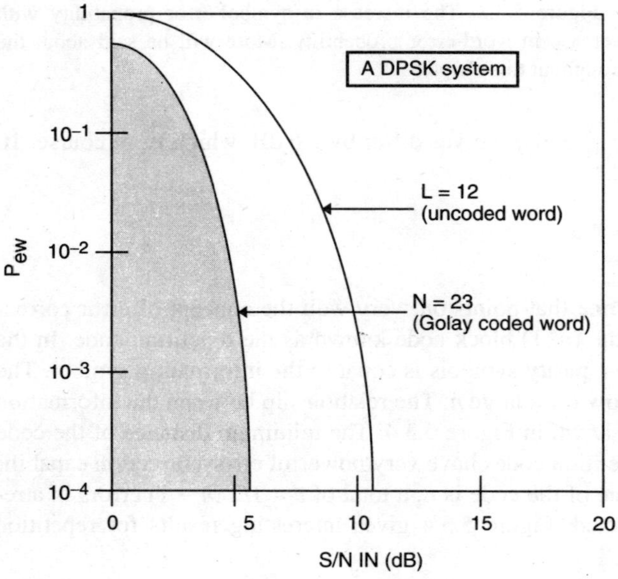

Figure 5.3.3 Word-error rates of a non-coded word and a Golay coded word in a Gaussian noise environment. (From *Mobile Communications Design Fundamentals,* William C.Y. Lee, Copyright © J. Wiley & Sons, 1993. Reprinted by permission of J. Wiley & Sons, Inc.)

5.3.3 Linear Block Codes

In the preceding section we saw that an encoder maps a *k*-symbol information sequence onto an *n*-symbol codeword:

$$\overline{Y} = (y_1, y_2, \ldots, y_n).$$

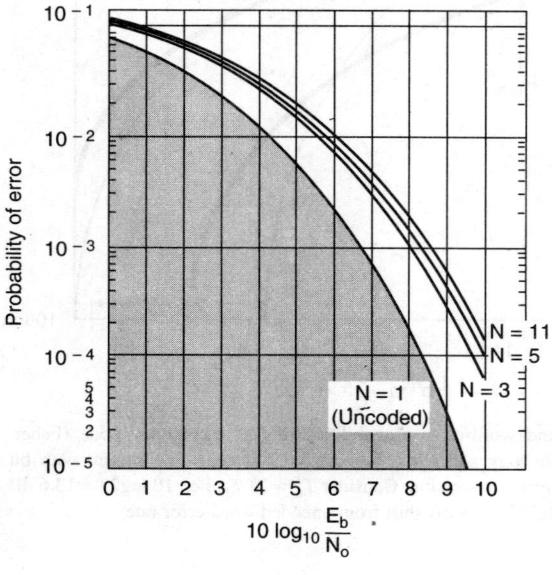

Figure 5.3.4 Error probability for repetition codes. Results for N = 1, 3, 5, and 11 are shown. (From Feher, 1983.)

A *linear code* is defined as one in which the ℓth component of $\overline{Y}$ can be written as a linear combination of the k information symbols. This is best expressed in matrix form as

$$\overline{Y} = \overline{X}\,\overline{G}$$

in which matrix $\overline{G}$ is known as the *generator matrix* of the code and $\overline{X}$ is the information sequence.

A *systematic code* is one in which the first k symbols of the codeword $\overline{Y}$ constitute the information sequence $\overline{X}$. A systematic code has a generator matrix of the form

$$\overline{G} = \begin{bmatrix} 1 & 0 & \cdots & 0 & g_{1,k+1} & \cdots & g_{1,n} \\ 0 & 1 & \cdots & 0 & g_{2,k+1} & \cdots & g_{2,n} \\ \vdots & \vdots & & \vdots & \vdots & & \vdots \\ 0 & 0 & \cdots & 1 & g_{k,k+1} & \cdots & g_{k,n} \end{bmatrix} \tag{5.3.7}$$

or

$$\overline{G} = \left[\overline{I}_k \vdots \overline{P}\right] \tag{5.3.8}$$

in which $\overline{I}_k$ is the $k \times k$ *identity matrix* and $\overline{P}$ represents the last $(n - k)$ columns of the generator matrix.

Closely related to the generator matrix is the parity check matrix. The parity check matrix, $\overline{H}$, is constructed from the generator matrix by writing

$$\overline{H} = \begin{bmatrix} \overline{P} \\ \cdots \\ \overline{I}_{n-k} \end{bmatrix} \tag{5.3.9}$$

so that the parity check matrix has the form

$$\overline{H} = \begin{bmatrix} g_{1,k+1} & \cdots & g_{1,n} \\ g_{2,k+1} & \cdots & g_{2,n} \\ \vdots & & \vdots \\ g_{k,k+1} & \cdots & g_{k,n} \\ 1 & & 0 \\ \vdots & & \vdots \\ 0 & \cdots & 1 \end{bmatrix} = \begin{bmatrix} \overline{P} \\ \cdots \\ \overline{I}_{n-k} \end{bmatrix}. \tag{5.3.10}$$

Note that for systematic codes the parity check matrix can be written by inspection from the generator matrix.

Decoding of a linear code takes place by first multiplying the received sequence at the receiver output, $\overline{Z}$, by the parity check matrix. This multiplication yields a vector $\overline{S}$,

$$\overline{S} = \overline{Z}\,\overline{H}, \tag{5.3.11}$$

known as the *syndrome*. Since binary codes are being considered, the received sequence

$\overline{Z}$ is the modulo-2 sum of the transmitted codeword $\overline{Y}$ and the n-symbol error sequence $\overline{E}$. In other words, the syndrome can be expressed

$$\overline{S} = (\overline{Y} \oplus \overline{E})\overline{H} = \overline{Y}\,\overline{H} \oplus \overline{E}\,\overline{H}.$$

In Feher (1983) it is demonstrated that for systematic codes the syndrome is given by

$$\overline{S} = \overline{E}\,\overline{H}. \tag{5.3.12}$$

Thus an all-zero syndrome denotes that the received sequence is a member of the set of codewords. This means that either no errors were made in transmission of the n-symbol codeword or that an error pattern occurred which mapped the transmitted codeword onto a different codeword. If the code has minimum distance $d_{\min}$, at least $d_{\min}$ errors are required to map the transmitted codeword onto a different codeword.

Decoding is accomplished by relating to each syndrome the minimum weight error pattern that satisfies $\overline{S} = \overline{E}\overline{H}$. This error pattern is then modulo-2 added to the received sequence in order to obtain the most likely transmitted codeword.

5.3.4 Single-Error-Correcting Hamming Codes

To illustrate a single-error-correcting code, consider the parity check matrix in the following form

$$\overline{H} = \begin{bmatrix} \overline{h}_1 \\ \overline{h}_2 \\ \vdots \\ \overline{h}_j \\ \vdots \\ \overline{h}_n \end{bmatrix} \tag{5.3.13}$$

in which $\overline{h}_j$ is an $(n-k)$ symbol row vector. With this representation, equation 5.3.12 becomes

$$\overline{S} = \begin{bmatrix} e_1 & e_2 & \cdots & e_j & \cdots & e_n \end{bmatrix} \begin{bmatrix} \overline{h}_1 \\ \overline{h}_2 \\ \vdots \\ \overline{h}_j \\ \vdots \\ \overline{h}_n \end{bmatrix}. \tag{5.3.14}$$

It follows that if the error sequence is all zero except for a 1 in the jth position, denoting a single error in the jth symbol of the n-symbol codeword, then

$$\overline{S} = \overline{h}_j. \tag{5.3.15}$$

Therefore a single error in the jth position of the received codeword yields the jth row vector of the parity check matrix for a syndrome. If all single errors are to be detected, it follows that all row vectors making up the parity check matrix must be distinct. The all-zero vector must be excluded, since an all-zero syndrome denotes an assumed correct transmission. Since there are $2^{(n-k)}$ different binary sequences of length $n - k$, it follows that the parity check matrix has $2^{(n-k)} - 1$ rows. Thus n and k satisfy the relationship

$$n = 2^{(n-k)} - 1 \tag{5.3.16}$$

where, of course, $n - k$ is the number of parity check symbols.

Example 5.3.3: The (7, 4) Hamming Code

Consider a code with $n - k = 3$ parity check symbols. There are $2^3 - 1 = 7$ possible sequences of length 3, excluding the all-zero sequence. These seven sequences of length 3 form rows of the parity check matrix. It follows that $n = 7$ and $k = 4$. For a (7, 4) systematic code, the first four rows of the parity check matrix are the four sequences having more than one binary 1. The order of these four rows is arbitrary and does not affect code performance. Thus one possible parity check matrix for a single-error-correcting code is

$$\overline{H} = \begin{bmatrix} 0 & 1 & 1 \\ 1 & 0 & 1 \\ 1 & 1 & 0 \\ 1 & 1 & 1 \\ 1 & 0 & 0 \\ 0 & 1 & 0 \\ 0 & 0 & 1 \end{bmatrix}. \tag{5.3.17}$$

For this choice of parity check matrix, the generator matrix is given by

$$\overline{G} = \begin{bmatrix} 1 & 0 & 0 & 0 & 0 & 1 & 1 \\ 0 & 1 & 0 & 0 & 1 & 0 & 1 \\ 0 & 0 & 1 & 0 & 1 & 1 & 0 \\ 0 & 0 & 0 & 1 & 1 & 1 & 1 \end{bmatrix}. \tag{5.3.18}$$

Assume an information sequence $\overline{X} = [1\ 0\ 1\ 1]$. The corresponding codeword is

$$\overline{Y} = \overline{X}\,\overline{G} = [1 \quad 0 \quad 1 \quad 1 \quad 0 \quad 1 \quad 0].$$

If a transmission error occurs in the fifth position, the received sequence is

$$\overline{Z} = \overline{Y} \oplus \overline{E} = [1 \quad 0 \quad 1 \quad 1 \quad 1 \quad 1 \quad 0]$$

and the syndrome is

$$\overline{S} = \overline{Z}\,\overline{H} = [1 \quad 0 \quad 1 \quad 1 \quad 1 \quad 1 \quad 0] \begin{bmatrix} 0 & 1 & 1 \\ 1 & 0 & 1 \\ 1 & 1 & 0 \\ 1 & 1 & 1 \\ 1 & 0 & 0 \\ 0 & 1 & 0 \\ 0 & 0 & 1 \end{bmatrix} = [1 \quad 0 \quad 0].$$

Since the syndrome is the fifth row of the parity check matrix, an error is indicated in the fifth position.

Now assume an error pattern consisting of errors in the second and fifth positions so that the error vector is given by

$$\bar{E} = [0 \;\; 1 \;\; 0 \;\; 0 \;\; 1 \;\; 0 \;\; 0].$$

The received sequence is

$$\bar{Z} = [1 \;\; 1 \;\; 1 \;\; 1 \;\; 1 \;\; 1 \;\; 0],$$

and the corresponding syndrome is

$$\bar{S} = \bar{Z}\bar{H} = [0 \;\; 0 \;\; 1],$$

indicating (incorrectly) an error in the seventh position. It should be noted that the syndrome is the modulo-2 sum of the second and fifth rows of the parity check matrix. The reason for the failure of the code is that it takes a distance 5 code to correct double errors, and the code generated by equation 5.3.17 is a distance 3 code. Note, however, that an incorrect transmission was detected. Figure 5.3.5 describes the encoding procedure for this code.

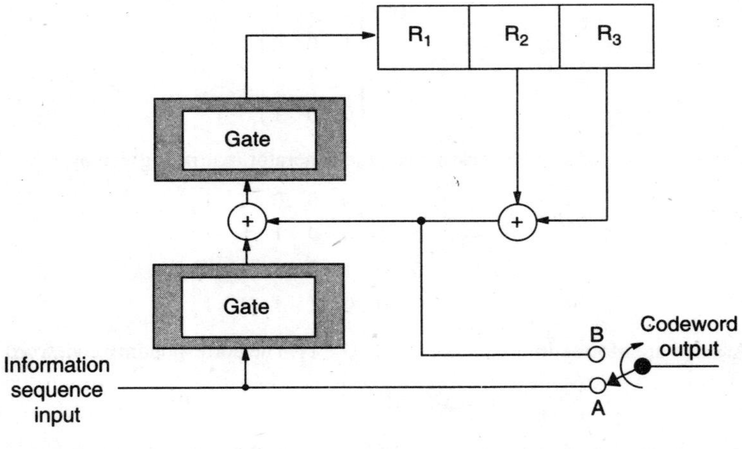

(a)

Shift	Input	Gate	Switch	R_1	R_2	R_3	Output
1	1	C	A	1	0	0	1
2	0	C	A	0	1	0	0
3	1	C	A	0	0	1	1
4	1	C	A	1	0	0	0
5	–	0	B	0	1	0	0
6	–	0	B	0	0	1	1
7	–	0	B	0	0	0	1

(b)

Figure 5.3.5 Encoding a (7, 4) cyclic code. (a), Example encoder for (7, 4) cyclic code. (b), Table of register contents for encoder. (From Feher, 1983.)

5.3.5 Cyclic Codes

Of all the linear block codes, the most useful and popular are the cyclic codes. A cyclic code is one for which an end-around shift of a codeword yields another codeword. In other words, if

$$(y_1, y_2, y_3, \ldots, y_n)$$

is a codeword, it follows that for a cyclic code,

$$(y_n, y_1, y_2, \ldots, y_{n-1})$$

is also a codeword. Note that only $n - 1$ codewords can be generated by cyclic shifts of a single codeword. Therefore it takes several different codewords to generate a complete set of codewords by cyclic shifts.

The principal reason that cyclic codes are of major importance is that encoding and decoding can be implemented using simple shift-register circuits and a small amount of additional logic. Encoding is accomplished by using either a k-stage shift register or an $(n - k)$-stage shift register. Syndrome calculation for decoding can also be accomplished using a k-stage or $(n - k)$-stage shift register.

A number of excellent treatments of cyclic codes are contained in the literature (Berlekamp, 1968; Clark and Cain, 1981; Lin, 1970; Peterson, 1961). Each of these textbooks provides the necessary mathematical background for implementing both the encoder and the decoder. Thus we shall merely illustrate the technique by means of a simple example.

Example 5.3.4

An encoder for a (7, 4) cyclic code using a three-stage shift register is illustrated in Figure 5.3.5. The operation of the encoder is summarized for the input word 1 0 1 0. As indicated in Figure 5.3.5, (b), the gates are closed (denoted by *C*) and the switch is in position *A* during the first four shifts. During this period the information sequence is shifted into the modulator and channel and into the register. The gates are then opened (denoted by *0*), and the switch is placed in position *B*. Three parity symbols are then output to complete the codeword. For the information sequence 1 0 1 0, the parity sequence 0 1 1 is generated. Thus the complete codeword is 1 0 1 0 0 1 1.

The operation of the decoder is investigated by assuming an error in the fourth position so that the sequence 1 0 1 1 0 1 1 is received. The decoder is illustrated in Figure 5.3.6, (a). Fourteen shifts are necessary for processing the complete received word. The state of the gate and all registers are given in Figure 5.3.6, (b), for all 14 shifts. The AND gate gives a binary 1 output only when all three inputs are binary ones. Thus the contents of the R register must be 1 0 0 in order for a 1 to be generated at the output of the AND gate. This condition exists on the eleventh shift and, as can be seen, this inverts the fourth symbol as the received sequence is being shifted out of the decoder.

If the generator and parity matrices are constructed for the given encoder, it is clear that an error in the fourth position generates a syndrome of 0 1 1. Thus the upper part of the decoder is actually a syndrome generator.

We now briefly turn our attention to an important and flexible class of cyclic codes, the BCH codes.

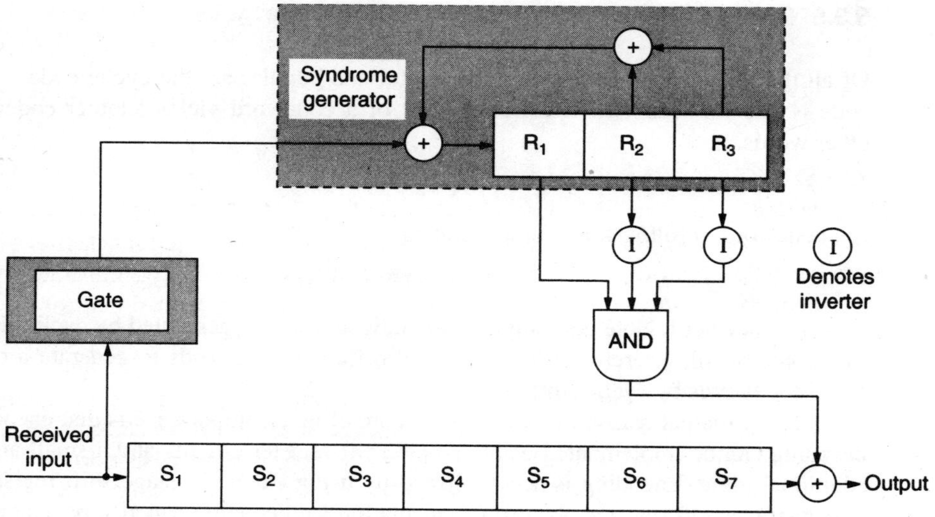

Shift	Input	Gate	R_1	R_2	R_3	AND	S_1	S_2	S_3	S_4	S_5	S_6	S_7	Output
1	1	C	1	0	0	–	1	–	–	–	–	–	–	–
2	0	C	0	1	0	–	0	1	–	–	–	–	–	–
3	1	C	0	0	1	–	1	0	1	–	–	–	–	–
4	1	C	0	0	0	–	1	1	0	1	–	–	–	–
5	0	C	0	0	0	–	0	1	1	0	1	–	–	–
6	1	C	1	0	0	–	1	0	1	1	0	1	–	–
7	1	C	1	1	0	–	1	1	0	1	1	0	1	–
8	–	0	1	1	1	0	–	1	1	0	1	1	0	1
9	–	0	0	1	1	0	–	–	1	1	0	1	1	0
10	–	0	0	0	1	0	–	–	–	1	1	0	1	1
11	–	0	1	0	0	1	–	–	–	–	1	1	0	0
12	–	0	0	1	0	0	–	–	–	–	–	1	1	0
13	–	0	1	0	1	0	–	–	–	–	–	–	1	1
14	–	0	1	1	0	0	–	–	–	–	–	–	–	1

(b)

Figure 5.3.6 Decoding a (7, 4) cyclic code. (a), Example decoder for (7, 4) cyclic code. (b), Table of register contents for decoding.

5.3.6 BCH, Bose-Chaudhuri-Hocquenghem Codes

The *Bose-Chaudhuri-Hocquenghem (BCH) codes* are perhaps among the most important codes in the class of cyclic codes. The design of these codes is straightforward, and for a given block length, *n*, codes can be designed with a wide range of rates and error-correcting ability. Specifically, if *e* is the number of correctable errors per codeword and *m* is an arbitrary integer, the number of symbols per codeword is

$$n = 2^m - 1 \qquad m > 2, \tag{5.3.19}$$

and the number of parity symbols per codeword is defined by the bound (Lin, 1970)

$$n - k \leq me. \tag{5.3.20}$$

Since e errors per codeword can be corrected, it follows that the minimum distance is given by

$$d > 2e + 1. \tag{5.3.21}$$

The relationship among n, k, and e is illustrated in Table 5.3.1 for a number of BCH codes. The value of k for given values of n and e is not easily determined. However, for small e equality holds in equation 5.3.20. Observation of Table 5.3.1 illustrates that for $n = 63$, equality in equation 5.3.20 holds for $e \leq 4$. It should be noted that for $e = 1$, the values of n and k define the Hamming code. Indeed, the Hamming code is a single-error-correcting BCH code.

Since the BCH codes are cyclic codes, encoding and decoding are accomplished using simple shift-register circuits. The performance of several BCH codes in an additive white Gaussian noise (AWGN) channel is illustrated in a subsequent section.

5.3.7 Golay Codes

The *Golay code* is important, since it is the only multiple-error-correcting code ($e > 1$) that is also a *perfect code.* The Golay code is a (23, 12) cyclic code that corrects all patterns of three or fewer errors. Closely related to the perfect (23, 12) Golay code is the (24, 12) Golay code, which is obtained from the (23, 12) Golay code by adding an overall parity check symbol. The (23, 12) Golay code has a minimum distance of 7, and the (24, 12) Golay code has a minimum distance of 8. Thus, in addition to correcting all patterns of

Table 5.3.1 BCH code illustrative parameters: Code length n, number of information symbols per code word k, and error-correcting capability e for BCH codes of lengths 7 to 255 (Peterson, 1961).

n	k	e	n	k	e	n	k	e	n	k	e
7	4	1									
15	11	1		10	13		8	31		115	21
	7	2		7	15	255	247	1		107	22
			127	120	1		239	2		99	23
31	26	1		113	2		231	3		91	25
	21	2		106	3		223	4		87	26
	16	3		99	4		215	5		79	27
	11	5		92	5		207	6		71	29
				85	6		199	7		63	30
63	57	1		78	7		191	8		55	31
	51	2		71	9		187	9		47	42
	45	3		64	10		179	10		45	43
	39	4		57	11		171	11		37	45
	36	5		50	13		163	12		29	47

three errors, the (24, 12) Golay code detects all patterns of four errors with a trivial reduction in code rate. The (24, 12) code is therefore popular for many applications.

The performance of a (23, 12) Golay code is illustrated in Figure 5.3.7. In this figure, the following are used:

P_{bec} = Probability of coded bit error (coded BER)
P_{wec} = Probability of word errors
k = Number of information symbols
n = Number of symbols in a coded word

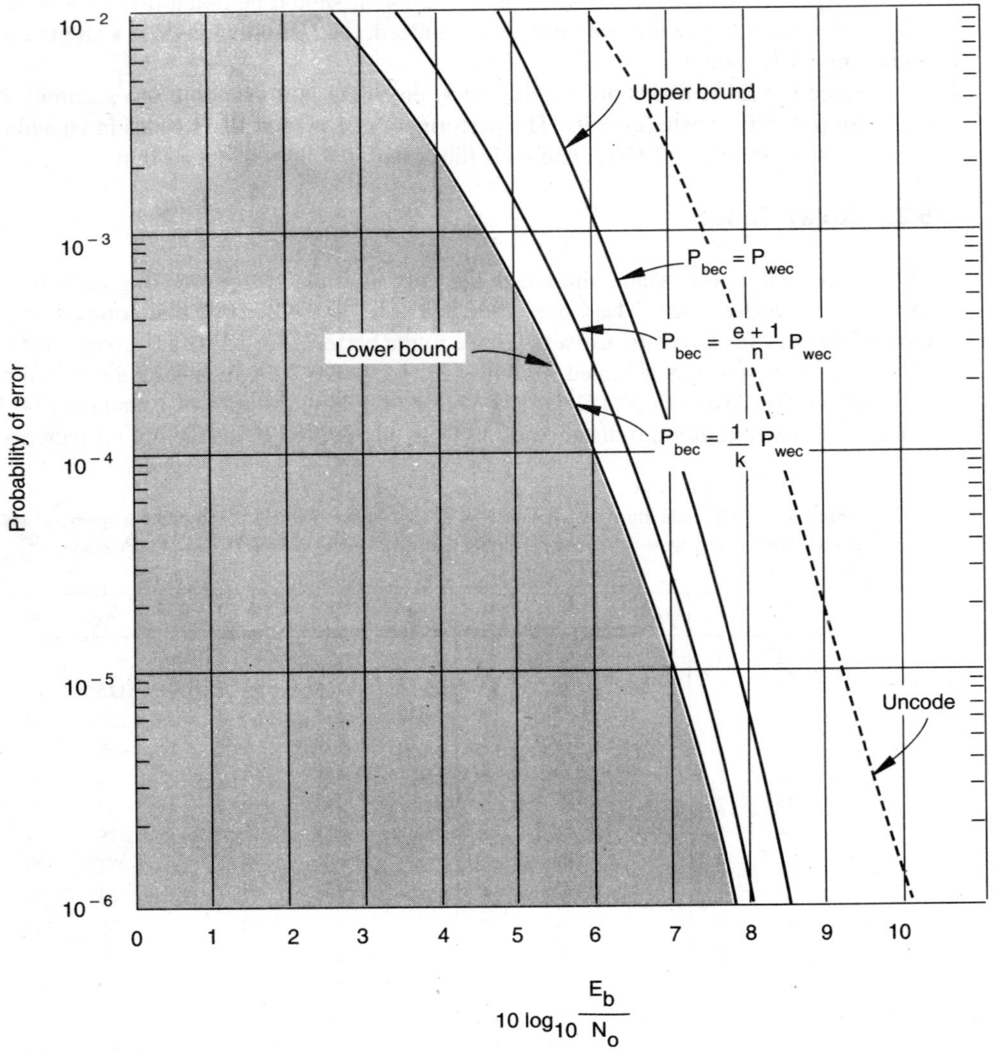

Figure 5.3.7 Bit-error probability for (23, 12) Golay code. [W.H. Tranter in Feher, K., 1983]

5.3.8 Reed-Solomon Codes

Among the nonbinary BCH codes, the most useful subclass is the one containing the Reed-Solomon (RS) codes. The encoder for an *(n, k, e)* RS code, with $n = 2^s - 1$, produces one of *n symbols* from the Galois field GF (2^s) for each group of *s* successive uncoded data bits. For each block of *k* such symbols, it generates a longer block of *n* symbols. After the symbols are interleaved, each symbol is converted back to its binary equivalent for transmission. Reed-Solomon codes achieve the largest possible code minimum-distance and error-correcting capability, *e,* for any linear code with the same *n* and *k*. In addition, they are especially effective in combating long strings of errors (burst errors) associated with channels that have memory. This is because of a given symbol error; the performance of the code is the same whether the symbol error is due to one bit being in error or *s* bits being in error. The probability of decoding an RS codeword in error is given by

$$P_E \le \sum_{i=e+1}^{n} \binom{n}{i} P_s^i \left(1 - P_s\right)^{n-i}$$

where P_s is the channel *symbol-error* probability, given by

$$P_s = \sum_{j=1}^{s} \binom{s}{j} q_c^j \left(1 - q_c\right)^{s-j}.$$

The probability of postdecoding symbol error is given by

$$P_e \le \frac{1}{n} \sum_{i=e+1}^{n} \binom{n}{i} (i + e) P_s^i \left(1 - P_s\right)^{n-i}.$$

If, in addition to the assumptions that the channel is memoryless (because of interleaving) and that successive bits are independent, we further assume that the RS code symbols are equally likely, then a channel error will convert the correct symbol into any one of the remaining $(n - 1)$ incorrect symbols with equal probability. Hence the postdecoding bit-error rate (Clark and Cain, 1987; Sklar, 1988) is.

$$P_{e(\text{bit})} \le \frac{2^{s-1}}{2^s - 1} P_{e(\text{symbol})}.$$

5.3.9 Comparative Performance of Block Codes

The performance of a number of block codes is illustrated in Figure 5.3.8. The assumption that a word error results in errors in all information symbols was used so that the illustrated performance represents "worst-case" bounds. The approximation of equation 5.3.6 was also used.

It can be seen from Figure 5.3.8 that the (7, 4) and (15, 11) codes, which are single-error-correcting Hamming codes, offer moderate improvement for values of energy of a bit (E_b) to noise density (N_o), E_b/N_o, greater than approximately 8 dB. The (127, 113) code is a

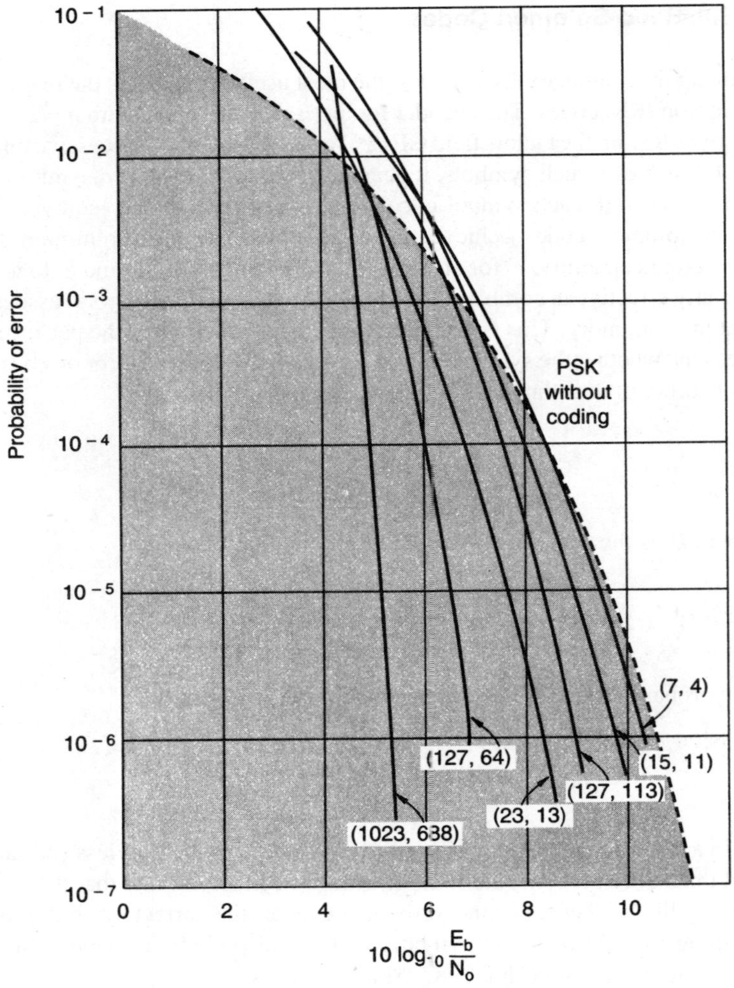

Figure 5.3.8 Comparison of codes. ("Worst-case" bounds are shown.)

double-error-correcting BCH code and improves performance by over an order of magnitude for a fixed value of E_b/N_o in excess of 8 dB. This rate 7/8 code has been specified for use in the 120-Mb/s rate INTELSAT-V time division multiple access (TDMA) system. The (23, 12) code is the triple-error-correcting Golay code. The (127, 64) and (1023, 688) codes are BCH codes capable of correcting 10 and 36 errors per codeword, respectively.

5.4 CONVOLUTIONAL CODING

We now consider a different type of encoder, in which the information symbols are not grouped together in blocks for encoding. This is the convolutional encoder, which has numerous successful applications in satellite communications (Berlekamp et al., 1987; Feher, 1983).

5.4.1 Encoding of Convolutional Codes

A convolutional encoder is shown in Figure 5.4.1. It consists of a K-stage shift register, v modulo-2 adders, a commutator, and a set of connections between the K stages of the shift register and the v modulo-2 adders. Operation of the basic convolutional encoder is simple. The information symbols are input to the shift register one symbol at a time. The outputs of the modulo-2 adders, determined by the connections to the shift register, are then sampled in turn by the commutator to produce v output symbols. Since v output symbols are produced for each input symbol, the rate of the code is $1/v$. For constant transmitter power and information rate, the symbol-error probability is increased through the use of convolutional encoding, just as with block codes. However, for a properly designed code, the redundancy induced by the encoder allows error correction and a net improvement in system performance.

Code rates greater than 1/2 can be accomplished by shifting k symbols into the k-stage shift register between the commutation operations. This obviously yields a code rate of k/v.

An important parameter in the consideration of convolutional encoding is the constraint span, which is defined as the number of output symbols that are affected by a given input symbol. If information symbols are input to the K-stage shift register in groups of k symbols, the register can hold K/k groups. Since each group yields v output symbols, the constraint span is $(K/k)v$. This is the memory time of the encoder.

To gain a better feeling for the convolutional encoding operation, consider the rate 1/3 encoder shown in Figure 5.4.2. For each information symbol, the sequence (v_1, v_2, v_3) is generated. It follows from Figure 5.4.2 that v_1, v_2, and v_3 are given by

$$v_1 = \mathbf{R}_1$$
$$v_2 = \mathbf{R}_1 \oplus \mathbf{R}_2 \oplus \mathbf{R}_3$$
$$v_3 = \mathbf{R}_1 \oplus \mathbf{R}_3$$

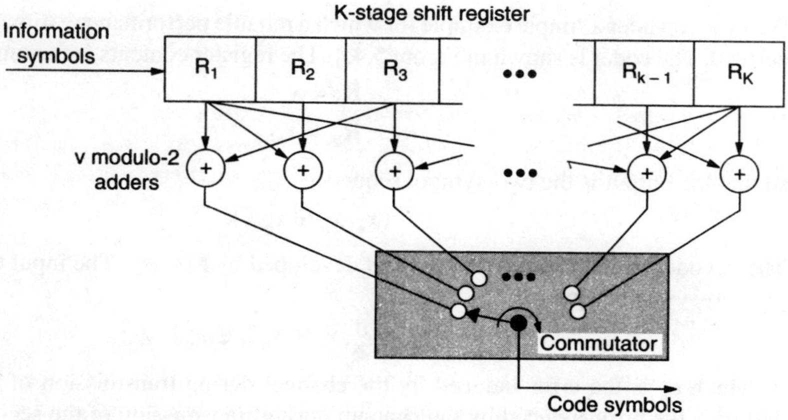

Figure 5.4.1 General convolutional encoder.

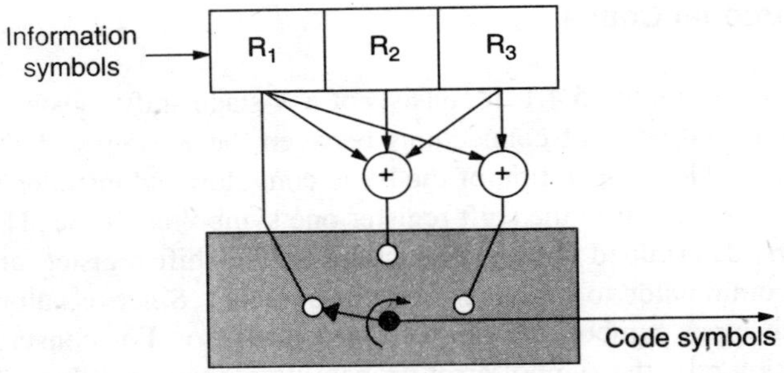

Figure 5.4.2 Example of a systematic rate $\frac{1}{3}$ convolutional encoder.

in which $\mathbf{R}_i$ denotes the contents of the ith register. Since the first symbol in the output sequence is the information symbol, this particular convolutional code is systematic. Thus v_2 and v_3 can be viewed as parity symbols.

The output sequence for an arbitrary input sequence is often determined with the aid of a code tree. The code tree for the encoder in Figure 5.4.2 is shown in Figure 5.4.3. The branches correspond to input symbols; a branch upward corresponds to an "input" 0, and a branch downward corresponds to an input 1. The three symbols on a given branch denote the output sequence corresponding to that branch. Thus the input sequence 1 0 1 1 generates the output sequence 1 1 1 0 1 0 1 0 0 1 0 1. Note that after nine output symbols the code tree is symmetrical about the dashed line. This results because the constraint length is 9.

Conceptually, decoding is accomplished by taking the received sequence and finding the path through the code tree that lies closest in Hamming distance to the received sequence. This is, of course, not practical for long sequences, since decoding a sequence of r symbols requires that 2^r branches of the code tree be searched for the minimum Hamming distance. Many algorithms have been developed to facilitate the decoding process. These are mentioned briefly later.

5.4.2 Threshold Decoding: An Example

We now consider a simple example for which a reliable performance estimate can be simply derived. The coder is shown in Figure 5.4.4. The register contents are assumed to be

$$\mathbf{R}_1 = x_n$$
$$\mathbf{R}_2 = x_{n-1}$$

so that the output is the two-symbol sequence

$$(x_n, x_n \oplus x_{n-1}).$$

The decoder is a threshold decoder first developed by Massey. The input to the decoder is the two-symbol sequence

$$(x_n \oplus e_n^1, x_n \oplus x_{n-1} \oplus e_n^2)$$

in which e_n^1 is the error induced by the channel during transmission of the first symbol and e_n^2 is the error induced by the channel during transmission of the second symbol. The

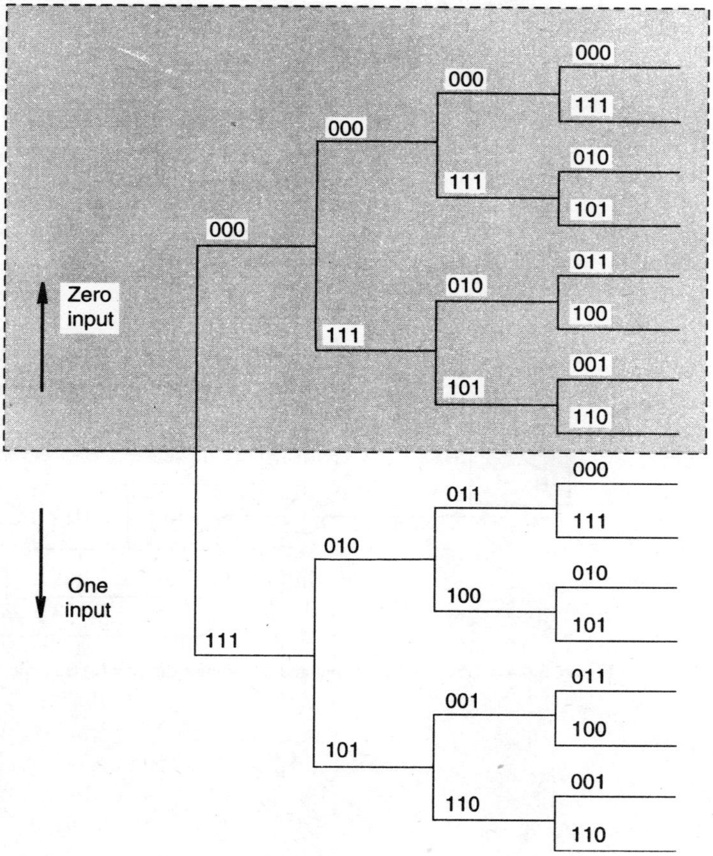

Figure 5.4.3 Code tree for encoder shown in Figure 5.4.2. (From J.A. Heller and I.M. Jacobs, "Viterbi decoding for satellite and space communication," *Proceedings of the IEEE*, (© 1971 IEEE).

switch on the decoder is in position A when the first symbol is input to the decoder and in position B when the second symbol is input to the decoder. Thus

$$D_1 = x_n \oplus e_n^1,$$

and it follows that

$$D_2 = x_{n-1} \oplus e_{n-1}^1.$$

Since the contents of D_3 is given by

$$D_3 = x_n \oplus x_{n-1} \oplus e_n^2 \oplus D_1 \oplus D_2,$$

it follows that

$$D_3 = e_n^1 \oplus e_{n-1}^1 \oplus e_n^2$$

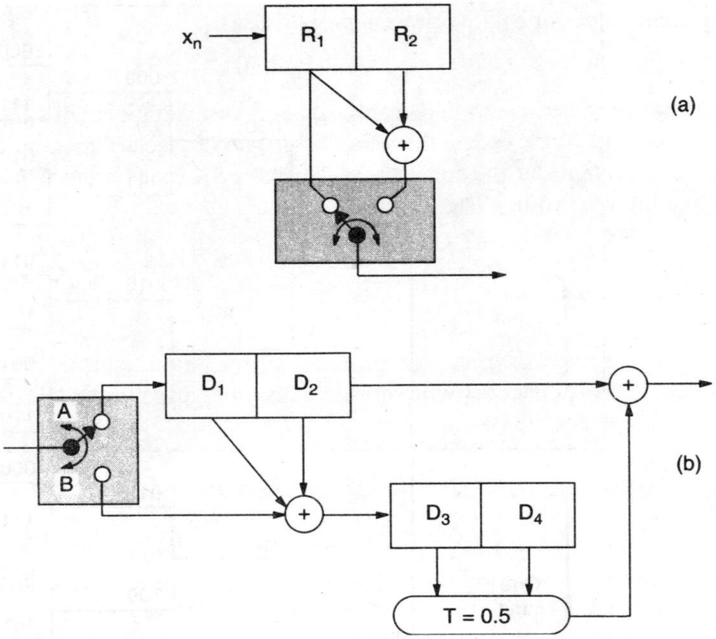

Figure 5.4.4 Threshold encoding and decoding example. (a), Encoder; (b), decoder.

and

$$D_4 = e^1_{n-1} \oplus e^1_{n-2} \oplus e^2_{n-1}.$$

In reasonable signal-to-noise ratio (S/N) environments, D_3 and D_4 provide sufficient information for making a reliable decision.

If D_3 and D_4 are *both* equal to 1, there are two possibilities. The first possibility is that the e^1_{n-1} is in error. The second possibility is that e^1_n or e^2_n is in error and e^1_{n-2} or e^2_{n-1} is in error. For small channel-error probability, q_c, the probability that e^1_{n-1} is 1 is approximately q_c. The other event requires that two errors are made in the sequence $e^1_n\, e^2_n\, e^1_{n-1}\, e^1_{n-2}$, and the probability of this event is q_c^2. Thus, with high probability, e^1_{n-1} is 1 if D_1 and D_2 are both 1. This determination is made by establishing a threshold level of 1/2 as shown. If the threshold is exceeded, an error is (with high probability) detected in the preceding information symbol. (Recall that the code is systematic.)

The probability of error is the probability that more than one error is made in the sequence $e^1_n\, e^2_n\, e^1_{n-1}\, e^2_{n-1} e^1_{n-2}$. The probability of this event is

$$P_E = \sum_{i=2}^{5} \binom{5}{i} q_c^i \left(1 - q_c\right)^{5-i}.$$

For small values of q_c, P_E can be approximated by

$$P_E \cong 10q_c^2.$$

The improvement in system performance is significant for small values of q_c.

As with block codes, the value of q_c must be determined by considering the code rate. For example, if the code rate is $1/v$ and PSK modulation is used, the symbol-error probability with coding is given by

$$q_c = \frac{1}{2} erfc\left[\sqrt{\frac{E_b}{vN_o}}\right].$$

The detailed diagram, the principal of operation, and the performance of the rate 3/4 convolutional encoder with threshold decoding used in the INTELSAT satellite is described in Feher (1983).

5.4.3 Performance of Convolutional Codes

At the present time, the most popular decoder for convolutional codes is the *Viterbi algorithm.* The Viterbi algorithm is a maximum-likelihood technique and was first published by Viterbi in 1967 (Viterbi and Omura, 1979). It is most practical for convolutional codes having a relatively short constraint length. A description of the algorithm is beyond the scope of this chapter, but excellent treatments are contained in the textbooks by Viterbi and Omura (1979) and Clark and Cain (1981). In addition, both of these textbooks contain descriptions of several other convolutional coding methods.

Computer simulation is a popular method for studying the performance of systems that utilize convolutional codes, and a large number of results have been published. Of

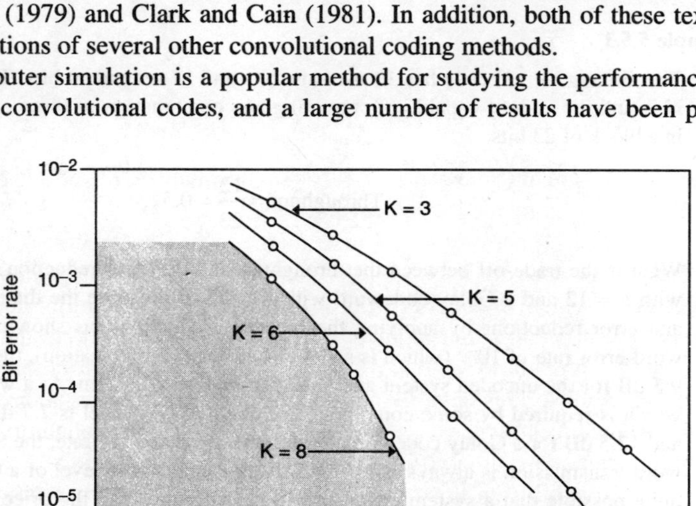

Figure 5.4.5 Performance of rate $\frac{1}{2}$ convolutional codes. (From Heller and Jacobs, 1971.)

particular note are the results published by Heller and Jacobs (1971), which were obtained by considering a power-limited satellite system with PSK modulation and Viterbi decoding. The authors considered both hard-decision and soft-decision decoders, and their results agree with the 2-dB performance penalty associated with hard-decision receivers that are discussed in Feher (1983).

An example of performance results obtained by Heller and Jacobs is illustrated in Figure 5.4.5. In these performance curves the parameter K represents the number of stages in the shift register, and the code rate is 1/2.

5.5 PRICE OF ERROR CORRECTION: REDUCED THROUGHPUT?

The price of having a t-error-correcting code on an L-digit message is to add N-L parity check bits for a binary cyclic code or to add N-L redundant bits for a linear block code. Usually the number of N-L bits is much greater than t bits,

$$\text{Throughput} = \frac{L}{N}.$$

A code with a Hamming distance d generally has an error-correcting capability of

$$t = \frac{d-1}{2}.$$

Example 5.5.1

The Golay (23, 12) code has 12 message bits and 11 redundant bits. The Hamming distance is 7, and the code is capable of correcting any combination of three or fewer random errors in a block of 23 bits:

$$\text{Throughput} = \frac{12}{23} = 0.52.$$

What is the trade-off between the throughput and the error reduction? Use a noncode word with $L = 12$ and a Golay codeword with $N = 23$ to illustrate the differences in throughputs and error reductions by applying the preceding equations, as shown in Figure 5.3.2. At a word-error rate of 10^{-3} (which is usually used for communication), the required S/N level is 9.5 dB for the uncoded system and 5 dB for the coded system. At a word-error rate of 10^{-7}, which is required by some computers, the required S/N level is 7.7 dB for a noncode word and 12.5 dB for a Golay codeword. With a given word-error rate, the S/N level of a noncode word transmission is always at least 4.5 dB higher than the level of a Golay code word. It is quite possible that a system designer will be willing to pay the price of increasing the S/N level 4.5 dB for a noncode word in order to keep the same word-error rate of the Golay codeword while doubling the throughput.

The following sections, 5.6 and 5.7, are based on the pioneering mobile communications system work of Dr. W. C. Y. Lee (1993) and several other references on coding technique and coding applications.

5.6 WORD-ERROR RATE, FALSE-ALARM RATE, AND PROBABILITY OF BIT ERROR

5.6.1 Definitions

False recognition among all the codes being assigned to different functions or addresses is annoying to the user and costly to the operating company. For example, if the probability of *false-alarm rate (FAR)* (explained later in this section) is high, the address number may be answered by the wrong party, an operational function such as *request for handoff* is made at the wrong time, or other signaling and channel access controls and functions may be executed at the wrong time and erroneously. Then the overall quality and reliability of the wireless network is degraded. This results in reduced capacity and revenues, including loss of dissatisfied customers.

The FAR should be minimized under all conditions, including the most difficult propagation, weak signal, and interference controlled environments.

Let P_e be the probability of bit error. The probability of having exactly m bits in error in a message of L bits is given by the binomial expansion

$$P_e(L,m) = \binom{L}{m}(1-P_e)^{L-m} P_e^m \tag{5.6.1}$$

where

$$\binom{L}{m} = \frac{L!}{(L-m)!\,m!}. \tag{5.6.2}$$

The *word-error rate* (P_{ew}) of a message-word having a length of L bits *without error correction* is

$$P_w = 1-(1-P_e)^L. \tag{5.6.3}$$

Word-error rate (P_{ew}) of a codeword consisting of N bits with an error-correction capability of correcting t errors or less can be expressed as

$$P_{ew} = 1-\sum_{k=0}^{t} C_k^N P_e^k (1-P_e)^{N-k} \tag{5.6.4}$$

where

$$C_k^N = \frac{N!}{(N-k)!\,k!}. \tag{5.6.5}$$

The word-error rate (P_{ew}) is the probability of erroneous codeword demodulation or reception.

The *FAR* (or P_f) is the probability of a falsely recognizable word. This corresponds to the event that the receiver recognizes a signal as one word (message), given that the transmitter had sent another word. If the two words (messages) differ from each other by d bits, then the probability of this event is

$$P_f = P_e^d (1 - P_e)^{L-d}. \tag{5.6.6}$$

The word-error rate *differs* from the false-alarm rate because one or more errors in a word occur more often then misinterpreted words. In an illustrative wireless telephony systems design, the word-error rate could be as high as 10^{-2}, whereas the false-alarm rate would have to be below 10^{-7}.

Example 5.6.1: A False-Alarm Rate

Observe two codewords of 9 bits. Let $L = 9$:

1 0 1 0 1 1 0 1 0

1 1 0 1 0 1 0 0 0

There are five places where the bits differ, so $d = 5$. Assume that the bit-error rate of each bit is 10^{-2}. Then substituting $L = 9$, $d = 5$, and $P_e = 10^{-2}$ into equation 5.6.6, P_f becomes

$$P_f = (0.01)^5 (1 - 0.01)^{9-5} = 10^{-7}.$$

The chance of a false alarm per user in this case is one in 10 million. If 10,000 users call the same area at the same time, then the probability of having a false alarm is 10^{-3}, which means one out of every thousand users will receive a false word. This, of course, is very undesirable. After codewords have been generated, they must be received virtually free of errors. If there are more than five erroneous bits in a codeword of nine bits, then the code detector interprets it as a correct word for some other user's identification or for another totally different operation or function.

5.6.2 Coded Word-Error-Rate Performance in Fast and Slow Rayleigh-Faded Environments

In this section we study the performance of coded word-error rate $\langle P_{cw} \rangle$ in slow and fast Rayleigh-fading environments. We assume that the (n, k) block code words have a t-error-correction capability. The average bit-error probability, denoted as $\langle P_e \rangle$ (the symbol $\langle\ \rangle$ represents average value in a faded environment), for most frequently used modulation techniques is described in Chapter 4.

In a Rayleigh-faded environment the *received modulated signal power fluctuates* over a large dynamic range, typically *10 dB to 50 dB*. The duration of the fades is related to the velocity of the mobile unit, radio frequency, and environment. When the velocity is high, the duration of the fades is short. Short fades, that is, short durations of weak signal receptions, lead to short time segments of low C/N or Carrier to Interference or (C/I) and thus to relatively short multiple-error intervals or short coded word-error or error-burst durations. When the velocity of the mobile (or of the environment) is low, the duration of the fades is long; thus the bit-error-rate and corresponding word-error-rate performance will be high for longer periods of time, that is, for long burst durations. The derivation of a general analytical expression for the word-error rate in terms of vehicle speed and propagation statistics is elaborate and beyond the scope of this book. Two extreme cases of fast-fading and slow-fading Rayleigh channels are illustrated in this section. These cases approximate several practical "fast" and "slow" faded system environments.

5.6.2.1 Fast-fading Rayleigh environment. When the speed of the mobile unit and/or the changes in the environment are fast the distribution statistics of the amplitude fades remain Rayleigh, but the duration of deep fades approaches a small fraction of the bit duration. Under such conditions there is no significant correlation between the performance of adjacent bits. For this reason, each bit is analyzed independently. The average bit-error rate $\langle P_e \rangle$ in a Rayleigh-faded environment is given in Chapter 4 equation 4.6.9 and Figure 4.6.3. The *(N, K)* error-correction-coded performance of the code word-error rate $\langle P_{cw} \rangle$ for *N*-bit-long coded words with *t*-bit error-correction capability is

$$\langle P_{cw} \rangle = 1 - \sum_{k=0}^{t} C_k^N \langle P_e \rangle^k (1 - \langle P_e \rangle)^{N-k} \tag{5.6.7}$$

where C_k^N is defined by equation 5.6.5. See Figures 5.6.1 to 5.6.3.

The word-error rate with $t = 0$ from (5.6.7) is:

$$\langle P_{cw} \rangle = 1 - [1 - \langle P_e \rangle]^N. \tag{5.6.8}$$

An illustrative result of this equation for $N = 22$ coded bits and ideal Differential Phase Shift Keying (DPSK) transmission, based on equation 4.6.9, is plotted in Figure 5.7.1 (Lee, 1993). In addition to the coded word-error rate (P_{cw}), we also plot the bit-error-rate (P_e) performance of a conventional DBSK system in a Rayleigh-faded environment. We recall that

$$\Gamma = \text{average } \frac{C}{N} = \frac{E_b}{N_o}. \tag{5.6.9}$$

for the Binary Phase Shift Keying (BPSK) system. Note that between the "dotted" $P_e = f(E_b/N_o)$ curve and the $t = 0$ (no error correction) $N = 22$ bit word there is a

$$10 \log \frac{22}{1} = 13.4 \; dB$$

shift. With a single-error-correction code ($t = 1$) from equation 5.6.7 we obtain

$$\langle P_{ew} \rangle = 1 - (1 - \langle P_e \rangle)^N - N(1 - \langle P_e \rangle)^{N-1} \langle P_e \rangle. \tag{5.6.10}$$

See Figure 5.6.1 for the $N = 22$ DBSK example. Note that the single-error-correction code has an improved P_{ew} performance. The performance improvement of the $t = 3$ error-correction code is very significant.

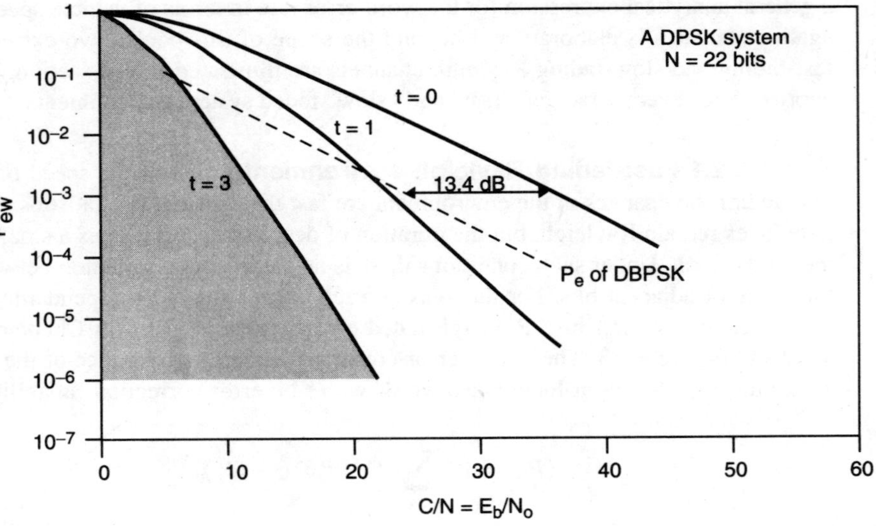

Figure 5.6.1 Error-corrected codeword error-rate P_{ew} and raw (uncoded) bit-error-rate probability (P_e) of a DPSK system in a Rayleigh-faded environment. The $P_e = f(E_b/N_o)$ performance is based on equation 4.6.9 and Figure 4.6.3 (see Chapter 4). The P_{ew} computation is based one equation 5.6.8 for $N = 22$ bit coded word length with $t = 0$, $t = 1$, and $t = 3$ error correction within one coded word. (From Lee, 1993.)

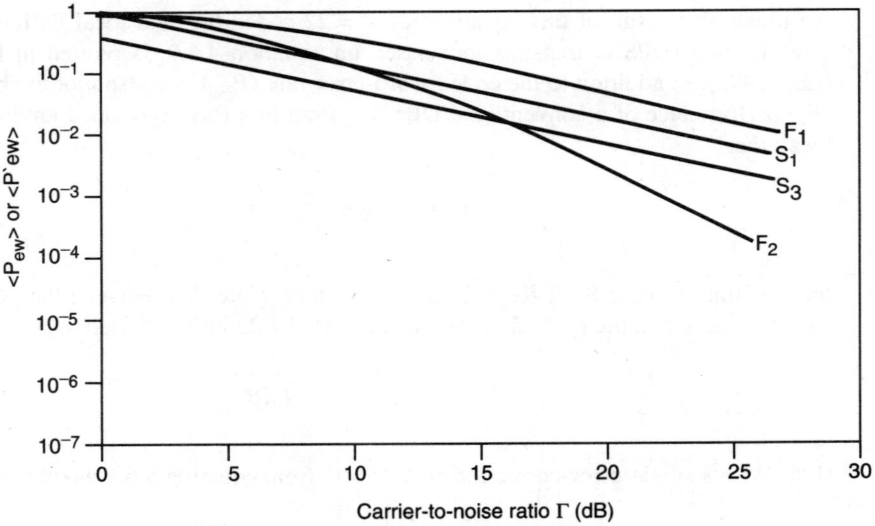

Figure 5.6.2 Word-error rates with and without repetition transmission. No-error correction code. A DPSK system (word length = 22 bits), S = slow-fading case, F = fast-fading case, S_1, F_1 = no repetition transmission, and S_2, F_2 = $\frac{2}{3}$ majority-voting process. (From *Mobile Communications Design Fundamentals,* William C.Y. Lee, Copyright © J. Wiley & Sons, 1993. Reprinted by permission of J. Wiley & Sons, Inc.)

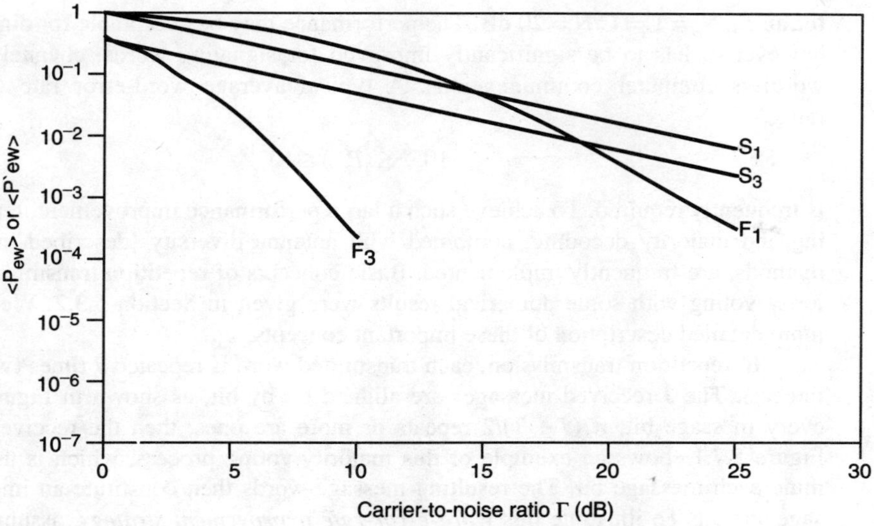

Figure 5.6.3 Word-error rates with and without repetition transmission. One-error correction code. A DPSK system (word length = 22 bits), S = slow-fading case, F = fast-fading case, S_1, F_1 = no repetition transmission, and $S_3, F_3 = \frac{3}{5}$ majority-voting process.

5.6.2.2 Slow-fading Rayleigh environment. The Rayleigh-fading environment is "slow fading" when the mobile unit is moving very slowly relative to the transmitted bit rate (Lee, 1993). In this case, we assume that all bits in a word are correlated, that is, all of them are either above the faded threshold (very low bit-error rate) or in the same deep fade (high bit-error rate). The entire word is treated like a single bit in a fast-fading case (Lee, 1993). For such a case the average word-error rate is

$$\langle P_{cw} \rangle = \int_0^\infty P_{ew}\, p(\gamma) d\gamma \qquad (5.6.11)$$

where $p(\gamma)$ is the Rayleigh probability density function (defined in Chapter 3).

By substituting equation 5.6.4 into equation 5.6.11, the word-error rate of the error-corrected code word is obtained. No-error-correction and single bit-error correction codes are illustrated in Figures 5.6.2 and 5.6.3. The performance curves with repetitive transmission and majority voting are explained in the next section.

5.7 REPETITION TRANSMISSION AND MAJORITY-VOTING SYSTEM: CONCEPTS AND PERFORMANCE

The single-error-corrected average word-error-rate $\langle P_{ew} \rangle$ performance of an illustrative DBSK system having a word length of $N = 22$ bits (see Figure 5.6.3) is in the range of

$$\langle P_{ew} \rangle = 10^{-2}$$

for an $E_b/N_o = \Gamma = C/N = 20$ dB. The performance may be acceptable for digitized voice; however, it has to be significantly improved for signaling words, channel access, and wordless computer communications. A typical average word-error rate $\langle P_{ew}\rangle$ in the range of

$$10^{-6} \le \langle P_{ew}\rangle \le 10^{-10}$$

is frequently required. To achieve such a large performance improvement, repetition coding and majority decoding, combined with antenna diversity (described in Chapter 7) methods, are frequently implemented. Basic concepts of repetition transmission and majority voting with some numerical results were given in Section 5.3.2. We now give a more detailed description of these important concepts.

In repetition transmission, each transmitted word is repeated J times (with J an odd integer). The J received messages are aligned bit by bit, as shown in Figure 5.7.1. For every message bit, if $(J + 1)/2$ repeats or more are ones, then the received bit is a 1. Figure 5.7.1 shows an example of this majority-voting process, which is used to determine each message bit. The resulting message-words then constitute an improved message stream. To illustrate this *word-error-rate improvement strategy,* assume that a single-bit error-correction code is used at the transmission end. Then at the receiving end, after the improved message stream is formed by applying the majority-voting process, the one-bit error-correction capability further improves the chances for obtaining an error-free message stream. Under fast-fading conditions, and on the assumption that no correlation exists between any two repeated bits among J repeats, the improved bit-error rate $\langle P_e'\rangle$ for J repeats with a majority-voting process can be expressed as

$$\langle P_e'\rangle = \sum_{k=(J+1)/2}^{J} C_k^J \langle P_e\rangle^k (1-\langle P_e\rangle)^{J-k}. \tag{5.7.1}$$

Equation 5.7.1 is plotted in Figure 5.7.1 for a two-out-of-three and three-out-of-five majority-voting process using a DPSK system. The improved bit-error rates of a repetition transmission are lower than those of the nonrepetition transmission, since in a fast-fading case all the message bits are uncorrelated. The bit-error rate in Rayleigh environment after the majority-voting process still cannot be lower than that in a Gaussian environment. Given a word length of N uncorrelated message bits, the bit-error rate that 1 or more bits will be in error can be expressed as

$$\langle P_{cw}'\rangle = 1-(1-\langle P_e'\rangle)^N \quad \text{(no-error correction)}. \tag{5.7.2}$$

Note the similarity to equation 5.6.8. Given a word length of N uncorrected message bits, the bit-error rate that more than t bits are in error can be obtained as

$$\langle P_{ew}'\rangle = 1-\sum_{k=0}^{t} C_k^N \langle P_e'\rangle(1-\langle P_e'\rangle)^{N-k}. \tag{5.7.3}$$

Equations 5.7.2 and 5.7.3 are plotted in Figures 5.6.2 and 5.6.3, where the performance of repetition transmissions is compared with that of nonrepetition transmissions. In contrast to the case of no-coding and nonrepetition transmission, the coding and repeti-

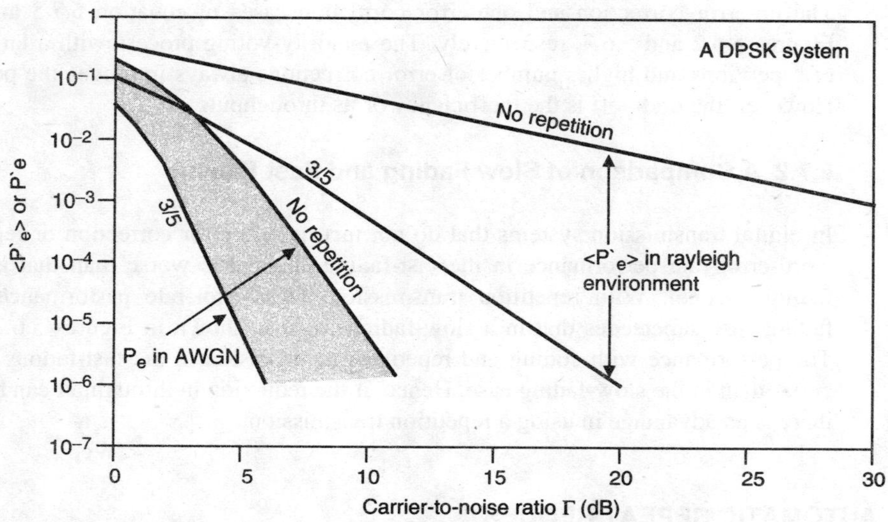

Figure 5.7.1 Comparison of improved bit-error rates in Rayleigh environment and in Gaussian (AWGN) environment (fast-fading case). (From Lee, 1993.)

tion transmissions provide considerable performance improvement, as shown in these two figures.

5.7.1 Repetition Transmission and Majority-Voting Process

After a majority-voting process over J-repetition transmission, the improved bit-error rate P'_e is given by

$$P'_e = \sum_{k=(J+1)/2}^{J} C_k^J P_e^k (1 - P_e)^{J-k} \qquad (5.7.4)$$

where P_e is the bit-error rate in the Gaussian environment. A DPSK system will be used to illustrate the performance. The P'_e of a fast-fading case is higher than that of a slow-fading case in both strategies of the majority-voting processes: two out of three and three out of five. The average word-error rate to come out of this repetition transmission is

$$\langle P'_{ew} \rangle = \int P'_{ew} p(\gamma) d\gamma \qquad (5.7.5)$$

where

$$\begin{aligned} P'_{ew} &= 1 - \sum_{k=0}^{t} C_k^N (1 - P'_e)^{N-k} P_e'^{k} \quad \text{(general form)} \\ &= 1 - (1 - P'_e)^N \quad (t = 0, \text{ case of no-error correction}) \qquad (5.7.6) \\ &= 1 - (1 - P'_e)^N - N(1 - P'_e)^{N-1} P'_e \\ &\quad (t = 1, \text{ case of one-error correction}). \end{aligned}$$

The no-error correction and one-error correction cases of equation 5.7.5 are shown in Figures 5.6.2 and 5.6.3, respectively. The majority-voting process with a larger number of repetitions and higher number of error corrections always improves the performance. However, the trade-off is the inefficiency of its throughput.

5.7.2 A Comparison of Slow Fading and Fast Fading

In digital transmission systems that do not incorporate error correction or repetition, the word-error-rate performance in the fast-fading channel is worse than that in the slow-fading channel. With repetition transmission, word-error-rate performance in a fast-fading case supersedes that in a slow-fading case, as shown in Figures 5.6.2 and 5.6.3. The performance with coding and repetition transmission in the fast-fading case is also better than in the slow-fading case. Hence, if the reduction in throughput can be tolerated, there is an advantage in using a repetition transmission.

5.8 AUTOMATIC REPEAT REQUEST

Automatic repeat request (ARQ) systems use a code with good error-detecting capability. The decoder computes the syndrome of the received vector. If the syndrome is not 0, the decoder decides that the received codeword contains errors. The receiver then requests the transmitter, over the return channel, to repeat the same codeword. Retransmission continues until the decoder decides that the received vector is error free. Hence the end user gets erroneous data only if the number of errors in the received codeword exceed the error-detecting capability of the code. Since a good number of codes with good error-detecting capabilities exist, the probability of this latter event can be made very small.

Of the many different types of ARQ techniques, the three most basic are the stop-and-wait ARQ, the go-back-N ARQ, and the selective-repeat ARQ. See Berlekamp et al. (1987) and Lin and Costello (1983) for details.

Automatic repeat request can be a very efficient technique for delivering highly reliable data. However, its biggest drawback is the reduced message throughput, because some messages are repeated. (If α is the probability that a received message will be detected to have errors, then the throughput is reduced by $1 - \alpha$, and the time required to transmit a given amount of information is increased by $1/(1 - \alpha)$ [Yacoub, 1993]). Even when a message is repeated, the repetition may still fail, and this causes a further reduction in throughput. In a wireless communications channel with its characteristically deep fades and their associated error bursts, ARQ can have an unacceptably low throughput. One solution is to shorten the ARQ block length. Another is to use a hybrid ARQ forward-error-correction (FEC) scheme. In a typical hybrid scheme the decoder initially determines the number of received bits that are in error. If this is within the error-correction capability of the code, the decoder will correct the errors. If the decoder cannot correct the errors, it requests the transmitter to repeat the message (Berlekamp et al., 1987; Lee, 1993).

CHAPTER 6

Spread-Spectrum Systems

6.1 INTRODUCTION

The term *spread-spectrum* (SS) has been used in a wide variety of military and commercial communication systems (Dixon, 1976; Pickholtz et al., 1982; Simon et al., 1985). In spread-spectrum systems each information signal requires significantly more radio frequency (RF) bandwidth than a conventional modulated signal would require. The expanded bandwidth provides certain desirable features and characteristics that could otherwise be difficult to obtain.

Spread-spectrum is a technique whereby a modulated wave form is modulated (spread) a second time in such a way as to generate an expanded-bandwidth wideband signal that does not significantly interfere with other signals. Bandwidth expansion is achieved by a second modulation means, a means that is independent of the information message. For this reason this expansion does not combat additive white Gaussian noise (AWGN), as does wideband frequency modulation (FM). Since spread-spectrum systems are not useful in combating white noise, we might ask ourselves, *"Why bother?"*

Applications and potential advantages of spread-spectrum systems include the following:

1. Improved interference rejection
2. Code division multiplexing for code division multiple access (CDMA) applications
3. Low-density power spectra for signal hiding
4. High-resolution ranging
5. Secure communications

6. Antijam capability
7. Increased capacity and spectral efficiency in some mobile-cellular personal communications system (PCS) applications
8. Graceful degradation of performance as the number of simultaneous users of an RF channel increases
9. Lower cost of implementation
10. Readily available IC (Integrated Circuit) components

Spread-spectrum systems have been classified by their architecture and modulation concepts. The most commonly employed SS modulation techniques are the following (Cooper, and McGillem, 1986; Dixon, 1976):

Direct-sequence (DS) spread-spectrum (DS-SS), including CDMA
Frequency hopping (FH), including slow frequency-hopping (SFH) CDMA and fast frequency-hopping (FFH) systems
Carrier sense multiple access (CSMA) spread-spectrum
Time hopping
Chirp
Hybrid spread-spectrum methods

In mobile radio systems and wireless local area networks (WLAN), direct-sequence, frequency-hopped CDMA, and CSMA methods have been extensively used. We describe these techniques in the following sections.

6.2 FUNDAMENTAL CONCEPTS OF SPREAD-SPECTRUM SYSTEMS

6.2.1 Direct-Sequence Spread-Spectrum

A conceptual diagram of *direct-sequence* spread-spectrum (DS-SS) system is given in Figure 6.2.1. The digital binary baseband information, $d(t)$, also known as *nonreturn to zero* (NRZ) data, having a source bit rate of $f_b = 1/T_b$, is phase shift key (PSK) modulated in the first modulator. To illustrate the fundamental concepts, we assume a simple unfiltered, constant-envelope (hard-limited) binary PSK modulation. The modulated binary PSK signal $s(t)$ is given by

$$s(t) = \sqrt{2P_s}\, d(t) \cos\omega_{IF} t \tag{6.2.1}$$

where $d(t)$ is an unfiltered binary signal having two states +1 or −1, ω_{IF} is the carrier frequency, and P_s is the corresponding carrier power. The spreading signal $g(t)$ is a pseudonoise (PN) signal having a chip rate of $f_c = 1/T_c$. The binary PSK (BPSK) modulated DS-SS is given by

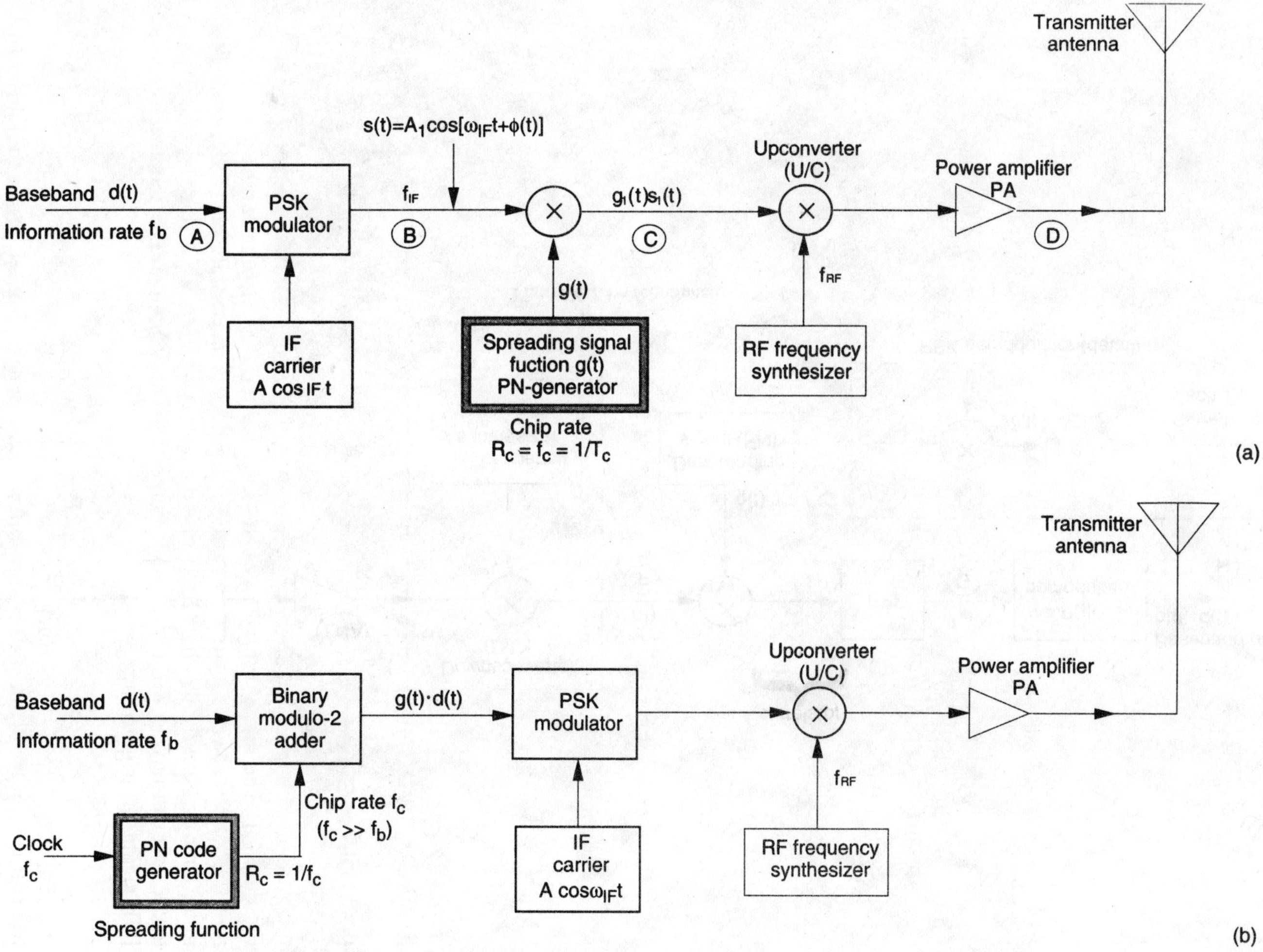

Figure 6.2.1 Direct-sequence spread-spectrum (DS-SS) block diagrams. (a); Transmitter with PSK modulation followed by spreading. (b); Equivalent transmitter to that shown in (a), except the spreading is performed first in the baseband. (c); Receiver. The despreading and demodulation sequence could be interchanged.

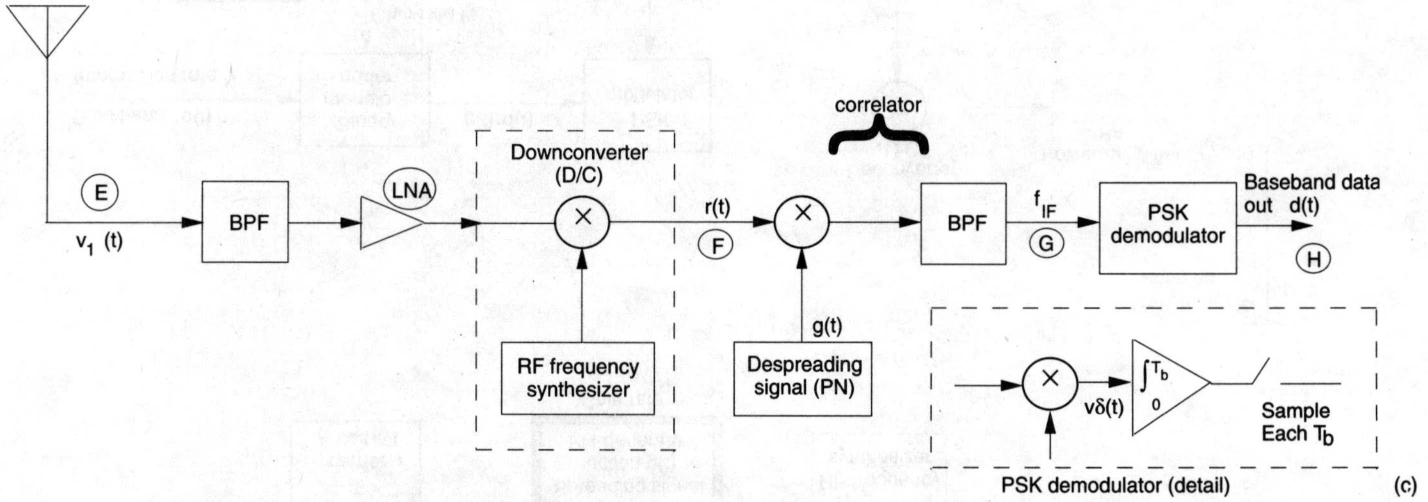

Figure 6.2.1 (continued)

$$v(t) = g(t)s(t) = \sqrt{2P_s}\, g(t)\, d(t) \cos \omega_0 t. \tag{6.2.2}$$

This intermediate frequency (IF) signal is upconverted by an RF synthesizer to the desired transmission frequency. In this notation, ω_0 corresponds to the IF frequency ω_{IF} or to the upconverted RF ω_{RF}.

We assume that in a wireless mobile system, within the same cell there are several simultaneous users. Each user is assigned the same RF carrier f_{RF} (or ω_{RF}) and occupies the same RF bandwidth B_{RF}. Measured power spectral densities are illustrated in Figure 6.2.2. The spread-spectrum generation process in a multiple-access system application involves two fundamental steps: modulation and spreading (or second modulation by a PN sequence). The second modulation is assumed to be an ideal multiplication, $g_1(t)\, s_1(t)$, (Figure 6.2.1). Ideal multiplication is equivalent to double-sideband suppressed-carrier (DSB-SC) amplitude modulation (AM) (Feher, 1983). The positions of the first and second modulators can be interchanged without any impact on the theoretical system performance.

The spread-spectrum signal $g_1(t)\, s_1(t)$ is upconverted to the desired RF frequency. The upconversion (U/C) and downconversion (D/C) process is a practical requirement in most system applications; however, it is not a fundamental step. In our discussion we assume that the $g_1(t)\, s_1(t)$ IF signal is transmitted and received; that is, we bypass the upcon-

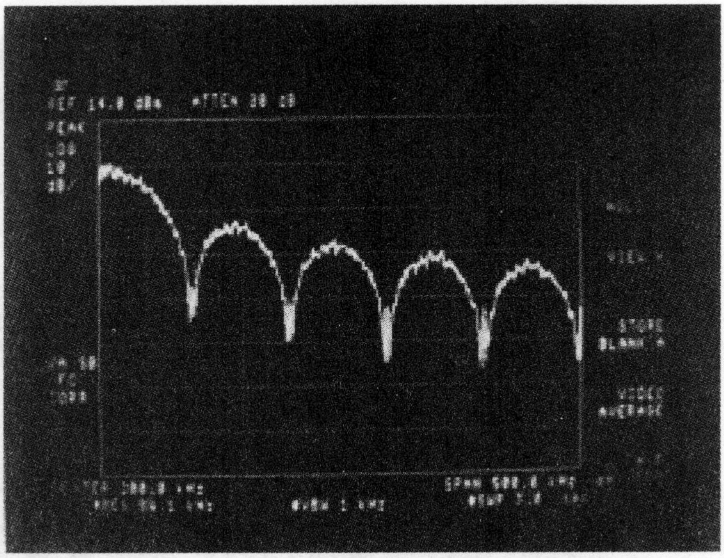

(a)

Figure 6.2.2 Measured power spectral densities related to the block diagram in Figure 6.2.1. In this case, a bit rate of f_b = 100 kb/s and a chip rate of f_c = 1 Mchips/second are illustrated. Measured at the University of California, Davis, Digital-Wireless Communication Research Laboratory. (a), Baseband spectrum of 100 kb/s nonreturn to zero (NRZ) random signal. Horizontal scale 100 kHz/division. (b), IF spectrum at 70 MHz center; chip rate, 1 Mchips/second. (c), RF spectrum at 900 MHz with an added unmodulated carrier (interference) tone.

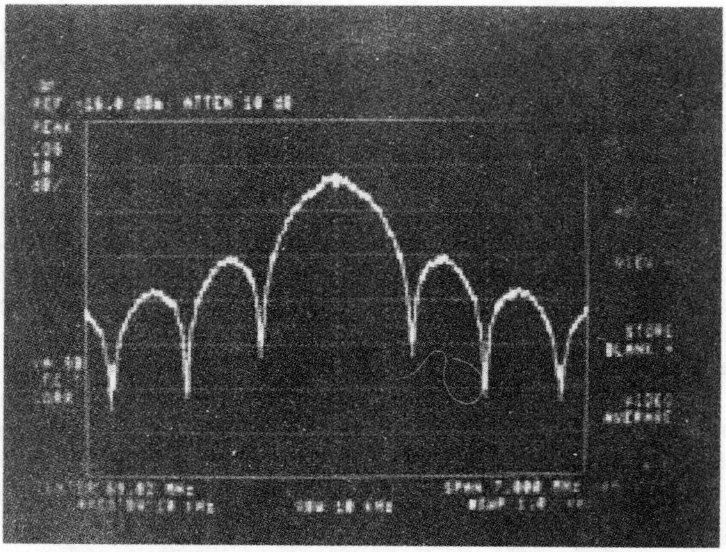

(b)

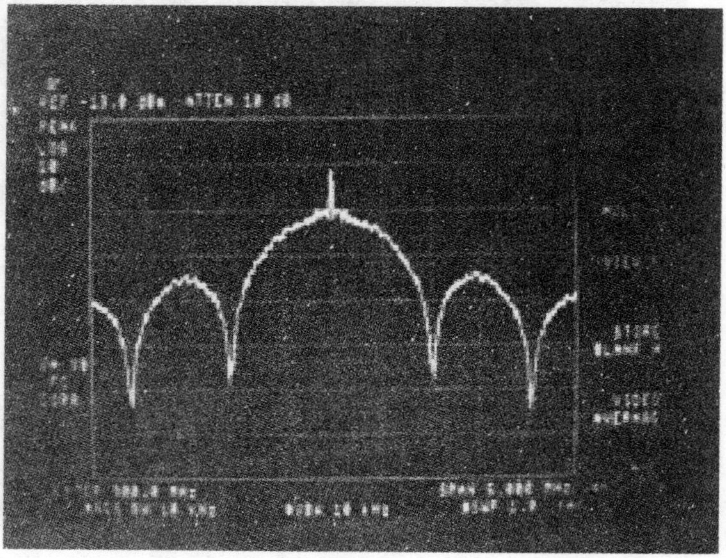

(c)

Figure 6.2.2 (continued)

version and downconversion subsystems. Thus the $g_1(t)\ s_1(t)$ spread-spectrum signal is transmitted, and at the receiver it is combined with other M independent spread-spectrum signals that use the same RF band (Bhargava et al., 1981). The combined received signal $r(t)$ is given by

$$r(t) = \sum_{i=1}^{M} g_i(t)s_i(t) + I(t) + n(t) \tag{6.2.3}$$

where M is the number of simultaneous users, $g_i(t)$ is the spreading function or PN code of the "i"-th transmitter/receiver pair, $s_i(t)$ is the modulated signal, $I(t)$ is interference (deliberate or self-noise), and $n(t)$ is AWGN.

At the receiver the intended user will have a synchronized $g_i(t)$ despreading function, which is the same PN sequence as that of the corresponding transmitter. The despread signal is PSK demodulated. In this basic treatment of spread-spectrum systems, binary PSK modulation/demodulation is assumed. Other modulation methods, described in Chapter 4, such as MSK, GMSK, GFSK, 4-FM, FBPSK, and FQPSK have also been implemented in spread-spectrum systems. See Appendix A.3 for Feher's patented/licensed modulation and filtering techniques.

If the chosen set of PN spreading waveforms is not cross-correlated, then after despreading only the desired modulated waveform $s_i(t)$ remains. All other waveforms are not correlated and are effectively spread over a much wider bandwidth than that of the final demodulator bandwidth. The whole process of spreading and despreading (correlation) is illustrated in a qualitative manner in Figures 6.2.3 and 6.2.4. In these conceptual time-domain and spectrum illustrations we have made several simplifications, including the omission of the carrier wave in the time domain.

Processing gain, G_p, or *process gain* is the relation of output and input signal-to-noise (S/N) or signal-to-interference (S/I) ratio. For instance, if the input S/N or S/I at point F in Figure 6.2.1, (c), is 5 dB, and after despreading with a matched PN sequence (matched to the transmit PN sequence) the desired signal collapses to its original narrow modulated bandwidth, and the output $(S/N)_0$ is 27 dB, then the processing gain is 22 dB. Thus processing gain G_p is defined by

$$G_p = (S/N)_0 : (S/N)_i. \tag{6.2.4}$$

The process gain available is frequently estimated by the following rule of thumb:

$$G_p = \text{processing gain} = \frac{BW_{RF}}{BW_{\text{mod}}} = \frac{BW_{RF}}{R_{\text{info}}} = \frac{BW_{RF}}{f_b} \tag{6.2.5}$$

where BW_{RF} is the RF bandwidth and BW_{mod} is the modulated signal bandwidth. This bandwidth equals $R_{\text{info}} = f_b$ = bit rate of the baseband signal if the spectral efficiency is 1 b/s/Hz.

Jamming margin, M_j, takes into account the practical required $(S/N)_0$ and allows for a system implementation loss L_{sys} (Dixon, 1976). Jamming margin is defined by

$$M_j = G_p - \left[L_{\text{sys}} + \left(\frac{S}{N}\right)_o \right]. \tag{6.2.6}$$

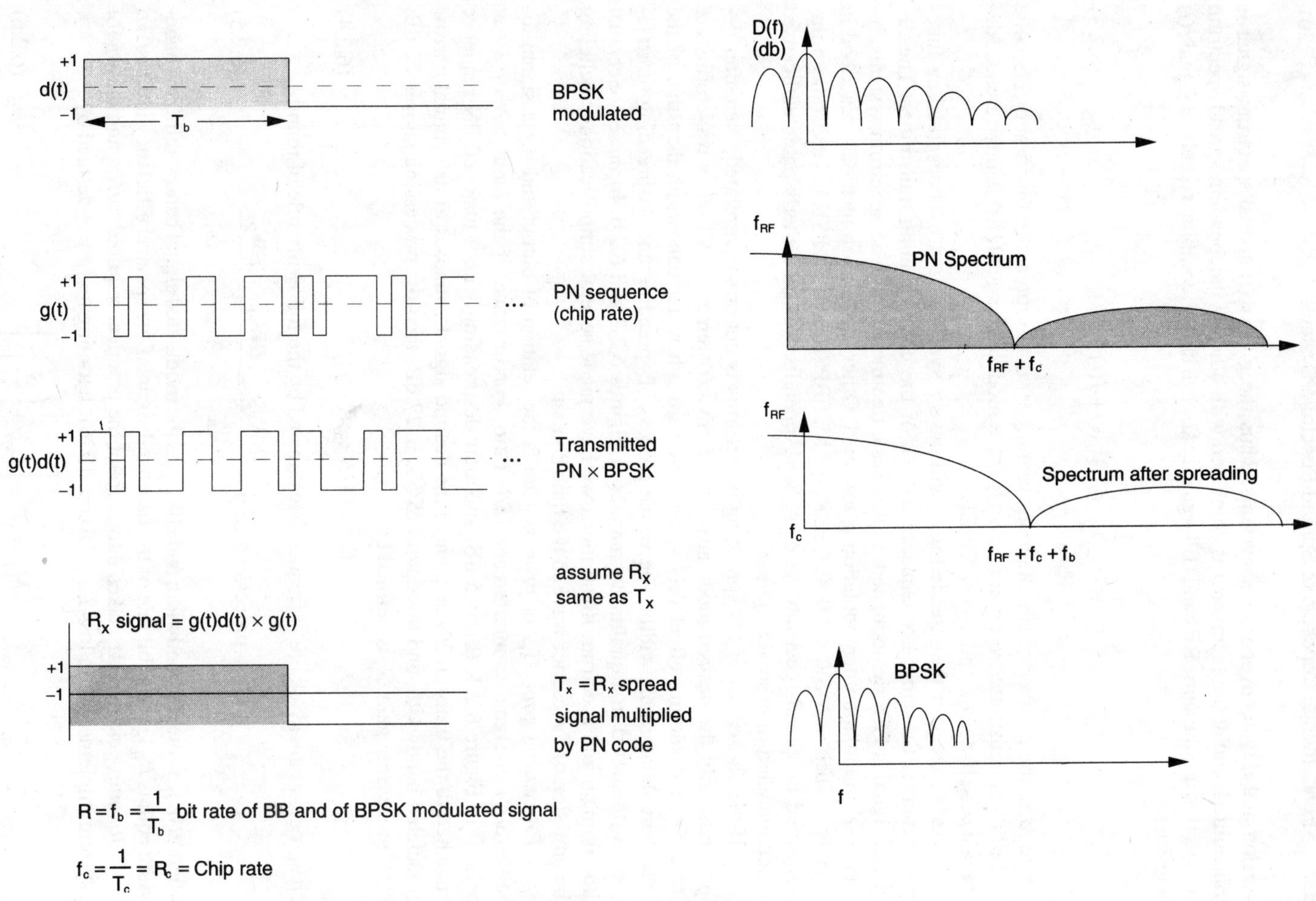

Figure 6.2.3 Process of spreading and despreading. A qualitative time-domain and power-spectrum illustration of a DS-SS system. (From Taub and Schilling, 1986.)

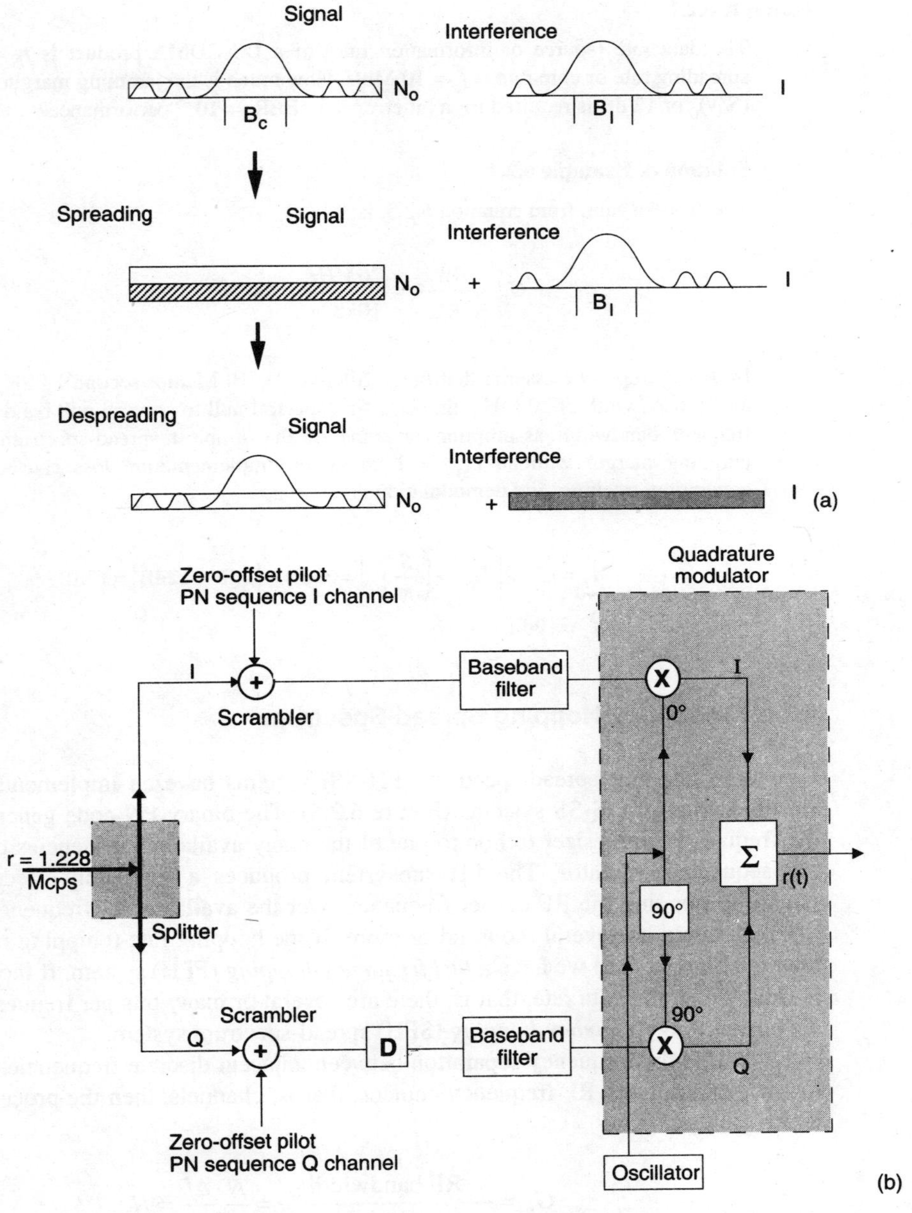

Figure 6.2.4 (a), Spreading-despreading of signal and interference in a DS-SS system. (b) Modulator and scrambler of offset QPSK quadrature modulated cross-correlated "IS-95" standardized CDMA system "reverse link". For a large class of Quadrature Cross-correlated implementations, see Feher's patented technologies in Appendix A.3. (From IEEE Globecom 90, Workshop 2, Qualcomm, Inc.)

Example 6.2.1

The data rate (source or information rate) of a DS-CDMA product is f_b = 10 kb/s. The spreading rate or chip rate is f_c = 10 Mb/s. How much is the jamming margin M_j if an output $(S/N)_0$ of 12 dB is required for a bit error rate (BER) = 10^{-6} performance?

Solution of Example 6.2.1

The process gain, from equation 6.2.5, is:

$$G_p = \frac{BW_{RF}}{R_{\text{info}}} = \frac{20MHz}{10\text{kb/s}} = 2000 \triangleq 33db.$$

In this example we assume that the unfiltered f_c = 10 Mchips/second BPSK signal requires an RF bandwidth of 20 MHz, that is, a first spectral null to spectral null bandwidth. This is a frequent bandwidth assumption in some of the simplest spread-spectrum systems. The jamming margin with an L_{sys} = 2 db system/implementation loss caused by imperfect generation, tracking, and demodulation is

$$M_j = G_p - \left[L_{\text{sys}} + \left(\frac{S}{N}\right)_o\right] = 33\text{dB} - [2\text{dB} + 12\text{dB}] = 19\text{dB}$$

$$M_j = 19\text{dB}.$$

6.2.2 Frequency-Hopping Spread-Spectrum

Frequency-hopping spread-spectrum (FH-SS) systems have an implementation concept similar to that of DS-SS systems (Figure 6.2.5). The binary PN code generator "drives" the frequency synthesizer to hop to one of the many available frequencies chosen by the PN sequence generator. The FH subsystem produces a spreading effect by pseudo-randomly hopping the RF carrier frequency over the available RF frequencies, $f_1 \ldots f_N$ where N could be several thousand or more. If the hopping rate (chipping rate) is higher than the bit rate, then we have a *fast frequency-hopping* (FFH) system. If the hopping rate is slower than the data rate, that is, there are several or many bits per frequency hop, then we have a *slow frequency-hopping* (SFH) spread-spectrum system.

If Δf is the frequency separation between adjacent discrete frequencies and N is the number of available RF frequency choices, that is, channels, then the processing gain of an FH-SS system is

$$G_p = \frac{\text{RF bandwidth}}{\text{message bandwidth}} = \frac{N \cdot \Delta f}{\Delta f} = N. \tag{6.2.7}$$

The most frequently used spread-spectrum techniques, DS and FH, require PN sequences for spreading, synchronization, and despreading; these are discussed in the following section.

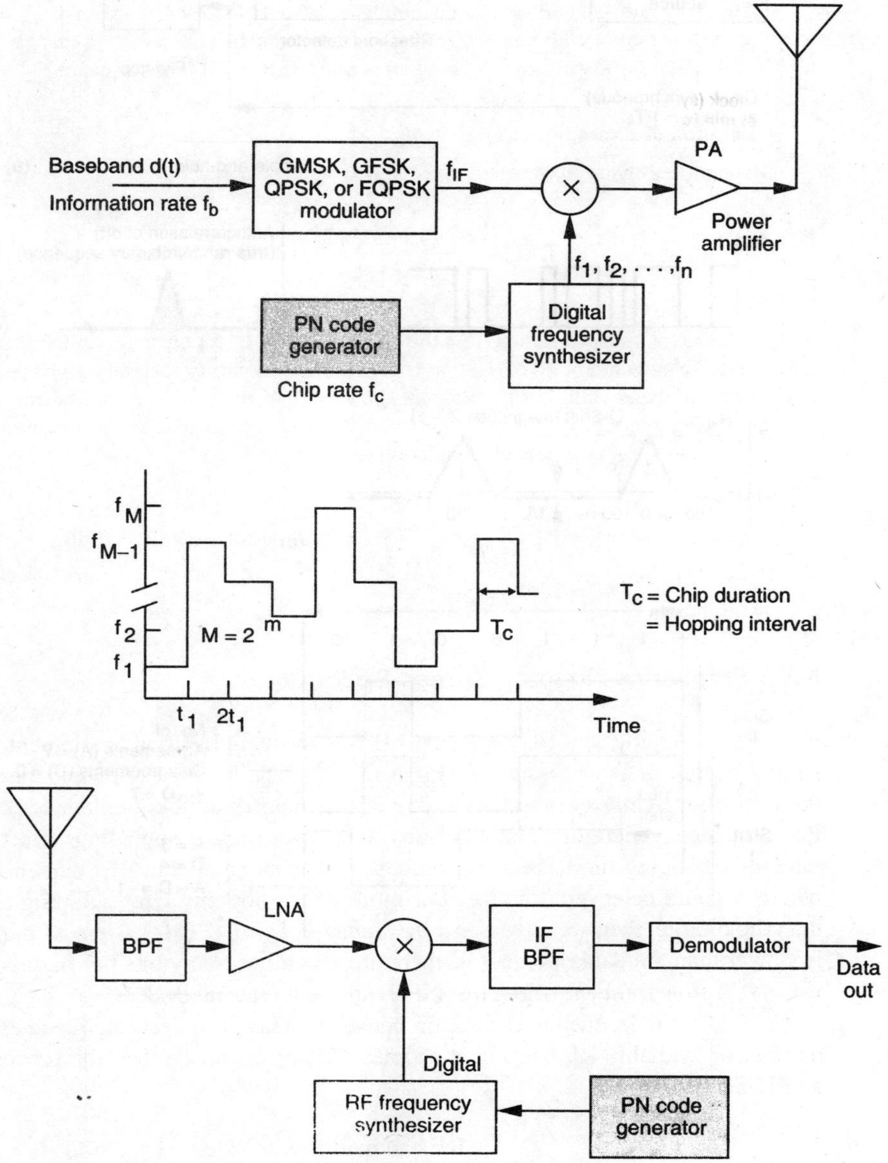

Figure 6.2.5 Frequency-hopping (FH) spread-spectrum transmitter/receiver. Basic block diagram.

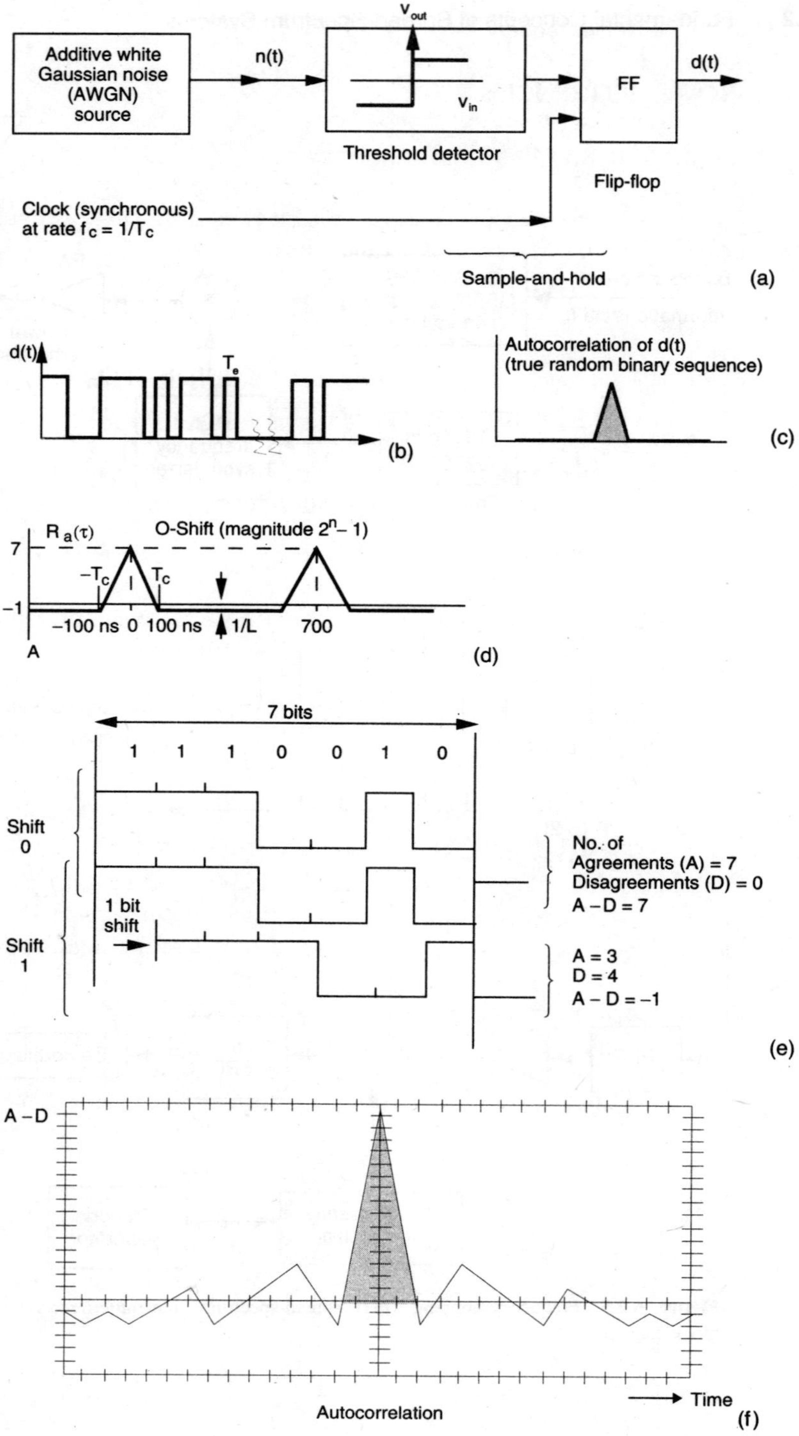

Additive white Gaussian noise (AWGN) source
n(t)
V_{out}
V_{in}
Threshold detector
FF
d(t)
Flip-flop
Clock (synchronous) at rate $f_c = 1/T_c$
Sample-and-hold
(a)
d(t)
T_e
(b)
Autocorrelation of d(t)
(true random binary sequence)
(c)
$R_a(\tau)$
O-Shift (magnitude $2^n - 1$)
7
−1
$-T_c$
T_c
−100 ns
0
100 ns
1/L
700
A
(d)
7 bits
1 1 1 0 0 1 0
Shift 0
No. of
Agreements (A) = 7
Disagreements (D) = 0
A − D = 7
1 bit shift
Shift 1
A = 3
D = 4
A − D = −1
(e)
A − D
Autocorrelation
Time
(f)

6.3 PSEUDO-NOISE SEQUENCES

6.3.1 Definitions and System Requirements

The major tasks of the pseudonoise (PN) sequences used in wireless digital or personal communications SS-CDMA systems are the following:

1. Spreading the bandwidth of the modulated signal to the larger transmission bandwidth
2. Distinguishing between the different user signals utilizing the same transmission bandwidth in a multiple-access scheme

To meet these tasks, the sequences need special correlation properties.

Autocorrelation, $R_a(\tau)$, in general, is defined by the integral

$$R_a(\tau) = \int_{-\infty}^{\infty} f(t) \cdot f(t-\tau)dt. \tag{6.3.1}$$

It is a measure of a similarity between a signal f(t) and a τ-second time-shifted replica of itself. The autocorrelation function is a plot of autocorrelation over all shifts (t–) of the $f(t)$ signal.

Cross-correlation, $R_c(\tau)$, is defined as the correlation between two different signals $f(t)$ and $g(t)$ and is given by

$$R_c(\tau) = \int_{-\infty}^{\infty} f(t) \cdot g(t-\tau)dt. \tag{6.3.2}$$

In the known wireless communications systems, the spreading signals are binary digital PN codes. Autocorrelation and cross correlation of code sequences are obtained by computing the number of agreements (A) minus the number of disagreements (D), when the codes are compared bit by bit for every discrete shift τ in the field of interest (Figure 6.3.1, (f).

To solve the spreading task and to occupy the transmission band equally, the power spectrum of a single sequence should be like white Gaussian noise. Such a sequence could be generated by the scheme shown in Figure 6.3.1, (a), where a noiselike digital data pattern is obtained by "sample and hold," a hard-limited analog AWGN signal. The sampling frequency corresponds to the chip rate $f_c = 1/T_c$. The autocorrelation function of

---

Figure 6.3.1 Pseudonoise (PN) binary data and random synchronous data sequence generation concept and autocorrelation functions. Autocorrelation is computed in Example 6.3.1 for an $L = 7(2^3 - 1)$ PN sequence length with $T_c = 1/f_c = 1/10$ Mc/s = 100ns. The following are shown:

(a) True random synchronous binary generator.

(b) Time-domain response of a true random sequence.

(c) Autocorrelation of an ideal random sequence.

(d) Autocorrelation of a short PN data sequence of 7 bits.

(e) Agreements/disagreements in aligned and 1-bit shifted sequences.

(f) Autocorrelation-agreements, (A), minus disagreements, (D), in a practical sequence. (From Kesteloot and Hutchinson, Editors, 1991).

this signal is shown in Figure 6.3.1, (c). The single sharp peak in the autocorrelation function at the time-shift $\tau = 0$ is a desired property and supports an easy receiver synchronization. If the sequence is repeated on a periodic manner after N chips, we get a pseudo-noise (PN) or pseudo-random type of sequence. For these PN-sequences we obtain a periodic autocorrelation function (see Chapter 9, Figure 9.3.1, (d)).

The second and more difficult task of the PN sequence for a multiuser CDMA system is to distinguish between the signals of the different users utilizing the same transmission bandwidth. The PN code is the "key" of each user to his or her intended signal in the receiver. For this reason the complete set of PN sequences has to be chosen with a small cross-correlation between the several sequences. This keeps the adjacent channel interference (ACI) small. Theoretically, a zero cross-correlation is maintained by every set of orthogonal spreading signals (such as the Fourier series and Walsh functions). However, in practical wireless systems one has to design for easy, coherent generation of the PN sequences, on both the transmitter and the receiver sides.

The best-known, best-described PN sequences are maximal-length sequences (*m-sequences*). They are suitable for single-user spread-spectrum systems and were widely used in military applications. Because of the cross-correlation demands, *Gold-sequences, Kasami-sequences,* or *Walsh-sequences* are more interesting for cellular or personal communication CDMA systems (Cooper and McGillem, 1986; Lüke, 1992). Sometimes they are combined with *m*-sequences. Some of these sequences and their major properties are next described.

6.3.2 *m*-Sequences

In this section maximal-length linear codes or maximal-length shift-register sequences (*m-sequences*) are described, since these codes are still of importance in digital communications and in spread-spectrum and ranging systems (Cooper and McGillem, 1986; Dixon, 1976; Bhargava et al., 1981). An illustrative, widely used hardware implementation of a PN-sequence generator and corresponding correlator or matched-data filter receiver is shown in Figure 6.3.2. The generator contains type D flip-flops and is connected so that each data input except D_0 is the Q output of the preceding flip-flop (Taub and Schilling, 1986). Not all Q flip-flop outputs need be connected to the parity generator (indicated by the dashed lines). The number of flip-flops L and the selection of which flip-flop outputs are connected to the parity generator determine the length and the characteristics of the generated PN sequence. The parity generator provides an output logic *O* when an even number of inputs are at logic *0* and generates logic 1 output when an odd number of inputs are at logic 1 state.

Sequence length. For maximal-length linear codes, it is always possible to find a set of connections from flip-flop outputs to the parity generator (Figure 6.3.2) that will yield a maximal (m) length sequence of

$$L = 2^N - 1 \tag{6.3.3}$$

bits (or chips) where N is the number of flip-flops. A specific connection diagram of flip-flop outputs to the parity generator input shown in Figure 6.3.2, (a), for $N = 3$ through N

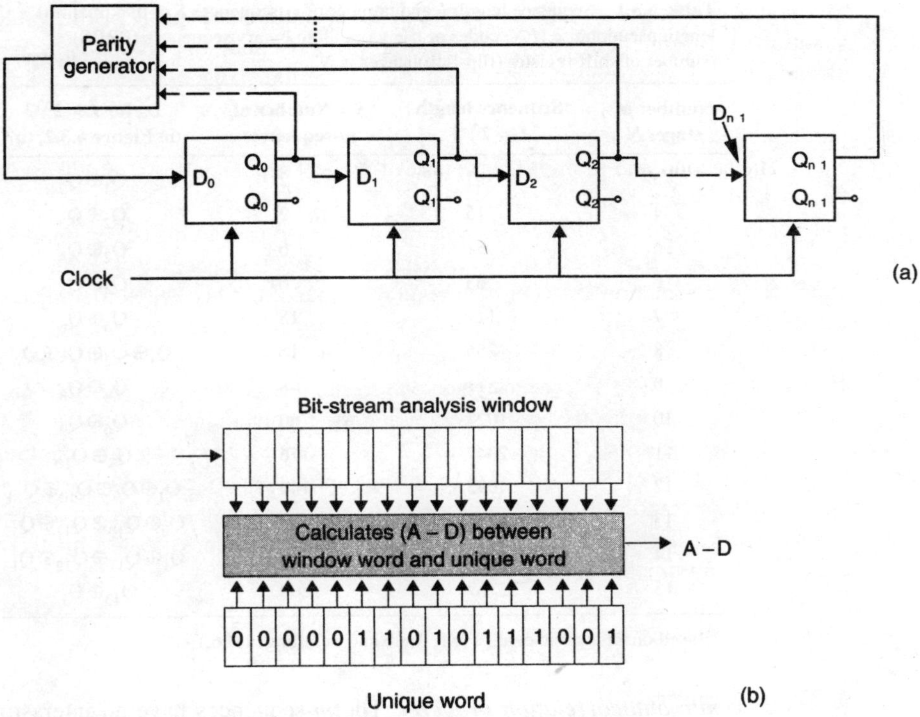

Figure 6.3.2 Hardware of (a), a pseudo random (pseudonoise or PN) generator and, (b), corresponding cross-correlator-matched data filter receiver. (From Taub and Schilling, 1986; Kesteloot and Hutchison, Editors, 1991.)

= 15 is illustrated in Table 6.3.1. The resultant maximal-length PN sequence L is between 7 and 32767 bits.

Independent sequences. One possible logic design connection is illustrated in Table 6.3.1. There are many possible connections to the parity generator, which have small correlation to one another. The upper bound S of the number of independent sequences is given by

$$S \leq \frac{L-1}{N}. \tag{6.3.4}$$

Numerical values are illustrated in Table 6.3.1.

Balance property. There are exactly $2^{L-1} - 1$ zeros and 2^{L-1} ones in one period of a maximal-length sequence.

Shift-and-add property. The modulo-2 sum of an m-sequence and any of its cyclic versions is another cyclic version of the original sequence with a phase different from either version.

Table 6.3.1 Sequence length L and number of m-sequences S of maximal (m) length pseudonoise (PN) codes or pseudorandom binary sequences (PRBS). Number of shift-register (flip-flop) stages is N.

Number of stages N	Sequence length $L = 2^{N-1}$	S = Number of m-sequences	D_0 for $L = 2^{N-1}$ in Figure 6.3.2, (a)
3	7	2	$Q_1 \oplus Q_2$
4	15	2	$Q_2 \oplus Q_3$
5	31	6	$Q_2 \oplus Q_4$
6	63	6	$Q_4 \oplus Q_5$
7	127	18	$Q_5 \oplus Q_6$
8	255	16	$Q_1 \oplus Q_2 \oplus Q_3 \oplus Q_7$
9	511	48	$Q_4 \oplus Q_8$
10	1023	60	$Q_6 \oplus Q_9$
11	2047	176	$Q_8 \oplus Q_{10}$
12	4095	144	$Q_1 \oplus Q_9 \oplus Q_{10} \oplus Q_{11}$
13	8191	630	$Q_0 \oplus Q_{10} \oplus Q_{11} \oplus Q_{12}$
14	16383	756	$Q_1 \oplus Q_{11} \oplus Q_{12} \oplus Q_{13}$
15	32767	1800	$Q_{13} \oplus Q_{14}$

(Based on Bhargava, et al., 1981; Taub and Schilling, 1986.)

Periodic autocorrelation property. The m-sequences have an interesting cyclic or periodic autocorrelation property. If we transform the binary (0,1) sequence of the shift-register output to the binary (+ 1, −1) sequence by replacing each zero by + 1, and each 1 by −1, then the periodic correlation function is given by

$$\theta(\tau) = N = \begin{cases} 2^m - 1, & \tau = 0 \\ -1, & \tau \neq 0 \end{cases},$$

and this is the best possible periodic correlation function in the sense that for no other binary sequence is the term "$\max_{\tau \neq 0} \theta(\tau)$" smaller. This is one of the main reasons for the use of m-sequences in preamble design for bit timing and synchronization (Bhargava et al., 1981).

Randomness property. Since a maximal-length sequence is a periodic sequence, it cannot be called random; yet it has a well-defined statistical distribution for the runs of ones and zeros. In fact, in each period, one half of the runs have length 1, one fourth of the runs have length 2, one eighth of the runs have length 3, and so on.

Example 6.3.1

Tabulate and plot the autocorrelation function for all shifts of an $L = 3$ stage shift-register generator, generating a 7-bit ($m = 2^{L-1}$) maximal-length pseudorandom code. Assume that the chip rate is $f_c = 10$ Mc/s (megachips per second) and that the 7-bit reference sequence is 1110010, based on Dixon (1976).

Solution for Example 6.3.1

First we tabulate the number of agreements (A) and disagreements (D) by lining up the shifted autocorrelation code sequence with the unshifted sequence in one-bit increments. We obtain the following data:

Reference sequence: 1110010

Shift	Sequence	Agreements (A)	Disagreements (D)	A – D
0	1110010	7	0	7
1	0111001	3	4	−1
2	1011100	3	4	−1
3	0101110	3	4	−1
4	0010111	3	4	−1
5	1001011	3	4	−1
6	1100101	3	4	−1

The resultant autocorrelation plot of this PN signal is shown in Figure 6.3.1, (d). Note: the net autocorrelation values $A - D$ are −1 for all shifts except for the 0th, 7th, and 14th, . . ., shifts, where it is 7.

The highest value of the autocorrelation function is also known as *correlation spike.* It is used for code or word synchronization. Between the 0 and + 1 or −1 bit shifts the correlation decreases linearly (Feher, 1981). Thus the autocorrelation function for an *m*-sequence is triangular, as shown in Figure 6.3.1.

Two or more independent signals can be transmitted simultaneously over the same bandwidth and successfully recovered if their codes are phase-shifted by more than 1 bit. In ranging systems an accurate range measurement, within one bit, is obtained by using a correlation peak as a marker.

6.3.3 Gold-Sequences

In contrast to simple *m*-sequences, Gold-sequences are suitable for multiuser CDMA systems. They offer a large number of sequence sets with good cross-correlation properties between the single sequences. Gold (1967) presented the design method.

The Gold-sequences are generated by modulo-2 addition of two *m*-sequences clocked by the same chip-clock (Figure 6.3.3). The most significant key in the Gold-sequence design is that only special pairs of *m*-sequences deliver the desired correlation properties. These preferred pairs of *m*-sequences are listed in tables, for example, in Dixon (1976) and Simon et al. (1985).

Since both *m*-sequences have equal length L and use the same clock, the created Gold-sequence is of length L as well; however, it is no longer maximal. Let n be the number of stages in each *m*-sequence generator. The Gold-sequence length will be

$$L = 2^n - 1$$

Let us look at the possible number of different Gold-sequences created with the two–*m*-sequence generator setup. It can be shown that for any shift in the initial conditions

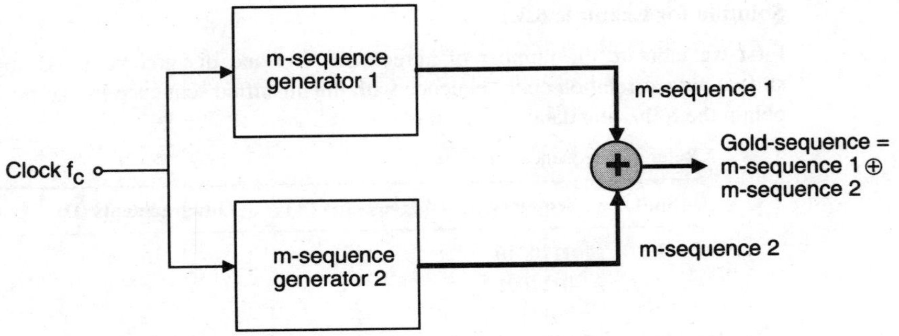

Figure 6.3.3 Block diagram of Gold-sequence generator. Two *m*-sequences are connected in parallel. The resulting sequence is no longer maximal length but has good cross-correlation properties for special pairs of *m*-sequences. (Based on Gold, 1967.)

between the two *m*-sequences a new Gold-sequence is generated (Gold, 1967). Since each *m*-sequence is of length *L*, the same number of different shifts between the two *m*-sequences is available. Thus a Gold-sequence generator combining two different *m*-sequences can create a number of different $L = 2^{n-1}$ Gold-sequences. With a proper choice of the *m*-sequence pairs the desired low cross-correlation can be maintained between all created Gold-sequences.

6.4 PERFORMANCE OF DIRECT-SEQUENCE SPREAD-SPECTRUM SYSTEMS

One of the advantages of spread-spectrum (SS) systems is the ability of these systems to reject interference that otherwise might prohibit useful communications. In this section we study relatively narrowband interference rejection capabilities and the performance in a thermal noise, that is, additive white Gaussian noise (AWGN) environment.

6.4.1 Thermal Noise *not* Rejected by Spread-Spectrum Techniques

A heuristic demonstration and physical interpretation of the performance of spread-spectrum systems in an AWGN environment is presented in this section. We follow the approach presented in Taub and Schilling (1986). For a more detailed treatment and derivation see Cooper and McGillem (1986). We observe from Figures 6.2.1 and 6.2.3 that spectral spreading is achieved by the second modulator's pseudonoise (PN)-spreading signal, $g(t)$, at a chip rate of $R_c = f_c = 1/T_c$. The spreading signal is independent of the $f_b = 1/T_b$ rate information signal.

Let us assume a simplest case where an unfiltered hard-limited BPSK modulator has instantaneous signal-state changes between +1 and −1 at a rate of $f_b = 1/T_b$ and the PN signal-chipping waveform has instantaneous voltage changes between +1 and −1 at a rate of

$f_c = 1/T_c$ (Figure 6.2.3). In the overall spread-spectrum systems, the baseband data signal $d(t)$ is twice multiplied by the spreading-despreading PN sequence $g(t)$. Since $g^2(t) = 1$, as $1^2 = 1$ and $(-1)^2 = 1$, there is no effect on the received despread output signal. The thermal noise or AWGN is introduced in the receiver part of the channel by the low-noise amplifier (LNA) and downconverter subsystems. AWGN is a wide-bandwidth noise (thus the term *white*), and its probability density function is approximately Gaussian. The noise bandwidth of the LNA-downcoverter (D/C) subsystem is at least as wide as that of the spread-spectrum signal. During the despreading process this noise is multiplied by the despreading PN signal. Multiplication reverses the polarity of the noise waveform at nominally random times at integer multiples of the chip duration $T_c = 1/f_c$. Polarity reversal has no impact on the power spectral density or the probability density function of the AWGN. Hence, based on our intuitive and somewhat heuristic physical derivation and reasoning, we conclude that the spreading-despreading operation does not affect the signal and does not affect the spectral and probability density functions of the noise. For this reason the overall bit-error ratio (BER) or probability of error, P_e, performance of the spread-spectrum system, in an AWGN-controlled channel, is the same as the BER $= f(E_b/N_o)$ performance of the modulated-demodulated system, without spread-spectrum. For example, the BER $= f(E_b/N_o)$ performance of a coherent binary PSK (BPSK) spread-spectrum system is

$$\text{BER} = P_e = \frac{1}{2} erfc\sqrt{E_b / N_o} \tag{6.4.1}$$

where

$E_b = CT_b$ = Average energy of a received bit
C = Average power of received carrier
N_o = Noise density = Noise power in 1 Hz of RF or IF bandwidth
T_b = Unit bit duration = $1/f_b$; f_b = Bit rate

The performance of this BPSK spread-spectrum system in an AWGN environment is identical to the performance of conventional coherent BPSK systems. The same conclusion applies to performance equivalence of other modulation methods.

6.4.2 Narrowband Interference Rejection

We assume that the AWGN power within the receiver bandwidth is much smaller than that of the interference. The narrowband signal. In Coqper and McGillem (1986) it has been demonstrated that a single-frequency (carrier wave [CW]) interference represents a "worst-case" narrowband interference. The derivation and notation are partially based on Taub and Schilling (1986). In Figure 6.2.1, (c), the input signal of the radio receiver is given by

$$v_r(t) = \sqrt{2P_s}\, d(t)g(t)\cos\omega_0 t + \sqrt{2P_J}\cos(\omega_0 t + \theta) \tag{6.4.2}$$

where

$d(t)$ is the baseband signal at the transmitter input and receiver output; $f_b = 1/T_b$ bit rate
f_c is the chipping rate $1/T_c$
$g(t)$ is the spreading pseudonoise (PN) sequence at a chipping rate of $f_c = 1/T_c$
ω_0 is the radio frequency (RF) or the downconverted intermediate frequency (IF)
P_J is the power of the interfering signal at the receiver RF input
P_s is the received, desired signal power at the receiver RF input
θ is a random variable, uniformly distributed over 0 to 360 degrees

The received input signal $v_r(t)$ contains the $g(t)$ spreading function. In the despreading operation $v_r(t)$ is multiplied by the synchronized $g(t)$ PN signal. Because in our simplified binary model $g^2(t) = 1$, we obtain the integrator input $v_0'(t)$ given by

$$v_0'(t) = \sqrt{P_s}\; d(t) + \sqrt{P_J}\; g(t) \cos\theta. \tag{6.4.3}$$

As the bit duration T_b is much longer than the period of the carrier frequency $T_0 = 1/f_0 = 2\pi/\omega_0$ and/or the bit duration is an integer multiple of the half period of the carrier, we obtain the demodulated interference at the integrator input $G_J(f)$, given by

$$G_J(f) = \frac{P_J \overline{\cos^2\theta}}{2f_c}\left(\frac{\sin \pi f / f_c}{\pi f / f_c}\right)^2. \tag{6.4.4}$$

This demodulated interference term has a wideband spectrum, with the first spectral null at f_C. In Figure 6.2.3 the equivalent spectral density around f_{RF} is indicated, and the first pair of spectral nulls is at $f_{RF} \pm f_c$. After the integrate sample-and-dump (ISD) filter, having a bandwidth of $f_b = 1/T_b$, we have

$$G_J(f) = \frac{P_J \overline{\cos^2\theta}}{2f_c}; \qquad |f| \le f_b \tag{6.4.5}$$

and since θ the phase of the relatively narrowband interference is a random variable, without any correlation between the interfering (jamming) signal and the desired carrier with a uniform distribution, having an average value $\overline{\cos^2\theta} = 1/2$, we obtain the final expression of the demodulated narrowband interference $G_J(f)$ at the demodulator baseband output given as

$$G_J(f) = \frac{P_J}{4f_c}; \qquad |f| \le f_b. \tag{6.4.6}$$

From equations 6.4.4 and 6.4.6, observe that the single-tone narrowband RF interference, having all of its power P_J in a single frequency tone at $\omega_0 = 2\pi f_0 = 2\pi f_{RF}$, is transformed into a wideband demodulated signal, having a uniform, practically "white" power spectral density of $G_J(f) = 1/4f_c$ or $I_J(f) = 2f_c$. The power spectral density of the demodulated interference $I_J(f)$ is inversely proportional to the chipping rate f_c.

The $G_J(f)$ interference is theoretically defined, in baseband, for the $-f_b \le f \le f_b$ range. For practical baseband systems we define $I(f)$ the baseband interference as

$$I(f) = 2G_J(f) \quad \text{and} \quad 0 \le f \le f_b \tag{6.4.7}$$

for only positive frequencies in the $0 \le f \le f_b$ range.

The relation for the BER in AWGN (equation 6.4.1) applies also to the interference-controlled situation, assuming that the demodulated baseband interference (I), before the decision-making point, resembles AWGN. For coherent PSK demodulation we have

$$\text{BER} = P_e = \frac{1}{2} erfc\sqrt{\frac{E_b}{N_o}} = \frac{1}{2} erfc\sqrt{\frac{E_b}{I(f)}}$$

$$= \frac{1}{2} erfc\sqrt{\frac{E_b}{2P_J/4f_c}} = \frac{1}{2} erfc\sqrt{\frac{P_s T_b 2 f_c}{P_J}} = \frac{1}{2} erfc\sqrt{\left(\frac{P_s}{P_J}\right)\left(\frac{f_c}{f_b}\right)} \tag{6.4.8}$$

$$\text{BER} = \frac{1}{2} erfc\sqrt{2\left(\frac{P_s}{P_J}\right)\left(\frac{f_c}{f_b}\right)}.$$

The quantity

$$P_{J_{1eff}} = \frac{P_J}{2(f_c / f_b)} \tag{6.4.9}$$

is known as the *effective jamming power*. The effective jamming power, in comparison with the signal power P_s, determines the BER of the spread-spectrum system.

From equation 6.4.8, note that the chipping-rate to bit-rate ratio, f_c/f_b, determines the reduction of the narrowband interference power. It is the processing gain G_P defined by

$$G_P \triangleq f_c / f_b. \tag{6.4.10}$$

In section 6.2 we defined process gain in equations 6.2.4 and 6.2.5 as

$$G_P = \frac{(S/I)_0}{(S/I)_i} = \frac{\text{RF Bandwidth} = (BW_{RF})}{\text{Bit Rate} = (f_b)}. \tag{6.4.11}$$

We reiterate that $(S/I)_0$ represents the output signal-to-interference (S/I) ratio at the demodulator output and $(S/I)_i$ represents the S/I ratio at the receiver RF input. In section 6.2 we used N for noise; here we replace it with I for interference, since it is a more representative annotation for an interference-controlled system.

6.4.3 Interference Rejection: Experimental Hardware Demonstration

To demonstrate the interference-rejection capabilities of a DS-SS system, we design a hardware test setup based on Figure 6.2.1. In this illustrative experiment we use an intermediate frequency (*IF*) of $f_{IF} = 70$ MHz, a baseband date rate of $f_b = 10$ kb/s and a chipping rate of $f_c = 2$Mc/s. These data and chip rates are approximately the same values as those used in Qualcomm's DS-CDMA cellular system (Gilhousen et al., 1991). A coherent BPSK modem has been designed at the University of California, UC Davis. The PSK modulation has no filters; it is an "infinite-bandwidth" or unfiltered BPSK transmitter. The demodulator has a very simple postdemodulation "roofing filter" to remove the second- and higher-order carrier products from the baseband signal. In the experiments a fourth-order Butterworth low-pass filter (LPF), having $f_{3dB} = 30$ kHz, is used. *Note:* The Nyquist minimum bandwidth would be only 5 kHz for a 10 kb/s data rate.

6.4.4 Wideband Interference Rejection

In principal, the mechanism of interference rejection described in section 6.4.2 for narrowband interferers also applies for wideband interfering signals. The total power of wideband interfering signals, such as that of "self-interference" created by approximately equal chip-rate f_c DS-SS systems having different PN spreading functions $g_1(t)$, $g_N(t)$, . . ., $g_N(t)$, is reduced in the despreading operation. The wideband interference power is reduced by the same quantity as for the relatively narrowband interference signals derived in the previous sections.

Wideband interference reduction has a physical mechanism similar to that for narrowband interference. The desired signal is spread in the transmitter and is despread in the receiver. Thus the total desired signal energy is reduced, that is, "collapsed," to the bandwidth of the demodulation bandwidth. This spectral collapsing occurs only for the desired signal, since the transmitted PN sequence $g_k(t)$ is correlated (multiplied) in the receiver by the same $g_k(t)$ sequence. The wideband interference is by multiplication with an independent $g_L(t)$ PN spreading signal. In the receiver the $g_k(t) \cdot g_L(t)$ product has a very wideband spectrum. It is filtered by the relatively narrowband demodulator filter; thus only an f_b/f_c fraction of the wideband interference energy reaches the demodulator output.

6.5 CODE DIVISION MULTIPLE ACCESS (CDMA): DIRECT-SEQUENCE (DS) AND FREQUENCY-HOPPED (FH) SPREAD-SPECTRUM SYSTEMS

6.5.1. CDMA: Principles of Operation

Code division multiple access (CDMA) systems are an extension of direct-sequence spread-spectrum (DS-SS) and frequency-hopped spread-spectrum (FH-SS) systems. They provide multiple-access communications capabilities. In CDMA each user is provided with an individual, distinctive pseudonoise (PN) code. If these codes are uncorrelated with each other, then *within the same mobile cell k independent users can transmit at the same time and in the same radio bandwidth.* The receivers decorrelate (despread) the information and regenerate only the desired data sequence $d_i(t)$ where $i = 1, \ldots k$. In Figure 6.5.1 a CDMA spectral overlay concept of $k = 10$ DS-SS carriers is illustrated. Assuming

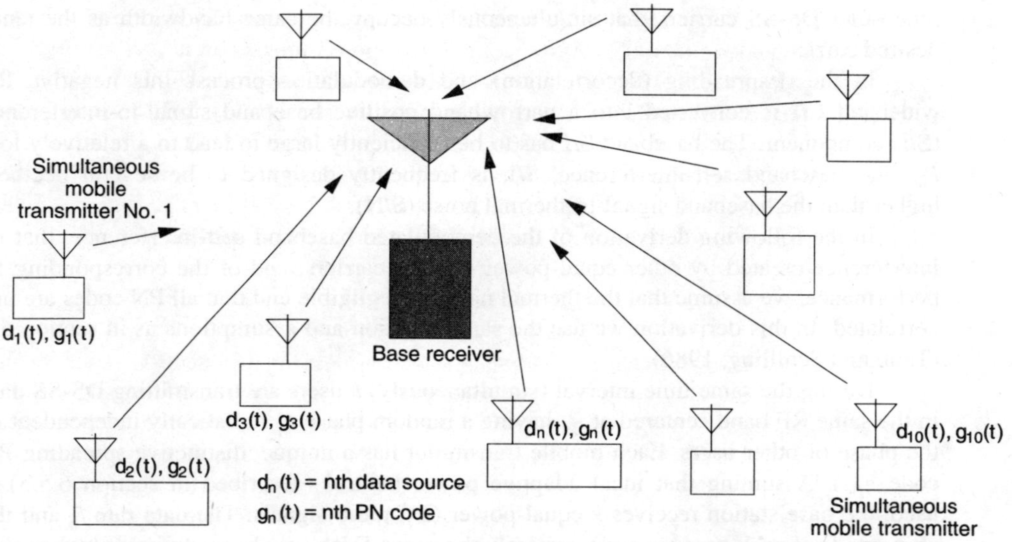

Figure 6.5.1 Code division multiple access (CDMA) with 10 active mobile users within the same mobile cell. Each mobile unit transmits a direct-sequence spread-spectrum (DS-SS) signal in the same RF bandwidth and at the same time as the other users. Adaptive power control, described in section 6.5.3, ensures that all received, overlayed signals at the base station have the same power. Uncorrelated Pseudonoise (PN) sequences are used by each transmitter. (Based on IEEE-Qualcomm, 1980 workshop.)

that $k = 10$ mobile units are transmitting at the same time, the base station receiver will have 10 spectrally overlapped and time-overlapped signals. The terms *base station* and *mobile* could be interchanged. If the received power of all these signals is the same, P_s, then any one of the desired signals will be interfered by nine other equal-power CDMA signals. Thus at the RF receiver port the desired carrier-to-interference (C/I) ratio will be 1/9, or C/I = −9.54 dB. This negative C/I is caused by "self-interference," that is, by the nine other DS-SS carriers that simultaneously occupy the same bandwidth as the tenth desired carrier.

In the despreading (decorrelation) and demodulation process this negative RF wideband C/I is converted into a narrowband positive baseband signal-to-interference (S/I) component. The baseband S/I has to be sufficiently large to lead to a relatively low P_e. The baseband self-interference, S/I, is frequently designed to be several decibels higher than the baseband signal-to-thermal noise (S/N).

In the following derivation of the demodulated baseband self-interference, that is, interference created by other equal-power CDMA carriers, and of the corresponding P_e performance, we assume that the thermal noise is negligible and that all PN codes are uncorrelated. In this derivation we use the same notation and assumptions as in section 6.4 (Taub and Schilling, 1986).

During the same time interval (simultaneously) k users are transmitting DS-SS data in the same RF band centered at f_0, having a random phase ϕ_i statistically independent of the phase of other users. Each mobile transmitter has a unique, distinctive spreading PN code $g_i(t)$. Assuming that ideal adaptive power control (described in section 6.5.3) is used, the base station receives k equal-power (P_s) radio signals. The data rate f_b and the chip rate f_c of each user are approximately the same. Each user has a different message or information to convey; thus $d_i(t)$ is different for all mobile transmitters. The base station RF receives $v(t)$, a composite RF signal defined by

$$v(t) = \sum_{i=1}^{k} \sqrt{2P_s}\, g_i(t)\, d_i(t) \cos(\omega_o t + \theta_i). \tag{6.5.1}$$

The base station receiver is required to correlate (despread) and demodulate the "k" independent DS-SS messages; k correlators are illustrated in Figure 6.5.2. A straightforward extension of the DS-SS receiver of Figure 6.2.1 to the multiple-correlator CDMA receiver is illustrated in Figure 6.5.2, (a). In this configuration the despreading occurs at IF. An alternative implementation is shown in Figure 6.5.2, (b). The composite overlapped RF signal is downconverted to a convenient IF frequency, for example, 70 MHz, and is demodulated in one common, coherent wideband demodulator. The low-pass filter of this demodulation is sufficiently wide to pass the f_c chipping rate signal. The k separate decorrelators are in the baseband output stage.

The following equations apply to both of the architectures illustrated in Figure 6.5.2. At the output of the demodulator in Figure 6.5.2, (a), following the low-pass effect of the integrator that is built into the PSK demodulator, we have

$$v'_{01} = \sum_{i=1}^{k} \sqrt{P_s}\, g_1(t)\, g_i(t)\, d_i(t) \cos(\theta_i - \theta_1) \tag{6.5.2}$$

$$= \sqrt{P_s}\, d_1(t) + \sum_{i=2}^{k} \sqrt{P_s}\, g_1(t)\, g_i(t)\, d_i(t) \cos(\theta_i - \theta_1). \tag{6.5.3}$$

These CDMA equations are similar to the DS-SS baseband output (equation 6.4.3), except that in equations 6.5.2 and 6.5.3 there are $k - 1$ interfering components. As for the derivation in section 6.4, it can be demonstrated (Taub and Schilling, 1986) that the total power spectral density $G_J(f)$ of the $k - 1$ interferers is

$$G_J(f) \simeq (k-1)\frac{P_s}{4 f_c} \qquad |f| \le f_b. \tag{6.5.4}$$

By defining the total interference power as

$$P_J = (k-1)P_s, \tag{6.5.5}$$

the probability of error (P_e) caused by the "self-interference" of the k simultaneous equal-power received signals is obtained. It is given by

$$P_e = \frac{1}{2}\, erfc \sqrt{2\left(\frac{1}{k-1}\right)\left(\frac{fc}{f_b}\right)} \tag{6.5.6}$$

where f_c is the chipping rate and f_b is the bit rate. To attain the desired P_e, the number of users k, the chipping, and bit rates have to be carefully selected. Two important assumptions in the derivation of the P_e expression (equation 6.5.6) are the following:

- Equal power received overlapped wideband DS-SS signals with uncorrelated codes for CDMA operation: Equal receive power requires accurate adaptive power control.
- Thermal noise is negligible; only self-induced or self-interference (noise) is considered.

6.5.2 Near-Far Interference Problems in DS-CDMA Systems

In a DS-CDMA system, all traffic channels within one cell simultaneously share the same radio bandwidth, that is, radio channel. Neighboring cells may be assigned the same frequencies or adjacent channels. Some of the mobile units are close to the base station, while others are far from it. A strong signal received at the base from a near-in mobile unit masks the weak signal from a far-end mobile unit. For example, assume that all 10 mobile units illustrated in Figure 6.5.1, (a), transmit the same RF power P_s = +30 dBm and that the propagation-loss from the far-end mobile unit, Unit 10, is 95 dB, while the loss from the near-in unit, Unit 4, is only 35 dB. In this case, at the base station the received power from Unit 4 is P_{R4} = +30 dBm – 35 dB = –5 dBm, while from the far-end

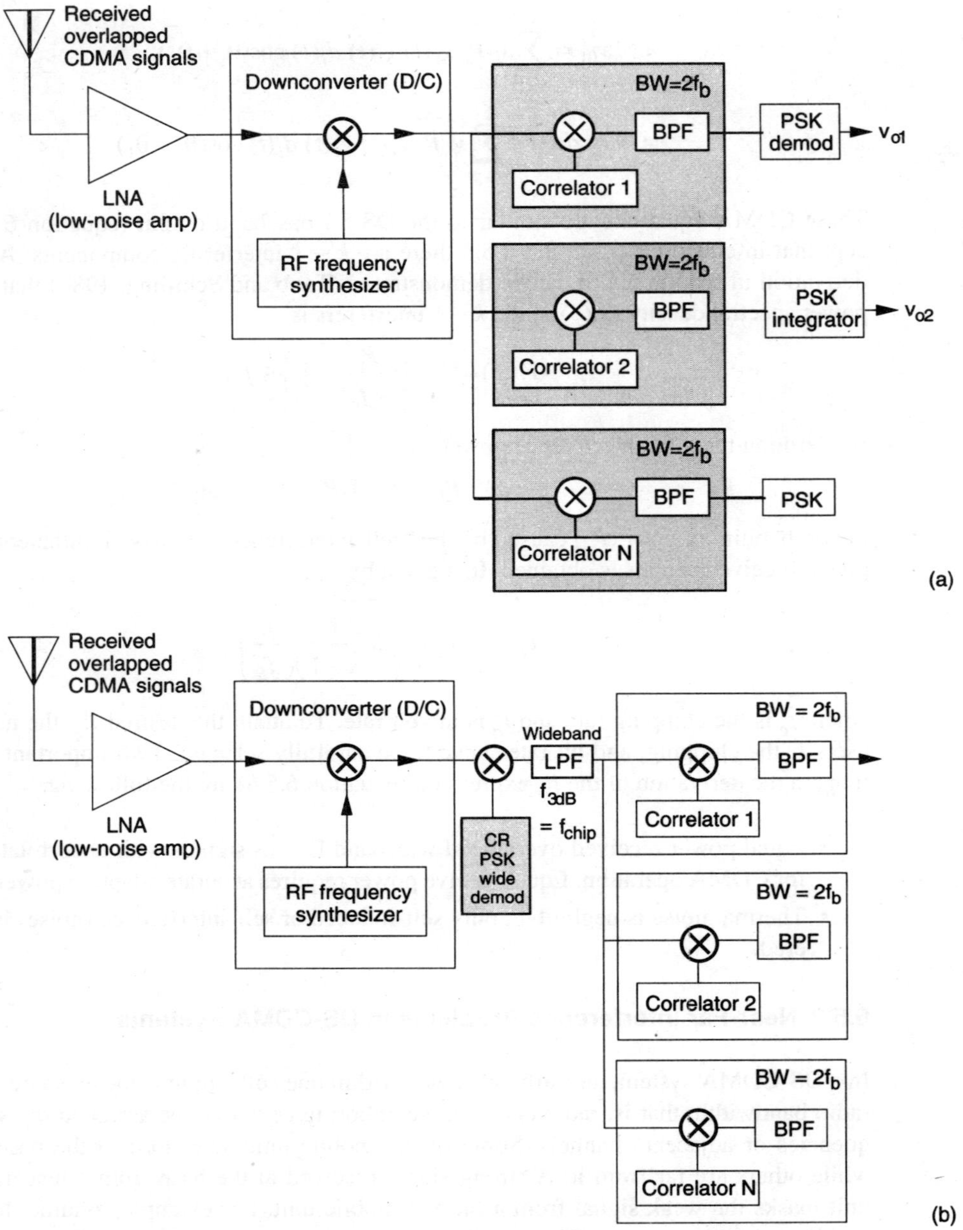

Figure 6.5.2 Implementation of equivalent CDMA receivers. (a), Despreading (correlation) followed by narrowband demodulation. (b), Wideband demodulation followed by correlation.

unit, Unit 10, the received power is P_{R10} = +30 dBm −95dB = −65 dBm. Thus we have an inband interference power, caused by the near-in unit, of the 60 dB higher than the received signal power from the far-end mobile unit. This masking effect, or inband interference created by the near-in units, is known as "near-far interference." It is a serious problem in CDMA applications and designs.

Equation 6.5.6 represents a mathematical relationship between the chipping rate f_C, bit rate f_b, and specified P_e, for k simultaneous users. In the derivation it is assumed that all received signals at the base station have the same power level. This requirement is essential to maximize the capacity of CDMA systems. From our discussion of "near-in" and "far-end" mobile units we note that this assumption is not valid in practical cellular-mobile systems without adaptive power control.

6.5.3 Adaptive Power Control in CDMA Spread-Spectrum Systems

To optimize the system capacity and spectral efficiency, adaptive power control schemes have been developed. Power control reduces the near-far interference ratio. An ideal power control scheme ensures that the signals received at the cell site from all the mobile units within a cell remain at the same power level, independent of the movement, propagation path loss, and/or location of the mobile units. Numerous power control schemes have been developed. Here we describe a simple, efficient adaptive power control method based on Kubota et al. (1992).

The *forward link* of the CDMA system originates at the base station transmitter, and it ends in the mobile receiver. The *reverse link* is in the opposite direction from the mobile unit to the base. In the open-loop transmit power control (TxPC) configuration, analog or digital pilot signals are transmitted in the forward link. The measured strength of the received pilot at the mobile unit provides an estimate of the path loss between the base transmitter and mobile receiver. Based on the path loss measurement, the mobile unit generates a transmit power control signal and sets the mobile transmitter to the desired power. This process is performed frequently; thus an adaptive open-loop control is achieved. It is assumed that the forward and reverse links have the same propagation path loss. However, such an open loop arrangement may not lead to sufficient precision and accuracy.

An improved arrangement is attained with the closed loop TxPC system (Figures 6.5.3 and 6.5.4, (b)). In this adaptive power control system the following sequence of events takes place:

1. The base station receiver detects the received RF power from the mobile unit (achieved through the reverse link).
2. Base station transmits through forward link (base to mobile) control bits to the mobile unit to adjust the transmit power of the mobile to the desired level.

The power control error of practical TxPC loops is about 1.5 dB. Ideally it should be 0 dB, that is, all transmitted signals from various mobile units should be received with 0 dB

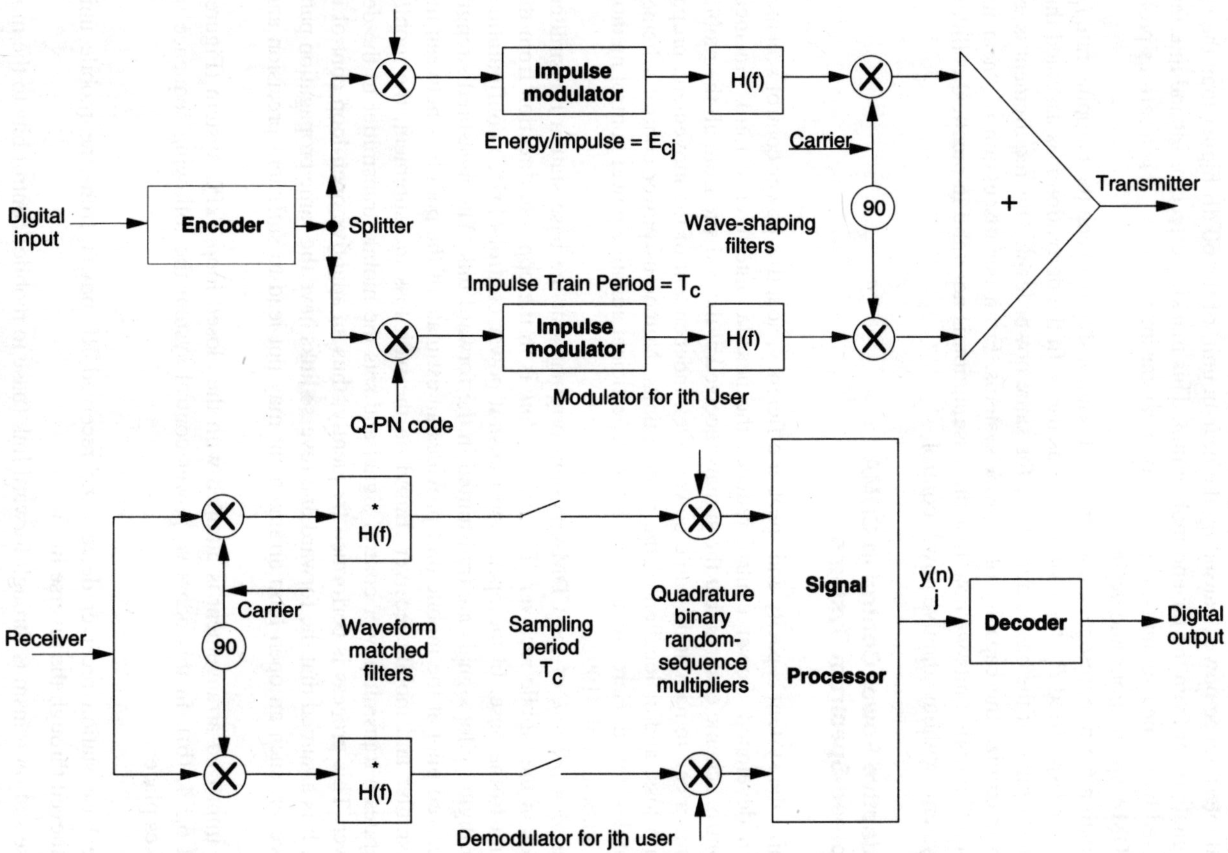

Figure 6.5.3 CDMA implementation architecture by Qualcomm, Inc., of the "IS-95" cellular standard (Based on IEEE-Globecom, 1990.) For Quadrature crosscorrelated I and Q systems and modulators see Appendix A.3 in regards to Dr. Feher Associates-Digcom Inc. licenced technologies, including USA Patent No. 4,567,602.

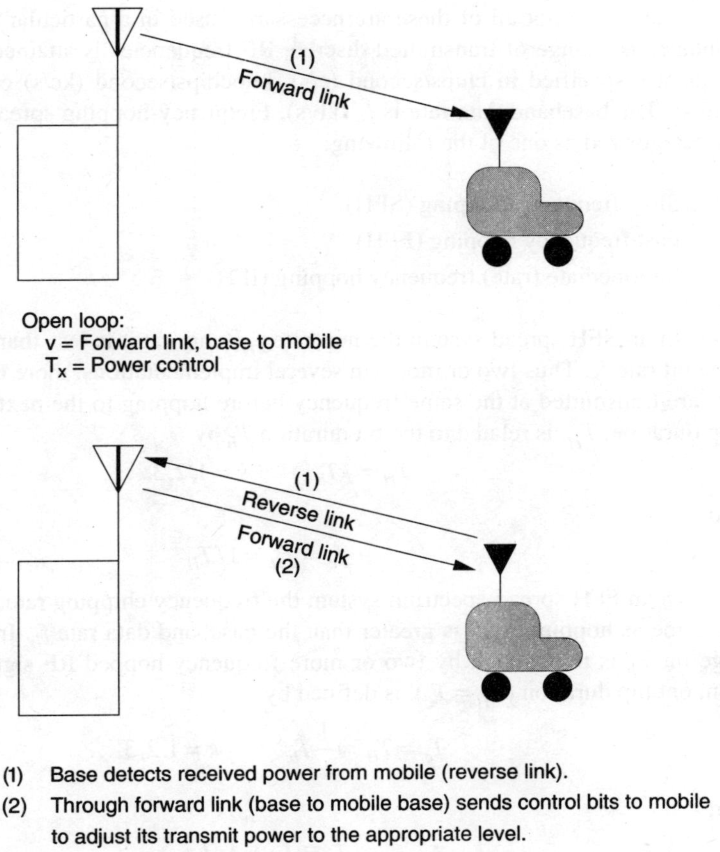

Figure 6.5.4 Transmit power control in open-loop and closed-loop arrangements.

differential at the base station. This would eliminate the near-far interference problem and optimize (maximize) the capacity of CDMA cellular systems.

6.6 FREQUENCY-HOPPING SPREAD-SPECTRUM SYSTEMS

6.6.1 Slow Frequency-Hopping Spread-Spectrum Systems

In frequency-hopping spread-spectrum (FH-SS) systems the transmitted radio frequency is constant in each chip that is in each frequency-hopping interval but is changed from chip to chip (Figure 6.2.5). The transmitted hopped frequencies are generated by a digital frequency synthesizer, which is controlled by serial or parallel "words," each containing m binary digits. These m-bit words produce one of $M = 2^m$ frequencies for each separate word or symbol combination of the digits (Cooper and McGillem, 1986). The number of radio frequencies available for a frequency hopper is frequently $M = 2^m$ where $m = 2, 3,$

4, . . ., although not all of these are necessarily used in a particular application. The instantaneous change of transmitted discrete RF frequencies is attained at the chip rate f_c, frequently specified in chips/second (c/s), kilochips/second (kc/s) or megachips/second (Mc/s). The baseband data rate is f_b (kb/s). Frequency-hopping spread-spectrum systems are categorized as one of the following:

Slow frequency hopping (SFH)
Fast frequency hopping (FFH)
Intermediate (rate) frequency hopping (IFH)

In an SFH spread system the hop rate f_H (chip rate) is less than the baseband message bit rate f_b. Thus two or more (in several implementations, more than 1000) baseband bits are transmitted at the same frequency before hopping to the next RF frequency. The hop duration, T_H, is related to the bit duration T_b by

$$T_H = kT_b \qquad k = 1, 2, 3, \ldots$$

and

$$f_c = f_H = 1/T_H. \tag{6.6.1}$$

In an FFH spread-spectrum system the frequency chipping rate, f_c, (chipping rate is the same as hopping rate) is greater than the baseband data rate f_b. In this case one message bit T_b is transmitted by two or more frequency-hopped RF signals. The hop duration, or chip duration ($T_H = T_c$), is defined by

$$T_c = T_H = \frac{1}{k}T_b \qquad k = 1, 2, 3, \ldots$$

and

$$f_c = f_H = 1/T_c. \tag{6.6.2}$$

In an intermediate hop-rate situation the hop rate and the message bit rate are of the same order of magnitude. This implementation is designated as intermediate rate frequency hopping (IFH). Most applications have been in the "slow hop" or "fast hop" categories.

In Figure 6.6.1 an illustrative frequency-hopping transmitter, a noncoherent frequency-hopping receiver, and related synchronization and error-correction coding/decoding subsystems are presented (Cooper and McGillem, 1986). This figure presents somewhat more functional details than does the basic frequency-hopped diagram in Figure 6.2.5. The source data signal $d(t)$ is encoded/decoded in a forward-error-correction (FEC) subsystem. If one or more hops are interfered with strong interfering signals, then one or more bits within that particular hop(s) could be destroyed. For this reason error correction, as demonstrated in a subsequent section, is required in many frequency-hopped spread-spectrum applications. The digital frequency synthesizer has m controlling input bits; one of these bits is the encoded message bit T_b, the other $m - 1$ bits (digits) are generated by the pseudonoise (PN) code generator. Digital frequency synthesizers are frequently implemented at a convenient intermediate frequency (IF) having a somewhat limited IF bandwidth. The frequency multiplier following the IF digital frequency synthe-

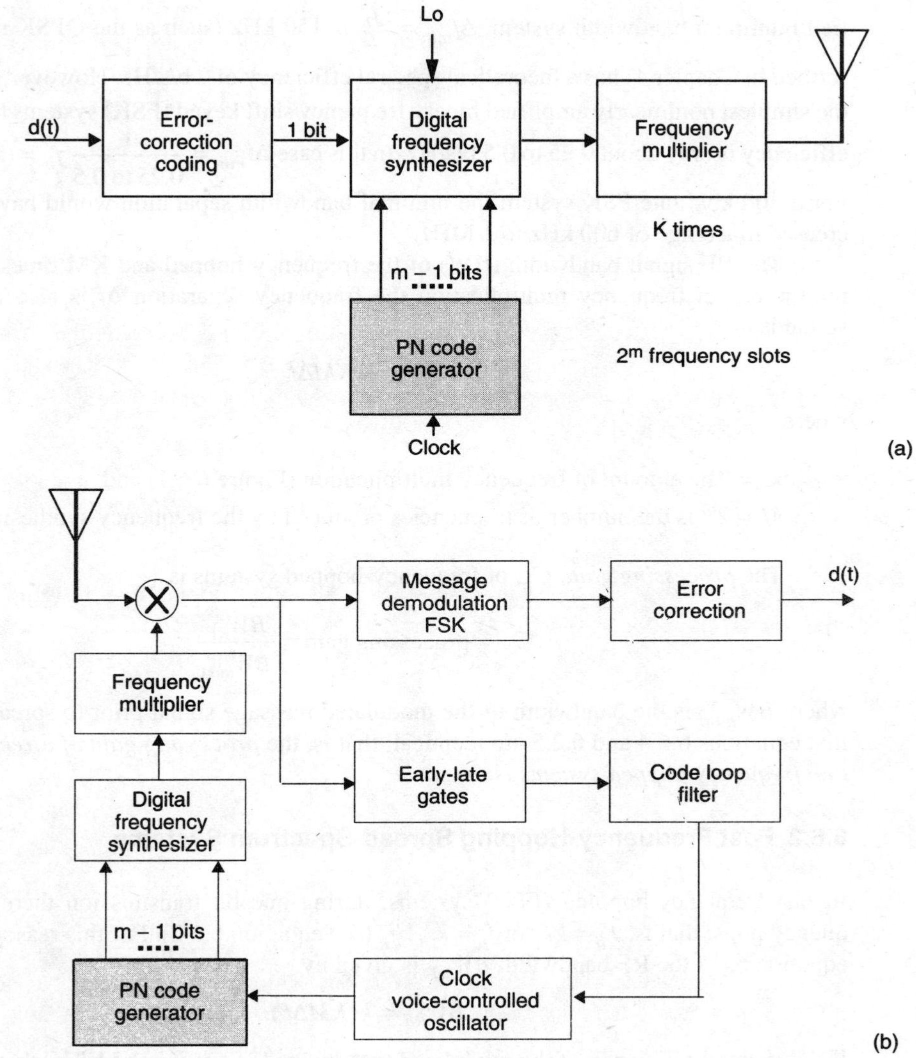

Figure 6.6.1 (a), Frequency-hopping (FH) transmitter and, (b), noncoherent frequency-hopping receiver with error correction coding/decoding and synchronization subsystems. (Based on Cooper and McGillem, 1986.)

sizer "multiplies up" the individual discrete frequency to RF, thus increasing the RF bandwidth; thereby an increased processing gain is achieved.

Let the frequency separation between adjacent discrete frequencies of the digital frequency synthesizer equal Δf. This minimal bandwidth separation Δf has to be larger than the f_b bit-rate modulated RF bandwidth of a carrier wave (CW) modulated, not-hopped system. For example, for an f_b = 300 kb/s – QPSK band-limited, linearly amplified minimum bandwidth system, $\Delta f_{min} = \frac{f_b}{2} = 150$ kHz (such as the QPSK modem described in Chapter 4) has a theoretical spectral efficiency of 2 b/s/Hz. However, in some of the simplest nonlinearly amplified binary frequency shift keyed (FSK) systems the spectral efficiency is only about 0.25 to 0.5 b/s/Hz. In this case $\Delta f_{min} = \frac{1}{0.25 \text{ to } 0.5} f_b = (2 \text{ to } 4) * f_b$. For a 300 kb/s rate FSK system the minimal bandwidth separation would have to be increased to a range of 600 kHz to 1 MHz.

The RF signal bandwidth (BW) of the frequency-hopped and KM times frequency multiplied (in frequency multiplication the frequency separation Δf is also multiplied) signal is

$$BW_{RF} \approx KM\Delta f \tag{6.6.3}$$

where

K = The amount of frequency multiplication (Figure 6.6.1) and
$M = 2^m$ is the number of frequencies produced by the frequency synthesizer

The *processing gain,* G_p, of frequency-hopped systems is

$$G_P = \text{processing gain} = \frac{BW_{RF}}{BW_{\text{mod}}} \tag{6.6.4}$$

where BW_{mod} is the bandwidth of the modulated message signal prior to spreading. Note that equations 6.6.4 and 6.2.5 are identical; that is, the *processing gain of direct-sequence and frequency-hopped systems is the same.*

6.6.2 Fast Frequency-Hopping Spread-Spectrum Systems

In fast frequency-hopping (FFH) systems, during one bit transmission there are k frequency hops; that is, $T_b = kT_c$ or $f_b = k \cdot 1/f_c$ (see equation 6.6.2). For this reason and from equation 6.6.3 the RF bandwidth BW_{RF} is given by

$$BW_{RF} = k(KM\Delta f). \tag{6.6.5}$$

If the spectral efficiency of the modulated (not-hopped) system is 1 b/s/Hz, then

$$BW_{\text{mod}} = f_b = 1/T_b = \Delta f, \tag{6.6.6}$$

and the processing gain in this case is

$$G_P \approx \frac{BW_{RF}}{BW_{\text{mod}}} = \frac{kKM\Delta f}{\Delta f} = kKM. \tag{6.6.7}$$

Thus the processing gain of this FFH system depends on the number of different frequencies employed (M), the number of hops per bit (k), and the frequency multiplication factor K.

In the frequency-hopping receiver (Figure 6.6.1), the received frequency-hopped signal is multiplied by a PN code-driven digital-frequency-synthesized, and frequency-multiplied signal. This PN-controlled frequency-hopped signal, locally generated in the receiver, stores the same PN code as the corresponding transmitter. If this receiver-generated PN code is "in step," that is, in synchronization with the transmitted code, then the multiplier despreads the RF-received signal (similar to the case in DS-SS) and the spread RF signal is "collapsed" into the modulated message bandwidth. Message demodulation using simple FSK receivers is frequently used. Evidently other modulation/demodulation techniques such as PSK could be employed. The demodulated baseband data is fed to the error-correction decoder. At the output an estimate equal to $\hat{d}(t)$ of the transmitted source data $d(t)$ is obtained. The early-late gates, code-loop filter, and clock voltage-controlled oscillator (VCO) are part of the synchronization subsystem described in Section 6.7. As long as synchronization is not attained, for example, initial phase of a burst-operated "on-off" CDMA transmitter/receiver, the spread signal is not "collapsed" to the bandwidth of the FSK demodulator. During this synchronization time the demodulator has a wideband noiselike spread-spectrum input and for this reason cannot demodulate (meaningfully) the desired $d(t)$ information signal.

6.6.3 Performance of Frequency-Hopped Systems in an Interference Environment

A simple intuitive derivation of the probability of error, P_e, performance of frequency-hopped spread-spectrum systems, presented in this section, provides an insight into the principles of operation and interference-rejection capabilities of these systems (Dixon, 1976). We assume that bit errors are caused by strong interfering signals and that thermal noise is negligible when compared with the strong interfering signal components. In such an interference-controlled and thermal "noise-free" system model, errors occur with a probability of 0.5 whenever the interference power within the bandwidth of a particular frequency-hopped channel (receiver bandwidth of the demodulation subsystem that is approximately the same as Δf the minimal spacing between adjacent hopped frequencies) exceeds the carrier power.

For a frequency-hopping system without any form of data redundancy, for example, no error coding/decoding, the average error rate P_e is

$$P_e = \frac{J}{M} \tag{6.6.8}$$

where

J = Number of interferers with power greater than or equal to the carrier power

M = total number of frequencies available

For example, in Figure 6.6.2 the number of high-power interfering signals is 2, ($J = 2$) and $M = 16$. Thus in such an interference environment the P_e would equal $2/16 = 1.25 \cdot 10^{-1}$, an unacceptably high P_e performance for most applications.

In a frequency-hopped system having built-in redundancy such as forward-error-correction coding or multiple chips per bit, the average probability of error P_e may be approximated by

$$P_e = \sum_{x=r}^{c} \binom{c}{r} p^x q^{c-x}, \tag{6.6.9}$$

where

P = J/M = error probability for a single trial
J = Number of interferers greater than the carrier power
M = Number of channels available to the frequency hopper
q = 1 − p = probability of no error for a single trial
c = Number of chips (frequencies) sent per bit of information
r = Number of wrong chip decisions necessary to cause a bit error

If three or more frequency chips (frequency hops) are transmitted for each information bit, T_b, and *majority decision* decoding (EIA, 1990; Bhargava et al., 1981) is used in the receiver, then the performance in an interference environment can be greatly enhanced (Dixon, 1976). We illustrate P_e performance improvement in the following example.

Example 6.2.1

How much is the average P_e of a frequency-hopped spread-spectrum system if 1000 frequency hops (frequencies) are available and the interference power of a single-tone jammer, measured at the receiver, exceeds the received carrier power of the desired frequencies by 4 dB? Assume (a) that one chip per bit is used, (b) that three chips (hops) per information bit are transmitted, and that a majority-decision decoding receiver algorithm, in which two out of three chips being correct lead to the right decision, is implemented.

Solution for Example 6.2.1

(a) One (hop) chip per bit case:
The average probability of error P_e based on equation 6.6.8 is given by

$$P_e = \frac{J}{M} = \frac{1}{1000} = 1 \cdot 10^{-3},$$

an unacceptably high P_e for many applications.

(b) Three chips (hops) per bit:
The average P_e of this redundant system is given by equation 6.6.9. Thus we have
$c = 3$ = The number of hops or chips sent per information bit
$r = 2$ = The number of wrong-chip decisions to cause a bit in error in a "two-out-of-three" based majority-decision rule
$p = 10^{-3}$ probability of error of a single trial, without majority decoding, as obtained in part (a) of the solution
$q = 1 - p = 1 - 10^{-3} = 0.999$ = probability of no error (single trial)

The following equations are obtained:

$$P_e = \sum_{x=r}^{c} \binom{c}{r} p^x q^{c-x} = \sum_{x=2}^{3} \binom{3}{2} (10^{-3})^x (1-10^{-3})^{3-x}$$
$$= 3 \cdot 10^{-6}(1-10^{-3})^1 + 3 \cdot 10^{-9}(1-10^3)^0$$
$$\approx 3 \cdot 10^{-6}$$
$$P_e = 3 \cdot 10^{-6}$$

From Example 6.6.2 we note that the P_e of the unprotected (not coded or not redundant) system is $P_e = 1 \cdot 10^{-3}$, while that of the redundant (increased to three chips per bit with majority decoding) system is only $P_e = 3 \cdot 10^{-6}$; thus an improvement of about 333 times in the average bit-error rate is obtained. However, the number of RF frequencies and the hopping rate had to be increased three times. If the minimum spacing Δf between frequency hops is specified (Δf equals the modulated bandwidth prior to frequency hopping), then the required RF bandwidth has to be increased in proportion with the chipping rate.

In Figure 6.6.2 the $P_e = f(J/M)$ with simple majority decoding rules is shown. In Figure 6.6.3 the number of interfering signals (or jammers [J]), the interference or jamming margin (J/M), and the number of hopped channels are plotted.

In these figures and our assumptions, *contiguous* frequency spacing has been used. In contiguous frequency-hopped frequency phases, the dehopped received signal does not overlap from one channel into another. To conserve RF bandwidth, significant overlap may be allowed between frequency-hopped channels, as illustrated in Figure 6.6.4 (Dixon, 1976).

6.6.4 Delay Spread: Multipath Robustness of Frequency-Hopping Systems

Delay-spread multipath mobile environments are studied in detail in Chapter 3 and illustrated in Figure 6.6.5. The direct (shortest) propagation path from the frequency-hopped (FH) base station transmitter to the mobile receiver is obstructed by a mountain. This direct

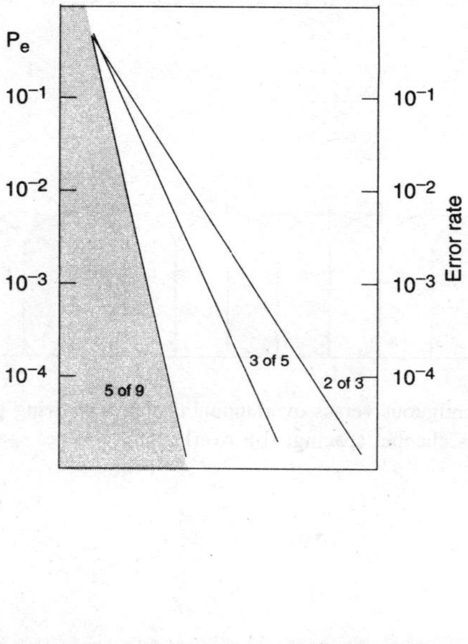

Figure 6.6.2 Error rate P_e versus fraction of channels jammed J/M for various chip decision criteria in multichip transmissions. (Dixon, 1976 [© IEEE].)

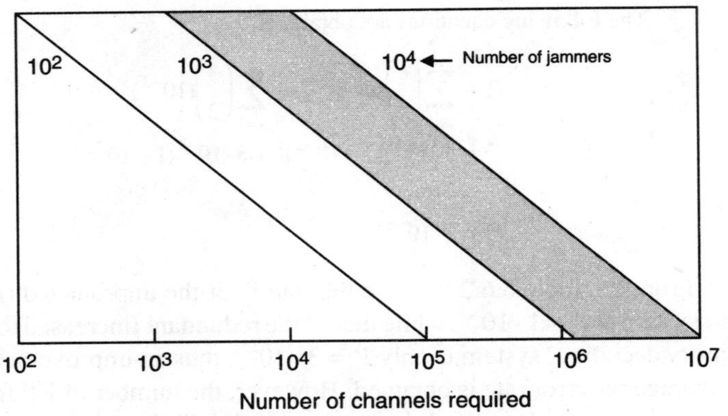

Figure 6.6.3 Number of channels required versus fraction of channels jammed J/M and number of jammers. (Dixon, 1976 [© IEEE].)

path has a propagation time τ_0 and a received signal strength comparable to the reflected signal power, which has a propagation time $\tau_1 + \tau_2$. The delayed signal is the cause of severe in-band interference unless the frequency synthesizer "hops" to another RF frequency before the arrival of the delayed signal. If the hopping (chipping) rate f_c is larger than the inverse of the delay difference between the reflected path and direct path, that is

$$f_c > \frac{1}{(\tau_1 + \tau_2 -)\tau_d}, \tag{6.6.10}$$

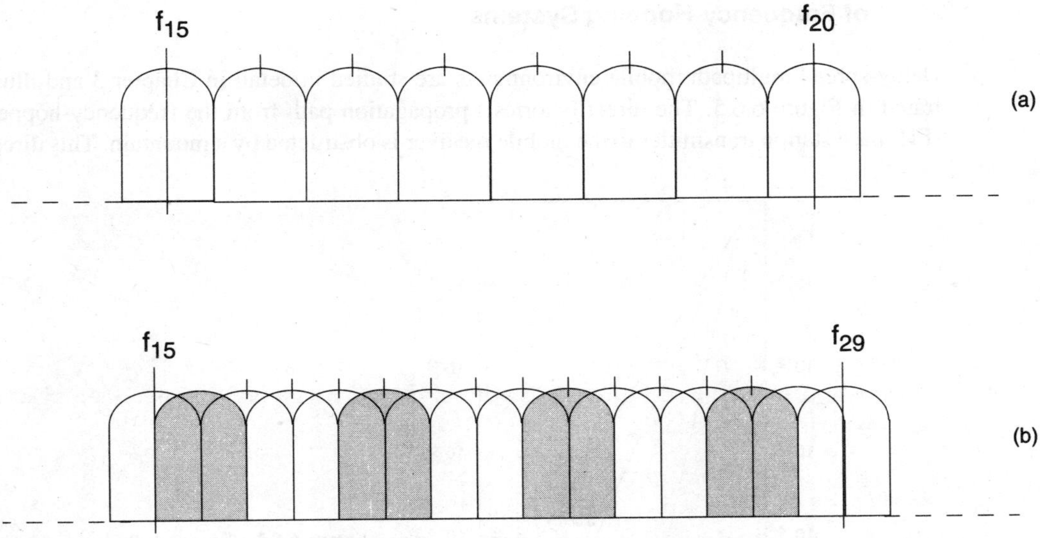

Figure 6.6.4 Illustration of contiguous versus overlapping channels showing gain in channels per unit bandwidth. (a), Contiguous channel spacing; (b), overlapping channel spacing. (Dixon, 1976 [© IEEE].)

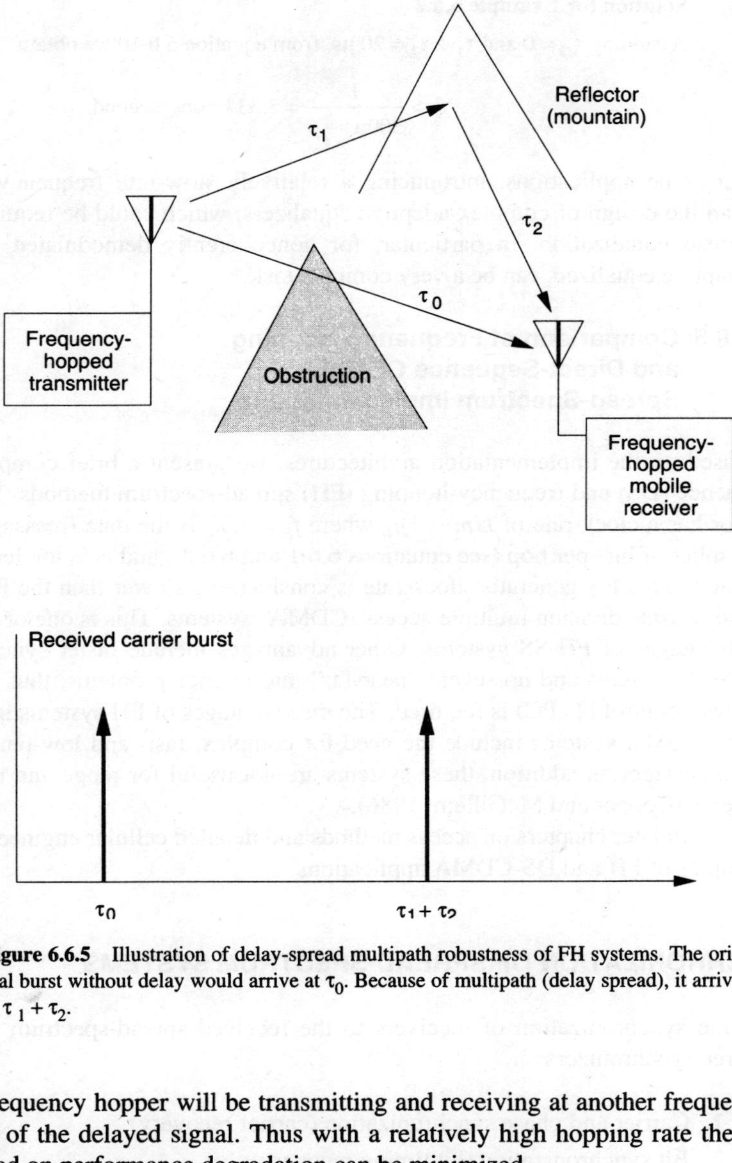

Figure 6.6.5 Illustration of delay-spread multipath robustness of FH systems. The original burst without delay would arrive at τ_0. Because of multipath (delay spread), it arrives at $\tau_1 + \tau_2$.

then the frequency hopper will be transmitting and receiving at another frequency before the arrival of the delayed signal. Thus with a relatively high hopping rate the impact of delay spread on performance degradation can be minimized.

Example 6.6.2

In a U.S. digital public land mobile radio (PLMR) system, an $f_b = 4.8$ kb/s rate QPSK type of modem/radio is used. If this time division multiple access (TDMA) system could be modified to include FH-SS, then what would be the minimum hop rate to mitigate the impact of larger than $\tau = 300$ μs delay spreads?

Solution for Example 6.6.2

Assuming $\tau_D = 0$ and $\tau_1 + \tau_2 = 20\ \mu s$, from equation 6.6.10 we obtain

$$f_c > \frac{1}{300\mu s - 0} = 3.33\,k \text{ hops/second.}$$

For some applications, introducing a relatively slow-rate frequency hopper is simpler than the design of complex adaptive equalizers, which could be required for large delay-spread equalization. In particular, for noncoherently demodulated systems, design of adaptive equalizers can be a very complex task.

6.6.5 Comparison of Frequency-Hopping and Direct-Sequence CDMA Spread-Spectrum Implementations

Based on the implementation architectures, we present a brief comparison of direct-sequence (DS) and frequency-hopping (FH) spread-spectrum methods. The PN code generator has a clock rate of $k(m-1)f_b$ where $f_b = 1/T_b$ is the data (message) bit rate, k is the number of bits per hop (see equations 6.6.1 and 6.6.2), and m is the length of the PN generator. This PN generator clock rate is considerably slower than the PN clock rate in DS and in code division multiple access (CDMA) systems. This is one of the implementation advantages of FH-SS systems. Other advantages include faster synchronization than in DS-SS systems and no severe "near-far" interference problems; thus no precise transmit power control (TxPC) is required. The disadvantages of FH systems in comparison to DS and CDMA systems include the need for complex, fast- and low-phase noise-frequency synthesizers; in addition, these systems are not useful for range and range-rate measurements (Cooper and McGillem, 1986).

In later chapters on access methods and detailed cellular engineering we present examples of FH and DS-CDMA applications.

6.7 SYNCHRONIZATION OF SPREAD-SPECTRUM SYSTEMS

Time synchronization of receivers to the received spread-spectrum signal may require three synchronizers:

1. Carrier and phase synchronization (carrier recovery)
2. Bit synchronization (bit timing recovery)
3. Pseudonoise (PN) or chipping waveform synchronizers

For noncoherent system applications, such as noncoherent FSK or DPSK demodulation, there is no need for a carrier-recovery circuit, since the demodulation process is accomplished by a discriminator detector or by a differential demodulator (described in Chapter 5). Coherent systems require all three synchronizers.

Time synchronization is attained in two phases:

1. Acquisition (initial coarse synchronization)
2. Tracking (fine synchronization)

In the following sections a brief description of some of the simplest synchronization *concepts* for DS and FH spread-spectrum applications are presented. A detailed presentation of spread-spectrum synchronization methods is given in Cooper and McGillem (1986), Dixon (1976), Kesteloot et al. (1991), and Simon et al. (1985).

6.7.1 Acquisition and Tracking of Direct-Sequence Spread-Spectrum Signals

To facilitate and shorten the initial synchronization, that is, "acquisition," of direct-sequence spread-spectrum (DS-SS) received signals, the baseband data signal, $d(t)$, is set to a constant value, $d(t) = 1$. A "pilot" unmodulated, but chipped, RF carrier is received during the acquisition time. It is defined by

$$v_i(t) = \sqrt{2P_s}\, g(t)\cos(\omega_0 t + \theta). \tag{6.7.1}$$

In the conceptual acquisition circuit (Figure 6.7.1) switch S initially is in position 1, connected to a positive voltage source (Taub and Schilling, 1986). The free-running voltage controlled oscillator (VCO) through the AND gate drives the PN or "despreading" generator of the receiver. This generator has a chipping rate of approximately f_c (chips/second or c/s) and generates the same PN sequence as the corresponding transmitter.

Prior to acquisition the transmit and receive PN generators are not in synchronism, that is, the time position of the chip patterns is not aligned. The output of the multiplier (mixer) $v_r(t)$ is given by

$$v_r(t) = v_i(t)\cdot g(t - iT_C) = \sqrt{2P_s}\, g(t)\cos(\omega_0 t + \theta)\cdot g(t - iT_c) \tag{6.7.2}$$

where

$$i = 0,\ 1,\ 2,\ 3,\ \ldots .$$
$$T_c = \text{Unit chip duration}$$

In this equation we assume an iT_c initial shift between the received pilot (unmodulated) spread-spectrum signal and the stored PN sequence in the receiver.

The product waveform $v_r(t)$, for $i \neq 0$ is a DS-SS signal. This wideband signal has a very low power spectral density; for this reason the relatively narrowband bandpass-filtered (BPF) and envelope-detected signal level is low. The integrator and comparator outputs are also in low states. The sample switch is switched every nT_c seconds to position 2. During the low-state output of the comparator and during the nT_c time when the switch is in position 2, the AND gate prevents the VCO signal from driving the PN generator. During this time the PN generator misses some chips (cycles); that is, effectively it is forced to step back with respect to the transmitter PN generator. Afterwards the integrated output is "dumped," and the switch is switched back every nT_c seconds to position 1. The acquisition attempt is starting all over. This repetitive trial-and-error process eventually leads to a state in which the received chipped signal $g(t)$ is aligned with $g(t - iT_c)$, that is, the relative shift $iT_c = 0$ (Taub and Schilling, 1986). At acquisition

$$g(t)g(t-iT_c) = g(t)g(t-0 \cdot T_c) = g^2(t) = 1; \qquad (6.7.3)$$

that is, the received "pilot" signal is despread and equation 6.7.2 becomes

$$v_r(t) = \sqrt{2P_s}\cos(\omega_0 t + \theta), \qquad (6.7.4)$$

an unmodulated or "pilot" tone. The BPF centered at f_0 transfers the complete received signal power to the envelope detector. Integration during nT_c chips leads to a high comparator output state, and acquisition or crude synchronization is now established. Tracking or fine synchronization is the next step in the overall synchronization process.

Delay-lock loops (DLLs) (Figures 6.7.1 and 6.7.2) are often used for tracking or fine synchronization of DS-SS and CDMA signals. The operation of the DLL starts immediately upon completion of coarse synchronization (acquisition). The receiver PN generator is now aligned within one chip with the transmitter; however, it could have a time lead or time lag relative to the received chipped waveform. For this reason the receiver generator output is $g(t + \tau)$ where $0 < \tau < T_c$. The waveforms $v_0 f(t)$, $v_A(t)$, V, and the filtered waveforms $v_{DF}(t)$ and $v_{AF}(t)$ (Figure 6.7.2) are given by Taub and Schilling (1986) as

$$v_D(t) = \sqrt{2P_s}\, g(t)g(t+\tau - T_c/2)d(t)\cos(\omega_0 t + \theta) \qquad (6.7.5)$$

$$v_A(t) = \sqrt{2P_s}\, g(t)g(t+\tau + T_c/2)d(t)\cos(\omega_0 t + \theta) \qquad (6.7.6)$$

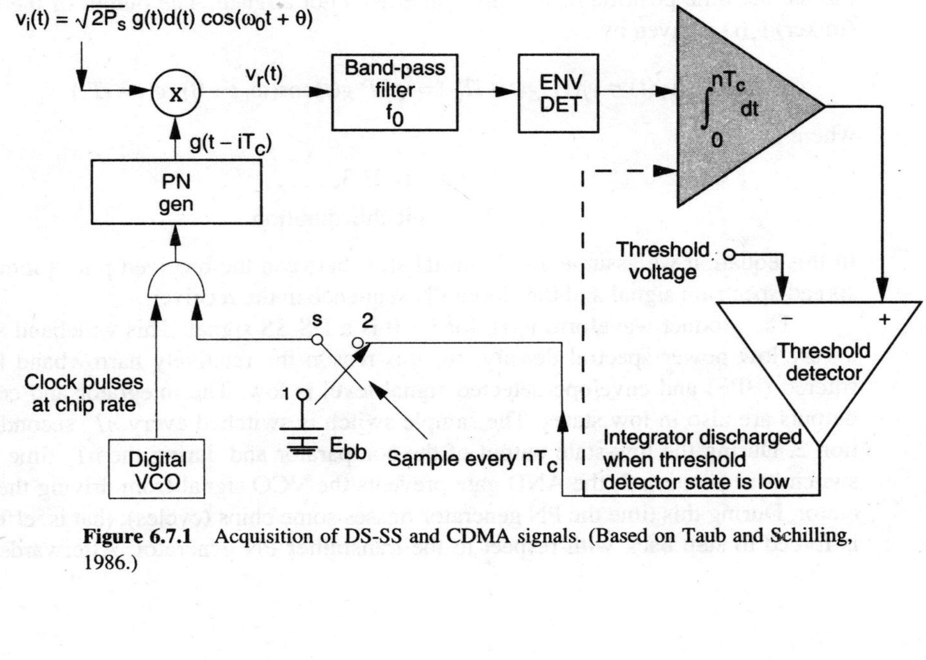

Figure 6.7.1 Acquisition of DS-SS and CDMA signals. (Based on Taub and Schilling, 1986.)

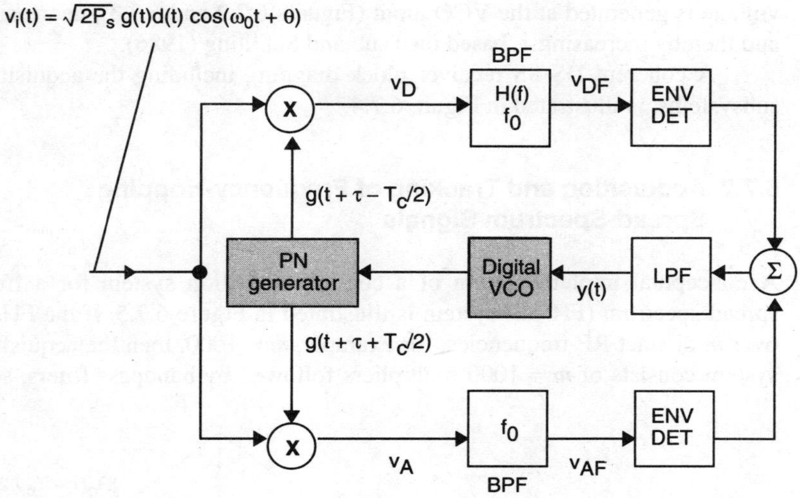

Figure 6.7.2 Delay-locked loop (DLL) for tracking of DS-SS (and CDMA) signals. (Based on Taub and Schilling, 1986.)

$$v_{DF}(t) \simeq \sqrt{2P_s}\,[\overline{g(t)g(t+\tau-T_c/2)}]\,d(t)\cos(\omega_0 t+\theta) \tag{6.7.7}$$

$$v_{AF}(t) \simeq \sqrt{2P_s}\,[\overline{g(t)g(t+\tau+T_c/2)}]\,d(t)\cos(\omega_0 t+\theta). \tag{6.7.8}$$

The bandwidth of the BPF is much narrower than the bandwidth required to allow the wideband PN sequence to be transferred to the envelope detectors. Only the average values of the $g(t)g(t + \tau + T_c/2)$ products are passed. The average value of the product of the received PN sequence and a shifted version of the same sequence is the autocorrelation function (Taub and Schilling, 1986) defined by

$$R_g(\tau \pm T_c/2) = \overline{g(t)\;g(t+\tau \pm T_c/2)}. \tag{6.7.9}$$

The envelope detectors extract the envelopes of $v_{DF}(t)$ and $v_{AF}(t)$ and thus remove the data $d(t)$. We obtain

$$v_D(t) = \left|R_g(\tau - T_c/2)\right| \tag{6.7.10}$$

and

$$v_A(t) = \left|R_g(\tau + T_c/2)\right|. \tag{6.7.11}$$

The input to the VCO is $y(t)$, given by

$$y(t) = \left|R_g(\tau - T_c/2) - R_g(\tau + T_c/2)\right|. \tag{6.7.12}$$

If τ is positive, a positive voltage appears at the VCO input and the VCO frequency is increased. This increased VCO frequency reduces τ. For negative values of τ a negative $y(t)$

voltage is generated at the VCO input (Figures 6.7.2 and 6.7.3), decreasing the VCO rate and thereby increasing τ, based on Taub and Schilling (1986).

A coherent DS-SS receiver block diagram, including the acquisition and tracking subsystems, is illustrated in Figure 6.7.4.

6.7.2 Acquisition and Tracking of Frequency-Hopping Spread-Spectrum Signals

A conceptual implementation of a coarse acquisition system for a frequency-hopping spread-spectrum (FH-SS) system is illustrated in Figure 6.7.5. If the FH transmitter hops over m distinct RF frequencies, for example, $m = 1000$, then the acquisition (correlation) system consists of $m = 1000$ multipliers followed by bandpass filters, square low detec-

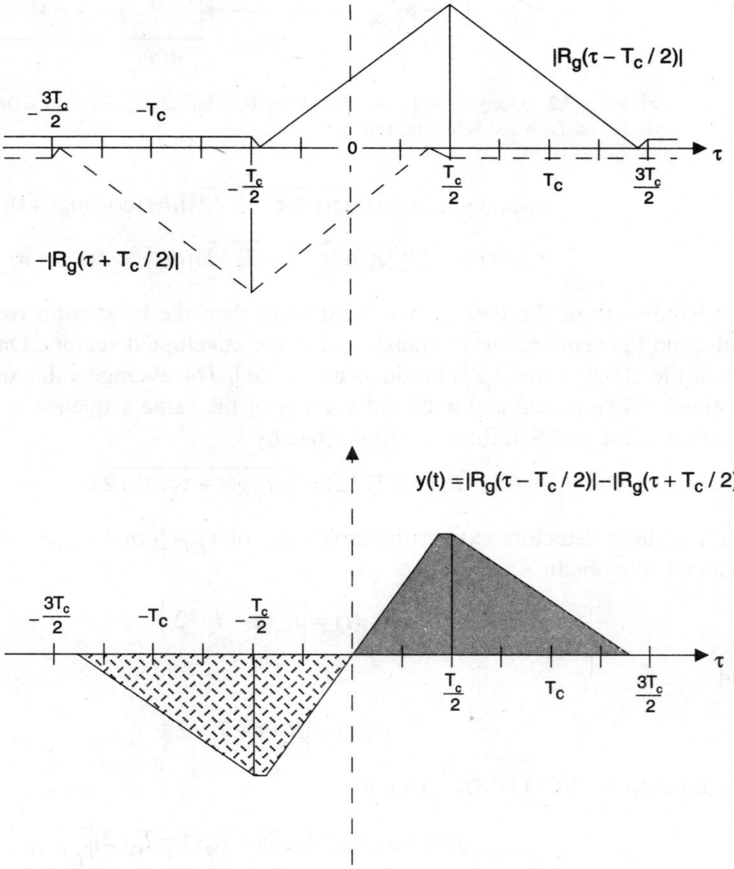

Figure 6.7.3 Delay-locked loop (DLL) input voltage of the voltage-controlled oscillator (VCO) in Figure 6.7.2. (Based on Taub and Schilling, 1986.)

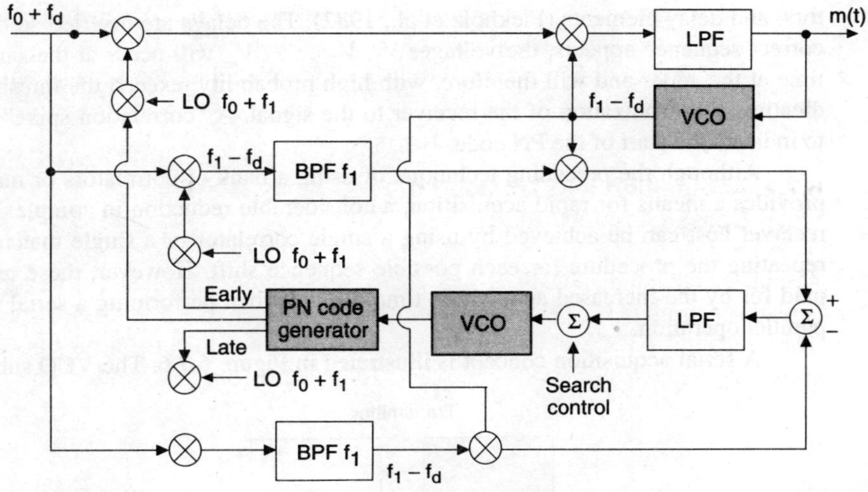

Figure 6.7.4 Coherent direct-sequence spread-spectrum (DS-SS) receiver. (Based on Cooper and McGillem, 1986.)

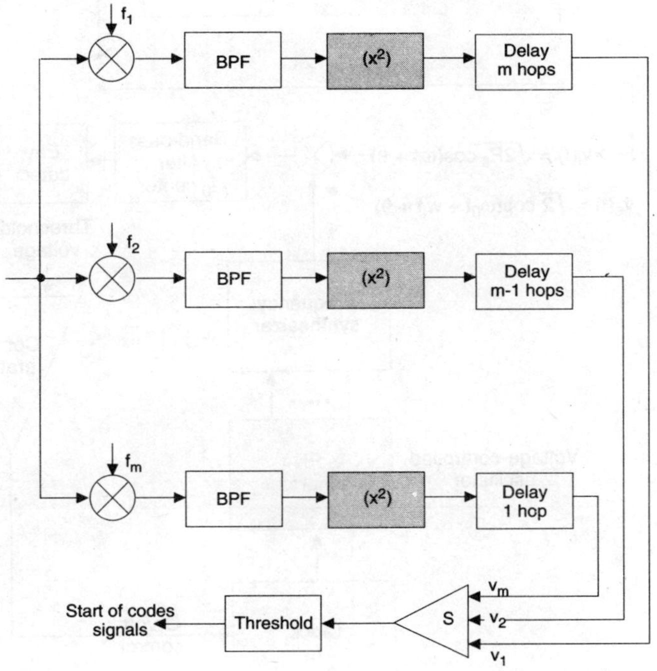

Figure 6.7.5 Frequency-hopping (FH) receiver coarse-parallel acquisition scheme with a passive correlator structure. (From R. L. Pickholtz, D. L. Schilling, and L. B. Milstein, "Theory of spread-spectrum communications—a tutorial," *IEEE Transactions on Communications,* [© 1982 IEEE].)

tors, and delay elements (Pickholz et al., 1982). The delays are inserted so that when the correct sequence appears, the voltages $V_1, V_2, \ldots, V_m$ will occur at the same instant of time at the adder and will therefore, with high probability, exceed the threshold level indicating synchronization of the receiver to the signal. A "correlation spike" is generated to indicate the start of the PN code.

Although the preceding technique of using a bank of correlators or matched filters provides a means for rapid acquisition, a considerable reduction in complexity, size, and receiver cost can be achieved by using a single correlator or a single matched filter and repeating the procedure for each possible sequence shift. However, these reductions are paid for by the increased acquisition time needed when performing a serial rather than a parallel operation.

A serial acquisition concept is illustrated in Figure 6.7.6. The VCO subsystem con-

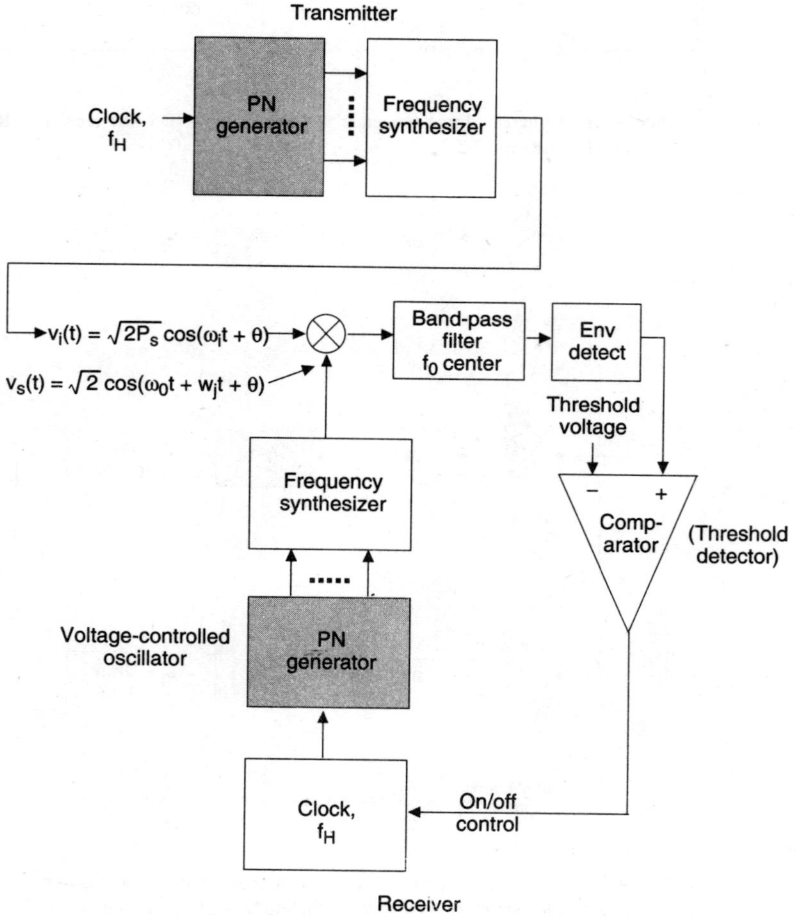

Figure 6.7.6 Coarse serial-acquisition diagram of a frequency-hopped spread-spectrum (FS-SS) receiver. This acquisition technique is also known as "camp-and-wait." (Based on Taub and Schilling, 1986.)

sists of a clock generator having a rate of f_H, that is, the hopping rate; a PN generator that has the same PN sequence as the corresponding transmitter; and a frequency synthesizer. The clock generator is either off or on, depending on the state of the control signal generated by the comparator output circuit. The frequency of the frequency synthesizer is controlled by the digital PN signal. As the PN generator moves through each of its states, the frequency synthesizer hops from frequency f_1 to f_2 to $f_3 \ldots$ to f_M and back to f_1 and so forth. The hopping rate of the synthesizer is $f_H = 1/T_H$ (Taub and Schilling, 1986).

Before acquisition the received RF frequency f_i and the frequency generated by the frequency synthesizer of the receiver f_j are not the same; that is, $f_i \neq f_j$. In this case, despreading or correlation is not achieved and the spectrum at the input of the BPF is a wideband spread-spectrum signal. The relatively narrowband BPF, having a bandwidth of approximately $2f_H$, will filter out most power of the wideband spectrum and will provide only a low signal power to the envelope detector. The comparator output is now in a low state and provides an "off" signal to the f_H (hopping rate) clock generator. The PN generator does not cycle through its states, and the receiver synthesizer holds at a frequency $f_0 + f_J$; that is, it remains in a *camp-and-wait* position. The transmit frequency hopping is ongoing. When finally the received frequency becomes f_j, the difference signal passes through the BPF. The envelope detector provides a higher voltage than the preset threshold, and the comparator provides a high "on" state to the clock generator. The PN generator advances in synchronism with the transmit FH generator. Thus coarse acquisition occurs.

Although acquisition has occurred, there is still an error of τ seconds between transitions of the received signal's RF frequencies and the locally synthesized frequencies. The next step in the synchronization process is to "fine tune" or track (minimize) the τ-second error signal. This can be achieved by a tracking loop such as the one illustrated in Figure 6.7.7. The bandpass filter is made sufficiently wide to pass the product signal $V_p(t)$ when $V_1(t)$ and $V_2(t)$ are at the same frequency f_i, but sufficiently narrow to reject $V_p(t)$ when $V_2(t)$ are at different frequencies f_i but sufficiently narrow to reject $V_p(t)$ when

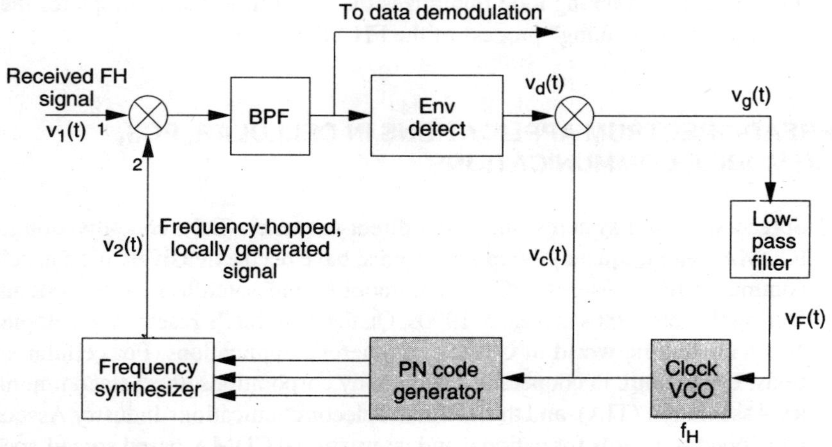

Figure 6.7.7 Tracking loop for FH signals. (Based on Pickholz et al., 1982.)

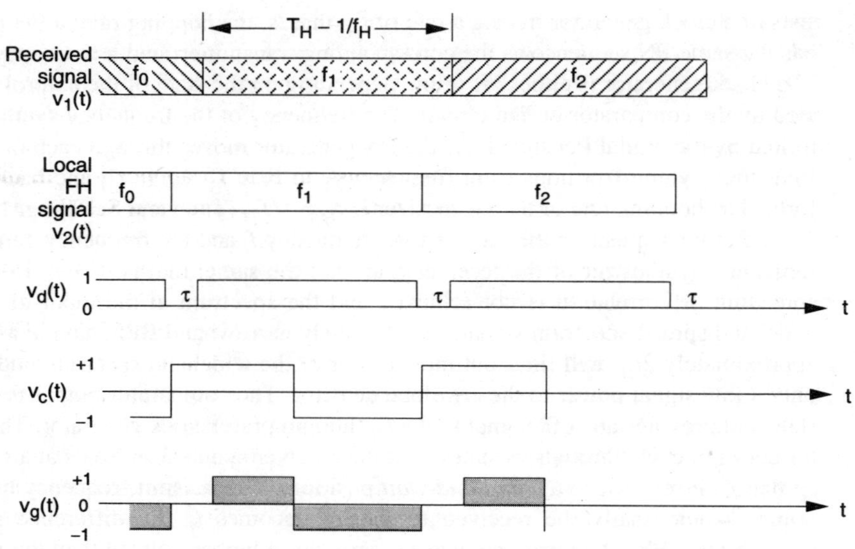

Figure 6.7.8 Waveforms for tracking an FH signal. (Based on Pickholz et al., 1982.)

$V_1(t)$ and $V_2(t)$ are at different frequencies f_i and $f_i + 1$. Thus the output of the envelope detector $V_d(t)$ (Figure 6.7.7) is unity when $V_1(t)$ and $V_2(t)$ are at the same frequency and is 0 when $V_1(t)$ and $V_2(t)$ are at different frequencies. From Figure 6.7.8 we see that $V_g(t) = V_d(t)\ V_c(t)$ and is a three-level signal. This three-level signal is filtered to form a direct-current voltage, which in this case presents a negative voltage to the VCO (Pickholz et al., 1982). When $V_2(t)$ has frequency transitions that precede those of the incoming waveform $V_1(t)$, the voltage into the VCO will be negative, thereby delaying the transition; if the local waveform frequency transitions occur after the incoming signal frequency transitions, the voltage into the VCO will be positive, thereby speeding up the transition. This tracking loop minimizes the offset time τ and completes the fine synchronization or "fine tuning" process of the FH-SS system.

SPREAD-SPECTRUM APPLICATIONS IN CELLULAR, PCS, AND MOBILE COMMUNICATIONS

Spread-spectrum systems, including direct-sequence (DS), code-division multiple access (CDMA), and frequency-hopping systems, have been extensively used in cellular, personal communication systems (PCS), land-mobile, and satellite-mobile systems applications. During the late 1980s and early 1990s, Qualcomm, Inc.'s research developments and products have led the world in CDMA commercial applications. For cellular system applications, Qualcomm, in cooperation with many corporations, the Telecommunications Industry Association (TIA), and the Cellular Telecommunications Industry Association (CTIA), developed standards for national and international CDMA-based spread-spectrum applications. A detailed description of these developments is included in several papers published in the *IEEE Transactions on Vehicular Technology* in a special issue (for example, Lee [1991] and Gilhousen et al. [1991]), in the TIA standard No. IS-95, and in many other journal and conference papers. The Qualcomm CDMA system is probably the best-documented commercial spread-spectrum system in the readily available literature.

For Federal Communications Commission Part 15 applications in the *902 to 928 MHz, 2.4 to 2.48 GHz,* and *5.4 to 5.6 GHz* ranges, numerous CDMA and frequency-hopped (FH) systems and products have been developed. Some of the most interesting papers on slow frequency-hopping (SFH) spread-spectrum systems for wireless applications include Dornstetter and Verhulst (1987) and Saleh and Salz (1983). Research by Saleh and Cimini (1989) at AT&T Bell Laboratories demonstrated that SFH-TDMA systems have an increased capacity and improved performance over conventional cellular TDMA systems. Inherent diversity, ability of SFH systems to combat interference, and delay-spread robustness are among the advantages of this system.

In Chapter 9, more applications and access methods, including FDMA, TDMA, SS, CDMA, and SFH, are described. Cellular systems and network engineering analysis design tools and methods are presented. Knowledge of this chapter, chapter 6, combined with comprehension of the foundation presented in Chapters 1 to 5, enable us to begin a detailed study of cellular engineering issues and comprehension of the newest and most challenging global developments in these revolutionary fields.

6.9 PROBLEMS

6.1 Describe the differences between the basic multiple access methods FDMA, TDMA, and CDMA. Explain their main properties.

6.2 Compare similarities and differences in the fundamental concepts of a direct-sequence spread-spectrum (DS-SS) system versus a frequency-hopping spread-spectrum (FH-SS) system.

6.3 Why is there a process gain in a spread-spectrum system? How is the process gain defined?

6.4 What are the tasks of PN sequences in multiuser wireless or personal communications CDMA systems?

6.5 Why are Gold-, Kasami-, or Walsh-sequences preferred over *m*-sequences in practical CDMA systems?

6.6 How much is the interference rejection of a BPSK direct-sequence spread-spectrum system (DS-SS) if $f_b = 10$ kb/s and $f_c = 2$ Mc/s (two megachips per second)? How much is the BER of this spread-spectrum system if the practical BPSK modem has a 1 dB degradation from the ideal theoretical performance? (a) Assume that 11 equal-power independent DS-SS signals occupy the same RF bandwidth and that the E_b/N_o ratio is $E_b/N_o = 25$ dB, that is, noise is negligible in such a high E_b/N_o system. (b) Assume that only three independent equal-power DS-SS signals are used and that the available $E_b/N_o = 12$ dB.

6.7 The "near-far interference" is a serious problem in a wireless cellular CDMA network. What is the reason for this?

6.8 Adaptive power control is the common solution to the near-far problem in a CDMA system. Describe two basic power-control concepts for CDMA.

6.9 The bit rate of a CDMA cellular system is 9.6 kb/s, and the chipping rate is 1.788 Mb/s (Figure 6.5.3). How many simultaneous users can be accommodated within one cell if a BER = 10^{-2} threshold performance is accepted for voice-quality mobile telephone systems and if it is assumed that the self-interference–caused BER has to be an order of magnitude lower, that is, BER = 10^{-2}? Note that in this implementation a quadrature binary modulation structure is used.

6.10 Assume that the received digital "pilot" power in a CDMA system is measured at the base with a ±1 dB error and at the mobile unit within ±1.5 dB. How much is the maximal error of the received signal if (a) open-loop and (b) closed-loop transmit power control are implemented?

6.11 A fast frequency-hopped system has a chipping (hopping) rate to bit ratio of 2000. The source bit rate is f_b = 10 kb/s. A 1/2 rate forward-error-correction (FEC) code is used. The modulation format is a nonlinearly amplified FQPSK or an FSK system having approximately (a) 1 b/s/Hz or (b) 0.5 b/s/Hz spectral efficiency. How much are the required RF bandwidth and the processing gain of this system? Comment on the advantages and disadvantages of the 1 b/s/Hz versus 0.5 b/s/Hz system, and compare the spread-spectrum performance of FQPSK and FSK or GFSK systems. *Hint:* In addition to the spectral efficiency advantage of the nonlinearly amplified FQPSK system, note that it has a 5 dB to 10 dB advantage in terms of power efficiency, that is, E_b/N_o requirement over standardized Gaussian filtered (IEEE 802.11) GFSK systems. Find the corresponding performance curves in Chapters 4 and 9.

CHAPTER 7

Diversity Techniques for Mobile-Wireless Radio Systems

7.1 INTRODUCTION

In previous chapters, we demonstrated that multipath Rayleigh fading severely degrades the average bit-error-rate (BER) or probability of error (P_e) performance of wireless digital mobile radio transmission systems. In order to achieve highly reliable digital data transmission without excessively increasing both transmitter power and cochannel reuse distance, it is indispensable to adopt an auxiliary technique that can cope with the fast multipath fading effect. Diversity reception is one of the most effective techniques for this purpose. Various diversity techniques have been proposed and studied, not only for high-frequency (HF) radio systems, but also for troposcatter and line-of-sight (LOS) microwave radio relay systems. Operational principles of diversity techniques were discovered in HF radio experiments in the 1930s (Schwartz et al., 1966). Diversity techniques for very high-frequency (VHF) and ultrahigh-frequency (UHF) and microwave land mobile radio applications have also been studied for many years (Jakes, 1974; Lee, 1982; Parsons and Gardiner, 1989). Most of these books describe analog mobile radio applications, but the techniques they describe can, in principle, also be applied to digital cellular-wireless radio systems. The benefits obtained by diversity techniques are gaining recognition with the increased demand for digital land mobile radio services, since digital transmission is more susceptible to fast multipath fading effects. This chapter, based on Chapter 10 by Dr. K. Hirade in Feher (1987) and other references, highlights the concepts, techniques, and performance of diversity systems for digital wireless applications.

7.2 CONCEPTS OF DIVERSITY BRANCH AND SIGNAL PATHS

A diversity technique requires a number of signal transmission paths, named *diversity branches,* that carry the same information but have uncorrelated multipath fadings and a circuit to combine the received signals or select one of them. Depending on the land mobile radio propagation characteristics, there are a number of methods to construct diversity branches. Generally, *branches* are classified into one of the following categories of diversity:

1. Space
2. Angle or direction
3. Polarization
4. Frequency
5. Time

Each of these methods will be reviewed briefly.

Space diversity, which has been widely used because it can be implemented simply and economically, has a single transmitting antenna and a number of receiving antennas. Spacing between adjacent receiving antennas is chosen so that multipath fading appear-

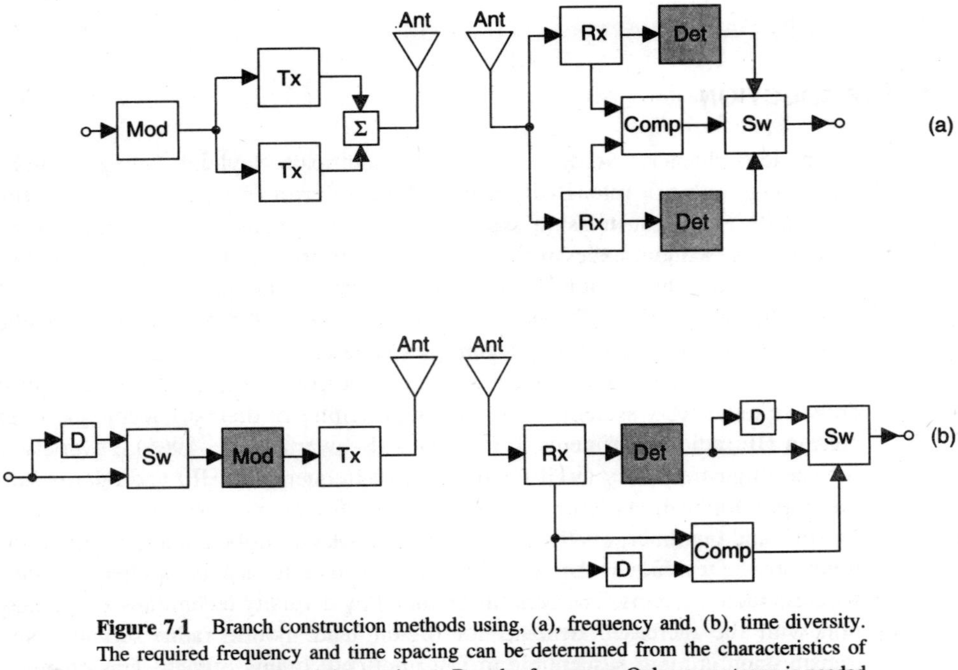

Figure 7.1 Branch construction methods using, (a), frequency and, (b), time diversity. The required frequency and time spacing can be determined from the characteristics of the time-delay spread and the maximum Doppler frequency. Only one antenna is needed at each end, but this simplicity comes at the cost of bandwidth. (Figures 7.1 to 7.10 are based on Dr. Hirade's chapter in Feher [1987a].)

ing in the diversity branches becomes uncorrelated. *Angle diversity,* which is also called *direction diversity,* requires a number of directional antennas. Each antenna responds independently to a wave propagating at a specific angle and receives a faded signal that it uncorrelated with the others. *Polarization diversity,* in which only two diversity branches are available, is effective because the signals transmitted through two orthogonally polarized propagation paths have uncorrelated fading statistics in the usual VHF and UHF land mobile radio environment (Jakes, 1971).

Difference in frequency and/or time can also be utilized to construct diversity branches with uncorrelated fading statistics. Figure 7.1 illustrates the block diagrams of two-branch *frequency* and *time diversity* techniques. The required frequency and time spacing can be determined from the characteristics of the time-delay spread and the maximum Doppler frequency. A common advantage of these two techniques compared with space, angle, and polarization diversity techniques is that the number of transmitting and receiving antennas can be reduced to one of each, with the disadvantage that a wider bandwidth is required. *Error-correction coding,* which is peculiar to digital transmission systems, can be regarded as a kind of time diversity technique.

In principle, with an exception for the case of polarization diversity, there exists no limit to the number of diversity branches. For example, several practical wireless applications in the 2.4 GHz band have used up to five receiver antennas to achieve space diversity.

.3 COMBINING AND SWITCHING METHODS

A number of methods have been studied for many years to combine or select uncorrelated faded signals obtained from the diversity branches. They are usually classified into the following three categories:

1. Maximal-ratio combining
2. Equal-gain combining
3. Selection

For the coherently demodulated case, there is no difference whether the combining is carried out in the predetection or in the postdetection stage. However, for noncoherently detected systems such as frequency modulation (FM) discriminator or differential detection schemes a difference in performance exists between predetection and postdetection combining methods (Adachi, 1981). Block diagrams of three predetection combining methods are shown in Figure 7.2.

Assuming ideal operation, predetection stage *maximal-ratio combining* achieves the best performance improvement compared with the other methods. However, it requires cophasing, weighting, and summing circuits, as shown in Figure 7.2,) (a), resulting in the most complicated implementation. Figure 7.2, (b), shows an *equal-gain combining* system diagram. It is similar to maximal-ratio combining, except that the weighting circuits are omitted. The performance improvement obtained by an equal-gain combiner is slightly inferior to that of a maximal-ratio combiner, since interference- and noise-

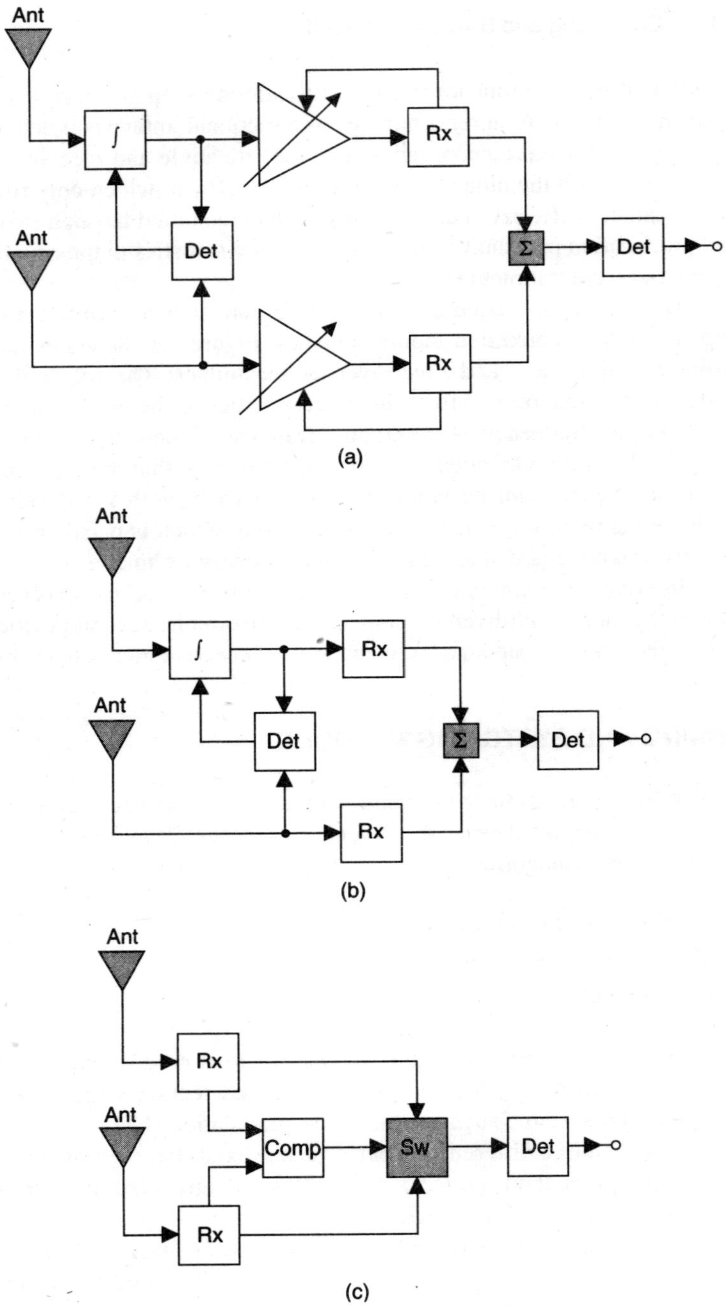

Figure 7.2 Typical combining methods. (a), Maximal-ratio combining gives the largest improvement in performance of the three, but results in the most complicated implementation. (b), Equal-gain combining omits the weighting circuitry and still achieves comparable performance, but will corrupt high-quality signals at one antenna with noise and interference from another. (c), Selection (or switching) is most suitable for mobile radio applications. (Hirade, Chapter 10 in Feher 1987 has been used for Fig. 7.1 to Fig. 7.10.)

corrupted signals may be combined with high-quality (noise- and interference-free) signals. For VHF, UHF, and microwave wireless/mobile radio applications, both the maximal-ratio and the equal-gain combining methods are unsuitable. It is difficult to realize a cophasing circuit having a precise and stable tracking performance in a rapidly changing, random-phase, multipath fading environment. Compared with these two combining methods, the *selection* method is more suitable for mobile radio applications because of its simple implementation. In this method the diversity branch having the highest signal level (or, in more advanced implementations, the branch having the lowest P_e) is selected (Figure 7.2, (c). In addition, stable operation is easily achieved, even in the fast multipath fading environments. It has been shown that the performance improvement obtained by the selection method is still only slightly inferior to the ideal one achieved by the maximal-ratio combining method (Feher and Chan, 1975).

The major disadvantage of the selection or switching method is that continuous monitoring of the signals requires the same number of receivers as the number of diversity branches. This redundancy can be alleviated by the use of a *switching* or *scanning* receiver (Parsons et al., 1973). Figure 7.3 illustrates such a receiver. In Figure 7.3, (a),

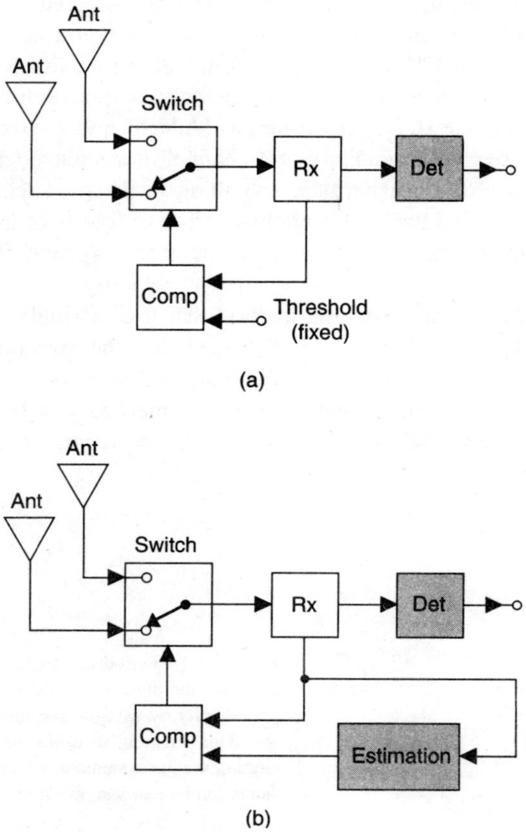

Figure 7.3 Switching methods with, (a), fixed and, (b), variable threshold. Although the former implementation is simpler and faster, it is not possible to choose a threshold value that is appropriate over the entire service area. Feedback solves this problem but may introduce envelope and phase transients.

switching from one branch to the other occurs when the signal level falls below a threshold. The threshold can be set at a fixed value within a small area, but this value is not necessarily the best over the entire service area. Therefore the threshold value should be adjusted dynamically as the vehicle moves, as shown in Figure 7.3, (b). The degree of improvement in performance obtained by the switching method depends on the choice of the threshold value, and the time delay that arises from the feedback loop of monitoring, estimation, decision, and switching. Furthermore, envelope and phase transients of a carrier, which may be caused by switching in the predetection stage, reduce the performance improvement. In angle modulation systems such as Global Special Mobile (GSM), phase transients cause errors in the detected data stream, whereas envelope transients can be removed by a predetection band-pass limiter. For robust GSM hardware and system design, see Appendix 3. Feher's patented GSM related technology is described in Appendix 3.

Figure 7.4 illustrates a simple implementation of the switching method, in which the diversity branches are selected periodically by using a conventional, free-running oscillator. This method is used in relatively low-speed, large-deviation digital FM systems in which phase transients caused by *periodic switching* can be suppressed. The switching rate, which is the only selectable parameter, is chosen to be minimally twice the height of the signaling bit rate, so that the signal of the better branch can be received in every signaling period. The same performance improvement as that of a conventional switching method can be achieved by using an FM discriminator followed by a suitable low-pass filter (LPF). The effectiveness of this method was experimentally demonstrated in a thermal noise and cochannel-interference (CCI) environment (Adachi and Parsons, 1988). However, the performance improvement in an adjacent-channel interference (ACI) environment may end up being reduced, since periodic switching in the predetection radio frequency (RF) stage could cause the adjacent-channel spectrum to fold over into the desired channel band. This overlap can be solved by an increase of the adjacent-channel selectivity of the receiver.

Another effective variation on the switching method that uses a single receiver is the *phase-sweeping* method, shown in Figure 7.5. Provided that the sweeping rate is higher than twice the highest frequency of the modulation signal, the same diversity improvement effect as that obtained by the periodic switching method can be achieved (Parsons and Gardiner, 1989). The phase-sweeping method can be regarded as a *mode-*

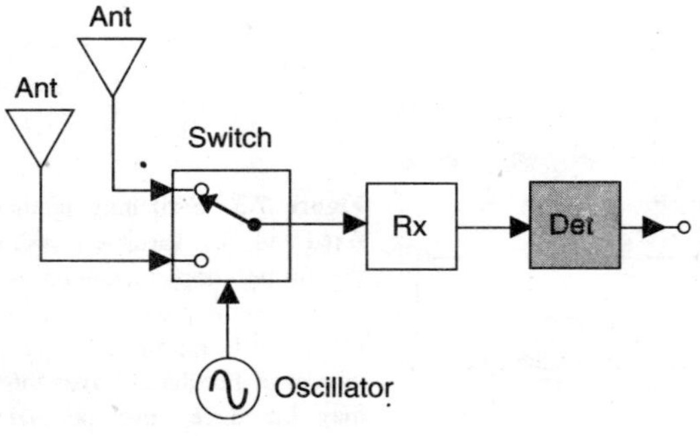

Figure 7.4 Periodical switching method, in which the diversity branches are selected periodically by using a free-running oscillator. This method is useful in low-speed, large-deviation systems in which phase transients can be easily suppressed.

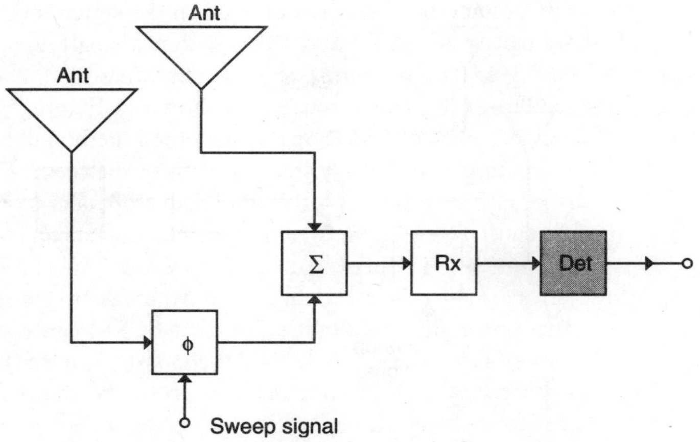

Figure 7.5 Combining method using phase-sweeping scheme, which achieves the same diversity improvement effect as periodic switching if the sweeping rate exceeds twice the highest frequency of the modulation signal.

averaging method using spaced antennas with electronically scanned directional patterns (Villard et al., 1972). Most of the studies related to this method are concerned with amplitude modulation (AM) systems. However, this method can also be applied to digital phase shift keyed (PSK) and FM systems. A *frequency-offset* method such as the one illustrated in Figure 7.6 is also useful, since the same improvement can be achieved as in the case of the linear phase-sweeping method. This method becomes even more attractive when there are multiple diversity branches.

The switching or selection method, illustrated in Figure 7.2, (c), is the most frequently used diversity technique in wireless communications systems applications.

7.4 CARRIER-TO-NOISE AND CARRIER-TO-INTERFERENCE RATIO PERFORMANCE IMPROVEMENTS

The performance improvement of two-branch ($N = 2$) and multiple-branch ($N = 3, 4, 5, \ldots$) diversity systems is expressed in terms of the permissible reduction of the minimum carrier-to-noise ratio (CNR) and carrier-to-interference ratio (CIR) that are required to obtain a specified P_e. For example, in Figure 7.10 we note that for a $P_e = 10^{-4}$, an average CNR of 40 dB is required for a single (nondiversity) system, while the CNR requirement is reduced to 22 dB for a two-branch, maximumal-ratio combining system. The average CNR and CIR statistical reduction of the fading dynamic range is evaluated in this section. In section 7.5 we study the average P_e performance improvement.

In the following study we investigate two-branch diversity systems that use predetection combining. These systems are very effective and useful for practical mobile radio applications. Let us first examine the statistics of CNR and CIR, without diversity, as-

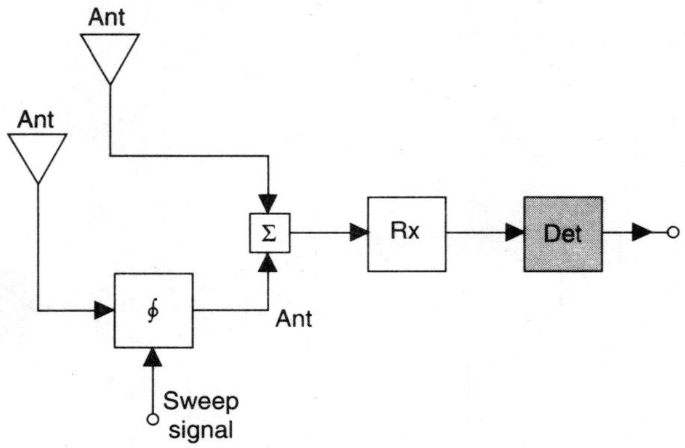

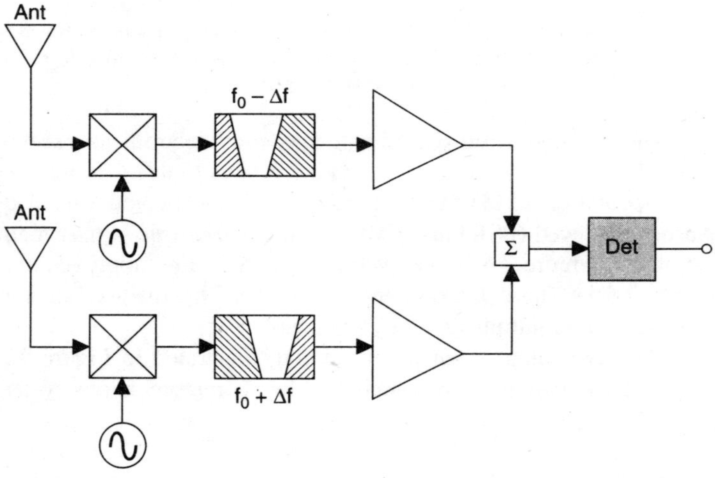

Figure 7.6 Combining method using frequency-offset scheme obtains the same improvement as methods in Figures 7.4 and 7.5 and is especially attractive for multiple-diversity branches.

suming a Rayleigh-fading model. Since the instantaneous CNR γ is proportional to the square of a Rayleigh-distributed signal envelope, the probability density function (pdf) of γ, where $\gamma \geq 0$, is given by the following exponential distribution:

$$p(\gamma) = \frac{1}{\Gamma} e^{-\gamma/\Gamma} \tag{7.1}$$

where Γ denotes the average value of γ. The instantaneous CIR λ is given by the ratio of squared signal envelope to squared interference envelope. These envelopes are mutually independent, Rayleigh-distributed random variables. The pdf of λ, where $\lambda \geq 0$, is then obtained as the following F-distribution:

$$p(\lambda) = \frac{\Lambda}{(\lambda + \Lambda)^2} \tag{7.2}$$

where Λ denotes the average value of λ.

Letting γi $(i = 1, 2)$ be the instantaneous CNR of each diversity branch and γ be the instantaneous CNR of the combined branch, the three combining methods may be described by

$$\begin{cases} \gamma = \gamma_1 + \gamma_2 & \text{for maximal-ratio combining,} \quad (7.3a) \\ \sqrt{\gamma} = \sqrt{\dfrac{\gamma_1}{2}} + \sqrt{\dfrac{\gamma_2}{2}} & \text{for equal-gain combining, and} \quad (7.3b) \\ \gamma = \begin{cases} \gamma_1 \ldots \gamma_1 > \gamma_2 \\ \gamma_2 \ldots \gamma_1 < \gamma_2 \end{cases} & \text{for selection/switching.} \quad (7.3c) \end{cases}$$

Assuming that the two Rayleigh fades that appear on the diversity branches are mutually independent and that both Rayleigh-faded signals have an equal average power, that is, $\Gamma_1 = \Gamma_2 = \Gamma$, where Γ_i $(i = 1, 2)$ denotes the average value of γi $(i = 1, 2)$, the *pdf*s of γ for the above three combining methods have been expressed (Jakes, 1974) by

$$\begin{cases} p(\gamma) = \dfrac{\gamma}{\Gamma^2} e^{-\gamma/\Gamma} \approx \dfrac{\gamma}{\Gamma^2} & \text{for maximal-ratio combining,} \\ p(\gamma) \approx \dfrac{4}{3} \dfrac{\gamma}{\Gamma^2} & \text{for equal-gain combining, and} \\ p(\gamma) = \dfrac{d}{d\gamma} \{(1 - e^{-\gamma/\Gamma})^2\} \approx 2 \dfrac{\gamma}{\Gamma^2} & \text{for selection/switching} \end{cases} \tag{7.4}$$

where the approximation holds for $\gamma << \Gamma$. The outage rates of γ, that is, the probabilities that γ does not exceed a specified value, γs, can be obtained by using the following integral:

$$\text{Prob}[\gamma \leq \gamma_s] = \int_0^{\gamma_s} p(\gamma)\, d\gamma. \tag{7.5}$$

Computed results of equation 7.5 for equations 7.1 and 7.4 are shown in Figure 7.7. We conclude from this figure that the fading dynamic range of γ may be reduced remarkably by the use of the diversity techniques and that there is only a slight difference among the performance improvements of the preceding combining methods. The *pdf*s of λ can be obtained in a similar manner, as derived in Arredondo et al. (1973). They are

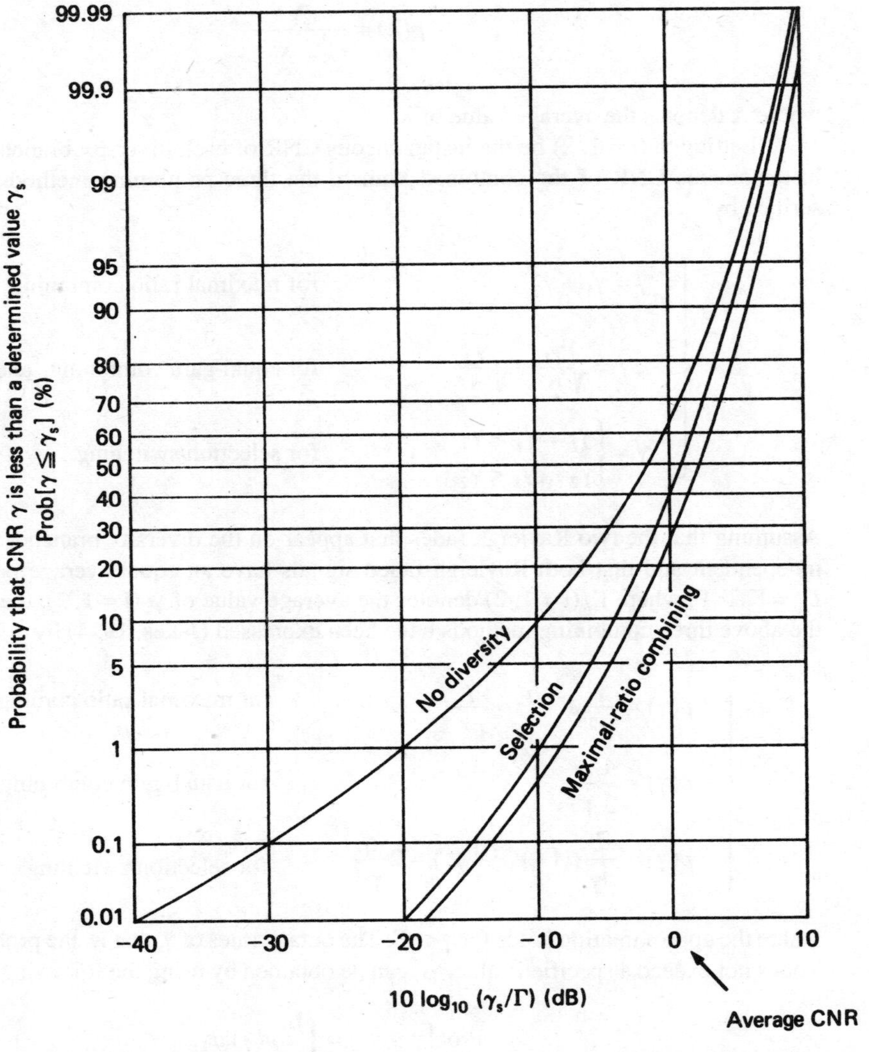

Figure 7.7 Cumulative probability distribution of CNR γ. Γ is the average CNR of each branch. γs is a specified γ. *Note:* Diversity techniques reduce the fading dynamic range of γ, and the choice of combining method is not as significant.

$$
\begin{cases}
p(\lambda) = \dfrac{d}{d\lambda}\left\{\left(\dfrac{\lambda}{\lambda + \Lambda}\right)^2\right\} & \text{for maximal-ratio combining,} \quad (7.6a) \\[2ex]
p(\lambda) \approx \dfrac{d}{d\lambda}\left\{\left(\dfrac{\gamma}{\gamma + \dfrac{\sqrt{3}}{2}\Lambda}\right)^2\right\} & \text{for equal-gain combining, and} \quad (7.6b) \\[2ex]
p(\lambda) = \left\{\dfrac{2\Lambda}{(\lambda + \Lambda)^2} - \dfrac{2\Lambda}{(2\lambda + \Lambda)^2}\right\} & \text{for selection/switching.} \quad (7.6c)
\end{cases}
$$

where a perfect-pilot cophasing scheme is assumed for both the maximal-ratio combining and the equal-gain combining methods and the larger desired signal-power algorithm is assumed for the selection method. The mutual correlation among the four Rayleigh fades appearing on the desired signals and the undesired interferences obtained from the respective branches are assumed to be negligible. It is also assumed that the average CIRs of the branches are equal to each other, that is, $\Lambda_1 = \Lambda_2 = \Lambda$. Computed values of the outage rate given by

$$
\text{Prob}[\lambda \le \lambda_s] = \int_0^{\lambda_s} p(\lambda)\, d\lambda \qquad (7.7)
$$

are shown graphically in Figure 7.8. This figure shows that the fading dynamic range of λ can also be reduced remarkably by diversity techniques. There is only a slight difference in the performance improvement of the various combining methods.

7.5 AVERAGE P_e PERFORMANCE IMPROVEMENT

The performance improvement of a diversity technique can also be assessed by its ability to reduce, for a specified P_e, the permissible values of CNR and CIR. Diversity improvement effects on the average P_e performance of digital radio transmission systems in multipath fading environments have been studied extensively (Prapinmongkolkarn et al., 1974). For digital land mobile radio transmission systems, diversity improvements have been analyzed by taking into account the effects of nonselective envelope fading. The impact of postdetection-selection diversity systems on the average P_e performance of minimum shift keyed (MSK) modulated wireless systems has been analyzed in detail.

In the following discussions, two-branch predetection diversity improvement effects on the average P_e performance of MSK wireless systems in the quasistatic, nonselective Rayleigh-fading environment are considered. The study of the simplest MSK diversity systems can be extended to more advanced modulated wireless diversity architectures.

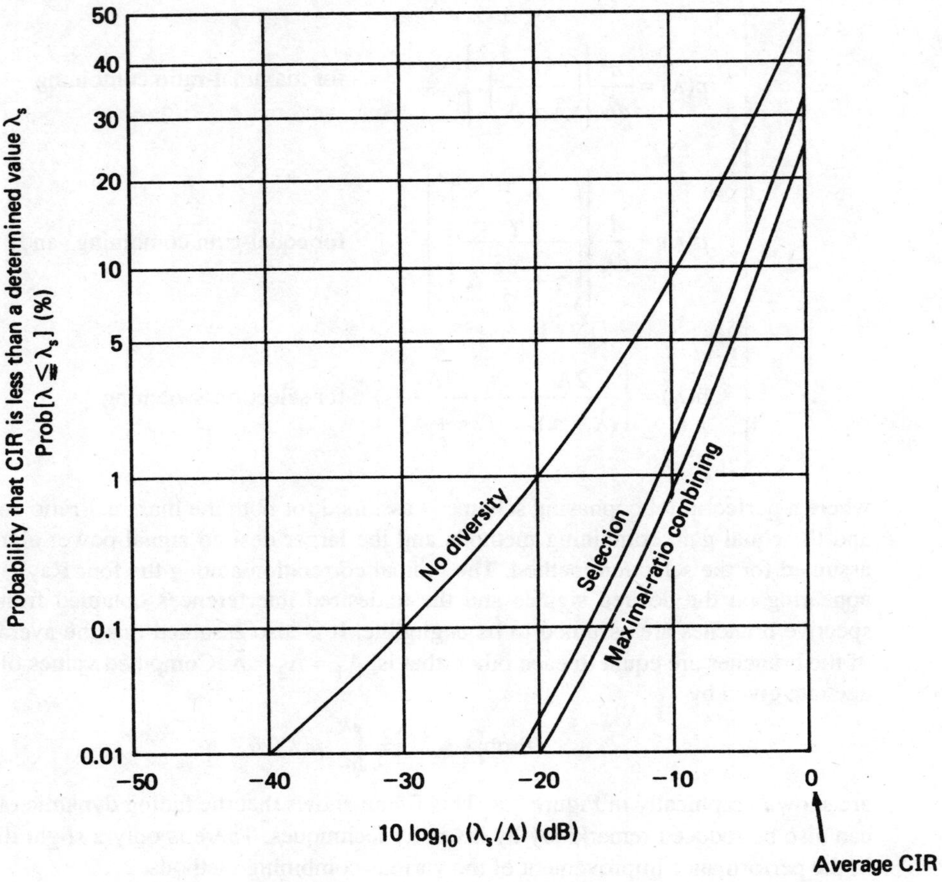

Figure 7.8 Cumulative probability distribution of CIR λ. Λ is the average CIR of each branch. λs is a specified λ. (See *Note*, Figure 7.7.)

7.5.1 P_e versus Carrier-to-Noise Ratio Performance Improvement

Let us first consider a case in which the effect of CCI can be disregarded. Provided that an ideal selection method is used, the average P_e versus CNR performances, with and without diversity, are denoted by $P_e^{(2)}(\Gamma)$ and $P_e^{(1)}(\Gamma)$, respectively. They can be obtained from equations 7.1 and 7.4c as

$$P_e^{(2)}(\Gamma) = \int_0^\infty P_e(\gamma) \frac{d}{d\gamma} \{(1 - e^{-\gamma/\Gamma})^2\}\, d\gamma \tag{7.8}$$

$$P_e^{(1)}(\Gamma) = \int_0^{\infty} P_e(\gamma)\frac{1}{\Gamma}e^{-\gamma/\Gamma}\,d\gamma \tag{7.9}$$

where $P_e(\gamma)$ denotes the static P_e-versus-CNR performance in the nonfading condition. Therefore the following relationship between $P_e^{(2)}(\Gamma)$ and $P_e^{(1)}(\Gamma)$ can be given by

$$P_e^{(2)}(\Gamma) = 2P_e^{(1)}(\Gamma) - P_e^{(1)}\left(\frac{\Gamma}{2}\right). \tag{7.10}$$

For the maximal-ratio combining method a similar relationship can be obtained from equation 7.3a as

$$P_e^{(2)}(\Gamma) = P_e^{(1)}(\Gamma) - \frac{1}{\Gamma}\frac{\partial}{\partial(1/\Gamma)}\{P_e^{(1)}(\Gamma)\}. \tag{7.11}$$

These relationships can be generalized to the case of M-branch diversity reception.

By using the relationships obtained in Feher (1987a) and $P_e^{(1)}(\Gamma)$ for nondiversity MSK modulation, we have

$$\begin{cases} P_e^{(1)}(\Gamma) = \dfrac{1}{2}\left\{1 - \dfrac{\Gamma}{[(\Gamma+1)(\Gamma+\frac{4}{3})]^{1/2}}\right\} & (7.12a) \\ \approx \dfrac{7}{12\Gamma} \quad \text{for discriminator detection} & \\ P_e^{(1)}(\Gamma) = \dfrac{1}{2}\left[1 - \dfrac{\Lambda}{(\Gamma+1)}\right] & (7.12b) \\ \approx \dfrac{1}{2\Gamma} \quad \text{for differential detection} & \\ P_e^{(1)}(\Gamma) = \dfrac{1}{2}\left(1 - \sqrt{\dfrac{\Gamma}{\Gamma+1}}\right) & (7.12c) \\ \approx \dfrac{1}{4\Gamma} \quad \text{for coherent detection.} & \end{cases}$$

By substituting equation 7.12 into equation 7.10, $P_e^{(2)}(\Gamma)$ for the selection method is obtained as

$$
\left\{
\begin{aligned}
P_e^{(2)}(\Gamma) &= \frac{1}{2}\left\{1 - \frac{2\Gamma}{[(\Gamma+1)(\Gamma+\frac{4}{3})]^{1/2}} + \frac{\Gamma}{[(\Gamma+2)(\Gamma+\frac{8}{3})]^{1/2}}\right\} && (7.13a)\\
&\approx \frac{11}{8\Gamma^2} \quad \text{for discriminator detection}\\
P_e^{(2)}(\Gamma) &= \frac{1}{(\Gamma+1)(\Gamma+2)} && (7.13b)\\
&\approx \frac{1}{\Gamma^2} \quad \text{for differential detection}\\
P_e^{(2)}(\Gamma) &= \frac{1}{2}\left(1 - 2\sqrt{\frac{\Gamma}{\Gamma+1}} + \sqrt{\frac{\Gamma}{\Gamma+2}}\right) && (7.13c)\\
&\approx \frac{3}{4\Gamma^2} \quad \text{for coherent detection.}
\end{aligned}
\right.
$$

In addition, by substituting equation 7.12 into equation 7.11, $P_e^{(2)}(\Gamma)$ for the maximal-ratio combining method is obtained as

$$
\left\{
\begin{aligned}
P_e^{(2)}(\Gamma) &= \frac{1}{2}\left\{1 - \frac{\Gamma}{[(\Gamma+1)(\Gamma+\frac{4}{3})]^{1/2}} - \frac{\Gamma(\frac{7}{6}\Gamma+\frac{4}{3})}{[(\Gamma+1)(\Gamma+\frac{4}{3})]^{3/2}}\right\} && (7.14a)\\
&\approx \frac{11}{8\Gamma^2} \quad \text{for discriminator detection}\\
P_e^{(2)}(\Gamma) &= \frac{1}{2(\Gamma+1)^2} && (7.14b)\\
&\approx \frac{1}{2\Gamma^2} \quad \text{for differential detection}\\
P_e^{(2)}(\Gamma) &= \frac{1}{2}\left(1 - \sqrt{\frac{\Gamma}{\Gamma+1}} + \frac{1}{2}\sqrt{\frac{\Gamma}{(\Gamma+1)^3}}\right) && (7.14c)\\
&\approx \frac{3}{16\Gamma^2} \quad \text{for coherent detection.}
\end{aligned}
\right.
$$

Curves obtained by computing equations 7.13 and 7.14 are shown in Figures 7.9 and 7.10, respectively. Moreover, curves representing equation 7.12 are also shown in both

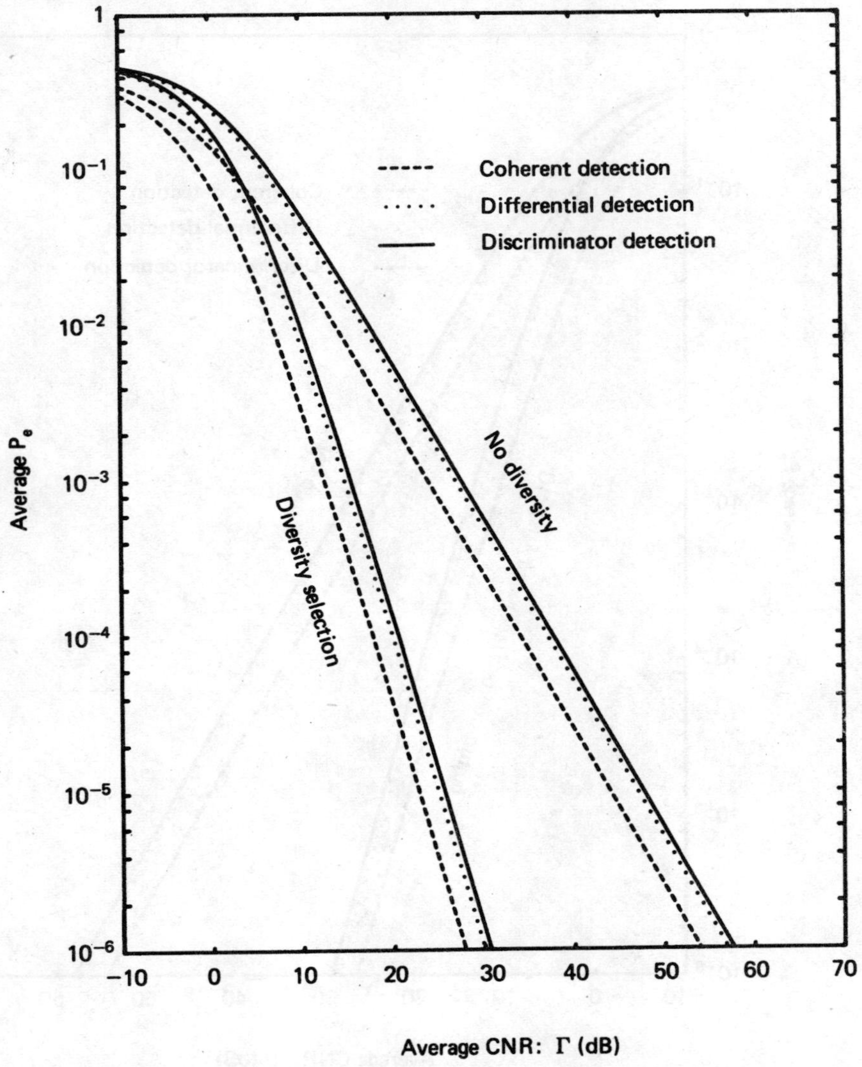

Figure 7.9 Diversity improvement effect on average P_e-versus-CNR performance of MSK modulated system in the quasistatic Rayleigh-fading environment. Two-branch predetection selection method is used. MSK, GMSK, and FQPSK systems, coherently demodulated, have practically (within 1dB) the same results.

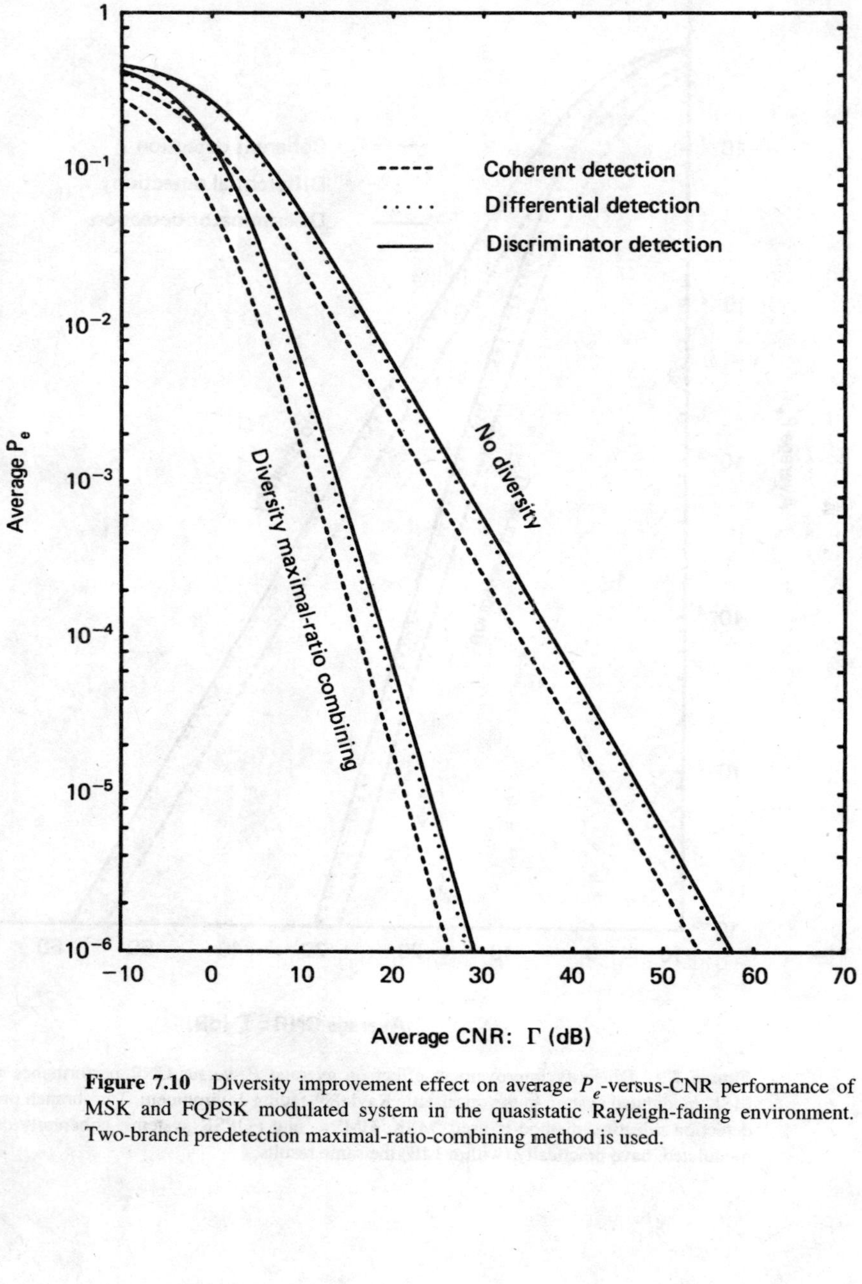

Figure 7.10 Diversity improvement effect on average P_e-versus-CNR performance of MSK and FQPSK modulated system in the quasistatic Rayleigh-fading environment. Two-branch predetection maximal-ratio-combining method is used.

figures. These figures indicate that in order to improve the average P_e 10 times, it is necessary to increase the average CNR by about 5 dB when two-branch diversity techniques are used, while up to a 10-dB increase is required in the case of single-branch reception.

7.5.2 P_e versus Carrier-to-Interference Performance Improvement

In this section we consider the case in which the effect of cochannel interference (CCI) is the major cause of errors. The derivation of the P_e-versus-CIR performance is similar to the derivation of the P_e-versus-carrier-to-noise ratio (CNR) performance. Details are presented in Dr. Hirade's chapter in Feher (1987). The final equations for ideal MSK systems with maximal-ratio combining methods are

$$\left\{\begin{aligned} P_e^{(2)}(\Lambda) &= \frac{1}{2(\Lambda+1)^2} \qquad \text{(7.15a)} \\ &\approx \frac{1}{2\Lambda^2} \quad \text{for discriminator detection} \\ P_e^{(2)}(\Lambda) &= \frac{1}{2}\left\{1 - \frac{2\Lambda}{[(\Lambda+1)^2-(1/\pi)^2]^{1/2}} + \frac{\Lambda^2(\Lambda+1)}{[(\Lambda+1)^2-(1/\pi)^2]^{3/2}}\right\} \qquad \text{(7.15b)} \\ &\approx \frac{1}{2\Lambda^2}\left(1+\frac{2}{\pi^2}\right) = \frac{1}{2\Lambda^2} \quad \text{for differential detection} \\ P_e^{(2)}(\Lambda) &= \frac{1}{2}\left[1 - \frac{3}{2}\sqrt{\frac{\Lambda}{\Lambda+1}} + \frac{1}{2}\sqrt{\frac{\Lambda^3}{(\Lambda+1)^3}}\right] \qquad \text{(7.15c)} \\ &\approx \frac{3}{16\Lambda^2} \quad \text{for coherent detection.} \end{aligned}\right.$$

In Figures 7.11 and 7.12, two-branch predetection selection and maximal-ratio-combining $P_e = f(C/I)$ results are presented where

$$\Lambda = C/I. \qquad (7.16)$$

As with the curves in Figures 7.9 and 7.10, these figures indicate that in order to improve the average P_e 10 times, it is only necessary to increase the average CIR by about 5 dB when two-branch diversity improvement is available, whereas an increase of 10 dB is required in the case of no-diversity reception.

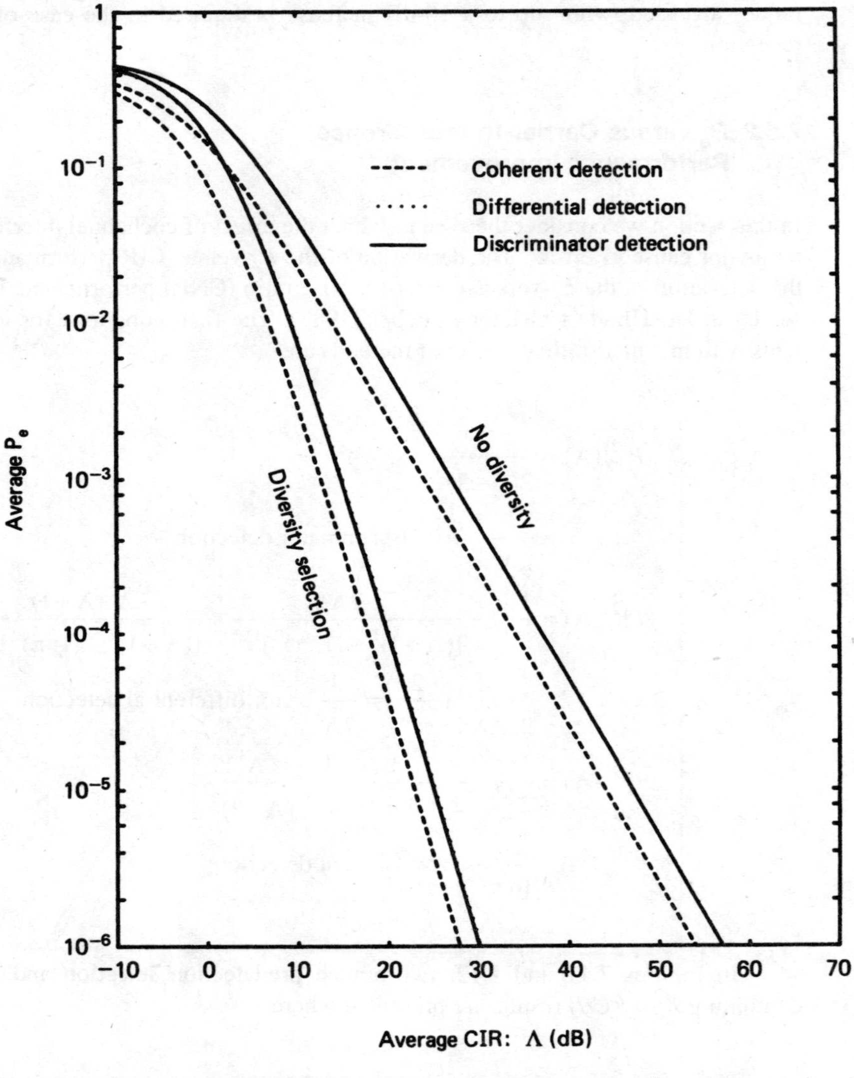

Figure 7.11 Diversity improvement effect on average P_e-versus-CIR performance of MSK and coherently demodulated GMSK and FQPSK modulated system in the quasistatic Rayleigh-fading environment. Two-branch predetection selection method is used. Accuracy within 1.5 dB. For FQPSK design, see Appendix A.3.

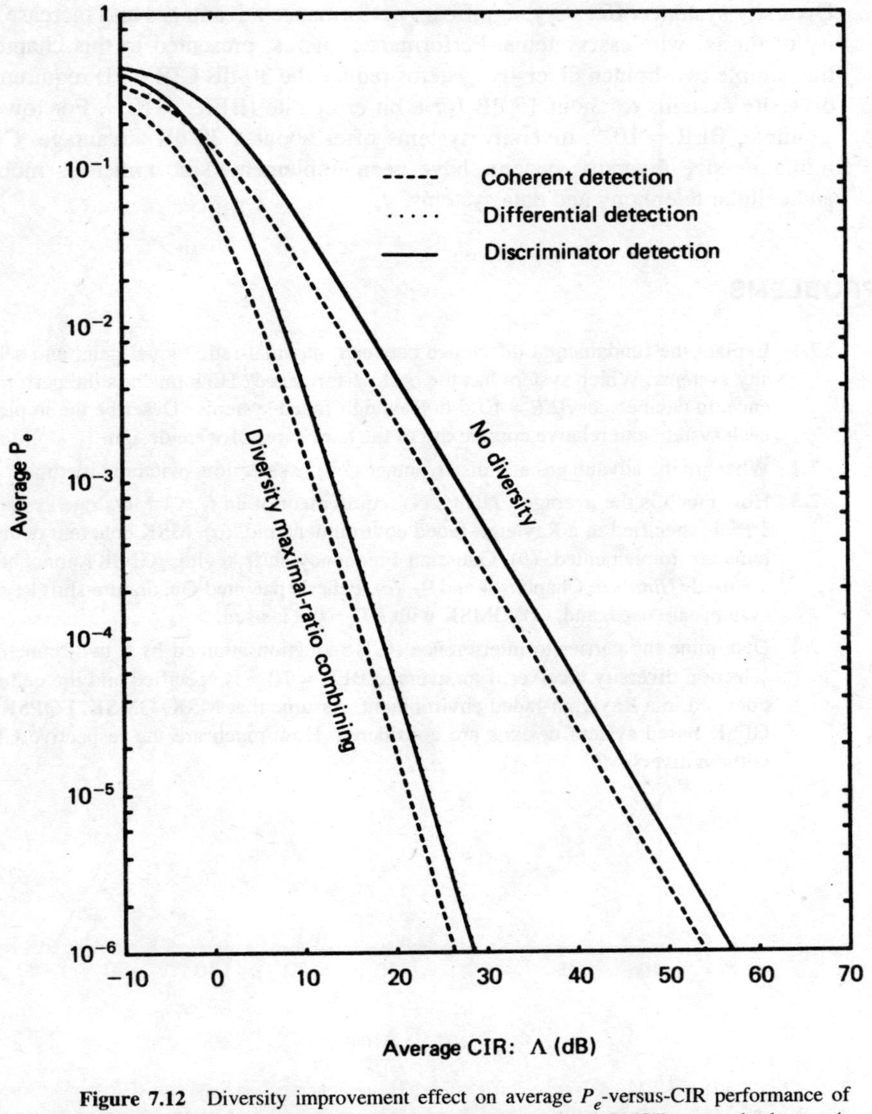

Figure 7.12 Diversity improvement effect on average P_e-versus-CIR performance of MSK and FQPSK, modulated and coherently demodulated GMSK system in the quasi-static Rayleigh-fading environment. Two-branch predetection maximal-ratio-combining method is used. (From Feher, 1987.)

7.6 SUMMARY

Diversity systems offer very significant performance advantages and increase the reliability of digital wireless systems. Performance curves, presented in this chapter, illustrate that simple two-branch diversity systems reduce the 30-dB CIR (C/I) requirement of non-diversity systems to about 15 dB for a bit-error rate (BER) = 10^{-3}. For lower BER, for example, BER = 10^{-6}, diversity systems offer about a 30-dB advantage. Cost-efficient miniature-size diversity systems have been implemented in numerous mobile-wireless and cellular telephony and data systems.

7.7 PROBLEMS

7.1 Explain the fundamental difference between maximal-ratio, equal-gain, and selection diversity systems. Which system has the best performance? How much is the performance difference, in decibels, at $BER = 10^{-5}$ in Rayleigh-faded systems? Describe the implementation of each system and relative complexity of the hardware software design.

7.2 What are the advantages and disadvantages of the selection-switching method?

7.3 How much is the average CNR (C/N) requirement of an f_b = 1 Mb/s rate system if a BER = 10^{-5} is specified in a Rayleigh-faded environment and, (*a*), MSK coherent demodulated systems are implemented, (*b*), Gaussian Frequency shift keying (GFSK) noncoherent systems are used (*Hint:* see Chapters 4 and 9), (*c*), Feher's patented Quadrature shift keying (FQPSK) systems are used, and, (*d*), GMSK with $BT_b = 0.3$ is used.

7.4 Determine the carrier-to-interference (C/I) reduction attained by a two-branch predetection selection diversity receiver if an average BER = 10^{-2} is specified and the cellular system is operated in a Rayleigh-faded environment. Assume that MSK, GMSK, FQPSK, 4-FSK, and GFSK based system designs are considered. How much are the respective CIRs with and without diversity?

CHAPTER 8

Personal Mobile Satellite Communications

8.1 INTRODUCTION

Satellites have the unique capability of providing both *multipoint-to-point,* that is, *multiple access,* and *point-to-multipoint,* that is, *broadcast* modes of transmitting voice, image, and other data simultaneously. This capability can in turn be used for multipoint-to-multipoint mobile (or permanent/stationary) communications systems applications by small and large users. However, most of the current *geosynchronous (GEO)* satellite systems are limited to "star-configured" networks (Feher, 1987a). In these star configurations, users of very small-aperture terminals (VSATs) communicate by satellite with larger earth stations, called *hubs* or *gateways.* End-to-end transmissions between small users are relayed by the central hub. This method results in double-hop mode transmission over the GEO satellite transponders. Because GEO satellites are about 40,000 km above the equator, the propagation delay of a two-hop link is approximately 500 ms. This delay is acceptable for television broadcasting and perhaps for relatively low-speed data transmission. However, it is not acceptable for "toll-grade-quality" two-way (2×500 ms = 1-second delay) voice communications and for higher-speed, interactive data communications services.

For small mobile personal communications terminals, a fully meshed network is required with significantly reduced transmission and processing delays. Such a service could be provided by *low earth orbit (LEO)* and *medium earth orbit (MEO)* satellite systems (Markovic, 1993).

Communications satellites may serve the emerging personal-wireless communications demands in several ways. One way is to serve in their traditional role as international hubs, thus providing a worldwide capability to existing localized networks, or extending a network to a mobile user (similar to INMARSAT's maritime coverage). Alternatively, satellite systems can provide direct personal-terminal-to-personal-terminal connectivity, thus being independent of permanent installations. Hybrid systems are also possible, requiring radios that can operate with multiple standards and switch seamlessly between systems as network and transmission conditions dictate (Golding and Palmer, 1992).

One of the most challenging satellite communications projects of the 1990s is the IRIDIUM™ project spearheaded by Motorola (Hatlelid and Casey, 1993). The IRIDIUM system has been designed to provide handheld personal communications between arbitrary locations around the world at any time and without prior knowledge of the location of the personal-mobile units.

The community of satellite, telephone, and portable computer manufacturers and satellite communications operating companies has been involved in the design of economically viable and technically feasible satellite mobile communications systems. Research and development proposals and studies indicate that the trend in mobile satellite communication is toward more sophisticated satellites with a large number of spot beams and onboard processing, providing worldwide interconnectivity. For example, studies performed by Hughes indicate that from a cost standpoint the GEO satellite is most economical, followed by the MEO satellite and then by the LEO satellite. From a system performance standpoint, this evaluation may be in reverse order, depending on how the public will react to speech delay and collision (Johannsen and Bowles, 1993).

The implementations of mobile personal communications services (PCSs) via satellite systems could demonstrate the benefits of integrated space- and terrestrial-based communications systems. Service tone overlap and complementarity between terrestrial

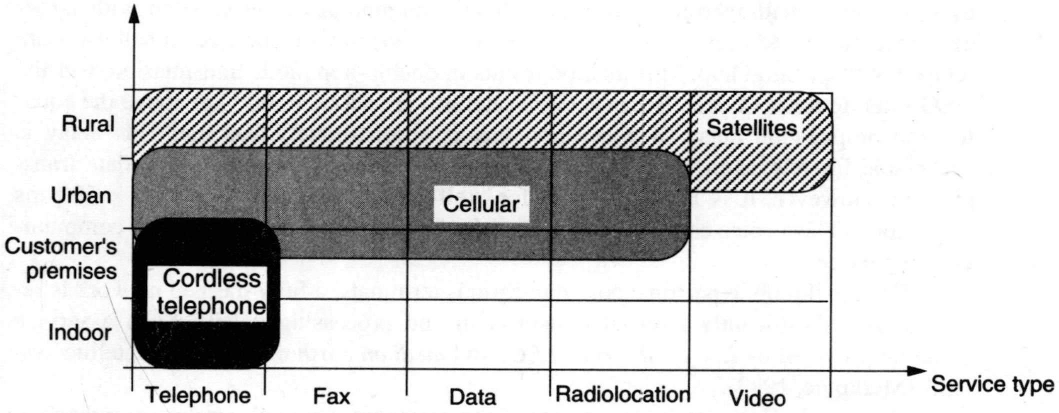

Figure 8.1.1 Complementarity between terrestrial and satellite personal communications system. (From Maral, 1994.)

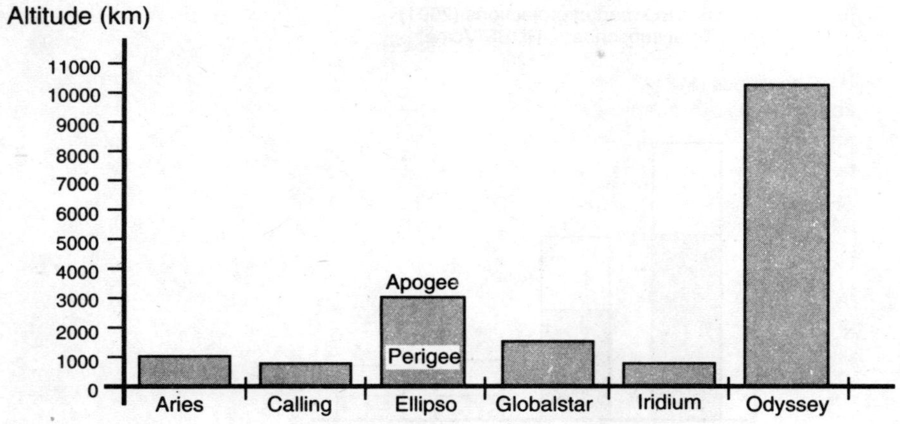

Figure 8.1.2 Orbit altitude comparison for proposed real-time personal communications satellite systems. Odyssey employs only 12 high-alttitude satellites, two of which are visible anywhere in the world at all times. (From Maral, 1994.)

and satellite wireless (personal-mobile) systems is depicted in Figure 8.1.1 (Maral, 1994). Orbit altitude and satellite mass for several proposed real-time personal LEO and MEO satellite systems are compared in Figures 8.1.2 and 8.1.3.

Market projections and service revenues of LEO satellite systems are indicated in Figure 8.1.4 (Hartsborn and Carter-Lome, 1993). Cost to the user is of utmost importance if large-volume commercial applications are anticipated. Indeed, low-cost terminals and service could be attained by nongeostationary systems (Table 8.1.1).

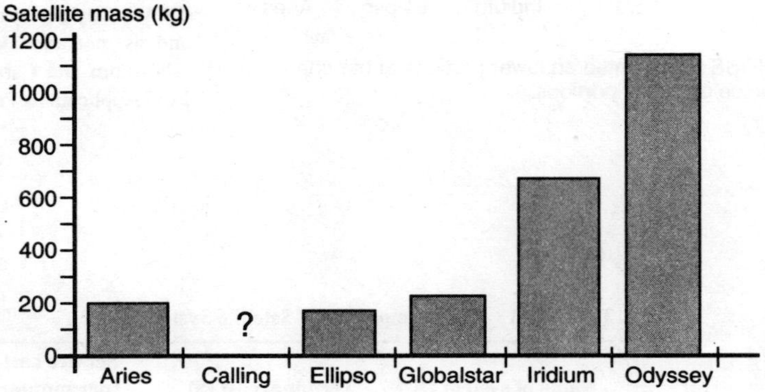

Figure 8.1.3 Satellite mass comparison for proposed real-time personal communications satellite systems. Although IRIDIUM satellites weigh 40% less than Odyssey satellites, there are almost seven times as many of them in the orbital constellation. (From Maral, 1994.)

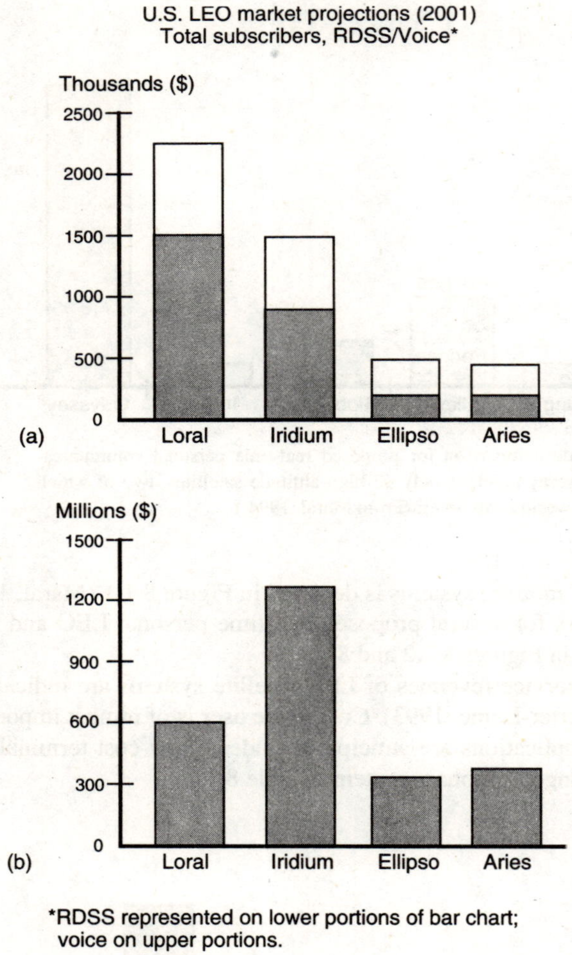

Figure 8.1.4 Market projections and service revenues of U.S. LEO satellite systems. TRW's Odyssey system is an MEO network and is not included in the comparison (Hartshorn and Carter-Lome, 1993). (From FCC Applications Press Reports.)

Table 8.1.1 Cost Comparison of Satellite Systems

Name of system	Terminal cost ($)	Service cost (perminute)
Globalstar	700	$0.30
IRIDIUM-Motorola	1000	$3
Odyssey-TRW	300	$0.65

From Maral, 1994.

8.2 INTEGRATION OF GEO, LEO, AND MEO SATELLITE AND TERRESTRIAL MOBILE SYSTEMS

Multimedia wireless data and personal telephony represents more than just a combination of radio, network, and data technologies. These disciplines have evolved in largely independent communities, and their fusion is neither obvious nor direct. Each has been spawned with separate technologies and in separate markets. It is only recently that combinations of these disciplines have merged. Figure 8.2.1, (a), shows how the overlaps of

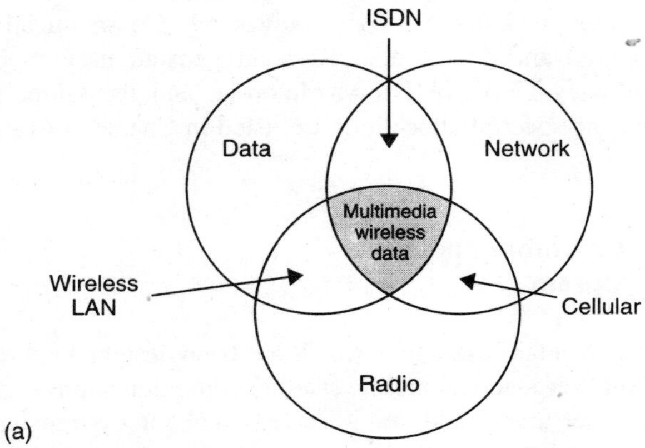

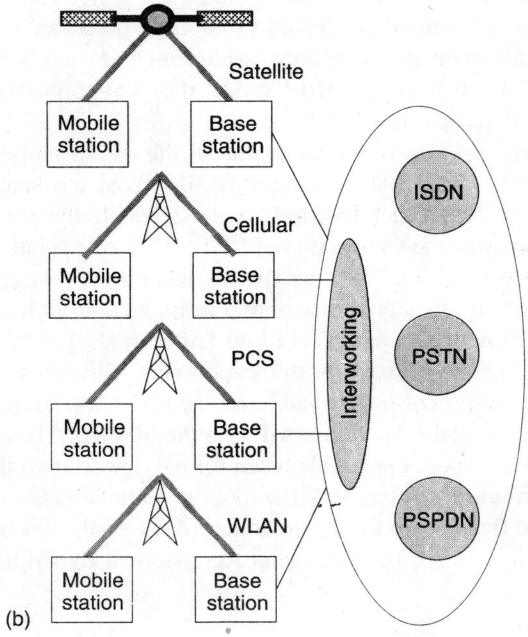

Figure 8.2.1 The three main terrestrial communication technologies and their application arenas. Each technology has been introduced in particular markets that remain hitherto unemerged. (a), Market and application areas. (b), System configuration architecture. (From Dean and Levesque, 1993.)

these areas have combined in new techniques and markets (Dean and Levesque, 1993). Figure 8.2.1, (b), presents an architectural view of various mobile services, including wireless local area networks (WLAN), personal communications services (PCSs), and cellular and satellite systems served by a common public network.

8.3 PERSONAL SATELLITE COMMUNICATIONS PROGRAMS

In this section several major personal satellite communications programs of the 1990s are briefly reviewed. These programs include NASA's Advanced Communications Technology Satellite (ACTS), an advanced Canadian Ka-band geostationary mobile satellite system, INTELSAT, Odyssey-TRW, IRIDIUM-Motorola, and the Globalstar programs. Additional applications and spectral allocations are listed in Chapter 1 (Tables 1.4 and 1.5).

8.3.1 ACTS: NASA's Advanced Communications Technology Satellite Program

The Broadband Aeronautical Experimental Program of ACTS has been designed not only to prove the feasibility of K/Ka-band aeronautical mobile satellite communications, but to design the overall system in a manner that would allow for easy technology transfer to U.S. industry. The aeronautical system configuration consists of a fixed (ground-based) terminal, ACTS itself, and an aircraft terminal, as shown in Figure 8.3.1. The fixed terminal consists of a communications terminal connected to the high burst-rate link-evaluation terminal (HBR-LET) radio frequency hardware, which includes a 4.7-m antenna. The ACTS antenna uses three fixed beams in HBR mode; they are pointed at the U.S. cities of Cleveland, Atlanta, and Tampa (Ince, 1992).

The aircraft terminal's architecture is similar to that of the ACTS mobile terminal (AMT). In the forward direction (fixed station-to-aircraft), the fixed terminal transmits data and a pilot signal to ACTS. ACTS then transmits these signals to the aircraft terminal while operating in the microwave switch matrix (MSM) mode of operation (a bent-pipe mode). The signal in the forward link has a maximum data rate of 384 kb/s. On the return link (aircraft-to-fixed station) the signal transmitted from the aircraft terminal consists of a data signal with a maximum data rate of 112 kb/s (Abbe et al., 1993).

Two transponders on ACTS are utilized for this experiment. One transponder supports the fixed station-to-aircraft forward-link signals, and the other, the aircraft-to-fixed station return link. The first transponder is configured with the 30-GHz Cleveland fixed beam for the uplink and a 20-GHz spot or steerable beam for the downlink to the aircraft. The second transponder is configured with a 30-GHz spot or steerable beam for the uplink and the 20-GHz Cleveland fixed beam for the downlink (Abbe et al., 1993).

The primary objectives for the ACTS Broadband Aeronautical Experiment are the following:

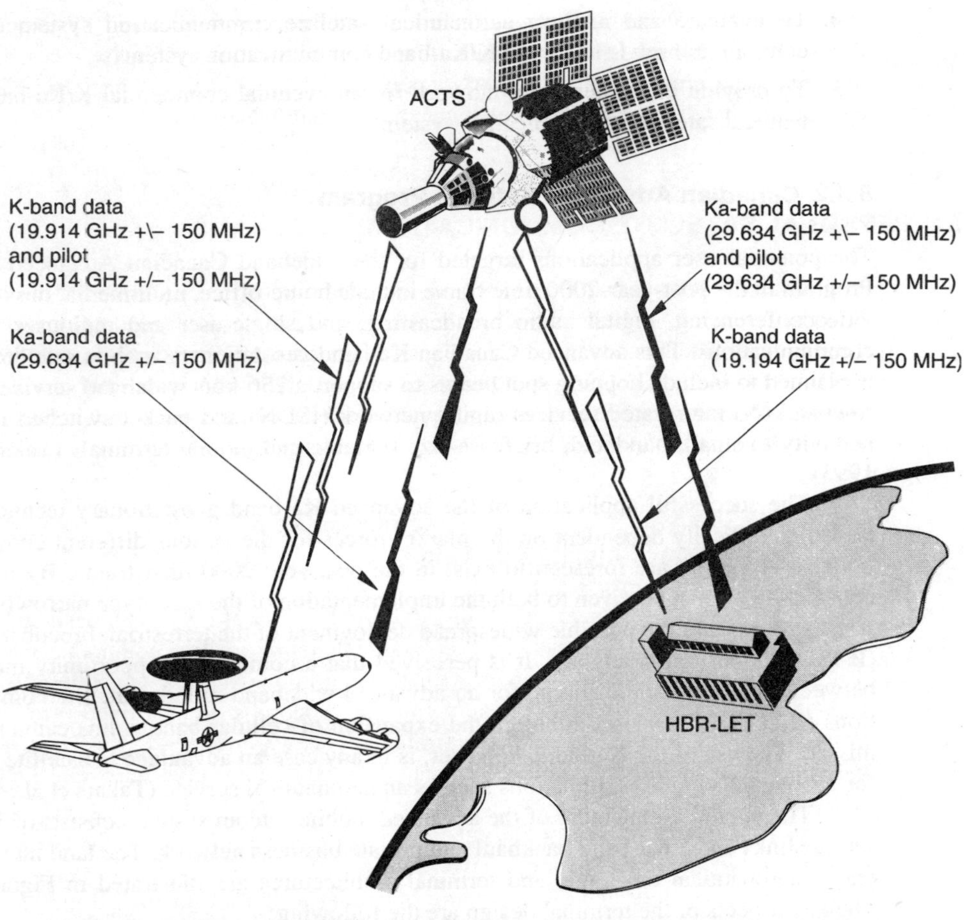

Figure 8.3.1 ACTS broadband aeronautical experiment setup. One ACTS transponder (30 GHz fixed beam, 20 GHz steerable beam) supports the fixed station-to-aircraft link, and the other transponder (20 GHz fixed beam, 30 GHz steerable beam) supports the return link. (From Abbe et al., 1993.)

1. To characterize and demonstrate the performance of the aircraft to ACTS-to-AMT K/Ka-band communications link for high data-rate aeronautical applications. This evaluation includes the characterization of full-duplex compressed video and multiple-channel voice and data links.
2. To evaluate and assess the performance of current video compression algorithms in an aeronautical satellite communications link
3. To characterize the propagation effects of the K/Ka-band channel for aeronautical communications during take-off, cruise, and landing phases of aircraft flight

4. To evaluate and analyze aeronautical satellite communication system concepts common to both L-band and K/Ka-band communication systems
5. To provide the systems groundwork for an eventual commercial K/Ka-band aeronautical satellite communication system

8.3.2 Canadian Advanced Satellite Program

The potential user applications targeted for the wideband Canadian Advanced Satellite Program in the post-year-2000 time frame include home-office, multimedia, desktop (PC) videoconferencing, digital audio broadcasting, and single-user and multiuser personal communications. This advanced Canadian Ka-band geostationary mobile satellite system is planned to include hopping spot beams to support a 256-kb/s wideband service for narrowband (N) intergrated services digital network (ISDN) and packet-switched interconnectivity to small, handheld, briefcase-size portable and mobile terminals (Takats et al., 1993).

The successful application of the advanced Ka-band geostationary technology is, however, critically dependent on the market forces for the various different communications services that are foreseen to exist in the post-year-2000 time frame. By that time, consideration must be given to both the implementation of the LEO-type narrowband personal systems and the possible widespread deployment of the terrestrial, broadband ISDN (B-ISDN) fiber optic network. It is perceived that a commercial opportunity may exist, between these two applications, for an advanced wideband mobile satellite communications (SATCOM) service, although the expansion of cellular bandwidths cannot be dismissed. The use of the Ka-band, however, is in any case an advantage to satellite systems for "above the clouds" applications such as an aeronautical service (Takats et al., 1993).

The overall architecture of the advanced mobile satcom system consists of Ka-band service links and a Ku-band backhaul and private business network. The land mobile coverage, aeronautical coverage, and terminal architectures are illustrated in Figure 8.3.2. The key aspects of the terminal design are the following:

- Selection of antenna types
- Selection of acquisition and tracking approaches
- Frequency control
- Flexibility of the terrestrial interface
- Low cost

Modulation-nonlinear amplification combined with spectral efficiency is also among the most important design parameters. The aeronautical link budget of this system is summarized in Table 8.3.1. During 1994, use of the quadrature amplitude modulation (SQAM) class of Feher's patented FQPSK modems and nonlinearly amplified transmitters (described in Chapter 4 and Appendix A.3) was recommended. The SQAM technology (Seo and Feher, 1987) and is described in Seo and Feher (1985, 1987, 1988, and

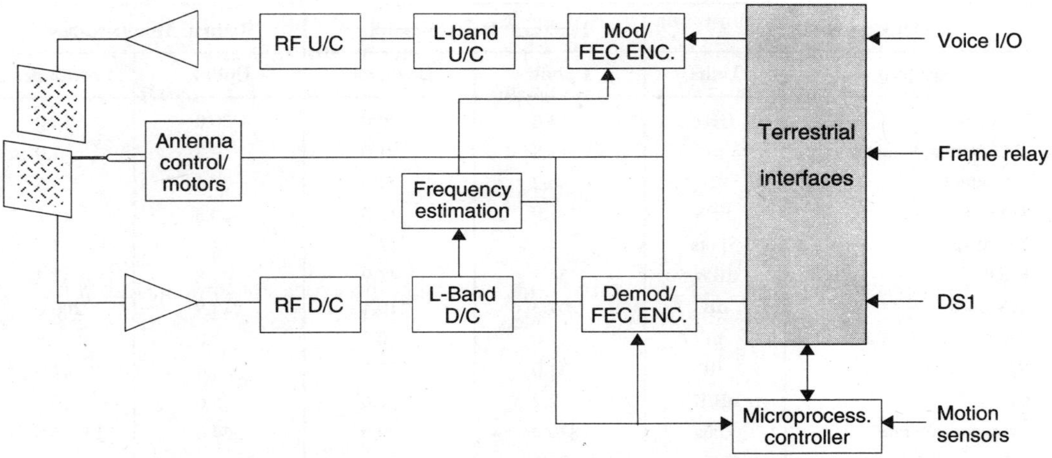

Figure 8.3.2 Canadian Advanced Satellite Program basic architecture. This system uses a class of FQPSK modulation known as SQAM. (From Takats et al., SPAR Aerospace, 1993.) The SQAM family of Dr. Feher's patented technologies is described in Chapter 4 and Appendix A.3 in the FQPSK and FQAM sections. Licensing is described in Appendix A.3.

1991). For technology transfer and licensing arrangements, interested organizations should contact Dr. Feher Associates-Digcom Consultants, Inc.

8.3.3 INTELSAT Ku Band

For personal communications applications via INTELSAT Ku-band transponders, a fully meshed network of very small terminals is involved. The double-hop delays, which are undesirable for voice communications between terminals, are avoided (Fang, 1992). The bandwidth and power resources of the satellite transponder are shared by users in a demand-assigned and code division multiple access (CDMA) architecture.

Voice, data, and facsimile are statistically multiplexed at each terminal. To minimize terminal costs, frequency-precorrected and level-preadjusted continuous-wave (CW) tones are sent from the central network control station in each beam. The terminals in each downlink beam can use these pilots as references for antenna acquisition and tracking, as reliable frequency sources, and as indicators of signal fade for uplink power control (ULPC). The potential CDMA "near-far" problem resulting from uplink fades is mitigated by using ULPC. Quasiburst-mode transmission is employed to minimize the potential loss of clock and pseudorandom number code synchronization. When these terminals are used only to interconnect into the public switched telephony networks (PSTNs) through large, hublike gateway stations, they can employ flat-plate antenna technology. The complete terminal can therefore be packaged into a briefcase so that it is easily transportable for personal use (Figure 8.3.3).

For ease of explanation, it is assumed that all PCTs are in the same uplink and downlink footprints of the satellite coverage, as depicted in Figure 8.3.3. Each terminal is

Table 8.3.1. Aeronautical link budget of the Canadian Advanced Satellite Program (Takats et al., 1993). For power-efficient (nonlinear, C-class amplification) and spectral-efficient systems, the SQAM subclass of FQPSK systems has been recommended. For licensing of this technology, see Appendix A.3.*

Link parameters		Forward: Base-to-mobile		Return: Mobile-to-base	
Description	**Units**	**Uplink**	**Downlink**	**Uplink**	**Downlink**
Frequency	GHz	14.0	20.0	30.0	12.0
TX antenna diameter	m	1.8	1.0	0.3	1.0
TX antenna gain1	dB	46.2	32.9	37.3	29.5
Transmit power	dBW	7.9	15.0	10.5	14.2
No. of spots[2]	Spots	4	12	12	4
EIRP	dBW	54.1	47.9	47.8	43.7
Space loss (39500 km)	dB	207.3	210.4	213.9	206.0
RX Antenna Diameter	m	1.0	0.3	1.0	1.8
RX antenna gain	dB	31.0	33.7	34.4	44.9
G/T	dB/K	2.2	7.8	5.6	20.7
Transmission rate	kbps	1870.0	1500.0	364.0	13900.0
C/N_o thermal	dB-Hz	77.6	74.0	68.1	84.9
Off-axis angle	deg.	2.0	8.0	8.0	2.0
Adjacent-set interference	dB	83.4	79.8	73.9	91.2
C/No unfaded	dB-Hz	76.6	73.0	67.1	84.0
Set pointing loss	dB	0.2	0.2	0.2	0.2
Atmos loss	dB	0.2	0.0	0.0	0.2
Ground pointing loss	dB	0.2	0.5	0.5	0.2
Multipath loss[3]	dB	0.0	0.0	0.0	0.0
Availability	%	99.95	100.0	100.0	99.95
Ottawa rain fade[4]	dB	5.1	0.0	0.0	5.1
Polarization loss	dB	0.1	0.5	0.5	0.1
System margin	dB	1.0	1.0	1.0	1.0
Faded C/N_o	dB-Hz	69.7	70.8	64.9	78.5
Faded E_b/N_o	dB-Hz	7.0	9.0	9.0	7.0
Demod impl. margin	dB	1.5	1.5	1.5	1.5
Nonlinearity degrad.	dB	0.0	0.0	0.2	0.0
Ideal E_b/N_o	dB-Hz	5.5	7.5	7.6	5.5
BER faded		8.8×10^{-8}	6.1×10^{-8}	8.9×10^{-7}	8.8×10^{-8}
Maximum BER faded		8.8×10^{-8}		8.9×10^{-7}	
Overall availability	%	99.95		99.95	

[1]Mobile TX gain is reduced by 1.0 dB for radome and rotary coupler, and satellite gain is reduced by 1.5 dB for RF filter/coupling. Mobile antenna is 30 cm microstrip patch.

[2]For ku band, 4 fixed beams, for ka band, 12 spots in one hopping beam group of 12.

[3]Multipath loss is assumed 0 for aeronautical service because of antenna directivity.

[4]Rain fading assumed 0 for operation "above clouds" at cruising altitude.

*For technology transfer and licensing, contact Dr. Feher and Associates.

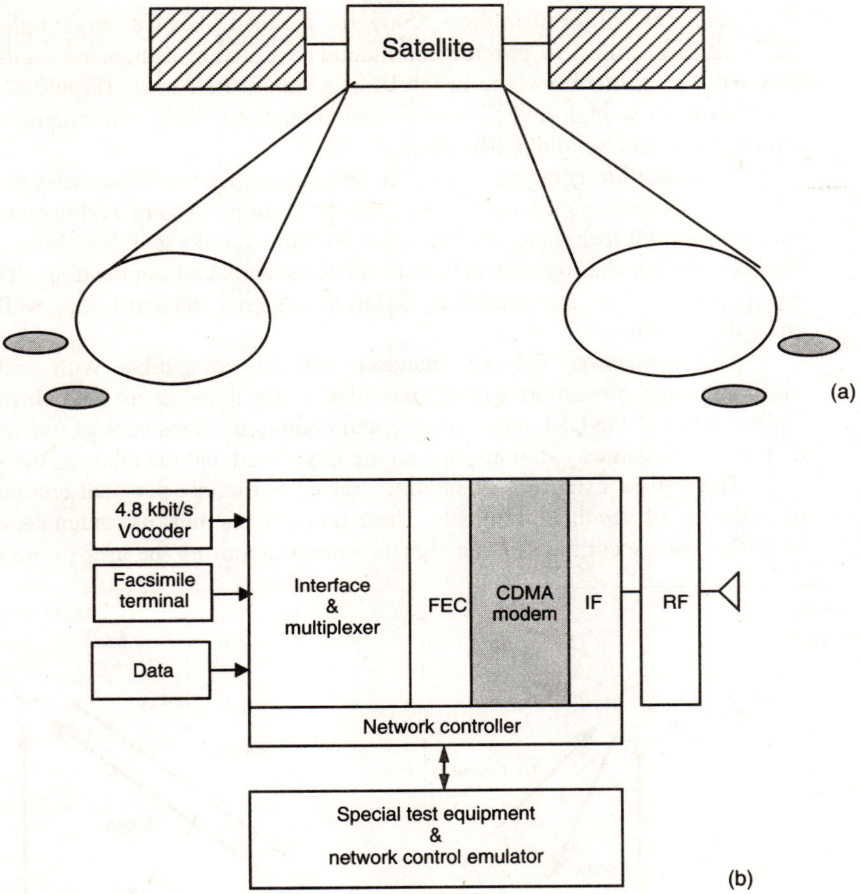

Figure 8.3.3 Overview of, (a), network concept and, (b), terminal concepts (block diagram) of the INTELSAT Ku-band PCN. Voice, data, and facsimile are statistically multiplexed at the transmitting terminal. (From Fang, 1992.)

given a unique pseudonoise (PN) code for reception. Thus, if terminal A wishes to communicate with terminal B, it uses terminal B's PN code to spread-spectrum modulate the information bit stream and transmit to terminal B over the satellite transponder. These PCTs access the transponder by using frequency-division multiple access (FDMA) and CDMA. Each frequency slot in the transponder generally supports one meshed network of PCTs, each of which accesses this frequency slot (Fang, 1992).

8.3.4 Odyssey-TRW

Odyssey will provide high-quality wireless communications services from satellites worldwide. These services will include voice, data, paging, geolocation, and messaging. Odyssey will be an economical approach to providing communications. A constellation of 12 satellites will orbit in three 55-degree inclined planes at an altitude of 10,354 km (5591 nautical miles) to provide continuous coverage of designated regions. Two satellites will be visible anywhere in the United States at all times (Figure 8.3.4). This dual visibility leads to high line-of-sight elevation angles, thereby minimizing obstructions by terrain, trees, and buildings (Rusch et al., 1992).

Each satellite generates a multibeam antenna pattern that divides its coverage area into a set of contiguous cells. The communications system architecture employs the spread-spectrum technique of CDMA on both the uplinks and downlinks. This signaling method permits sharing of bands with other systems and applications. The "bent-pipe" transponders could accommodate different regional standards, as well as signaling changes over time.

The low-power Odyssey handset will be compatible with cellular systems. Multipath fade protection will be provided in the handset as well. In the continental United States (CONUS), most satellite and communications control function will be embodied in two gateway stations, one on the East Coast and the other on the West Coast.

The logical extension of satellite service to include personal communications implies the use of handheld terminals. These transceivers must use antennas with broad patterns that can detect the satellite signals without requiring the user to orient them. Since

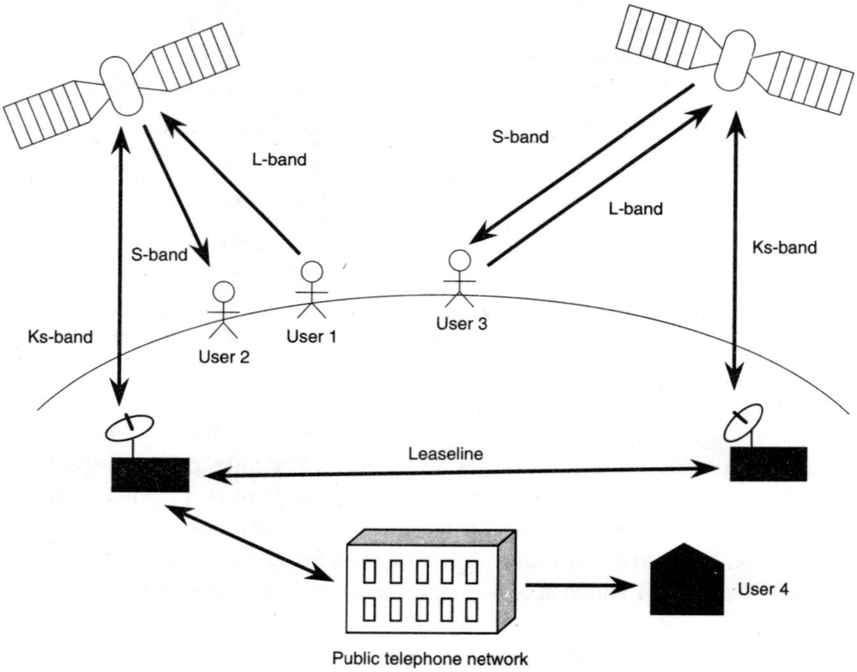

Figure 8.3.4 TRW's Odyssey network provides dual coverage of the continental United States and, many other areas of the world, with only 12 MEO satellites. (From Rusch et al., 1992.)

an omnidirectional handset antenna is able to contact satellites in any region of the sky, the satellites do not need to be geostationary! This breakthrough in thinking permits consideration of orbits nearer to Earth, thus reducing both path loss and propagation delay, simplifying satellite design, and reducing the cost of the space segment.

8.3.5 IRIDIUM-Motorola

The IRIDIUM system is designed to provide handheld personal communications between diverse locations around the world at any time and without *a priori* knowledge of the location of other personal units. The system will provide a digitally switched telephone network and a global dial tone, allowing the user to place a call to or be called by any other telephone in the world. A user will have the convenience of calling a portable telephone number and talking directly to an individual. Global roaming is designed into the system so that one calls the handheld phone of a particular person, not just the place where a fixed phone is located (Hatlelid and Casey, 1993).

A key feature of the system is the use of a constellation of 77 low-altitude satellites, which will prevent the annoying delays that presently occur during conversations. The low-altitude satellites also allow the use of low-power, handheld telephones in this personal communication system. Earth-based gateways provide the interface to the public switched telephone networks and determine the routing as a call is placed. The system will have its own operational control system for command and control of the communications system and the constellation of satellites.

The IRIDIUM system will provide the full range of communication services that are expected in a modern system. Enabling high-quality voice transmission with the use of a pocket-sized telephone is the driving requirement. The system will also have provisions for paging, data exchange, messaging, facsimile, and geolocation.

System operation is similar to that for existing ground-based cellular systems (Ince, 1992). In fact, the dual-mode handset will have the capability to operate on both cellular and IRIDIUM frequencies and with both communication architectures. When a call is dialed and sent, the system will first try to use a cellular channel from the local terrestrial system. IRIDIUM will transmit to a satellite on an IRIDIUM channel only if ground-based cellular system is not available. The gateways will route the calls through the constellation in the most economical fashion and will use existing terrestrial infrastructure when necessary. As such, the IRIDIUM system will complement existing systems, not replace them (Hatlelid and Casey, 1993).

CHAPTER 9

Cellular and Wireless Systems Engineering

9.1 INTRODUCTION

Analog cellular systems are the first generation of cellular systems. Several *incompatible analog standards* have been developed and implemented worldwide. These systems use analog frequency modulation (FM) and have a frequency division multiple access (FDMA) based media access control (MAC) architecture. The available radio spectrum is shared by a relatively large number of FM modulated signals, as shown in Figure 9.2.1.

Second-generation cellular systems primarily use digital modulation and processing techniques and have several incompatible air-interface standards. The first goal, to use digital techniques, has been achieved, whereas the second goal, to have a single digital cellular-wireless global standard, is unlikely to be achieved. Numerous incompatible digital mobile wireless and cellular standards have been developed. Some of these techniques use FDMA; others use time division multiple access (TDMA). The physical layer (radio) bit rates are as low as 1.2 kb/s for narrowband, land mobile radio applications, while some of the wireless local area network (WLAN) applications are in the high-bit-rate (1 Mb/s to 40 MB/s) range. Frame alignment, error correction, digital modulation, and overall MAC and physical layer (PHY) radio transmission specifications are significantly different in these systems.

Third-generation systems such as several spread-spectrum (SS) systems, CDMA, collision sense multiple access (CSMA), direct-sequence (DS), and frequency-hopped (FH) spread-spectrum systems have also been standardized. The various spread-spectrum standards are not compatible and are not interoperable with each other.

First-generation cellular systems were briefly reviewed in Chapter 1. In this chapter, Chapter 9, second- and third-generation systems are described.

9.2 ACCESS METHODS: TDMA (TDD AND FDD) FDMA; SPREAD-SPECTRUM FREQUENCY-HOPPING; DIRECT-SEQUENCE CDMA AND CSMA

Several standardized and nonstandardized digital cellular radio access methods are described in this section.

The *media access control (MAC)* unit determines the access method and the radio channel (frequency, time, and space) assignment. In the case of FDMA, the available radio spectrum is divided into channels 1, . . . , N, as shown in Figure 9.2.1. The bandwidth of each modulated channel is set by the emission mask of the radio transmitter, as illustrated in Figure 9.2.2. The FDMA architecture is also known as "narrowband mobile radio," as the bandwidth of the individual data or digitized analog signal (voice, facsimile, and so forth) is relatively narrow compared with TDMA and CDMA applications. From the illustrative example of Figure 9.2.2, we note that the modulated nonlinearly amplified FQPSK 22 kb/s rate signal power is contained in a narrower bandwidth than the Federal Communications Commission (FCC)-specified emission, an essential FCC requirement. To meet this requirement, frequency spacing is required between adjacent channels. This argument has been put forward several times by opponents of FDMA (and proponents of TDMA) to claim that FDMA is not as efficient in spectrum use as TDMA or CDMA. However, proponents of the FDMA solutions claim that FDMA is as efficient as or even more efficient than TDMA. In particular, slow frequency-hopped spread-spectrum (FH-SS) FDMA systems, combined with power- and spectrally-efficient modulation techniques such as FQPSK could have significantly increased capacity over other access methods.

In several FCC-authorized frequency bands, particularly those below 470 MHz, the authorized bandwidth per channel is limited to the 5 kHz to 12.5 kHz range. In these narrowband mobile or cellular systems, digital FDMA could offer the most spectrally efficient and cost-efficient solutions.

The major U.S. and international standards of the 1990s use TDMA access methods. As of 1995, several million TDMA digital cellular subscriber units are operational. These highly advanced standardized, second-generation cellular-wireless systems include the following:

- GSM: Global System for Mobile Communications
- ADC: American Digital Cellular (IS-54 standard)
- JDC: Japanese Digital Cellular

An overview of these TDMA systems is presented in sections 9.7 and 9.8.

Code division multiple access (CDMA) and *collision sense multiple access (CSMA)* spread-spectrum systems have also been standardized and are operating in numerous countries. The **CDMA system, pioneered by Qualcomm, Inc., of San Diego,** was standardized and is known as the IS-95 standard of the Electronic Industries Association (EIA IS-95). For higher-speed data and wireless computer communications, the IEEE standardization committee known as IEEE 802.11 developed several spread-spectrum of CSMA-

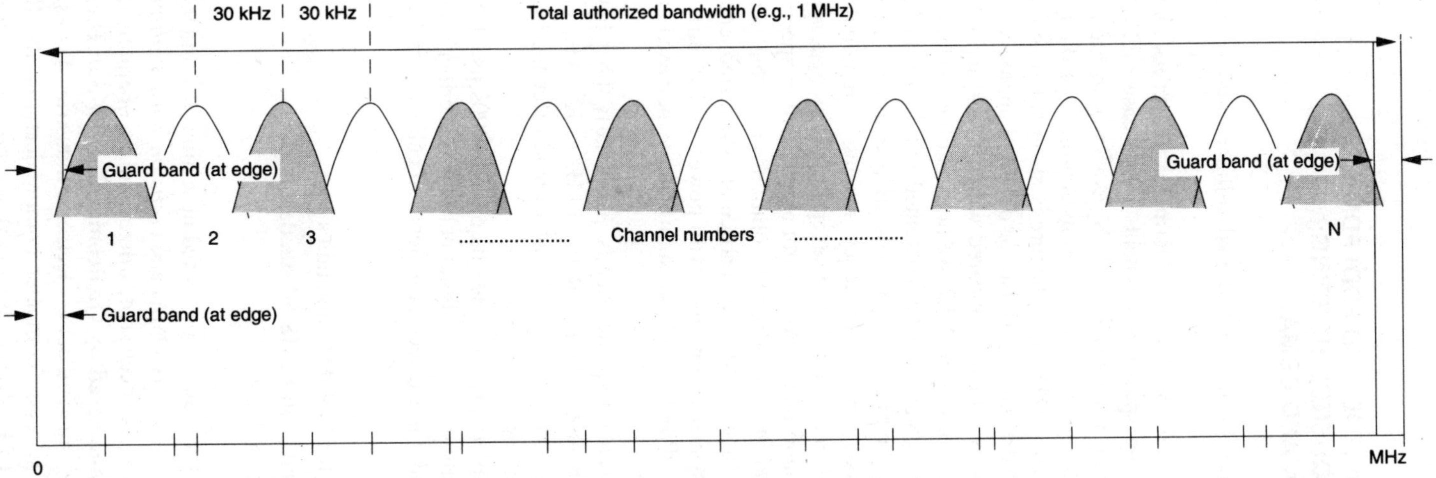

Figure 9.2.1 Mobile communications spectral use for a narrow band national application FDM-FH-FQPSK composite spectrum for 15 channels, having an 8 kHz spacing (bandwidth) and 2.5 kHz at the edge for FCC-125 kHz authorization. Total bandwidth is (15 × 8 kHz) + 2 × 2.5 kHz. Each FQPSK channel has a rate of 8 kHz × 1.4 b/s/Hz = 11.2 kb/s (for ACI-integrated-20 dB). 15 channels × 11.2 kb/s = 168 kb/s. For Dr. Feher Associates-Digcom, Inc. patented/licensed FQPSK technology see Appendix A.3.

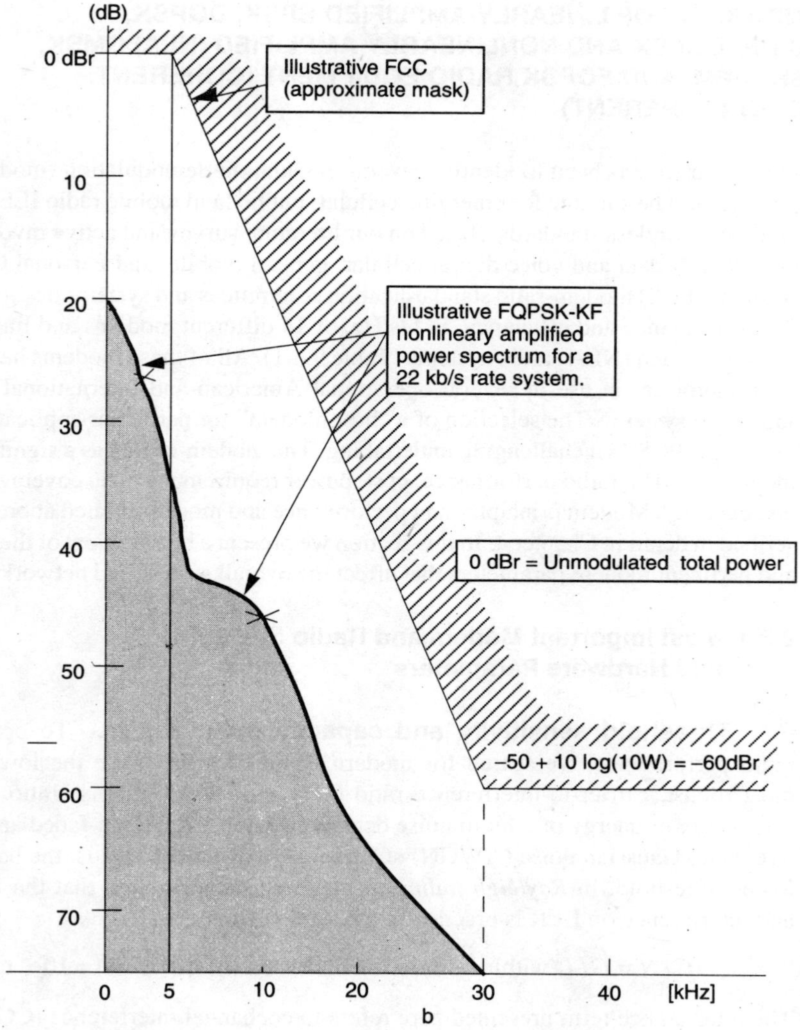

Figure 9.2.2 Edge of FCC-band and FQPSK at $f_b = 11.2$ kb/s per 8 kHz FDM channel. [Based on FBPSK and FQPSK Consortium, 1994 and patented technology transfer described in Appendix A.3.]

based standards for wireless radio and for wireless infrared (IR) applications. In later sections of this chapter, illustrative parameters of standardized systems are presented.

The terms *time division duplex (TDD)* and *frequency division duplex (FDD)* refer to the fact that the radio frequency band is time division and frequency division multiplexed, respectively. Both TDD and FDD techniques have been used in TDMA systems.

For WLAN higher-data-rate (1 Mb/s to 10 Mb/s range) computer communications applications, the IEEE 802.11 PHY and MAC standardization committee standardized several radio (900 MHz to 928 MHz and 2.4 GHz to 2.48 GHz band) and infrared systems.

9.3 COMPARISON OF LINEARLY AMPLIFIED BPSK, DQPSK, AND Π/4-DQPSK AND NONLINEARLY AMPLIFIED (NLA) GMSK, GFSK, 4-FM, AND FQPSK RADIO EQUIPMENT (COHERENT AND NONCOHERENT)

Our objective has been to identify several modulation-demodulation (modem) techniques which could be suitable for emerging cellular, public land mobile radio IEEE 802.11 PHY, and other wireless standards. Based on our literature survey and active involvement in several WLAN data and voice digital cellular, general mobile, and Personal Communication Systems (PCS) modem-ratio standardization committees and systems designs, we highlight the performance and efficiency, in b/s/Hz, of 14 different modems and linearly or nonlinearly amplified (NLA) radio systems (Table 9.3.1). All of these modems have been considered and/or are in use in several operational American and International (European and Japanese) systems. The selection of a "best modem" for particular applications, for example, a new PCS, is a challenging undertaking. The modem-radio has a significant impact on the overall PHY radio performance, cost, power requirement, size, coverage area, and system capacity. Modem principles and performance and modem-related abbreviations are described in detail in Chapter 4. In this section we present a brief review of the most important and pertinent modem parameters that affect the overall system and network design.

9.3.1 Most Important Modem and Radio System and Hardware Parameters

Threshold sensitivity and capacity optimization. To optimize modem-radio performance, we search for modern techniques that have the lowest, that is, the most robust, carrier-to-interference ratio (*C/I*) and carrier-to-noise ratio (*C/N*) or E_b/N_o (bit energy or energy of a bit to noise density ratio) in a Rayleigh-faded and/or in an additive white Gaussian noise (AWGN)-stationary environment, that is, the best sensitivity or lowest threshold. In *Rayleigh fading,* it has been demonstrated that the impact of noise and interference on BER is practically the same, that is:

$$C/N = C/I \text{ (within 1 dB)} \qquad \text{for bit-error rate (BER)} = 10^{-2} \text{ to } 10^{-5}.$$

The interference term presented here refers to cochannel interference (CCI), whether it is caused by interference of our own cellular radio system or by another Rayleigh-faded, external interference in the cochannel band, that is, external cochannel interference (ECI).

Spectral efficiency, in terms of *b/s/Hz* with a defined integrated out-of-band adjacent channel interference (ACI), is important from a capacity point of view. Spectral efficiency should be *jointly* maximized with *C/I* sensitivity to attain the largest capacity objectives in b/s/Hz/m^2.

LIN-NLA **Linear amplification and nonlinear amplification power amplifier** issues relate to hardware size, required power, FCC regulations, and cost. In most systems, *nonlinear amplifiers (NLAs)* have a lower cost and smaller size and are more RF power efficient than *linear amplifiers (LIN)*. Using NLA instead of LIN amplifiers and devices, inexpensive, portable units can be produced with a longer battery life.

Table 9.3.1 Comparison of digital mobile radio modems, radio, and diversity systems in AWGN and Rayleigh-faded environments. Approximate values are indicated to establish trend and first-order estimates. For details see Appendix A.3 and Fig. A.3.9.

				Rayleigh fading C/N = C/I							
		Approx. b/s/Hz	E_b/N_0 AWGN	10^{-1}		10^{-2}		10^{-3}		10^{-4}	
Modem/BER	Amp.*	Pract.	10^{-4}	Th	Div	Th	Div	Th	Div	Th	Div
FSK-MAN; Amps	NLA	0.33	—	10	—	20	—	30	—	40	—
Digital cellular π/4-DQPSK	LIN	1.7	—	—	—	—	17	—	—	—	—
FSK-NRZ	NLA	0.5 ?	11.4	8	—	20	—	30	—	—	—
BPSK	LIN	0.7	8.4	3	—	14	8	24	14	34	19
BPSK with pilot	LIN	0.7	9	4	—	15	—	25	—	35	—
QPSK coherent	LIN	1.6	8.4	5.5	—	17	12	27	17.5	37	22
π/4-DQPSK	LIN	1.7	10.5	—	—	20	15	30	20	40	25
FQPSK	NLA	1.5	9.4	—	—	17	12.5	27	16	37	—
QPRS with pilot	LIN	2.1	11.2	14	17	20	15	29	30	40	25
C-GMSK ($BT_b = 0.5$)	NLA	0.9	9.3	—	—	—	—	—	—	—	—
C-GMSK ($BT_b = 0.3$)	NLA	1.02	10.5	7.5	—	19	14	30	20	40	25
Noncoherent 4CPM-FM discrim.	NLA	1.2	22.5	—	—	22?	—	32?	—	42?	?
16-QAM	LIN	3.1	13 dB	—	—	22	15	32	21	42	25

*Key: *LIN* = Linear, *NLA* = nonlinear amplification; *Th* = theoretical performance; *Div* = diversity system theory.

9.3.2 Four-Level FM, 16-QAM and QPSK

A generic or "universal" quadrature coherent modem architecture is presented in Figure 4.3.29 and 4.3.30. These illustrative block diagrams are suitable for QPSK, π/4-QPSK, and 16-QAM as well as FQPSK, GMSK, and FBPSK implementations.

From Table 9.3.1 (a rough estimate of modem parameters), we note the following:

$$\boxed{\text{C / N of 4 CPM-FM} = \text{C / N of 16-QAM} = \text{C / N of QPSK} + 5\text{ dB}}$$

For example, for a BER = 10^{-2} in a Rayleigh-faded environment, coherent QPSK requires $C/N = C/I = 17$ dB, while coherent 16-QAM requires $C/I = C/N = 22$ dB for the same BER. In other words, conventional QPSK is 5 dB more robust than 16-QAM to CCI and/or noise. Additionally, 16-QAM requires very linear amplifiers, Automatic Gain Control (AGC) circuits, and mixers at both the receiver and the transmitter, leading to a low RF power/battery efficiency. A potential advantage of 16-QAM, on the other hand, is that it has a 3 b/s/Hz practical spectral efficiency, as compared with the 1.6 b/s/Hz of linearly amplified QPSK.

Four-level FM or 4 CPM-FM, noncoherently detected, with 1.2 to 1.4 b/s/Hz, also has an approximately *5-dB worse* BER = $f(C/I)$ performance than QPSK-type systems (see Chapter 4, and Appendix A.3).

9.3.3 GMSK Modulation

Gaussian-MSK (GMSK) is the modulation format used in the GSM system standard, as well as in other standards. This modulation technique has been used with coherent and noncoherent implementations and is well described in many references. In GMSK systems the BT_b product refers to the cut-off frequency of the premodulation Gaussian filter. A $BT_b = 0.3$ will lead to an increased spectral efficiency, as compared with $BT_b = 0.5$. However, this improvement results in a more complex implementation and increased sensitivity to C/I and to radio propagation (for example, delay-spread) and equipment-caused imperfections (Leung, 1994).

The principal advantages of GMSK are power-amplifier efficiency (because of the use of NLA) and reasonably robust performance: BER = 10^{-3} for $C/N = 30$ dB. Both coherent and noncoherent demodulation are possible. Several European standards use GMSK, and single-chip VLSI implementations are readily available. For Feher's patented GMSK see Appendix A.3.

However, GMSK has several disadvantages in practice. The relatively wideband main lobe results in a lower spectral efficiency than with QPSK-type modems. GMSK is less robust than FQPSK (by 2 dB), yet it requires a more complex baseband processor in order to implement the Gaussian low-pass filter (G-LPF) and digital signal processor (DSP). GMSK with $BT_b = 0.3$ is more sensitive than QPSK to system-caused imperfections, another disadvantage of GMSK (Leung, 1994; Leung and Feher, 1993). A detailed study of GMSK systems, as well as of other modulated systems, has been presented in Chapter 4.

9.3.4 π/4-DQPSK Modulation: The Standard in the United States and Japan

The π/4-rotated DQPSK modulation requires linear amplifiers, even though it has a somewhat reduced envelope fluctuation as compared with conventional QPSK. The principal advantage of π/4-DQPSK is that it can be coherently or noncoherently demodulated and has somewhat reduced spectral spreading and BER degradation as compared with conventional QPSK in "linearized" or "quasilinear" channels. Noncoherent detection was the preferred approach several years ago for fast-moving (for example, 100 km/hour) large Doppler-shift systems. Later it was found that because of predominant delay, spread-coherent receivers must be used.

Filtered π/4-QPSK and conventional QPSK systems have an envelope fluctuation in the range of 3 dB to 5 dB. The linear RF amplifiers that these modulation schemes require have a gain and output power variation of 1 dB to 3 dB. Because of imperfect linearization, an additional output backoff (OBO) of 2 dB is common. For these reasons, the **OBO of digital π/4-DQPSK** cellular systems is

$$\boxed{\text{OBO} = 6\ \text{dB to } 10\ \text{dB},}$$

and the overall power efficiency of some of the simplest π/4-DQPSK amplified systems is only 5% to 15%. Linearized advanced amplifiers have a power efficiency (for π/4-DQPSK) in the 30% to 40% range.

π-4-DQPSK could be a reasonable choice for systems that require coherent and/or noncoherent reception, with spectral efficiency not greater than 1.6 b/s/Hz, and in which power efficiency (linearly amplified RF power/direct-current [dc] power ratio) is not too critical. The receiver baseband processor of π/4-DQPSK is slightly more complex than that of conventional QPSK or offset QPSK (O-QPSK). In nonlinearly amplified systems, offset-QPSK with specific filtering (baseband processing) has significant spectral advantages. For this reason, we investigate in further detail a family of O-QPSK systems that have been patented and licensed by Dr. Feher Associates–Digcom, Inc. These systems are known as FQPSK and FBPSK.

9.3.5 FQPSK and FBPSK: Feher's Patented Family of O-QPSK, QPSK, BPSK, and GMSK Systems

Simple, patented baseband processors and filters in an offset-QPSK structure lead to an intersymbol interference- and jitter-free (IJF) eye diagram. We call this type of QPSK modulator ***FQPSK*** **(*F* for Feher's patented signal processors,** and QPSK-based family of modems) (Feher 1982 to 1994). The I and Q baseband FQPSK signal-generation concept is described in many references, including Chapter 4 of this book. It is a very simple concept, with a simple, "smooth-baseband-drive" signal. The implementation of FQPSK is practically identical to that of a quadrature GMSK modulation, except that FQPSK has a simpler baseband processor (see detailed description in Chapter 4).

In Figures 9.3.1 to 9.3.8 and Tables 9.3.2 to 9.3.4, several FQPSK waveshapes, applications, and modulated system and overall performance charts are presented and compared with other digital modulated wireless systems.

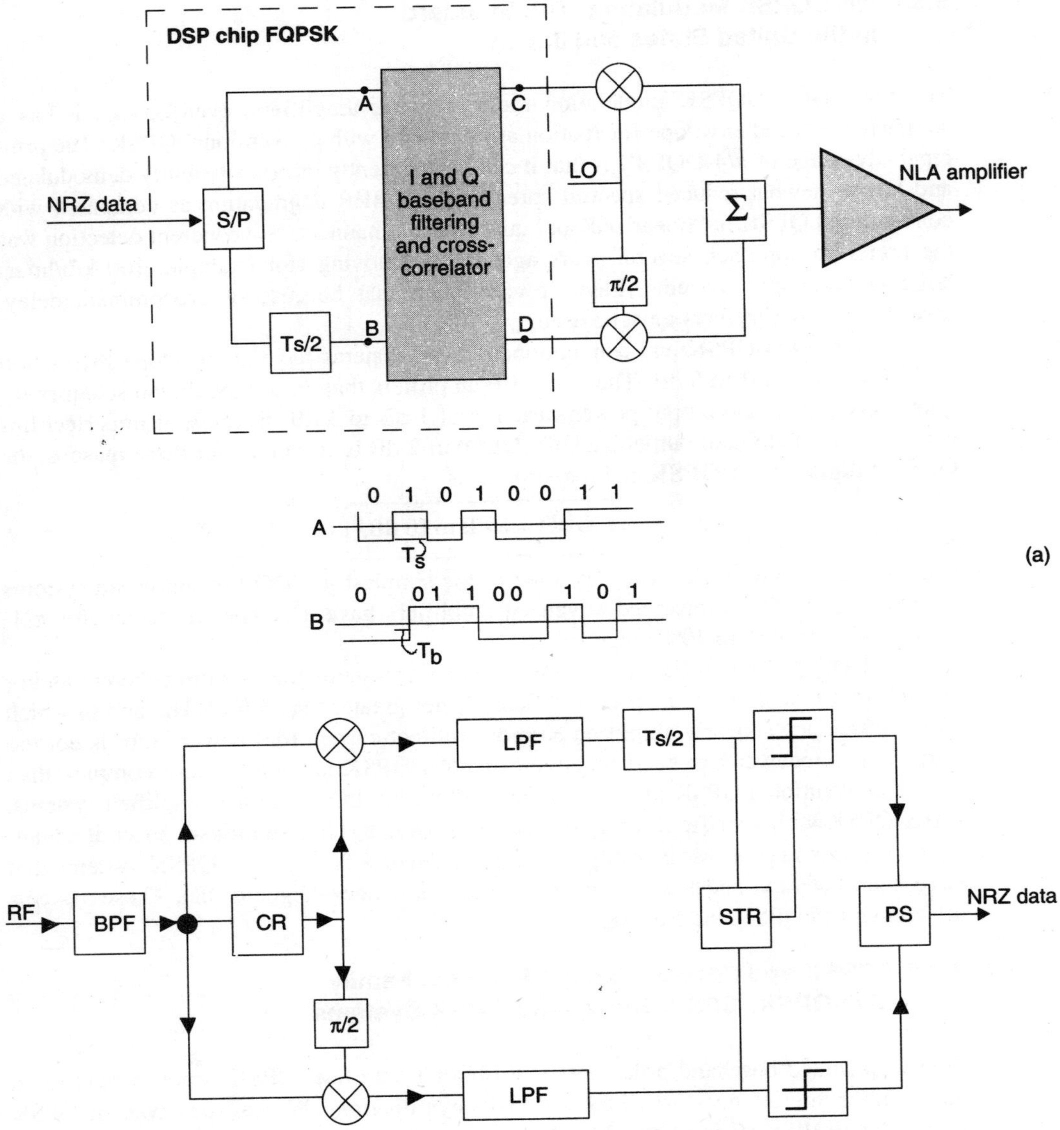

Figure 9.3.1 (a), FQPSK nonlinearly amplified (NLA) tranceiver/modem. Several I and Q cross-correlated signals of the FQPSK family are illustrated in Figure 9.3.1b. (b), FQPSK crosscorrelated signal examples of FBPSK and FQPSK. For technology transfer and patent licensing information, contact Dr. Feher Associates, Digcom, Inc. (Kato and Feher, patent, 1986). The cross-correlated FQPSK and GMSK invention described in Appendix 3, is "against" the well-established theory of linear communications.

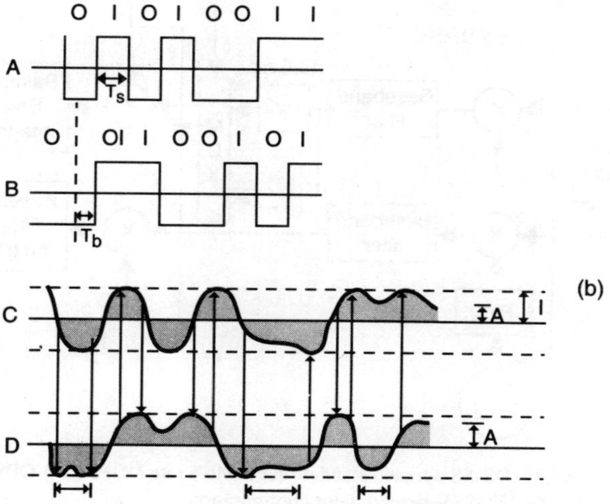

Signal after cross-correlation based on
Dr. Feher Associates patented technologies (see Appendix A.3)

Figure 9.3.1 (continued)

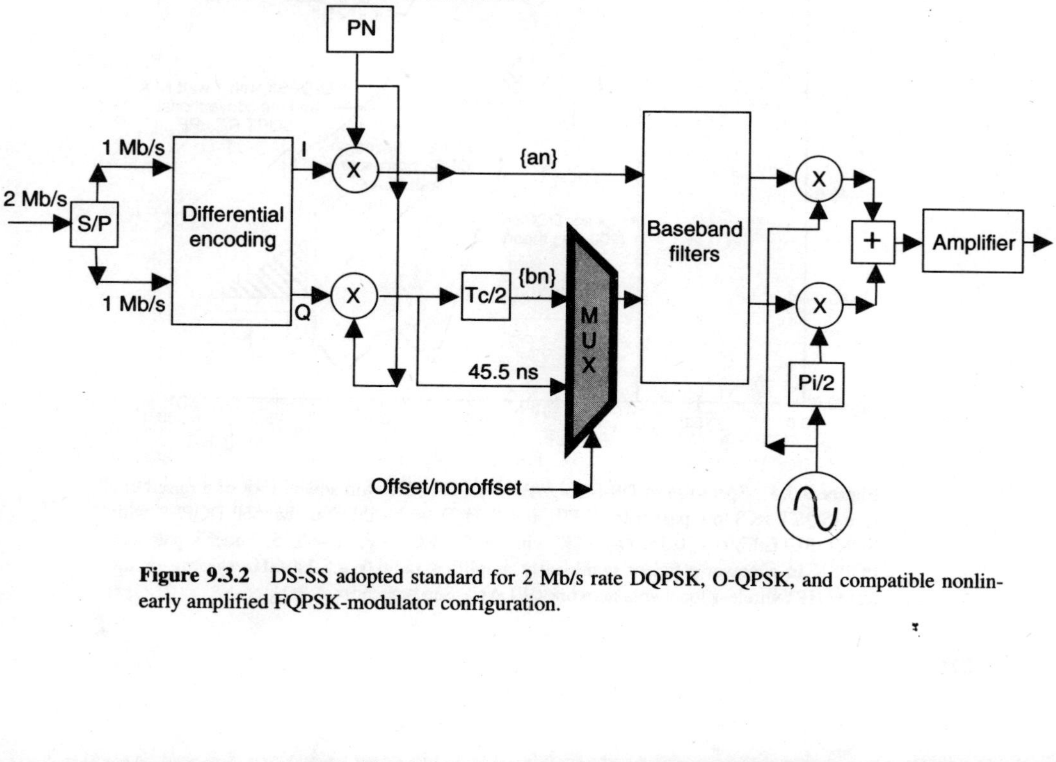

Figure 9.3.2 DS-SS adopted standard for 2 Mb/s rate DQPSK, O-QPSK, and compatible nonlinearly amplified FQPSK-modulator configuration.

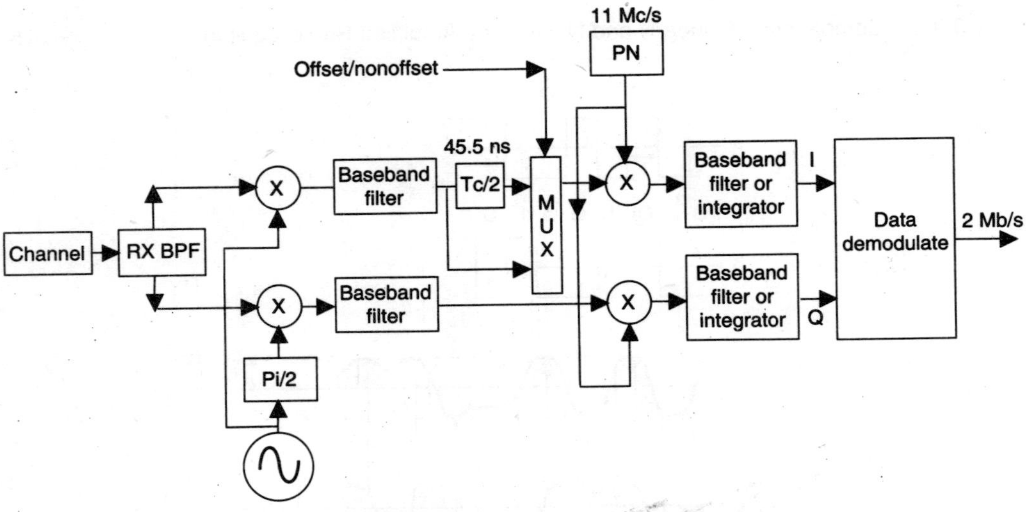

Figure 9.3.3 DS-SS adopted standard for 2 Mb/s rate DQPSK, O-QPSK, and interoperable nonlinearly amplified FQPSK-demodulator configuration.

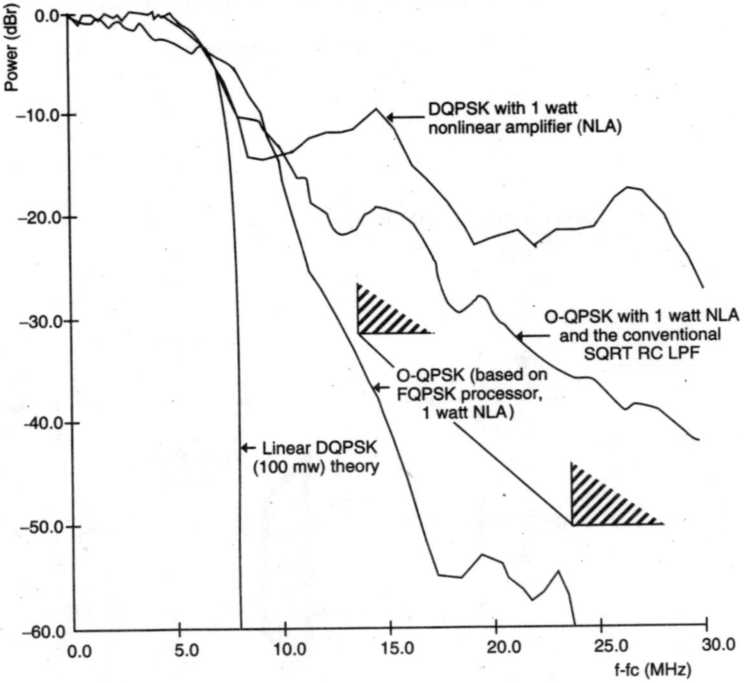

Figure 9.3.4 Spectrum of DS-SS signals with, DQPSK with square root of a raised cosine (SQRT-RC) low-pass filter (LPF), $\alpha = 0.35$, in an ideal linear channel; DQPSK with SQRT RC LPF, $\alpha = 0.35$; O-QPSK with SQRT RC LPF, $\alpha = 0.35$; Feher's patented FQPSK in a power-efficient nonlinearly amplified radio, e.g., 2.4-GHz system, or infrared (IR) wireless local area network (WLAN). See Appendix A.3.

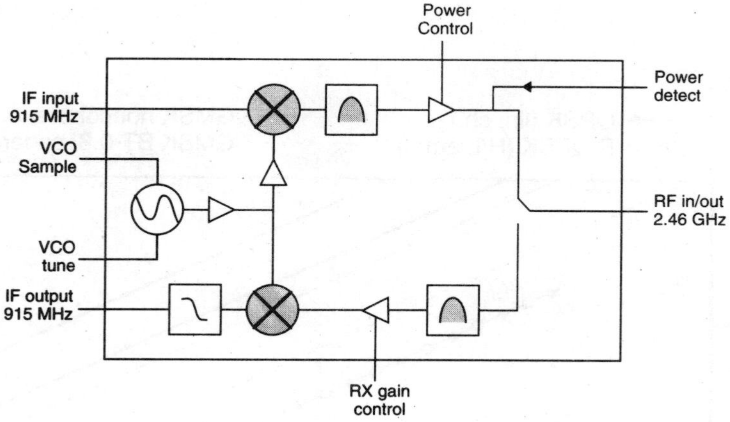

Figure 9.3.5 Transceiver chip (2.4 GHz) block diagram of the TELEDYNE TFE-1050 chip set.

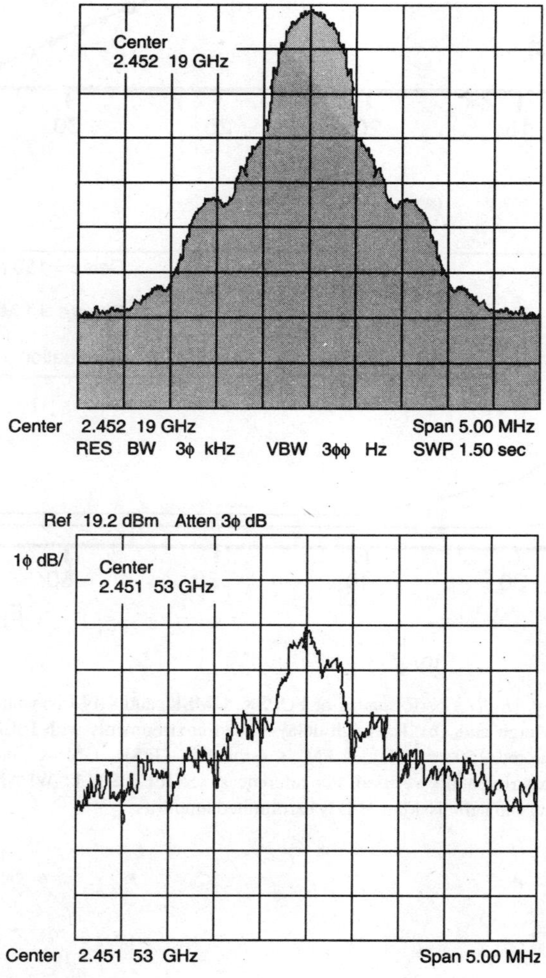

Figure 9.3.6 GaAs 2.4-GHz MMIC-Teledyne TAE-1010A measurements of newest RF amplifier chip and TAE-TFE transceiver FQPSK, (*top*), and DQPSK, (*bottom*), modulated spectra. The FQPSK spectrum (28.5 dBm with 5 V) meets the requirements, while the linearly amplified (24.3 dBm with 5 V) output DQPSK spectral spreading does not meet IEEE 802.11 standard specifications. The saturated (nonlinearly amplified) FQPSK system has a 4-dB power advantage over that of the conventional standardized DBPSK. Normalized f_b = 1Mb/s rate experiments.

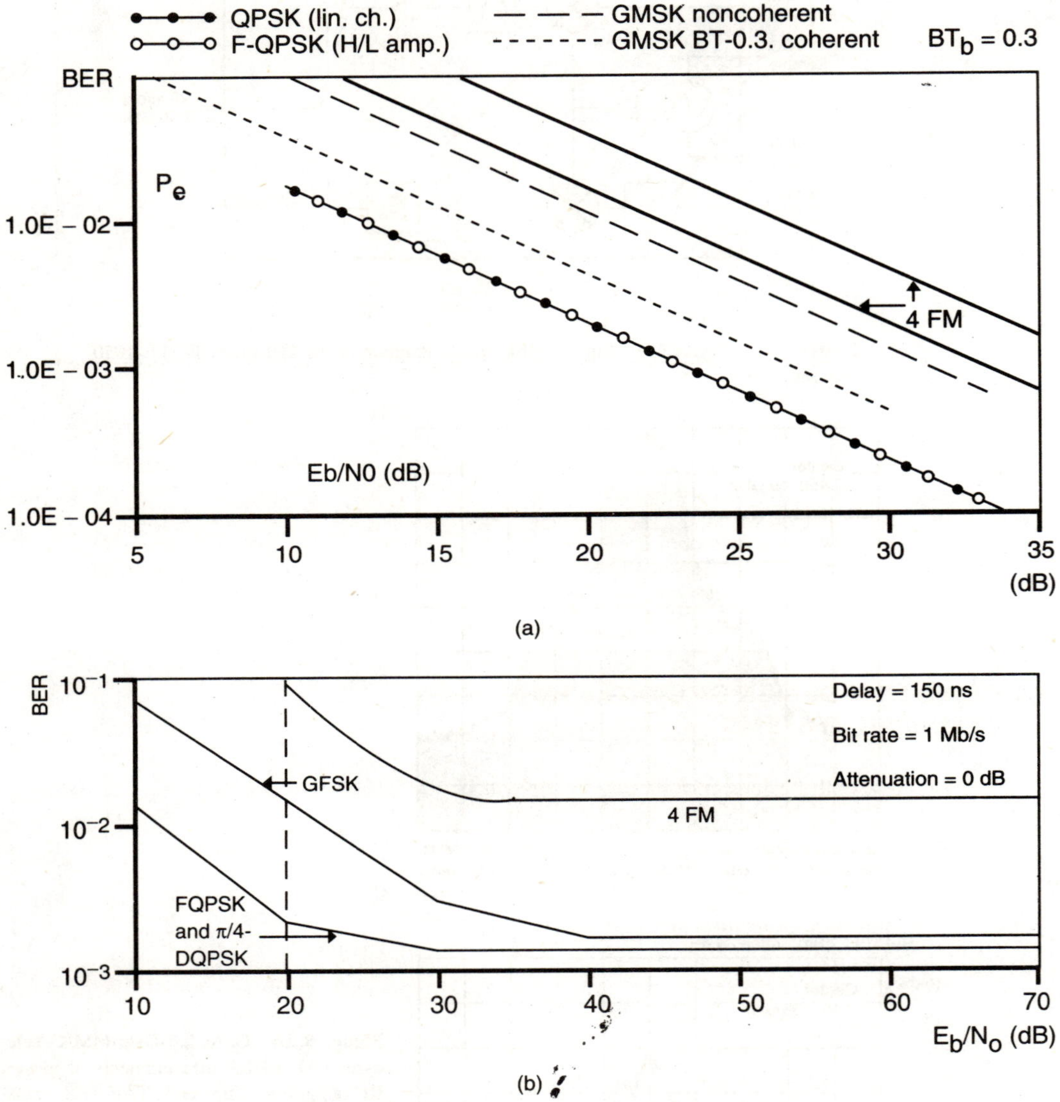

Figure 9.3.7 (a), BER = $f(E_b/N_o)$ performance of FQPSK, GMSK, and 4-FM constant envelope systems in Rayleigh and, (b), Rayleigh delay-spread environments with IEEE 802.11 measured and quoted 150 ns delay; 4-FM is estimated. GFSK, GMSK, and FQPSK computed and experimentally verified. For references, see IEEE 802.11-WLAN standardization documents and submissions. H/L is hardlimited amplifier.

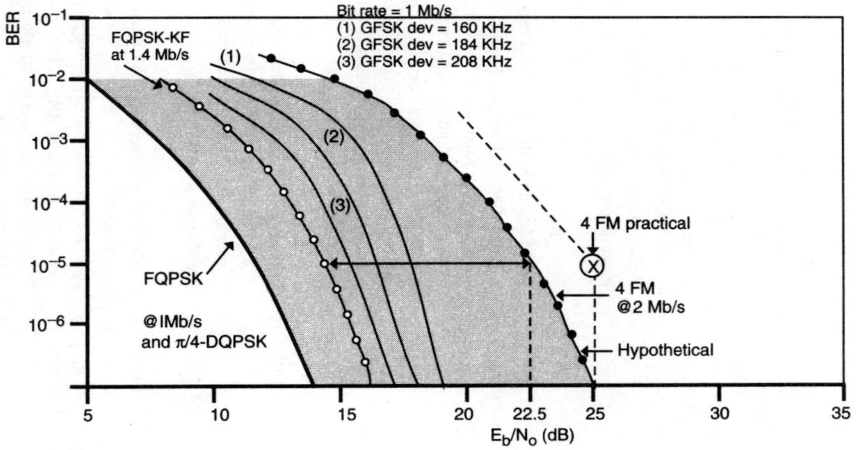

Figure 9.3.8 BER of FQPSK, GFSK, and 4-FM in an AWGN environment. For BER = 10^{-5}, FQPSK requires 4 to 6.5 dB less E_b/N_o than the GFSK systems shown, and 13 dB less than 4-FM for AWGN (the exact improvement depends on the frequency deviation). For slow frequency-hopped spread-spectrum systems, the IEEE 802.11 Standardization Committee adopted GFSK and 4-FM during 1994. These f_b = 1 Mb/s and 2 Mb/s rate systems have to operate with low deviation in order to meet the spectral requirements.

9.4 RADIO LINK DESIGN OF DIGITAL WIRELESS CELLULAR SYSTEMS

Wireless cellular land mobile radio propagation is frequently modeled by the following:

1. Fast multipath Rayleigh fading
2. Slow log-normal shadowing
3. Path-loss variation with distance

In Chapter 3 we presented a detailed description of the propagation environment. Radio link design, one of the most important problems for wireless and cellular system engineers, must be carried out by taking these effects into account. Fundamental parameters of radio link design for cellular land mobile radio systems are transmitter power and cochannel reuse distance. These parameters are determined for a specified *transmission quality,* that is, a specified bit-error rate (BER), and *allowable outage.* Outage is defined as the fraction of the service area over which the required transmission quality cannot be maintained within the service area. A comprehensive design approach, suitable for cellular land mobile radio systems, is presented in this section. For the system design, transmission quality requirement is obtained from a knowledge of the transmission performance in a pure multipath Rayleigh-fading environment without log-normal shadowing. Thermal noise and CCI are also taken into account. Outage is approximated under the as-

Table 9.3.2 Specification highlights and critical parameters of wireless local area networks (WLAN) standardization committee IEEE 802.11, as of March 1994.

Parameter	Specification	FQPSK	DQPSK	4-FM	Comments
Transmitted power levels	1000 mW, max	1000 mW	150 mW	1000 mW	Technology/size/power/cost limit of $\pi/4$-DQPSK to 150 mW
Maximum radiated EIRP	FCC 15.247 USA; ETS 300-328 Europe; TBD Japan		8 dB peak disadvantage		Peak radiation of $\pi/4$-DQPSK ? Regulation limits?
Receiver minimum input level sensitivity	−80 dBm @10^{-5} BER			8 dB problem; no	4-FM has an 8 dB higher C/N requirement than FQPSK and $\pi/4$-DQPSK; requires an 8 dB lower noise figure to meet specs; could be very expensive.
Occupied bandwidth @20 dB	±500 kHz		?	?	$\pi/4$-DQPSK marginal because of nonlinearity of amplifiers or mixers/modulators; 4-FM extremely sensitive to modulation index
Modulation		FQPSK	$\pi/4$-DQPSK	4-FM	
Channel data rate and increments		1.4 Mb/s 2.8 Mb/s 4.2 Mb/s	1.5 Mb/s	2 Mb/s	FQPSK could handle 1 Mb/s, 1.5 Mb/s, 2 Mb/s, 3 Mb/s and 4 Mb/s; best performance for indicated rates
BER at specified E_b/N_o (Gaussian model assumed)	10^{-5} @ E_b/N_o = 19 dB	E_b/N_o = 15 dB	15 dB	23 dB	4-FM does not meet specs
BER with 150 ns delay-spread B; E_b/N_o requir.	10^{-2} @ E_b/N_o = 21 dB	15 dB	17 dB	50 dB?	4-FM does not meet specs; extremely sensitive
Channel availability	99.5%	99.5%; 3	90%; no	90%; no	$\pi/4$-DQPSK lower availability because of low Tx power (1 dB). 4-FM lower availability because of 10 dB higher C/N that is required

(From Feher, 1994b.)

Table 9.3.3a GFSK, FQPSK-1, FQPSK-KF, FQPSK 4*4, and FQPSK 8*8 comparison.

	Standardized	Proposed higher speed			
	GFSK	FQPSK-1	FQPSK-KF	FQPSK 4*4	FQPSK 8*8
Maximum bit rate in 1 MHz	1 Mb/s	1.0 Mb/s	1.5 Mb/s	2.8 Mb/s+	4.2 Mb/s
Required E_b/N_0 for BER = 10^{-5} in Gaussian noise	19.3 dB (15.5*)	10.5 dB	15.7 dB	15 dB	19.8 dB

*With more complex reciever baseband processor.

Table 9.3.3b BER = f(C/I) in Rayleigh fading and BER = $f(E_b/N_0)k$ in AWGN (stationary) for GFSK, FQPSK and 4-FM constant envelope NLA systems. The π/4-DQPSK BER performance is similar to that of FQPSK; however, it requires linear amplifiers.

	GFSK	FQPSK	QPSK	4-FM
Bit rate in 1 MHz (–20 dB)	1.0 MB/s	1.6 Mb/s	1.6 Mb/s	2 Mb/s
RF power @ 2.4 GHz (max)	1 Watt (NLA)	1 Watt (NLA)	150 mW (linear)	1 Watt (NLA)
Required C/I for BER = 10^{-2} Rayleigh	20 dB	16 dB	16 dB	23 dB
Increase in peak radiation	0 dB	0 dB	5 to 10 dB	0 dB
Capacity (relative to GFSK)	100%	300%	300%	50?%

Table 9.3.3c GaAs MMIC, 2.4GHz power efficiency; newest generation of power amplifiers (Teledyne TAE-1010a) measurement result with 3 V dc battery power. Amplifier measured at Teledyne during March 1994 to meet IEEE 802.11 spectrum mask.

	Efficiency	RF out
FQPSK saturated (NLA)	19.8%	+24 dBm
DQPSK linear*	8.6%	+21 dBm

*With more complex receiver baseband processor.
(From Feher, 1994b.)

sumptions of log-normal shadowing and path-loss variation with distance. The material in this section is based on Feher (1987a).

9.4.1 Outage and Margin

Thermal noise and cochannel interference (CCI) are two factors that have the most significant impact on the transmission quality, expressed in terms of bit-error rate (BER) of mobile systems. A simple model of geographical cochannel reuse is illustrated in Figure 9.4.1. The outage and required CNR and CIR margin derivations, presented in section 9.4.1.1, are related in Figure 9.4.1.

Table 9.3.4 Comparison of coherent and noncoherent GMSK and FQPSK. (From Feher, 1993.)

Maximal bit-rate and delay-spread τ_{rms} issues	Coherent QPSK or FQPSK (or GMSK-similar, but worse, performance)	DQPSK (or DGMSK)
τ_{rms} "worst-case" 1 μs		
τ_{rms} 200 ns		
BER = 10^{-2} floor due to τ_{rms}/T_s	$\tau_{rms}/T_s = 0.2$	$\tau_{rms}/T_s = 0.15$
P_e = C/I degrad (addit) of 1 dB due to τ_{rms}/T (4 times more sensitive than for "floor")	$\tau_{rms}/T_s = 0.075$ QPSK; higher by about 50% for F-QPSK	$\tau_{rms}/T_s = 0.05$
Maximum bit rate f_b		
For 10^{-2} error floor 1 μs (200 ns)	600 kb/s (3 Mb/s)	
For 1 dB τ_{rms} caused degradation 1 μs (200 ns)	150 kb/s (750 kb/s)	300 kb/s (1.5 Mb/s) 75 kb/s (375 kb/s)
Capacity issues based on C/I = 3 dB (CCI advantage)	BER = 10^{-2}; C/I = 15 dB	BER = 10^{-2} C/I = 18 dB
Normalized relat. capacity		
Based on k = 9 to k = 7 reuse	100%	70% (30% loss)
Based on WER and throughput	100%	20% (80% loss)
Spectral efficiency ACI and BPF versus LPF caused advantage, i.e., lower noise BW-coherent receiver (normalized to coherent)	100%	60%
Increased bit rate or cell coverage/adaptive equalization	Relatively simple, low cost DSP/SW adaptive equalizer could increase rate (coverage)	Very costly if at all feasible; adaptive equalization technology and theory not well understood and require original research
Bit rate (PHY) change, without loss of performance (within range)	Automatic, software controlled in BBP	Very difficult and could require change of IF-BPF
Spectral efficiency for ACI = −20 dB nonlinearly amplified radio	FQPSK = 1.42 b/s/Hz GMSK = 0.94 b/s/Hz $BT_b = 0.5$ and 0.98 b/s/Hz for $BT_b = 0.3$	Approximately 0.7 b/s/Hz depending on BPF complexity
Synchronization time (CR) (relative to no CR-differential loss of frame efficiency for 1000 or 10,000 bit word (packet)	50 bits: 1000 = 5% (max 100 bits = max 10%); 50 bits: 10,000 = 0.5% (max 100 bits for CR = max); 1%—a disadvantage; parallel CR and STR design could eliminate this drawback	Potential of 1% to 10% packet/synch time advantage (?) However, could be lost because of BPF transient ringing; Synch. time advantage could be lost because of DC comp. to sat. time requirement
Threshold capture effect (discriminator-impulse noise)	No problem	Potential problem in the critical BER = 10^{-2} range with discriminator
Tools (prediction)	Well known	Much more involved, since IF-BPF imperfect; impact of frequency tolerance GMSK $BT_b = 0.3$, very difficult

(continued)

Table 9.3.4 Continued

Maximal bit-rate and delay-spread τ_{rms} issues	Coherent QPSK or FQPSK (or GMSK-similar, but worse, performance)	DQPSK (or DGMSK)
Normalized relat. capacity		
RF oscillator drifts include synthesizer, impact on BER, DC restoration	Simple	Very costly; potential danger as in DECT
Additional down conversion/filters	Not required	Very costly, extra stage could be required because of lower IF and BPF problems
Carrier recovery requirements	Yes. Simple pilot in band and other costs, well-known techniques; no Doppler problem; low-power solution; GSM, ADC, and other cellular have it	No need for CR; advantage
DC power, extra for CR	Could be marginally higher for demand alone	Discriminator power requirement is smaller than coherent; however, DC battery power advantage could be lost because of LO or synthesizer-DC compensation requirement
IC chips, trend	Most manufacturing companies developing QUAD (coherent structure)	Noncoherent discrimination today cheaper; however, overall radio, extra IF, BPF, and DC compensation not evident
Overall cost, DC power estimate	About the same as noncoherent receiver (total radio) with new technology	About the same
Radio frequency 900 MHz, 1.9 GHz, 2.4 GHz; bit rate variation	Same architecture for both radio frequencies; flexible bit rate	Could require some applications, extra-expensive IF stage (space/cost), and does not lead to software-driven bit-rate change

9.4.1.1 Derivation of outage and margins for CNR and CIR.

In reference to Figure 9.4.1 (Feher, 1987, Chapter 10 by Hirade), let X and Y be the *local means* of the desired signal and the undesired interference, respectively. Assuming that X and Y are subjected to mutually independent log-normal shadowing, the joint probability density function (PDF or pdf) of X and Y is given by

$$p(X,Y) = \frac{1}{2\pi\sigma^2 XY} e^{-(1/2\sigma^2)[ln^2(X/X_m)+ln^2(Y/Y_m)]} \qquad (9.4.1)$$

In equation 9.4.1, σ is the standard deviation, whose value in decibels was empirically shown to be 5 to 12 dB in a typical urban area (Okomura et al., 1968), and X_m and Y_m are the *area means* of X and Y, which are given, respectively, by

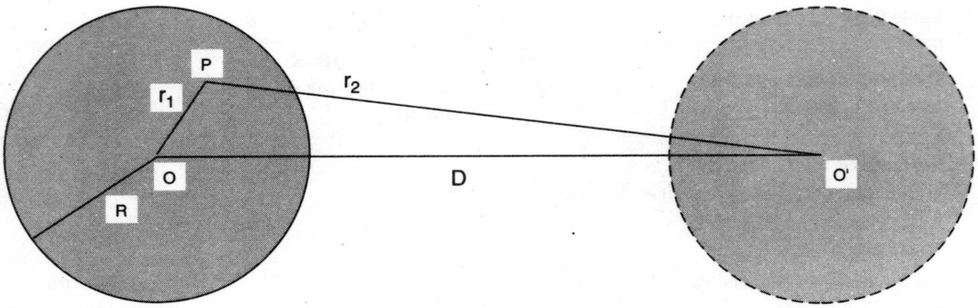

Figure 9.4.1 Simple model of geographical cochannel reuse. R is cell radius, and D is intercell distance. r_1 and r_2 are distances from the mobile unit to each base station. (Printed by permission of the IEEE [Hansen, 10.108], copyright, 1982, IEEE).

$$\begin{cases} X_m = X_m(r_1) = A \cdot r_1^{-\alpha} \\ Y_m = Y_m(r_2) = A \cdot r_2^{-\alpha} \end{cases} \tag{9.4.2}$$

where A and α are the propagation parameters and the value of α is about 3 to 4 in an urban area. As shown in Figure 9.4.1, r_1 and r_2 are the distances from a moving vehicle to the desired and undesired base stations, respectively. Letting the local means of the CNR and the CIR be Γ and Λ, respectively, and changing the variables in equation 9.4.1 such that $X = \Gamma$ and $X/Y = \Lambda$, the joint pdf of Γ and Λ is given by

$$p(\Gamma, \Lambda) = \frac{1}{2\pi\sigma^2\Gamma\Lambda} e^{-(1/2\sigma^2)[ln^2(\Gamma/\Gamma_m)+ln^2(\Lambda/\Lambda_m \cdot \Gamma_m/\Gamma)]} \tag{9.4.3}$$

where $\Gamma_m = \Gamma_m(r_1) = \Lambda_m = \Lambda_m(r_1, r_2)$ are the area means of CNR and CIR, respectively. The "threshold" values or levels of the CNR (Γ_{th}) and of the CIR (Λ_{th}) are the lowest values that lead to an acceptable BER.

For the threshold level Γ_{th} and Λ_{th} specified by the required transmission quality, the probability that $\Gamma \le \Gamma_{th}$ or $\Lambda \le \Lambda_{th}$ is expressed as

$$\begin{aligned} &\text{Prob}[\Gamma \le \Gamma_{th} \quad \text{or} \quad \Lambda \le \Lambda_{th}] = \\ &\text{Prob}[\Gamma \le \Gamma_{th}] + \text{Prob}[\Lambda \le \Lambda_{th}] - \text{Prob}[\Gamma \le \Gamma_{th} \quad \text{and} \quad \Lambda \le \Lambda_{th}] \end{aligned} \tag{9.4.4}$$

where

$$\text{Prob}[\Gamma \le \Gamma_{th}] = \int_0^{\Gamma_{th}} \int_0^{\infty} p(\Gamma, \Lambda)\, d\Gamma\, d\Lambda \tag{9.4.5}$$

$$\text{Prob}[\Lambda \le \Lambda_{th}] = \int_0^{\infty} \int_0^{\Lambda_{th}} p(\Gamma, \Lambda)\, d\Gamma\, d\Lambda \tag{9.4.6}$$

$$\text{Prob}[\Gamma \le \Gamma_{th} \quad \text{and} \quad \Lambda \le \Lambda_{th}] = \int_0^{\Gamma th} \int_0^{\Lambda th} p(\Gamma, \Lambda)\, d\Gamma\, d\Lambda. \tag{9.4.7}$$

Substituting equation 9.4.3 into equations 9.4.4 through 9.4.7 and making some modifications, equation 9.4.4 becomes

$$\begin{aligned}\text{Prob}[\Gamma \le \Gamma_{th} \quad \text{or} \quad \Lambda \le \Lambda_{th}] \\ = \frac{1}{2} erfc\left\{\frac{ln(\Gamma_m/\Gamma_{th})}{\sqrt{2}\sigma}\right\} + \frac{1}{2} erfc\left\{\frac{ln(\Lambda_m/\Lambda_{th})}{\sqrt{2}\sigma}\right\} \\ -1\frac{1}{2\sqrt{\pi}}\int_{-\infty}^{ln(\Gamma_{th}/\Gamma_m)/\sqrt{2}\sigma} e^{-t^2} erfc\left\{t + \frac{ln(\Lambda_m/\Lambda_{th})}{\sqrt{2}\sigma}\right\}dt\end{aligned} \tag{9.4.8}$$

where *erfc* is the complementary error function:

$$erfc(x) = \frac{2}{\sqrt{\pi}}\int_x^{\infty} exp(-u^2)du.$$

Equation 9.4.8 indicates that the outage, which takes into account thermal noise and CCI, is a function of the required CNR and CIR margins, that is, Γ_m/Γ_{th} and Λ_m/Λ_{th}. In other words, equation 9.4.8 presents the required area means of CNR and CIR Γ_m and Λ_m for the threshold levels Γ_{th} and Λ_{th} and the allowable outage $\text{Prob}[\Gamma \le \Gamma_{th} \text{ or } \Lambda \le \Lambda_{th}] = F_f$.

Figure 9.4.2 shows the required margins for CNR and CIR computed from equation 9.4.8, where the dashed lines are the asymptotes, and $\sigma_0 = 10\sigma\log_{10}e$. The lines parallel to the horizontal axis represent the CIR margin when the CNR margin is infinite, and the lines parallel to the vertical axis represent the CNR margin when the CIR margin is infinite. From this figure, the following conclusions can be drawn.

1. Allotment of the outage for thermal noise and CCI can be made according to the system scale or system grade. For example, when the total allowable outage is 10%, it is possible to make a link design for point A which gives priority to thermal noise or for point B which gives priority to CCI. The former link design is suitable for realizing large-cell systems, whereas the latter one is for smaller-cell, high-capacity systems.

2. When the outage is allotted separately for the respective factors, the required margins for CNR and CIR can be calculated separately. For example, assuming that the total specified outage is 5% and that 1% is allotted for thermal noise and 4% for CCI, the required margins for CNR and CIR are determined from the point marked by the star in this figure. As the point lies a little above the 5% curve, this design requires a slightly larger margin for the specified outage. The same relation generally holds for other allotted values. This procedure always leads to a good performance.

Based on the relationship between outage and margin, the transmitter power and the cochannel reuse distance, both of which are fundamental parameters of a mobile radio link design, can be determined.

Threshold values for the local mean of CNR, Γ_{th}, and the local mean of CIR, Λ_{th}, are assumed to be specified separately based on the transmission-quality requirement in a pure Rayleigh-fading environment without log-normal shadowing. The allowable outage for thermal noise and CCI and be determined separately. Thus the transmitter power and the cochannel reuse distance can be determined as follows.

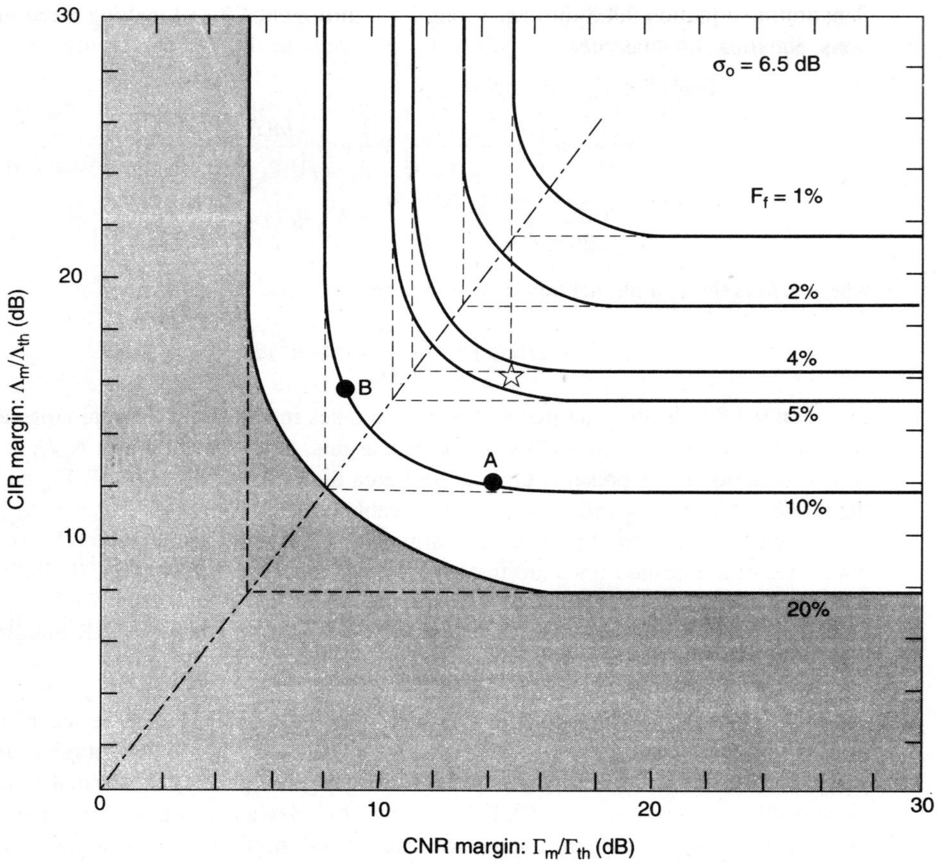

Figure 9.4.2 Required margins for CNR and CIR for several outage probabilities F_f, that is, F_f = Prob ($\Gamma \le \Gamma_{th}$ or $\Gamma \le \Gamma_{th}$). Lines parallel to the horizontal axis represent the CIR margin when the CNR margin is infinite; lines parallel to the vertical axis represent the CNR margin when the CIR margin is infinite. (Printed by permission of the IEEE [Hansen, 10.108], copyright 1982, IEEE).

9.4.2 Determination of Transmitter Power and Cochannel Reuse Distance

Let F_f^1 be the outage at some point P in the desired cell as shown in Figures 9.4.1 and 9.4.2. The relation between F_f^1 and the required CNR margin Γ_m/Γ_{th} is calculated from equations 9.4.3 and 9.4.5 and results in

$$
\begin{aligned}
F_f^1 &= \text{Prob}[\Gamma \le \Gamma_{th}] \\
&= \int_0^{\Gamma_{th}} \frac{1}{\sqrt{2\pi}\sigma\Gamma} e^{-(1/2\sigma^2)ln^2(\Gamma/\Gamma_m)} d\Gamma \\
&= \frac{1}{2} erfc\left\{\frac{ln(\Gamma_m/\Gamma_{th})}{\sqrt{2}\sigma}\right\}.
\end{aligned} \tag{9.4.9}
$$

The obtained numerical values are shown in Figure 9.4.3. As Γ_m is a function of the distance between the base station and a moving vehicle, Γ_m/Γ_{th} represents the minimum CNR margin at some point on the cell fringe.

When planning a system, the outage must be specified within the whole cell. Therefore, it is necessary to make clear the relation between the outage at the cell fringe and the outage within the whole cell. Letting $r_1 = r$ and using equation 9.4.2, the outage within the whole cell F_a^1 can be obtained as

$$\begin{aligned} F_a^1 &= \frac{1}{\pi R^2}\int_0^R F_f^1(r)2\pi r\,dr \\ &= \frac{1}{2}erfc(X_0) = \frac{1}{2}e^{(2X_0Y_0+Y_0^2)}erfc(X_0+Y_0) \end{aligned} \tag{9.4.10}$$

where

$$X_0 \equiv \frac{ln(\Gamma_m(R)/\Gamma_{th})}{\sqrt{2}\sigma} \quad \text{and} \quad Y_0 \equiv \frac{\sqrt{2}\sigma}{\alpha}. \tag{9.4.11}$$

The first term of equation 9.4.10 is equal to the outage F_f^1. (R) at the cell fringe given by equation 9.4.9 with r = R, and the second term is the correction term. The numerical results obtained by equation 9.4.10 are shown in Figure 9.4.4. This figure shows that the radio link can be designed based on the outage at the cell fringe. Consequently, the required CNR margin can be computed by equation 9.4.9.

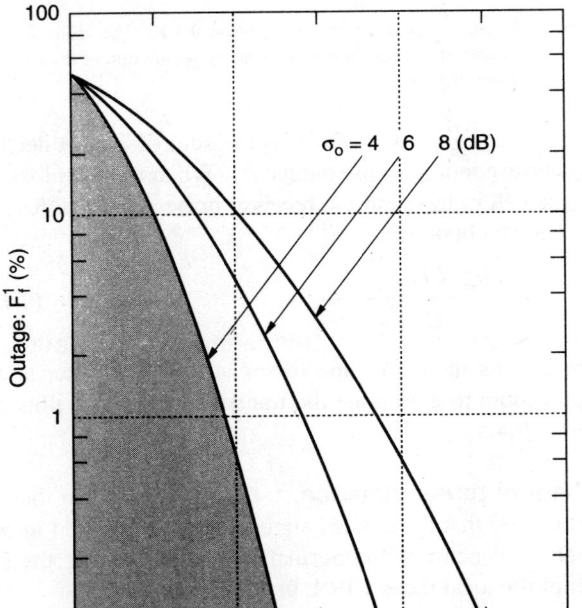

Figure 9.4.3 Relation between outage and required CNR margin as described in equation 9.4.9; F_f^1 = Prob[$\Gamma \le \Gamma_{th}$). (Printed by permission of the IEEE [Hansen, 10.108]; copyright 1982, IEEE).

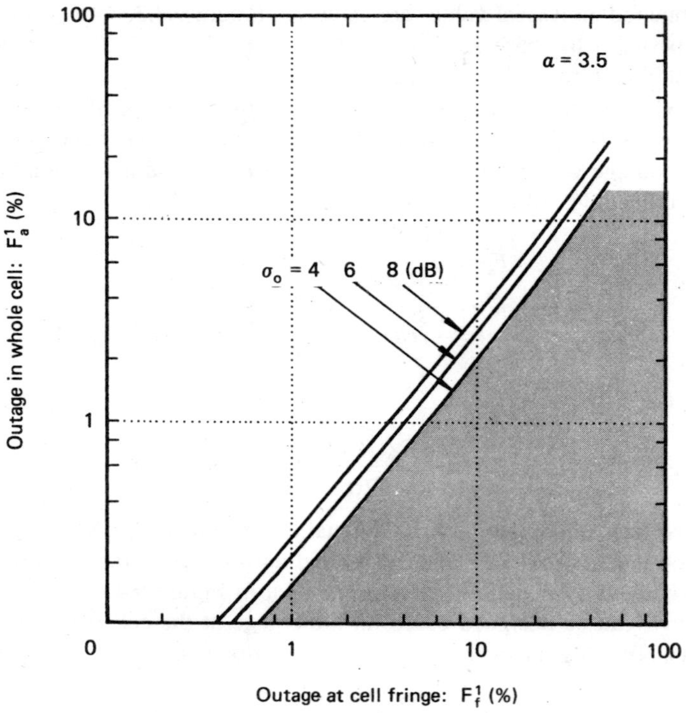

Figure 9.4.4 Relation between F_f^1 and F_a^1 as described in equation 9.4.10. The radio link can be designed based on the outage at the cell fringe. (Printed by permission of the IEEE [Hansen, 10.108]; copyright 1982, IEEE).

The required area mean of CNR, Γ_m, is then given as the sum of Γ_{th} (in decibels) and margin Γ_m/Γ_{th} (in decibels) corresponding to the outage F_f^1. When the path loss with distance L_p, which is related to the cell radius, and the receiver noise power, $kTBN_F$, are given, the transmitter power, P_t, can be obtained as

$$P_t = \frac{\Gamma_m \cdot kTBN_F \cdot L_p}{G_t \cdot G_r} \tag{9.4.12}$$

where G_t and G_r are the antenna gains including line losses at the transmitter and receiver, respectively. A design procedure to determine the transmitter power is illustrated in the form of a flowchart in Figure 9.4.5.

Determination of cochannel reuse distance. Let us assume that there exists a single interfering base station and that the desired signal and the undesired interference are subjected to the mutually independent log-normal shadowing having the same standard deviation. Then the pdf of the local mean CIR L becomes

$$p(\Lambda) = \frac{1}{2\sqrt{\pi}\sigma\Lambda} e^{-1/4\sigma^2 ln^2(\Lambda/\Lambda_m)}. \tag{9.4.13}$$

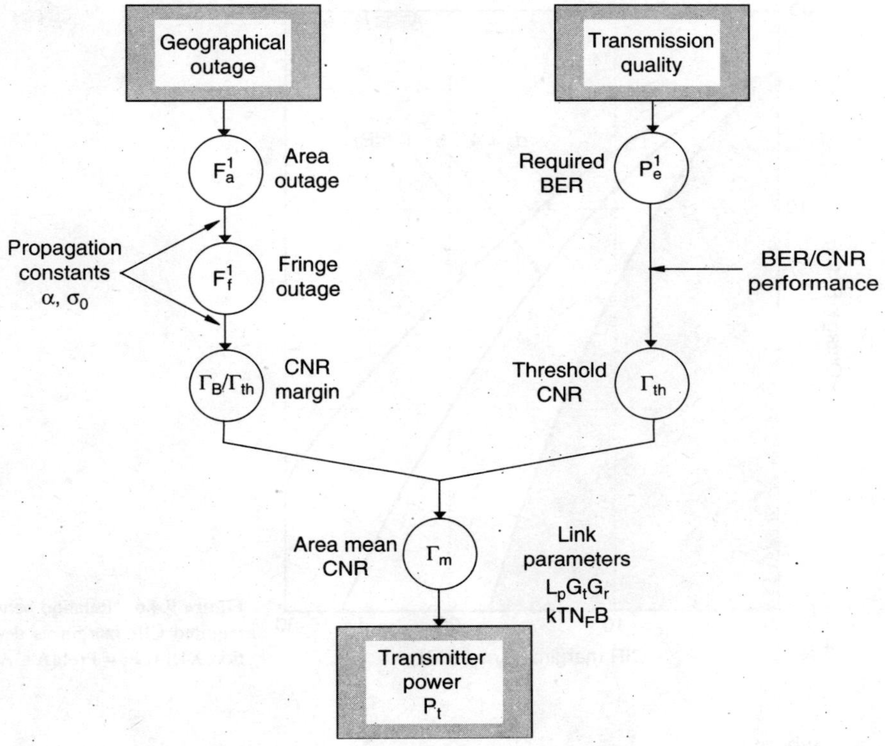

Figure 9.4.5 Design procedure to determine the required transmitter power. (Printed by permission of the IEEE [Hansen, 10.108]; copyright 1982, IEEE).

Letting F_f^2 be the outage at the point P in the desired cell, the relationship between outage F_f^2 and the required CIR margin Λ_m/Λ_{th} can be obtained as

$$\begin{aligned} F_f^2 &= \text{Prob}[\Lambda \le \Lambda_{th}] \\ &= \int_0^{\Lambda_{th}} \frac{1}{2\sqrt{\pi}\sigma\Lambda} e^{-(1/4\sigma^2)ln^2(\Lambda/\Lambda_m)} \, d\Lambda \\ &= \frac{1}{2} erfc\left\{\frac{ln(\Lambda_m/\Lambda_{th})}{2\sigma}\right\}. \end{aligned} \tag{9.4.14}$$

The results are shown in Figure 9.4.6.

Letting $r_1 = r$ and $r_2 \cong D - r$, the outage within the whole cell F_a^2 can be approximately expressed as

$$\begin{aligned} F_a^2 &= \frac{1}{\pi R^2} \int_0^R F_f^2(r) 2\pi r \, dr \\ &= \frac{1}{2} erfc(X_0') - \frac{1}{2} e^{(2X_0'Y_0' + Y_0'^2)} erfc(X_0' + Y_0') \end{aligned} \tag{9.4.15}$$

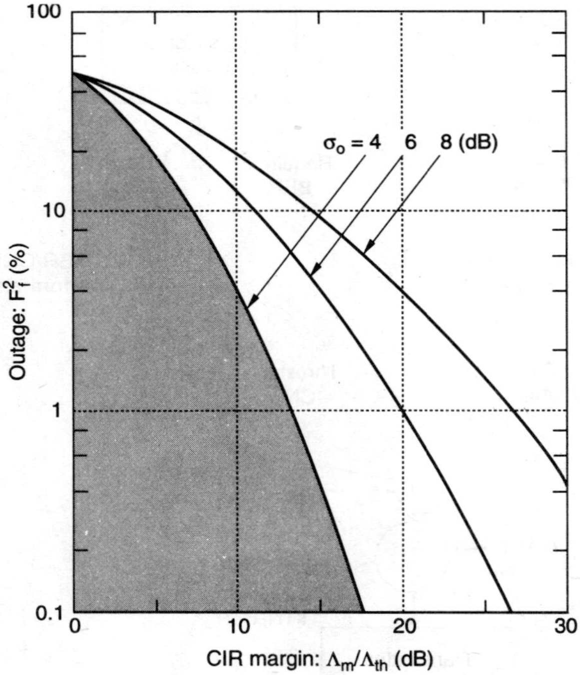

Figure 9.4.6 Relation between outage and required CIR margin as described in equation 9.4.14; $F_f^2 = \text{Prob}[\Lambda \le \Lambda_{th}]$.

where

$$X_0' \equiv \frac{ln[\Lambda_m(R)/\Lambda_{th}]}{2\sigma} \quad \text{and} \quad Y_0' \equiv \frac{2\sigma}{\alpha} \tag{9.4.16}$$

assuming Λ_m, Λ_{th}>> 1. The first term of equation 9.4.15 is equal to equation 9.4.14, and the second term is the correction term. The computed results of equation 9.4.15 are shown in Figure 9.4.7.

The area mean of CIR Λ_m at the worst point on the cell fringe $r = R$ (see Chapter 7, equation 7.2) is given by

$$\Lambda_m = \left(\frac{R}{D-R}\right)^{-\alpha} \equiv \Lambda_m(R). \tag{9.4.17}$$

This can be rewritten as

$$\frac{D}{R} = 1 + \Lambda_m(R)^{1/\alpha}, \tag{9.4.18}$$

and the results obtained are shown in Figure 9.4.8. The ratio D/R is the minimum cochannel reuse distance normalized by the cell radius because $\Lambda_m(R)$ is given by the sum of Λ_{th} (dB) and the minimum CIR margin Λ_m/Λ_{th} (decibels), which corresponds to the fixed

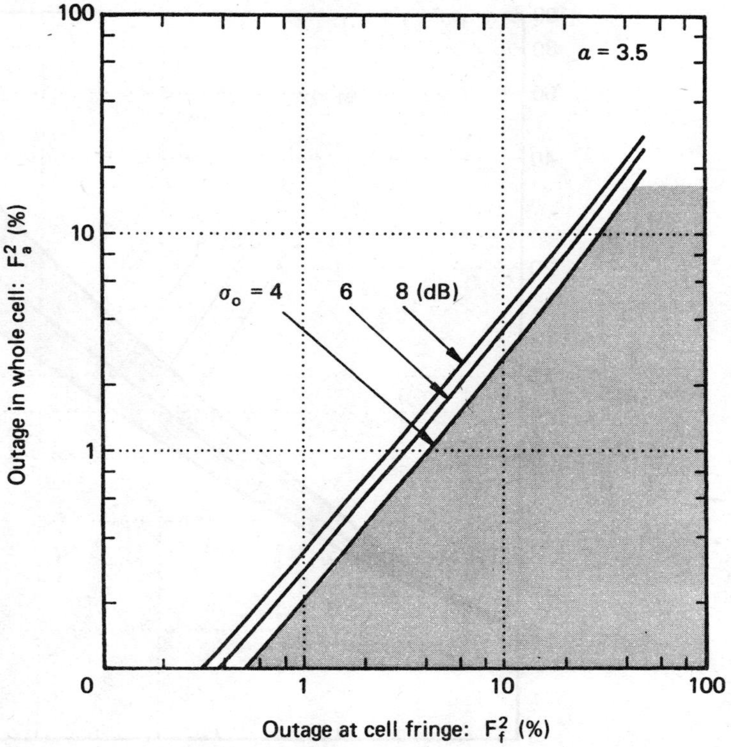

Figure 9.4.7 Relation between F_f^2 and F_a^2 as described in equation 9.4.15. (Printed by permission of the IEEE [Hansen, 10.108]; copyright 1982, IEEE).

outage F_f^2. A suggested design procedure to determine the cochannel reuse distance is shown in a flowchart form in Figure 9.4.9. In the preceding derivation it is assumed that the desired signal and the undesired interference are subjected to mutually independent log-normal shadowing. However, in practical land mobile radio propagation, shadowing may be partially correlated because the shadowing is caused by buildings or the terrain near the vehicle. Taking the correlation effect into account, the pdf of the local mean of CIR can be shown as

$$p(\Lambda) = \frac{1}{\sqrt{\pi}\sigma\sqrt{1-\rho}\Lambda} e^{-1(1/4\sigma^2(1-\rho))ln^2(\Lambda/\Lambda_m)} \tag{9.4.19}$$

where ρ is the correlation coefficient. The results are shown in Figure 9.4.10. Comparing equation 9.4.13 with equation 9.4.19, we conclude that the correlation effect is equivalent to decreasing the standard deviation from σ to $\sigma\sqrt{1-\rho}$. Therefore we may state that Figure 9.4.10 presents the worst-case interference probability.

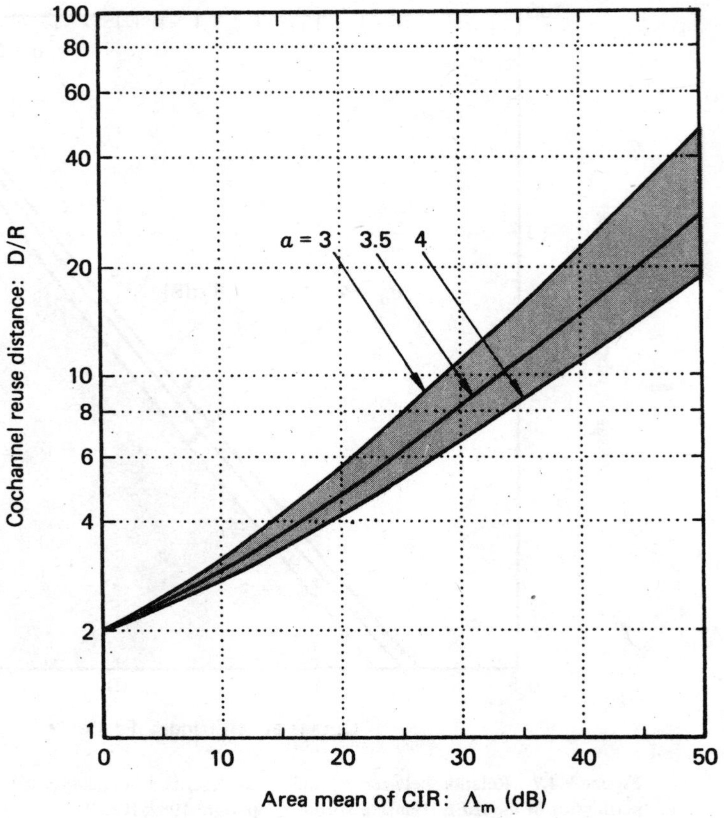

Figure 9.4.8 Relation between cochannel reuse distance and area mean of CIR. (Printed by permission of the IEEE [Hansen, 10.108]; copyright 1982, IEEE).

9.4.3 Example of a Digital Mobile Radio Link Design

According to our described procedure, let us determine the transmitter power and the cochannel reuse distance for a digital mobile radio link.

The following conditions are assumed:

1. The frequency band of the system is 900 MHz, and the cell radius $R = 3$ km. Standard deviation of the log-normal shadowing is $\sigma_0 = 6$ dB, and the propagation constant is $\alpha = 3.5$.
2. An average P_e of 1×10^{-3} and an outage F_a of 10% are required, and these values are allotted equally for thermal noise and cochannel interference.
3. MSK with differential detection is adopted as the modem scheme. The required transmission bandwidth for a 16-kb/s bit rate is $B = 16$ kHz. A two-branch selection diversity technique is applied.

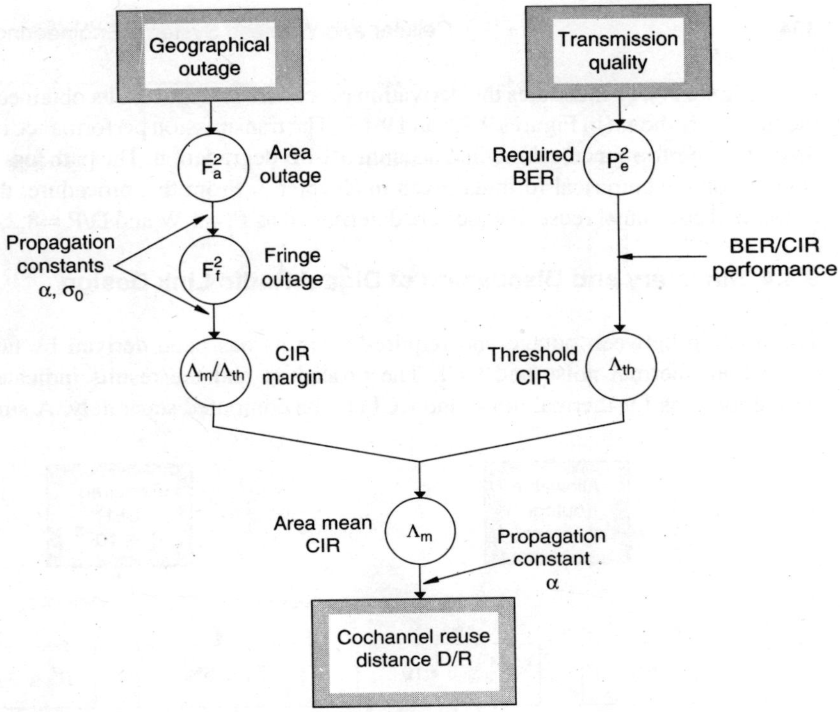

Figure 9.4.9 Design procedure to determine the cochannel reuse distance. (Printed by permission of the IEEE [Hansen, 10.108]; copyright 1982, IEEE).

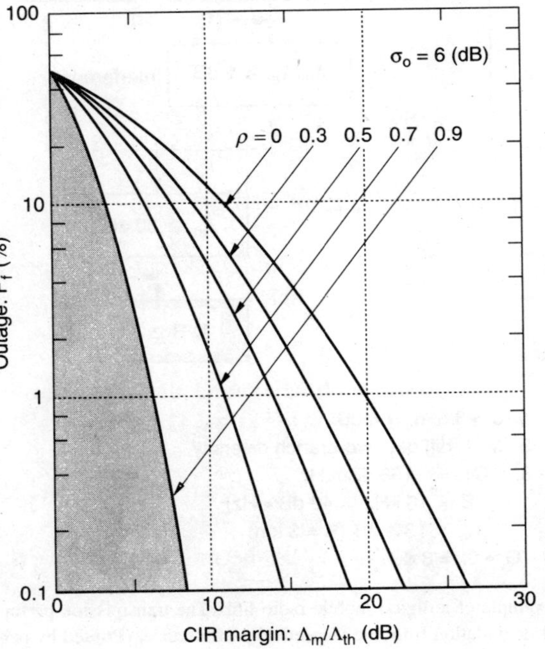

Figure 9.4.10 Correlation effect on the relation between outage and required CIR margin. The correlation effect is equivalent to decreasing the standard deviation from σ to $\sigma\sqrt{1-\rho}$), where ρ is the correlation coefficient. The worst-case interference probability.

Figure 9.4.11 illustrates the derivation procedure and the results obtained according to the flowchart shown in Figures 9.4.5 and 9.4.9. The transmission performance is based on the theoretical performance, taking into account a 2-dB degradation. The path loss with distance is based on the empirical formula given in Chapter 3. From this procedure, the transmitter power and cochannel reuse distance are determined as $P_t = 1$ W and D/R = 8.2, respectively.

9.4.4 Summary and Discussion of Digital Radio Link Design

The relation between outage and required margins has been derived by taking into account both thermal noise and CCI. The procedure and the results indicate that the required margins for thermal noise and CCI can be computed separately. A simple and use-

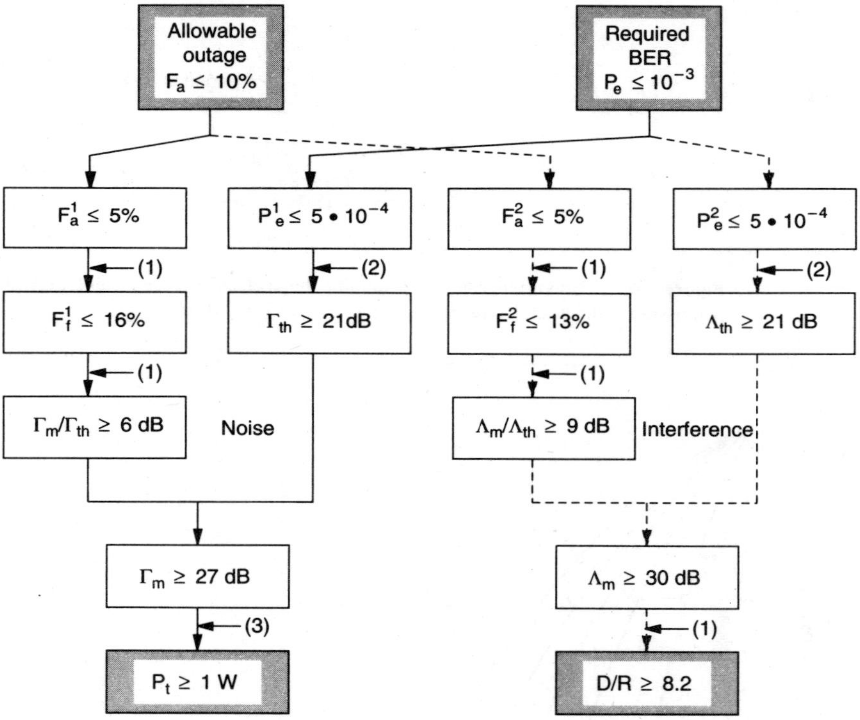

1. $\alpha = 3.5$, $\sigma_o = 6$ dB
2. MSK diff det, two-branch diversity
3. $kTN_F = -168$ dBm/Hz
   B = 16 kHz (= 42 dB • Hz)
   L_p = 137 dB (R = 3 km)
   $G_t \cdot G_r$ = 8 dB

Figure 9.4.11 Design example of a digital mobile radio link. The transmission performance is based on a 2-dB degradation from the theoretical performance. (Printed by permission of the IEEE [Hansen, 10.108]; copyright 1982, IEEE).

ful procedure to determine the transmitter power and the cochannel reuse distance is presented in a flowchart form. The procedure can be applied to digital as well as analog mobile radio link designs.

To obtain a more accurate specification of required transmitter power, it is necessary to take other degradation factors, such as manufactured noise or terrain factors, into account. These factors should be treated as additional margin or propagation loss. In a cellular system, it is also necessary to design the cochannel reuse distance more accurately because of the presence of multipath interfering base stations. If we wish to have a conservative (safe) design, then we should add 8 dB, which corresponds to six interfering base stations, to the area mean of the CIR determined by our procedure.

As shown in the mobile ratio link design example, the space diversity effect, which mitigates the fast multipath Rayleigh fading, effectively decreases the permissible local means of CNR and CIR. On the other hand, the site diversity effect, which is obtained by the hand-off technique and is effective for mitigating the shadowing, decreases the required CNR and CIR margins.

9.5 SPECTRUM UTILIZATION IN DIGITAL WIRELESS MOBILE SYSTEMS

In line-of-sight (LOS) microwave, satellite, and many other cable systems, spectral efficiency is defined in terms of bits/second/Hertz (*b/s/Hz*). We use the (b/s/Hz) term frequently in Chapter 4 on modulated systems. For cellular non–line-of-sight (NLOS) applications, we extend the basic (b/s/Hz) spectral efficiency concept of modulated systems to the spectral efficiency of a complete geographic coverage or service area in terms of (b/s/Hz/m^2) or (erl/Hz m^2) (Feher, 1987a, Chapter 10 by Hirade).

9.5.1 Definition of Spectral Efficiency of Cellular Systems

Let us first define the spectral efficiency of a cellular land mobile radio system. In this system the entire service area is covered with many small cells, and the same set of frequencies is geographically reused in every cluster of cells, as shown in Figure 9.5.1. We use the following definitions:

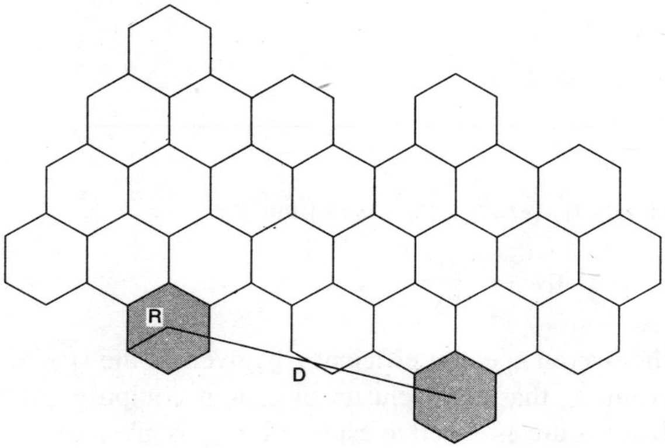

Figure 9.5.1 An example of small cell layout (hexagonal cell structure, N = 13). The shaded cells share the same frequency because they occupy the same position within their respective clusters.

DEFINITIONS FOR CAPACITY AND SPECTRAL EFFICIENCY

A	$\text{ERLANGS} = \dfrac{\text{avg. calling time (minutes)} \times \text{total customers}}{60 \text{ minutes}}$
α	Propagation exponential attenuation factor (3 to 4)
a_c	Carried traffic per channel or ERLANGS (erl/channel)
a_{cell}	Offered traffic per cell (erl/cell)
a_{sub}	Traffic per subscriber during a busy hour (erl/sub)
B	Blocking rate of calls
D	Cochannel reuse distance
Δ_f	Carrier frequency drift
erl	ERLANG
f_b	Bit rate of source code
f_s	Channel spacing, that is, bandwidth in Hz per RF channel (Hz/chan)
η_f	Spectral efficiency with respect to frequency
η_s	Spectral efficiency with respect to space
η_T	Overall spectral efficiency (erl/Hz/m^2)
η_t	Spectral efficiency with respect to time
Λ_{th}	CIR (C/I) at threshold for given BER or P_e
m	Bandwidth efficiency
M_f	Fade margin against allowable geographic outage due to log-normal shadowing
N	Number of cells per cluster ($N = 4, 7, 9, 13, \ldots$)
n_{cell}	Number of channels assigned to each cell (chan/cell)
N_{sub}	Number of subscribers accommodated by the system in a unit area = system capacity (sub/m^2)
n_{sys}	Number of channels assigned for total system
R	Radius of unit cell
R_c	Coding rate
S	Cell coverage area (m^2/cell)
W	Bandwidth of total system (Hz)

The overall spectral efficiency η_T ($erl/Hz \cdot \text{m}^2$) is defined by

$$\eta_T = \frac{n_{cell} a_c}{WS}. \tag{9.5.1}$$

This definition indicates that the overall spectral efficiency is given as the spatial traffic density per unit bandwidth. Assuming that every cluster of cells is composed of N cells and that the same number of channels are assigned to each cell, n_{cell} is given by

$$n_{cell} = \frac{n_{sys}}{N} \tag{9.5.2}$$

where n_{sys} (channels) is the total number of channels assigned for the system and is given by

$$n_{sys} = \frac{W}{f_s} \tag{9.5.3}$$

where f_s (Hz/channel) is the channel spacing. By substituting equations 9.5.2 and 9.5.3 into equation 9.5.1, η_T is obtained as

$$\eta_T = \frac{1}{NS} \cdot \frac{1}{f_s} \cdot a_c. \tag{9.5.4}$$

This representation means that the overall spectral efficiency η_T is given as the product of the following three factors:

$$\eta_s = \frac{1}{NS} \tag{9.5.5}$$

$$\eta_f = \frac{1}{f_s} \tag{9.5.6}$$

$$\eta_t = a_c \tag{9.5.7}$$

where η_s, η_f, and η_t are the elementary spectral efficiencies with respect to space, frequency, and time, respectively.

Capacity and Erlangs. The number of subscribers accommodated by the system, or the system capacity, is another useful measure of efficient spectrum utilization. Assuming that the geographical distribution of traffic is uniform within the service area, the system capacity is proportional to the number of subscribers in a unit area.

Erlang, the international, dimensionless unit of telephone traffic, is frequently used in capacity computations. The terms *Erlang* and *Erlang/subscriber* have been used in the honor of a Danish telephony traffic engineer, A. K. Erlang. One Erlang is defined as a circuit occupied for one hour, thus (Macario, 1993).

$$1 \text{ Erlang} = 1 \text{ call} - \text{hour} / \text{hour}.$$

Recall that the number of Erlangs per busy hour is calculated as follows (call-holding time expressed in hours):

$$\text{Erlangs} = (\text{calls} / \text{busy hour}) \times (\text{mean call-holding time}).$$

Example 9.5.1

A telephony connection has a duration of 23 minutes. This connection is maintained continuously for computer-to-computer communications at a bit rate of $f_b = 9600$ b/s. How much is the amount of traffic, in Erlangs, of this computer communications link?

Solution for Example 9.5.1

The traffic of this data communications link in Erlangs is

$$\begin{aligned}\text{Traffic} &= (1\ \text{call})(23\ \text{minutes}/1\ \text{hours}) \\ &= (1\ \text{call})(23\ \text{minutes}/60\ \text{minutes}) \\ &= 0.383\ \text{Erlangs}.\end{aligned}$$

The data rate is immaterial in the traffic computation, expressed in Erlangs. The traffic is solely based on the call duration.

Letting busy-hour traffic per subscriber and offered traffic per cell be a_{sub}(erl/sub) and a_{cell}(erl/cell), respectively, the number of subscribers in a unit area N_{sub} (sub/m^2) is given by

$$N_{sub} = \frac{a_{cell}}{a_{sub}} \cdot \frac{1}{S}. \tag{9.5.8}$$

The offered traffic per cell, a_{cell}, is related to the carried traffic per cell, $n_{cell} \cdot a_c$ by the following equation:

$$a_{cell} = \frac{n_{cell} \cdot a_c}{1 - B} \tag{9.5.9}$$

where B denotes the blocking rate of calls. Substituting equation 9.5.9 into equation 9.5.8 and using equation 9.5.1, N_{sub} can be obtained as

$$N_{sub} = \frac{W}{a_{sub}(1 - B)} \eta_T. \tag{9.5.10}$$

Since W, a_{sub}, and B are already-defined system parameters, maximizing system capacity can be reduced to the problem of maximizing η_T. This problem is considered here in detail.

9.5.2 Effective Spectral Utilization Methods

Equation 9.5.4 indicates that efficient spectrum utilization can be achieved by increasing η_s, η_f, and η_t. For this purpose, the following three methods are used, respectively: (1) high-density geographical cochannel reuse (reducing N and S); (2) narrowband transmission (reducing f_s); and (3) demand-assignment multichannel access (increasing a_c). We now consider each method in more detail.

9.5.2.1 Geographical cochannel reuse. In the case of an ideal hexagonal layout of cells, as shown in Figure 9.5.1, the number of cells, N, in a cluster of cells is given by

$$N = \frac{1}{3}\left(\frac{D}{R}\right)^2 \tag{9.5.11}$$

where R and D are the radius of a unit cell and the cochannel reuse distance, respectively. Under the assumption that both signal and interference are subjected to uncorrelated multipath fading and have a local mean proportional to the inverse αth power of the propagation distance, the ratio of (D/R) is determined from the following relationship:

$$\left(\frac{D-R}{R}\right)^{\alpha} = M_f \Lambda_{th} \tag{9.5.12}$$

where M_f and Λ_{th} denote fading margin against allowable geographical outage due to log-normal shadowing and threshold CIR for a specific P_e, respectively. Experimental field test results indicate that α equals 3 to 4 in the usual V/UHF land mobile radio environment. Using equations 9.5.11 and 9.5.12, the relationship between N and $M_f \Lambda_{th}$ is obtained as

$$N = \frac{1}{3}[1 + (M_f \Lambda_{th})^{1/\alpha}]^2 \tag{9.5.13}$$

where N takes on a discrete value of 3, 4, 7, 9, 12, 13,. . . . Reduction of N is therefore achieved by ensuring a high CCI protection by reducing Λ_{th}.

Space or polarization diversity technique, which can mitigate the multipath fading effect without transmission bandwidth expansion, is the most effective one for this purpose. Forward-error-correction (FEC) coding, which can be regarded as a certain kind of time diversity, is also effective, although it introduces some redundancy into the transmitted data stream and requires an expansion of the transmission bandwidth. Consequently, there exists an optimum coding rate with respect to the maximal spectral efficiency, which is achieved by a trade-off between high-density geographical cochannel reuse and narrowband transmission.

Moreover, it is self-evident that smaller cell layout with lower transmitter power is effective for reducing the area of a unit cell S in equation 9.5.5. However, it is necessary to place more base stations in order to make S smaller. Accordingly, the area of a unit cell S should be optimized from the system cost viewpoint.

9.5.2.2 Narrowband transmission. Provided that source coding with bit rate f_b, modulation with bandwidth efficiency m, and FEC coding with rate R_c $(0 < R_c \le 1)$ are adopted in a digital land mobile radio system, the channel spacing f_s is obtained as

$$f_s = \frac{f_b}{mR_c} + 2\Delta f \tag{9.5.14}$$

where Δf is the carrier frequency drift. To achieve narrowband transmission, or to increase η_f, low bit-rate source coding (reduction of f_b), bandwidth-efficient modulation (increase of m), high-rate FEC coding ($R_c \to 1$), and stabilized carrier-frequency sources ($\Delta f \to 0$) are required.

For efficient spectrum utilization, low bit-rate source coding that does not require a very good P_e performance is needed, since an excessively low P_e transmission requirement leads to excessively high CCI protection.

Thus, high-density geographical cochannel reuse becomes a difficult requirement. For voice coding, a number of low bit-rate (less than 32 kb/s) coding techniques, each of which requires only a moderate P_e (10^{-2} to 10^{-4}) performance to obtain high-quality telephone service, are currently being developed.

It is effective to increase the bandwidth efficiency m of the modulation technique for narrowband transmission, that is, to increase η_f. However, this requires higher CCI protection, or larger Λ_{th} in equation 9.5.11, which results in decreasing η_s. Therefore bandwidth efficiency m should be optimized to achieve a trade-off between narrowband transmission (increasing η_f) and high-density geographical cochannel reuse (increasing η_s).

To achieve narrowband transmission, it is desirable not to introduce any FEC coding (that is, to set $R_c = 1$). However, FEC coding, which can improve the P_e-versus-CIR performance or strengthen cochannel interference protection, is effective for achieving high-density geographical cochannel reuse, that is, increasing η_s at the sacrifice of transmission bandwidth. Therefore the coding rate R_c should be optimized in order to maximize the overall spectral efficiency.

Needless to say, carrier-frequency drift should be kept as small as possible in order to increase η_f. It is one of the most important and difficult problems to realize a *miniaturized, frequency-agile mobile radio transceiver* having a highly stabilized carrier-frequency source. A frequency-agile mobile radio transceiver is necessary for achieving demand-assignment multichannel access, which is effective for increasing η_f (equation 9.5.6). Phase-locked frequency synthesizers are widely used for this purpose.

9.5.2.3 Multichannel access. Demand-assignment multichannel access, which enables time-shared use of a channel and increases the traffic a_c carried by a channel, is effective for increasing η_t in equation 9.5.7. An electronic central processor using a stored-program-control scheme and a microprocessor-controlled, frequency-agile mobile radio transceiver may be used for achieving multichannel access. By an application of Erlang's B-formula (Lee, 1989), it is easy to attain $a_c = 0.7$ to 0.9 by conventional multichannel access control schemes, while its maximum limit is $a_c = 1$.

9.5.3 Optimization of Spectral Efficiency for GMSK

By substituting equations 9.5.13 and 9.5.14 into equation 9.5.4, the overall spectral efficiency η_T can be obtained as

$$\eta_T = \frac{3a_c}{S[1+(M_f\Lambda_{th})^{1/\alpha}]^2[f_b/mR_c + 2\Delta f]}. \tag{9.5.15}$$

If the carrier frequency drift and the log-normal shadowing are negligible, that is, $\Delta f = 0$ and $M_f = 1$, then η_T becomes

$$\eta_T = \frac{3a_c mR_c}{Sf_b[1+(\Lambda_{th})^{1/\alpha}]^2}. \tag{9.5.16}$$

In the following discussion, we assume that (1) $\alpha = 3.5$, (2) S, f_b, and a_c in equations 9.5.15 and 9.5.16 are constants, and (3) the premodulation Gaussian-filtered MSK (GMSK) modulation technique described in section 9.3 is used. Under these assumptions, bandwidth efficiency m is given as a function of the normalized 3-dB bandwidth BT_b of the premodulation Gaussian LPF. Moreover, the threshold CIR Λ_{th} for a specific P_e is given as a function of BT_b and R_c. Therefore the optimization problem can be reduced to the problem of obtaining BT_b and R_c to maximize η_T. Let us now consider this problem.

9.5.3.1 Relationship between bandwidth efficiency *m* and BT_b in GMSK systems. By assuming that no FEC coding is introduced and that the carrier-frequency drift can be disregarded, or $R_c = 1$ and $\Delta f = 0$, bandwidth efficiency m is derived from equation 9.5.14 as the transmission bit rate normalized by the channel spacing ($m = f_b/f_s$). In GMSK-modulated systems, m is increased by reducing BT_b, where the ACI suppression is a parameter. Figure 9.5.2 shows computed results of the relationship between m and BT_b for an ACI of –70 dB, which is a general requirement for single-channel per carrier (SCPC) land mobile radio systems. The ACI is defined as the relative power that falls into an adjacent channel having an ideal rectangular bandpass characteristic whose bandwidth equals the transmission bit rate.

9.5.3.2 Relationship between CIR threshold (Λ_{th}) and BT_b. To clarify the relationship between the required carrier-to-interference threshold Λ_{th} and BT_b, it is necessary to obtain the average P_e-versus-CIR performance of a GMSK transmission system in a multipath fading environment. To simplify our investigation, let us assume that coherent detection is used. Noise-free and interference-limited conditions are assumed. A GMSK signal is assumed to be subjected not only to ISI because of the premodulation Gaussian LPF, but also to CCI caused by geographical reuse of the same frequency while intersymbol interference (ISI) due to the predetection bandpass filter (BPF) in the re-

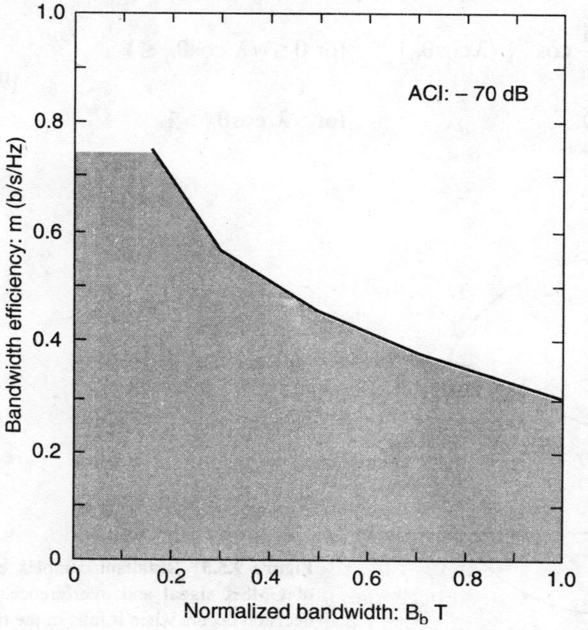

Figure 9.5.2 Relationship between m and BT_b (computed) for an ACI of –70 dB, general requirement for signal channel per carrier (SCPC) land mobile radio systems.

ceiver side is not taken into account. Under these assumptions, let us first consider the P_e versus CIR performance in a nonfading environment.

Figure 9.5.3 shows a vector diagram of the resultant complex envelope for a GMSK signal $s(t)$ and CCI $i(t)$ at a decision instant $t = 0$, where correct decision occurs when the resultant complex envelope $s(0) + i(0)$ falls onto the right half-plane. The carrier-phase difference ψ between between $s(0) = i(0)$ is a random variable with a uniform distribution. Moreover, $\theta_0 = \theta(0)$ is the modulation-phase deflection due to ISI effect of the premodulation Gaussian LPF. For the worse signal pattern, . . . , 0, 0, 0, 1, 1, 1, . . . , which is the cause of maximal ISI, the modulation phase change $\theta(t)$ is given by

$$\theta(t) = \frac{\pi}{2T}\left[\int_0^t erf(\beta\tau)d\tau + \frac{1}{\beta\sqrt{\pi}}\right] \tag{9.5.17}$$

where T is the signaling period and β is given by

$$\beta = \pi B_b\sqrt{\frac{2}{ln2}}. \tag{9.5.18}$$

Here, B_b is the 3-dB bandwidth of a premodulation Gaussian LPF. The reference phase is defined as the modulation phase change at $t = 0$ of a simple MSK, that is, $BT_b \rightarrow \infty$, without the ISI effect. By substituting $t = 0$ into equation 9.5.17, θ_0 is obtained as

$$\theta_0 = \theta(0) = \frac{\sqrt{ln2}}{2\sqrt{2\pi}B_bT}. \tag{9.5.19}$$

Letting the instantaneous CIR by λ, the probability of decision error, $P_e(\lambda)$, is obtained as

$$P_e(\lambda) = \begin{cases} \frac{1}{\pi}\cos^{-1}[\sqrt{\lambda}\cos\theta_0] & \text{for } 0 \le \sqrt{\lambda}\cos\theta_0 \le 1 \\ 0 & \text{for } \sqrt{\lambda}\cos\theta_0 > 1. \end{cases} \tag{9.5.20}$$

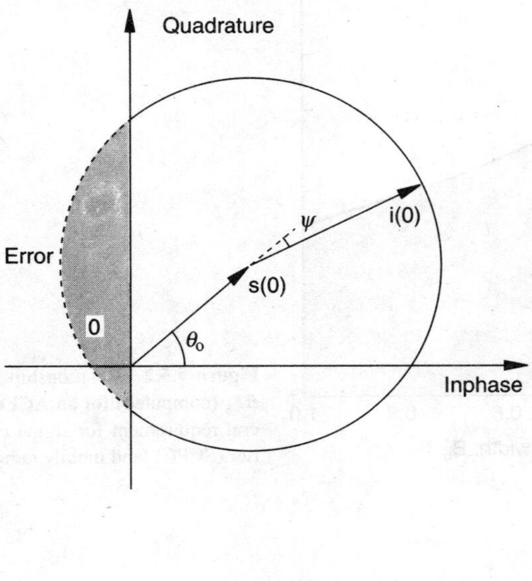

Figure 9.5.3 Resultant complex envelope of GMSK signal and interference. Correct decision occurs when it falls in the right half plane. ψ is a random variable.

Averaging $P_e(\lambda)$ over the fading dynamic range of λ, the average P_e-versus-CIR performance in the quasistatic multipath fading environment is obtained is

$$P_e(\Lambda) = \int_0^{\infty} P_e(\lambda)p(\lambda)d\lambda \tag{9.5.21}$$

where Λ and $p(\lambda)$ are the average CIR and the pdf of λ, respectively. Assuming that both the desired GMSK signal and the undesired CCI are subjected to mutually independent quasistatic Rayleigh fadings and that an ideal two-branch diversity technique that has a perfect-pilot, maximal-ratio combining method in the predetection stage is adopted, $p(\lambda)$ may be derived as

$$p(\lambda) = \begin{cases} \dfrac{\Lambda}{(\lambda+\Lambda)^2} & \text{for no diversity} \\ \dfrac{\lambda\Lambda}{(\lambda+\Lambda)^3} & \text{for diversity.} \end{cases} \tag{9.5.22}$$

By substituting equations 9.5.19, 9.5.20, and 9.5.22 into equation 9.5.21, $P_e(\Lambda)$, the P_e as a function of Λ = CIR for GMSK systems, is obtained as

$$P_e(\Lambda) = \begin{cases} \dfrac{1}{2}\left[1 - \sqrt{\dfrac{\Lambda \cos^2\theta_0}{\Lambda \cos^2\theta_0 + 1}} \approx \dfrac{1}{4\Lambda\cos^2\theta_0}\right] & \text{for no diversity} \\ \dfrac{1}{2}\left[1 - \dfrac{3}{2}\sqrt{\dfrac{\Lambda \cos^2\theta_0}{\Lambda \cos^2\theta_0 + 1}} + \dfrac{1}{2}\sqrt{\dfrac{(\Lambda\cos^2\theta_0)^3}{(\Lambda\cos^2\theta_0+1)^3}}\right] \approx \dfrac{3}{16\Lambda^2\cos^4\theta_0} & \text{for diversity.} \end{cases} \tag{9.5.23}$$

For the particular case of $\theta_0 = 0$, and $BT_b \to \infty$, the derived results for GMSK correspond to MSK.

The threshold CIR, Λ_{th}, for a specific P_{es} can be obtained in the following approximate form:

$$\Lambda_{th} \cong \begin{cases} \dfrac{1}{4P_{es}\cos^2\theta_0} & \text{for no diversity} \\ \dfrac{\sqrt{3}}{4\sqrt{P_{es}}\cos^2\theta_0} & \text{for diversity.} \end{cases} \tag{9.5.24}$$

Since θ_0 is given by equation 9.5.19 as a function of BT_b, the relationship between Λ_{th} and BT_b is shown in Figure 9.5.4.

9.5.3.3 Relationship between carrier-to-interference threshold, Λ_{th}, and coding rate of FEC codecs, R_c. Now, let us assume that a self-orthogonal convolutional FEC coding technique with a two-bit error-correction capability is used along with some auxiliary technique to randomize long burst errors caused by deep fading. Improvement of the average P_e versus-CIR performance can be approximated as follows:

$$P_e(\Lambda, R_c) \approx c(R_c)P_e^3(\Lambda) \tag{9.5.25}$$

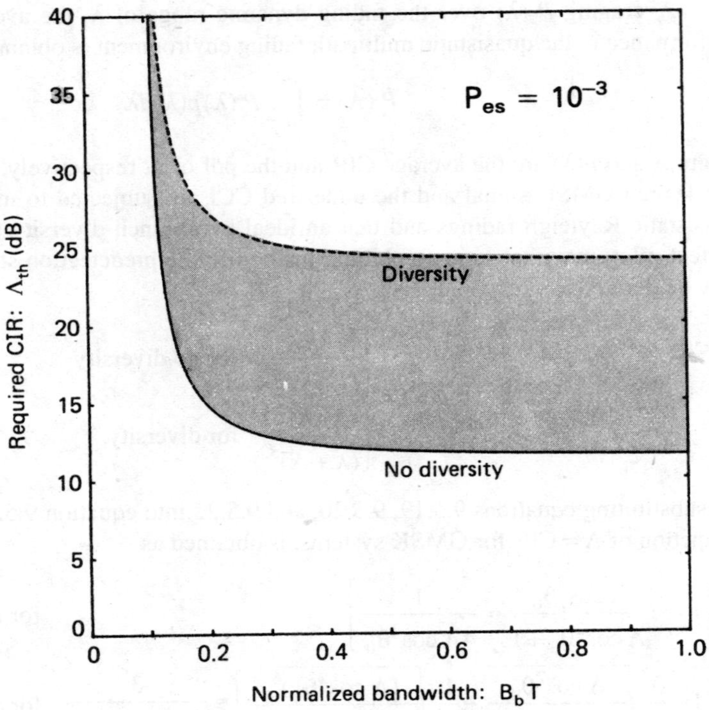

Figure 9.5.4 Relationship between Λ_{th} and BT_b for $P_{es} = 10^{-3}$, for GMSK and FQPSK in a quasistatic Rayleigh-faded environment.

where $P_e(\Lambda)$ is given by equation 9.5.23 and $c(R_c)$ is an approximation constant dependent on R_c and is listed in Table 9.5.1. By using equations 9.5.23 and 9.5.25, the threshold CIR Λ_{th} for a specific P_{es} can be obtained as

$$\Lambda_{th} = \begin{cases} \dfrac{\{c(R_c)\}^{1/3}}{4(P_{es})^{1/3}\cos^2\theta_0} & \text{for no diversity} \\ \\ \dfrac{\sqrt{3}\{c(R_c)\}^{1/6}}{4(P_{es})^{1/6}\cos^2\theta_0} & \text{for diversity.} \end{cases} \tag{9.5.26}$$

The relationship between Λ_{th} and R_c can therefore be obtained as shown in Figure 9.5.5, where $BT_b = 0.25$, which will be demonstrated later to be near optimum.

9.5.3.4 Optimization of BT_b and FEC coding rate, R_c, of GMSK systems. Let us first consider a simple case without FEC coding, that is, $R_c = 1$. The relationship of η_T versus BT_b for $P_{es} = 10^{-3}$ and $\alpha = 3.5$ is shown in Figure 9.5.6, which has

Table 9.5.1 Approximation constant $c(R_c)$ for self-orthogonal convolutional codes.

R_c	$c(R_c)$
$\frac{1}{2}$	151
$\frac{2}{3}$	807
$\frac{3}{4}$	2227
$\frac{5}{6}$	8192
$\frac{6}{7}$	14,000

been obtained by substituting the calculated results of m shown in Figure 9.5.2 and equation 9.5.24 into equation 9.5.16. The ordinate of this figure is normalized by the value of η_T for the simple MSK ($BT_b \to \infty$) without diversity. This figure shows that $BT_b = 0.25$ is a near-optimum value in the sense of maximizing the spectral efficiency. An optimum channel spacing for a specific transmission bit rate is usually determined from this opti-

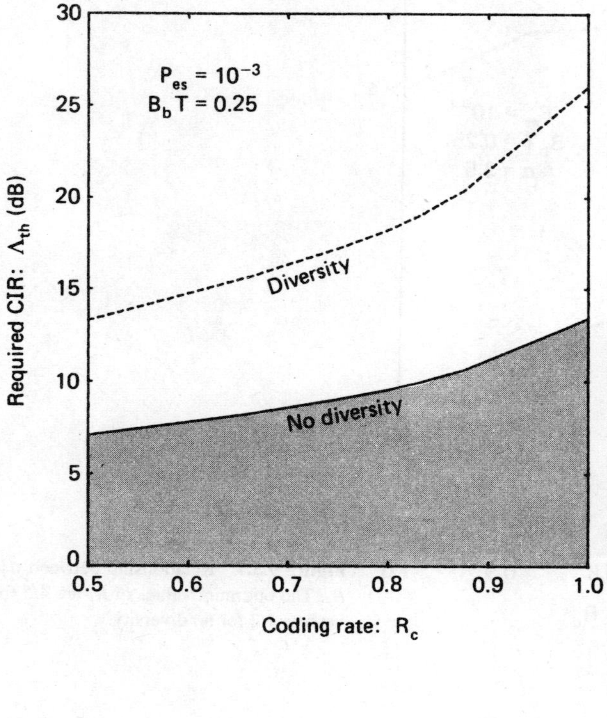

Figure 9.5.5 Relationship between Λ_{th} and R_c for $P_{es} = 10^{-3}$. A self-orthogonal, convolutional FEC coding technique with a two-bit correction capability is assumed.

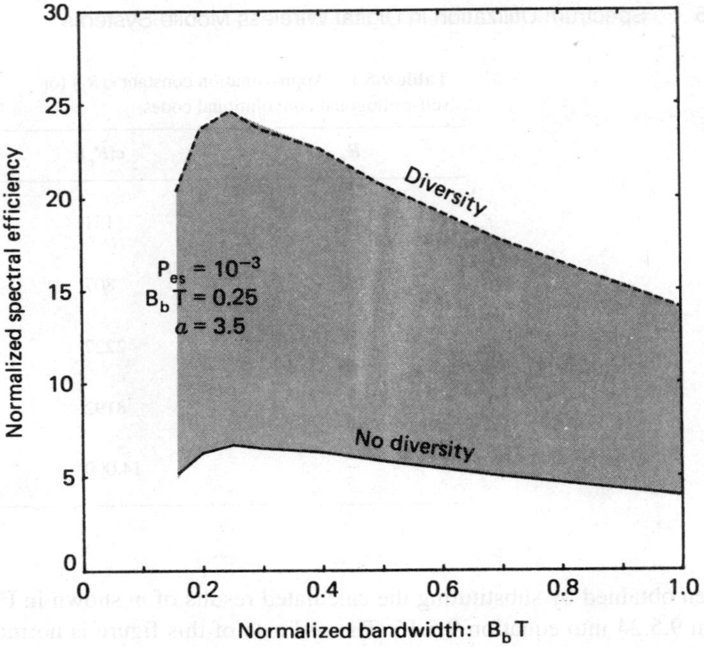

Figure 9.5.6 Relationship between η_T and BT_b. η_T has been normalized by the value of η_T for simple MSK without diversity.

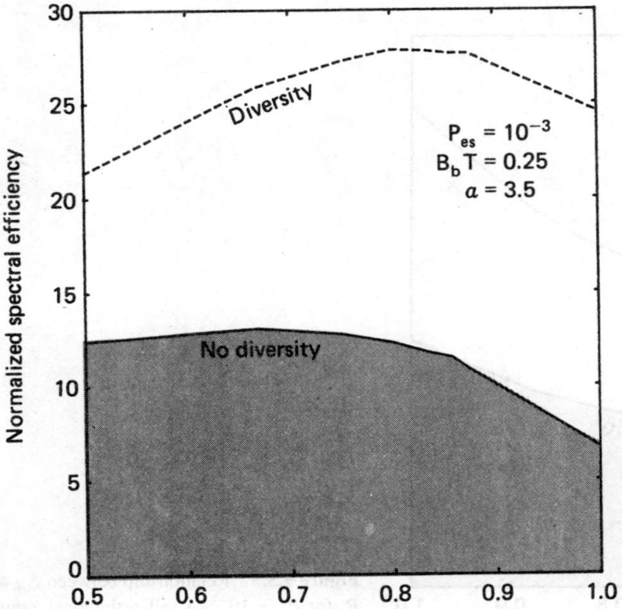

Figure 9.5.7 Relationship between η_T and R_c. The optimum values of R_c are 4/5 for diversity, 1/2 for no diversity.

mum BT_b by using the parameter m (shown in Figure 9.5.2). However, the channel spacing may have to be determined before hand by some other reasons. In such cases an optimum transmission bit rate is determined.

Example 9.5.2

When channels are assigned every 25 kHz, a transmission bit rate of f_b = 16 kb/s can be determined as near optimum with BT_b = 0.25, where the ACI is suppressed as much as −70 dB.

Solution of Example 9.5.2

Let us then solve an optimum value of R_c for the FEC coding. The dependency of η_T upon R_c for $BT_b = 0.25$, $P_{es} = 10^{-3}$, and $\alpha = 3.5$ is shown in Figure 9.5.7, which has been obtained by substituting m = 16/25 = 0.64 for BT_b = 0.25 and equation 9.5.26 into equation 9.5.16. The ordinate of this figure is normalized by the value of η_T for R_c = 1 without diversity. Optimum values of R_c are those at which η_T attains a local maximum: R_c = 4/5 for diversity and R_c = 1/2 for no diversity, approximately.

9.6 CAPACITY AND THROUGHPUT (MESSAGE DELAY) STUDY AND COMPARISON OF GMSK, GFSK, AND FQPSK MODULATED WIRELESS SYSTEMS

In this section we demonstrate that in typical cellular networks, including voice and data PCS applications, coherent systems have a 30% to 100% advantage in capacity and/or throughput over noncoherent systems. The basic advantage of coherent systems is demonstrated in a CCI-limited, k = 7 reuse (cluster) cellular configuration. Their noncoherent (GMSK and/or FQPSK) counterparts would require a k = 9 (minimum) frequency reuse, and thus a loss in available channels of 9/7 = 1.3 or 30%.

The significant ACI-1 advantage of FQPSK (narrow lobe, with −20 dB ACI-1) enables a 1.35 b/s/Hz efficiency with k = 7, while the GMSK BT_b = 0.5 system has a 1.04 b/s/Hz. For this reason, coherent FQPSK has a 30% higher spectral efficiency than coherent G-MSK. Thus coherent FQPSK has an approximately 60% higher capacity potential than noncoherent GMSK.

These are some of the most conservative estimates. With a second method using estimated automatic repeat query (ARQ) overhead requirements, we demonstrate that coherent FQPSK has even greater advantages, in the order of 100% to 200%, over noncoherent GMSK.

9.6.1 Impact of ACI and CCI Cellular Capacity and Performance

In this section we propose uniform ACI (integrated ACI) criteria and specifications for cellular PCS systems. Systems such as Digital European Cordless Telephone (DECT), GSM, IS-54 (U.S. digital cellular), and Japan's digital cellular all have different criteria. We could not find in the readily available literature the criteria and principles for the specifications of the first ACI, second ACI, and so forth. For this reason, we hope that this section will provide, through illustrative examples, some clarification on this critical cellular engineering issue. For definitions and illustrations of ACI, refer to to Figures 9.6.1 through 9.6.3.

We demonstrate that for a $k = 7$ omnicell reuse pattern, having a CCI or $I_c = -15$ dB (due to D/R = 4.6 reuse), the first ACI (integrated) should be in the −20 dB to −26 dB

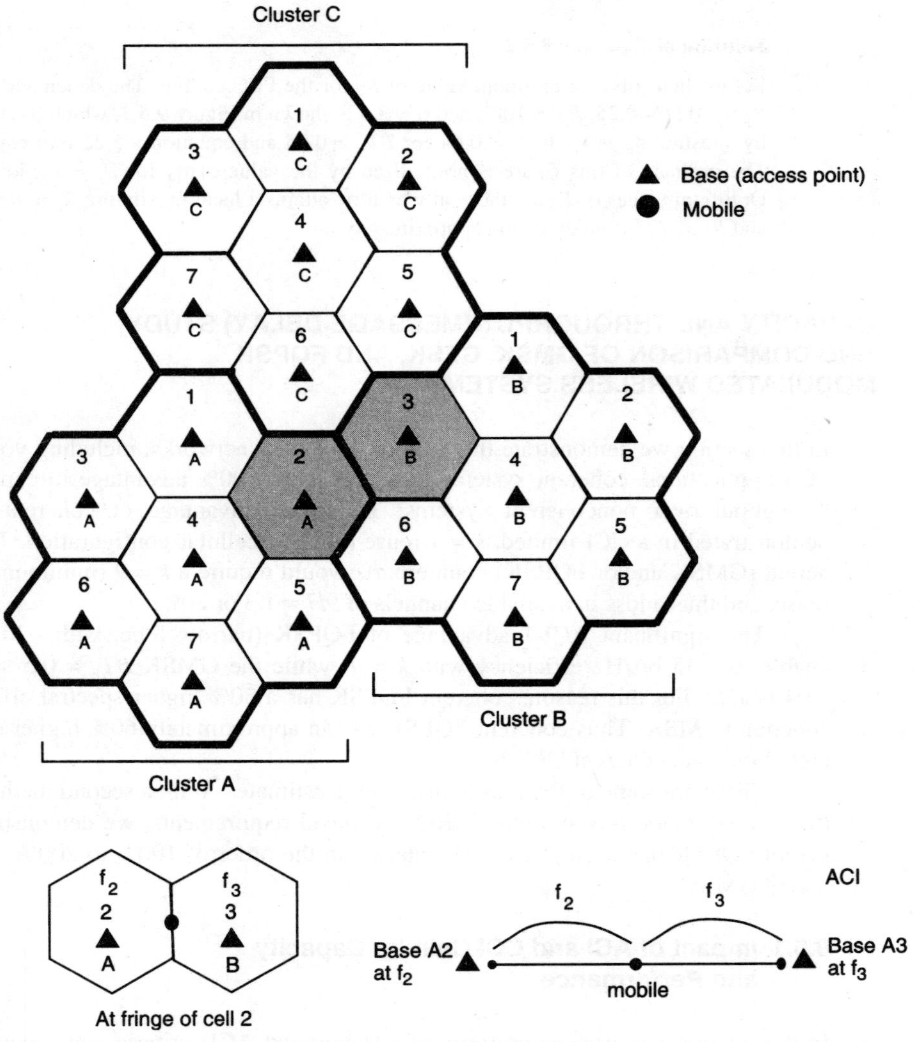

Figure 9.6.1 Impact of ACI on CCI from first neighboring cells. Assume first ACI is used in cells A2 and B3, designated ACI-1. N = 1 . . . 7 base station numbers within a cluster of 7 cells (reuse pattern) having center frequencies $f_1, f_2 \ldots f_7$. Clusters A, B and C are illustrated.

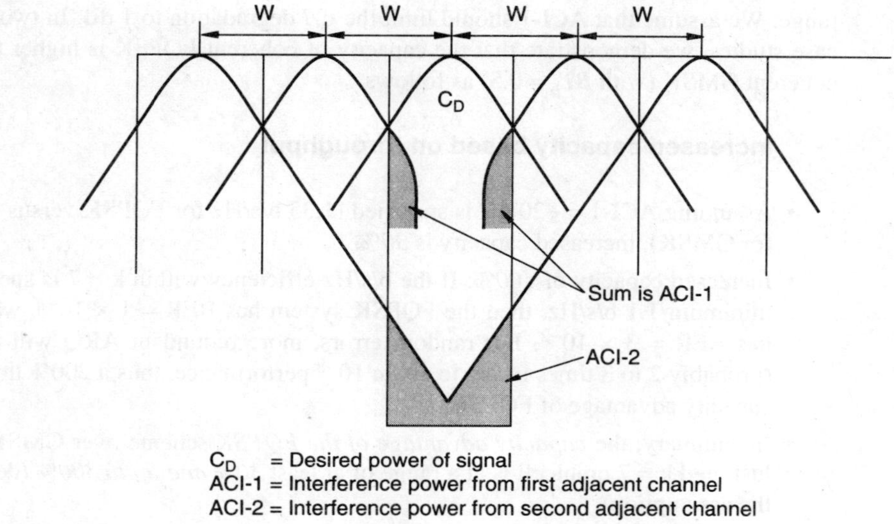

Figure 9.6.2 Illustration of the interference that adjacent channels introduce into a given channel.

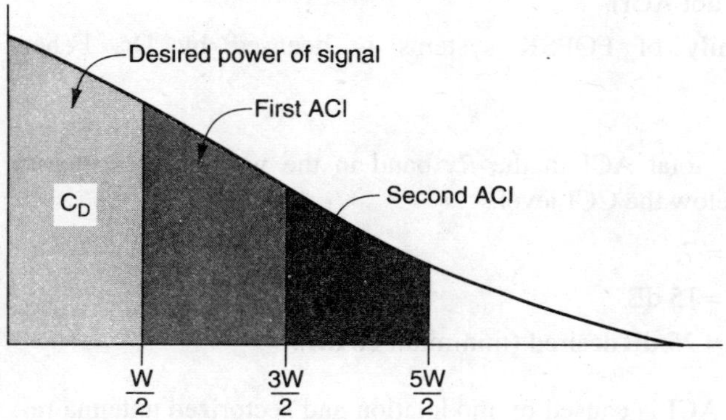

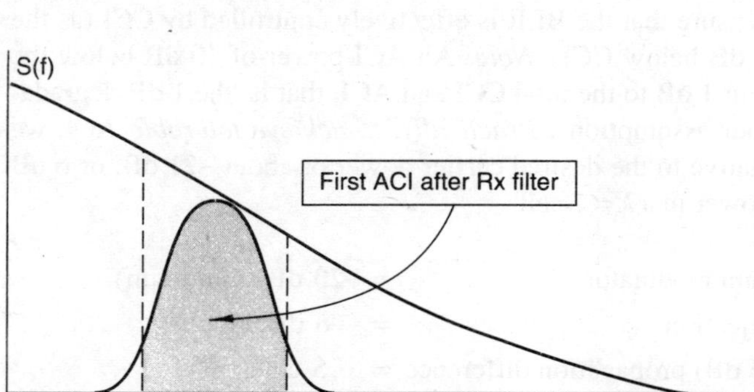

Figure 9.6.3 Illustration of the interference that an individual channel causes in adjacent channels. We define ACI-1 as the integrated interference power in the first adjacent channel, after the Rx filter.

range. We assume that ACI-1 should limit the *C/I* degradation to 1 dB. In two illustrative case studies, we demonstrate that the capacity of coherent FQPSK is higher than that of coherent GMSK (with $BT_b = 0.5$) as follows.

Increased capacity based on throughput

- Assuming ACI-1 = –20 dB is specified (1.35 b/s/Hz for FQPSK versus 1.04 b/s/Hz for GMSK), increased capacity is *30%*.
- Increased capacity of *100%*: If the b/s/Hz efficiency within k = 7 is specified to be minimum 1.1 b/s/Hz, then the FQPSK system has BER = 1×10^{-2}, while GMSK has BER = 3×10^{-2}. For random errors, more redundant ARQ will be required (probably 2 to 3 times more) to attain 10^{-8} performance, thus a 200% throughput or capacity advantage of FQPSK.
- In summary, the *capacity advantage of the FQPSK* scheme over GMSK for the illustrated k = 7 omnicell is at a range of at least *30% and up to 300%* (depending on the assumption).
- The most conservative capacity advantage (minimum 30% increased capacity) is based on specified ACI. The more optimistic capacity advantage (100% plus) is based on specified b/s/Hz (not ACI).
- *Note:* The patented family of FQPSK systems is licensed by Dr. Feher Associates–Digcom, Inc.

Design guideline The total ACI in the *Rx* band in the worst-case scenario should be about 5 dB to 10 dB below the CCI level:

For k = 7,

C/I_c = 15 dB

$C/I_{ACI_{TOT}}$ = 25 dB desired (minimum 20 dB).

The ACI_{TOT} assumes that ACI is caused by modulation and sectorized antenna reduction. This scenario would ensure that the BER is effectively controlled by CCI (as the ACI total is about 5 dB to 10 dB below CCI). *Note:* An ACI power of 10 dB below the CCI power will contribute about 1 dB to the total CCI and ACI, that is, the 1 dB degradation permitted previously in our assumptions. *Practically, to achieve tolerable* ACI, we should have an ACI power relative to the desired carrier power of about –21 dB, or 6 dB less than the CCI = –15 dBr power in a $k = 7$ cell.

Integrated ACI-1 (from modulator)	= –20 dB (minimum)
Sectorized antenna rejection	= –6 dB
Increased ACI (σ = 5 dB) propagation difference	= 5 dB
Total ACI - 1	= –21 dB

Hence, the total interference is as follows:

From ACI - 1,* $\dfrac{C}{\mathrm{ACI}_{TOT}} = 21\text{ dB}$

$k = 7$ cluster C/I, $\dfrac{C}{\mathrm{CCI}} = 15\text{ dB}$

$$\frac{C}{I_{TOT}} = \frac{C}{\mathrm{ACI\text{-}1}} + \frac{C}{\mathrm{CCI}} = \underline{\underline{14\text{ dB}}},$$

as next explained. Assuming unmodulated carrier power $C = 0$ dB, then

$$\frac{C}{I_{TOT}} = \frac{C}{\mathrm{ACI\text{-}1} + CCI} \approx 14\text{ dB}.$$

To obtain the result of 14 dB, remember to convert from dB to linear units. Assumptions:

$k = 7$ reuse (cluster)

omnidirectional antenna

$C/I_c = 15$ dB due to $q = D/R = 4.6$.

ACI is caused by the closest cell in the first adjacent cluster, see Figure 9.6.1. The mobile unit is at the cell fringe, equidistant from Base No. 2 in Cluster A and from Base No. 3 in Cluster B. We assume that the total ACI ending up in the desired receiver bandwidth is 20 dB below the received carrier level, C.

This ACI-1 = −20 dB (maximum) is assumed to meet the BER = 10^{-2} specification of a typical system

$$\frac{C}{ACI-1} = 20\text{ dB}.$$

Total in-band interference (ACI-1 + CCI)

$$C/I_{TOT} = C/(ACI-1+CCI)$$
$$= (20\text{ dB}) + (15\text{ dB})$$
$$C/I_{TOT} = 13.8\text{ dB} \approx \underline{\underline{14\text{ dB}}}.$$

The assumed ACI-1 = −20 dB could be achieved with FQPSK or GMSK having the spectral efficiencies and resultant BER (caused by C/I_{TOT}), as shown in Tables 9.6.1 to 9.6.3. In conclusion, for the same BER (practically), the FQPSK system will have a spectral efficiency of 1.35 b/s/Hz, compared with GMSK having 1.04 b/s/Hz. Thus capacity advantage of FQPSK is 30% over coherent GMSK. FQPSK also has a somewhat better BER performance.

*ACI-2 is calculable by the same method, that is, limited ACI-caused degradation.

Table 9.6.1 Spectral efficiency η in b/s/Hz. *Note:* FQPSK-1 is 51% more efficient than GMSK (at 20 dB).

	ACI = –15 dB	ACI = –20 dB	ACI = –26 dB	ACI = –30 dB
FQPSK-1	1.63 (147%)	1.42 (151%)	1.23 (156%)	1.10 (155%)
GMSK BT = 0.3	1.16 (105%)	0.98 (104%)	0.83 (105%)	0.74 (104%)
GMSK BT = 0.5	1.11 (100%)	0.94 (100%)	0.79 (100%)	0.71 (100%)

(From Feher, 1993c.)

Table 9.6.2 Capacity (geographic spectral efficiency) comparison of FQPSK-1 and noncoherent GMSK as in DECT.

	ηf	λ for $P_e = 10^{-2}$	K	ηT
FQPSK-1	1.42	15.7 dB	7	0.203 (195%)
GMSK BT = 0.5	0.94	18.2 dB	9	0.104 (100%)

Table 9.6.3 Capacity comparison of FQPSK-1 and coherent GMSK as in DCS1800.

	ηf	λ for $P_e = 10^{-2}$	K	ηT
FQPSK-1	1.42	15.7 dB	7	0.203 (186%)
GMSK BT = 0.3	0.98	16.7 dB	9	0.109 (100%)

Table 9.6.4 Capacity improvement of FQPSK-1 over GMSK as in the current PCS standards DECT and PCS1800.

	DECT	PCS-1800
FQPSK-1	195%	186%
GMSK	100%	100%

Table 9.6.5 Comparison between FQPSK-1 and π/4-DQPSK.

	Power efficiency	Capacity (12)
FQPSK-1	0 dBr	100%
π/4-DQPSK	–6 to –8 dBr	100%

(From Feher, 1993c.)

9.6.2 How Much Should the ACI Specification Be?

Assume that ACI is not specified. We wish to design for a minimum specified spectral efficiency within a $k = 7$ frequency reuse factor cluster. From simulated results, some of which are shown in Tables 9.6.1 to 9.6.5, we have the following ACI-1 values:

Spectral Efficiency	**1.1 b/s/Hz**	**1.35 b/s/Hz**
FQPSK-1	−26 dB	−20 dB
GMSK ($BT_b = 0.5$)	−17 dB	−15 dB

In the calculations we assumed the use of the simplest FQPSK-1 patented technique. More advanced FQPSK techniques licensed by Dr. Feher Associates have additional advantages.

With ACI-1 from the neighbor cluster having the same power, C, as desired carrier, we have that $C/I_c = 15$ dB. The following are some additional C/I_{TOT} calculations for various values of ACI.

$$\begin{aligned} C/I_{TOT} &= (-15 \text{ dB}) + (-15 \text{ dB}) = 12 \text{ dB} \\ &= (-15 \text{ dB}) + (-17 \text{ dB}) = 13 \text{ dB} \\ &= (-15 \text{ dB}) + (-20 \text{ dB}) = 14 \text{ dB} \\ &= (-15 \text{ dB}) + (-16 \text{ dB}) = 15 \text{ dB} \end{aligned}$$

With this assumed C/I_{TOT}, the following bit-error rates can be calculated. BER of unprotected (nondiversity) signaling:

$\frac{C}{I_{TOT}}$	**BER, FQPSK**	**BER, GMSK**
12 dB	4×10^{-2}	3×10^{-2}
13 dB	2×10^{-2}	3×10^{-2}
15 dB	10^{-2}	1.5×10^{-2}

Thus because ACI = −15 dB, the C/I_{TOT} is only 12 dB, and the raw BER increased from 10^{-2} to 4×10^{-2}.

9.6.3 Capacity Advantage of Coherent Versus Noncoherent Systems

We now consider two realistic scenarios in which the higher transmission capacity of a coherently demodulated scheme, such as FQPSK, over a noncoherent scheme, such as GMSK, makes itself apparent. Assumptions include the following:

Omnidirectional antenna NLOS propagation, with propagation constant $\alpha = 4$ (the CCI is lower from $\alpha = 3.5$) and Rayleigh fading q = D/R = 4.6 reuse factor

CCI = 15 dB (approximately 90% coverage)

Method 1. Assume that a worst-case (threshold) BER of unprotected, raw data is specified as 10^{-2}. Then,

$$\text{for } k = 7, C/I = 15 \text{ dB};$$
$$\text{for } k = 9, C/I = 19 \text{ dB};$$
$$\text{for } k = 12, C/I = 23 \text{ dB}.$$

From our previous discussion and from Table 9.6.2, the minimum *C/I* required for BER = 10^{-2} is 15 dB for coherent FQPSK, as compared with 18 dB for noncoherent GMSK. Now, the noncoherent system requires a BPF (compared with the LPF of coherent systems). Since the "steepness" factor of an IF or RF filter is not as large as that of a baseband filter, the ACI of a noncoherent receiver is much larger than the ACI of a coherent receiver with the same b/s/Hz efficiency. Also assume there is 1 to 2 dB of additional degradation because of the imperfect BPF-noise bandwidth. Taking this practical BPF-caused degradation into account, the GMSK noncoherent modem will require a *C/I* = 19 to 20 dB. The coherent, $k = 7$ systems could have equivalent or even better BER than the less efficient, noncoherent system with $k = 9$. While $k = 7$ reuse is sufficient for the previously mentioned coherent system, it is not sufficient for the noncoherent system; for the latter we will have to use a larger number of clusters, raising k to 9. Since 9/7 = 1.28, the *capacity loss* of the noncoherent system, compared with the coherent system, is *≈30%*, just based on the increased sensitivity to CCI.

Method 2. A cell reuse with $k = 7$ is specified and the *C/I* is given as 15 dB. In this case, we have the following BERs:

	Coherent FQPSK	Noncoherent GMSK
BER	10^{-2}	3×10^{-2} (or worse)

To obtain BER = 10^{-8}, a powerful automatic repeat request (ARQ) or FEC technique would be required with a combined redundancy in the 500% range, while for the noncoherent system the redundancy could be 1000% or more (since improving the BER from 3×10^{-2} to 10^{-8} is much more difficult than from 1×10^{-2} to 10^{-8}). In this case, the *capacity throughput advantage of the coherent system over the noncoherent system is 100%.*

9.6.4 Capacity and Spectral Efficiency Comparison of GMSK, GFSK, and FQPSK-1 Wireless Systems

In this section we study the overall geographic spectral efficiency of constant envelope methods, particularly those of GMSK, GFSK, and FQPSK. The spectral efficiency is directly proportional to capacity. Therefore we use both terms in comparisons of system efficiency. We study these frequently used digital radio transmission methods, based on the theoretical concepts presented in sections 9.4 through 9.6. A brief review and the computed results are presented next.

In microcellular PCS and WLAN systems, frequencies are reused in geographically separate cells to achieve greater network capacity. In this environment we need to include the frequency reuse factor K when comparing modulations. Overall spectral efficiency η_T (in b/s/Hz/m^2) of a modulated system in a cellular environment is given by:

$$\eta_T = \eta_f \times \frac{1}{K} \times \frac{1}{S} \qquad (9.6.1)$$

where η_f is the modulation's spectral efficiency with respect to frequency (in b/s/Hz) and S is the coverage area of a cell (m^2). The frequency reuse factor K (cells per cluster) is an integer

$$K = \frac{1}{3}\left[1 + (M_f \lambda)^{1/\alpha}\right]^2 \qquad (9.6.2)$$

where λ is the C/I ratio required for a given BER performance, α is the propagation constant whose value ranges between 2 and 4, and M_f is the C/I margin. $K = 1, 3, 7, 9, 12,$ and so forth. (See Chapter 3 and section 9.5.)

In this analysis, we assume the following:

1. A BER of 10^{-2} for acceptable quality voice and/or raw data in a Rayleigh-faded environment (at threshold)
2. $\alpha = 3.5$
3. A fade margin of $M_f = 3$ dB

This margin corresponds to a geographical outage probability of approximately 10%. Furthermore, without loss of generality, we let $S = 1\ m^2$. The total spectral efficiency η_T of the proposed FQPSK-1 scheme and GMSK in a microcellular mobile PCS environment is compared in Tables 9.6.1 and 9.6.2. This comparison serves as an indicator of the system capacity. Table 9.6.2 shows that the combined spectral efficiency η_f of FQPSK and its CCI advantage over the noncoherent GMSK BT = 0.5 leads to a 95% increase of the overall spectral efficiency η_T in a cellular mobile environment. This fact indicates that our proposed FQPSK-1 modem radio solution can nearly double (95% increase) the capacity of DECT. Likewise, Table 9.6.3 shows that FQPSK-1 can improve the capacity of the current PCS standard DCS-1800 by 86%. The advantages of FQPSK-1 are further summarized in Tables 9.6.4 and 9.6.5.*

*More advanced variations of FQPSK have been licensed by Dr. Feher and Associates to wireless radio, infrared (IR) wireless LAN, and digital cable TV-telephone users. The advanced versions of FQPSK and FBPSK have been developed by members of the FQPSK worldwide consortium. See Appendix A.3.

9.7 TIME DIVISION MULTIPLE ACCESS WIRELESS CELLULAR SYSTEMS

An alternative to frequency division multiple access (FDMA) (Figure 9.2.1) is the time division multiple access (TDMA) technique. In TDMA, each user has access to the whole authorized radio frequency (RF) band for a short time to transmit a preamble and a traffic burst. During the allocated burst time the unit transmits the data much faster than the source information rate of the user. All users share the authorized frequency spectrum with all other users who have time slot-burst allocations at other preassigned times.

If the available spectrum is only partially allocated to a particular user group, this access method is known as *narrowband TDMA* (Figure 9.7.1). If all of the authorized spectrum is allocated to each user during the users time slot (burst duration), the system is known as a *wideband TDMA*. In this case each user has to transmit data at a very high rate, as the time slots have very short durations. Many users access the same RF spectrum, so each user is assigned a short time slot. An indication of the number of users per group and frame length can be ascertained from Table 9.7.1 (Macario, 1993).

In Figure 9.7.2, N_f channels per frame are shown. The convention is to start with number 0. Each user's time slot is made up of the following parts:

Header message, which contains carrier recovery, bit timing recovery, unique words, and channel identity

Control and signaling (C and S)

Traffic, which is the message part to the subscriber; typically, it would be encoded

Guard space (G) to allow for time-distance delay, because of cell size

From Figure 9.7.2 it can be seen that many bits within a frame of a TDMA system are taken up with what is called "identification and authentication." The overall bit rate allocated to

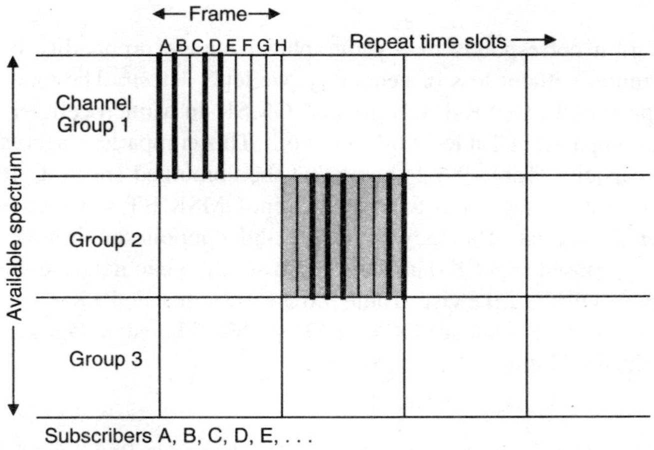

Figure 9.7.1 The TDMA mode of operation. Each channel group of eight subscribers (A . . . H) sends and receives messages as bursts. The number of base-station transmitters is equal to the number of groups. (From Macario 1993.)

Table 9.7.1 FDMA to TDMA changes. In this table, we assume 10 MHz of spectrum available for each service in a frequency division duplex mode.

System	TACS	ADC	GSM
Multiple access	**FDMA**	**TDMA**	**TDMA**
Channels per carrier	1	3	8
Carrier spacing (kHz)	25	30	200
Number of carriers	400	333	50
Number of channels	400	999	400
Frame period (ms)	No limit	40	4.6
Channel data rate (kb/s)	10	48	270

(From Macario, 1990.)

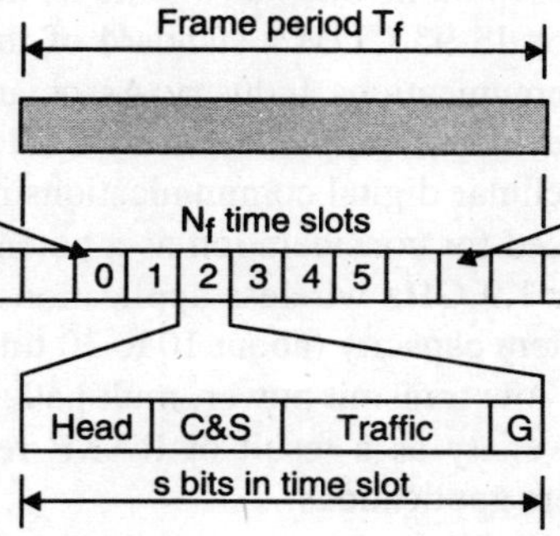

Figure 9.7.2 The frame, time slot, and message relationship in TDMA. The header message and control and signal (C&S) portions contain transmission overhead. *Traffic* is the actual message and is followed by guard space to allow for propagation delays. (From Macario, 1993.)

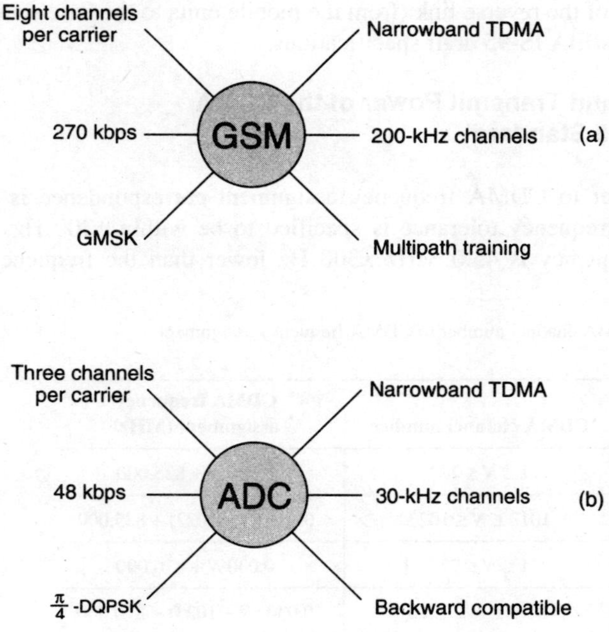

Figure 9.7.3 Features of narrowband TDMA digital cellular radio, (a) refers to the GSM standard also known as Group Speciale Mobile or Global Mobile System Standard, (b) refers to American Digital Cellular (ADC), also known as IS-54 Standard (From Macario, 1993).

each user is only a percentage of that available in a single-person-per-carrier scheme, such as in FDMA. On the other hand, no channels are uniquely allocated as control channels.

A brief overview of critical features of two well-documented narrowband systems, GSM and ADC, is illustrated in Figure 9.7.3. The features of the JDC ADC systems are quite similar.

9.8 CODE DIVISION MULTIPLE ACCESS SPREAD-SPECTRUM DIGITAL CELLULAR IS-95 SYSTEM

Code division multiple access (CDMA) spread-spectrum (SS) system and implementation concepts and techniques are presented in Chapter 6. One of the most advanced and best-documented CDMA standards is IS-95 CDMA standard of the Electronic Industry Association (EIA) and the Telecommunications Industry Association (TIA) (EIA/TIA, 1993). The system and equipment development, pioneered by Qualcomm, Inc., led to the adoption of the IS-95 standard for cellular digital communications in the "900 MHz" frequency band, and it has been proposed for consideration as a potential personal communications system (PCS) standard for 1.9 GHz wireless applications. Some of the unique features of CDMA, such as high system capacity (about 10 to 30 times higher than that of the analog standard AMPS system), low transmit power, multipath mitigation, soft handoff, uniform coverage, and path diversity as a result of RAKE receiver, make CDMA suitable for new generations of system applications.

In the following section we highlight important features of the IS-95 standard CDMA system, particularly of the reverse link (from the mobile units to the base station). The material is based on TIA/EIA IS-95 draft specifications.

9.8.1 Radio Frequency and Transmit Power of the CDMA Reverse Link (IS-95 Standard)

The CDMA channel number to CDMA frequency assignment correspondence is specified in Table 9.8.1. The frequency tolerance is specified to be within ±300 Hz. The mobile station transmit frequency is 45.0 MHz ±300 Hz lower than the frequency of

Table 9.8.1 CDMA channel number to CDMA frequency assignment correspondence.

Transmitter	CDMA channel number	CDMA frequency assignment (MHz)
Mobile station	$1 \leq N \leq 777$	$0.030\,N + 825.000$
	$1013 \leq N \leq 1023$	$0.030\,(N - 1023) + 825.000$
Base station	$1 \leq N \leq 777$	$0.030\,N + 870.000$
	$1013 \leq N \leq 1023$	$0.030\,(N - 1023) + 870.000$

(From EIA, 1990.)

Table 9.8.2 Effective radiated power at maximum output power.

Mobile station class	ERP at maximum output shall not exceed	ERP at maximum output shall not exceed
I	1 dBW (1.25 Watts)	8 dBW (6.3 Watts)
II	−3 dBW (0.5 Watts)	4 dBW (2.5 Watts)
III	−7 dBW (0.2 Watts)	0 dBW (1.0 Watts)

the base station transmit signal as measured at the mobile station receiver (EIA/TIA, 1993).

All power levels are referenced to the mobile station antenna connector unless otherwise specified. The absolute maximum effective radiated power (ERP) with respect to a half-wave dipole for any class of mobile station transmitter shall be 8 dBW (6.4 W). Effective radiated power measured during a transmitted power control group for each mobile station class when commanded to maximum output power shall be within the limits given in Table 9.8.2.

9.8.2 CDMA Reverse Link Orthogonal Modulation and Quadrature Spreading

The reverse CDMA channel is composed of access channels and reverse traffic channels. These channels share the same CDMA frequency assignment using direct-sequence CDMA techniques. In Figure 9.8.1 an example is given of all of the signals received by a base station on the reverse CDMA channel. Each traffic channel or access channel is identified by a long, distinct user code. Multiple reverse CDMA channels may be used by a base station in a frequency-multiplexed manner.

The modulation process for the reverse CDMA channel is as shown in Figure 9.8.2. Data transmitted on the reverse CDMA channel is grouped into 20-ms frames. All data transmitted on the reverse CDMA channel is convolutionally encoded, block-interleaved, modulated by means of 64-ary orthogonal modulation, and direct-sequence spread prior to transmission. Data frames may be transmitted on the reverse CDMA channel at a data rate of 9600, 4800, 2400, or 1200 b/s. The reverse traffic channel may use any of these data rates for transmission. The transmission duty cycle on the reverse traffic channel

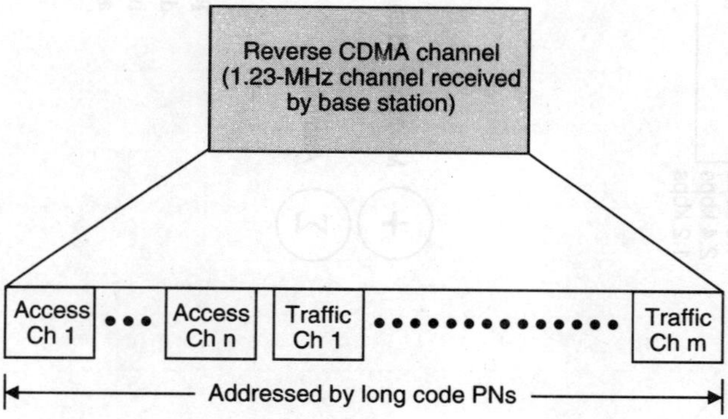

Figure 9.8.1 Example of logical reverse CDMA channels received at a base station. [EIA/TIA-IS-95, Draft Standard].

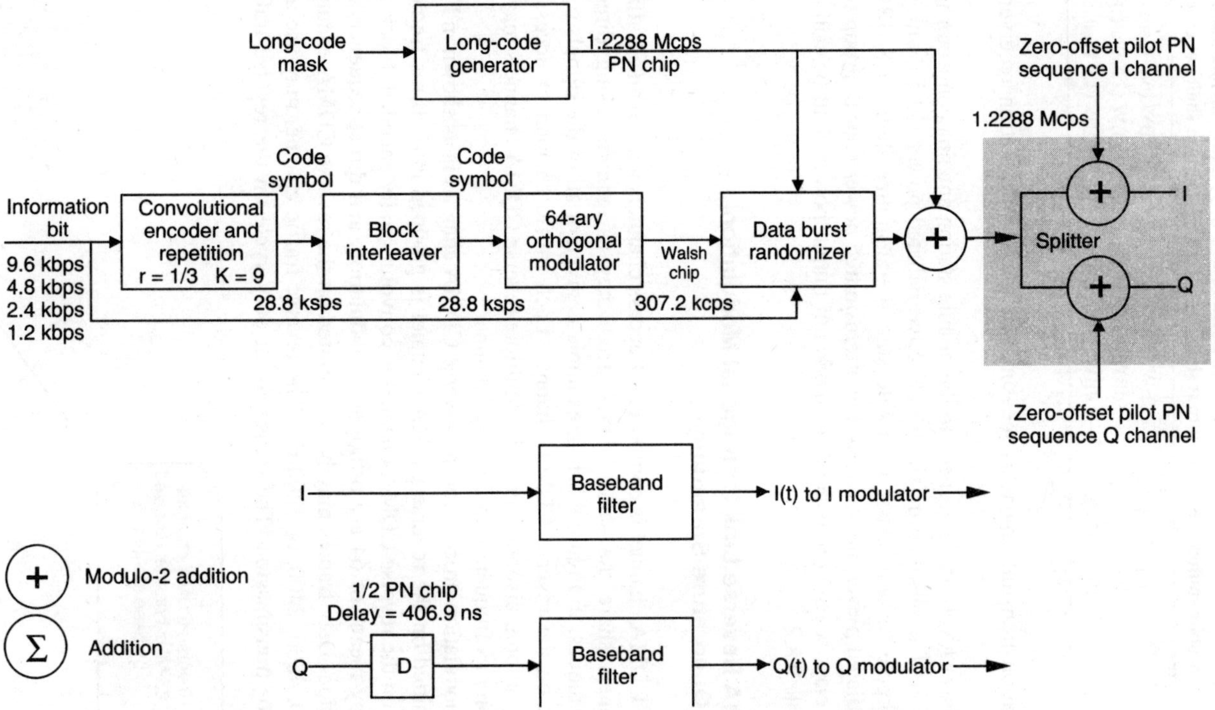

Figure 9.8.2 Reverse CDMA channel modulation process pioneered by Qualcomm, Inc., and standardized in the U.S.A. (From EIA/TIA, 1993.) Note that the above offset QPSK modulator structure is cross-correlated. Several cross-correlated patented quadrature structures of Dr. Feher Associates are described in Appendix 3.

Table 9.8.3 Reverse traffic channel modulation parameters

	Data Rate (bps)				
Parameter	**9600**	**4800**	**2400**	**1200**	**Units**
PN chip rate	1.2288	1.2288	1.2288	1.2288	Mcps
Code rate	1/3	1/3	1/3	1/3	Bits/code sym
Tx duty cycle	100.0	50.0	25.0	12.5	%
Code symbol rate	28,800	28,800	28,800	28,800	sps
Modulation	6	6	6	6	Code sym/Walsh sym
Walsh symbol rate	4800	4800	4800	4800	sps
Walsh chip rate	307.20	307.20	307.20	307.20	kcps
Walsh symbol	208.33	208.33	208.33	208.33	μs
PN chips/code symbol	42.67	42.67	42.67	42.67	PN chip/code sym
PN chips/Walsh symbol	256	256	256	256	PN chip/Walsh sym
PN chips/Walsh chip	4	4	4	4	PN chips/Walsh chip

(From EIA/TIA, 1993.)

varies with the transmission data rate. Specifically, the transmission duty cycle for 9600-bps frames is 100%, the transmission duty cycle for 4800-bps frames is 50%, the transmission duty cycle for 2400-bps frames is 25%, and the transmission duty cycle for 1200-bps frames is 12.5% as shown in Table 9.8.3. As the duty cycle for transmission varies proportionately with the data rate, the actual burst transmission rate is fixed at 28,800 code symbols per second. Since six code symbols are modulated as one of 64 Walsh symbols for transmission, the Walsh symbol transmission rate is fixed at 4800 Walsh symbols per second. This results in a fixed Walsh chip rate of 307.2 kcps. The rate of the spreading pseudonoise (PN) sequence is fixed at 1.2288 Mcps, so that each Walsh chip is spread by four PN chips. Table 9.8.3 defines the signal rates and their relationship for the various transmission rates on the reverse traffic channel.

The numerology is identical for the access channel except that the transmission rate is fixed at 4800 b/s, each code symbol is repeated once, and the transmission duty cycle is 100%. Table 9.8.4 defines the signal rates and their relationship on the access channel.

Orthogonal modulation. Modulation for the reverse CDMA channel is 64-ary orthogonal modulation. One of 64 possible modulation symbols is transmitted for each six code symbols. The modulation symbol shall be one of 64 mutually orthogonal waveforms generated by using Walsh functions. These modulation symbols are numbered 0 through 63. The modulation symbols shall be selected according to the following formula:

$$\text{Modulation symbol number} = c_0 + 2c_1 + 4c_2 + 8c_3 + 16c_4 + 32c_5,$$

where c_5 shall represent the last (or most recent) and c_0 the first (or oldest) binary-valued ("0" and "1") code symbol of each group of six code symbols that form a modulation symbol.

The 64-by-64 matrix can be generated by means of the following recursive procedure:

Table 9.8.4 Access channel modulation parameters.

Parameter	Data Rate (bps) 4800	Units
PN chip rate	1.2288	Mcps
Code rate	1/3	Bits/code sym
Code symbol repetition	2	Symbols/code sym
Tx duty cycle	100.0	%
Code symbol rate	28,800	sps
Modulation	6	Code sym/Walsh sym
Walsh symbol rate	4800	sps
Walsh chip rate	307.20	kcps
Walsh symbol	208.33	μs
PN chips/code symbol	42.67	PN chips/code sym
PN chips/Walsh symbol	256	PN chips/Walsh sym
PN chips/Walsh chip	4	PN chips/Walsh chip

(From EIA/TIA, 1993.)

$$H_1 = [0], \quad H_2 = \begin{bmatrix} 0 & 0 \\ 0 & 1 \end{bmatrix},$$

$$H_4 = \begin{bmatrix} 0 & 0 & 0 & 0 \\ 0 & 1 & 0 & 1 \\ 0 & 0 & 1 & 1 \\ 0 & 1 & 1 & 0 \end{bmatrix}, H_{2N} = \begin{matrix} H_N & H_N \\ H_N & \overline{H_N} \end{matrix},$$

where N is a power of 2. The period of time required to transmit a single modulation symbol is referred to as a Walsh symbol interval, equal to 1/4800 second (208.333 . . . μs). The period of time associated with one sixty-fourth of the modulation symbol is referred to as a Walsh chip and is equal to 1/307200 second (3.255 . . . μs). Within a Walsh symbol, Walsh chips are transmitted in the order 0, 1, 2, . . . , 63.

Quadrature spreading. Following the direct sequence spreading, the reverse traffic channel and access channel are spread in quadrature, as shown in Figure 9.8.2. The sequences used for this spreading shall be the zero-offset I and Q pilot PN sequences used on the forward CDMA channel. These sequences are periodic with period 2^{15} chips and are based on the following characteristic polynomials:

$$P_I(x) = x^{15} + x^{13} + x^9 + x^8 + x^7 + x^5 + 1$$

for the in-phase (I) sequence and

$$P_Q(x) = x^{15} + x^{12} + x^{11} + x^6 + x^5 + x^4 + x^3 + 1$$

for the quadrature-phase (Q) sequence.

The maximum-length, linear feedback shift-register sequences, $\{i(n)\}$ and $\{q(n)\}$, based on the above polynomials, are of period $2^{15}-1$ and can be generated by using the following linear recursions:

$$i(n) = i(n-15) \oplus i(n-10) \oplus i(n-8) \oplus i(n-7) \oplus i(n-6) \oplus i(n-2)$$

based on $P_I(x)$ as the characteristic polynomial and

$$q(n) = q(n-15) \oplus q(n-12) \oplus q(n-11) \oplus q(n-10) \oplus q(n-9) \oplus q(n-5) \oplus q(n-4) \oplus q(n-3)$$

based on $P_Q(x)$ as the characteristic polynomial, where $i(n)$ and $q(n)$ are binary-valued ("0" and "1") and the additions are modulo-2. To obtain the I and Q pilot PN sequences (of period 2^{15}), a 0 is inserted in $\{i(n)\}$ and $\{q(n)\}$ after 14 consecutive 0 outputs. (This occurs only once in each period.) Therefore the pilot PN sequences have one run of 15 consecutive 0 outputs instead of 14.

The mobile station shall align the I and Q pilot PN sequences such that the first chip on every even second mark as referenced to the transmit time reference is the 1 after the 15 consecutive 0s.

The pilot PN sequences repeat every $2^{15}/1228800$ seconds (26.666 . . . ms). There are exactly 75 repetitions in every 2 seconds. The spreading modulation is offset quadrature phase shift keying (O-QPSK). The data spread by the Q pilot PN sequence is delayed by half a chip time (406.901 ns) with respect to the data spread by the I pilot PN sequence (Figures 9.8.3 and 9.8.4 and Table 9.8.5).

9.8.3 Baseband Filtering of the Modulated CDMA System

Following the spreading operation, the I and Q data are applied to the inputs of the I and Q baseband filters as shown in Figure 9.8.2. The baseband filters are specified to have linear phase. The baseband filters shall have a frequency response $S(f)$ that satisfies the

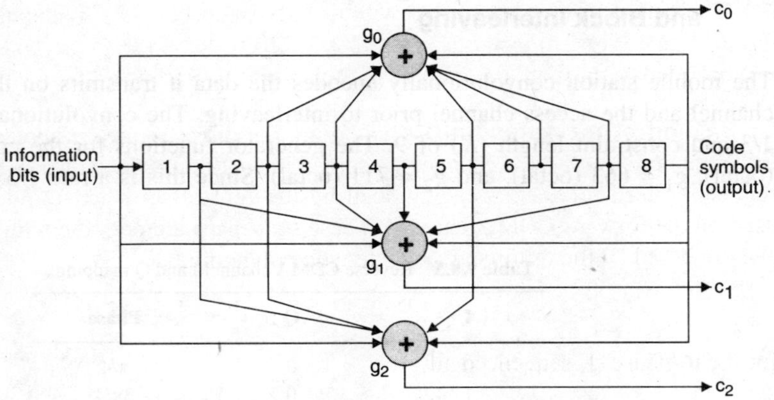

Figure 9.8.3 K = 9, rate 1/3 convolutional encoder of the IS-95 EIA/TIA standard for CDMA systems. (From EIA/TIA, 1993.)

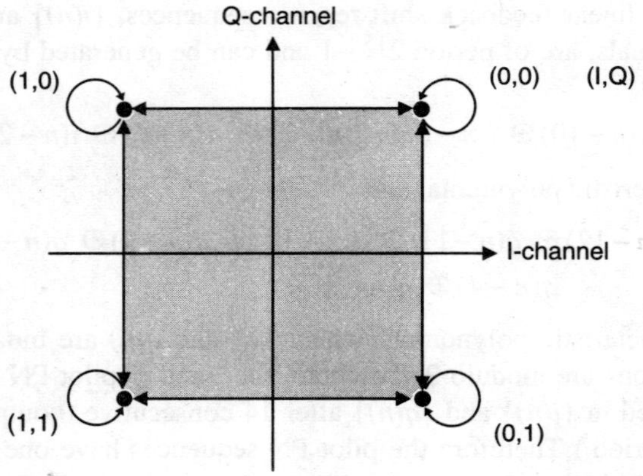

Figure 9.8.4 Reverse CDMA channel signal constellation and phase transition of the offset QPSK standardized architecture. Chapter 4 and Appendix 3 describes Dr. Feher Associates patented technologies of offset QPSK with cross-correlated I and Q channels.

limits given in Figure 9.8.5. Specifically, the normalized frequency response of the filter is contained within $\pm\delta_1$ in the passband $0 \le f \le f_p$, and is less than or equal to δ_2 in the stopband $f \ge f_s$. The numerical values for the parameters are $\delta_1 = 1.5$ dB, $\delta_2 = -40$ dB, $f_p = 590$ kHz, and $f_s = 740$ kHz.

Let *s(t)* be the impulse response of the baseband filter. Then *s(t)* satisfies the following equation:

$$\text{Mean squared error} = \sum_{k=0}^{47} [\alpha s(kT_s - \tau) - h(k)]^2 \le 0.03,$$

where the constants α and τ are used to minimize the mean squared error. The constant T_s is equal to 203.451 . . . ns, which equals one quarter of a PN chip. The values of coefficients *h(k)* are given in Table 9.8.6. Note that *h(k)* equals *h*(47 – *k*). See Figure 9.9.1.

9.8.4 Convolutional Encoding Repetition and Block Interleaving

The mobile station convolutionally encodes the data it transmits on the reverse traffic channel and the access channel prior to interleaving. The convolutional code has a rate 1/3 and constraint length (*K*) of 9. The generator functions for the code are $g_0 = 557$ (octal), $g_1 = 663$ (octal), and $g_2 = 711$ (octal). Since this is a rate 1/3 code, three code

Table 9.8.5 Reverse CDMA channel I and Q mapping.

I	Q	Phase
0	0	$\pi/4$
1	0	$3\pi/4$
1	1	$-3\pi/4$
0	1	$-\pi/4$

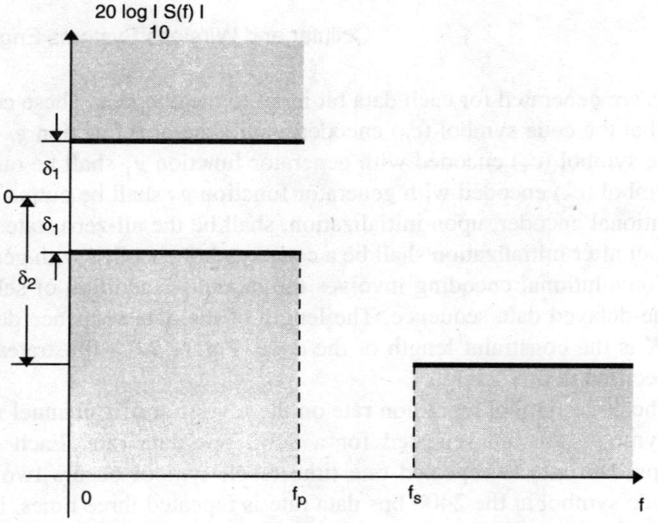

Figure 9.8.5 Baseband filters of the CDMA draft standard (IS-95) frequency response limits.

Table 9.8.6 CDMA baseband filter.

k	h(k)
0, 47	−0.025288315
1, 46	−0.034167931
2, 45	−0.035752323
3, 44	−0.016733702
4, 43	0.021602514
5, 42	0.064938487
6, 41	0.091002137
7, 40	0.081894974
8, 39	0.037071157
9, 38	−0.021998074
10, 37	−0.060716277
11, 36	−0.051178658
12, 35	0.007874526
13, 34	0.084368728
14, 33	0.126869306
15, 32	0.094528345
16, 31	−0.012839661
17, 30	−0.143477028
18, 29	−0.211829088
19, 28	−0.140513128
20, 27	0.094601918
21, 26	0.441387140
22, 25	0.785875640
23, 24	1.0

(From EIA/TIA, 1993.)

symbols are generated for each data bit input to the encoder. These code symbols are output so that the code symbol (c_0) encoded with generator function g_0 shall be output first, the code symbol (c_1) encoded with generator function g_1 shall be output second, and the code symbol (c_2) encoded with generator function g_2 shall be output last. The state of the convolutional encoder, upon initialization, shall be the all-zero state. The first code symbol output after initialization shall be a code symbol encoded with generator function g_0.

Convolutional encoding involves the modulo-2 addition of selected taps of a serially time-delayed data sequence. The length of the data sequence delay is equal to $K-1$, where K is the constraint length of the code. Figure 9.8.3 illustrates the encoder for the code specified in this section.

The code symbol repetition rate on the reverse traffic channel varies with data rate. Code symbols are not repeated for a 9600 bps data rate. Each code symbol at the 4800 bps data rate is repeated one time (each symbol occurs two consecutive times). Each code symbol at the 2400 bps data rate is repeated three times. (Each symbol occurs four consecutive times.) Each code symbol at the 1200 bps data rate is repeated seven times (each symbol occurs eight consecutive times). For all of the data rates (9600, 4800, 2400, and 1200 bps) this results in a constant code symbol rate of 28800 code symbols per second. On the reverse traffic channel these repeated code symbols are not transmitted multiple times. rather, the repeated code symbols are input into the block interleaver function, and all but one of the code symbol repetitions are deleted prior to actual transmission because of the variable transmission duty cycle. See Figure 9.9.1.

Each code symbol on the access channel, which has a fixed data rate of 4800 bps, is repeated one time. (Each symbol occurs two consecutive times.) On the access channel, both repeated code symbols are transmitted.

The mobile station interleaves all code symbols on the reverse traffic channel and the access channel prior to modulation and transmission. A block interleaver spanning 20 ms is used. The interleaver is an array with 32 rows and 18 columns (that is, 576 cells). Code symbols (repeated code symbols when at data rates lower than 9600 bps) are written into the interleaver by columns filling the complete 32 by 18 matrix.

9.9 STANDARDS FOR WIRELESS LOCAL AREA NETWORKS

For higher data rate (higher rate is defined as a minimum of 1 Mb/s) wireless computer communications, particularly for wireless local area network (WLAN) computer communications, the IEEE established an international standardization committee known as the IEEE P802.11 Wireless Access Methods and Physical Layer Specifications Committee (IEEE 802.11). It was established during 1989 by several engineers, and in 1994 there were 105 voting and 108 aspirant voting members from manufacturers of computers, infrared and radio equipment, and microelectronics, as well as governments, and universities (Hayes, 1994). Represented nations span the globe and include the United States, Canada, several European countries, Taiwan, and Israel.

Whereas other IEEE P802 committees require the 4-kbit media access control (MAC) service data unit (MSDU) loss rate to be less than 4×10^{-5}, this requirement is an unsuitable specification for a wireless medium where occasional data loss is inevitable. The IEEE

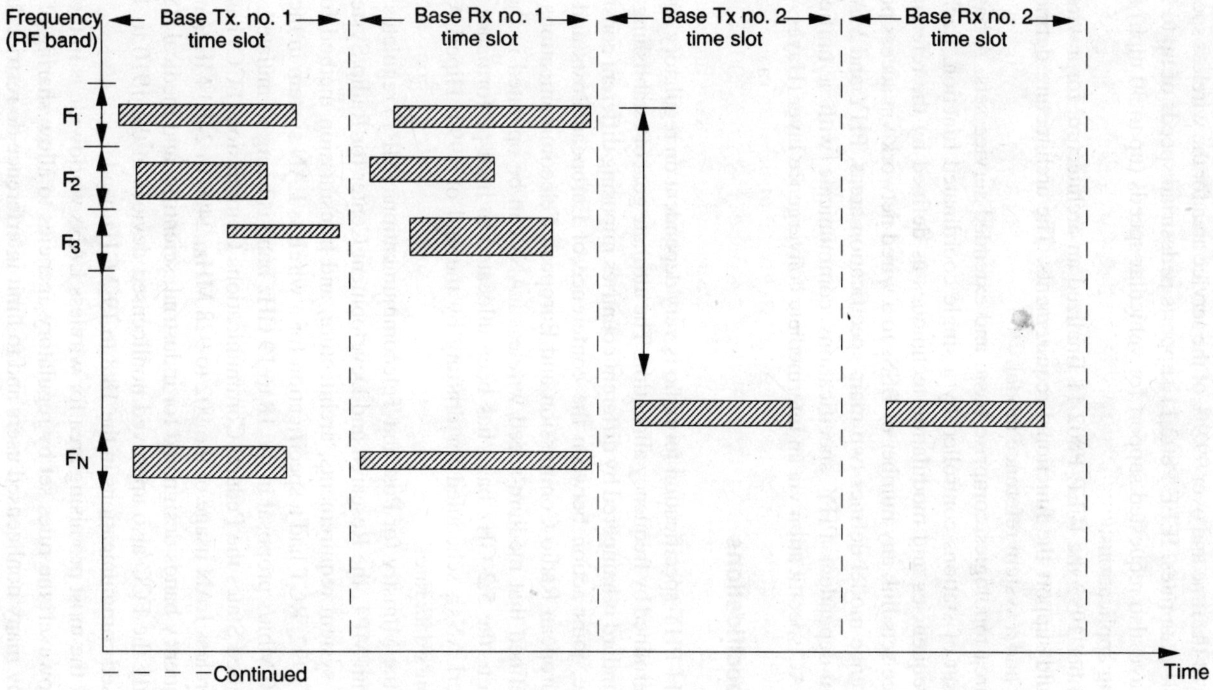

Figure 9.9.1 Time-frequency diagram illustration for an SS-SFH TDMA-TDD system at a base station (cell site). For the transmitted blocks it is assumed that the time duration and the RF bandwidth of the base station is dynamically controlled by the MAC. The RF bandwidth is always within the preassigned maximal RF band.

P802.11 committee has therefore accepted that an MSDU loss rate of 4×10^{-5} is acceptable if met over 99.9% of the time and over 99.9% of the service area for the wireless specification.

For mobile data rates, IEEE P802.11 supports pedestrian speeds of up to 2 mph; industrial users have also requested support for vehicular speeds (up to 30 mph) for factory and warehousing applications.

In November 1992 the IEEE P802.11 finalized an architecture for a wireless LAN system that could support the functional requirements. The architecture defines service-area topologies and a system reference model.

Service-area topologies comprise basic and extended service sets. A basic service set (BSS) is a set of stations controlled by a single coordinated function. Each BSS can use different frequencies and modulation techniques as defined by the reference model. Extended service sets link any number of BSSs to a wired network via access points.

The reference model defines two main specification areas: PHY and MAC specification. Medium-dependent PHY specifications communicate with a unified, media-independent MAC specification via an intermediate convergence layer (Hayes, 1994).

9.9.1 PHY Specifications

The IEEE 802.11 PHY specification for radio is very dependent on regulatory agencies and is primarily determined by frequency allocation. The ultimate goal of establishing a common international standard is hampered by different countries imposing different constraints.

In Europe, joint action between the conference of European Posts and Telecommunications European Radio Commission and European Telecommunications Standards Institute has defined that medium-speed wireless LANs can be operated in the 2.4 GHz band. In addition, the 5.2 GHz band has been allocated to high-performance local area networks (HiperLANs), scheduled for drafting by the end of 1994. HiperLANs aim at wireless 20 Mbit/s data rates.

In Japan the Ministry for Post and Telecommunications (MPT) regulates frequency resources. Within MPT, the Research and Development Center for Radio Systems (RCT) is studying the system requirements, architecture, and transmission method for wireless LANs. In May 1992, RCT had a specification for a wireless LAN system in the 2.4 to 2.5 GHz band. A 10 Mbit/s proposal in the 18 to 19 GHz band is being formulated.

In the United States the Federal Communications Commission (FCC) has approved nonlicensed wireless LAN usage of the 902 to 928 MHz, 2400 to 2483 MHz, and 5725 to 5875 MHz frequency bands designated for industrial, scientific, and medical (ISM) applications. Recently the FCC also approved nonlicensed devices in the 1910 to 1930 MHz band and licensed communications in the 18.8 to 19.2 GHz band.

Currently the most promising area for wireless LANs worldwide is in the 2.4 to 2.5 GHz region. However, the rules set by regulatory agencies to allow sharing of those frequency bands by many nonlicensed users and to limit interference do restrict data rates to the low-Mbit/s range.

Table 9.9.1 shows the specifications now in place for the IEEE 802.11 direct-sequence spread-spectrum (DS-SS) and frequency-hopping spread-spectrum (FH-SS) standards (Hayes et al., 1994). The extensions of this table for higher-speed FHSS and for

Table 9.9.1 WLAN International Standardization Committee "IEEE 802.11 Wireless Access Methods and Physical Layer Specifications" standard specification highlights based on Hayes et al., AT&T/NCR, Chair 802.11 committee, Electronic Engineering Times, February 21, 1994. Entries for higher-speed (HS) FH-SS and infrared (IR) standards are based on IEEE committee documentation as of May 1994.

802.11 PHY SPEC'S GOAL: COMMON INTERNATIONAL STANDARD (frequency-allocation regulatory-requirement disparities imposing constraints)	
Parameter	**Value**
For both frequency-hopping spread-spectrum (FH-SS) and direct-sequence spread-spectrum (DS-SS) modulation	
Frequency range	U.S.: 2.402 to 2.482 GHz; Europe: 2.4 to 2.498 GHz; Japan: 2.471 to 2.497 GHz
Transmitted power levels	U.S.: 1 W; Europe: 100 mW; Japan: 10 mW; 100 mW for DS-SS; 10 mW for FH-SS
Transmitter minimum power level	10 mW
Receiver minimum input level sensitivity	−80 dBm @ 10^{-5} BER
Channel availability	99.5 %
Antenna port impedance	50Ω
For FH-SS only	
Minimum hops/second	2.5
Minimum modulation frequency deviation	ΔF = 160 KHz
Occupied bandwidth @ 20 dB	± 500 KHz
Occupied channel bandwidth	20 dBc @ $\Delta F = \pm 0.5$ MHz; 45 dBc @ $\Delta F = \pm 2$ MHz; 60 dBc @ $\Delta F = \pm 3$ MHz
Receiver center frequency acceptance range	±25 ppm
Modulation	Two-level GFSK with BT = 0.5
BER at specified E_b/N_o	10^{-5} @ E_b/N_o = 19 dB
PHY supplied clock jitter	0.0625 μs
Channel data rate	1 Mbit/s
Preamble length	106 bit times
For DS-SS modulation only	
Spreading sequence	11 chips Barker sequence (1,−1,1,1,−1,1,1,1,−1,−1,−1)
Adjacent channel rejection	37 dB
Occupied channel bandwidth	30 dB @ $\Delta f = \pm 11$ MHz changing linearly to 50 dBc @ $\Delta f = \pm 22$MHz
Modulation	DQPSK and/or DO-QPSK
BER at specified E_b/N_o	10^{-5} @ E_b/N_o = 17 dB
Channel data rate	2 Mbit/s
Fallback data rate	1 Mbit/s
Preamble length	160 symbols (160 μs)
For higher-speed FH-SS; For infrared (IR)	
IR wavelength	880 nm
Electronic (BB) bands	0–6 MHz baseband; 6–15 MHz coexistence; 15–30 MHz modulated
Baseband encoding	4-PPM for 2 Mb/s and 16-PPM for 1 Mb/s
Modulation	FQPSK for 4 Mb/s and 10 Mb/s
BER at specified E_b/N_o	10^{-5} at 13 dB

infrared (IR) wireless local area network IEEE 802.11 standards were inserted by the author, based on IEEE committee data and specifications as of May 1994.

The DO-QPSK modulation format as of February 1994 was included in the DS-SS specifications based on Dr. Feher and Associates' proposals to enable the compatible use of FQPSK and/or nonlinearly amplified power efficient applications. With conventional DQPSK, the technology limit (for 3V-PCMCIA card size implementations) is about 18 dBm, while with the patented FQPSK (compatible with O-QPSK and GMSK), it is 23 dBm, as nonlinear saturated RFICs can be used with FQPSK.

The infrared WLAN diffused system can achieve high bit rates at the 4 Mb/s and 10 Mb/s rates by the use of FQPSK modulation nonlinear IR diodes. See Chapter 4 and section 9 for FQPSK details.

At the IEEE P802.11 November 1993 meeting, the committee reviewed all of the preceding proposals. That month, the committee selected distributed foundation wireless MAC (DFWMAC) as the IEEE P802.11 foundation protocol for media access control. DFWMAC contains 95% of the functionality of NCR's and Symbol's original WMAC proposal, adding support from Xircom's proposal for hidden nodes.

Overall, DFWMAC is a distributed-access protocol based on *carrier-sense, multiple access collision avoidance with acknowledgment (CSMA-CA-ACK*). The MAC-level ACK allows for data recovery at a low level. Low-level recovery is essential in a wireless environment to resolve reliability problems arising from access collisions and interference.

In DFWMAC, time-bounded services are also available via an optional point coordination function (PCF). The PCF runs on top of the basic-access protocol to ensure coexistence. Time-bounded services are critical in applications requiring transmission of real-time data, such as digital voice, digital video, and process control. As such, the IEEE P802.11 MAC protocol is well positioned to suit the needs of future products and applications, as well as being usable now for current-generation wireless LAN systems.

The entire IEEE P802.11 standard is aimed at becoming a global standard. Plans are underway to have an International Standards Organization (ISO)/International Electrotechnical Commission adoption of these IEEE P802.11 WLAN standards by November 1995.

9.10 WIRELESS PERSONAL COMMUNICATIONS

A personal communications network (PCN) extends the definition of a telephone call to the establishment of a connection to a particular person rather than a particular residence, workplace, or automobile. In a PCN a telephone number correspondes to the lightweight, personal transceiver a subscriber carries everywhere. Outside of being an upgraded, digital cellular system for the masses that achieves reduced transmitter power levels and cell areas, a true PCN allows data other than real-time audio to be sent. The expansion of the mobile unit's role to include appropriately decoding nonvoice transmissions, screening calls, and delivering messages reflects changes in a society's communication habits that have taken place even since the adoption of AMPS in the 1980s.

Each "microcell" of a PCN has a radius of only 1 to 300 meters (Lipoff, 1994). The antenna's coverage area remains fixed for the lifetime of the system, unlike first-generation cellular base stations that were arranged sparsely until increased subscriber count warranted more available channels. Both receiver and transmitter average power levels can be reduced, from the approximately 30 dBm of conventional cellular systems to only 10 dBm (Newell, 1991). Guidelines for acceptable outage fraction are more stringent as well, only 5% as compared with 10% (Raychaudhuri and Wilson, 1993).

One low-cost version of the PCN is the Telepoint system, which essentially puts a "pocket payphone" into a mobile pager unit (Newell, 1991). The personal unit will indicate an incoming call anywhere in the service area, but to transmit via the reverse link, one must be near a designated antenna. Interspersing fewer base stations over the service area means not only a lower startup cost for the provider, but also negligible ACI and CCI because of the lower frequency reuse factor. Hand-off of calls is clearly not a concern, either.

However, the public's expectations of accessibility have pushed the PCN trend towards full-coverage voice-and-data networks. The different characteristics of the two types of transmission require increased flexibility, and thus complexity, on the part of the mobile unit. Voice conversations must occur in real time, but since the information is not stored, they can tolerate a greater packet loss rate than data transmissions can, approximately 10^{-4} versus 10^{-9} (Raychaudhuri and Wilson, 1993). Low-bit-rate speech coding to reduce transmission bandwidth has the cost of lower perceived quality.

Four viable RF interfaces for PCN have been proposed so far (Lipoff, 1994). CT-2, a U.K. standard that uses GFSK, and Japan's $\pi/4$-DQPSK-based Personal Handyphone (PHP) both achieve simple handset design and long battery life but require at least 75 kHz of spectrum per voice channel. Bellcore's Universal Digital PCS uses the same 32 kb/s ADPCM speech coder as the previous two, but obtains the same 1.07 b/s/Hz spectral efficiency of analog AMPS. The more efficient Qualcomm CDMA interface uses a variable-rate speech coder so that as more users come onto the system during high-traffic hours, the speech resolution of all conversations degrades imperceptibly. However, the spread-spectrum techniques necessary for this dynamic allocation of bandwidth require advanced signal processing capability in the handheld unit.

The challenge is to strike a compromise between handset complexity and affordability. At the very least, consumers will expect support for auxiliary types of transmissions such as voice mail and text messages, as well as the "secret arial" tasks of call identification and screening. Since PCN is intended to serve a broader subscriber base than cellular telephony and relies on a large number of low-power base stations, the traditional networks that act as its "backbone" experience greater demands as well.

In Tables 9.11.1 to 9.11.5, several proposed PCN air interface standards (proposals during the first part of 1994) and several already standardized cellular systems are illustrated.

Table 9.11.1 Candidate air interface proposal attributes to JTC-TIA Committee 1994.

	GSM-based proposal			
System attribute	**DCS 1900**	**DCS 1800**	**PCS 1900**	**D 1900**
High/low mobility support	Both?		Both	
Frequency band:uplink/downlink (MHZ)	1930 to 1970, 2180 to 2200 1850 to 1890, 2130 to 2150			
Duplex method	FDD	FDD	FDD	FDD
RF channel spacing	200 mHz	200 mHz	200 mHz	200 mHz
Baseband mod. tech.: forward or reverse	GMSK	GMSK	GMSK	GMSK
Access technology	TDMA	TDMA w/ freq. hopping	TDma/FDM	TDMA/FMDA
Voice encoding rate	6.5, 13 kbps	16 kbps	6.3, 13, 14.5 kbps	13 kbps
Voice channels per RF channel per sector	16, 8	8	16, 8	8
Channel bit rate	270.833 kbps	270.833 kbps	270.833 kbps	270.833 kbps
As for IS-54/7X	40 W MAX	20 W	63 W	100 W
Terminal transmit power	1 W	1 W	1 W/.25W	1 W/.25W
Maximum user bit rate	9.6, 13 kbps	9.6 kbps (aggr. to 76 kbps)	182.5 kbps	9.6 kbps
Receiver threshold (mobile/base)	−100/−m104 dBm	−100/−108 dBm	−100/−104 dBm	−105/−113 dBm
Handover	Yes, MAHO	Yes, MAHO	Yes	Yes
Related system technology or standards	DCS 1800	DCS 1800	DCS 1800, T1.602/607	DCS 1800

Note: This table presents information contained in documentation provided by the candidate system proponents, with limited interpretation. Blank entries indicate insufficient or missing information in the proposal.

Table 9.11.2 Candidate air interface proposal attributes to JTC-TIA Committee 1994.

System attribute	IS-54-based proposal			WACS-based proposal	
	PCS 2000	PCS 1800	WACS-8+	WACS-8+	PPS 1800 LT
High/low mobility support	High		High	Low	Low
Frequency band:uplink/downlink (MHZ)	18050 to 1970, 2130 to 2200 MHzMHz		PCS bands	PCS bands	1805 to 1809, 2130 to 2150 1930 to 1970, 2180 to 2200
Duplex method	FDD		FDD	FDD	FDD
RF channel spacing	30 kHz	30 kHz	60 kHz	300 kHz	300 kHz
Baseband mod. tech.: forward or reverse	DQPSK	DQPSK OR 8 PSK	DQPSK	DQPSK	QPSK
Access technology	TDMA	TDMA	TDMA	TDM/TDMA	TDMA
Voice encoding rate	8, 16, 24 kbps	7.95, 16 kbps	4,8,26 kbps	8,16,32 kbps	32 kbps
Voice channels per RF channel per sector				7-31 (for 32 kbps codec)	7
Channel bit rate	97.2 kbps			400 kbps	400kbps
As for IS-54/7X	As for IS-54/7X		40 mW	800 mW	800 mW
600 mW max	600 mW max		4, 1.6, .6 W ERP	20 mW max	100 mW max
Maximum user bit rate	24 kbps	29 kbps (async)		32 kbps (to 224 kbps)	256 kbps
Receiver threshold (mobile/base)	TBD	−105/−110 dBm	−107 dBm	−103 dBm	−101/−103 dBm
Handover	Yes, as for IS-54/7X	Yes		ALT	MDHO
Related system technology or standards	IS-54/7X, Q931./932, G.728	IS-54/7X	IS-54	G.721	G.721

Note: This table presents information contained in documentation provided by the candidate system proponents, with limited interpretation. Blank entries are due to insufficient information in the proposal.

Table 9.11.3 Candidate air interface proposal attributes to JTC-TIA Committee 1994.

System attribute	CDMA-based proposal			
	W-CDMA	**IW-CDMA**	**CMDA PCS**	**A-CDMA**
High/low mobility support	Both	Both		Both (incl. local loop)
Frequency band:uplink/downlink(MHz)	1850 to 1890	1850 to 1880, 1880 to 1890, 2130 to 2150	Same as Interdigital	Same as Interdigital
	1930 to 1970	1930 to 1960, 1960 to 1970, 2180 to 2220	"	"
Duplex method	FDD	FDD	FDD	FDD
RF channel spacing	5 MHz	NA, one RF chan. per band	25 MHz	
Baseband mod. tech.: forward or reverse	BPSK/GMSK	QPSK/QPSK	BPSK OR QPSK/???	QPSK
Access technology	DS CMDA	B-CDMA (DS=CMDA)	CDMA	CDMA
Voice encoding rate	Rates up to 64 kbps	34 kbpd voice, 64 kbps voicelike	13.3 kbps and 32 kbps	32/34 kbps
Voice channels per RF channel per sector		231	3-43 and 7-90	28 (5 MHz) and 256 (10 MHz)
Channel bit rate			1.229 Mcps and 2.458 Mcps	38.4 kbps
Base transmit power per RF (MAX)		100 W	5 W	12/.25 W (1/.3 k radius)
Terminal transmit power	220 mW per user	200mW portable, 2W mobile MAX	600 mW	95/2 mW (1/.3 k radius)
Maximum user bit rate	64 kbps	64 kbps (144 kbps in 18 mo.)	38.4 kbps and 76.8 kbps	144 kbps
Receiver threshold (mobile/base)	TBD	−106 dBm		
Handover	Soft and hard	Soft, mobile, and base-initiated	Soft, hard	Make before break
Related system technology or standards	IS-95/9X, G.721/728		IS-95, IS-41-B	IS-41 Rev. B

Note: This table presents information contained in documentation provided by the candidate system proponents, with limited interpretation. Blank entries indicate insufficient information in the proposal.

Table 9.11.4 Candidate air interface proposal attributes to JTC-TIA Committee 1994. Various systems contained in Tables 9.11.1 to 9.11.4 were proposed in 1994 by Alcatel, AT&T, Ericsson, Hughes, Interdigital, Motorola, Northern Telecom, Omnipoint, Oki, Qualcomm, Panasonic, PCSI, and Siemens. Dr. Feher Associates–Digcom, Inc., and the University of California at Davis.

System attribute	CDMA/TMDA/FMDA proposal	Low-Power TMDA Proposal		
		DCT 1800	PHPS	PHP
High/low mobility support	Both	Low	Low	Low
Frequency band:uplink/downlink (MHz)	1850 to 1990 MHz, 2.4 to 2.483 GHz	1880 to 1900	1850 to 2200	U.S. PCS bands
Duplex method	TDD	TDD	TDD	TDD
RF channel spacing	5 MHz	1.728 MHz	300 kHz	300 kHz
Baseband mod. tech.: forward or reverse	CPM	GFSK	QPSK	DQPSK
Access technology	CDMA, TDMA, FDMA	TDMA	TDMA	TDMA
Voice encoding rate	8–64kbps	32 kbps	32 kbps	32kbps
Voice channels per RF channel per sector	Up to 64; depends on codec	12 (per RF and per base station)	4	4
Channel bit rate	781.25 kbps	1152 kbps	384 kbps	384 kbps
Base transmit power per RF (max)	300 mW to 100 W	<315 mW	500 mW	10 mW AVG
Terminal transmit power	100 mW to 1 W EIRP	250 mW max	500 mW max	80 mW max (300 mW opt.)
Maximum user bit rate	256 kbps	880 kbps (async), 480 kbps (sync)	140.8 kbps (aggregate)	128 kbps
Receiver threshold (mobile/base)	TBD/–100 dBm	–83 dBm?		–97 dBm
Handover	Hard and soft, terminal controlled	Continuous dynamic ch. selection	Term and base initiated	Term and base initiated
Related system technology or standards	B.7265	ETSI DECT, G.721	RCR-28, G.721	RCR-28, G.721, IS-54/41

Note: This table presents information contained in documentation provided by the candidate system proponents, with limited interpretation. Blank entries indicate insufficient information in the proposal.

Table 9.11.5 Analog and digital cellular telephone standard attributes based on Phillips Semiconductor data and publications by other corporations.

	Analog cellular telephones			Digital cellular telephones			
Standard	**AMPS: advanced mobile phone service**	**TACS: total access communication system**	**NMT: Nordic Mobile Telephone**	**ADC: IS-54: North American Digital Cellular**	**IS-95: North American Digital Cellular**	**GSM: Global System for Mobile Communications**	**JDC: PDC: Japanese Digital Cellular; Personal Digital Cellular**
Mobile frequency range (MHz)	Rx: 869-894 TX: 824-849	ETACS Rx: 916-949 Tx: 871-904 NTACS: Rx: 860-870 Tx: 915-925	NMT-450 Rx: 463-468 Tx: 453-458 NMT-900 Rx: 935-960 Tx: 890-915	Rx: 869-894 Tx: 824-849	Rx: 869-894 Tx: 824-849	Rx: 935-960 Tx: 890-915	Rx: 940-956 Tx: 810-826 Rx: 1477-1501 Tx: 1429-1453
Multiple access method	FDMA	FDMA	FDMA	TDMA/FDM	CDMA/FDM	TDMA/FDM	TDMA/FDM
Duplex method	FDD	FDD	FDD	FDD	FDD	FDD	FDD
Number of channels	832	ETACS: 1000 NTACS: 400	NMT-450: 200 NMT-900: 1999	832 (3 users/ channel)	10 (118 users/ channel)	124 (8 users/ channel)	1600 (3 users/ channel)
Channel spacing	300 kHz	ETACSL: 25 kHz NTACS: 12.5 kHz	NMT-450: 25 kHz NMT-900: 12.5 kHz	30 kHz	1250 kHz	200 kHz	25kHz
Modulation	FM	FM	FM	π/4 DQPSK	BPSK/OQPSK	GMSK (0.3 Gaussian Filter)	π/4 DQPSK
Bit rate	n/a	n/a	n/a	48.6 kb/s	1.2288 Mb/s	270.833 kb/s	42 kb/s

9.11 PROBLEMS

9.1 Assuming the conditions listed in Figure 9.4.11, design a digital mobile radio link that has a successful bit transmission rate of 99.99% over three fourths of the service area. Give requirements for transmitter power and the minimum cochannel reuse distance.

9.2 Assume the conditions listed in Figure 9.4.11 and that available transmitter power is 25 dBm. Predict the outage fraction for the cell if 25 km separate the base stations broadcasting on the same channel. Estimate the BER as well.

9.3 With reference to section 9.4.2, assume that the receiver noise power $KTB = 4 \times 10^{-15}$ W, receiver noise figure $N_F = 2.27$ dB, area mean of CNR $\Gamma_m \geq 13$ dB, and path loss with distance $L_p = 160$ dB. Let the antenna gains at the Tx and *Rx*, including line losses, be 9 dB and 2 dB, respectively. Use equation 9.4.12 to find the minimum required *Tx* power, P_t.

9.4 Refer to section 9.4. If it is required that a transmitted bit will be in error no more often than once in every 1000 transmitted bits (on the average) and that $F_a^2 \leq 5\%$ and $\Lambda_{th} \geq 21$ dB, find the permissible normalized cochannel reuse distance, D/R.

9.5 If the number of channels assigned to each cell is 123, the carried traffic per channel is 0.42 Erlang, bandwidth of total system $W = 300$ KHz, and the cell radius is 1 Km, find the overall spectral efficiency η_T.

9.6 Assume that a typical telephone conversation in a given rural area has an average length of 8.3 minutes. Assume that the bandwidth of the telephone channel extends from 300 Hz to 3 KHz. Further, assume that BER $\leq 10^{-3}$ is required. Find the amount of traffic of this telephone channel.

9.7 Assume that the total ACI power and total CCI power rate 17 dB and 15 dB, respectively, below the unmodulated carrier power. Find the carrier to total-interference ratio, C/I_{TOT}.

APPENDIX 1

Statistical Communication Theory: Terms, Definitions, and Concepts

A.1.1 INTRODUCTION

Wireless signal transmission, reception, and demodulation are disturbed by signal distortion and by the presence of undesired waves. These waves can be generated by the thermal motion of electrons in the front-end receiver of a radio system, by adjacent radio transmitters, or by any other means, including deliberate jamming.*

The receiver of a radio system has at its input the received radio signal, front-end noise, and undesired adjacent or cochannel interference waves. This composite signal is random. To evaluate the quality of this radio system, probabilistic solutions have to be sought. The final performance of a digital wireless system, in addition to the conventional specifications of transmitter power, radiated spectrum, and receiver noise, is frequently specified in terms of the *probability of error* P_e, or *bit-error rate* (BER) and *word-error rate* (WER), and the availability time, in which P_e is smaller than a predetermined number. These quantities are calculated or measured by means of statistical measurement techniques and are the "bread and butter" of the digital transmission engineer. Essential definitions and equations of statistical communications theory required for the understanding of the performance of digital wireless systems are summarized in this appendix. Whenever possible, the physical significance of the mathematical equations is stressed. For an in-depth study of statistical communications theory, see Gardiner (1986), Proakis (1989), or other textbooks.

*Material in this appendix is based on Feher (1981).

A.1.2 PROBABILITY DENSITY FUNCTION AND CUMULATIVE PROBABILITY DISTRIBUTION FUNCTION

One of the most important statistical properties of a random variable, for example, random voltage (current or power), is the likelihood of that variable having a specified value or being within a specified range. The concept and definition of the *probability density function* (pdf) and the *cumulative probability distribution function* (CPDF) are introduced by means of the following examples, which are illustrated in the time, frequency (spectrum), and probability domains.

In Figure A.1.1, (a), the output signal of a random binary data generator is illustrated. In the time domain this signal has two discrete states, $v(t) = +100$ mV and $v(t) = -100$ mV. These voltages represent the $L = 1$ and $L = 0$ logic states, respectively. In Figure A.1.1, (b), the corresponding power spectral density is shown in the frequency domain. In synchronous random data-transmission systems the unit pulse (bit) duration is T_b seconds; that is, a transition can only occur at integer multiples of T_b seconds.

In most practical systems the source is random and equiprobable; thus the probability of occurrence of a +100 mV signal state is the same as the probability (p) of occurrence of a –100 mV signal state. Mathematically stated,

$$p[v(t) = -100 \text{ mV}] = p[v(t) = +100 \text{ mV}] = 0.5 \quad \text{or} \quad p(L = 0) = p(L = 1) = 0.5.$$

The corresponding pdf is shown in Figure A.1.1, (c). The magnitude of this pdf is zero for all values of the random variable v, with the exception of $v = \pm 100$ mV.

The area that is obtained by multiplication of the pdf by an infinitesimal width dv represents the probability that the signal (or noise) has a value of an interval of infinitesimal width.

The probability that the value of a signal or noise sample is less than a predetermined numerical value is known as the **cumulative probability distribution function** (CPDF) and is illustrated in Figure A.1.1, (d), for this example. This means that the CPDF represents the probability that the signal $v(t)$ has a value $V < x$, where x has a specified value. In this example there are no levels below –100 mV. Thus the value of the CPDF for $V < -100$ mV is 0; that is,

$$F(v) = P(V < v) = P(V < -100 \text{ mV}) = 0$$

The probability that the generator output voltage $v(t) < 100$ mV is 0.5; the probability that $v(t) \leq 100$ mV is 1.

The cumulative probability distribution function, $P\ (V \leq v)$, also known in the literature as distribution function and the probability density function, $p(v)$, are related (for a continuous random variable) by the following equations:

$$\text{CPDF:} \qquad F(v) \triangleq P(V \leq v) = \int_{-\infty}^{\infty} p(v) dv \qquad \text{(A.1.1)}$$

$$\text{pdf:} \qquad p(v) = \frac{dP_v(v)}{dv} \qquad \text{(A.1.2)}$$

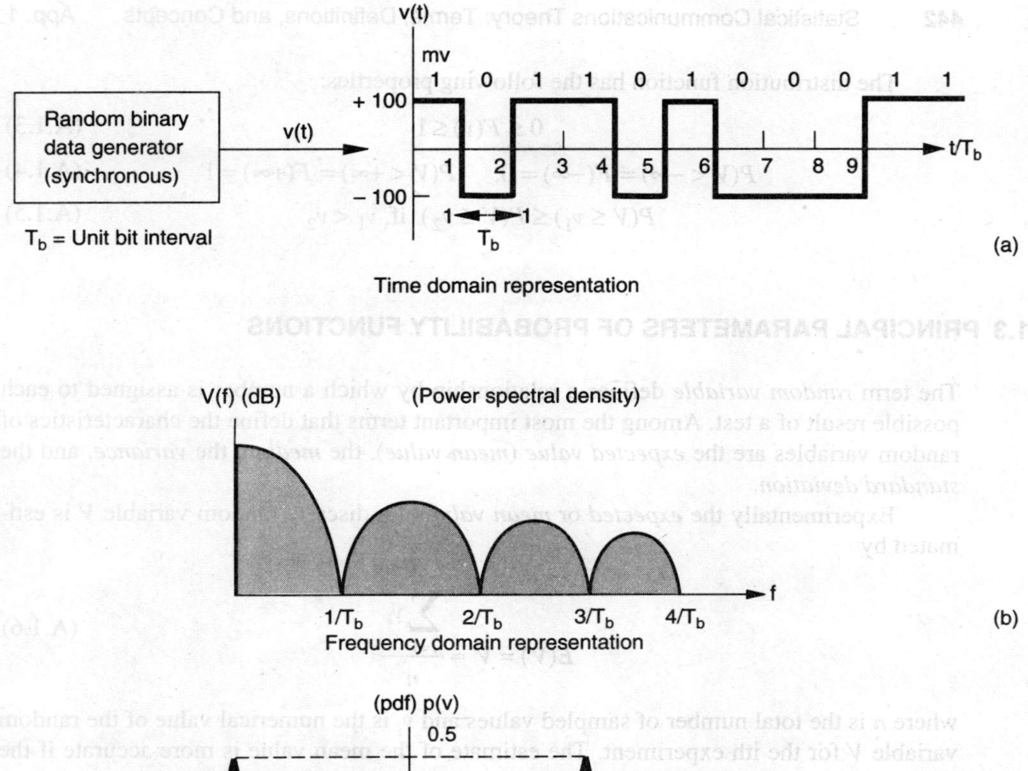

Figure A.1.1 (a), Time, (b), frequency, (c), probability density, and (d), distribution functions of a binary synchronous random data source. (From Feher, 1981.)

The distribution function has the following properties:

$$0 \le F(v) \le 1 \tag{A.1.3}$$

$$P(V < -\infty) = F(-\infty) = 0, \quad P(V < +\infty) = F(+\infty) = 1 \tag{A.1.4}$$

$$P(V \le v_1) \le P(V \le v_2) \text{ if } v_1 < v_2 \tag{A.1.5}$$

A.1.3 PRINCIPAL PARAMETERS OF PROBABILITY FUNCTIONS

The term *random variable* defines a relationship by which a number is assigned to each possible result of a test. Among the most important terms that define the characteristics of random variables are the *expected value* (*mean value*), the *median*, the *variance*, and the *standard deviation*.

Experimentally the *expected* or *mean value* of a discrete random variable V is estimated by

$$E(V) = \overline{V} \approx \frac{\sum_{i=1}^{n} v_i}{n} \tag{A.1.6}$$

where n is the total number of sampled values and v_i is the numerical value of the random variable V for the ith experiment. The estimate of the mean value is more accurate if the number of sampled values is larger. The expected value can also be obtained from

$$E(v) = \overline{V} = \sum_{i=1}^{n} v_i P(V = v_i) \tag{A.1.7}$$

where v_i represents the discrete values that the random variable V can assume.

For continuous random signals the *expected value* is defined by

$$m = E(V) = \overline{V} = \int_{-\infty}^{\infty} v p(v) dv. \tag{A.1.8}$$

In this equation, $E(V)$ is the mathematical expected value, and $p(v)$ is the pdf of the random variable V. If a very large number of samples is taken in a stationary (time invariant) system, then the limit approached by the measured mean is the expected value. The mean value is frequently measured with dc voltmeters. Physically, $[E(V^2)]$—that is, $\overline{V^2}$—represents the normalized power measured across a 1-ohm load.

The *expected value* of *any function* $g(V)$ is

$$E[g(V)] = \int_{-\infty}^{\infty} g(v) p(v) dv. \tag{A.1.9}$$

The *median* of a random variable is defined as the point at which the cumulative probability distribution function $F(v) = 0.5$.

The *mean square* value is obtained from equation A.1.9 if $g(v) = v^2$. It is given by

$$E(V^2) = \int_{-\infty}^{\infty} v^2 p(v)dv = \overline{V^2}. \qquad \text{(A.1.10)}$$

If v is the noise (or random signal) voltage across a resistance of *R* ohms, then the average power dissipated in this resistor equals $E(V^2)/R$. This power includes the ac and dc terms. In a number of applications, if the load resistance is *normalized* to $R = 1$ ohm, then $E(V^2)$ represents the average power in this load.

The *variance* is defined by

$$\sigma^2 = \int_{-\infty}^{\infty} (v - \overline{V})^2 p(v)dv$$

$$= \int_{-\infty}^{\infty} v^2 p(v)dv - 2\overline{V} \int_{-\infty}^{\infty} vp(v)dv + \overline{V}^2 \qquad \text{(A.1.11)}$$

$$\int_{-\infty}^{\infty} p(v)dv = 1 \text{ since probability of entire sample space } = 1$$

$$= \overline{V^2} - 2\overline{V}^2 + \overline{V}^2$$

$$\sigma^2 = \overline{V^2} - \overline{V}^2 \qquad \text{(A.1.12)}$$

The variance σ^2 represents the ac power dissipated in a 1-ohm normalized load. It equals the difference between the mean square value and the square of the mean voltage. The square root of the variance is the root-mean-square (rms) value of the ac wave, given by

$$\sigma = \sqrt{\overline{V^2} - \overline{V}^2}\,. \qquad \text{(A.1.13)}$$

When measuring random noise or random signal sources, special attention must be given to the rms voltage measurement. In general, probability density functions are not dependent on units. However, here the units of volts have been assumed, since these frequently are measurable quantities. A number of commercially available voltmeters that have peak detectors might lead to large inaccuracies of several decibels in the measurement of the rms voltage. To avoid measurement errors, only true power or true rms voltmeters should be used.

A.1.4 FREQUENTLY USED PROBABILITY DENSITY FUNCTIONS AND CUMULATIVE PROBABILITY DISTRIBUTION FUNCTIONS IN WIRELESS COMMUNICATIONS

A.1.4.1 The Gaussian (Normal) Distribution

The *Gaussian* pdf is the function used for the description of noise and random signal sources. This pdf represents with high accuracy the noise sources of a number of thermal noise generators, as well as the front-end noise of radio receivers.

The Gaussian pdf is given by

$$p(v) = \frac{1}{\sigma\sqrt{2\pi}} e^{-(v-m)^2/2\sigma^2} \tag{A.1.14}$$

where v is a chosen value of the random variable, and the dc component m and the rms value σ were defined in equations A.1.8 and A.1.13, respectively. The corresponding CPDF is

$$F(v) \triangleq P(V \le v) = \frac{1}{\sigma\sqrt{2\pi}} \int_{-\infty}^{v} e^{-(u-m)^2/2\sigma^2} du. \tag{A.1.15}$$

If the average value (dc component) of the noise source is 0 then the pdf and the CPDF of the Gaussian noise are given by

$$p(v) = \frac{1}{\sigma\sqrt{2\pi}} e^{-v^2/2\sigma^2} \tag{A.1.16}$$

$$F(v) = P(V \le v) = \frac{1}{\sigma\sqrt{2\pi}} \int_{-\infty}^{v} e^{-u^2/2\sigma^2} du. \tag{A.1.17}$$

The normalized Gaussian pdf of a noise source is obtained if it is assumed that this source does not have dc component ($m = 0$) and that it has a 1-V rms voltage ($\sigma = 1$ V rms). This normalized pdf is known as the *unit normal* or *standardized Gaussian density function* and is given by

$$p(v) = \frac{1}{\sigma\sqrt{2\pi}} e^{-v^2/2}, \qquad (m = 0, \sigma = 1). \tag{A.1.18}$$

The CPDF corresponding to the unit normal pdf is

$$F(v) = P(V \le v) = \frac{1}{\sqrt{2\pi}} \int_{-\infty}^{v} e^{-u^2/2} du \tag{A.1.19}$$

where u represents the dummy variable of integration. The unit normal density and cumulative distributions are shown in Figures A.1.2 and A.1.3, respectively. The values of the pdf are computed directly from equation A.1.18.

The distribution function (equation A.1.19) is not expressible in terms of elementary functions. It is customary to relate this function to the error function *erf* (v), which has been numerically computed and appears in most mathematical handbooks. It is defined by

$$erf(v) \triangleq \frac{2}{\sqrt{\pi}} \int_{0}^{v} e^{-u^2} du. \tag{A.1.20}$$

Some authors define *erf* (v) as

$$erf(v) = 1/(\sqrt{2\pi} \int_{0}^{v} e^{-u^2/2} du.$$

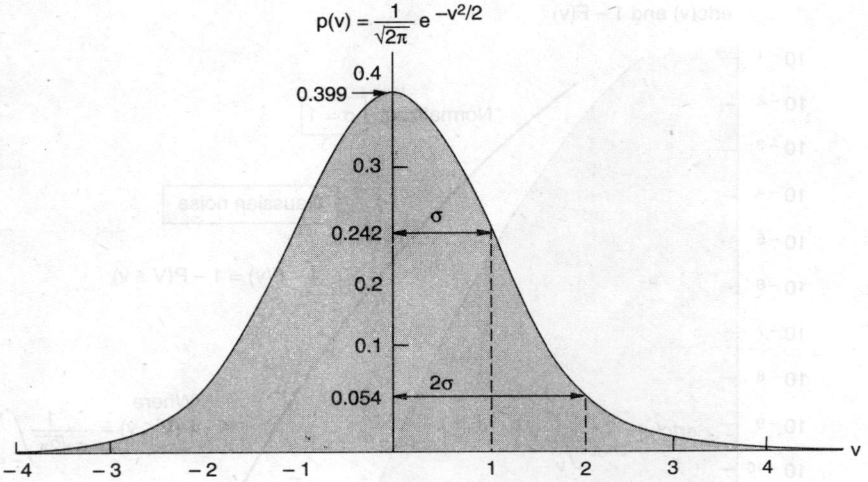

Figure A.1.2 Gaussian unit normal probability density function (pdf).

These two definitions coexist in the literature but should not cause any confusion. The complementary error function *erfc* (*v*) is defined by

$$erfc(v) \triangleq 1 - erf(v) = \frac{2}{\sqrt{\pi}} \int_{v}^{\infty} e^{-u^2}\, du. \tag{A.1.21}$$

In Figure A.1.4 *erfc* (*v*) is plotted on a logarithmic scale for the $0 < v < 5$ range. The cumulative distribution function $F(v)$ may be expressed in terms of the complementary error function as

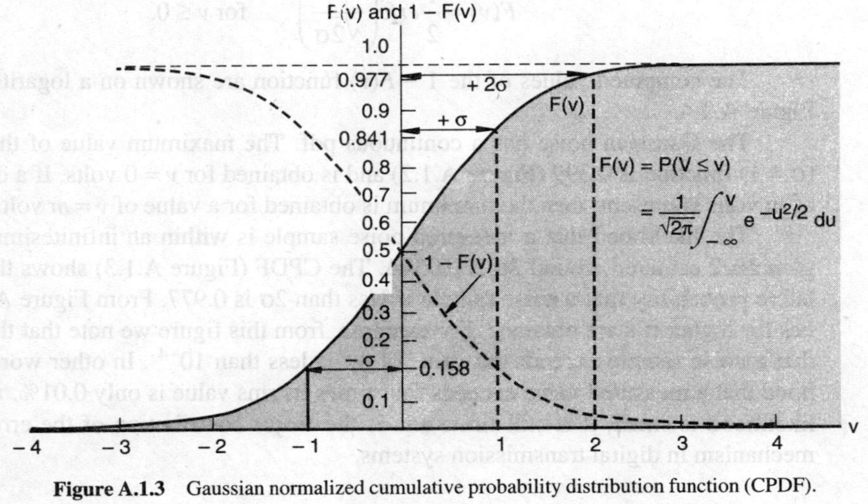

Figure A.1.3 Gaussian normalized cumulative probability distribution function (CPDF).

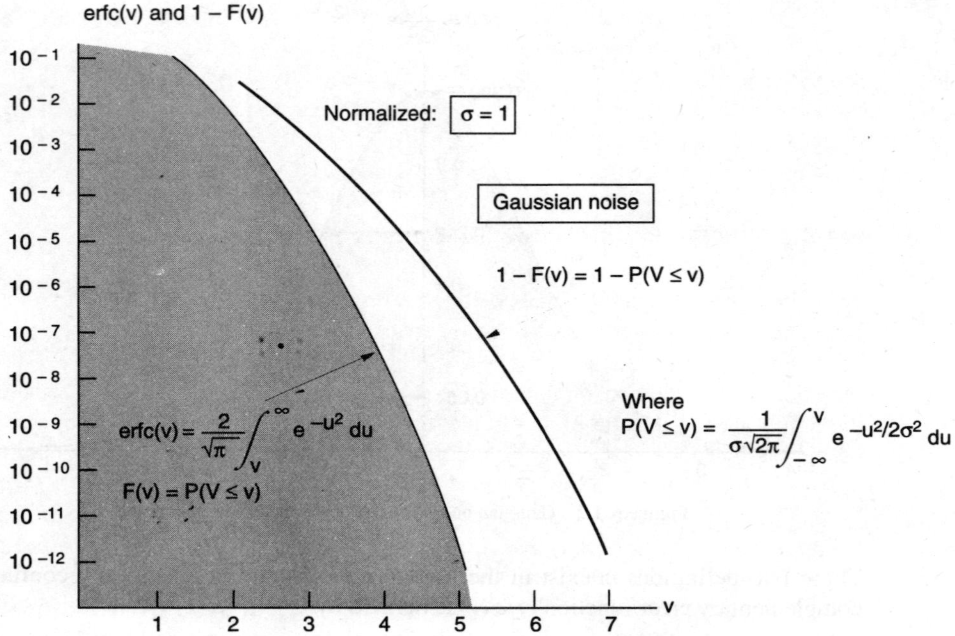

Figure A.1.4 Logarithmic plot of the complementary error function *erfc*(*v*) and of the 1 – *F*(*v*) function.

$$F(v) = 1 - \frac{1}{2}\,erfc\left(\frac{v}{\sqrt{2}\sigma}\right) \quad \text{for } v \geq 0$$

$$F(v) = \frac{1}{2}\,erfc\left(\frac{|v|}{\sqrt{2}\sigma}\right) \quad \text{for } v \leq 0. \tag{A.1.22}$$

The computed values of the 1 – $F(v)$ function are shown on a logarithmic scale in Figure A.1.4.

The Gaussian noise has a continuous pdf. The maximum value of the normalized ($\sigma = 1$) function is 0.399 (Figure A.1.2) and is obtained for $v = 0$ volts. If a dc component of m volts is present, then the maximum is obtained for a value of $v = m$ volts.

The likelihood that a measured noise sample is within an infinitesimally small region $\pm\Delta/2$ centered around 2σ is 0.054Δ. The CPDF (Figure A.1.3) shows that the cumulative probability that a noise sample is less than 2σ is 0.977. From Figure A.1.4, the values for higher σ's are obtained. For example, from this figure we note that the probability that a noise sample exceeds the value of 4σ is less than 10^{-4} . In other words, the likelihood that a measured value exceeds four times its rms value is only 0.01%. Although this likelihood is small, it is still finite and is the major contribution of the error-generating mechanism in digital transmission systems.

Theoretically an ideal Gaussian noise process has infinitely high peaks; that is, there is a finite likelihood that a peak as high as 7σ or even higher will occur. This theoretical probability that a peak of 7σ occurs is only 10^{-12} (Figure A.4). *Practical Gaussian noise generators resemble the theoretical Gaussian density and distribution functions closely*, up to $\pm 4\sigma$ or $\pm 5\sigma$ *values* (*within* 1%). Above these voltages, most generators clip and thus do not follow the theoretical Gaussian curve.

A.1.4.2 The Rayleigh Probability Density Function

The *propagation* of radio signals through fading media can be described by the Rayleigh probability density function. If a radio carrier is incident on the medium and this medium produces scattered beams caused by multiple reflections or by atmospheric variations, then the transmitted constant amplitude signal is converted into one with randomly varying amplitude. This random amplitude term at the input of the receiver appears as multiplying the radio wave. For this reason, this random fluctuation is known as *multiplicative noise*, and its pdf is given by equation A.1.23.

The front end of a radio receiver is considered to be *narrowband* if the receiver bandwidth is small as compared with the radio frequency. The Gaussian noise generated in the front-end amplifier of a narrowband receiver has the appearance of a sinusoidal carrier amplitude modulated by a low-frequency wave. This wave has a low-frequency envelope. The probability density function of this envelope is also described by the *Rayleigh density*, it is defined by

$$p(v) = \begin{cases} \dfrac{v}{\alpha^2} e^{-(v^2/2\alpha^2)}, & (0 \le v \le \infty) \\ 0, & (v < 0) \end{cases}, \tag{A.1.23}$$

and the corresponding CPDF is

$$F(v) = P(V \le v) = \begin{cases} 1 - e^{-v^2/2\alpha^2}, & (0 \le v \le \infty) \\ 0, & (v < 0) \end{cases}. \tag{A.1.24}$$

Curves for these functions are shown on a linear scale in Figure A.1.5 and on a logarithmic (dB) scale in Chapter 3 (see Figure 3.2.5).

The average (mean) value of the Rayleigh density function is given by

$$E(v) = \int_0^\infty \frac{v^2}{\alpha^2} e^{-v^2/2\alpha^2}\, dv = \sqrt{\frac{\pi}{2}}\alpha. \tag{A.1.25}$$

The rms ac component is 0.655α.

From the CPDF shown in Chapter 3 (see Figure 3.2.5) we note that the received

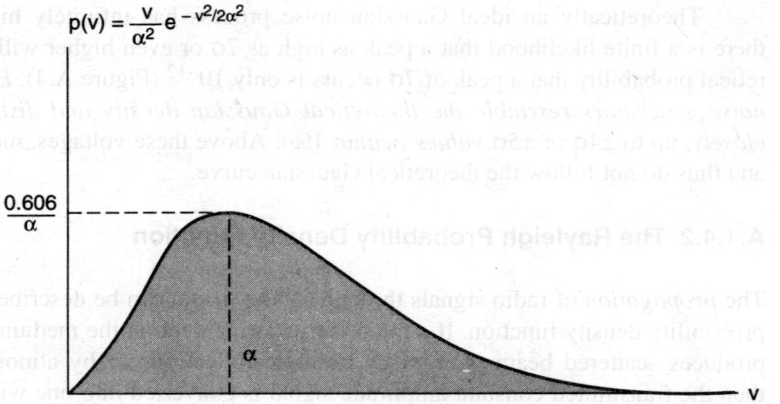

Figure A.1.5 Rayleigh probability density function linear scale display, for logorithmic (dB) plot see Figure 3.2.5. (From Feher, 1981.)

radio signal has a smaller attenuation (less severe fade) than 18 dB from its median value during 99% of the time and a less severe fade than 28 dB during 99.9% of the time. In other words, the Rayleigh signal fade depth exceeds 28 dB only in 100% − 99.9% = 0.1% of the reception time. The probability distribution is an order of magnitude higher for a received signal value that is 10 dB lower.

APPENDIX 2

Software Package of CREATE-1 (Disk Enclosed)

INSTRUCTION MANUAL FOR THE "CREATE-1" SOFTWARE PACKAGE FOR PCS (DOS VERSION)

Summary Description of CREATE-1

The CREATE-1 software package has been developed at the University of California, Davis based on several programs previously developed at the University of Ottawa, Canada, and other institutions (universities and corporations), under the direction of the author of this text.[1]

CREATE-1 software (disk enclosed) enables you to compute and plot the baseband waveform, eye diagram, modulated linearly or nonlinearly amplified power spectral density (PSD), and integrated adjacent channel interference (ACI) characteristics of well-known digital communications modems such as the following:

QPSK (raised-cosine Nyquist filtered)

O-QPSK (raised-cosine Nyquist filtered)

O-QPSK (asymmetric)

GMSK

FQPSK-1*

FQPSK (FQAM, previously known as SQAM*)

*FQPSK, FBPSK, and FQAM are abbreviations for Dr. Feher and Associates patented QPSK, BPSK, and QAM. Note that GFSK and GMSK systems may be implemented by Feher's patents. See Appendix A.3.

FQPKS-KF (double-jump-filtered FQPSK)

FQPSK (self-created)

The program also allows you to analyze modems which use baseband waveforms designed by yourself (henceforth referred to as self-designed modems). See Figure A.2.1.

Bit error rate (BER) performance is available only for FQPSK and Nyquist OQPSK in an Additive White Gaussian Noise (AWGN) environment.

Several band pass filters at the receiver could be selected for some of the above modems. The transmitted system can be hardlimited [nonlinearly amplified (NLA)] to represent "C" class practical power-efficient amplifiers or linearly amplified (LNA).

Disclaimer

This software package provides examples of modulated, linearly and nonlinearly amplified wireless systems. It is provided only as an illustrative educational tool to accompany *Wireless Digital Communication: Modulation and Spread Spectrum Applications*, by Dr. K. Feher. We also disclaim all responsibility for the accuracy of the models and results. The scope of the software is only to illustrate and qualitatively compare some of the modulation techniques described in [1]. It should not be used as a substitute for professional software packages available commercially. For Feher's patented filters, GFSK and GMSK implementations, see Appendix A.3.

Restrictions (patented material), technology transfer, and licensing. *Important: The FQPSK, FBPSK, and FQAM (also known as SQAM types of systems (modem/radio) have been patented or are in patent disclosure stages* (see references 1 to 6 of

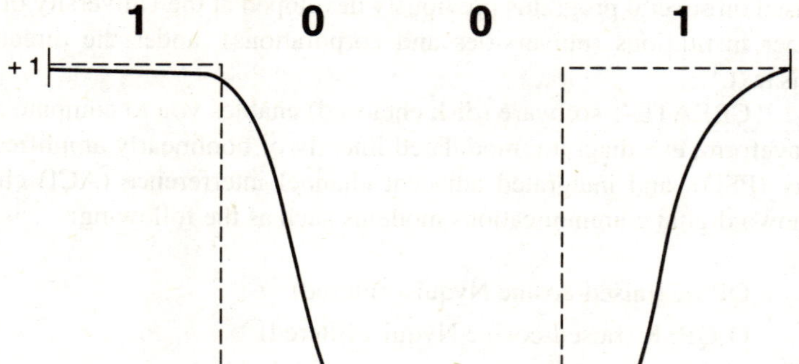

Figure A.2.1 CREATE-1 software. Illustration of four combinations (two bits) of unfiltered NRZ (nonreturn to-zero; *dotted line*) and FQPSK-1 (Feher's patented QPSK, subclass 1) baseband signal. For details see Chapter 4 and Appendix 3 of this book.

this appendix). Before any commercial use, implementation or production of FQPSK, FBPSK, or FQAM (SQAM) signals, you should verify with Dr. Feher whether the signals you created are protected by his patents.* *Note:* In some publications, for example, in Feher,[5] some of Dr. Feher's patents and the FQPSK and FBPSK family of modems and radio systems were described under the old names, IJF-O-QPSK and SQAM.

At the University of California at Davis we are developing more comprehensive and accurate software tools for wireless systems research. These tools are for workstations. Interested organizations and individuals may wish to write to the author, if they are willing to consider joint use and/or further development of more advanced simulation packages.

Getting Started

Before you attempt to run CREATE-1, we recommend that you read Chapter 4 in Feher[1] and this appendix in their entirety. Read also the 'README.DOC' file (available on the diskette).

In this manual, C:\> and A:\> refer to DOS prompts. In what follows, type only the letter in boldface, and follow *all* your commands by pressing the <enter> key.

Please make sure that you have at least 550 kbytes of RAM memory to run CREATE. To check if you have the necessary 550 kbytes of RAM memory, type the following:

C:>**mem** <enter>.

Check the number appearing on the line "largest executable programm size." To run CREATE, this number has to be larger than 550 kbytes. Additionally, you will need at least 3 Mbytes of hard-disk space and a math coprocessor. Your DOS version should be 3.3 or higher.

To abort the program, press <ctrl> <break> simultaneously. *To install CREATE, insert the diskette in drive A and type the following:*

C:\>**A:** <enter>

A:\>**install A: C:** <enter>

To Run CREATE

First, type the command *graphics* followed by your printer type. For example, if your printer is an HP Laserjet II, type the following:

C:\>**graphics laserjetii** <enter>

*Mailing address: ECE Department, University of California, Davis, CA 95616. Telephone: (916) 752–8127. Fax: (916) 752–8428. Also, contact Dr. Kamilio Feher, President, Dr. Feher and Associates, a unit of Digcom, Inc., 44685 Country Club Drive, El Macero, CA 95618. Fax: (916) 753–1788.

Refer to the DOS command ***graphics*** for more information. Consult your computer manual or type ***help graphics*** at the DOS prompt. Then type the following:

```
C:\>cd \create <enter>
C:\CREATE> create <enter>
```

The MAIN MENU gives you the following options.

A. self-designed modems. Under this option, you can create your own baseband waveform (BBW), then test the performance of a modem that uses your baseband signal. You can enter your baseband waveform from the keyboard, or you can store the data points for the waveform in data files, one file for the I channel and one for the Q channel (DATAI.INP and DATAQ.INP, respectively.) Then you can choose to plot your baseband signal, its eye diagram, power spectral density (PSD), adjacent channel interference (ACI), and bit-error rate (BER).

To create your own baseband waveform, you will need to specify the transition region of each of the four combinations of two consecutive bits (1 to 1, 1 to −1, −1 to −1, −1 to 1.) A transition region is defined as the region starting at the start of the right-most half of a bit and ending at the start of the right-most half of the bit that is immediately to the right. You can enter 8 samples or 16 samples per each transition region. The followings are examples of NRZ and FQPSK signals with 8 samples per transition. See Figure A.2.1.

An example of NRZ follows:

```
For 1 to 1 transition (1 volt to 1 volt):*
1
1
1
1
1
1
1
1
For 1 to 0 transition (1 volt to -1 volt):*
1
1
1
1
-1
-1
-1
-1
```

*Do not include this line in the files.

For 0 to 0 transition (-1 volt to -1 volt):*

-1

-1

-1

-1

-1

-1

-1

-1

For 0 to 1 transition (-1 volt to 1 volt):*

-1

-1

-1

-1

1

1

1

1

Example for FQPSK-1 (see [1–6] for the FQPSK-1 waveform):

(for 1 to 1 transition):*

1

1

1

1

1

1

1

1

(for 1 to 0 transition):*

0.923

0.707

0.383

0

-0.383

-0.707

-0.923

-1

(for 0 to 0 transition):*

-1

-1

*Do not include this line in the files.

```
-1
-1
-1
-1
-1
-1
(for 0 to 1 transition):*
-0.923
-0.707
-0.383
0
0.383
0.707
0.923
1
```

B. Conventional modems. When you choose this option, you will be able to compute and plot the EYE diagram, PSD and ACI for FQPSK-1, Nyquist O-QPSK, DJ-O-QPSK, asym-O-QPSK, GMSK, and SQAM. Additionally, you will be able to compute and plot the BER for FQPSK-1 and Nyquist O-QPSK.

Additional things you need to know include the following:

1. Be aware that the BER program is Time-consuming.
2. Input files:
   a. For *self-designed modem:*
      I-channel: "DATAI.INP"
      Q-channel: "DATAQ.INP"
   b. For *conventional modem:* None
   c. The following example input files are available on the diskette; each contains 8 samples per transition region:
      $NRZ: data file for NRZ data
      $FQPSK: data file for FQPSK-1
3. Output files:
   a. EYE diagram: "EYE.BLK"
   b. PSD: "PSD.BLK"
   c. ACI: "ACI.BLK"
   d. Baseband waveform: "BBW.BLK"

*Do not include this line in the files.

e. BER: "BER.BLK"

f. User-entered info.: "INFO.BLK" (for PSD, ACI, EYE, BBW)

g. User-entered info.: "INFOB.BLK" (For BER)

REFERENCES FOR APPENDIX 2

1. K. Feher: *Wireless Digital Communications: Modulation and Spread Spectrum Applications*, Englewood Cliffs, NJ, Prentice-Hall, 1995.
2. K. Feher: *Filter,* U.S. Patent No. 4,339,724, issued July 13, 1982. Canada No. 1130871, issued August 31, 1982.
3. S. Kato, K. Feher: *Correlated Signal Processor*, U.S. Patent No. 4,567,602, issued January 28, 1986. Canada No. 1211–517, issued September 16, 1986.
4. K. Feher: "F-modulation", patent disclosure files, confidential and proprietary, Digcom, Inc., 44685 Country Club Dr., El Macero, CA 95618, January, 1995.
5. J. S. Seo, K. Feher: *Superposed Quadrature Modulated Baseband Signal Processor*, U.S. patent No. 4,644,565, issued February 17, 1987. Canada Patent No. 10265-851, issued February 13, 1990.
6. K. Feher, Ed.: *Advanced Digital Communications: Systems and Signal Processing Techniques*, Prentice-Hall, Englewood Cliff, NJ, 1987 (available from Dr. Feher Assoc.-Digcom, Inc).

APPENDIX 3

Dr. Feher Associates Patented Filter, Digital Signal Processing, and Correlated Modulation/RF Amplification Means: GMSK, GFSK, FBPSK and FQPSK Implementations of Digcom, Inc. Licensed Technologies

ABSTRACT

The extraordinary impact of two landmark inventions on filter, modulation, linear and nonlinear amplification and overall digital wireless system design is described in this appendix. Feher's "Filter" (*FF*) patent led to new generations of reduced power/size, cost-efficient, and increased speed Field Programmable Gate Array (FPGA) and Read Only Memory (ROM) look-up table-based filter designs and to more spectral- and power-efficient modulated GFSK, FQPSK, and FBPSK systems. The abbreviations *F*QPSK and *F*BPSK are for *F*eher's patented QPSK and BPSK systems. New generations of GMSK quadrature modulator IC baseband processor chips use the "Correlated Signal Processor" means of the Kato/Feher (*KF*) patent. The described patented/licensed technologies have been used in the Global Mobile System (GSM), DECT, PCS-1900, and other standardized and non-standard wireless and cable system applications. Standard compatible and interoperable FQPSK and FBSK inventions increase the power and spectral efficiency of conventional QPSK, $\pi/4$-DQPSK, and GMSK systems by 300%.

Material contained in this Appendix No. 3 is based on and is closely related to previously copyrighted material by Dr. Feher-Digcom, Inc. It is published on a "non-exclusive" basis in this book, by permission of Dr. Feher-Digcom, El-Macero, CA.

A.3 INTRODUCTION

Filter and Digital Signal Processing (DSP) theory, development and design techniques have been documented in numerous authoritative publications and books. Many patents have been issued for original and truly outstanding principles, implementations, and design structures/architectures and/or "means" (a term frequently used in patents). Until the 1980s inventors devoted their attention to "linear" filter implementation means, including analog (passive and active) and digital DSP filters. The DSP filters are based on Infinite Impulse Response (IIR) and Finite Impulse Response (FIR) designs. These "linear transversal filter structures" are in extensive use.

In this appendix, two inventions (patents) are highlighted. The *Feher "Filter"* patent, or *"FF"* for short, contains a **new and completely different non obvious** principle from that of linear filter theory and design. Feher's Filter Patent includes "nonlinear" or "synthesized wave" store-readout/switching filter and comparison means.

Another extraordinary discovery described in this appendix is the Kato/Feher or *"KF" "Correlated Signal Processor"*. This invention could be described as **an invention which is "against" the well-established wisdom of classical linear communication system theory and principles**. Digital communications textbooks and prestigious research publications contain detailed justifications in regard to the need of having *independent or uncorrelated* in-phase (I) and quadrature (Q) baseband signals. Independent I and Q signals lead to optimum quadrature modulated performance. Cross-correlation between the I and Q baseband transmit signals would be a cause of crosstalk and thus detrimental to performance. Therefore communication theory, developed for linear systems, demonstrates that cross-correlation is not desired and that for optimum performance it must not exist.

The KF Correlated Signal Processor patent demonstrates, **contrary** to previous theoretical and practical achievements, that correlation between the I and Q channels can be of substantial benefit.

A.3.1 A Review of Two of Dr. Feher Associates' Patents

Some of the reasons for the worldwide impact of these inventions/patents, technology transfer, consulting and professional training courses, and license arrangements on new generations of products are discussed. These include digital and analog filters, Digital Signal Processing (DSP), correlated baseband processsor, combined modulation and Radio Frequency (RF), Integrated Circuit (IC), cable and other wireless technology, and continued Research and Development (R&D). An informal discussion follows. This appendix is merely a brief description of some of the patent claims. **It is not a legal and contractual licensing arrangement or technical/legal interpretation of the patents described herein.** For a complete text of these patents and of **other** Dr. Feher Associates patents a detailed study of the complete patents and disclosure documentation is recommended.

We limit this Appendix to the informal discussion of only two patents and only one claim per patent. Detailed study of the entire patents will give you an insight into the value of these technologies for your research, ongoing product developments, and licensing. For licensing and technology transfer arrangements contact:

Dr. Feher Associates/Digcom, Inc.-Digital and Wireless Communications
U.S. and International Consulting/Training and Licensing-FQPSK Consortium
44685 Country Club Drive, El Macero, CA 95618, USA
Tel: 916–753–0738, Fax: 916–753–1788 or
Dr. K. Feher at University of California, Davis; UC Davis Tel: 916–752–8127

A.3.2 Patents: Feher: "Filter", USA No. 4,339,724, July 13, 1982, Abbreviated "FF" and Kato/Feher: "Correlated Signal Processor" USA No. 4,567,602, Issued January 28, 1986, Abbreviated "KF"

Our patent claims, as well as patent claims of inventors include a text related to other embodiments and variations which utilize the principles described in the awarded patents. Such a text may state: . . . "A person understanding this invention may now conceive of changes or other embodiments or variations, which utilize the principles of this invention. All are considered within the sphere and scope of the invention as defined in the claims appended hereto . . ."

A.3.3 A Brief Historical Perspective of the FF (Feher Filter) Patent Technology and of Other Signal Filtering Methods

Assume that around 1980 you were given a task to design a "Gaussian" or "raised-cosine" filter having a 3 dB bandwidth of approximately 500kHz for a 1Mb/s rate digital communication system. Probably you would accomplish this task by means of analog (active or passive) traditional filter design or by transversal IIR or FIR filters which use mixed digital and analog components (flip-flops and discrete resistors or other gain coefficients served as multipliers). For your power and cost-efficient design during 1980 it would not be obvious to use a filter with several thousand logic gates instead of one operational amplifier or a couple of low-cost LC components.

Transversal filter structures include "IIR" or Infinite Impulse Response and "FIR" or Finite Impulse Response digital and/or mixed analog-digital implementations. Design of these types of digital filters has been extensively covered in numerous references and is briefly reviewed in Section 4.9 of this book. Many Digital Signal Processing (DSP) IIR and FIR filters/DSP Integrated Circuits have been manufactured during the late 1980s and 1990s. These IIR and FIR architectures have a drawback, namely that they may require a relatively large number of "multiplier" coefficients and adders. Each multiplier requires many gates. For high speeds, such DSP-based filters, could be very "power hungry," require far too many gates, and can be expensive.

Principles of the more efficient ROM look-up table and/or FPGA nonlinearly synthesized or switched filters are described in Chapter 4 of this book, in Feher's previous books and publications (see detailed list of more than 20 references) and in the original discoveries/patents.

During the 1990s, Feher's Filter (FF) family products have been implemented with ROM and FPGA control-based DSP architectures. The scheme may work at a sampling rate nf_b where n is an integer and f_b is the bit rate. Thus, n is the number of samples per bit period. To have an acceptably small aliasing error "n" is frequently chosen to be larger than 4. In the ROM various signal shapes, e.g., $s_1(t) \ldots, s_{16}(t)$ are stored or it is arranged that the ROM is used as a waveform selector/generator/switch. Depending on the data input, the difference between data patterns, these stored waveforms are "read out" or switched to the D/A converter, converted into an analog wave and transmitted.

A.3.4 An Interpretation of the Principles and/or of Claim No 1 (of 7 claims) Based on the "FF" (Feher's Filter) USA Patent No. 4,339,724:

I claim:

"A filter having an input for receiving a pulse signal form of binary information and an output for providing a synthesized output signal correlated to the input signal comprising:

a. means for comparing the output signal with the input signal one bit at a time

b. means connected to said comparing means and said output for generating a first predetermined output signal waveform when the output signal bit is different from that of the input signal and the input signal is binary "1,"

c. means connected to said comparing means and said output for generating a second predetermined output signal waveform when the output signal bit is different from that of the input signal and the input signal is binary "0,"

d. means connected to said comparing means and said output for generating a third predetermined output signal waveform when the output signal bit is the same as that of the input signal and the input signal is binary "1,"

e. means connected to said comparing means and said output for generating a fourth predetermined output signal waveform when the output signal bit is the same as that of the input signal and the input signal is binary "0,"

in which the predetermined output signals are continuous, whereby the spectra and sidelobes of the output signal which is correlated to the input signal are controlled to a predetermined extent."

In Claim No. 1, means for comparing the output signal with the input signal one bit at a time are claimed. In a sequence of serial bits at the input of a processor the **first input bit**, relative to the **second input bit**, which has been previously processed is defined as the **"output signal"** or output bit. As described in the body of the patent consecutive bits A_i and A_{i-1} are compared. This comparison is interpreted as a *1 or multibit memory system.* Based on the bits which are being processed, various predetermined signals are "read-out" to the transmission system. In particular, means for generating four (4) distinct and separate time-limited pulses

$$S1(t),\ S2(t),\ S3(t) \text{ and } S4(t)$$

are generated. Whether we choose the "first or second" or other signals depends on the logic control bits. Extension of the "four" (4) signal "storage" or "generation" and "read-out" principle to "eight" (8) or more signals generated, and read out from a memory, is obvious.

The first embodiment of this "FF" patent was described in the Canadian priority date filing during 1979 and even earlier in the inventor's recorded reference. This embodiment, as described in the patent, uses nonlinearly switched and thus synthesized waveforms dependent on the comparing means of correlated bits. The switched waveforms are read out from separately stored or generated functions by means of selection. Means for Intersymbol Interference and Jitter Free **(IJF)** waveshape generations are also claimed in this patent.

The means of the Feher Filtering (FF) can be achieved through the use of a ROM and digital-to-analog converter (ROM-DAC filter). In this implementation of the filter, the possible amplitude or possible phase-transitions and values of the transmit data are stored in a ROM and read out based on addresses formed by the transmit data. The addresses are based on comparative means of input data patterns. For example, with 2 bits, 4 different signal patterns can be read-out from the memory, with 3 bits, 8 pulse shapes are synthesized, et cetera.

In Figures A.3.1 to A.3.8, GFSK, GMSK architectures, Gaussian and "FQPSK-1," Intersymbol Interference and Jitter Free (IJF) circuit diagrams, time domain response, and eye diagrams are illustrated. The bit-by-bit "comparing means" of the Feher Filter (FF) patent led to many implementations. The circuit diagrams illustrate that by the FF comparing means the number of stored signals of a Gaussian $BT_b = 0.5$ filter can be reduced from $s_1(t) \ldots s_8(t)$ to only two signals, thus a **4 times (400%) hardware/memory saving is obtained.**

A careful and thorough study of the awarded claims of the FF patent and of ROM or other stored waveform and controlled read-out means of input data patterns leads to the conclusion that the ROM or FPGA based filter implementation is a non-linear filter waveform synthesis method. It has not received nearly as much attention in the literature as the so-called IIR (infinite impulse response) and FIR (finite impulse response) DSP implementation which has also been known under the category of "transversal filters." These types of filters have been implemented by several corporations since 1984. It is our belief that the ROM-based filter implementation is more cost and power efficient than the conventional IIR and FIR "transversal" DSP structures, and leads to significant reduction of gate counts because this approach does not require multipliers and is based solely on ROM-driven waveform synthesis. Survey of some leading DSP and filter IC products indicates that the trend and particularly for higher speed systems is towards the implementation of nonlinearly switched waveform-synthesized filters which are implemented by the ROM or FPGA technology and means of the FF patent.

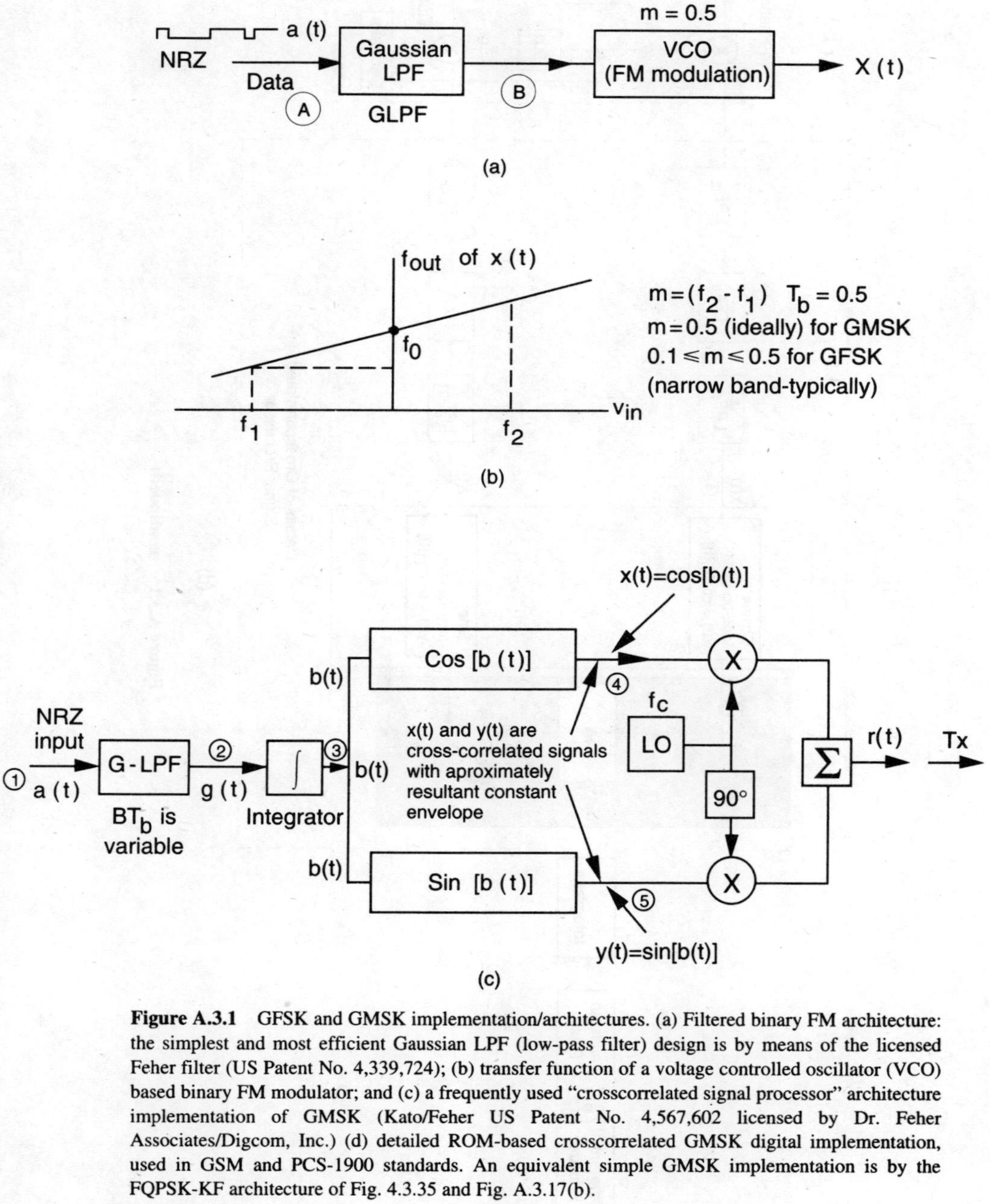

Figure A.3.1 GFSK and GMSK implementation/architectures. (a) Filtered binary FM architecture: the simplest and most efficient Gaussian LPF (low-pass filter) design is by means of the licensed Feher filter (US Patent No. 4,339,724); (b) transfer function of a voltage controlled oscillator (VCO) based binary FM modulator; and (c) a frequently used "crosscorrelated signal processor" architecture implementation of GMSK (Kato/Feher US Patent No. 4,567,602 licensed by Dr. Feher Associates/Digcom, Inc.) (d) detailed ROM-based crosscorrelated GMSK digital implementation, used in GSM and PCS-1900 standards. An equivalent simple GMSK implementation is by the FQPSK-KF architecture of Fig. 4.3.35 and Fig. A.3.17(b).

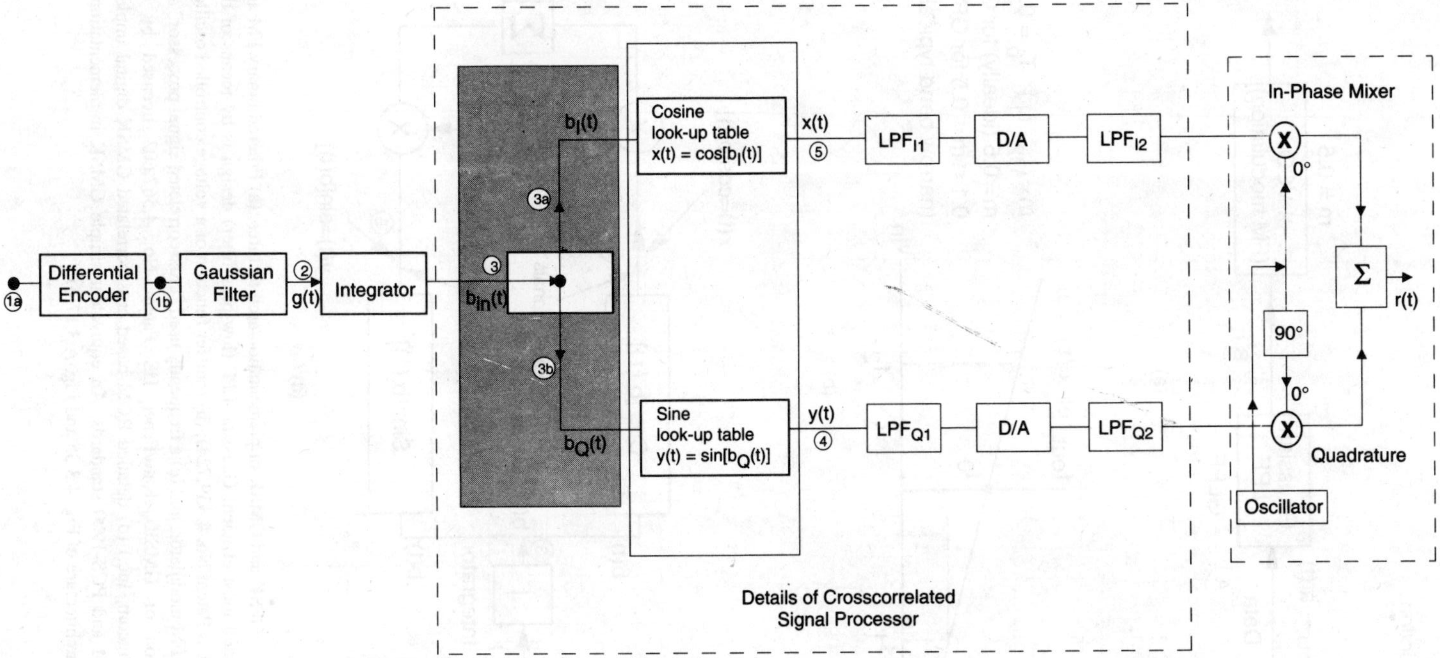

(d)

Figure A.3.1 (continued)

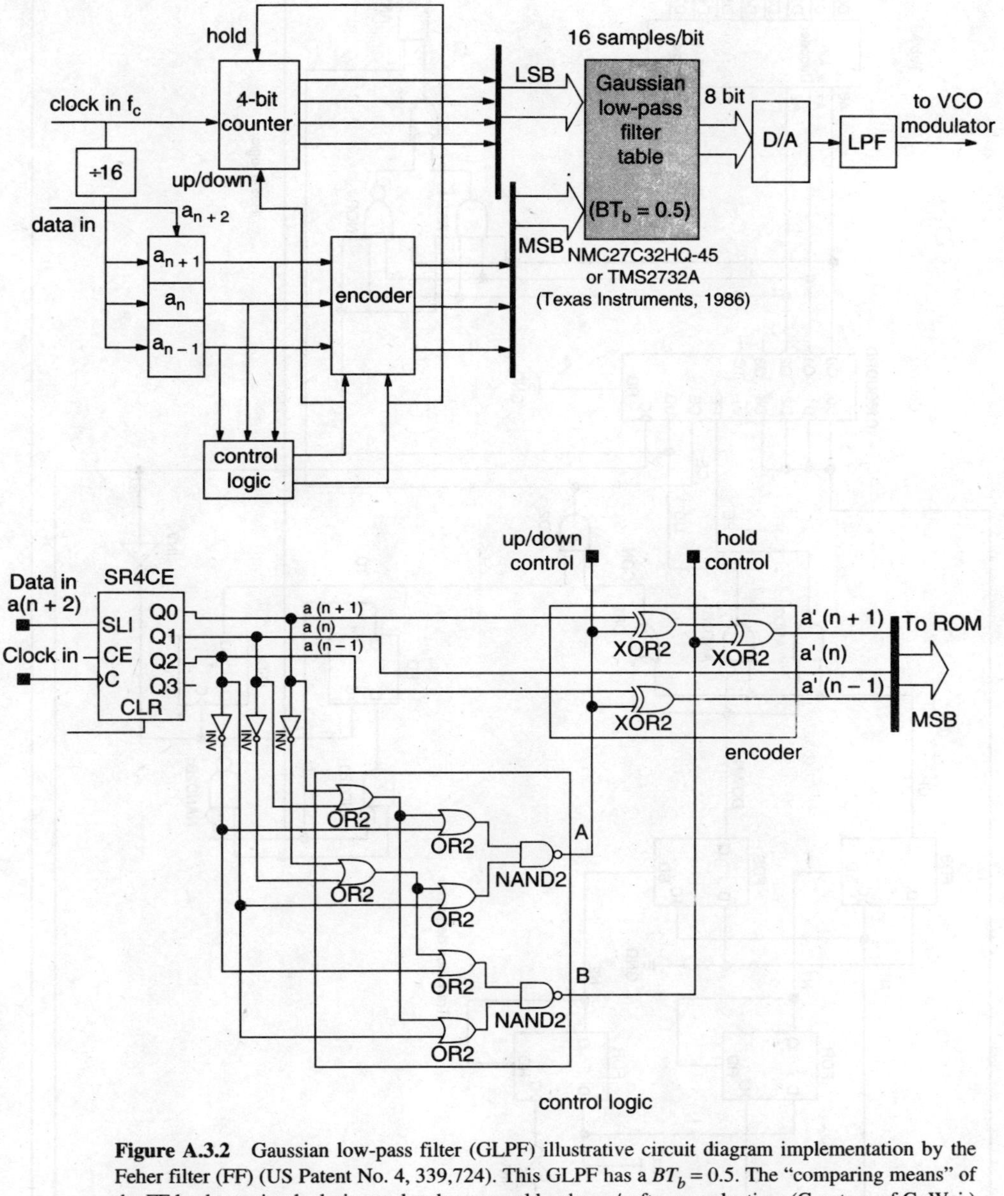

Figure A.3.2 Gaussian low-pass filter (GLPF) illustrative circuit diagram implementation by the Feher filter (FF) (US Patent No. 4, 339,724). This GLPF has a $BT_b = 0.5$. The "comparing means" of the FF lead to a simple design and a phenomenal hardware/software reduction. (Courtesy of G. Wei.)

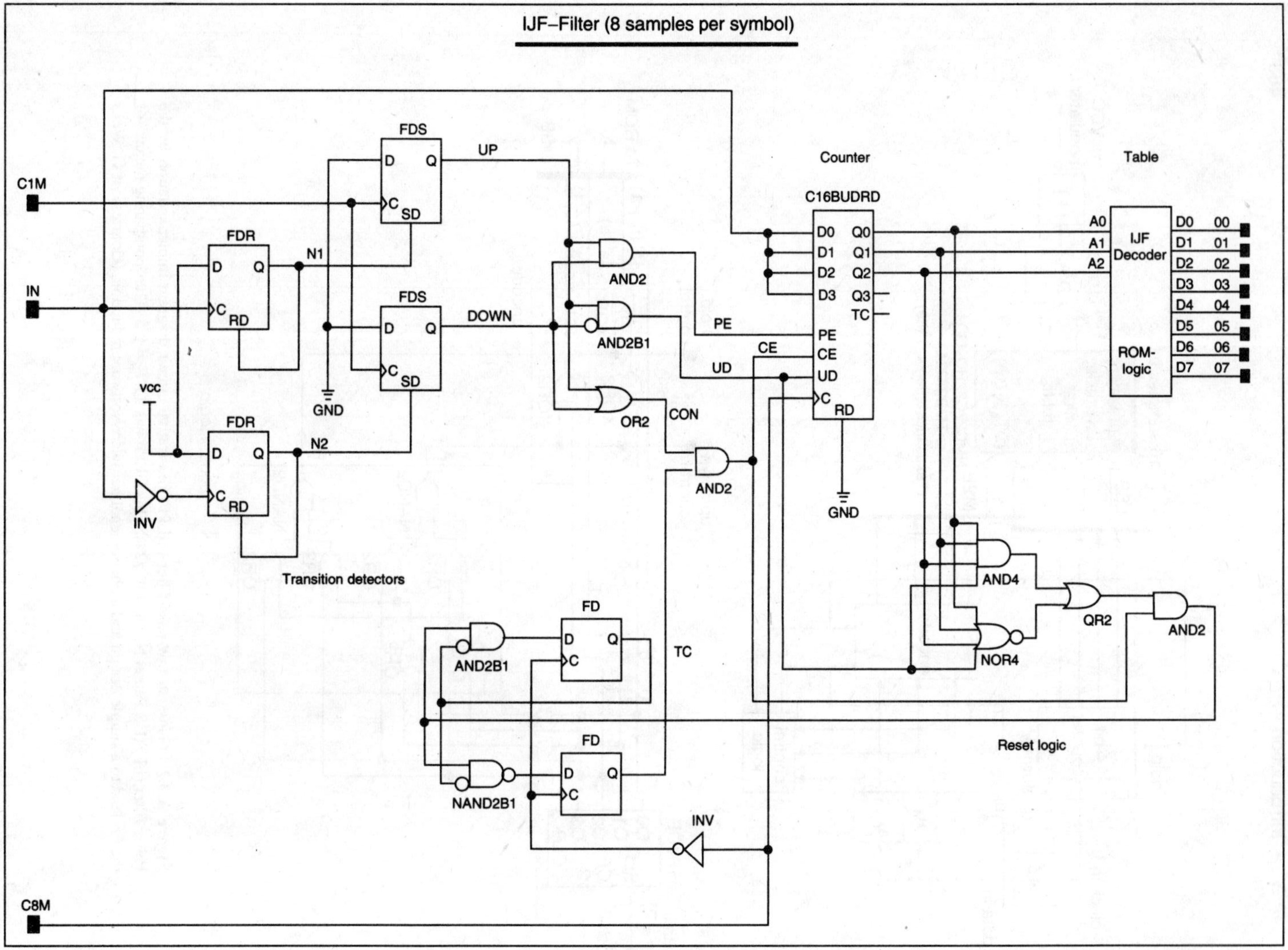

Figure A.3.3 Circuit diagram of an illustrative FQPSK-1 baseband processor by means of the Feher filter. Intersymbol Interference and Jitter Free (IJF) read only memory (ROM)-based implementation example.

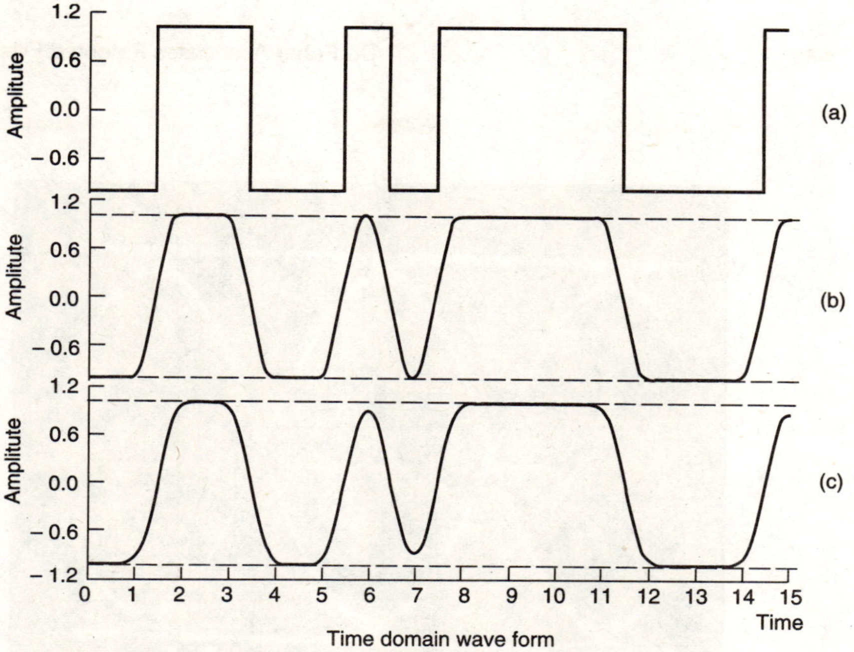

Figure A.3.4 GFSK and FQPSK-1 signal patterns generated by Feher's filter (FF) (US Patent No. 4,339,724). (a) NRZ unfiltered sample data pattern; (b) "FQPSK-1" of the I-channel baseband modulator or of FGFSK (Feher patent—means based GFSK-equivalent generator); and (c) Gaussian filtered ($BT_b = 0.5$) signal generated by the FF patent. In both digital ROM based implementations, only one- and two-bit memory comparison circuits were required.

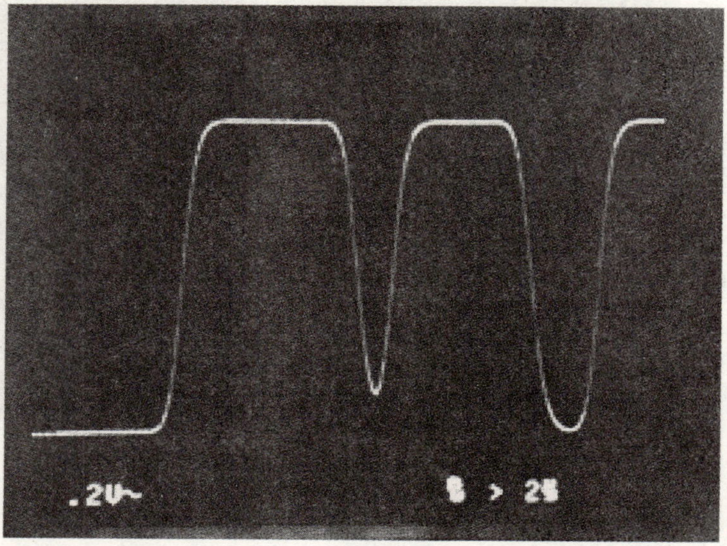

(a)

Figure A.3.5 GFSK experimental "eye diagrams" and sample filtered (Gaussian $BT_b = 0.5$) pulse pattern responses. (a) National's LMX 2411 at DECT standardized $f_b = 1.152$ Mb/s rate, and (b), (c) implementations based on Feher filter (FF) (US Patent No. 4,339,724) with reduced gate count, reduced power.

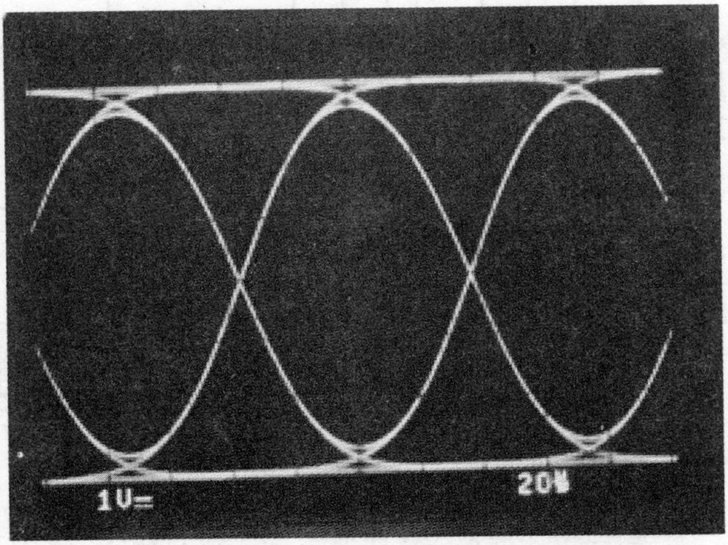

(b)

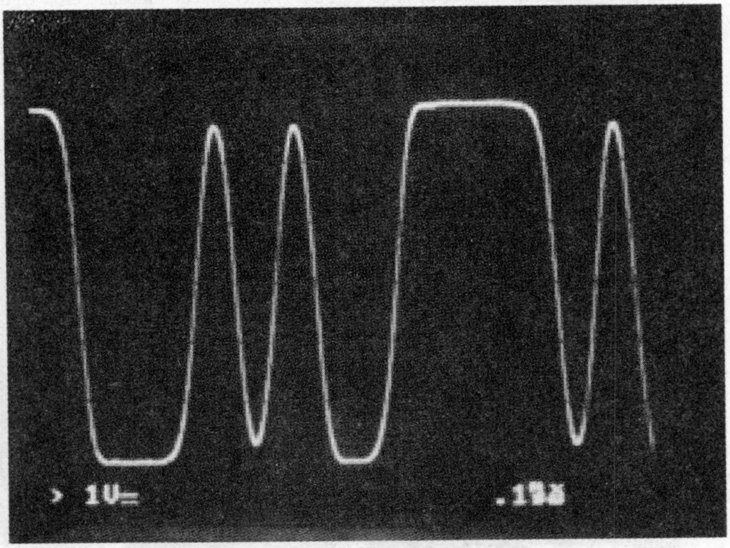

(c)

Figure A.3.5 (continued)

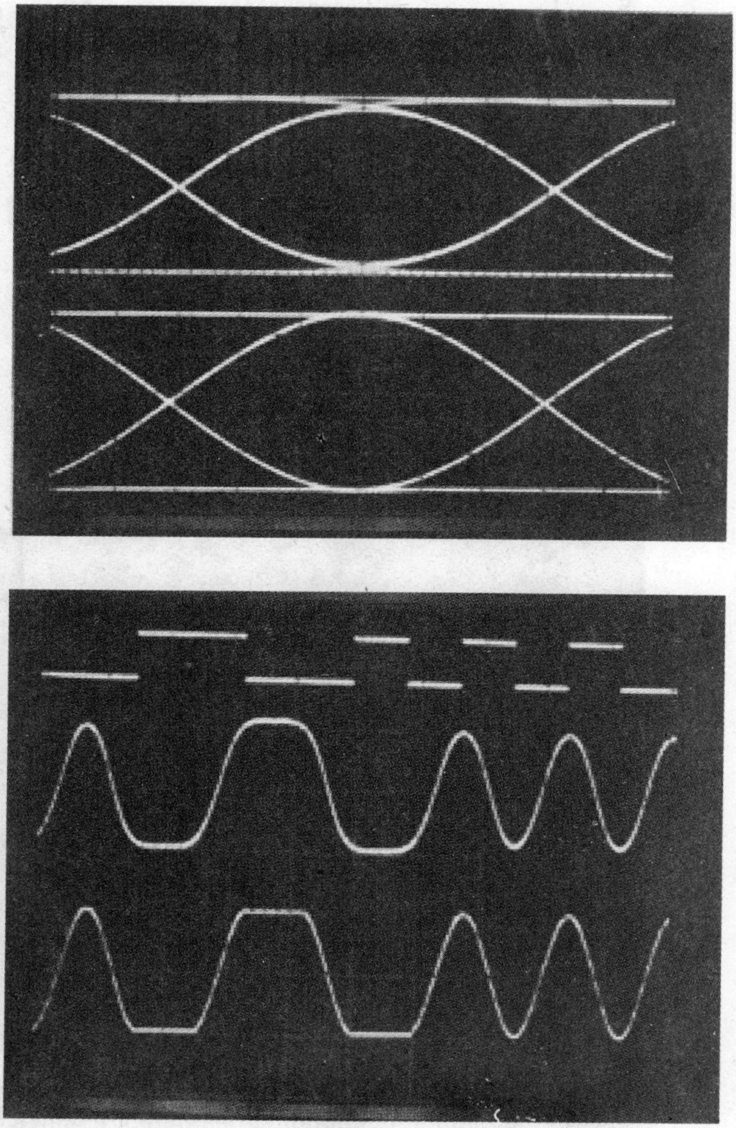

Figure A.3.6 Eye diagrams and sample data pattern diagrams of Gaussian ($BT_b = 0.5$) filtered and of "FQPSK-1" baseband processed signals. The upper eye diagram and time response of GFSK has approximately 10% ISI (intersymbol interference). The lower diagrams correspond to FQPSK-1 and are intersymbol interference and jitter free (IJF). Both implementations are simple and use the technology and principles of the Feher filter (US Patent No. 4,567,602).

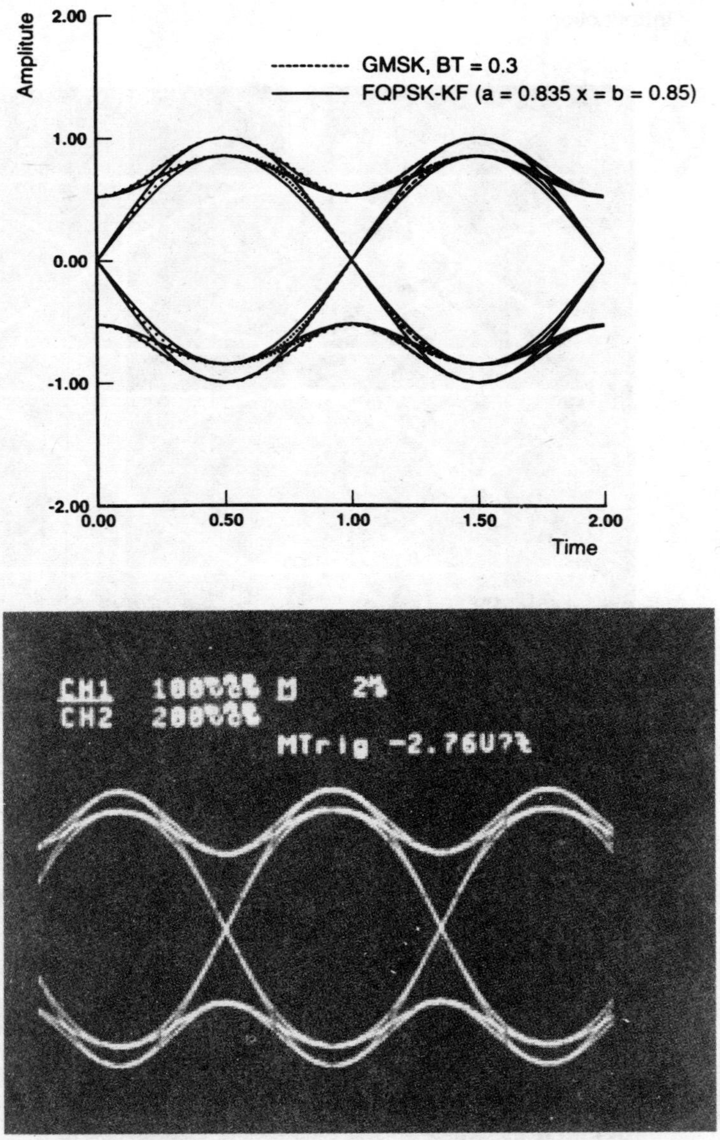

(a)

(b)

Figure A.3.7 GMSK ($BT_b = 0.3$) and FQPSK-KF equivalent eye diagrams. The GMSK (dotted lines) as well as the FQPSK-KF (solid lines) are generated by the Kato/Feher (KF) (US Patent No. 4,567,602). The licensed KF technology, for GMSK as well as FQPSK applications, leads to simpler hardware than alternative GMSK implementations. The KF patent enables simple I and Q quadrature based GMSK designs. Generated by Hongying Yan. (a) Computer generated results. (b) Hardware experimental results at $f_b = 270.833$ kb/s rate measured on the Phillips PCD-5071 chip, manufactured for the Global Mobile System (GSM) internationally standardized markets (Courtesy of E. Fu, UC Davis). The computer generated results and the hardware results are practically the same. See Figures A.3.1(c), 4.3.35, and A.3.14.

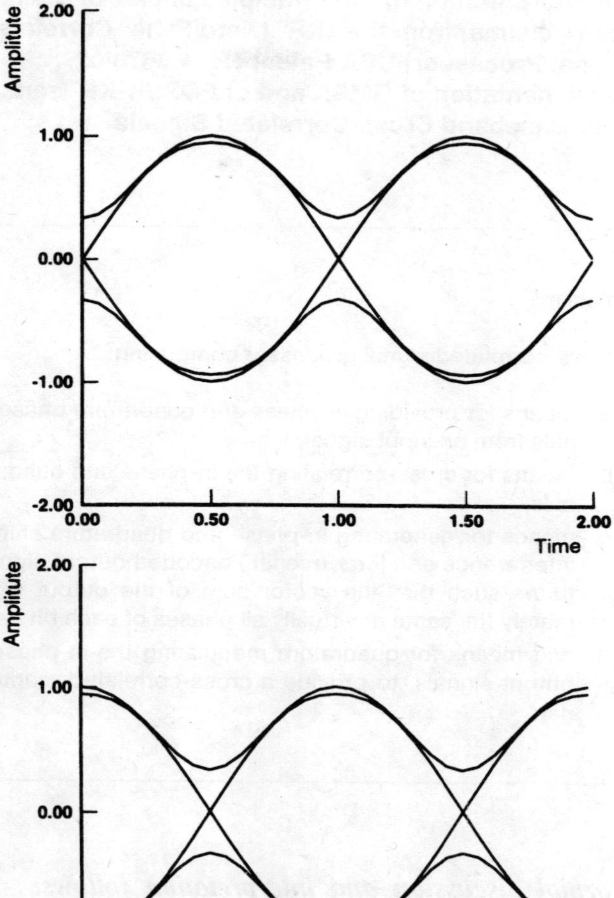

Figure A.3.8 GMSK eye diagrams with $BT_b = 0.5$ of a quadrature modulator generated by the Kato/Feher (KF) (US Patent No. 4,567,602). Note from Figure A.3.1(c) that the I and Q signals are crosscorrelated, are virtually intersymbol interference and jitter free (IJF), and that their quadrature modulated signal has a constant envelope. These specifications are identical to some of the claims of this patent.

A.3.5 An Interpretation of the Principles and/or of Claim No. 6 (of 14 claims) from the "KF" (Kato/Feher Correlated Signal Processor) USA Patent No. 4,567,602. Implementation of GMSK and of FQPSK-KF Transmitters with Baseband Cross-Correlated Signals

We claim:

A cross-correlated signal processor comprising:

a. means for providing in-phase and quadrature phase shifted NRZ signals from an input signal,
b. means for cross-correlating the in-phase and quadrature shifted signals,
c. means for generating in-phase and quadrature shifted intersymbol -interference and jitter free(IJF) encoded output signals having amplitudes such that the vector sum of the output signals is approximately the same at virtually all phases of each bit period,
d. and means for quadrature modulating the in-phase and quadrature output signals, to provide a cross-correlated modulated output signal.

An informal discussion and interpretation follows:

A simplified tutorial or "academic" interpretation of one of the independent claims, Claim #6 of the "KF" patent, indicates that we were awarded claims for principles and implementations of cross correlation between the in-phase and quadrature channels of a quadrature (QUAD) modulation structure and the generation of bandlimited signals of constant modulated envelope with intersymbol interference and jitter-free (IJF) crosscorrelated capability.

A closer examination of some of the modern quadrature GMSK and FQPSK-KF integrated circuit architectures and products indicates that the I and Q baseband signals are obtained from an original NRZ signal which is Gaussian filtered and integrated (e.g., see Figures A.3.1c and 3.1d). This resultant filtered signal is split into a "cos ( ) and sin ( )" ROM-based look-up table and in turn is used as the I and Q baseband drives of the quadrature modulator. One of the key principles is that the final I and Q outputs are cross-correlated over an interval of bits. In fact the Q signal is mathematically related or "cross-correlated" to the I signal. You may note that the term **"correlated" means "predictable, calculable."** In a Quadrature (QUAD)-based ROM implementation, the I and Q signals are cross-correlated and they lead to a constant envelope signal which is bandlimiting the original NRZ signal. Additionally this constant envelope transmitted signal, after demodulation, has a practically IJF property and in particular if the BTb product is 0.5. Illustrative experimental photographs demonstrate this fact in several well-known references and also Fig. A.3.8.

Bandwidth product $BT_b = 0.5$ is specified in systems such as the European Standard DECT, CT-2 and others. For a reduced $BT_b = 0.3$, such as specified for the *GSM Standardized* and PCS-1900 systems, the GMSK modulated systems have *I and Q cross-correlated eye diagrams and exhibit Intersymbol Interference,* see Fig. A.3.7 and Fig. A.3.16. Claims of the KF patent (U.S. Patent No. 4,567,602 Kato/Feher) include signals with Intersymbol Interference, e.g., "When the in-phase channel signal is non-zero, the maximum magnitude of the quadrature shifted signal is reduced from normalized to A, where $1/\sqrt{2} \leq A \leq 1$."

GMSK implementations based on traditional passive component Gaussian filter design, followed by FM modulator (VCO) do not necessarily use the means of the FF and KF patents. However, GMSK structures which implement the bit comparison ROM-based Gaussian filter, integrator, and Quadrature Crosscorrelated architecture use the claims of the FF patent. Additionally the sin ( ) and cos ( ) derived from the same input signal to drive the IQ processors has cross correlation and in particular correlation to attain fully-constant envelope. Careful examinations of the claims as well as of the text of the KF patent may reveal that our claims in the KF patent have also been used.

A.3.6 What are Feher's FQPSK, FBPSK, FQAM, FGFSK, and FGMSK? Are All of These Systems Patented?

Conventional (coincident transition or "non-offset") and offset QPSK as well as other filtered systems which use one or more of Dr. Feher and Associates' patented filters and correlators are part of the **FQPSK family of inventions** and products. The broad "FQPSK" term may include Feher's patented BPSK or FBPSK, patented baseband, and/or FSK signals. The implementation of Feher's filter or processors is much simpler than that of conventional raised-cosine, Gaussian, Chebychev, and Butterworth filters. FF patented filters operate with less DSP power and they lead to dramatic combined modem-RF system advantages (see Figure A.3.9). The ROM and FPGA based "Feher Filter (FF)" patent advantages were discussed previously in this appendix.

The implementations of conventional FSK systems (coherent or noncoherently demodulated) including GFSK and GMSK may or may not be patented. For example, if a GFSK transmitter utilizes a filtered ROM generated signal, then the conventional GFSK system may be protected by Intellectual Property. In the case of BPSK-compatible FBPSK, which is suitable for power-efficient low-cost nonlinear amplifications with a 5dB to 7dB power advantage, the implemented BPSK may also be in the category of our patented systems, see Table A.3.1 and Figure 4.3.40. If a conventional GMSK system is

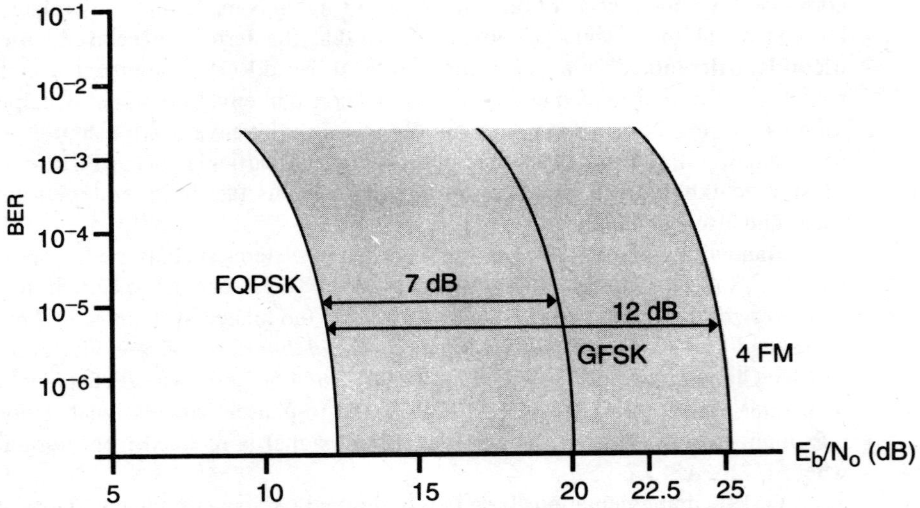

Figure A.3.9 Measured BER = $f(E_b/N_o)$ curves of several "C-class" RF IC-nonlinearly amplified modulated systems at f_b = 1 Mb/s and 2 Mb/s rate. FQPSK, GFSK with 160 kHz deviation, and digital 4FM shown. Illustrative experimental data as submitted to WLAN and PCS standardization committees such as IEEE 802.11 and TIA/JTC. The experimental data show that at the specified BER = 10^{-5}, FQPSK is 7 dB and 12 dB more robust than GFSK and 4FM, respectively. Such dramatic performance improvement in an interference controlled environment, e.g., FCC-15, can increase the throughput rate about 100 to 1000 times. Relatively small 160 kHz deviation is specified in order to meet the FCC-15 and IEEE 802.11 spectral efficiency and out of band attenuation requirements.

implemented based on one of our patents, e.g., ROM-based filter and/or I and Q transmit quadrature baseband correlation (quadrature) then the product, **has to be licensed from Digcom, Inc.**

To designate that GFSK, GMSK, BPSK, QPSK, or QAM systems use the means and claims of *F*eher Associates patents we call them "*F*GFSK," "*F*GMSK," "*F*BPSK," "*F*QPSK," or "*F*QAM". See Figure A.3.10.

Table A3.1 Maximal output power of illustrative 2.4 GHz integrated circuit amplifiers, suitable for PCMCIA cards with 3 V battery supplies and power efficiency comparison of DBPSK, DQPSK, π/4-DQPSK vs. FQPSK and FBPSK.

	DBPSK, DQPSK and π/4-DQPSK	**FQPSK and FBPSK**	**Improvement achieved by FQPSK and FBPSK**
Measured maximum RF output power at 2.4 GHz	18.5 dBm	23.5 dBm	300%
Power efficiency	10%	20%	100%

A.3.7 Correlated and crosscorrelated in-phase (I) and quadrature (Q) signals of GMSK and of FQPSK-KF transmitters. An informal tutorial discussion in regards to the use of Kato/Feher U.S. Patent for GMSK applications and in particular of the GSM standard.

A demonstration of the fact that the in-phase (I) and Quadrature (Q) signals in a GMSK transmitter are crosscorrelated (Kato/Feher, U.S. Patent No. 4,567,602) follows. In Figure A.3.1(c), we refer to the input NRZ signal a(t) at point 1, Gaussian low-pass filtered signal $g(t)$ at point 2, integrated and Gaussian filtered signal $b(t)$ at point 3, and cosine and sine values of the $b(t)$ signal, designated as $x(t)$ and $y(t)$ at points 4 and 5 of Fig. A.3.1(c). Signals for the implementation means of Fig. A.3.1(c) have been generated for the **Global Mobile System (GSM) international standard specifications.** These specifica-

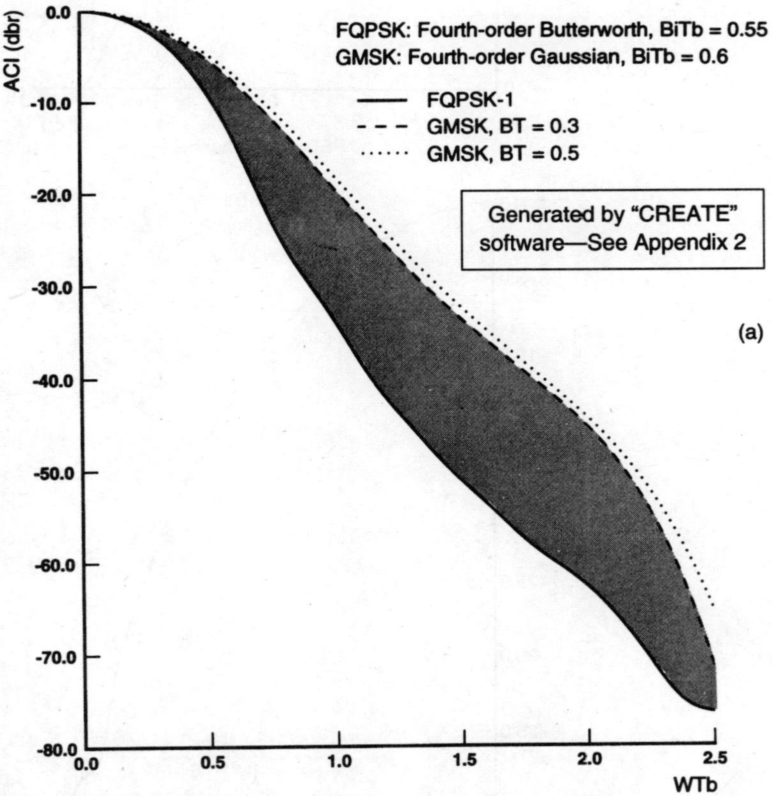

Figure A.3.10 Power spectral density advantage of "FQPSK-1" over GMSK. Integrated adjacent channel interference (ACI) is illustrated in Fig. A.3.10(a). Even more significant spectral compression and efficiencies can be attained with FQPSK-KF, as illustrated in Fig. A.3.10(b) and Fig. A.3.10(c). Nonlinearly amplified data.

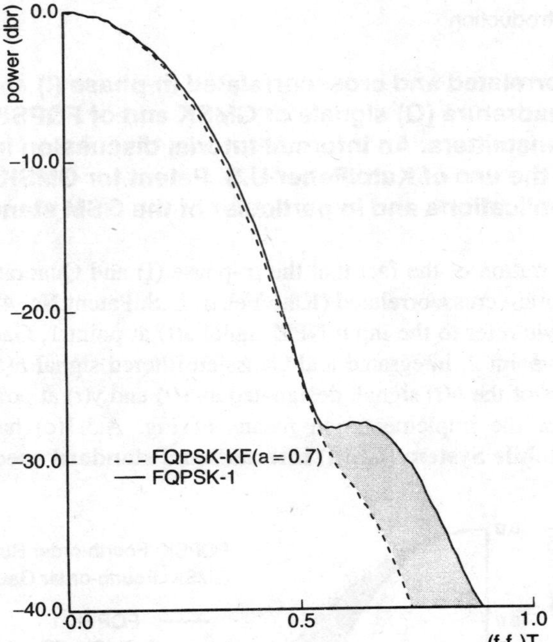

PSD in HL Channel (b)

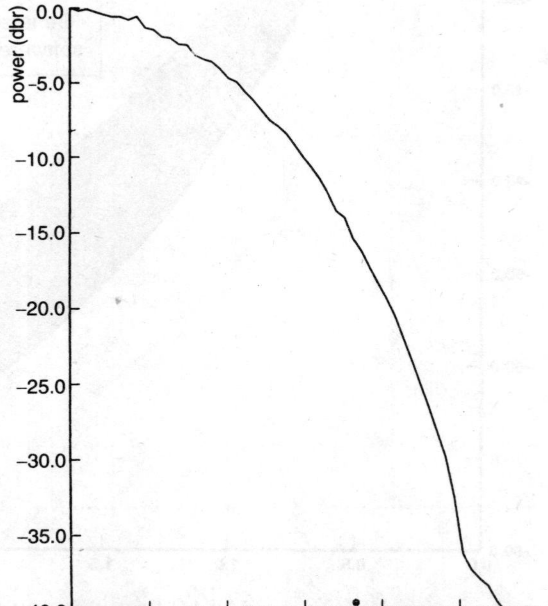

PSD of FQPSK-KF (a = 0.5, DJ, alpha = 1.0, jr = 0.01) (c)

Figure A.3.10 (continued)

tions stipulate a GMSK modulator with $BT_b = 0.3$. A brief explanation of the generated signals of Fig. A.3.1(c) and of the corresponding eye diagrams follows.

The Gaussian ($BT_b = 0.3$) filtered output signal at point 2 in Fig. A.3.1(c) of an input Non-return to Zero (NRZ) signal for a typical random pattern is illustrated in Fig. A.3.11. Note that this Gaussian filtered NRZ signal pattern, designated $g(t)$, exhibits substantial Intersymbol Interference (ISI). The ISI-free maximal amplitude values are normalized to +1 and −1. After integration, the filtered and integrated signal at point 3 is shown in Fig. A.3.13. This random-like data signal, signal $b(t)$, is **not a** "sinusoidal" signal. At point 3, this signal is split into the "in-phase" (I) and "quadrature" (Q) channels. Thus the **same** $b(t)$ signal appears in the I and Q channels. The presence of the "same" I and "Q" is a difference between MSK, OQPSK, QPSK, and GMSK quadrature imple-

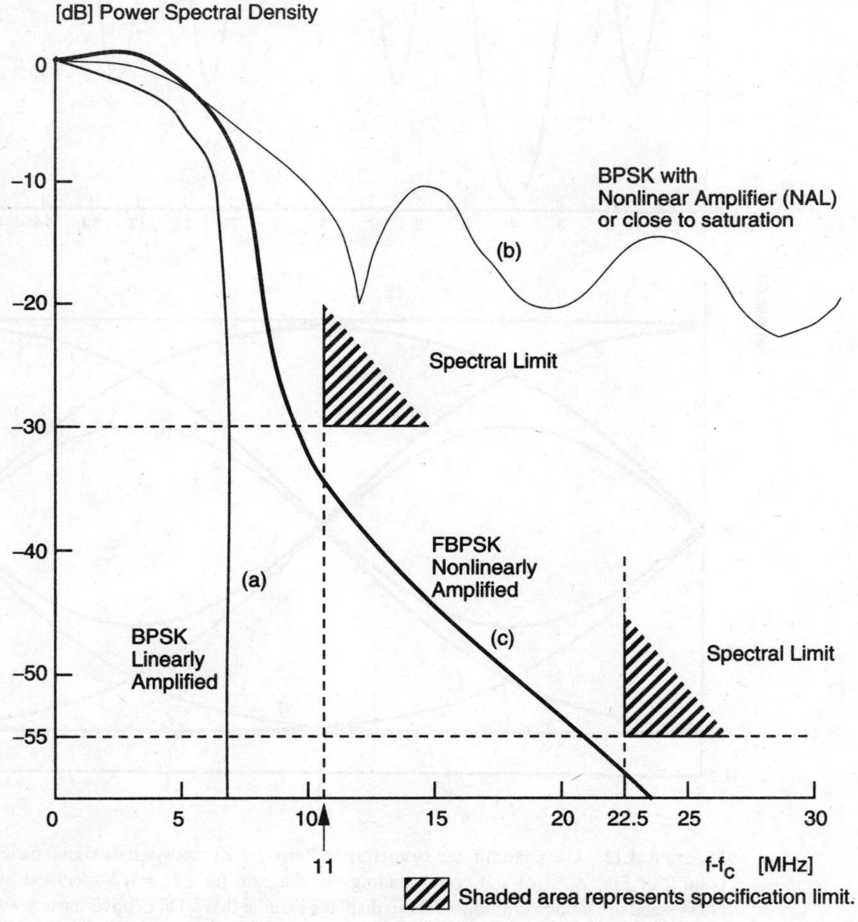

Figure A.3.11 Power spectral density of $f_c = 11$ Mchip/second rate direct sequence spread spectrum BPSK systems. (a) BPSK-bandlimited, linearly amplified. (b) BPSK-bandlimited and nonlinearly amplified. (c) FBPSK-bandlimited and nonlinearly amplified.

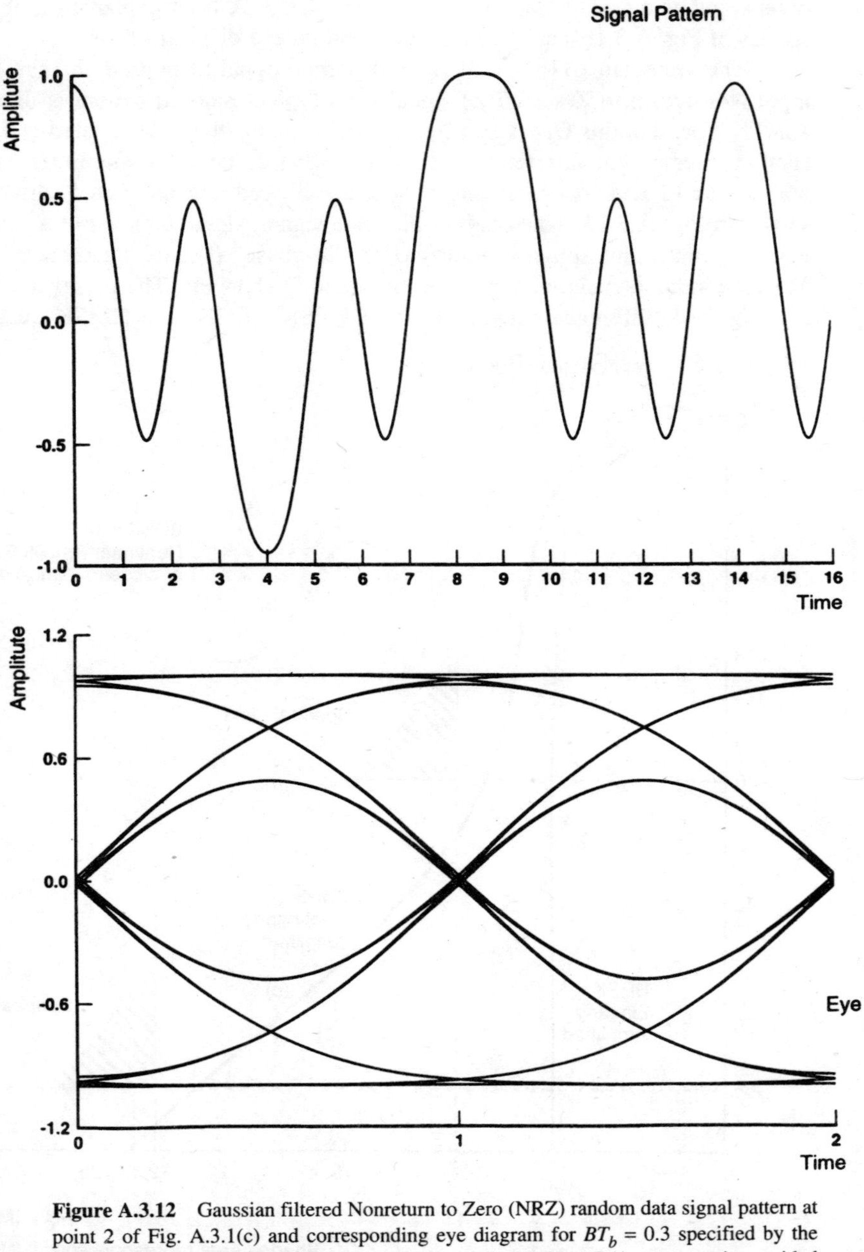

Figure A.3.12 Gaussian filtered Nonreturn to Zero (NRZ) random data signal pattern at point 2 of Fig. A.3.1(c) and corresponding eye diagram for $BT_b = 0.3$ specified by the GSM standardization committee. These displays assume that a D/A converter is provided for the case of DSP.

mentations in which a serial to parallel converter provides independent and **not correlated** binary data into the I and Q branch of the modulator. Thus splitter, point 3, with its connecting wires provides the same $b(t)$ signal into I and Q. Evidently these I and Q signals are **correlated and crosscorrelated** as they are the same. An interesting implementation means (to **split** the **same** signal into I and Q).

Following the $\cos[b(t)]$ and $\sin[b(t)]$ processors at points 4 and 5, the generated signal patterns are shown in Fig. A.3.14 and on an expanded time scale in Fig. A.3.15. These resultant bandlimited processed NRZ signals are designaled $x(t)$ and $y(t)$ in Fig. A.3.1(c). Points 4 and 5 serve as the in-phase and quadrature drives of quadrature modulators. These $x(t)$ and $y(t)$ random data signal patterns are "nonsinusoidal" in nature, i.e., they are not periodic sinusoidal waves. The $x(t)$ and $y(t)$ signals are crosscorrelated, in fact, they are related by equations.

$$x(t) = \cos[b(t)] \tag{1}$$

$$y(t) = \sin[b(t)] \tag{2}$$

Thus, the "predictability" or crosscorrelation of $y(t)$ from $x(t)$ is defined. In this case,

$$y(t) = \sin[\cos^{-1}x(t)] \tag{3}$$

In other words, to generate $x(t)$ and $y(t)$ we use a mathematical relation of "crosscorrelation" between these terms.

In Fig. A.3.16, the respective "eye diagrams" of these crosscorrelated $x(t)$ and $y(t)$ signals are displayed. Note that these crosscorrelated signals are data transition jitter free

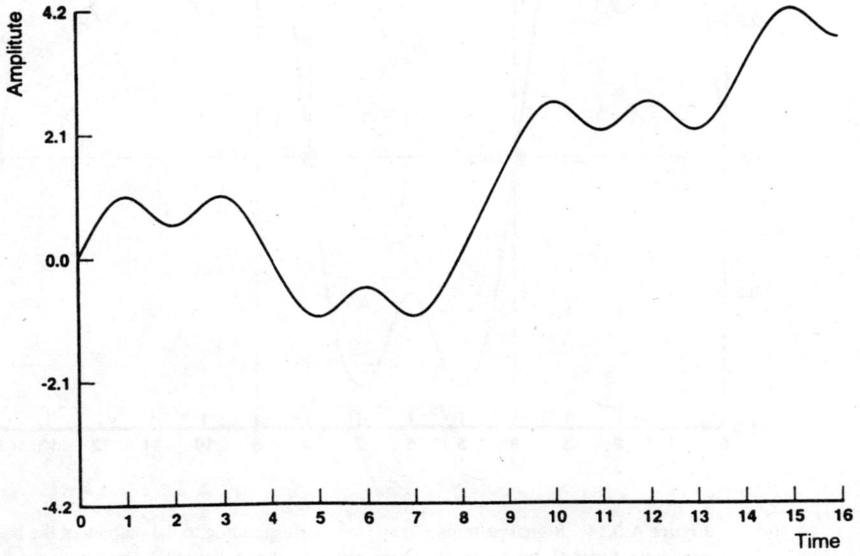

Figure A.3.13 Integrated Gaussian ($BT_b = 0.3$) filtered signal pattern $b(t)$ at point 3 of Fig. A.3.1(d). This analog "looking-like" signal is only a concept in DSP-ROM-based implementations. It could be measured if a D/A converter was provided.

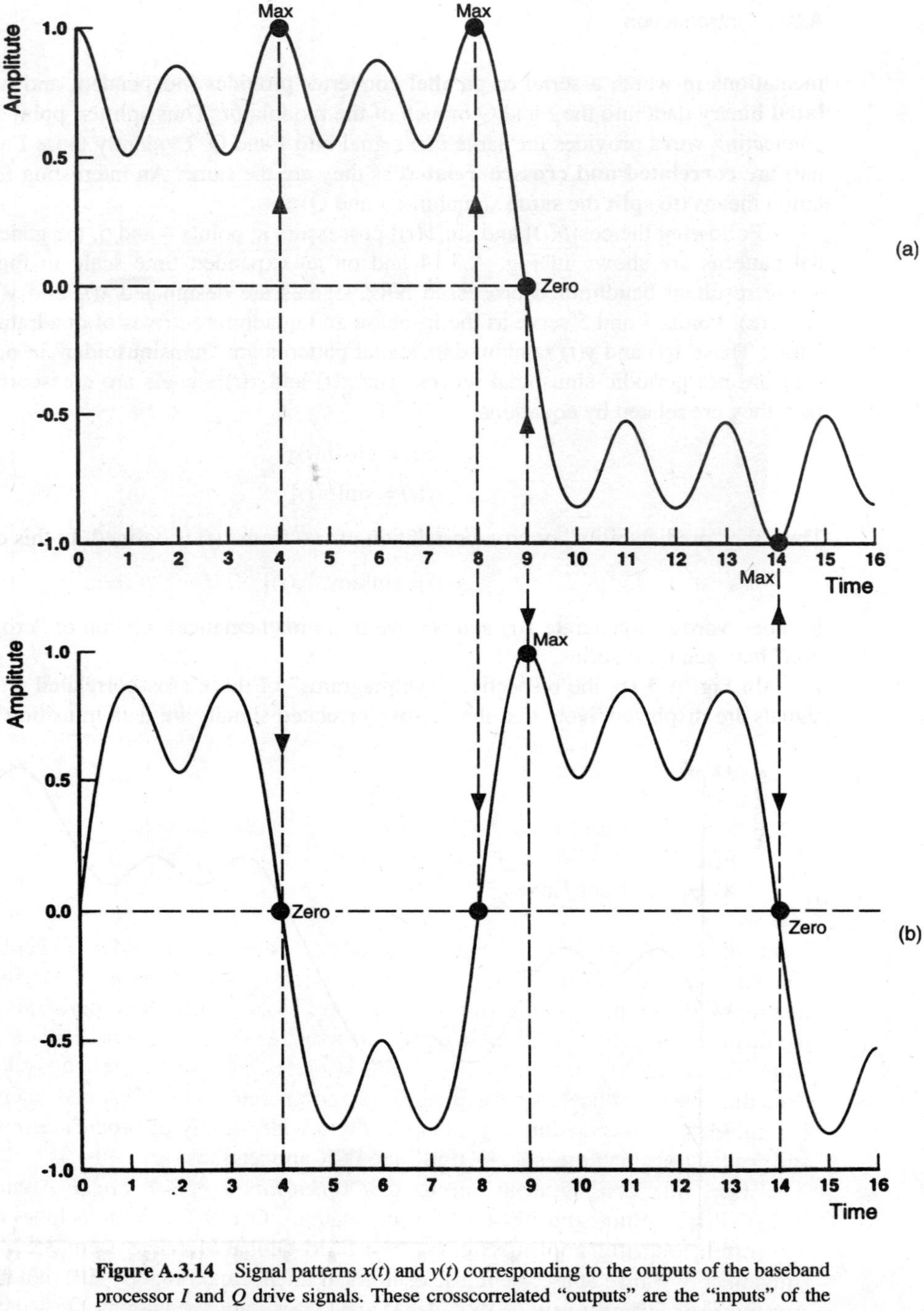

Figure A.3.14 Signal patterns $x(t)$ and $y(t)$ corresponding to the outputs of the baseband processor I and Q drive signals. These crosscorrelated "outputs" are the "inputs" of the quadrature modulator, see points 4 and 5 in Fig. A.3.1(c). (a) and (b) computer generated; (c) experimental on a GSM standard chip at 270.833 kb/s (Phillips PCD-5071). Virtually identical signal patterns, eye diagrams, and specifications were generated by the simpler FQPSK-KF structure of Figures 4.3.35(a) and A.3.17(b). See Figure A.3.7.

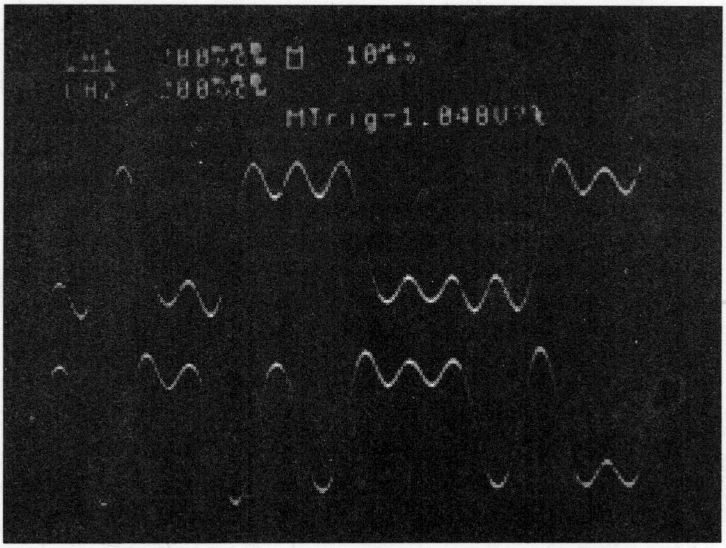

f_b = 270.833 kb/s
PCD-5071
GSM Standard
GMSK

(c)

Figure A.3.14 (continued)

and the maximum magnitude of the quadrature (alternatively in-phase) signal is reduced when the in-phase channel signal is non-zero. A careful examination of U.S. Patent No. 4,567,602 leads to a conclusion that these GMSK system quadrature implementations use the means of this invention.

A.3.8 Field-Proven? Can We Get Patented GFSK, GMSK, FBPSK, FQPSK, or FQAM Technology Transfer? IC Chips? Bit Rates?

Since the early 1980s, generations of products benefited from Dr. Feher Associates patented/licensed technologies. Many products have been developed. During the first quarter of 1995, one of the largest and most profitable American corporations completed the design of FQPSK-based systems for a production run of *several million subscriber units.* For power efficient *satellite* systems at 6GHz and 14GHz, relatively low bit rate (less than 500kb/s) have been implemented and operate in the USA and internationally. For cable systems including digital *cable TV,* a wide variety of products use these filter and processor technologies for FQPSK and FSK applications.

Our filter "FF" patent meets the *Token-Passing Bus Local Area Networks* ISO/IEC/**IEEE Standard 802.4**-1990 specifications. Our "KF" patent includes the quadrature correlation based implementation of the GSM-Global Mobile System (GSM) specified equipment. We have other patent disclosures and Intellectual Property (IP) (not listed in this Appendix) which is for new FBPSK, 4-FM and GFSK implementations. On Motorola, Teledyne, MiniCircuits, and other RF ICs at 900MHz and 2.4GHz we demonstrated at 1Mb/s and 2Mb/s the spectral and power performance advantages of our wireless technologies (e.g., see

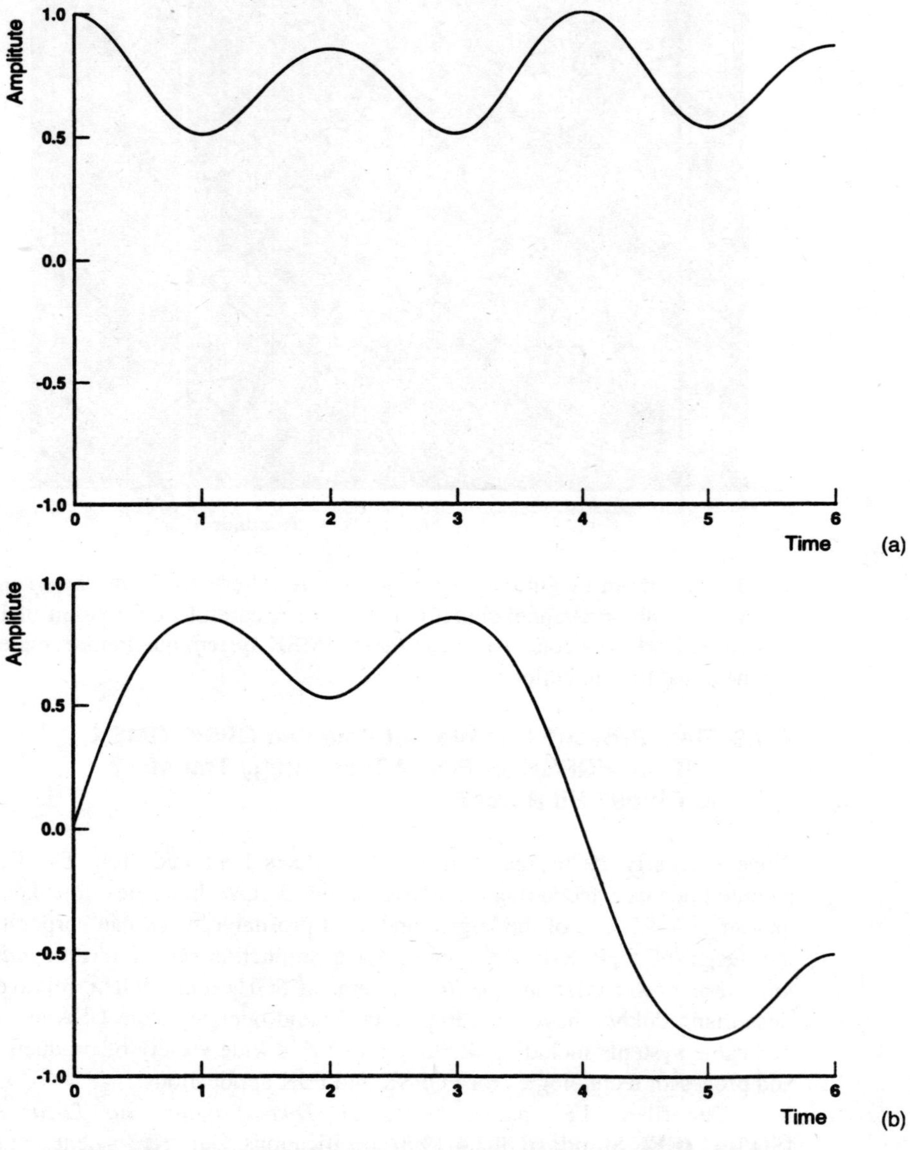

Figure A.3.15 Time scale expanded signal outputs of $x(t)$ and $y(t)$ (otherwise same as Fig. A.3.14). Generated by the GMSK—Figure A.3.1(c) and the FQPSK-KF cross-correlated structure of Figure A.3.17(b).

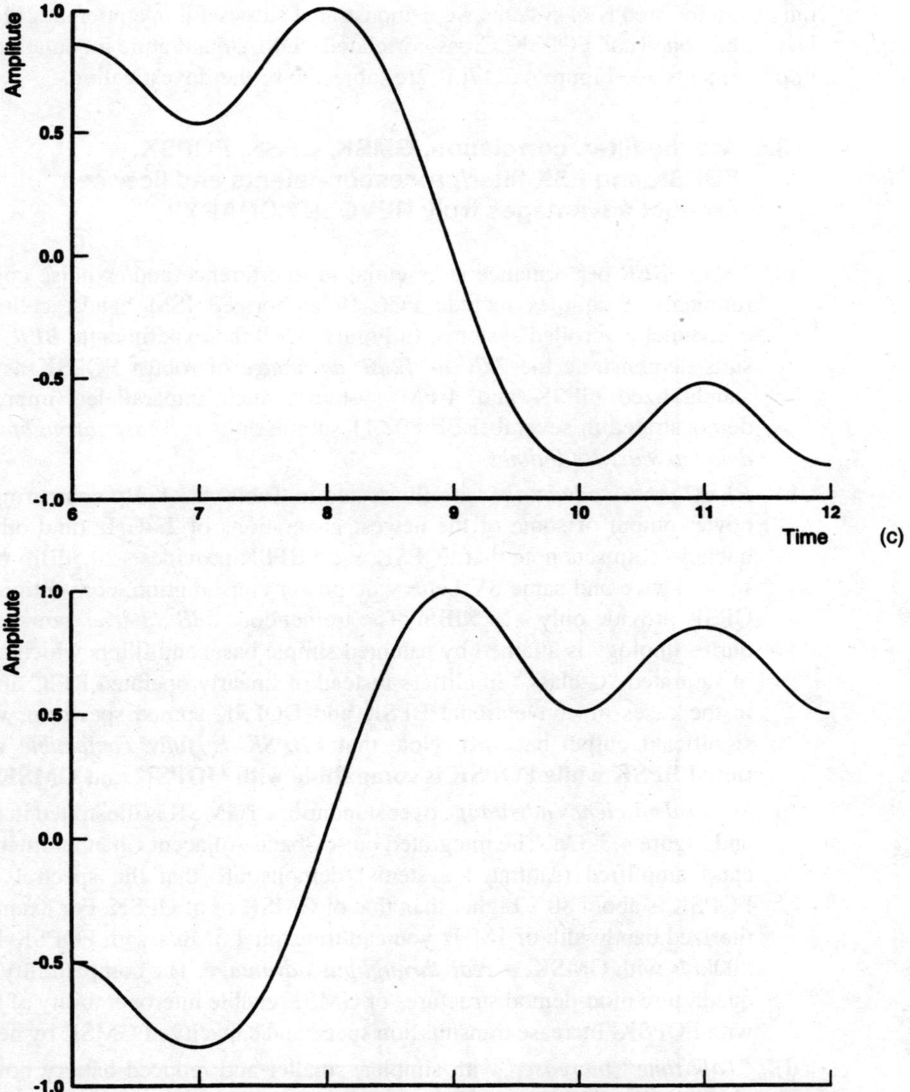

Figure A.3.15 (continued)

Table A.3.1, page 472). FQPSK, FBPSK, FGFSK and FGMSK technology transfers is available to members of the **FQPSK Consortium.** Chips operate in the 64kb/sec to 10Mb/sec range. On infrared (IR) systems we demonstrated successful operation at 2Mb/s to 10Mb/s bit rate baseband and FQPSK. Cross-correlated CDMA-quadrature modulation and possible improvements, see Figure A.3.17(a), are subject to further investigation.

A.3.9 Are the filter, correlation, GMSK, GFSK, FQPSK, FBPSK and FSK filter/processor patents and licensed product advantages truly REVOLUTIONARY?

a) *Robust BER* performance is essential in interference and/or noise controlled environments. Examples include FCC-15 authorized ISM bands, cellular and PCS cochannel controlled systems. In Figure A.3.9 the experimental $BER = f(E_b/N_o)$ results demonstrate the ***7dB to 12dB advantage*** of robust FQPSK as compared to standardized GFSK and 4-FM systems. Such unparalleled improvements, as demonstrated in several IEEE 802.11 submissions *increase throughput and reduce delay at least 1000 times.*

b) *RF IC power advantages* are illustrated in Table A.3.1. By comparing the average power output of some of the newest generations of 2.4GHz (and other RFIC frequency) chip sets note that FQPSK and FBPSK provides +23.5dBm while with the same device and same 3V battery dc power consumption, conventional BPSK and QPSK provide only +18.5dBm. The tremendous ***5dB (300%) power advantage*** of our technology is attained by patented simple baseband filters which enable the use of saturated "C-class" amplifiers instead of linearly operated RFIC amplifiers used in the cases of conventional BPSK and DQPSK spread spectrum, which require significant output back-off. Note that ***FBPSK is fully compatible*** **with conventional BPSK while FQPSK is compatible with OQPSK and GMSK.**

c) *Spectral efficiency advantage* over standardized GMSK is illustrated in Figure A.3.10 and Figure 4.3.32a. The integrated out-of-band Adjacent Channel Interference of C-class amplified (saturated systems) demonstrate that the spectral efficiency of FQPSK is about 80% higher than that of GMSK or of GFSK. For example, in an authorized bandwidth of 1MHz you can transmit 1.5Mb/s with FQPSK-KF instead of 800kb/s with GMSK, ***a real throughput advantage.*** The compatibility and identical quadrature mod-demod structures of GMSK enable interoperability of these systems with FQPSK. Increase transmission speed and capacity of GMSK by nearly 200%!

d) *"Talk time" increased* with simpler, smaller and reduced battery power filter implementations and more efficient RF IC operation.

e) *Radiation is reduced.* Nonlinearly amplified FQPSK and FBPSK wireless systems have a 6dB to 8dB lower peak radiation than standardized DBPSK, DQPSK and $\pi/4$-DQPSK.

f) *Gate count reduction of over 500% with Feher's Filter/Correlation* look-up table ROM or FPGA enables design of much simpler quadrature implementations, see Figure A.3.18.

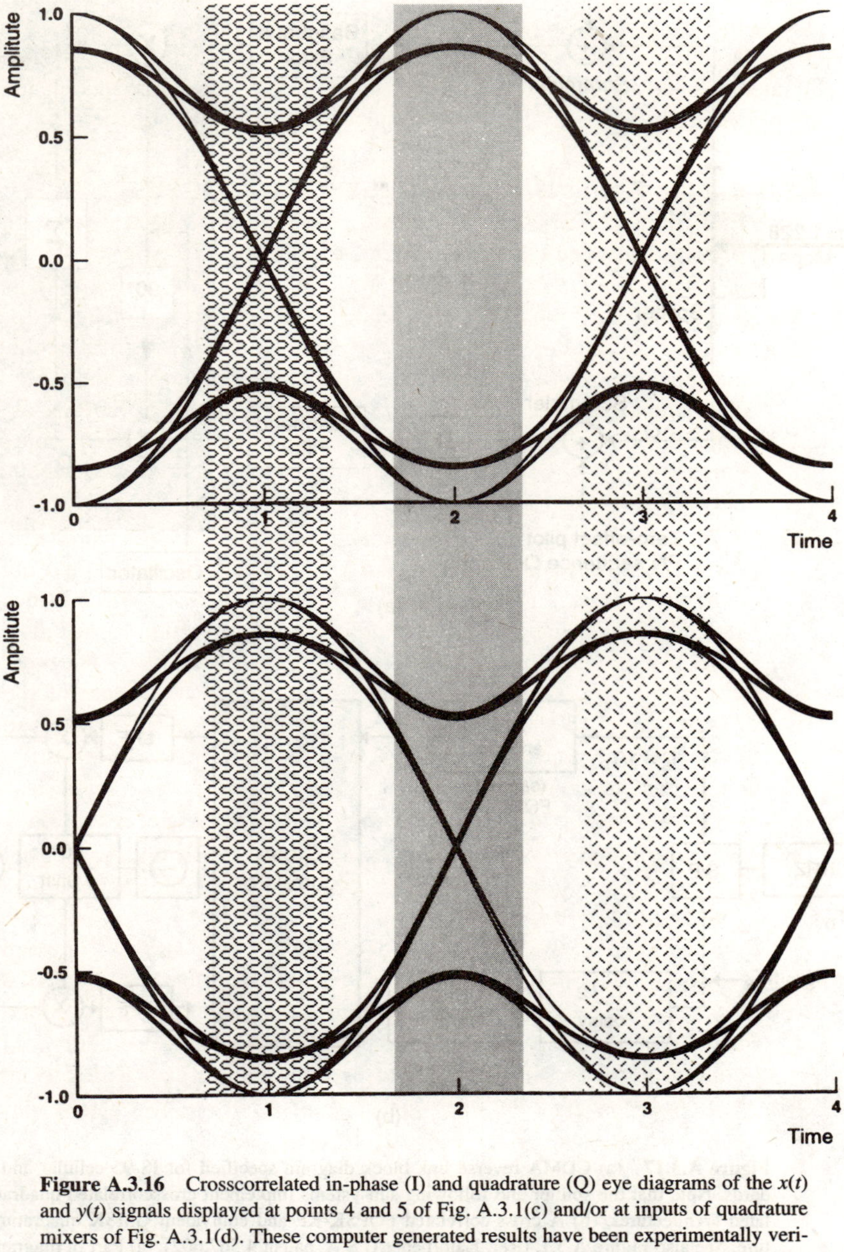

Figure A.3.16 Crosscorrelated in-phase (I) and quadrature (Q) eye diagrams of the $x(t)$ and $y(t)$ signals displayed at points 4 and 5 of Fig. A.3.1(c) and/or at inputs of quadrature mixers of Fig. A.3.1(d). These computer generated results have been experimentally verified, see Fig. 4.3.24(c) for GSM standardized chips. Same eye patterns generated by means of simpler FQPSK-KF, see Figure 4.3.17(b).

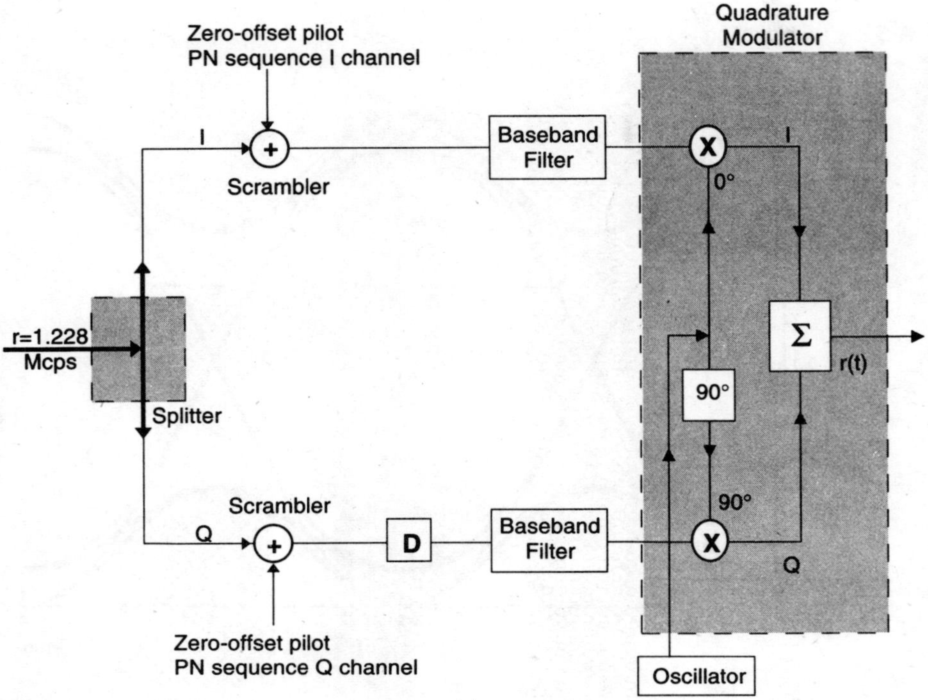

(a)

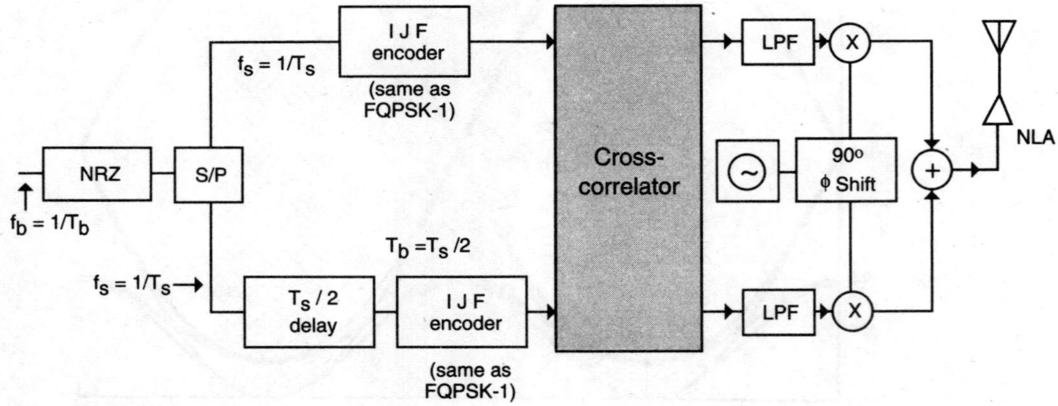

(b)

Figure A.3.17 (a) CDMA reverse link block diagram specified for IS-95 cellular and PCS standards. Note that the splitter and following subsystems implement crosscorrelated quadrature modulated architectures, (b) A cross-correlated FQPSK-KF and equivalent GMSK quadrature architecture. See also Figure A.3.1. (Ref. Kato/Feher U.S.A. patent 4,567,602). (a) Part of diagram extracted from standard.

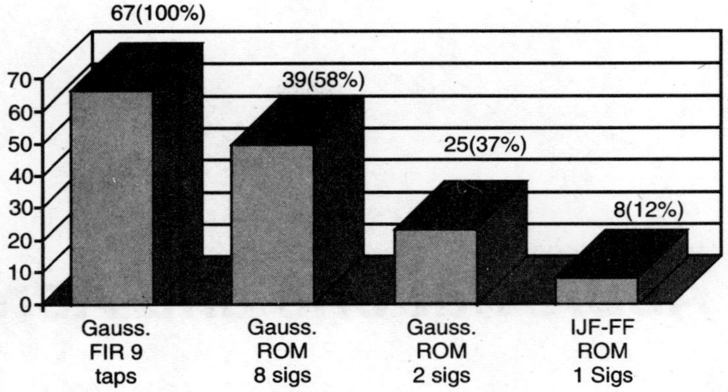

Figure A.3.18 FPGA (Field Programmable Gate Array) implementation of Gaussian and of "FQPSK-1" Intersymbol Interference and Jitter Free (IJF) filters by means of Dr. Feher Associates-Digcom, Inc. patented/licensed technologies. The number of packed configurable logic blocks (CLB) required for the implementation of filters is reduced from 67 to 9—an extraordinary reduction achieved by Feher's invention. [Ref. Yan, Borowski, IEEE 802.11, Jan. 95].

A.3.10 Is Reduced Peak Radiation an Essential Requirement?

New PCS and wireless regulations could stipulate limits on peak radiation. For such applications you could transmit with the FQPSK family of radio systems 6dB or more power than with conventional QPSK because of the **reduced peak factor** and envelope fluctuation of our technologies. FQPSK's reduced peak radiation is an additional advantage of this powerful technology.

A.3.11 Benefits of Joining the International FQPSK Consortium. Contact: Dr. Feher Associates-Digcom, Inc.

To introduce, manufacture and market power and spectrally efficient cost-competitive wireless -RF, cable, infrared satellite microwave and other systems and components, you may wish to become knowledgeable and have the license to participate in some of the most exciting technical achievements and product implementations including FQPSK, GFSK, GMSK, and FBPSK designs. You could obtain technology transfer and license for FPGA and ROM based "FF" and Kato/Feher "KF" correlation, e.g., GMSK design and "know-how" details. By joining the FQPSK Consortium your products could become compatible with standardized wireless systems and be ahead of the "just barely meets" standard requirements. Your organization may also benefit from potentially new "de facto" leading and emerging standards which could have significantly superior performance, increased speed, longer "talk time" (reduced battery power consumption) than compatible conventional systems.

Abbreviations and Acronyms

3VPCMCIA

4-FSK 4-level frequency shift keying

A Ampere(s)

A Erlangs $= \dfrac{\text{average calling time (minutes)} \times \text{total customers}}{\text{60 minutes}} =$ [ERLANGS]

α Propagation exponential attenuation (3 to 4)

A/D Analog to digital

AC or ac Alternating current

$\mathbf{a_c}$ Carried traffic per channel or ERLANGS (erl/channel)

$\mathbf{a_{cell}}$ Erl/cell = offered traffic per cell

ACG Automatic gain control

ACI Adjacent-channel interference

ACT Adaptive carrier tracking

ACTS Advanced Communications Technology Satellite

ADC American Digital Cellular

ADM Adaptive delta modulation

ADPCM Adaptive differential pulse-code-modulation

AGC Automatic gain control

AIN Advanced intelligent network

ALT Automatic link transfer

AM Amplitude modulation

AMPS Advanced Mobile Phone Service

AMSC American Mobile Satellite Corporation

AMT Advanced Communications Technology Satellite (ACTS) Mobile Terminal

AND AND logic function

ANSI American National Standards Institute, Inc.

AP Access point

APC American Personal Communications

ARQ Automatic repeat query or automatic repeat request

ASCII American National Standard Code for Information Interchange

a_{sub} Erl/sub ERLANG/subscriber during the = busy hour traffic

ATSR Automatic time-slot reassignment

AWGN Additive white Gaussian noise

B Blocking rate of calls

B-ISDN Broadband-integrated services digital network

b/s Bits per second

b/s/Hz Bits per second per Hertz-spectral efficiency

BBP Baseband processor

BBRELP Baseband residual-excited linear predictive

BBC Bellcore Client Company

BCD Binary coded decimal

BCH Bose-Chaudhuri-Hocquenghem code

BER Bit-error rate or bit-error ratio

BPF Band-pass filters

BPF_T Transmit bandpass filter

BPSK binary phase shift keying (see also Feher's FBPSK)

BSE Basic spectral efficiency

BSS Basic service set

BW Bandwidth

C/D Ratio of average received carrier power to average delayed carrier power

C/I Carrier-to-interference ratio

C/N Carrier-to-noise ratio; also CNR

CAI Common air interface

C_B Coherence bandwidth

CCI Cochannel-interference

CCIC Cochannel interference control

CCIR International Radio Consultative Committee

CCITT International Telegraph and Telephone Consultative Committee

CCS Common channel signaling

ccs Hundred call seconds

CDMA Code division multiple access

CELP Code excited linear predictive

CEPT Standard compression law in Europe

CIR Carrier-to-interference ratio

CMOS Complementary metal oxide semiconductor

CNR Carrier-to-noise ratio, also C/N

CO Central office

codec Coder/decoder

CONUS Continental United States

CPDF Cumulative probability distribution function

CPE Customer-provided equipment

CPFSK Continuous phase frequency shift keying

CPM Continuous phase modulation

CPM-FM Continuous phase modulation-frequency modulation

CR Carrier recovery

CSMA Collision sense multiple access, carrier sense multiple access

CSMA-CA-ACK Carrier-sense, multiple access collision avoidance with acknowledgment

C_T Coherence time

CT Cordless telephone

CT-2 Cordless telephone-2

CTIA Cellular Telecommunications Industry Association

CW Carrier wave or continuous wave

D Cochannel reuse distance

D/A Digital to analog

D/C Downconversion

D/R Distance (separation) to radius ratio

dB Decibel(s)

dBm Decibel(s) referred to 1 milliwatt

DBPSK Differential binary phase shift keying

DC or dc Direct current

DCA Dynamic channel allocation

DEBPSK Differential encoded binary phase shift keying

DECT Digital European Cordless Telephone

DES Data encryption standard

Δf Carrier frequency drift

DFWMAC Distributed foundation wireless MAC

DLL Delay lock loops

DM Delta modulation

DO-QPSK Differential offset-quadrature phase shift keying

DPCM Differential pulse code modulation

DPSK Differential phase shift keying

DQPSK Differential QPSK

DS Direct-sequence

DS-CDMA Direct sequence-code division multiple access

DS-SS Direct-sequence spread-spectrum

DSB Double-sideband

DSB-SC Double side band suppressed carrier

DSB-SC-AM Double-sideband suppressed-carrier amplitude modulators

DSP Digital signal processor or processing

DTMF Dual-tone multifrequency

E_bN_o Bit energy to noise density

EC European Commission

ECI Externally caused interference

EIA Electronics Industries Association

ERL Erlang = average calling time per hour (e.g., 1.5 min/hour)(Lee, p. 3)

ERP Effective radiated power

ESN Electronic serial number

FA Framework technical advisory

FAR False alarm rate

f_b Bit rate of source code

FBPSK Feher's patented constant envelope BPSK licensed product

FCC Federal Communications Commission

f_D Doppler spread

FDD Frequency-division duplex

FDI Feeder distribution interface

FDM Frequency-division multiplexing

FDMA Frequency-division multiple access

FEC Forward error correction

FF Feher's filter patent

FF Flip-flop

FFH Fast frequency-hopping

FH Frequency-hopping

FH-SS Frequency-hopped spread-spectrum

FIR Forward impulse response

FM Frequency modulation

FPLMTS Future Public Land Mobile Telecommunications System

FQAM Feher's patented QAM, nonlinear amplification

FQPSK Feher's patented family of QPSK licensed products

f_s Channel spacing (Hz/channel), i.e., bandwidth in Hz for RF channel [Hz/chan]

FSK Frequency shift keying

ft Foot/feet

G-LPF Gaussian-low-pass filter

GEO Geosynchronous

GFSK Gaussian frequency shift keying

GHz Gigahertz

GLPF Gaussian low-pass filter

GMSK Gaussian-minimum shift keying

GSM Group Special Mobile or Global Mobile Standard

HBR-LET High burst-rate link-evaluation terminal

HCMTS High capacity mobile telephone system

HDSL High digital subscriber line

HF High-frequency

ηf Spectral efficiency with respect to frequency

HLR Home location register

HPF High-pass filter

η_s Spectral efficiency with respect to space

ηT Overall spectral efficiency [erl/Hz m^2]

η_t Spectral efficiency with respect to time

Hz Hertz

IAM Initial address message

IC Integrated circuit

ICAO International Civil Aviation Organization

IEEE Institute of Electrical and Electronics Engineers

IF Intermediate frequency

IIR Infinite impulse response

IJF Interference- and jitter-free

INMARSAT International Maritime Satellite Organization

IR Infrared

IS-54 United States Standard 54

ISD Integrate-sample-and-dump

ISDN Integrated services digital network

ISI Intersymbol interference

ISM Industrial, scientific, and medical

ISO International Standards Organization

ISUP ISDN users part (message)

ITU International Telecommunications Union

IWP Interim Working Party

JDC Japanese Digital Cellular

JSAC Journal on Selected Areas in Communications

kb/s Kilobits per second

kcps kilo cycles per second

KF Kato/Feher patented crosscorrelator processor

kHz Kilohertz

LATA Local access and transport area

LCD Liquid crystal display

LEC Local exchange carrier

LEO Low earth orbit

LIDB Line information data base

LIN Linear amplifiers

LMS Least-mean-squared

LNA Low-noise amplifier

LO Local oscillator

LOS Line-of-sight

LPC Linear predictive coding

LPF Low-pass filter

LPF_T Transmit low-pass filter

Λ_{th} **CIR** (C/I) at threshold for given BER or P_e

m Bandwidth efficiency

M-ary Multiple level modulation

M-QAM Multistate quadrature amplitude modulation

MAC Media access control

MAP Mobile application part (CCITT)

M_{cps} Mega cycles per second

MEO Medium earth orbit

M_f Fade margin against allowable geographic outage due to log-normal shadowing

MHz Megahertz

min Minute(s)

MIP Millions of instructions per second

MIPS Millions of instructions per second

MNRU Modulated noise reference unit

MODEM Modulation/demodulation

mph Miles per hour

MPT Ministry of Post and Telecommunications of Japan

ms Millisecond(s)

MSDU Media Access Control (MAC) Service Data Unit

MSE Mean squared error

MSK Minimum shift keying

MSM Microwave switch matrix

MTS Message telephone service

MUX Multiplexer

mW Milliwatts(s)

N Number of cells per cluster (N = 4, 7, 9, 13, . . .)

N-ISDN Narrowband-integrated services digital network

NADC North American digital cellular

NAMTS Nippon Advanced mobile Telephone System

NARUC National association of regulatory utility commissioners

n_{cell} Number of channels assigned to each cell (chan/cell)

NCF National communications forum

NCO Numerically controlled oscillator

NE Network elements

NEBS Network equipment-building system

NETZ-C Germany's mobile telephone system

NLA Nonlinearly amplified

NLOS Non–line-of-sight

NMT Nordic Mobile Telephone

NMTS Nordic Mobile Telephone System

NOI Notice of inquiry (by FCC)

NOP Null operation

NRZ Nonreturn-to-zero

ns Nanosecond(s)

N_{sub} Capacity = number of subscribers accommodated by the system in a unit area = system capacity [sub/m^2]

n_{sys} Number of channels assigned for total system

NTM Network traffic management

O-QPSK Offset-keyed quaternary phase shift keyed

OBO Output backoff

OF Optical fiber

OOB Out-of-band

P(e) Probability of error, same as P_e or BER

π/4-DQPSK Differential quadrature phase shift keying

PA Power amplifier

PB Blocking probability

PBX Private branch exchange

PC Personal computer

PCF Point coordination function

PCIA Personal Communications Industry Association

PCM Pulse code modulation

PCMCIA Personal Computer Memory Card International Association

PCN Personal communications network(s)

PCS Personal or portable communications system(s) or personal communications services

PDF Probability density function

pdf Probability density function

P_e Probability of Error, same as P(e) or BER

pel Picture element

PELP Pulse-excited linear predictive

P_{ew} Work error rate (also P_F)

P_F Work error rate (also P_{ew})

PHP Presonal handyphone

PHY Physical layer

PIN Personal indentification number

PLL Phase-locked loop

PLMR Public land mobile radio

PMR Private mobile radio

PN Pseudonoise

ppm Parts per million

PRBS Pseudorandom binary sequence

PSD Power spectral density

PSI Pilot-symbol inserted

PSK Phase-shift keying

PSTN Public-switched telephone networks

QAM Quadrature amplitude modulation

QDU Quantization distortion unit

QPSK Quadrature phase shift keying

QUAD Quadrature

R Radius of unit cell

RACE Research on Advanced Communications in Europe

RACF Remote access to call forward

RAM Random access memory

RC Raised cosine

R_c Coding rate

RCT Research and Development Center for Radio Systems

RDSS Radio Determination Satellite System

RELP Residual-excited linear predictive

RF or rf radio frequency

RFICs Radio frequency integrated circuit

rms Root-mean-square

ROM Read only memory

RPCU Radio Port Control Unit

RPE Regular Pulse Excited

RS Reed-Solomon code

RSA Rural service area

Rx-LPF Receive low-pass filter

RZ Return-to-zero

S Area of unit cell (m^2) or (msq)

s second(s)

S/D Signal-to-distortion; also signal-to-distortion ratio

S/I Signal-to-interference

S/N Signal-to-noise; also signal to noise ratio

SAC Special access code (routing)

Satcom Satellite communication(s)

SCP Service control point

SCPC Single channel per carrier

SFH Slow frequency-hopping

SFH-CDMA Slow frequency hopped-code division multiple access

SFH-SS Slow frequency hopping spread spectrum

SFR Structured frequency reuse

SNR Signal-to-noise ratio

SQAM Superposed quadrature amplitude modulation

SS Signaling system; also, spread-spectrum

SS Spread-spectrum

SS7 Signaling system number 7

STR Symbol timing recovery

T/R Transmitter/receiver (transceiver)

TACS Total Access Communications System

TCAP Transaction capabilities application part

TCM Trellis-coded modulation

TDD Time division duplex

TDM Time division multiplexing

TDMA Time division multiple access

TIA Telecommunications Industry Association

TMI Telesat Mobile Inc.

TR Technical reference

TSA Time-slot assignment

TSGR *Transport System Generic Requirements*, Bellcore TR-TSY-000499

TWT Traveling wave tube

Tx Transmit

Tx-LPF Transmit low-pass filter

TxPC Transmit power control

U.S. United States

U/C Upconversion

UHF Ultrahigh-frequency

ULPC Uplink power control

V Volt(s)

VCO Voltage-controlled oscillator

VCXO Voltage controlled crystal oscillators

VHF Very high-frequency

VLSI Very large scale integration

VQ vector quantization

VSAT Very small aperture terminals

VSELP Vector sum excited linear prediction

VTC Vehicular Technology Conference

W Bandwidth of total system (Hz)

W Watt(s)

WARC World Administrative Radio Conference

WER Word-error-rate

WLAN Wireless local area network

ZF Zero-forcing

Bibliography

ABBE, B. S., T. C. JEDREY, P. ESTABROOK, and M. J. AGAN: "ACTS broadband aeronautical experiment," *Proceedings of the Third International Mobile Satellite Conference, IMSC 93,* Pasadena, Calif., June 16–18, 1993.

ADACHI, F.: "Selection and scanning diversity effects in a digital FM land mobile radio with discriminator and differential detections," *Trans. IECE of Japan,* Vol. 64-E, p. 398, June 1981.

ADACHI, F., J.D. PARSONS: "Unified analysis of postdetection diversity for binary digital FM mobile radio," *IEEE Transactions on Vehicular Technology,* Vol. 37, No. 4, pp. 189–198, November 1988.

ADAMS, B.K., D.M. WUTHNOW: "Microcellular demonstration," *IEEE-VTC-91,* St. Louis, Mo, 1991.

ADAMS, D.E., C.R. FRANK: "WARC embraces PCN," *IEEE Commun. Mag.,* Vol. 30, No. 6, pp. 44–46, June 1992.

AKAIWA, Y., Y. NAGATA: "Highly efficient digital mobile communications with a linear modulation method," *IEEE Transactions on Selected Areas in Communications,* Vol. 5, No. 5, pp. 890–895, June 1987.

ANG, H.P., P.A. RUETZ, D. AULD: "Video compression makes big gains," *IEEE Spectrum,* October 1991.

ARIYAVISITAKUL, S., T-P. LIU: "Characterizing the effects of nonlinear amplifiers on linear modulations for digital portable radio communications," *IEEE Globecom,* pp. 12.7.1–12.7.6, 1989.

ARNOLD, H.W., W.F. BODTMAN: "Switched diversity FSK in frequency selective Rayleigh fading," *IEEE Journal on Selected Areas in Communications,* Vol. 2, No. 4, pp. 540–547, July 1984.

ARREDONDO, G., W. CHRISS, E. WALKER: "A multipath fading simulator for mobile radio," *IEEE Transactions on Vehicular Technology,* November 1973.

ARREDONDO, R.: "AMPS-advanced mobile phone system," *Bell Syst. Tech J.,* January 1979.

ATAL, B.S., M.R. SCHROEDER: "Predictive coding of speech signals and subjective error criteria," *IEEE Transactions of ASSP,* June 1979.

AUSTIN, M.C., M.U. CHANG: "Quadrature overlapped raised cosine modulation," *IEEE Transactions on Communications,* Vol. 29, No. 3, pp. 237–249, March 1981.

BAKER, P.A.: "Phase-modulation data sets for serial transmission at 2000 and 2400 bits per second," Part I, *AIEE Transactions on Communications Electronics,* pp. 166–171, July 1962.

BELLCORE: "Generic framework criteria for universal digital personal communications systems (PCS)," *Bellcore, Technical Advisory FA-NWT-001013,* Issue 2, December 1990.

BELL TELEPHONE LABORATORIES: *Transmission Systems for Communications,* Ed. 5, 1982.

BENNET, L.: "Mobile automation buyer's guide," *California Business,* September 1992.

BENNETT, W.R., J.R. DAVEY: *Data Transmission,* McGraw-Hill, New York, 1965.

BERLEKAMP, E.R.: *Algebraic Coding Theory,* McGraw-Hill, New York, 1970.

BERLEKAMP, E.R., R.E. PEILE, and S.P. POPE: "The application of error control to communications," *IEEE Comm. Mag.,* April 1987.

BHARGAVA, V.K., D. HACCOUN, R. MATYAS, and P. NUSPL: *Digital Communications by Satellite,* Wiley-Interscience, New York, 1981.

BIGLIERI, E., D. DIVSALAR, P.J. MCLANE, and M.K. SIMON: *Introduction to Trellis-Coded Modulation with Applications,* Macmillan Publishing Co., New York, 1991.

BLACKARD, K.L. ET AL.: "Path loss and delay spread models as functions for antenna height of microcellular system design," *VTC-92,* pp. 333–337, 1992.

BLAHUT, R.E.: *Theory and Practice of Error Control Codes,* Addison Wesley Publishing Co., 1984.

BLOMEYER, P.: "EXIRLAN: A multichannel, high speed, medium range IR-local area network," *IEEE P.802.11- 93/217,* November 1993.

BLOMEYER, P. (ANDROMEDA): "Structural needs for an IR-standard," *IEEE P.802.11-94/24,* January 1994.

BLOMEYER, P.: "Revised version of the combined baseband and multichannel IR-PHY EXIRLAN," *IEEE P.802.11- 94/62.*

BLOMEYER, P.: "Implementation of EXIRLAN multichannel IR-PHY using existing commodity components," *IEEE P.802.11-94/63.*

BLOMEYER, P.: "Compatibility issues between existing IR techniques and present/future requirements," *IEEE P.802.11-94/64.*

BLOMEYER, P.: "EXIRLAN Template," *IEEE P.802.11-94/65,* March 1994.

BOER, J.: "Proposal for 2 Mb/s DSSS PHY," *IEEE 802.11-93/37,* March 1993.

BOER, J. and P. STUHSAKER: "Establishment of DSSS PHY Parameters," *IEEE 802.11-93/145,* September 1993.

BOER, J. (AT&T, EDITOR): "Draft proposal for a direct sequence spread spectrum PHY standard," *IEEE P.802.11-93/232r1,* January 26, 1994.

BORTH, D.E., P.D. RASKY: "An experimental RF link system to permit evaluation of the GSM air interface standard," *Proceedings of the Third Nordic Seminar on Digital Land Mobile Radio Communication,* Copenhagen, Denmark, September, 1988.

BROWN, C. (INTEL): "Wireless communications building blocks: a new approach with programmable logic," Draft of submitted and anticipated publication in *EE Times,* April 1, 1994.

CALHOUN, G.: *Digital Cellular Radio,* Artech House, Norwood, Mass., 1988.

CALHOUN, G.: *Wireless Access and the Local Telephone Network,* Boston, Artech House, 1992.

CASAS, E., C. LEUNG: "A simple digital fading simulator for mobile radio," *IEEE Transactions on Vehicular Technology,* August 1990.

CAVERS, J.K.: "Phase locked transparent tone-in-band: an analysis," *Proceedings of IEEE 39th Vehicular Technology Conference,* pp. 73–77, San Francisco, Calif. May 1989.

CAVERS, J.K.: "A linearizing predistorter with fast adaptation," *IEEE VTC,* Orlando, Fla. 1990.

CCITT: "32 kb/s Adaptive differential pulse code modulation (ADPCM)," *Recommendation 6.721, Blue Book,* CCITT, Geneva.

CHENNAKESHU, S.: "Time delay spread measurements," GE Corporate Research and Development, Schenectady, N.Y., 12301, *Report,* December 21, 1988.

CHEUNG, W.W., A.H. AGHVAMI: "Performance of 16-ary DEQAM signaling with a prerotated constellation through nonlinear satellite channels," *IEEE ICC,* pp. 51.6.1–51.6.6, 1988.

CHUANG, J.C.I.: "The effect of time delay spread on portable radio communications channels with digital modulation," *IEEE Journal on Selected Areas in Communications,* Vol. 5, No. 6, pp. 879–889, June 1987a.

CHUANG, J.C.I.: "The effect of multipath delay spread on timing recovery," *IEEE Transactions on Vehicular Technology,* Vol. 36, No. 3, pp. 135–140, August 1987b.

CHUANG, J.C.I.: "The effect of time-delay spread on QAM with nonlinearly switched filters in a portable radio communications channel," *IEEE Transactions on Vehicular Technology,* Vol. 38, No. 1, pp. 9–13, February 1989.

CLARK, B.L.: "Comments of the Hewlett-Packard Company to the FCC," *Redevelopment of Spectrum to Encourage Innovation, ET Docket 92-9,* Hewlett Packard, Mobile Communications Group, RND, Roseville, Calif., June 1992.

CLARK, G.C., JR., and J.B. CAIN: *Error Correction Coding for Digital Communications,* Plenum Press, 1981.

CLARK, R.H.: "A statistical theory of mobile-radio reception," *Bell Syst. Tech. J.,* Vol. 47, pp. 957–1000, July-August 1968.

COLMENARES, N.J.: "The FCC on personal wireless," *IEEE Spectrum,* May 1994.

COOPER, G.R., C.D. MCGILLEM: *Modern Communications and Spread Spectrum,* McGraw-Hill, New York, 1986.

COX, D.C.: "Delay Doppler characteristics of multipath propagation at 910-MHz in a suburban mobile radio environment," *IEEE Transactions on Antennas and Propagation,* Vol. AP-20, No. 5, pp. 625–635, September 1972.

COX, D.C.: "Multipath delay spread and path loss correlation for 910-MHz urban mobile radio propagation," *IEEE Transactions on Vehicular Technology,* Vol. 26, No. 4, pp. 340–344, November 1977.

COX, D.C.: "A radio system proposal for widespread low-power tetherless communications," *IEEE Transactions on Communications,* Vol. 39, No. 2, pp. 324–335, February 1992.

COX, D.C., MURRAY, W. NORRIS: "800 MHz Attenuation measured in and around suburban houses," *AT&T Bell Labs Technical Journal,* July/August 1984.

COX, D.C. ET AL.: "Correlation bandwidth and delay spread multipath propagation statistics for 910-MHz urban mobile radio channels," *IEEE Transactions on Communications,* Vol. COM-23, NO. 11, pp. 1271–1280, November 1975.

CREVISTON, E. (TELEDYNE), R. ATIENZA, G. WEI and Y. GUO: "Experimental evaluation of DQPSK and FQPSK for DS-SS, FH-SS and IR applications," *IEEE 802.11-94/52.*

CT-2: "Second generation cordless telephone (CT-2)," *Common Air Interface Specifications,* Dept. of Trade and Industry, London, May 1989.

D'ARIA, G., ET AL.: "Adaptive baseband equalizers for narrowband TDMA-FDMA mobile radio," *CSELT Technical Reports,* Vol. 16, No. 1, pp. 19–27, February 1988.

DAVARIAN, F., "Mobile digital communications via tone calibration," *IEEE Transactions of Vehicular Technology,* Vol. 36, No. 2, pp. 55–62, May 1987.

D'AVELLA, R., ET AL.: "Adaptive equalization in TDMA mobile radio systems," *IEEE Vehicular Tech. Conference,* Tampa, FL, 1987, pp. 385–392.

DEAN, R.A., A.H. LEVESQUE: "Transparent data service with multiple wireless access," *Proceedings of the Third International Mobile Satellite Conference, IMSC 93,* Pasadena, CA June 16–18, 1993.

DE JAGER, F., C.B. DEKKER: "Tamed Frequency Modulation: A method to achieve spectral economy," *IEEE Transactions on Communications,* May 1978.

DECT: "Radio Equipment and Systems: Digital European Cordless Telecommunication," *European Telecommunications Standards Institute, ETSI,* Valbonne, Cedex, France, May 1991.

DEL RE, E. ET AL.: "Architectures and protocols for an integrated satellite-terrestrial mobile system," *Proceedings of the Third International Mobile Satellite Conference, IMSC 93,* Pasadena, CA June 16–18, 1993.

DEVASIRVATHAM, D.M.J.: "Multipath time delay spread in the digital portable radio environment," *IEEE Comm. Mag.,* Vol. 25, No. 6, pp. 13–21, June 1987.

DIVSALAR, D., M.K. SIMON: "The Power Spectral Density of Digital Modulations Transmitted Over Nonlinear Channels," *IEEE Transactions on Communications,* vol. 30, No. 1, pp. 142–151, January 1982.

DIVSALAR, D., M.K. SIMON: "Combined trellis codes with asymmetric modulations," *Proceedings of the IEEE Globecom,* pp. 21.2.1–21.2.7, 1985.

DIXON, R.C.: *Spread Spectrum Systems,* Wiley- Interscience, J. Wiley & Sons, New York, 1976.

DJEN, W.S., N. DANG, K. FEHER: "Performance Improvement Methods for DECT and other Noncoherent GMSK Systems," *Proceedings of the IEEE VTC-92,* May 11–13, 1992, Denver, CO.

DONALDSON, R.W. and A.S. BEASLEY: "Wireless CATV network access for personal communications using simulcasting," *IEEE Transactions on Vehicular Technology, Part II,* August 1994.

DORNSTETTER, J.L., D. VERHULST: "Cellular efficiency with slow frequency hopping analysis of the digital SFH 900 mobile system," *IEEE Journal on Selected Areas in Communications,* June 1987.

DRUCKER, E.: "Delay spread measurements from Salt Lake City," *Contribution by US West to TR-45.3 W.G. III, contribution #: TR-45.3.3/88.11.30.1,* Dallas, TX, November 30–December 1, 1988.

EDNEY, J. (SYMBIONICS): "Proposal for a higher data rate frequency hopping modulation scheme," *IEEE P.802.11-94/34, January i994.*

EIA: *Dual-Mode Subscriber Equipment Compatibility Specification, Electronic Industries Association Specification IS-54,* EIA Project Number 2215, Washington, D.C., May 1990.

EIA/TIA-QUALCOMM, INC.: "Spread spectrum digital cellular system dual-mode mobile station-base station compatibility standard," *Proposed EIA-TIA Inerim Standard, April 21, 1992; TIA Distribution TR 45.5, April 1992.*

EIA/TIA: "Mobile station-base station compatibility standard for dual-mode wideband spread spectrum cellular system," *TIA/EIA IS-95,* 1993.

FAGUE, D., K. FEHER: "Experimentally optimized narrowband FM system for TDMA operated mobile radio environment," *Proceedings of the Twenty-Fourth Asilomar Conference on Signals, Systems and Computers,* Pacific Grove, CA, November 5–7, 1990, (4 pp.).

FANG, R. J. F: "Personal communications via Intelsat ku-band transponders," *International Journal of Satellite Communications,* Vol. 10, 1992.

FBPSK and FQPSK: Consortium and licensing information pamphlets. Dr. Feher and Associates a division of Digcom, Inc. 44685 Country Club Dr., El Macero, CA 95618. Contact the author of this book at the University of California, Davis.

FCC: "Part 15-Radio Frequency Devices," *CFR Ch. 1 (10-1-90 Edition), Federal Communications Commission,* Washington, D.C., October 1990.

FCC: "Notice of Proposed Rule Making and Tentative Decision," in regards to personal communications services (PCS), *Federal Communications Commission (FCC), General Docket No. 90–314,* ET Docket No. 92–100, FCC-92-333, released August 14, 1992, Washington, D.C. 20554.

FEHER, K., ED.: *Advanced Digital Communications: Systems and Signal Processing Techniques,* Prentice-Hall, Inc., Englewood Cliffs, NJ, 1987a. (To order copies, see "Series" page.)

FEHER, K. and ENGINEERS OF HEWLETT-PACKARD: *Telecommunications Measurements, Analysis and Instrumentation,* Prentice-Hall, Inc., NJ, 1987. (To order, see "Series" page.)

FEHER, K., D. CHAN: "PSK Combiners for Fading Microwave Channels," *IEEE Transactions of Communications,* May 1975, pp. 554–558.

FEHER, K., G.S. TAKHAR: "A new symbol timing recovery technique for burst modem applications," *IEEE Transactions on Communications,* January 1978, pp. 100–108.

FEHER, K., H. MEHDI: "Modulation/microwave integrated digital wireless developments," *IEEE Transactions on Microwave Theory and Techniques, (invited paper) Special Issue on Wireless Communications,* July 1995.

FEHER, K., K.T. WU, J.C.Y. HUANG, D.E. MACNALLY: *Improved Efficiency Data Transmission Technique,* U.S. Patent No. 4-720-839, Washington, D.C. Issued Janaury 19, 1988.

FEHER, K., M. MORRIS: "Simultaneous transmission of digital Psk and of analog television signals," *IEEE Transactions on Communications,* December 1975, pp. 1509–1514.

FEHER, K., M. SATO: "A new generation of modems for power efficient radio systems," *International Journal of Satellite Communications,* a Wiley-Interscience Publication, Vol. 9, May-June 1991, pp. 137–147.

FEHER, K., R. DECRISTOFARO: "Transversal filter design and application in satellite communications," *IEEE Transactions on Communications,* November 1976, pp. 1262–1267.

FEHER, K., R. GOULET, S. MORRISSETTE: "Performance evaluation of hybrid microwave systems," *IEEE Transactions on Communications,* June 1974, pp. 873–877.

FEHER, K.: "1 Mb/s and higher data rate PHY-MAC: GFSK and FQPSK," *IEEE 802.11-93/138,* September 1993d.

FEHER, K.: "1024-QAM and 256-QAM coded modems for microwave and cable system applications," *IEEE Journal on Selected Areas in Communications,* Vol. SAC-5, No. 2, April 1987, pp. 357–368.

FEHER, K.: "A new generation of 90 Mb/s SATCOM systems: bandwidth efficient field tested 16-QAM," *IEEE Transactions on Broadcasting,* March 1989, Vol. 35, No. 1, pp. 23–30.

FEHER, K.: "Comparison between coherent and noncoherent mobile systems in large Doppler shift delay spread and C/I environment," *Proceedings of the Third International Mobile Satellite Conference,* Pasadena, CA, June 16–18, 1993b.

FEHER, K.: *"Digital Modulation Techniques in an Interference Environment,"* Encyclopedia on EMC, Vol. 9, Don White, Inc., Gainsville, Virginia, 1977.

FEHER, K.: *"Filter: Nonlinear Digital,"* U.S. Patent No. 4,339,724. Issued July 13, 1982. Canada No. 1130871, August 31, 1982a. Licensor is Digcom, Inc.—Dr. Feher Associates.

FEHER, K.: "FQPSK, GMSK, and QPSK compatible proposed air interface standards for TDMA, FDMA, and CDMA," JTC (AIR)/94.01.19-035, Jan. 1994a.

FEHER, K.: "FQPSK: A modulation power efficient RF amplification proposal for increased spectral efficiency and capacity GMSK and π/4-QPSK compatible PHY standard," *Document IEEE P.802.11-93/97,* Denver, CO, July 13, 1993c.

FEHER, K.: "HS-FH and IR FQPSK-based proposed standards for 1.4 Mbit/s to 4.2 Mbit/s," *IEEE 802.11-94/51,* March, 1994b.

FEHER, K.: "Infrared EXIRLAN-FQPSK proposed flexible standard," *IEEE 802.11-94/55,* March 1994c.

FEHER, K.: "JTC Modulation Standard Group-FQPSK Consortium: Spectrum utilization with compatible/expandable GMSK, QSPK, and FQPSK," *JTC TR 46.3.3/TIPI.4 Telecommunications Industry Association.*

FEHER, K.: "Modem/radio for nonlinearly amplified systems," patent disclosure files in preparation, Digcom, Inc. Confidential and proprietary, Digcom, Inc. 44685 Country Club Dr., El Macero, CA 95618, December 1992b.

FEHER, K.: "Modems for Emerging Digital Cellular Mobile Radio Systems," (Invited paper), *IEEE Transactions on Vehicular Technology,* Vol. 40, No. 2, May 1991, pp. 355–365.

FEHER, K.: "Notice of Patent Applicability," *Document IEEE P.802.11-93/139,* Atlanta, September 1993e.

FEHER, K.: *"Time Jitter Determining Apparatus,"* U.S. Patent No. 4,350,879. Issued September 21, 1982b.

FEHER, K.: *"Timing Technique for NRZ Data Signals,"* U.S. Patent No. 3,944,926. Issued March 16, 1976.

FEHER, K.: Delay spread measurements and Feher's bound for digital PCS and mobile cellular systems," *Proceedings of the Wireless Symposium and Exhibition,* San Jose, CA, January 12–15, 1993a.

FEHER, K.: *Digital Communications: Microwave Applications,* Prentice-Hall, Inc., Englewood Cliffs, NJ, 1981. (To order this book, see "Series" page.)

FEHER, K.: *Digital Communications: Satellite/Earth Station Engineering,* Prentice-Hall, Inc., Englewood Cliffs, NJ, 1983. To order copies of this book write to the author: Dr. K. Feher at University of California, Davis; CA 95616 or at DIGCOM, Inc.; 44685 Country Club Drive; El Macero, CA 95618 or see "Series" page in this book.

FEHER, K.: "Comparative study of digital modulation techniques for mobile, cellular and PCS systems," *UC Davis, ECE-DCRL, file S-1,* for publication in IEEE, February 1992a.

FORNEY, G.D.: "Burst correcting codes for the classic burst channel," *IEEE Trans. Comm.,* Oct. 1971, pp. 772–781.

FORNEY, G.D.: "The Viterbi Algorithm," *Proceedings of the IEEE,* Vol. 61, No. 3, March 1973, pp. 268–278.

GALLAGER, R.G.: *Information Theory and Reliable Communication,* Wiley, New York, 1968.

GANESH, R. and K. PAHLAVAN: "On the modeling of fading multipath indoor radio channels," *IEEE GLOBECOM '89,* Dallas, TX, pp. 1346–1350, November 1989.

GANS, M.J.: "A power-spectral theory of propagation in the mobile-radio environment," *IEEE Trans. Veh. Technol.,* Vol. VT-21, February 1972, pp. 27–38.

GARDINER, J.G.: "Satellite services for mobile communication," *Telecommunications,* August 1986.

GARDINER, W.A.: *Introduction to Random Processes with Applications to Signals and Systems,* MacMillan, New York, 1986.

GERGEZ, R.: "IVHS System Integration Issues," *Proceedings of the 6th Intelligent Vehicle and Highway Systems Seminar,* Berkeley, CA, June 1992. (Author is with CALTRANS, NTMO R/ATMIS, Sacramento.)

GILHOUSEN, K.S., I.M. JACOBS, R. PADOVANI, A.J. VITERBI, L.A. WEAVER, JR. and C.E. WHEATLEY, "On the capacity of a cellular CDMA system," *IEEE Transactions on Vehicular Technology,* Vol. 40, No. 2, May 1991, pp. 303–312.

GINN, S.: "Personal Communications Services: Expanding the Freedom to Communicate," *IEEE Communications Magazine,* Vol. 29, No. 2, February 1991, pp. 30–39.

GIRARD, H., K. FEHER: "A new baseband linearizer for more efficient utilization of earth station amplifiers used for QPSK transmission," *IEEE Journal on Selected Areas in Communications,* January 1983, Vol. SAC-1, No. 1, pp. 45- 56.

GOLANBARI, M.: "Channel coding for coherent lightwave FSK communications," *Master's thesis, University of Texas at Dallas,* 1991.

GOLANBARI, M., E. FU, H. MEHDI and H. YAN: "CCA (Clear Channel Assessment) proposed solutions for 1 Mbit/s GFSK and higher rate FQPSK systems," *IEEE 802.11-94/53.*

GOLANBARI, M., N. DANG, P. LEUNG and H. MEHDI: "Performance study of GFSK and of 4FM, FQPSK, p/4-DQPSK in a delay spread environment," *IEEE 802.11-94/54.*

GOLD, R.: "Optimal binary sequences for spread spectrum multiplexing," *IEEE Transactions on Information Theory,* October 1967.

GOLDING, L.S. and L.C. PALMER: "Personal communications by satellite," *International Journal of Satellite Communications,* Vol. 10, 1992.

GOODMAN, D.J.: "Trends in cellular and cordless communications," *IEEE Communications Magazine,* Vol. 29, No. 6, pp. 31–40, June 1991.

GOSSACK, L.L.: "Cellular Radio Telephone Systems," *U.S. Industrial Outlook 1992: Radio Communications and Detection Equipment,* publisher: U.S. Department of Commerce, Washington, D.C., 1992a.

GOSSACK, L.L.: "Wireless Personal Communications," *U.S. Industrial Outlook 1992: Radio Communications and Detection Equipment,* publisher: U.S. Department of Commerce, Washington, D.C., 1992b.

GRAU, J. (PROXIM): "High speed frequency hopping PHY proposal," *IEEE P.802.11-94/8,* January 1994.

G.S.M.: "Channel Coding," *Group Special Mobile Standard Committee,* 1988–1990.

G.S.M.: "Physical Layer on the radio-path," *Vol. G, Group Special Mobile (GSM-Europe).* Recommendation 05.02; GSM Committee 1990.

G.S.M.: "Physical layer on the Radio Path: G.S.M. System," *G.S.M. Recommendation 05.02,* Vol. G, G.S.M. Standard Committee, July 1988.

GUO, Y. and K. FEHER: "Power and spectrally efficient SFH-FQSPK for PCS applications," *IEEE Transactions on Vehicular Technology,* August 1994

GUO, Y., H. YAN and K. FEHER: "Proposed modulation and data rate for higher speed frequency hopped spread spectrum (HS-FH-SS) standard," *IEEE 802.11–94/03, Wireless Access and Physical Layer Specifications,* January 1994.

GURUNATHAN, S.: "Pilot tone and pilot symbol aided QPRS modems for mobile and cellular systems," *Doctoral Thesis, Dept. of Electrical and Computer Engineering, University of California, Davis* (supervisor: Professor K. Feher), September 1992, Davis, CA.

GURUNATHAN, S., K. FEHER: "Pilot tone aided QPRS systems for digital audio broadcasting," *IEEE Transactions on Broadcasting,* March 1992, pp. 1–6.

GURUNATHAN, S., K. FEHER: "Multipath simulation models for mobile radio channels," *Proceedings of the IEEE VTC- 92,* May 11–13, 1992, Denver, CO.

GURUNATHAN, S., K. FEHER: "Pilot symbol aided QPRS for digital land mobile applications," *Proceedings of the IEEE-International Conference on Communications,* ICC-92, Chicago, IL, June 15–17, 1995, 5 pages.

HANSEN, F. and F.I. MENO: "Mobile fading-Rayleigh and lognormal superimposed," *IEEE Trans. Veh. Technology,* Vol. VT-26, November 1977.

HARBIN, S., C. PALMER, B.K. RAINER: "Measured propagation characteristics of simulcast signals in an indoor microcellular environment," *Proceedings of the IEEE VTS- 92 Conference VTC-92,* p. 608, Denver, May 1992.

HARTSHORN, D. and M. CARTER-LOME: "Cellular vs. and satellite," *Satellite Communications,* February 1993.

HATA, M.: "Empirical formula for propagation loss in land mobile receivers," *IEEE Transactions on Vehicular Technology,* August 1980.

HATELID, J.E. and L. CASEY: The IRIDIUM™ system personal communications anytime, anyplace," *Proceedings of the Third International Mobile Satellite Conference, IMSC 93,* Pasadena, CA June 16–18, 1993.

HAYES, V., W. DIEPSTRATEN, C. LINKS: "Wireless LAN standards making strides," *Electronic Engineering Times,* February 21, 1994.

HAYES, V., ET AL.: "Article on IEEE 802.11 standardization status," *Electronic Engineering Times,* February 21, 1994.

HAYKIN, S.: *Digital Communications,* J. Wiley & Sons, New York, 1988.

HELLER, J.A. and I.M. JACOBS: "Viterbi decoding for satellite and space communication," *IEEE Trans. Commun. Technol.,* October 1971.

HILL, T., K. FEHER: "A Performance study of NLA-64 state QAM," *IEEE Transactions on Communications,* June 1983, pp. 821–826.

HIRADE, K.: "Mobile-Radio Communications," in K. Feher: *Advanced Digital Communication System and Signal Processing Techniques,* Prentice-Hall, Englewood Cliffs, NJ, 1987. Available from Dr. K. Feher & Associates/Digcom, 44685 Counry Club, El Macero, CA 95618: 1994.

HOLDEN, T.P., K. FEHER: "A spread spectrum based synchronization technique for digital broadcast systems," *IEEE Transactions on Broadcasting,* Vol. 36, September 1990, pp. 185–194.

HOLMES, J.K.: *Coherent Spread Spectrum Systems,* J. Wiley & Sons, New York, 1982.

IEEE: "FCC to allocate 220MHz of spectrum to new telecommunication technologies," *IEEE Vehicular Technology Society Newsletter,* Vol. 39, No. 2, May 1992, pp. 38–59.

INCE, A.: *Digital Satellite Communications Systems and Technologies: Military and Civil Applications,* Kluwer Academic Press, Boston, 1992.

ISHIZUKA, M., Y. YASUDA: "Improved coherent detection of GMSK," *IEEE Transactions on Communications,* Vol. COM-32, No. 3, March 1984, pp. 308–311.

JAKES, W.C., ED: *Microwave Mobile Communications,* J. Wiley, New York, 1974.

JAKES, W.C., JR.: "A comparison of specific diversity techniques to reduction of fast fading in UHF mobile radio systems," *IEEE Transactions on Veh. Tech.,* Vol. VT-20, November 1971, p.81.

JAYANT, S.N.: "Digital coding of speech waveforms: PCM, DPCM and DM Quantizers," *Proceedings of the IEEE,* May 1975.

JOHANNSEN, K.G. and M.W. BOWLES: "Trends in mobile satellite communications," *Proceedings of the Third International Mobile Satellite Conference, IMSC 93,* Pasadena, CA June 16–18, 1993.

JOHANSON, G.A. and N.G. DAVIES: "Implementation of a system to provide mobile satellite services in North America," *Proceedings of the Third International Mobile Satellite Conference, IMSC 93,* Pasadena, CA June 16–18, 1993.

JORDAN, E.C., K.G. BALMAIN: *Electromagnetic Waves and Radiating Signals,* Prentice-Hall, Inc., Englewood Cliffs, NJ, 1968.

KATO, S. and K. FEHER: "XPSK: A new cross-correlated phase-shift-keying modulation technique," *IEEE Transactions on Communications,* May 1983.

KATO, S. and K. FEHER: *"Correlated Signal Processor,"* U.S. Patent No. 4,567,602. Issued January 28, 1986. (Licensor is Digcom, Inc.—Dr. Feher Associates).

KATO, S., S. KUBOTA, K. SEKI, T. SAKATA, K. KOBAYASHI, and Y. MATSUMOTO: "Implementation architectures, suggested preambles and VLSI components or FQPSK, offset QPSK and GFSK standard 1 Mb/s rate and for higher bit rate WLAN," a submission by NTT-Japan, *Document IEEE P.802.11- 93/137,* 1993a.

KATO, S. (NTT-JAPAN) ET AL.: "Implementation architectures, suggested preambles and VLSI components for FQPSK, offset QPSK and GFSK standard 1 Mb/s rate and for higher bit rate WLAN," a submission by NTT-Japan, *Document IEEE P802.11-93/137,* 1993b.

KATO, S. (NTT-JAPAN) ET AL.: "Performance of OQPSK and equivalent FQPSK-KF for the DS-SS system," *IEEE p.802.11 93/189,* November 1993d.

KATO, S. (NTT-JAPAN) ET AL.: "Preamble specifications for the standard 1 Mb/s FH-SS system and for higher speed systems," *IEEE p.802.11 93/188,* November 1993c.

KATOH, H., K. FEHER: "SP-QPSK: A new Modulation technique for satellite and land-mobile digital broadcasting," *IEEE Transactions on Broadcasting,* Vol. 36, September 1990, pp. 195–202.

KESTELOOT, A., C.L. HUTCHISON, EDITORS: *The ARRL Spread Spectrum Sourcebook,* The American Radio Relay League, 1991.

KIM, D.Y.: "On the Implementation of a GMSK Modem," *Digital Communications Research Report,* University of California, Davis, April 20, 1988.

KIM, D.Y., K. FEHER: "Power suppression at the Nyquist frequency for pilot-aided PAM and QAM systems," *IEEE Transactions on Communications,* Vol. 37, No. 9, September 1989, pp. 984–986.

KINGSBURY, N.G.: "Transmit and receive filters for QPSK signals to optimise performance in linear and hard-limited channels," *IEEE Proceedings,* Vol. 133, Pt. F, No. 4, pp. 345–355, July 1986.

KINOSHITA, K., M. KURAMOTO, N. NAKAJIMA: "Development of a TDMA digital cellular system based on Japanese standard," *IEEE-VTC-91,* St. Louis, Mo., 1991.

KUBOTA, S., S. KATO, K. FEHER: "Inter-channel interference cancellation technique for CDMA mobile personal communication base stations," *Proceedings of the Third International*

Symposium on Personal, Indoor and Mobile Radio Communications, IEEE, Boston, October 19–21, 1992.

KUCAR, A., K. FEHER: "Practical performance prediction techniques for spectrally efficient digital systems," *RF Design,* (Cardiff Publishing Company) Vol. 14, No. 2, February 1991, pp. 58–66, p. 5.

LABEDZ, G.P., P.L. REILLY: "Network and radio receiver simulation studies of the Pan-European digital cellular system," *IEEE-VTC-91,* St. Louis, MO.

LARSSON, G., B. GUDMUMDSON, K. RAITH: "Receiver performance for north american digital cellular," *Proceedings of the IEEE Vehicular Technology Conference,* St. Louis, MO, May 1981.

LE-NGOC, T., K. FEHER: "A digital approach to symbol timing recovery systems," *IEEE Transactions on Communications,* December 1980, pp. 1993–1999.

LE-NGOC, T., K. FEHER: "Performance of IJF-OQPSK modulation schemes in a complex interference environment," *IEEE Transactions on Communications,* January 1983, pp. 137–144.

LE-NGOC, T., K. FEHER, H. PHAM VAN: "New modulation techniques for low-cost power and bandwidth efficient satellite earth stations," *IEEE Transactions of Communications,* January 1982.

LEBOWITZ, E.A., S.A. RHODES: "Performance of coded 8-PSK signalling for satellite communications," *International Conference on Communication, ICC,* Denver, CO, June 1981.

LEE, E.A., D.G. MESSERSCHMITT: *Digital Communication,* Kluwer Academic Press, Boston, 1988.

LEE, W.C.Y.: "Antenna spacing requirement for mobile radio base station diversity," *Bell Systems Technical Journal,* Vol. 50, No. 6, pp. 1859–1876, July/August 1971.

LEE, W.C.Y.: "Applying the intelligent cell concept to PCS," *IEEE Transactions on Vehicular Technology, Part II,* August 1994.

LEE, W.C.Y.: "Estimate of channel capacity in Rayleigh fading environment," *IEEE Transactions on Vehicular Technology,* Vol. 39, No. 3, pp. 187–189, August 1990.

LEE, W.C.Y.: "Lee's Model," *Proceedings of the IEEE Vehicular Technology Society 42nd VTS Conference,* Denver, CO., May 1992.

LEE, W.C.Y.: "Overview of cellular CDMA," *IEEE Transactions on Vehicular Technology,* Vol. 40, No. 2, May 1991.

LEE, W.C.Y.: "Spectrum efficiency in cellular," *IEEE Transactions on Vehicular Technology,* Vol. 38, No. 2, pp. 69–75, May 1989b.

LEE, W.C.Y.: *Mobile Cellular Telecommunication Systems,* McGraw-Hill, New York, 1989a.

LEE, W.C.Y.: *Mobile Communications Design Fundamentals,* Howard W. Sams, Indianapolis, IN, 1986. Second Edition published by J. Wiley & Sons, New York, 1993.

LEE, W.C.Y.: *Mobile Communications Engineering,* New York, MacGraw-Hill, 1982.

LEE, W.C.Y., Y.S. YEH: "Polarization diversity system for mobile radio," *IEEE Transactions on Communication Technology,* Vol. 20, No. 5, pp. 912–923, October 1972.

LEI, Z., M.X. CHAN, K. FEHER: "Burst interference in TDMA radio systems," *International Journal on Satellite Communications,* A Wiley Interscience Publication, Vol. 3, No. 4, October–December 1985 (pp. 249–258).

LEUNG, P.S.K.: "GMSK and F-QPSK for high capacity cellular mobile radio and microcellular personal communications systems," *Doctoral Thesis, Dept. of Electrical and Computer Engineering, University of California, Davis* (supervisor: Professor K. Feher), January 1991, Davis, CA.

LEUNG, P.S.K.: "Performance of FQPSK and coherent QPSK modulation in indoor PCS communications environment with time delay spread," *IEEE P.802.11-94,* Vancouver, March 1994.

LEUNG, P.S.K., K. FEHER: "Block inversion coded QAM systems," *IEEE Transactions on Communications,* Vol. 36, No. 7, July 1988, pp. 797–805.

LEUNG, P.S.K., K. FEHER: "A novel scheme to aid coherent detection of GMSK signals in fast rayleigh fading channels," *Proceedings of the Second International Mobile Satellite Conference,* Ottawa, Canada, June 17–20, 1990, pp. 605–611.

LEUNG, P.S.K., K. FEHER: "F-QPSK: A superior modulation for future generations of high-capacity microcellular PCS systems," *Proceedings of the IEEE-VTC-93,* May 18–20, 1993a, Secaucus, NJ.

LEUNG, P.S.K., K. FEHER: "F-QPSK: A superior modulation technique for mobile and personal communications," *IEEE Transactions on Broadcasting,* Vol. 39, No. 2, June 1993b, pp. 288–294.

LIN, S.: *An Introduction to Error-Correcting Codes,* Prentice-Hall, Englewood Cliffs, NJ, 1970.

LIN, S. and D.J. COSTELLO: *Error control coding,* Prentice-Hall, Englewood, NJ, 1983.

LIPOFF, S.J.: "Personal communications networks bridging the gap between cellular and cordless phones," *Proceedings of the IEEE,* Vol. 82, No. 4, April 1994.

LIU, C.L.: "Fade-Compensated and Anti-Multipath π/4-QPSK in Dipersive Fast Rayleigh Fading Channels," *Doctoral Thesis, Dept. of Electrical and Computer Engineering, University of California, Davis* (supervisor: Professor K. Feher), December 1992, Davis, CA.

LIU, C.L., K. FEHER: "Pilot symbol aided coherent M-ary PSK in frequency-selective fast Rayleigh fading channels," *UC Davis report, Digital Communications Research Laboratory, No. S-68, Submitted to the IEEE Trans. on Communic,* September 1990.

LIU, C.L., K. FEHER: "π/4-QPSK modems for satellite sound/data broadcast systems," *IEEE Transactions on Broadcasting Technology,* Vol. 37, pp. 1–8, 1991a.

LIU, C.L., K. FEHER: "A new filtering strategy to combat the delay spread," *Proceedings of the IEEE Vehicular Technology Conference, VTC-91,* St. Louis, MO, May 19–21, pp. 776–779, 1991b.

LIU, C.L., K. FEHER: "Bit-error-rate performance of π/4-DQPSK in a frequency selective fast Rayleigh fading channel," *IEEE Transactions on Vehicular Technology,* Vol. 40, No. 3, August pp. 558–568, 1991c.

LIU, C.L., K. FEHER: "Proposed π/4-CQPSK with increased capacity in digital cellular systems," *Proceedings of the IEEE-International Conference on Communications, ICC-92,* Chicago, IL, June 15–17, 1992, 5 pages.

LOO, C.: "A statistical model for a land mobile satellite link," *IEEE Transactions on Vehicular Technology,* Vol. 34, No. 2, pp. 122–127, August 1985.

LORENZ, R.W., H.J. GELBRICH: "Bit error distribution in digital mobile radio communication: Comparison between field measurements and fading simulation." For exact date and reference see Peter Kriessen's paper at VTC-90 reference no. 4.

LOTSE, F. ET. AL.: "Indoor propagation measurements at 900 Mhz," (Ericsson Radio, Stockholm), *Proceedings of the IEEE-VTC-92-IEEE-Vehicular Technology Conference,* Denver, May 1992, pp. 629–632.

LUCKY, R.W., J. SALZ and J. WELDON: *Principles of Data Communication,* McGraw-Hill, New York, 1968.

LÜKE, H.D.: *Korrelationssignale,* Springer-Verlag, Berlin, 1992.

MACARIO, R.C.V., ED.: *Personal and Mobile Radio Systems,* Peter Peregrinus Ltd., London, 1990.

MACARIO, R.C.V.: *Cellular Radio Principles and Design,* McGraw-Hill, New York, 1993.

MACDONALD, J.: "Discussion of modulation parameters for the 2.4 GHZ FH PHY," a submission by Motorola, *Document IEEE P.802.11–93/76,* Denver, CO, July 1993.

MACDONALD, J., R. DEGROOT, C. LAROSA: "Discussion of 0.39 GMSK modulation for frequency hop spread spectrum," a submission by Motorola. Submission to IEEE 802.11 Wireless Access Methods and Physical Layer Specifications, *Document IEEE P.802.11 93–97,* May 1993.

MACDONALD, V.H.: "Advanced mobile phone service: the cellular concept," *Bell System Technical Journal,* Vol. 58, No. 1, pp. 15–41, January 1979.

MACIEJKO, R.: "Digital modulation in Rayleigh fading in the presence of cochannel interference and noise," *IEEE Transactions on Communications,* Vol. COM-29, No. 9, pp. 1379–1386, September 1981.

MALARKEY TAYLOR ASSOCIATES: "Top 20 international cellular markets estimated as of June 30, 1993," MIA-EMCI, 1130 Connecticut Avenue, NW, Suite 325, Washington, D.C. 20036, *Cellular Marketing,* September 1993.

MARAL, G.: "The ways to personal communications via satellite," *International Journal of Satellite Communications,* Vol. 12, No. 1, January/February 1994.

MARINHO, J.: "Digital Standards Crossroads to the Future," *Cellular Business,* September 1992.

MARKOVIC, Z.: "Satellites in non-geostationary orbits." Chapter 9 in M. Miller, B. Vucetic, and L. Berry, *Satellite Communications: Mobile and Fixed Services,* Kluwer Academic Press, Boston, 1993.

MARTIN, P.M., A. BATEMAN, J.P. MCGEEHAN and J.P. MARVILL: "The implementation of a 16 QAM mobile data system using TTIB-based fading correction technique," *Proceedings of IEEE 38th Vehicular Technology Conference,* pp. 71–76, Philadelphia, PA, June 1988.

MATHIOPOULOS, P., K. FEHER: "Pilot Aided Techniques for System Caused Phase Jitter Cancellation," *IEEE Transactions on Broadcasting,* Vol. 34, No. 3, September 1988, pp. 356–366.

MATSUMOTO, T., A. HIGASHI: "Performance analysis of RS-coded M-ary FSK for frequency-hopping spread spectrum mobile radios," *IEEE Trans. Vehic. Technol.,* August 1992.

MCCARROLL, T.: "The humongous hookup: New AT&T McCaw System," *Time Magazine,* August 30, 1993.

MCGEEHAN, J.P. and A.J. BATEMAN: "Phase locked transparent tone-in-band (TTIB): A new spectrum configuration particularly suited to the transmission of data over SSB mobile radio networks," *IEEE Transactions on Communications,* Vol. 32, No. 1, pp. 81–87, January 1984.

MEHDI, H. and K. FEHER: "Compatible power efficient NLA technique (1 Watt) for DS-SS," *IEEE 802.11–94/04,* Wireless Access and Physical Layer Specifications, Jan. 1994.

MESSER, D: "Worldwide survey of direct-to-listener digital audio delivery systems development since WARC-92," *Proceedings of the Third International Mobile Satellite Conference, IMSC 93,* Pasadena, CA June 16–18, 1993.

MIKULSKI, J.J.: "A system plan for a 900-MHz portable radio telephone," *IEEE Transactions on Vehicular Technology,* Vol. 26, No. 1, pp. 76–81, February 1977.

MILLER, J.M., B. VUCETIC, and L. BERRY: *Satellite Communications: Mobile and Fixed Services,* Kluwer Academis Publishers, Boston, 1993.

MOHER, M.L. and J.H. LODGE: "TCMP-A modulation and coding strategy for Rician fading channels," *IEEE Journal on Selected Areas in Communications,* Vol. 7, No. 9, pp. 1347–1355, December 1989.

MOLKDAR: "Review on radio propagation into and within buildings," *IEEE Proceedings-H,* Vol. 138, No. 1, pp. 61–73, February 1991.

MORAIS, D.H., K. FEHER: "Bandwidth efficiency and probability of error performance of MSK and QKQPSK systems," *IEEE Transactions on Communications,* December 1979 (pp. 1794–1801).

MORAIS, D.H., K. FEHER: "NLA-QAM: A method for generating high power QAM signals through nonlinear amplification," *IEEE Transactions on Communications,* March 1982 (pp. 517–522).

MOREIRA, A.J.C., R.T. VALAOLAS and A.M. DE OLIVEIRE DUARTE: "Modulation-encoding techniques for wireless infrared transmission," *IEEE P.802.11-93/79,* May 1993.

MOREIRA, A.J.C., R.T. VALAOLAS and A.M. DE OLIVEIRE DUARTE: "Infrared modulation method: 16 pulse position modulation," *IEEE P.802.11-93/154,* September 1993.

MUROTA, K.: "Spectrum efficiency of GMSK land mobile radio," *IEEE Transactions on Vehicular Technology,* Vol. 34, No. 2, pp. 69–75, May 1985.

MUROTA, K., K. HIRADE: "GMSK modulation for digital mobile radio telephony," *IEEE Transactions on Communications,* July 1981.

NAGATA, Y.: "Linear amplification technique for digital mobile communications," *IEEE VTC,* pp. 159–164, Orlando, FL, 1990.

NAKAJIMA, A., M. KURAMOTO, K. WATANABE, M. EGUCHI: "Intelligent digital mobile communications network architecture for universal personal telecommunications (UPT) services," *IEEE-VTC-91,* St. Louis, MO.

NEWELL, R.P.: "Personal communication networks," *Radio-Electronics,* Vol. 62, No. 5, May 1991, p. 61–64.

NGUYEN, J., R. TAM, T. WATTS, A. ISIDORO: "Personal communications service-concept and architecture," *IEEE-VTC-91,* St. Louis, MO.

NYQUIST, H.: "Certain topics in telegraph transmission," *Transactions A.I.E.E.,* Vol. 47, No. 2, pp. 617–644, April 1928.

O'NEAL, J.B.: "Waveform encoding on voiceband data signals," *Proceedings of the IEEE,* February 1980.

OHNISHI, H., M. MAKIMOTO, K. FEHER: "Spectrally efficient digital broadcast systems operated in a phase noise environment, *IEEE Transactions of Broadcasting,* Vol. 35, No. 1, March 1989. (pp. 31–39)

OKOMURA, Y., E. OHMORI, T. KAWANO, and K. FUKUDA: "Field strength and its variability in VHF and UHF land mobile radio service," *Rev. Elec. Communic. Lab.,* Vol. 16, September–October 1968.

OPPENHEIM, A.V., R.W. SCHAFER: *Digital Signal Processing,* Prentice-Hall, Inc., Englewood Cliffs, NJ, 1975.

PARSONS, J.D., J.G. GARDINER: *Mobile Communications Systems,* Halsted Press, John Wiley, New York, 1989.

PARSONS, J.D., P.A. RATLIFF, M. HENZE, and M.J. WITHERS: "Single-receiver diversity system," *IEEE Trans. Commun.,* Vol. COM-21, November 1973, p. 1276.

PCMCIA, B. MCGUIRE: *"PCMCIA Backgrounder: Background Information on Personal Computer Memory Card International Association (PCMCIA) and the PC Card Standard for Mobile Computing,"* published by *PCMCIA,* Sunnyvale, CA, 1995.

PERK, J.M., L. BIALOK: "A chip set for the US digital cellular mobile," *IEEE-VTC-91,* St. Louis, MO.

PETERSON, W.W.: *Error Correcting Codes,* MIT Press, Cambridge, MA, 1961.

PHAM-VAN, H., K. FEHER: "A class of two-symbol interval modems for non-linear radio systems," *IEEE Transactions on Communications,* March 1983, pp. 433–441.

PICKERING, L.W., E.N. BARNHART, M.L. WITTEN, R.C. LU: "Trends in multipath delay spread from frequency domain measurements of the wireless indoor communications channel," *Proceedings of the Third IEEE International Symposium on Personal, Indoor and Mobile Radio Communications,* Boston, October 1992.

PICKHOLTZ, R.L., L.B. MILSTEIN and D.L. SCHILLING: "Spread spectrum for mobile communications," *IEEE Transactions of Vehicular Technology,* Vol. 40, No. 2, pp. 313–322, May 1991.

PICKHOLTZ, R.L., D.L. SCHILLING, L.B. MILSTEIN: "Theory of spread-spectrum communications: A tutorial," *IEEE Transactions on Communications,* May 1982.

PRAPINMONGKOLKARN, P., N. MORINAGA, and T. NAMEKAWA: "Performance of digital FM systems in a fading environment," *IEEE Trans. Aerosp. Electron. Syst.,* Vol. AES-10, September 1974, p. 698.

PRISCOLLI, F.D. and F. MURATORE: "Assessment of a public mobiel satellite system compatible with the GSM cellular network," *International Journal of Satellite Communications,* Vol. 12, No. 1, January/February 1994.

PROAKIS, J.G.: *Digital Communications:* Ed. 5, New York: McGraw-Hill, 1989.

PROAKIS, J.G.: "Adaptive equalization for TDMA systems," *IEEE Transactions on Vehicular Technology,* Vol. 40, No. 2, pp. 333–341, May 1991.

RAITH, K., J. UDDENFELDT: "Capacity of digital cellular TDMA systems," *IEEE Transactions on Vehicular Technology,* May 1991.

RAMSEY, J.L.: "Realization of optium interleavers," *IEEE Trans. Info. Theory,* May 1970, pp. 338–345.

RAPPAPORT, T.S.: "Characterization of UHF multipath radio channels in factory buildings," *IEEE Transactions on Antennas and Propagation,* August 1989.

RAPPAPORT, T.S., S. SCOTT, Y. SEIDEL, and R. SINGH: "900-Mhz multipath propagation measurements for US digital cellular radiophone," *IEEE Transactions on Vehicular Technology,* Vol. 39, No. 2, pp. 132–139, May 1990.

RAYCHAUDHURI, D. and N. WILSON: "Multimedia personal communication networks (PCN): system design issues," *Wireless Communications: Future Directions,* Kluwer Academic Publishers, Dordrecht, Netherlands, 1993, pp. 289–304.

RICE, S.O.: "Mathematical analysis of random noise," *Bell System Technical Journal,* July 1974.

RUSCH, R.J., P. CRESS, M. HORSTEIN, R. HUANG, and E. WISWELL: "ODYSSEY: a constellation for personal communications," *Proceedings of the 14th AIAA International Communications Satellite Systems Conference,* Washington, D.C. March 22–26, 1992.

RUSH, C.M.: "Summary of Conclusions of the 1992 World Administrative Radio Conference," *IEEE Antennas and Propagation Mag.,* Col. 34, pp. 7–14, June 1992.

RUSH, C.M.: "How WARC'92 will affect mobile services," *IEEE Communications Magazine,* October 1992.

SAITO, S. and T. TAKAMI: "Adaptive carrier tracking (ACT) demodulation for QPSK mobile radio transmission," *Electronics & Communications in Japan, Part 1, Vol. 76,* No. 8, 1993.

SALEH, A., L.J. CIMINI: "Indoor radio communications using time-division multiple access with cyclical slow frequency hopping and coding," *IEEE Journal on Selected Areas in Communications,* January 1989.

SALEH, A.A.M., J. SALZ: "Adaptive linearization of power amplifiers in digital radio," *Bell Systems Technical Journal,* Vol. 62, No. 4, pp. 1019–1033, April 1983.

SALMASI, A., K.S. GILHOUSEN: "On the system design aspects of code division multiple access (CDMA) applied to digital cellular and personal communications networks," *IEEE-VTC-91,* St. Louis, MO. (Authors are with Qualcomm.)

SAMPEI, S.: "Performance of trellis coded 16-QAM/TDMA system for land mobile communications," *Proceedings of the IEEE Globecom,* pp. 906.1.1–906.1.5, 1990.

SAMPEI, S.: "Development of Japanese adaptive equalizing technology toward high bit rate data tranmission in land mobile communications," *IEICE Transactions,* Vol. E74, No. 6, June 1991.

SAMPEI, S., K. FEHER: "A method for universal link budget for computation for PCS systems: Several aspects and computation approaches," *Digital Communications Research Laboratory, public file S-70XX, ECE Dept., University of California, Davis, CA,* March 1992.

SAMPEI, S., K. FEHER: "Adaptive DC-offset compensation algorithm for burst mode operated direct conversion receivers," *Proceedings of the IEEE VTC-92,* May 11–13, 1992, Denver, CO.

SCALES, W.: "Potential use of spread spectrum techniques in non-government applications," *MITRE, Report No. MTR-80W335,* Submitted to the FCC, December 1980 (as printed in reference [KE-B1]).

SCHILLING, D.L.: "Wireless communications going into the 21st century," *IEEE Transactions on Vehicular Technology, Part II,* August 1994.

SCHNEIDERMAN, R.: "For offshore wireless markets, the accent is on rapid growth," *Microwave & RF,* August 1994.

SCHWARTZ, M., W.R. BENNETT, S. STEIN: *Communication Systems and Techniques,* McGraw-Hill, New York, 1966.

SEIDEL, S.Y., ET AL.: "The impact of surrounding buildings on propagation for wireless in-building personal communications system design," *VTC-92,* pp. 814–818.

SEO, J.S., K. FEHER: *"Superposed Quadrature Modulated Baseband Signal Processor,"* U.S. Patent No. 4,644,565, issued February 17, 1987a.

SEO, J.S., K. FEHER: "Bandwidth compressive 16-state SQAM modems through saturated amplifiers," *IEEE Transactions on Communications,* Vol. COM-35, No. 3, March 1987b, pp. 339–345.

SEO, J.S., K. FEHER: *"Superposed Quadrature Modulated Baseband Signal Processor,"* Canadian Patent No. 1–265–851; issued February 13, 1990.

SEO, J.S., K. FEHER: "Bandwidth compressive 64-state SQAM modems for nonlinearly amplified SATCOM systems," *International Journal of Satellite Communications,* Vol. 9, May–June 1991, pp. 149–154.

SEO, J.S., K. FEHER: "SQAM: A new superposed QAM modem technique," *IEEE Transactions on Communications,* March 1985, pp. 296–300.

SEO, J.S., K. FEHER: "Performance of SQAM systems in an nonlinearly amplified multichannel interference environment," *IEEE Proceedings: F, Communications, Radar and Signal Processing,* June 1985, pp. 175–180.

SEO, J.S., K. FEHER: "Performance of 16-state SQAM in a nonlinearly amplified multichannel interference environment," *IEEE Transactions on Communications,* Vol. 36, No. 11, November 1988, pp. 1263–1267.

SHANNON, C.E.: "A mathematical theory of communications," *Bell Sys. Tech. Jour.,* 1948.

SHIMIZU, I., S. URABE, K. HIRADE, K. NAGATA, S. YUKI: "A new pocket-size cellular telephone for NTT high-capacity land mobile communication system," *IEEE-VTC-91,* St. Louis, MO.

SILBERMAN, N. (ED.): "Draft proposal for a higher data rate frequency hopping spread spectrum PHY standard," (known as "TEMPLATE" document), *IEEE P.802.11-93/210a,* January 10, 1994.

SILBERMAN, N. and J. BOER: "Draft proposal for a frequency hopping and direct sequence spread spectrum PHY standard," *IEEE 802.11-93/83rl,* July 1993.

SILBERMAN, N.: "Proposal for a modulation technique for frequency hopping spread spectrum PHY standard," a submission by California Microwave, Inc., *IEEE P.802.11-93/94,* May 10, 1993.

SIMON, M.K.: "Dual-pilot tone calibration technique," *IEEE Transactions on Vehicular Technology,* Vol. 35, No. 2, pp. 63–70, May 1986.

SIMON, M.K., C.C. WANG: "Differential detection of Gaussian MSK in a mobile radio environment," *IEEE Transactions on Vehicular Technology,* Vol. VT-33, No. 4, pp. 307–320, November 1984.

SIMON, M.K., ET AL.: *Spread Spectrum Communications,* Vols. 1–3, Computer Science Press, Rockville, MD, 1985.

SKLAR, B.: *Digital Communications Fundamentals and Applications,* Prentice-Hall, Englewood Cliffs, NJ, 1988.

SMULDERS, P.F.M., A.G. WAGEMANS: "A statistical model for the MM-wave indoor radio channel," *Proceedings of the Third IEEE International Symposium on Personal, Indoor and Mobile Radio Communications,* Boston, October 1992.

SOCCI, J.: "GFSK as a modulation scheme for a frequency hopped PHY," a submission by National Semiconductor, *Document IEEE P.802.11-93/76,* Denver, CO., July 1993.

SODERSTRAND, M., ET AL. (WITH FEHER): "DS-SS and higher speed FH-SS modem VLSI implementation," *IEEE 802.11-94/06,* Wireless Access and Physical Layer Specifications, Jan. 1994.

STALLINGS, W.: *ISDN: An Introduction,* Macmillan Publishing Co., New York, 1989.

STEELE, R.: *Mobile radio communications,* Pentech Press, 1992.

STEIN, S.: "Fading channel issues in system engineering," *IEEE Journal on Selected Areas in Communications,* Vol. 5, No. 2, pp. 86–89, February 1987.

SUBASINGHE-DIAS, D.,: "New techniques for the improvement of capacity of digital mobile communications systems," *Doctoral Thesis, Dept. of Electrical and Computer Engineering, University of California, Davis* (supervisor: Professor K. Feher), May 1992, Davis, CA.

SUBASINGHE-DIAS, D., K. FEHER: "Miller coded pilot aided modulation schemes for digital mobile radio," *Proceedings of the IEEE Vehicular Technology Conf., VTC-90,* Orlando, FL, May 7–9, 1990.

SUBASINGHE-DIAS, D., K. FEHER: "Coded 16 QAM with channel state-derived decoding for fast fading mobiie channels," *UC Davis: DCRL Report No. SC-7,* October 1990.

SUBASINGHE-DIAS, D., K. FEHER: "π/4-CTPSK: A new modem technique for mobile satellite radio systems," (Invited paper), *IEICE Transactions on Communications Electronics Information and Systems,* The Institute of Electronics, Information and Communications Engineers, Tokyo, Japan, Vol. E74, No. 8, August, 1991, pp. 2247–2257.

SUBASINGHE-DIAS, D., K. FEHER: "A coded 16-QAM scheme with space diversity for cellular systems," *Proceedings of the IEEE-International Conference on Communications, ICC-92,* Chicago, IL, June 15–17, 1992, 5 pages.

SUBASINGHE-DIAS, D. and K. FEHER: "Baseband pulse shaping for π/4-FQPSK in nonlinearly amplified mobile channels," *IEEE Transactions on Communications,* October 1994.

SUZUKI, H., K. MOMMA, and Y. YAMAO: Digital portable transceiver using GMSK modem and ADM codec," *IEEE JSAC, Vol. SAC-2, No. 4,* pp. 604–610, July 1984. (Also in *IEEE Veh. Techn.,* Vol. VT-33, pp. 220–226, August 1984.)

SUZUKI, H., Y. YAMAO, and H. KIKUCHI: "A single-chip MSK coherent demodulator for mobile radio transmission," *IEEE Trans. Veh. Techn.,* Vol. VT-34, No. 4, pp. 157–168, November 1985.

TAKASAKI, Y.: *Digital Transmission Design and Jitter Analysis,* Artech House, Boston, 1991.

TAKATS, P., M. KEELTY, and H. MOODY: "A system architecture for an advanced Canadian wideband mobile satellite system," *Proceedings of the Third International Mobile Satellite Conference, IMSC' 93,* Pasadena, CA, June 1993.

TAUB, H., D. SCHILLING: *Principles of Communication Systems,* 2nd Ed., McGraw-Hill, New York, 1986.

TAYLOR, D.P., H.C. CHAN: A simulation study of two bandwidth efficient modulation techniques," *IEEE Transactions on Communications,* March 1981.

TEZCAN, I., K. FEHER: "Performance evaluation of differential MSK (DMSK) systems in an ACI and AWGN environment," *IEEE Transactions on Communications,* Vol. COM-34, No. 7, July 1986, pp. 727–733.

THOMAS, J.B.: *An Introduction to Statistical Communication Theory,* John Wiley, New York, 1968.

TOWNSEND, A.P.R.: *Digital Line-of-Sight Radio Links: A Handbook,* Prentice-Hall International, England, 1988.

TREMAIN, T.E.: "The government standard linear productive coding algorithm: LPC-10," *Speech Technology,* April 1982.

TRÖNDLE, K. and G. SÖDER: *Optimization of Digital Transmission Systems,* Artech House, Boston, 1987.

TUCH B.: "Comments and measurements on the physical layer," *NCR Corporation, Netherlands, Document IEEE,* p. 802.11/91-69, July 1991.

TUCH, B.: "An engineer's summary of an ISM band wireless LAN," *NCR Corporation, Netherlands, Document IEEE,* p. 802.11/91-69, July 1991.

TURIN, G.L. ET. AL.: "A statistical model of urban multipath propagation," *IEEE Transactions on Vehicular Technology,* Vol. VT-21, No. 1, pp. 1–9, February 1972.

TURIN, G.L., ET.AL.: "A statistical model of urban multipath propagation," *IEEE Transactions on Vehicular Technology,* February 1992.

TURKMANI, A.M.D., P.F. DE TOLEDO: "Radio transmission at 1800MHz into and within multistory building," *IEEE Proceedings, Part I,* Vol. 138, No. 6, December 1991.

TUTTLEBEE, W.H., ED.: *Cordless Telecommunications in Europe,* Springer Verlag, London, 1990.

UNGERBOECK, G.: "Channel coding with multilevel/phase signals," *IEEE Transactions on Information Theory,* January 1982.

VAISNYS, A., D. BELL, J. GEVARGIZ, N. GOLSHAN: "Direct broadcast satellite-radio receiver development," *Proceedings of the Third International Mobile Satellite Conference, IMSC 93,* Pasadena, CA June 16–18, 1993.

VANNUCCI, G., R.S. ROMAN: "Measurement results on indoor radio frequency re-use at 900 MHz and 18 GHz," *Proceedings of the third IEEE International Symposium on Personal, Indoor and Mobile Radio Communications (PIMRC '92),* Boston, October 1992.

VILLARD, O.G., JR., J.M. LOMASNEY, and N.M. KAWACHIKA: "A noise-averaging diversity combiner," *IEEE Trans. Ant. Prop.,* Vol. AP-20, July 1972, p. 463.

VITERBI, A.J.: "The evolution of digital wireless technology from space exploration to personal communication services," *IEEE Transactions on Vehicular Technology, Part II,* August 1994.

VITERBI, A., J.K. OMURA: *Principles of Digital Communication and Coding,* McGraw-Hill, New York, 1979.

WALKER, J., ED.: *Mobile Information Systems,* Artech House, Boston, 1990.

WAN, Z., K. FEHER: "Improved efficiency CDMA by constant envelope SQAM," *Proceedings of the IEEE VTC- 92,* May 11–13, 1992, Denver, CO.

WAN, Z. and K. FEHER: "Modulation specifications for 2 Mb/s, DS-SS system, *IEEE 802.11-94/02, Wireless Access and Physical Layer Specifications,* January 1994.

WATERS, P.H. and D.C. SMITH: "A comparison of decision feedback and Viterbi equalisers for UHF mobile radio communication," *Land Mobile Radio. Fourth International Conference (Publ. No. 78),* pp. 73–79, 1987.

WIEDEMAN, A.R., A.J. VITERBI: "The GLOBALSTAR mobile satellite system for worldwide personal communications," *Proceedings of the Third International Mobile Satellite Conference, IMSC 93,* Pasadena, CA June 16–18, 1993.

WILSON, S.G., H.A. SLEEPER, P.J. SCHOTTLER, M.T. LYONS: "Rate 3/4 convolutional coding of 16-PSK: Code design and performance study," *IEEE Transactions on Communications,* December 1984.

WIMMER, K.A. and J.B. JONES: "Global development of PCS," *IEEE Commun. Mag.,* Vol. 30, No. 6, pp. 22–27, June 1992.

WOLFF, R.S. and D. PINCK: "Internetworking satellite and local exchange networks for personal communications applications," *Proceedings of the Third International Mobile Satellite Conference, IMSC 93,* Pasadena, CA June 16–18, 1993.

WU, G., K. FEHER: "The impact of delay spread on multilevel FM systems in a Rayleigh fading, CCI and AWGN environment," *Proceedings of the IEEE VTC-92,* May 11–13, 1992, Denver, CO.

WU, K.T., K. FEHER: "Digital Modulation Techniques," Chapter in *The Froehlich/Kent Encyclopedia of Telecommunications, Vol. 6. Digital Microwave Link Design to Electrical Filters,* Marcel Dekker, Inc., New York, NY, 1993, pp. 51–167.

YACOUB, M.D.: *Foundations of Mobile Radio Engineering,* CRC Press, Inc., Boca Raton, Florida, 1993.

YANG, J., K. FEHER: "An improved π/4-QPSK with nonredundant error correction for satellite mobile broadcasting," *IEEE Transactions on Broadcasting Technology,* Vol. 37, March 1991, pp. 9–16.

YONGACOGLU, A., D. MAKRAKIS, K. FEHER: "Differential detection of GMSK using decision feedback," *IEEE Transactions on Communications,* Vol. 36, No. 6 June 1988, pp. 641–649.

ZOGG, A.: "Multipath delay spread in a hilly region at 210 MHz," *IEEE Transactions on Vehicular Technology,* Vol. VT-36, No. 4, pp. 184–187, November 1987.

Index